The Diaries of John Gregory Bourke

Volume 1

The Diaries of John Gregory Bourke

VOLUME 1
November 20, 1872–July 28, 1876

Edited and Annotated by
Charles M. Robinson III

University of North Texas Press
Denton, Texas

Permissions:
University of North Texas Press
P.O. Box 311336
Denton, TX 76203-1336

The paper used in this book meets the minimum requirements of the American National Standard for Permanence of Paper for Printed Library Materials, z39.48.1984. Binding materials have been chosen for durability.

Library of Congress Cataloging-in-Publication Data

Bourke, John Gregory, 1846-1896.
  The diaries of John Gregory Bourke / edited and annotated by Charles M. Robinson III.
    p. cm.
Includes bibliographical references and index.
  ISBN 1-57441-161-6 (cloth, alk. paper)
  ISBN 1-57441-935-1 (paperback, alk. paper)
  ISBN 1-57441-426-4 (ebook)
1. Bourke, John Gregory, 1846-1896—Diaries. 2. Soldiers—West (U.S.)—Diaries. 3. Indians of North America—Wars—1866-1895—Personal narratives. I. Robinson, Charles M., 1949- II. Title.

  E83.866 .B75 2003
978'.02'092—dc21

                          2002152293

Design by Angela Schmitt
All illustrations are held by United States Military Academy Library, West Point, N.Y. Cover photo of John Gregory Bourke is courtesy of the National Park Service, Little Bighorn Battlefield National Monument.

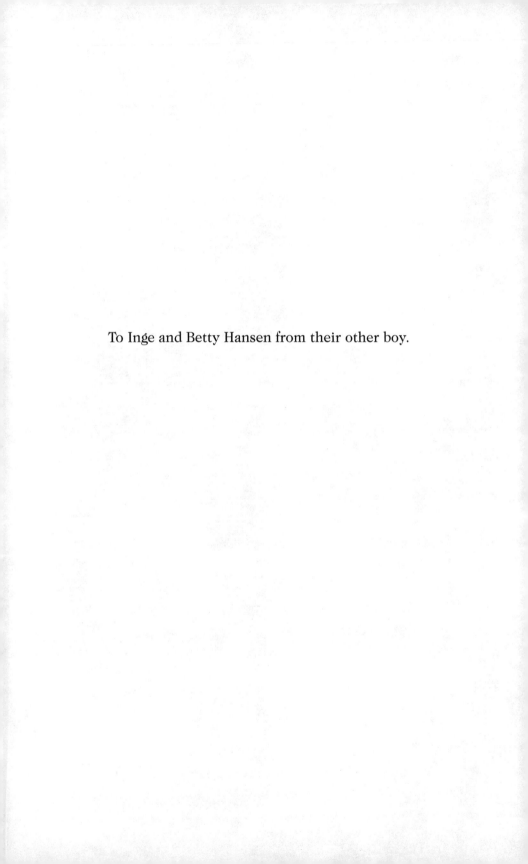

To Inge and Betty Hansen from their other boy.

Contents

Acknowledgments

Transcribing a set of nineteenth century diaries is a lonely task. However, certain people and institutions contributed to the completion of the project, and in some cases were responsible to the extent of making it possible.

Lieutenant Colonel Thomas T. Smith, U.S.A., garrison commander, Carlisle Barracks, Pennsylvania, and a notable historian in his own right, and Frances Vick, retired director of the University of North Texas Press, endorsed the significance of this project when it was still in the early stages of an idea, and promoted it with the UNT Press' academic advisors. Thanks also go to two very special people at UNT Press, who suffer through the project itself, and my occasional foul temper as it progresses: Ronald Chrisman, the current director, and Karen DeVinney, managing editor.

Kim Frontz, librarian/archivist, Arizona Historical Society, Tucson, provided information on some of the more obscure aspects of Arizona in the second half of the nineteeth century. Greg Lalire, editor of *Wild West Magazine*, gives me steady encouragement through the pages of the magazine. Another source of continuing moral support is the kind people of the Center for Western Studies, Augustana College, Sioux Falls, South Dakota, particularly Dr. Arthur Huseboe, director, Dr. Harry Thompson, Dean Schueller, and my good friend Richard Haase, former member of the CWS board.

I also wish to acknowledge the United States Army Military History Institute, Carlisle Barracks, Pennsylvania, holding institution for the Eugene A. Carr Papers, and the American Heritage Center, University of Wyoming at Laramie, holding institution for the Thaddeus Capron Diary. The Newberry Library, Chicago, Illinois, gave permission to quote from the Black Hills Expedition Journals of Lt. Col. Richard Irving Dodge.

Last, but not least, thanks to my "superior officers" at South Texas Community College, McAllen, Texas, who tolerate my quirks and who have created an environment that allows me to handle all my projects: Dr. Shirley A. Reed, president; Dr. Frank Williams, vice president of academic affairs; Jean Rodgers Swartz, associate dean of instruction; Dr. Thomas Cameron, dean of the Division of Liberal Arts and Social Sciences; and Bryant Morrison, chairman of the Department of History, Government and Philosophy.

Introduction

❖

❖

❖

❖

John Gregory Bourke:
The Man and His Work

J
ohn Gregory Bourke was one of the most prolific and influential authors to write about the nineteenth century American West. An officer of the 3rd Cavalry, he is most famous as Brig. Gen. George Crook's aide-de-camp for fourteen years, serving in every major campaign in Arizona and on the Northern Plains. His memoir, *On the Border With Crook*, written over a century ago and often reprinted, is one of the great military classics of the Indian Wars, and established Bourke's reputation as "Crook's Boswell."[1]

Yet Bourke was more than simply a writer of military memoirs. His long service on the frontier led to an interest in Indian life, and he became a devoted scholar of their beliefs, customs, and traditions. His interest and his constant note-taking prompted the Apaches to call him *naltsus-bichidin*, or "Paper Medicine Man."[2] Ultimately, he became a respected ethnologist, and it is a tribute to his work that some of his Indian studies, such as *Apache Medicine-Men*, remain standard works. Even *On the Border With Crook*, and *An*

1. O'Neal, *Fighting Men*, 48.
2. Porter, *Paper Medicine Man: John Gregory Bourke and His American West*, 181. Much of the material in this section is taken from Porter's biography. For a discussion of Bourke's contributions to Southwestern ethnology, see Turcheneske, "Historical Manuscripts."

Apache Campaign in the Sierra Madre, which deal primarily with military operations, contain observations about prehistoric sites, and contemporary Indian life and culture. His views on the settlement of the West were far more critical than those of other scholars of his era, such as Theodore Roosevelt and Frederick Jackson Turner. Like them, he saw it as a great national adventure, but devoid of much of the glory that Turner and Roosevelt gave it.

John Gregory Bourke was born in Philadelphia on June 23, 1846. His parents, Edward Joseph Bourke and Anna Morton, were well-to-do Irish immigrants. Edward Bourke, who owned a bookstore, knew Greek, Latin, French, and Gaelic, and was a student of Irish Gaelic folklore; his wife was grounded in English literature, history, and liberal arts. One of seven children in a staunchly Roman Catholic family, John attended parochial school, and was tutored in Latin, Greek, and Gaelic by a Jesuit. From this, John Gregory acquired an appreciation for the classics that becomes evident throughout his diary.

In 1862, the sixteen-year-old Bourke got caught up in the patriotic euphoria of the Civil War and, lying about his age, enlisted in the 15th Pennsylvania Volunteer Cavalry. He earned the Medal of Honor for unspecified "gallantry in action" at Stones River (Murfreesboro), Tennessee, served in the Battles of Chickamauga and Chattanooga, and was part of Sherman's army that invaded Georgia. Mustered out in July 1865, he entered West Point, graduating eleventh in a class of thirty-nine in June 1869.

As a newly commissioned second lieutenant, Bourke was posted to Fort Craig, New Mexico.[3] In March 1870, he was assigned to a company at Camp Grant, Arizona, the heart of Apache country.[4] For the next eighteen months, he was more or less continually in the field. On May 26, 1870, he was sent with a detachment to the scene of an attack on a wagon train, and saw his first example of Apache warfare. "It was a ghastly sight," he remarked of a mutilated corpse.[5]

3. Fort Craig was established on the Rio Grande, to provide protection against Apaches and guard the road along the Rio Grande. It was abandoned and transferred to the Interior Department in 1885. Frazer, *Forts of the West*, 98.

4. Camp Grant was established in 1865 on the San Pedro River near its confluence with Aravaipa Creek. Located on the site of the abandoned post of Fort Breckenridge, it guarded the road between Tucson and Sacaton. An Indian reservation was established briefly at Grant in 1872, but after the Indians were reconcentrated at San Carlos later that year, the post was no longer necessary. It was abandoned in 1873, a new Camp Grant having been established at the head of Sulphur Springs Valley. Ibid., 4-6, 8; Altshuler, *Starting With Defiance*, 28-30.

5. Bourke, *On the Border*, 25.

Like many soldiers exposed to such depredations, Bourke initially saw nothing wrong with repaying the Indians in kind, and when a scout presented him with the scalp and ears of a dead Apache, he had them mounted as trophies. But when a visitor nearly fainted at the sight, Bourke later recalled, "I saw at once how brutal and inhuman I had been and ordered them buried."[6] To divert his attention from warfare and the monotony of garrison life, he began studying the history and culture of Arizona's Spanish-Mexican population. This ultimately expanded to all the people of the West, particularly the Indians. The last may have been prompted by General Crook's belief that much of the Indian trouble rose from ignorance of Indians as human beings. Consequently, Crook implemented a policy that officers in Arizona were to make every effort "to acquire knowledge of the rites and ceremonies, the ideas and feelings, of the Indians under their charge."[7] Bourke carried out that policy with unbridled enthusiasm.

George Crook assumed command of the Department of Arizona in June 1871, and on September 1, Bourke was named aide-de-camp. His broad interests and his wide range of reading made him the scholar of Crook's official family. As such he helped shape the general's views, or gave intellectual justification to ideas Crook already held. His copious notes on Crook's official conferences and private conversations provide a detailed view of what was going through the general's mind in Arizona during the Apache campaigns, on the northern plains during and after the Great Sioux War, and again in Arizona during the closing campaigns against Geronimo, Naiche, and other famous Apache leaders.

Unlike Robert G. Carter, whose classic *On the Border With Mackenzie*, is part memoir, part embellishment, and part fabrication, Bourke's account rings true. Except for rare intervals, he was at Crook's side more or less continually during the entire fourteen years he served as aide-de-camp.[9] His loyalty was sorely tried during

6. Bourke, Diaries, 92:64-65.
7. Bourke, *On the Border*, 234.
8. See Appendix 2.
9. Robert Goldthwaite Carter served under Col. Ranald S. Mackenzie in the Fourth Cavalry during the Kiowa and Comanche wars in Texas in the early 1870s. Although Carter wrote *On the Border With Mackenzie* as a memoir, he often fabricated and embellished, describing virtually every event as an eyewitness, although he was not always present. A comparison of *On the Border With Mackenzie*, published in 1935, and *On the Border With Crook*, published in 1891, shows how much Carter was trying to emulate Bourke, even so far as using an almost identical title.

the infamous "Starvation March" or "Horse Meat March" of 1876, one of the bitterest tests of endurance ever imposed on United States soldiers in the field. A six-week trek through the wilderness of Montana and the Dakotas, its purported purpose was to catch the scattering bands of Indians, and save the Black Hills settlements from what Crook considered potential massacre. The summer-clad soldiers faced the onset of an early winter, and were exposed to weeks of rain, sleet, and mud. Food ran out, and the men were reduced to eating the worn-out cavalry horses. Even the infantrymen, accustomed to long treks, were so exhausted they could barely put one foot in front of another, and troopers had to be prodded along at bayonet point.[10] Years later, in *On the Border With Crook*, Bourke wrote:

> There was scarcely a day. . . for nearly a month that my note-books do not contain references to storms. . . the exposure began to tell upon officer, men, and animals, and I think the statement will be accepted without challenge that no one who followed Crook during those terrible days was benefited in any way.
>
> I made out a rough list of the officers present on this expedition, and another of those who have died, been killed, died of wounds, or been retired for one reason or another, and I find that the first list had one hundred and sixteen names and the second sixty-nine; so it can be seen that of the officers who were considered to be physically able to enter upon that campaign in the early summer months of 1876, over fifty per cent. are not now answering to roll-call on the active list, after about sixteen years' interval.[11]

Aside from his military memoirs, Bourke's published writings on Indian life and culture brought him international acclaim as an ethnologist. His work was encouraged by John Wesley Powell, head of the American Bureau of Ethnology, and the prominent historian

10. Robinson, *General Crook*, 190ff. The wastage of animals was so great that on September 10, Crook requisitioned five hundred remounts, indicating that about *forty percent* of his total cavalry strength had been reduced to walking. Crook to Sheridan, September 10, 1876, RG 393, Special File, Military Division of the Missouri, Sioux Wars, hereafter referred to as "Special File—Sioux."

11. Bourke, *On the Border*, 359-60. Bourke's account of the Horse Meat March will appear in Volume 2 of this series.

Francis Parkman, Jr. Crook, who enjoyed his company, kept Bourke on his staff as aide-de-camp, but allowed him ample time to pursue his ethnological studies. In 1885, however, he became uncomfortable with this obvious favoritism and requested reassignment. He was given command of Camp Rice (later Fort Hancock), Texas,[12] a position he held until March 1886, when, at Crook's insistence, he was returned to Arizona for the general's march into the Mexican Sierra Madre. At the conclusion of that campaign, he requested a transfer, and Secretary of War William Endicott assigned him to Washington so that he could continue his ethnological studies.

Despite his reputation, Bourke never advanced farther than captain, and as he grew older he began to resent the lack of promotion. When a vacancy for major opened, he sought Crook's support, but the general, affronted that Bourke would not return to his staff, was indifferent, and the promotion went elsewhere. Henceforth, Bourke avoided Crook whenever possible, although it must be said that after Crook's death, he abandoned his animosity and worked to glorify the general's memory.[13] By now, however, Bourke had other problems. During his lifetime, the irascible Crook had made many enemies, some of whom now were among the most important men in the army. Bourke's long association with Crook virtually assured that his comfortable tenure in Washington was over, and there would be no more "plum" assignments that might offer advancement beyond captain.

In 1891, Bourke was given command of Fort Ringgold, Texas,[14] on the lower Rio Grande, about 150 miles above its mouth. Here,

12. Fort Hancock was established on the Rio Grande about forty miles downriver from El Paso, in 1882. It was upgraded to a fort in 1886, and protected the area from Indians and bandits. The post was abandoned and transferred to the Interior Department in 1885. Although the town of Fort Hancock grew up adjacent to the site, nothing remains of the post itself. Frazer, *Forts of the West*, 151.

13. Theoretically promotion, at least until 1890, was based on a seniority system. However, the support of a well-connected general could do much to help a junior officer circumvent the system and attain higher rank. In fact, Crook had interceded with his old friend and admirer, President Rutherford Hayes, to secure a promotion to major and assistant adjutant general for his senior aide-de-camp, Azor Nickerson, one of more than seventy captains seeking the position. Undoubtedly his support at least would have added weight to Bourke's case, had Crook chosen to use it. See Robinson, *General Crook*, 220-21; Bourke, Diaries, 23:34-35; Crook to Hayes, June 16, 1878, copy in Bourke, Diaries, 23:35-36.

14. Fort Ringgold was established in 1848 at Davis's Landing (now Rio Grande City), as part of a chain of posts built along the Rio Grande following the Mexican War. Although there was some Indian campaigning in the early days, its primary function was to protect the border. It was deactivated in 1944, and transferred to the War Assets Administration for disposal. The post, which is largely intact, now belongs to the Rio Grande City Independent School District. See Robinson, "Fort Ringgold."

his career appears to have reached its lowest point. He had little use for or sympathy with the local *tejano* population, which he described as "so far behind those of the same race on the Mexican side [of the river]."[15] His ill-disposition was aggravated because of the outbreak of a revolt against the dictatorial rule of Mexican President Porfirio Díaz. As often happened during this period, the trouble spilled over into Texas, and Bourke's high-handed response earned the enmity of much of the local population. He was accused of sending troops into private homes "without warrant of law, at all hours of the day and night" to search for weapons, and of threatening to shoot prisoners if they did not name those engaged in the outbreak.[16]

With complaints to state and federal authorities mounting, Bourke's tenure at Ringgold was short-lived. He was reassigned to the Columbian Exposition, and to Chicago during the Pullman strike. His final post was Fort Ethan Allen, Vermont. During 1895 and 1896, Bourke's health deteriorated, and some modern scholars believe he became yet another casualty of the infamous Horse Meat March. On May 21, 1896, he was admitted to the Polyclinical Hospital in Philadelphia, where he died on June 8, just two weeks short of his fiftieth birthday. He is buried in Arlington National Cemetery.

The Bourke Diaries

Bourke's published work was largely based on notes in his extensive diaries. At this time 124 volumes and several subvolumes are known to exist, all preserved in the United States Military Academy Library at West Point. The earliest, designated Volume 1 in the West Point collection, begins on November 20, 1872. It is one of three extant volumes and two subvolumes from 1872 through 1875 that primarily consist of sporadic, disconnected narratives of specific expeditions or campaigns. Bourke occasionally mentioned other volumes as far back as his arrival in the Southwest in 1869, but by 1880 these had been, in his words, "mislaid, destroyed or stolen." One later volume covering the six-week period of July 28 to September 8, 1876, also was among those lost, and was

---

15. Bourke, "The American Congo," 21.

16. "War Against Peace," 49, 51. The violence centered around a rebellion led by Catarino Garza against the Porfirio Diaz regime in Mexico, which, like so many rebellions, spilled over into the Texas. This phase of Bourke's career is discussed in Robinson, "On the Border With Bourke."

reconstructed by Bourke from memory in two separate notebooks, now designated as Volumes 7 and 8 at West Point. With this exception, however, the diaries beginning in February 1876 form a more or less continuous daily journal until two weeks prior to his death in 1896. Bourke became so conscientious that if he ran out of space in one notebook, he immediately would start another, sometimes in mid-sentence, without interrupting the flow. Thus there is continuity in the text itself, even if it is disrupted by the switch to a new volume.[17]

The earliest volumes contain many monotonous descriptions of terrain, vegetation, measurements, and bearings of interest primarily to the geographer. Nevertheless, they also include some accounts of Indian tribal life and customs, as well as fights in which Bourke participated. Even the mundane is instructive of the problems facing people in the West during that era, because it shows a preoccupation with such things as availability of grass for the animals, and water for all concerned. As the diaries progress over time, they turn into a running narrative of army life in post, camp, and field, Indian fights, and Indian life. Bourke's own words are supplemented with hand-drawn maps and illustrations, photographs, newspaper clippings, orders, and copies of correspondence. Maps and sketches of the terrain are particularly abundant. Much of Arizona was unknown, and to facilitate his campaigns, Crook "directed that each scouting party should map out its own trail, and send the result on to the headquarters, to be incorporated in the general map of the territory. . . ."[18] The final volume consists of thirty-one water color sketches. Taken together, they are probably the most complete personal narrative of the Indian Wars, particularly notable because they are an insider's view from within the command structure.

Bourke used the language of the times. Indian warriors were "bucks," women were "squaws," children often were called "pappooses," and Indians as a whole were "savages" or "redskins." Nevertheless, his attitude toward the Indians was no more malicious than that of any soldier toward the enemy in time of war, and often far more tolerant. His real venom was reserved for whites—traders, contractors, and politicians who robbed and corrupted Indians. He

17. Bloom, "Bourke on the Southwest, vol. 10, no. 2:38, and, vol. 10, no. 3:289; Bourke, Diaries, 7:705.
18. Bourke, *On the Border*, 234.

also detested government officials whose well-intentioned meddling seemed (in his view at least) to prolong the agony of Indian war for both Indians and settlers. Early in his writings, he went so far as to call Vincent Colyer, secretary of the Board of Indian Commissioners, "that spawn of hell."[19] Ironically, as he grew older, he would assist men like Colyer in their efforts to secure for the Indians recognition of their proper rights and dignity as residents of the United States.

The diaries show Bourke's development, not only as soldier and scholar, but as a human being. The earlier volumes convey a certain amount of Victorian disdain, viewing Indians as savage relics of a primordial age in human development, and blaming much of the strife on their ability to manipulate a naive government. In 1876, for example, as the army prepared to subjugate the Lakota Sioux and Cheyennes of the northern plains, he commented in his diary:

> We are now on the eve of the bitterest Indian war the Government has ever been called upon to wage: a war with a tribe that has waxed fat and insolent on Gov't bounty, and has been armed and equipped with the most improved weapons by the connivance or carelessness of the Indian Agents.[20]

As time passed and he came to know the Indians, his attitude changed from condescension to profound respect. He began to attribute much of the problem to avarice, ignorance, and intolerance on the part of the whites. Commenting on the same war fourteen years later, he wrote:

> Much of our trouble with these tribes could have been averted, had we shown what would appear to them as a spirit of justice and fair dealing. . . . It is hard to make the average savage comprehend why it is that as soon as his reservation is found to amount to anything he must leave and give up to the white man. Why should not Indians be permitted to hold mining or any other kind of land? The whites could mine on shares or on a royalty, and the Indians would soon become workers in the bowels of the earth. . . . The policy of the American people has been to vagabondize the Indian, and throttle every

19. Bourke, Diaries, 1:91.
20. Ibid., 3:1-2.

ambition he may have for his own elevation. . . .[21]

Although he realized that their ancient tribal ways must ultimately yield to the modern world, he began to believe the process must be a gradual adaptation rather than a sudden, forced assimilation.

Yet even in his earliest entries, Bourke often demonstrated more interest and open-mindedness than many of his contemporaries. In 1872, he recorded a victory celebration among the army's Apache scouts that had homosexual overtones.

> Some of the young bucks arrayed themselves in muslin & calico captured in the Rancheria yesterday and feigning the manners of women, received their *male* companions a few singing in concert, though not in harmony, supplied the necessary music, and the dancing once commenced was continued with undiminished vigor until near midnight. I was unable to learn the purpose of the chorus, but to the best of my belief, it referred to past exploits against their enemies and promises of what might be expected in the future.[22]

His tolerance was reminiscent of the great British explorer, Sir Richard Burton, who also allowed his interest in other cultures to take priority over the moral and social prejudices of his own society. But where Burton went so far as to adapt himself to native customs (often with enthusiasm), Bourke always retained his own cultural identity.[23]

After Bourke left Crook's staff, the diaries expanded to include firsthand accounts of visits with Apache prisoners of war at Fort Marion, Florida, and Mount Vernon Barracks, Alabama, Bourke's involvement with the Indian rights movement, disturbances on the Texas-Mexican border, and labor unrest in Chicago. A lesser known, but equally important aspect is his descriptions and sketches of

---

21. Bourke; *On the Border*, 244; see also Porter, *Paper Medicine Man*, 65-67.

22. Bourke, Diaries, 1:43. Soldiers used "rancheria," derived from the Spanish, to indicate a more or less permanent Apache encampment.

23. Burton, who was twenty-five years older than Bourke, entered the Indian service at a time when the British East India Company still condoned officers who "went native." Bourke, on the other hand, served at the height of the Victorian era, and the United States Army was far less tolerant. Even if he had been inclined to emulate Burton, he would have been ostracized from both society and career had he done so. See Rice, *Captain Sir Richard Francis Burton*.

Arizona topography, particularly in the early volumes. On May 3, 1887, after Bourke departed from Arizona for good, the region he had known was struck by a great earthquake that shook some 720,000 square miles of the southwestern United States and northwestern Mexico. Consequently, his sketches depict many features that no longer exist or have been substantially altered.[24]

The diaries were donated to the West Point Library by Bourke's daughter, Mrs. Sara Bourke James, with the stipulation that they be in the public domain. They have been copied on microfilm by Bell & Howell, which offers them as a complete set of ten reels. These microfilms are in manuscript form only. Despite the fact that the Bourke Diaries are consulted (generally through microfilm) by virtually every scholar studying the Apache or Sioux Wars, no effort has been made to publish them as a whole. Since the mid-1940s, several persons have discussed it, but nothing has developed due, no doubt, to the sheer enormity of the project. Only with the development of electrostatic copying has a full, annotated edition of Bourke's diaries become feasible.

While the complete diaries have never before been published, portions have. The first efforts, and undoubtedly the most ambitious, were from 1933 to 1938, and again in 1944, when extracts dealing with Bourke's service in the Southwest were published in the *New Mexico Historical Review* under the title "Bourke On the Southwest." The series was edited by Lansing B. Bloom, co-editor of the *Review*. Because Bourke jumped from one topic to the next, and sometimes would reminiscence about an event years after, Bloom arranged the entries thematically and chronologically, rather than in the order in which they were written, to provide a smoother narrative.

Some fifty years after Bloom, an extract largely concerning the Horse Meat March, was published in La Miranda, California, in 1986. Titled *Bourke's Diary: From Journals of 1st Lt. John Gregory Bourke, June 27–Sept. 15, 1876*, it was annotated and published by James Willert, and today is very scarce. Much of the material in the Willert edition, however, comes from the notebooks that Bourke reconstructed from memory from the missing volume.

---

24. The earthquake was centered near Bavispe, Sonora, some forty miles south of Douglas, Arizona. Bavispe, which figures prominently in Bourke's writings about Crook's Sierra Madre Campaign in 1883, was totally destroyed, with forty-two killed. The quake is discussed in Farnsworth, "The Day the Southwest Shook."

Format for the Edited Diary

This is the first of a projected six volumes. In order to facilitate editing, I have undertaken a basic format to preserve as much as possible the flavor of the manuscript, while still making it intelligible to the reader and without being cumbersome.

Orders and Clippings. In the early volumes, Bourke kept his daily records only on the right-hand, odd-numbered pages of his notebook, using the even-numbered pages on the left for illustrations, hand-drawn maps, incidental information not part of the text, or for pasting official, printed copies of orders, organizational lists, or newspaper clippings. I seldom have included maps or sketches of the terrain, unless they add particular value to the text. Likewise, because the number of official papers and newspaper clippings is so extensive, and the fact that most are available from other sources, I have included only those that, again, add particular value to the text, and deleted any reference to others with (. . . .). Most of the clippings and other papers, together with miscellaneous extraneous notes that do not form part of the continuing narrative, have been placed in the appendices at the rear of this volume. On occasion, however, Bourke uses a clipping to elaborate on the narrative without disrupting the flow, and these have been left in place. The appendices themselves are arranged and numbered by category. All orders relevant to a particular subject or situation are grouped together; likewise correspondence; reports, etc. Among the extraneous notes was an Apache vocabulary. Because of its limited appeal outside of the field of linguistics, and for space considerations, it has been deleted.

Abbreviations, Spelling, and Grammar. Bourke used many abbreviations. The @ symbol often appears as a substitute for the word "or." While I have tried to remain as faithful as possible to the original text, for the sake of clarity I have spelled out the more common abbreviations, such as cardinal directions, "left," "right," "miles," and "road," as well as those he used frequently, such as "good grass and water," "creek," and "Sierra." For those that are less common or obvious, I have inserted the missing letters in [brackets], except when the abbreviations are scattered, requiring several sets of brackets within one word; in such cases, I have spelled out the word in brackets. When a word is illegible, but the meaning can be inferred, I have placed the probable word with a question mark in [brackets?]. If the meaning cannot be inferred, I have written it as [*illegible*]. Except for the works of Mark Twain, an "American" form of spelling and punctuation had not yet fully developed in Bourke's era. Consequently, he used British forms, which are retained. Even so, spelling and grammatical errors are so numerous that I have refrained from using the standard [*sic*] following misspelled words and errors in grammar except in the most extreme cases. In some isolated instances, I have corrected Bourke, such as with "campe" and "tanke" obviously written by light of a campfire after a long day's march. Otherwise, I have transcribed the text as is. Thus place names like Chevelon, Aravaipa, and Mazatzal are spelled several different ways. Names of individuals suffered in the same fashion. Among others, Capt. Emil Adam usually was rendered "Adams," Capt. James Burns was given the Irish spelling "Byrnes" or "Byrne," and Cochise was spelled several different ways. All such instances have been noted in the biographical sketches in Appendix 1.

Arcane References. As noted in the biographical sketch at the beginning of this section. Bourke's early education was grounded in the classics. His upper level education was at West Point, essentially an engineering school, with emphasis on geology and mathematics, with some heavy doses of French thrown in for good measure. From there, he went to the Southwest, where English and Spanish words, even now, are often used interchangeably. Consequently, there is a plethora of information on measurements and geology, often accompanied by technical words. He also made occasional references to classical subjects, and used French or Spanish words. Wherever possible, I have tried to provide an explanation of terminology and classical references, and a translation of foreign terms.

Punctuation and Capitalization. Punctuation in the diary was rudimentary. Bourke often used a dash (—) in lieu of punctuation. In most cases, I have substituted the punctuation marks, unless the dash appears more appropriate. In cases where Bourke did use punctuation, it was erratic, although he tended to use periods and commas *outside* quotation marks rather than within. I lean toward leaving Bourke's punctuation intact except for cases where it renders the text absolutely confusing. Capitalization was erratic. For example, in giving times of day, he might use a.m./p.m., A.M./P.M., or am./pm. I have preserved his capitalization as much as possible.

Emphasis. Bourke emphasized words by underlining them. Most of the time (but not always), he underlined names of people and places, dates, and geographical features of interest. Yet some of his emphasis seems little more than whimsy and, more than a century later, appears to have had no practical reason. In an effort to make it more readable, I have deleted the emphasis. Bourke occasionally annotated the entries after the fact, as new information came to hand. His notes are indicated by an asterisk (*) while mine are numbered. I have replaced Bourke's brackets with parentheses, to avoid confusing his texts with mine.

Names. Often individuals are named with no explanation as to who they were. Bourke was, after all, writing for his own future reference and knew the people in question. I have attempted, in Appendix 1, to identify as many as possible, and in the case of army officers, have been relatively successful. After more than a century, however, it has not always been possible to identify enlisted soldiers or civilians. Where Bourke uses the local name for plants, or names that might not be widely known, I have attempted to identify them and put the botanical name in the notes; I did not do so for commonly known plants. Bourke's designations of the territories have been preserved, and when they do not reflect the modern name of the state, I have inserted the state in [brackets]. In my own commentaries, I have used the modern state names.

Military Ranks. One of the more confusing aspects of the text is Bourke's inconsistencies in rank. For example, Andrew Sheridan Burt is sometimes referred to as "Major Burt," and other times as "Captain Burt." The same applies to Thaddeus Stanton, Joseph J. Reynolds, George Morton Randall, and many other officers. The reason is the system of brevet ranks used by the army during the nineteenth century. The brevet was bestowed to honor gallant and/or meritorious service, and generally was higher than the officer's active rank. During the Civil War, when many officers of the Regular Army transferred to the Volunteer Service, one individual might have as many as three ranks simultaneously, viz., active rank in the Regular Army, brevet rank in the Regular Army, and brevet rank in the Volunteers. When the Union Army was demobilized after the war, these officers reverted to their most recent active rank in the Regular Army. Nevertheless, the brevet remained on the officer's record, and as a courtesy he ordinarily would be addressed by the brevet. Again, using Andrew Burt as one of the many examples, the expedition roster would carry him by his active rank as captain, but outside of official documents and lists, but Bourke often referred to him by his brevet as major. The biographical sketches of officers in Appendix 1 includes both active and brevet ranks.

Introductory Material. Generally, I have tried to limit introductory material to the beginning of each part of the diary, specifically, Arizona, the Department of the Platte, and the Great Sioux War. Occasionally, however, a particular chapter is so much at variance with the rest of the narrative, or is of enough importance on its own, to require a separate introduction. I have used *italics* for introductions to distinguish them from Bourke's material.

Part 1
Arizona
1872–1875

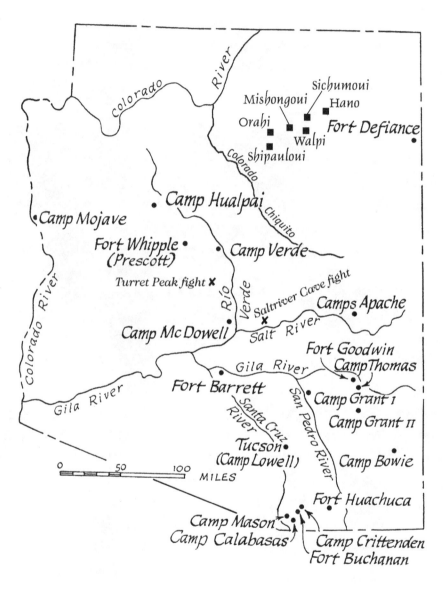

Camps upgraded to forts in 1879–81

Background

A pachería is the vast area encompassing what is now Arizona, most of New Mexico, and portions of the Mexican states of Sonora and Chihuahua. It is so called because it is the traditional land of the Western Apaches. For centuries, the Apaches had fought the people of the south, first the Spaniards, and then the Mexicans. Their initial contact with U.S. soldiers in 1846, however, was cordial. The United States was then at war with Mexico, and because of their own hatred for the Mexicans, the Apaches assumed the Americans must have some good qualities. In fact, when a U.S. expeditionary force crossed Apachería en route to Mexican-held California, the great Apache chief Mangas Coloradas suggested to the American commander, Brig. Gen. Stephen Watts Kearny,[1] that they should combine forces, and invade Sonora and Chihuahua. Kearny declined, and continued on his march.

Trouble appears to have begun with the discovery of gold in California. Apaches were disturbed by the large number of

1. Stephen Watts Kearny (1794-1848), army officer, explorer, and Mexican War hero, gave his name to Fort Kearny, Nebraska. The Fort Kearny, Wyoming, so frequently mentioned by Bourke in this volume, refers to Fort Phil Kearny named for Bvt. Maj. Gen. Philip Kearny, killed at Chantilly, Virginia, in 1862. Bourke and others have tended to erroneously render the name as "Kearney." There is no second "e." Heitman, *Historical Register*, 1:586, 2:514, 533.

Americans crossing their country en route to the gold fields. Additionally, because the Mexican jurisdictions offered a bounty on Apache scalps, some of these gold seekers offset their expenses by scalp hunting. The situation worsened early in 1851, when a boundary commission entered Apachería with a military escort. Mangas Coloradas' reaction seems to have been mixed. Initially outraged at the military presence, he ultimately realized that his warriors' bows and arrows were no match for the soldiers' firearms, and therefore expressed a guarded friendship. Nevertheless, trouble broke out when one band ran off a herd of cattle belonging to a mining camp not far from the boundary commission's camp. A detachment of soldiers pursued, and after a fight, recovered the cattle.

As more Americans settled the Territory of New Mexico (which then included Arizona), clashes erupted between the settlers and the Apaches. The temptation to plunder isolated ranches was too great for the Apaches, who had already established a raiding economy by their depredations against the Mexicans. Some Americans fueled it by wantonly killing any Indian they saw. The problem was exacerbated by a rotgut alcohol known as "Taos lightning," provided to the Indians not only by unscrupulous traders, but by settlers who used it to purchase protection from marauding bands. The government in Washington appeared largely uninterested in the problem, and different authorities often were at odds with each other over the gravity of the situation, and possible solutions. Already jealousy between civil and military authorities—a prominent theme in Bourke's diaries two decades later—was hindering attempts to control the situation. Efforts to force the freedom-loving Apaches onto reservations, while in some cases successful, by and large made matters worse.

In the late 1850s, the Apaches stole large herds of Mexican stock for sale in the United States, and large herds of U.S. stock for sale in Mexico. By 1860, they were in a full-scale war with both countries. They not only plundered, but also took captives for ransom. The abduction of a boy named Felix Ward[2] in 1860, would have lasting repercussions. Determined to get him back, Second Lt. George Bascom and a detachment of soldiers met with a band of Chiricahua

2. Felix Ward ultimately became a guide for the military, under the assumed name of Mickey Free.

warriors under Cochise, son-in-law and protégé of Mangas Coloradas, at Apache Pass, on February 4, 1861. When Cochise denied any knowledge of the boy, Bascom had the Indians surrounded and informed them they would be hostages until Felix was returned. Pulling a knife, Cochise managed to slash his way out, but six of his warriors were seized.

After a couple of days, Cochise appeared and advised Bascom that he had other prisoners to exchange, and was working to obtain Felix's release from the Apache band that held him. Bascom agreed, but the arrival of additional troops under First Lt. Isaiah Moore apparently convinced Cochise that a military expedition was being mounted against him. He murdered his own prisoners and left their mutilated bodies where the troops could find them. In retaliation, the six original Indian prisoners, along with three more captured by the soldiers, were hanged. They included Cochise's brother and two of his nephews. Cochise went on a rampage, and over the next two months, 150 whites were killed.

By this time, all movement through Apache territory was hazardous, unless it entailed large numbers of troops. In July 1862, Mangas and Cochise, with five hundred warriors, attempted to block Apache Pass. On July 15, however, Brig. Gen. James Carleton forced his way through with three hundred troops, and beat back the Apaches. Mangas received a severe chest wound, and was taken into Mexico for medical treatment. After his recovery, he hoped to arrange a peace. Carleton, however, had no intention of negotiating. In January 1863, Mangas was murdered by a detachment of troops whom he had met under a flag of truce.[3]

Mangas' death prompted Cochise to fight with a new fury. Over the next eight years, little progress was made either in subduing the Apaches or arranging a peace. To facilitate operations, the War Department created the Department of Arizona as a jurisdiction within the Military Division of the Pacific, and appointed Col. George Stoneman as commander. This did little to ease the situation, partly because Stoneman, who hated Arizona, maintained his headquarters at Drum Barracks, near Los Angeles, California, too far removed for effective command, and partly

3. The opening of the Apache Wars is discussed in Worcester, *Apaches*, Chapter 3; Faulk, *Crimson Desert*, Chapter 6; and Thrapp, *Conquest of Apacheria*, Chapter 2. A brief, but excellent summary of Mangas Coloradas' life and career is found in Hoxie, *Encyclopedia of North American Indians*, 354-55.

because Apachería extended into New Mexico, which was in an entirely different military jurisdiction.[4]

Additionally, Stoneman had no real stomach for handling the Apache depredations. He appears to have supported the Peace Policy implemented by President U.S. Grant, which called for settling the Indians on reservations, feeding and clothing them, and educating them. The goal was to make them productive citizens by the nineteenth century white definition, a goal that was alien to their own culture. Although Stoneman established a line of picket posts in the country of the Pinal and Tonto Apaches (which did little more than reduce the strength of the main garrisons), his overall view of the situation was totally unrealistic. He asked that the government send peace commissioners to negotiate a truce with the Apaches, and relieve the army of the burden of defending the department. When depredations continued, and complaints reached the president, Stoneman blamed the complaints on corrupt contractors, when, in fact, the ordinary farmers and ranchers were suffering from the raids.

The last straw, as far as local citizens were concerned, was a series of "feeding stations" that Stoneman established for Apaches who agreed to maintain the peace. The citizens contended they harbored renegades and would only encourage more depredations. At dawn, April 30, 1871, a group of Anglos, Hispanics, and Apache-hating Papago Indians attacked the feeding station at Camp Grant, near Tucson, massacring several dozen Aravaipa Apaches, raping women, and carrying off children. Blaming the massacre on Stoneman's policies, Arizona Territorial Gov. Anson P. K. Safford demanded his removal, and urged he be replaced by Lt. Col. George Crook, 23rd Infantry, who had gained a reputation as a successful Indian fighter in the Pacific Northwest. President Grant complied.[5]

A native of Ohio, Crook had served on the Indian frontier of northern California before the Civil War, and during the war attained the brevet rank of major general. When the war ended, he was

4. The Department of Arizona was formally established on April 5, 1870. New Mexico was attached to the Department of the Missouri, headquartered at Fort Leavenworth, Kansas, and itself an administrated jurisdiction of the Military Division of the Missouri, with headquarters in Chicago. Consequently, coordination of Apache operations in Arizona had to go first through Los Angeles and then through divisional headquarters in San Francisco, while New Mexico operations had to go through Fort Leavenworth and Chicago.

5. Altshuler, *Chains of Command*, 185ff.; Thrapp, *Conquest of Apacheria*, 80ff. The exact number of people killed at Camp Grant has never been determined, but probably was in the eighties.

commissioned to the active rank of lieutenant colonel and posted to Idaho, where he effectively ended Indian depredations. This led to his appointment as commanding officer of the Department of the Columbia, encompassing much of Washington, Oregon, and Idaho. Because his command responsibilities often exceeded the nominal authority of a lieutenant colonel, the War Department invoked his brevet rank of major general, both in the Columbia and in Arizona.[6]

After a brief stop at Drum Barracks, Crook continued to Tucson, the territorial capital. He brought two associates from the Columbia, Capt. Azor H. Nickerson, 23rd Infantry, who would serve as departmental adjutant, and Archie McIntosh, a civilian scout, who had performed ably in Indian campaigns in the Northwest, and would serve him again in Arizona. The remainder of his staff was chosen from officers already on station, whom he interviewed upon arrival. Bourke described the process in *On the Border With Crook*:

> He arrived in the morning, went up to the residence of his old friend, Governor Safford, with whom he lunched, and before sundown every officer within the limits of what was then called the southern district of Arizona was under summons to report to him. . . .
>
> From each he soon extracted all he knew about the country, the lines of travel, the trails across the various mountains, the fords where any were required for the streams, the nature of the soil, especially its products, such as grasses, character of the climate, the condition of the pack-mules, and all pertaining to them, and every other item of interest a commander could possibly want to have determined. But in reply not one word, not one glance, not one hint, as to what he was going to do or what he would like to do.

Crook selected Bourke and Second Lt. William J. Ross, 21st Infantry, as his aides-de-camp. He also decided to relocate departmental headquarters from Drum Barracks to Whipple Barracks at Prescott, Arizona, in order to exercise more effective command.[7]

6. Crook's story is told in Schmitt, ed., *General George Crook, His Autobiography*; and in Robinson, *General Crook*.

7. Bourke, *On the Border*, 108-09; Headquarters, Department of Arizona, General Orders No. 18, September 1, 1871, see Appendix 2.

Determined to carry the war to the Apaches, Crook inaugurated a series of expeditions to scour southern Arizona. Taking advantage of internal strife among the Indians, he employed disaffected Apaches as scouts, placing them under whites who could gain their respect and confidence. Although no decisive actions occurred, the expeditions were enough to convince Crook that with proper support, he could force hostile bands to take the defensive, keeping them away from the settlements and gradually wearing them down. His main goal appears to have been Cochise, but he was frustrated, in part because of that chief's tactical gifts, and in part by government interference.[8]

The first instance was in September, with the arrival of Vincent Colyer, secretary of the Board of Indian Commissioners, a quasi-official citizens' committee designated by congress to oversee the Department of the Interior's Indian Bureau. Charged with monitoring $70,000 that Congress had appropriated to establish reservations and provide the Apaches with subsistence, Colyer designated temporary reservations near military posts, and managed to get some four thousand Indians to move onto them. He also exposed corruption in the administration of the Indian Bureau. This success, however, appears to have strengthened his already naïve and simplistic view of the situation. Totally ignoring the warrior heritage and tradition of the Apaches, he believed they were a peaceful people who merely were retaliating for white outrages. While this might have been true of some Apaches, others enjoyed murder and pillage as much as some of the worst white riff-raff. Unwilling to consider any views that conflicted with his own, Colyer refused to meet with citizens who desired to present their cases. He also took a disdainful view of any Indians who did not fit his preconceived notions of how an Indian should be.

Although Colyer had no credibility in the West, his views nevertheless carried credence among Easterners, who accepted his claim that victims of Indian raids were bloodthirsty settlers being repaid in kind. His visit forced a prolonged suspension of military operations and, freed from pressure by the army, hostile bands stepped up their depredations. The turning point came November 5, when a band probably composed of Indians with white marauders attacked a stagecoach near the town of Wickenburg, killing six

8. Crook to AG USA, September 4, 1871, I, pp. 1-4, George Crook Letter Books, The Rutherford B. Hayes Library (microfilm edition); Crook to AAG, Military Division of the Pacific, December 7, 1871, I, p. 10, ibid.; Schmitt, *General George Crook*, 166-67; Bourke, *On the Border*, 144ff.

passengers and mortally wounding a seventh. Among the passengers was Bostonian Frederick W. Loring, whose background and Harvard education discredited Colyer in the East, and brought demands for retribution against the Indians.[9]

In response, Crook issued General Orders No. 10, requiring all Indians to report to reservations immediately, or be regarded as hostile. To avoid the appearance of being eager for war, he postponed action until February 1872. Before he could take the field, however, the government once again intervened by sending Brig. Gen. O. O. Howard to investigate the situation and, once again, try to find a solution. More practical than Colyer, Howard visited Arizona several times during 1872, determined to gather as much information as possible. He endorsed Crook's operations against hostile bands, while he worked to reassure those who were friendly. He negotiated a peace between the Apaches and their ancient enemies, the Pimas and Papagoes. At Howard's behest, President Grant abolished the scattered reservations created by Colyer, replacing them with two vast reservations at San Carlos on the Gila River, and at Camp Apache.[10] And finally, Howard achieved what many had deemed impossible—he ended the war with Cochise. Meeting personally with the Chiricahua chief, Howard gained a guarantee of peace, in turn giving the Chiricahuas a reservation in their homeland in the Dragoon Mountains. Not consulted about the treaty, Crook resented Howard's agreement, and never completely trusted Cochise. Even so, the peace lasted until the chief's death in 1874.[11]

Free from further government interference, Crook once again prepared to move against the Apaches. After several successful

9. The Board of Indian Commissioners was a citizens' group created by Congress in 1869 to oversee distribution of the Indian appropriation. Its members, who were appointed by President Grant, served without pay. With the president's support, the board assumed almost cabinet level status, and usurped the powers of Commissioner of Indian Affairs Ely S. Parker, eventually forcing him out of office. The board also dealt directly with Grant, rather than going through the secretary of the interior, who was legally responsible for Indian matters. However high minded, its members were not qualified for their roles, and based their actions largely on preconceived assumptions rather than reality. Thus the board only succeeded in further complicating an already chaotic situation. See Altshuler, *Chains of Command*, 198ff.; also Faulk, *Crimson Desert*, 168; Schmitt, *General George Crook*, 167-68; U.S. Department of the Interior, *Peace with the Apaches*, 28-29; Bancroft, *History*, 562-63.

10. Camp Apache was established in 1870 on the Mogollon Plateau to guard a proposed reservation in the White Mountains (later the Fort Apache Reservation). Upgraded to a fort in 1879, the fort was pivotal during the Apache campaigns of the 1870s and 1880s. The post was abandoned and transferred to the Indian Service in 1922. Altshuler, *Starting with Defiance*, 12.

11. Bancroft, *History*, 563-64. Howard's efforts are described in his autobiography, *My Life and Experiences Among Our Hostile Indians*, and in Sweeney, *Making Peace with Cochise*.

preliminary scouting expeditions in the summer and early fall of 1872, he reinvoked General Orders No 10. In November, three columns, each composed of cavalry and Indian scouts, were sent out from Camp Hualpai, and two more from Camp Date Creek.[12] His plan was to encircle the hostile bands, driving them into the Tonto Basin where the converging columns would crush them. His orders, as summarized by Bourke in *On the Border With Crook*, were clear and concise.

> Briefly, they directed that the Indians should be induced to surrender in all cases where possible; where they preferred to fight, they were to get all the fighting they wanted, and in one good dose instead of a number of petty engagements, but in either case were to be hunted down until the last one in hostility had been killed or captured. Every effort should be made to avoid the killing of women and children. Prisoners of either sex should be guarded from ill-treatment of any kind. When prisoners could be induced to enlist as scouts, they should be enlisted, because the wilder the Apache was, the more he was likely to know of the wiles and stratagems of those still out in the mountains, their hiding-places and intentions. No excuse was to be accepted for leaving a trail; if horses played out, the enemy must be followed on foot, and no sacrifice should be left untried to make the campaign short, sharp, and decisive.[13]

This campaign, a series of scouting expeditions designed to seek out, engage, and destroy, was so effective that Dan Thrapp, one of the leading historians of the Apache Wars, later named it "The Grand Offensive." This Grand Offensive, which to some degree sustained Crook's image as an Indian fighter for the rest of his life, marks the beginning of Bourke's diary.[14]

12. Camp Hualpai was established in 1869 at the toll gate on the road between Prescott and Fort Mojave, about forty miles northwest of Prescott. Troops from the post scouted against Yavapai Indians. The post was no longer necessary after Crook's offensive of 1872-73, and was abandoned in August 1873. Camp Date Creek, originally designated Camp McPherson, was established sixty miles southwest of Prescott to guard the reservation for the Yavapais, Mojaves, and affiliated groups. It was abandoned after the reservations and military posts were consolidated. Altshuler, *Starting with Defiance*, 25-26, 32-33, Frazer, *Forts of the West*, 10.

13. Bourke, *On the Border With Crook*, 182.

14. The Grand Offensive is discussed in Thrapp, *Conquest of Apacheria*, Chapter 10, and Robinson, *General Crook*, Chapter 9.

Field Notes,
Scouts in
Arizona Territory

Bvt Maj Genl George Crook

Commanding.

From Nov 18th 1872

to April 8th 1873.

John G. Bourke,

2nd Lieut, 3rd Cav,

A.D.C.

Preceding page. Title page of the first volume of Bourke's manuscript. This volume actually commences on November 20, 1872, and ends April 7, 1873.

Chapter 1

❖

❖

❖

❖

❖

Crook's Offensive

Nov 20th 1872

Left [Camp] Verde,[1] 9 a.m. Crossed [Verde] river and passed north about 5 1/2 miles in a general north and north x east direction, climbed a mesa and halted for pack-train. Ground [is] Lava, vegetation, cactus and palo verde.[2]

Still north x east 3 miles. Keeping in a very hilly country. Rio Verde to left, Beaver Creek to right. The perpendicular distance between these two streams cannot be much over 6 miles, but very high & rough hills intervene. Red-Rock country dead ahead.

Passed north 1 mile, east 3 miles to Beaver Creek.

Camp. Wood. Water and Grass. Beaver Creek here flows nearly east and west—making a small bend from its general north & south course. Had a first class supper of wild-duck, antelope steak & fried fish.

1. Camp Verde was established in 1865 on the Rio Verde to protect a nearby farming community. Initially called Camp Lincoln, it was renamed in 1868 to avoid confusion with other posts named in memory of Abraham Lincoln. With the arrival of additional troops for a permanent garrison in 1871, Camp Verde outgrew its site, and a year later was relocated to a larger area away from the river. The Rio Verde Reservation was established nearby, but was closed in 1875 when the Indians were reconcentrated at San Carlos. Verde was upgraded to fort in 1879, and abandoned in 1890. Altshuler, *Starting with Defiance*, 59-62; Frazer, *Forts of the West*, 14.

2. Palo verde (*parkinsonia aculeata*), also called paloverde, retama, and horsebean, is a thorny shrub or tree that can grow as high as thirty feet. It has long, delicate leaves, and blooms of small yellow flowers. Loughmiller, *Texas Wildflowers*, 134.

11 1/2 miles

Thursday, Nov. 21st, 1872   4 miles.

Left Beaver Creek northeast along the Creek until we joined the New Mexico Road at the cross[in]g—then north x east for 15 miles passing through a juniper country and up grade all day—passed over an open grass country about north—then rather more east for 2 miles up grade and in pine woods. Camped at Stoneman's Lake on left side of road.

Met broken down wagons from Santa Fe 6 miles west by south from this Camp—22 miles

Wood, Water and grass.

33 1/2 miles

Friday, Nov 22nd, 1872

Broke Camp at sun up—Marched northeast, up grade for 10 miles— then east for 3 miles about 2 1/2 miles from Camp, road crossed little spring—stopped at Saute Sp[ring]S for the train to close up— moved East for 6 miles and east x south for 3 miles—stopped at Jones Camp—Tanks on left of Road—

21 o[r] 22 miles

Country all day was grazing land—very elevated with some pine and occasionally, a little white poplar. Indian signals seen all day to South   21 miles

About 8 miles out from Camp of 21st there is a spring on right of road, about 300 or 400 yds from it; in a copse of cottonwood. Genl Crook says this spring has an abundance of good cold water. Camp this night (22nd) had plenty of wood and grass, but no water for the animals, the tank being frozen—water for cooking was obtained by melting ice. Ground all day was a lava soil. General Crook shot a fine, fat goose this morning.

Saturday Nov 23d Camp aroused at 3 A.M. Made coffee, breakfasted and started about one hour before dawn—Moved South one mile South East one mile. South x East half mile East half mile North West half mile, then around corner of big mesa (about 500 yds long) and a general North East and North x East course for about 18 miles, passing between two large mesas with timbered sides (juniper) and perpendicular crests, halted and made camp—Water in tank in deep arroyo on right. Ice six and eight inches thick. Arroyo is a feeder of the Colorado Chiquito. San Francisco Mountain on our left and rear, all day, about 60 miles distant.

Ground all day has been gravelly and sandy. Ant hills along road have been disturbed by diamond hunters. Indian signs plenty and fresh. Wood, Water & Grass plenty. Country generally open along trail, with good grass. Plenty of wood, juniper all day.

About one and a half miles from this camp, on left hand side of the road there is a dry tank, which evidently has plenty of water in rainy season.

Distance marched	25 miles
(on Morrow's Sketch)	18 miles

Sunday, Nov 24th, 1872

Broke camp one hour before Sunrise—Marched North East across an elevated table-land, well grassed for 7 miles* passed between two low mesas of shale; ground now became less fertile, grass and wood more and more scanty until we reached the Colorado Chiquito, 18 miles; after crossing, we turned East, marched 5 miles, and camped. Wood, drift cottonwood plenty: water, from river good, but full of sediment. Grass poor. Saw no game to-day, and no fresh Indian signs.

Saw the country of the Moquis [Hopis] to the North and North North West.

Distance to-day	25 miles

Monday, Nov 25th

Broke camp at daylight—East South East for 22 miles keeping in sight of river all day—river very sinuous in its course—about 19 miles from camp passed a ruined house on river bank, passed between two sandstone buttes, turned East, went three miles, along river, crossed it and camped. Wood and water plenty & good—grass fair. Saw no camp & no signs of Indians.

Total distance about 25 @ 26 miles

Note—There is a drywash on this road about 3 [miles] from to-days Camp.

Tuesday Nov 26th 1872

Broke camp at daylight—Weather extremely cold—Moved in a general Southerly direction all day to Chevelon's Fork (?)† about 3 miles out from Col[orado] Chiq[ito] passed between 2 sandstone buttes—country barren about 15 miles, passed between 2 other buttes; country now became more hilly covered with juniper—road

---

* Water on right hand in tanks, about one mile from road.
† Silver Creek.

sandy and from time to time rocky—road sinuous about 30 miles from Col Chiquito struck the Chevelon's Fork (?) and camped— Water plenty, grass & wood scarce.

Chevelon's Fork here flows from South South West to North North East.

Total march of the day   30 miles

Wednesday Nov 27th, 1872.

Broke camp before daylight. Weather very cold. Last night was the coldest by far, since leaving Prescott. Breakfasted on wild duck shot last evening.

Moved South East, 7 miles, passed what is known as Stoneman's Camp, no water—moved South East 5 miles struck the lower end of the stream flowing from Silver Sp[rings]. This water pours into Shevelon's Fork. Still South East 3 miles further to Silver Sp[rings], where we are camped. Grass on adjacent hills, plenty of wood (cedar or juniper) in vicinity and the water good. This is one of the largest springs I have ever seen in Arizona. Road to-day sandy in places. First 3 miles out from Camp had Shevelon's Fork on our Left, crossed it just after leaving camp. Saw flocks of ducks on left. Weather moderated about miday.

Total distance,   15 miles

Genl. Crook killed thirty eight wild ducks and Lt. Ross and Mr. McCoy killed a black tailed deer, which dressed about 175 o[r] 200 lbs. Weather moderated. This night was not very cold.

Thursday, Nov. 28th, 1872.

Camp aroused at 3 1/2 A.M. Had coffee and a fine breakfast of juicy venison, wild duck, ham, &&. Marched at 6.30—about half an hour before sun-rise. Moved East South East and South East all day going up grade till about 11 a.m. Country getting very hilly—ground of a basaltic formation, but covered with rich grasses. Entered dense pine forest and commence[d] going down grade. Came to forks of New Mexico Road. Saw camp fire still burning and fresh wagon tracks 22 miles. Kept up same general direction, going down grade—found no water at the Spring indicated in Morrow's Map. About 33 miles, found water in a Spring on left of road—Camped.

Wood in abundance (pine forest). Water plenty and good. Grass d[itt]o.

Total distance   33 miles

Marched 8 hours and over, at 4 miles per hour

An excellent spring at Forks of Road

Weather very fine—clear sky

The vicinity of this camp is very mountainous. Genl C reported finding a number of springs to the East and Lieut Ross found some to West of Camp—name of camp is Pleasant Grove.

Friday. Moved in a general direction to Camp Apache, 23 miles, found water about 3 or 4 miles out—frozen—about 5 miles from Apache crossed one fork of Rio Sierra Blanca, passed over divide, crossed the other fork of same river and entered post near the Brewery. Came through a pass in the Mogollon Range about 6 miles from Camp—23 miles.

Saturday, Nov 30th. Rem[aine]d at Apache

Men employed fixing aparejos &ct.[3]

Sunday, Dec 1st, D[itt]o. D[itt]o.

Camp Apache is probably one of the most beautiful sites in the U.S. The post is at present ably commanded by Capt. Randall 23[rd] U.S. Infantry.

Monday, Dec 2. Remained at Post.

Tuesday, Dec 3d. Left Post, going South x a little West, passed High Mesa on our right just after leaving Post. High hills on left. Hills break away in potreros,[4] crossed Sierra B[lanca] river about 1 1/2 miles from Camp. Kelly's Peak about due West from Apache. Turned West and went up on top of divide—trail rocky—springs to Right. On top of trail met two Indians from Grant with letters from Apache. Marched South West [by] West, over a grassy mesa land. Conical peak in front. Before going on the mesa had river on our right for about one mile. Went about 10 miles from Apache and then commenced the descent to the Rio Prieto. Trail very rough, filled with lava boulders. Camped on left bank of river. Wood, Water and Grass. The river flows with a very rapid current, water pure & clear, oak & pine trees on bank. Rapids in river just below Camp. Distance 12 @ 14 [miles].

Genl. C. shot a shell drake.

Wednesday, Dec 4th—Broke camp at sun-up. Went South West x

3. The *aparejo* is a packing rig of ancient and obscure origin, still used in the Middle East, Spain, and Mexico. It was brought to the Western Hemisphere by the early Spaniards. Essentially it consists of two leather pads stuffed with straw and stiffened at the front and rear edges by hardwood sticks. They hang down the sides of the mule, joined at the top by a leather gusset. The pads spread the load evenly over the mule's back and sides to avoid stress or soreness. See Hicks, "Aparajo."

4. Meadows, pastures.

West for 500 yds, then turned to ascend hill. Wound our way up a very bad and rocky trail to summit. Mesa cov[ere]d. with coarse grass and timber. Saw little stream on our right emptying into Rio Prieto, below our Camp. Went over mesa about 6 miles and then commenced to descend. Went down about 2 miles crossed over dry bed of a stream, probably head of east fork San Carlos. [P]assed on down grade. Struck a cañon coming from North East to South West with water. Saw a spring in the solid rock on left of trail. Country filled with Lava blocks. Timber principally oak and Juniper. Some pine. Saw a Bear on High Hill to left about 8 miles. Moved down this cañon to South. High hills on right & left. Cañon filled with scrub oak & juniper. Passed an old mescal pit 3 miles. Kept down cañon still going east for 5 miles. River now commences to run water. Saw place where there must be a spring on mountain side to left. Saw where little streams come in on right & left—passed all this time through oak grove—trails became very rocky & difficult—emerged from cañon, saw Pa. S. Carlos [San Carlos Peak] dead ahead—Mt. Trumbull and Green's P[ea]k beyond—Pinal Mountains to South West. Apache Mountains to West—Sierra S[ant]a Catalina West South West—Mt. Graham East South East—Turned South West and went over rough lava mesa. The plateau was now badly broken by cañons and trail wound more to South. Went South West about 5 miles—came to a cañon, with Lava sides & bed, very bad—water at bottom. Also passed tank about 1 mile from last place.

5 miles Passed down into cañon; trail very rough—one of the worst I have ever seen—after much labor reached the bottom. Found two cañons—one from North East, with plenty of water—one from North with a small amount, after junction, water flows South West. This is a very large stream and is probably the main East Fork of San Carlos and, if so, maps are all wrong. Sides of cañons, nearly vertical and precipices of basalt on all sides. Turned back on our trail and went North East for about 8 miles until we struck a small creek tributary of San Carlos, coming from East same one we left at noon, [it is the] main branch—crossed creek and turned West, went along creek for about 3 miles, crossed, turned South West, climbed high mesa, crossed over and found stream coming from North West, made by spring in rocks, turned South, passed long this stream about a mile turned East, climbed high hills and commenced descent on other side. Trail very steep and rocky, going North East about 2 miles

came into valley of San Carlos on left of high butte, turned and came down river about 5 miles above the junction of East and West forks and made a dry camp, no supper.

Total distance about   60 miles.

Thursday Dec 5th Marched to Camp on Gila about five miles below junction of San Carlos to which camp we marched this morning. Plenty of cottonwood, water from river and good grass on mesa.

10 miles.

Friday Dec 6. [18]72 Moved from camp about daybreak due West five hundred yards to small range which we crossed turning South and passing arroyo and going South East, passing along the arroyo (Ventana)⁵ about 5 miles, crossed high and rocky divide turning somewhat our course to South. Entered Cañon Gabilau⁶ South East about 3 miles found no water but saw plenty of cottonwood. Green's Peaks ahead and to East South East. Saw large mountain on right and large flat-topped peak in front. Turned to right crossing over this mountain, passed on left hand cañon flowing into cañon Galibau, and kept along range divd [dividing] waters of Galibau from those [of] San Carlos. Saw a big mesa in front. Crossed water of Deer Creek, here flowing West by little North, turned South— and going South by East reached camp, about 1 pm, Tanks in Rocks. Wood (cedar) scarce. Water sufficient. Grass, plenty but coarse, camp very poor. Day cold & windy. Lost (2) horses this morning.

18 Miles

Satd [Saturday] Dec 7th Left Camp 7.30 am. Rained very badly. Wind cold [from] North East. Marched South x East about 4 miles, getting to top of mesa—country very rough—turned South and South South West for 5 miles, going across water flowing South—passed down steep hill to Aravaypa cañon—turned West x North (2p[oin]ts) to [Camp] Grant.⁷ 11 miles, down Cañon—;—20 miles—Aravaypa runs dry within 3 miles [of] post. Took up our [quarters in?] Maj Royal's House. Found that 112 Bucks were reported present at Grant. Found Maj. Brown.

20 miles

Rained all night—

Dec 8th. Remained at Grant.

5. "Window."
6. Galibau Canyon.
7. Because of references to Aravaipa Creek, Bourke obviously means the old location of Camp Grant.

Monday. Dec 9th. Remained at Grant.

Conference with Indians and Genl Crook explains his policy.

Es-kim-in-zin promised to aid in the extermination of hostile Apaches. (31) Apaches enlisted as Scouts. The rest of the day occupied in providing them with clothing, arms &ct.

Tuesday Dec 10th. Enlisted ten more Indian Scouts. Padre Antonio arrived from Tucson, with news of general interest. Cochies Band in Drago[o]n Mountains. An escaped captive reports that Cochis intends to break out in early spring.

Capt Leib preparing to move out to Mt Graham to build new post.[8]

Wednesday, Dec 11th. Genl. C. rem[aine]d at Camp Grant, but expedition under command of Maj. Brown, Insp. [Inspector] Genl. left Grant, consisting of (31) Indian Scouts, under the Indian Chief Bocon,[9] Co. "L" 5th Cav. Capt. Taylor, Co. M 5th Cav 1[st] Lt. Almy. Lt. Ross ADC & Lt Bourke accompanied exped[ition]. Pack-train of 60 mules under charge of Mr. Bartlett and Mr. Hewitt. Guides, Antonio, Joe Felmer and Jose Maria (the latter did not join). Mr. Daly came along as a volunteer bacon chawer. Left camp at 4 P.M. travelled along San Pedro, North North West for about 4 miles. Halted and camped. Sent back for more amm[unitio]n. Have now 4800 R[oun]ds. of extra cartridges. Genl Crook has now an exped[itio]n. out from [Camp] Hualpai of 3 Cos. 5th Cav., under B[reve]t Col Mason, one from Verde, under care of the 1st, of 2 cos 5[th] & 1 of 1st [Cavalry], one from Apache, under Randall, 23d Inf[antry].; of 2 of 1st Cav. and one of 23d Inf and the present one. Each Command is amply equipped and provided with from 30 to 100 Indian guides. The common objective point is the Tonto basin, arriving in which country the Com[man]d's are so arranged as to divide and scatter in all directions.

I am afraid we shall miss much of the fun as the other Comd's being in the field earlier than we, may have all the work to themselves. If we clean out the Tonto this winter we shall give Cocheis hell in the spring.

One of the Indians got sick during the night and was sent back to Grant.

8. The new post of Camp Grant in Sulphur Spring Valley, about two miles from Mount Graham. The post was upgraded to fort in 1879. It was abandoned in 1905 because of a water shortage, and turned over to the State of Arizona in 1912. Altshuler, *Starting with Defiance*, 30-32.

9. Literally "Big Mouth," the Spanish nickname for the Apache scout leader Esquimasquin, not to be confused with Eskiminzin.

Mem[orandum]. We haven't enough Surgeons in Arizona. There should be one for each scouting command in the field.

Thursday, Dec 12th, Broke Camp about 8 a.m., moved North West along San Pedro 2 miles then North & North East towards the Saddle Mountain & went about 1 or 2 more [miles].

Country passed—alluvial.

Heavy dew last night. Weather to day clear and mild. Kept on North for about 4 miles leaving the San Pedro (flowing North West) to left, trail going over hills. Came to an Arroyo. Indians scraped away sand and found water in small quantity under a bluff of conglomerate, rock. Passed North about 3 miles. "Dos Narices"[10] or Saddle Mountain on right then into an arroyo which soon became a feeble stream, joining Deer Creek, coming in from North and bending to West, soon joining Gila [River], above junction of San Pedro. Passed Sp[ring]. at or near [the] head of the arroyo. The 1st water is laid down on map as Saddle Mountain Creek, the spring is one at which I saw a fight between a tarantula & a tarantula hawk in 1870.

Turned West & North, going over a small divide and coming down into cañon of Rock Creek. The Creek, where we touched it, was flowing but soon ran dry. Its direction was South West and then West, through a gorge, to Gila. High mountains to South, bordering on Gila, and South of Rock Creek Started again, going West across high hills 9 miles to Rio Gila, which we crossed and camped. Wood, Water & Grass. Our general direction to day has been about North. Day's march. . . . . 18 miles.

Friday Dec 13th. Broke Camp at day-break. Moved about due West 2 or 3 miles, going over a small divide and coming down into a dry bed of a stream (flowing East South East) which I think is Disappointment Creek. Country level. High mountains to left and right. Gila flows on other side of mountains to right. Kept on West about 2 or 3 miles, up mountain side. High hills on right & left and Pina Mountain directly on our Front. Indians left us, going to the right hand, following 2 fresh horse tracks (5) Indians remained with us. Kept North, keeping between High Hills. Came down into a potrero, where we camped. Good grass on hill side, cottonwood, scrub oak & a little cedar in vicinity. Saw some little pine to day. Water of Camp flowing South. Water scarce. Just before reaching

10. "Two Noses."

camp saw direction and indications (trees) of a water course coming in from North West.

Distance to-day. . . 16 miles

Saturday, Dec 14th Broke camp at daylight. Moved North up Disapp[ointmen]t Creek about 2 miles, crossed hills and turned North East after marching among elevated hills, came to H[ea]dwaters of West fork of San Carlos. Country well grassed. Plenty scrub oak—Manzanita[11]—Juniper—and on hill top—Pine. Ascertained that the Mountains we are now in are the Pinal, with which the Mescal Range must connect. Courier from Es-qui-mas-quin now came in to say that he had followed trail of yesterday and ascertained whither the hostile Apaches had gone. Command halted on brow of a hill—one of the foot hills of Pinal Range. . . .10 m

Triplets to East North East   Natana Butte North East   Mt Trumbull East East North East. Open country to our front and beyond that the Sierra Apache. Marched West North West and South West for about 4 miles. Going to a little cañon in Pinal Range on North side. 12 miles.

Wood in great quantities—Pinal, oak, manzanita, juniper and some few cottonwoods in close proximity to camp. Water in cañon, flowing at intervals. H[ea]d Waters of San Carlos Westfork, Grass—fine gramma.

Sierra San Carlos East North East. Natanas Butte North East.

Es-qui-mas-quin rejoined us at this Camp, bringing information as to the Indians whose trail he had followed yesterday. They have evidently gone in the direction of the West end of Sierra Pinal or to Superstition Mountains.

Sunday, Dec 15th Broke camp 7 a.m. Marched West, one mile, North West 2 miles and South West about 2 miles, the last turn taking us down through a smooth valley—passed a small dry arroyo with cottonwoods, running toward North West possibly a branch of Pinal Creek are now behind Mountains in front of which we camped last night. It and the entire range (Pinal) on left are covered with pine on summits. Hills to-day well grassed with blue & white gramma. Saw large Indian trail going North and North East. Women & children evidently with this party about 40 in no.[number.] Mountains to

11. Manzanita (*Arctostaphylos var.*) A member of the heath family. Bourke may have been referring either to *A. uva-ursi*, sometimes called kinnikinnick or bearberry, or *A. nevadensis*, also known as pinemat manzanita. Spellenberg, *National Audubon Society Field Guide*, 478-79.

Right, about 15 miles away, across open country, probably part of Sierra Apache. Kept South West going 4 miles passing a number of dry arroyos, which in rainy season are confluents of Pinal Creek. Made camp on a creek flowing North. Are now about West end of Sierra Pinal.

Wood, water & grass abundant. . . .In pursuance of a plan made last night Esquimasquin with Mr. Felmer, Macintosh, Antonio and 25 Indians, started this morning to follow the trail spoken of yesterday. This party was to move one day in advance of the main body, sending us back word each morning at what point we are to camp and also one of their party to guide us to the exact spot so as to avoid all possibility of mistake. In case the advance party suddenly came upon a rancheria or a band of hostile Indians beyond their strength, they are to halt, send messages to Major Brown and we are to join them by night and then united we will creep upon the enemy. From the number and variety of fresh tracks seen during to day's march, it is evident, the hostile Apache are much alarmed at our presence in their country and are seeking safety in hasty flight. I still adhere to the opinion that we shall encounter a very large band in the Sierra Superstición[12] or the extreme North West corner of the Sierra Pinal. If the troops from Hualpai, [Camp] Date Creek, Verde, Apache and [Camp] McDowell[13] only do half their duty we shall be able to inflict upon the hitherto incorrigible Apaches a chastisement from the effects of which they can never recover.

8 PM Rec[eive]d a dispatch from Archie MacIntosh stating that the advance guard had found a rancheria of Indians and had exchanged shots, wounding one Apache who however, managed to escape through the thick undergrowth on top of the Mountain. Also stated that the Indians know our Com[man]d was in their country & had detailed spies to watch our movements from the tops of the Mountain Ranges. Retreating Indians had fallen back in direction of the Superstition Mountains. A camp was also designated for to-morrow night. Indians who came as courriers [sic] brought some trophies left by the hostile Indians in their retreat and said that (12) horse-tracks had been counted on the trail. Weather to-night clear and warm.

12. Superstition Mountains. Bourke used the English and Spanish interchangeably.
13. Camp McDowell was established in 1865, and designated a fort in 1870. Troops from McDowell, with the assistance of Pima scouts, successfully campaigned against Apaches. Fort McDowell was transferred to the Interior Department in 1890. Altshuler, *Starting with Defiance*, 37-38; Frazer, *Forts of the West*, 11.

Monday Dec 16th Broke camp 6.35 a.m. Moved northerly across foothills of Pinal Mountain for about 2 miles, then for same distance down on other side—came down into valley of Pinal Creek (dry at this point) flowing to North turned North West and crossed over low hills—7 miles. While going down the sides of the high Mountain which forms one edge (North East) of Pinal saw to the north and in valley of Pinal Creek about 8 miles ahead of us, a great cloud of smoke resting over some cottonwood trees, where the Creek was evidently a running stream. Indian boys with us said this was the Camp of an American scouting party and it is more than probable we are now within easy communicating distance of the Comd. from Apache or Verde, or both. Country this morning finely grassed with gramma. Saw a small turret-shaped, barren peak to East of north about 8 miles, one of foot hills of Sierra Apache. From the Mountain tops to day saw the Sierra Matizal[14] to West by a little North. Travelled over the hills, trail very winding, but keeping in a general West & North direction, about 2 miles. Hills covered with fine grass—came down upon North fork of Pinal, flowing from High Mountain on our left—to the North—about 2 miles to North, joins with other branch flowing North West and the main stream in North West direction, passing to the West of the high pointed Mountain (Sierra Apache) which last night was to North of our camp. This High Mountain, I think, is the Western end of Sierra Apache. Pinal Creek also flows to West of the Turret Butte, already spoken of, and which is a spur from this high conical Mountain. Sierra Apache seen to North West & North. Turned South West marching up bed of Western branch of the Pinal—went about a mile—turned South and went about 2 1/2 miles. Saw trail made by a scouting party of Pima & Papago Indians this morning. Camped in a little cove on West end of Sierra Pinal. Wood, water & grass. Indications of Gold & Silver. Water in cañon. . . . 10 or 12 miles.

630 P.M. McIntosh, Felmer, Esquimasquin and the rest of the advanced guard, returned to camp, reporting that shortly after daybreak this morning they came upon the rancheria of the party they were pursuing yesterday; that owing to their being discovered by the hostile Apache, they were unable to surround the wickyups,[15]

14. Mazatzal.

15. The wickiup, or "wickyup" as Bourke spelled it, was a shelter used by the westernmost Apaches. It was a domed or vaulted structure made by poles or saplings bent over and tied together in the center, and covered with brush, grass, canvas, skin, or whatever other material

but that upon making a spirited attack, the hostile party fled, leaving everything behind—our Indian allies pursued for (5) miles, but were unable to overtake the flying enemy. Upon desisting from the pursuit, our men gathered up and destroyed everything belonging to the band of Chunts (who they ascertained was in command of those opposed to them). This is the man who lately killed in cold blood a Mexican boy at Camp Grant [*See Appendix 1 "Chunz"*]. Altogether the movement has been very successful because, at the present season, these incorrigible devils must feel keenly every deprivation, and [the] more that they are without an article of clothing, a particle of food, or any necessaries, the better winter winds will cause them to perish upon the tops of the Mountains. The Indians fled to the South West towards the point where the Sierra Superstición abuts upon the Rio Gila; our advanced guard reports camping last night at a spring—El ojo de "Chuparosa" (Humming Bird Springs) on the summit of the Pinal Mountains where no white man had hitherto been. [T]welve families comprise the band of Chunts, because there were that number of fires in his Camp.

Tuesday, Dec 17th. Remained in camp. I have reason to regret my inability to describe in fitting terms the beauty of the place in which we now are situated; at the extreme North West corner of the Sierra Pinal, we find ourselves surrounded by the lofty foothills of that range—upon the summits we can just discern forests of pine and cedar, while in closer proximity to us are noble oak, scattered in clusters of twos & threes, giving shade to our men and animals. Luxuriant grasses carpet the hills, delicious water trickles down over the rocks in the cañon to our left. In places, we have a running stream; in others the water buries itself beneath the sands or collects in tanks of considerable depth and capacity. Everything seems quiet, nothing disturbs the stillness of the evening, but the tinkling of the bells in the pack trains or the neighing of animals in the herds of the cavalry companies.

This night the Indians had a great war dance, of which, the general arrangement was similar to those of the Hualpais who accompanied us last year. Some of the young bucks arrayed themselves in muslin & calico captured in the Rancheria yesterday and feigning the manners of women, received their male companions a few singing

---

was available. The size and quality of construction depended largely on the availability of materials. See Haley, *Apaches*, 80.

in concert, though not in harmony, supplied the necessary music, and the dancing once commenced was continued with undiminished vigor until near midnight. I was unable to learn the purpose of the chorus, but to the best of my belief, it referred to past exploits against their enemies and promises of what might be expected in the future. The name of Chunts was frequently heard from which I infer that a dismal future awaits that refractory cuss, and those who adhere to his fortunes.

A messenger [was] sent to night to Genl. Crook.

Wednesday Dec 18th Broke camp at 6[:]35 a.m. Moved back on our own trail and afterwards on a generally North trail, from the point where we reached Pinal Creek yesterday to the place where it joins with East Branch, then West entering West end of the Sierra Apache and going up a small cañon which contained water flowing from the North—passed up this cañon about 3 miles turned East x North at [a] point where a tributary came in from North—marched about 4 miles in new direction and camped on running stream (branch of Pinal) Wood. Water. and Grass.

Weather cold. Rained and snowed all day. No fresh signs

Distance to-day. . . . . 15 miles

Thursday, Dec 19th On acc[oun]t. Of the rainy weather yesterday and the inclemency last night, the Comd. rem[aine]d in camp this morning rather later than usual, the early morning hours being devoted to inspecting aparajoes ascertaining and repairing damages, and drying blankets & clothing. Men were not aroused until 6 a.m. altho' the packers were busily at work long before that hour. Marched at 8.45 am. Going North over the Mountains, passed down a cañon, over another hill down the West side and then followed an arroyo, which was running from North to South. After going in the general Northerly direction about 3 miles, halted to allow the packers to close up. Hills covered with snow—weather cool but mild, sun shining brightly, but sky filled with low hanging clouds. We may expect more bad weather. Felmer, Antonio and the greater part of the Indians left us, going to North East they will scout the country on our left and join us to-morrow at a warm spring this side of the Rio Salado. Marched in a general Northerly direction varying not more than two or three points to East or West for about 9 miles, the last six being in a cañon, enclosed by high hills, came to a stream bubbling out of the rocks flowing from

South to North. Camped. Wood, Water & Grass in plenty. On our left we had a peak which is the cone I called Yeaston Peak in my notes of a previous scout, made in these Mountains in July 1870.[16] Saw great quantities of fine granite to day, also some prophyry and beautiful conglomeration. The stream we are now on is an effluent of Rio Salado. Saw the Sierra Ancha, to North and West distant in a right line about 8 miles.   Today's march not more than. . . . . .12 miles.

The maps of the Engineer Bureau do not correctly lay down the Sierra Apache, making it too narrow from North to South. There fore we have had excellent luck in the location of our camps, that of to-day being no exception to the general rule. Maj. Brown now proposes to cross the Rio Salado, push up Tonto Creek, or some other tributary, and, if any hostile bands be in that vicinity, it is evident we must certainly catch them or drive them into the hands of the parties operating from the North, who, by the way, seem to have experienced some obstacles in the performance of their duties, as we can see no signs of them.

Weather fine. Sky cloudy.

Passed through a little pine timber to day. Also some juniper. Both kinds rather small. Sombrero Butte due north of us. Night clear and cold. Hard frosting.

Friday Dec 20th. Broke camp 7.45, crossed High Hills to West of camp (about 1/2 mile): then turned South by a little West for about 2 miles, West one half mile passing among high hills, with rocky tops (running about East and West) turned West opposite little butte put down in map. Country hilly. 3 miles.

Moved West by a little South and then by a little North, so that we described an arc of a circle, passing through a very rough country, high Mountains on both sides; going down grade about 5 miles, until we came to a little stream flowing from the Mountains on left— turned to right going up hill until we came to summit where we overlooked countryside to North and North West. Saw the four peaks of Sierra Matzitzal to West. 8 miles.

N.B. The little creek we left to South a few hundred yds. Below us, at base of Mountain flows about West and must empty into Rio Salado. That on which we camped last night also joined that River. Marched about North West for one or two miles further, crossing

16. These notes are among those lost.

Salt River[17] and camping on right Bank. Wood. Water and Grass plenty. This camp is not so secluded as others have been. Rio Salado here about South West but just to right of where we crossed it, flows more in a due North and South direction. Sierra Ancha directly in front of our Camp.

Distance to day. . . . . .9 or 10 miles

Saturday Dec 21st Rem[aine]d in Camp to day. No Indian signs have been seen for two or three days; weather pleasant, but indications of another storm. Day devoted to overhauling aparajoes inspecting condition of animals and rest. A scout is to start to day towards Tonto Creek the country about old Camp Reno[18] unless some fresh trails might occasion a change of direction. 3 PM a scout party consisting of Felmer, Antonio, 15 soldiers and Esquimisquin [sic] with 25 Indians started for the country to the North West and North of us. They will rout out any bands they may find on the East of Pinto Creek unless they should happen to encounter a greatly superior force. It is also expected that when they join us at or near the site of old Camp Reno, they will bring us information upon which to base our calculations as to whereabouts of the Commands operating from the posts to the North of us. I do not doubt the ability and enthusiasm of the officers serving with the other expeditions, but the absence of signs of alarm on the part of the hostile Indians— there being no signal fires seen from the summits of Ranges overlooking or bordering upon the Tonto Basin since our departure from Grant—all this leads me to apprehend that something must have occured to obstruct the movements of Randall and Carr. It will be remembered that previous to our arrival at Camp Apache, alarm signals were seen showing from the Mountains to the South and South East of Camp Verde; then only one party, Mason's, was moving out. Now there are eleven companies of soldiers and about 200 or perhaps 250 Indians, in the Tonto Basin, these numbers being exclusive of any operating from McDowell or Prescott.

The beans issued to day and yesterday as rations to the Indians and soldiers were found to be over two thirds dirt. F. L. Austin is contractor at Grant and for this item of rascality his name should

17. Rio Salado.
18. Camp Reno was a temporary post formerly located in the Tonto Valley thirty-four miles from Camp McDowell. Reno was established in 1868, but the site proved impractical. It was abandoned in 1870. Altshuler, *Starting with Defiance*, 49-50; Heitman, *Historical Register*, 2:537.

never again by allowed to appear as an army contractor in Arizona. The officer who rec[eive]d such stuff should be cashiered.

Sunday Dec 22 Broke camp 7.45 am

Marched in a general Westerly direction for about 2 miles, crossing high hills, leaving Rio Salado to our left. Halted to allow packs to close up. By compass are now about 10° South of West from last night's camp. Scenery beautiful, grass very nutritious. Sierra Matizal [sic] dir[ectly] West. Sierra Superstición South West South 8°. . . . . .2 or 3 miles.

Marched in a Westerly course down the Salt River, crossing it twice, but returning to the right hand side. Just as we were ([after a march of] 7 miles) preparing to go into camp, heard shots to north—several volleys being fired in quick succession. Started at a gallop in the direction of the sound and after travelling about 10 miles or more, we crossed to the head of a little cañon which I think is the same as that laid down on maps as Racoon Creek, camped the command and sent out scouting parties in all directions. Soon found a rancheria, abandoned this morning, and carried off or destroyed everything they had left behind—Tobacco, meal, baskets &c&. Indians had been preparing to plant at this point, where the stalks of last year's corn are still standing. Just at this point Felmer and party returned bringing three prisoners—two women and (1) child—reported having attacked a party of Apaches with the above results. I omitted to state that I found a descriptive list, issued at Camp Apache, showing that some of these Indians had drawn rations at that post, Sept. 16, 1872, Signed "M Soule, Act'g Indian Agent" What our next move may be depends on the information to be extracted from the captives.

Found the ruins of an old fortification next to our camp. It is built on a hill over looking the country to South South West & South East, for miles, the location being such that surprise was impossible. A part of the wall in one place is still about 3 feet high.

Monday, Dec 23d Broke camp about daylight, moved South down the hill from camp about 3 miles, turned to West, climbed, up mesa and then South West 2 miles South and South South West about one more, crossed Rio Salado at mouth of a dry creek, which some of us took to be the Pinal—others the Pinto Creek. Went up stream (going South) for 2 miles then South West and South South West for 2 miles—d[itt]o 1/2 mile. Halted in dry bed of stream to allow pack train to close up. Sky cloudy windy, and every indication of a storm. Have now determined this to be Pinto Creek.

> 11 miles

Went South up creek one mile. Halted and camped. Wood. Water. and Grass. We are now about due South from last night's camp. Perhaps a little West of a due North and South line.

Distance   12 miles.

Tuesday, Dec 24th. 14th Day. Broke camp at day-break, moving West over a mesa about 2 1/2 or 3 miles, passed down, into a dry arroyo, turned South, went half a mile, halted to allow pack train to close up. 3 1/2 miles. Day bright and cold. Last night, contrary to expectations, we had only a slight rain, early in the evening, the stars coming out about midnight. Went South West about half a mile. South same. South West and South South West one mile. West one mile passing up this arroyo & getting into high hills. Found Water running from rocks but soon sinking into sand. Passed trail of Pimas and Papagoes going South about two months old. Saw many beautiful varieties of granite conglomerate and porphyry. Esquimisquin left us this a.m. going on scout. He is to rejoin us to-morrow. No fresh Indian signs, no signal fires. The captives state that they saw no signs of scouting parties from any direction, until seized upon by our advance guard. This may be interpreted either as showing a commendable secrecy in the movements of those dispatched by Genl. Crook from the other sides of Tonto Basin, or else they have not advanced with much energy and we are not to receive any benefit from their co-operation.

Distance   6 miles.

Stream not laid down on maps.

Wednesday Dec 25th Xmas comes but once a year. The day opened bright and genial just such a one as I hope our folks at home are having with the addition of good cheer, which we have not. Rations beginning to shorten. Broke camp at 8.45 a.m. Moved West by South going up cañon about 500 yds and then climbing very high & steep hills. Went one mile. Halted. Saw our camp on Salt River to North x East 5°. We are now in foot hills of Sierra Superstición and I incline to the opinion we have some climbing to do in the coming week. Marched South West 2 miles and West half a mile, passing three deep and rocky cañons and climbing steep mountains. Halted on top of high hill, well grassed. Saw Mountains on West of Phoenix* in distance. Directly in front of us and in very close proximity (South West) saw the portion of this range (Sierra Superstición) visible from the road as you pass from Rowell's Station on the Rio Salado to Stiles' on the Rio Gila. Moved down Mountain going about 2 miles; time occupied in descent 46 minutes. Found trail to be very good, but steep. Saw deep cañon on our left, running from South East to North West. When we reached foot of High Mountain, found ourselves in a cañon of granite walls, bottom sloping at very heavy grade. Still going South West and West South West, marched about 2 miles passing over rolling country for nearly the entire distance, reached the cañon of which I have just written. This has at this point a general South East to North West course. On left Bank of the stream, dry at this point; there is a high slender peak, which is most probably Weaver's Needle. The formation to-day is nearly all granite of inconceivable variety and beauty: some sandstone, porphyry &c. Went up cañon (South East) 500 yds struck running water clear and cold. Distance to day, nearly 8 miles.

Just as we made camp, a Sergeant of Capt. Burn's [sic], Co. "G" 5th Cav, came to inquire of Maj. Brown whom we were going after, Capt. Burns and Lt Thomas came into camp. Reported having left McDowell, Dec 20th, with 40 men "G" Co 5th Cav and ninety eight Pima Indians. Had captured one squaw, same date. Capt Hamilton 5th Cav, had left McDowell with 40 men, scouting to the North East North and North West. Each command was rationed for (12) days. Capt. Randall's command killed twenty-five Indians near head of Tonto Creek. Such good news served to enliven us all. We also ascertained that Montgomery had one fight and Adams two with the Apache-Mojaves, Killing two[,] Eleven[,] and thirteen respectively, besides captives. If we can only make a good strike the war, as far as the Tontos and Apache-Mojaves are concerned, will be at an end. Capt. Burns' captive boy Mike, gave an acc[oun]t. to night of three rancherias—one corresponding in location & character to that already described by Bocon, another in a cañon on Rio Salado and 3d on top of the four peaks—all inaccessible save by circuitous routes and all strong in numbers. By sneaking upon them in the night we can, by good luck, make our attacks at day-

---

* Later in day, found that these mountains are on West side of Gila, where it makes its Big Bend. John G.

dawn and kill their warriors whilst asleep.

Thursday, Dec 26th. Awaited in camp the arrival of messengers from
Es-qui-mis-quin, who sent 3 men in to Maj. Brown, about 9 o'clock.
A fresh trail had been struck, leading in the direction of Delt-chay's
strong-hold, our command is to go to-day to the Rio Salado and
camp in a cañon, to morrow we are to follow down the river and
make a camp at a point secluded from observation & from thence
we are to go on foot to surprise the rancheria. 11.45 Midday. Broke
camp going back on our trail. North West for about 300 yds, then
West to the camp of Captain Burns, about half a mile from our camp,
then West, a little South over hills for a total distance of 2 or 2 1/2
miles, halting on a hill about due West from the high Mountain we
descended yesterday, Hills are now covered with saguaros. We then
proceeded down a steep, but not bad grade to the Rio Salado, which
we reached at 1.05 P.M.   4 miles

Rio Salado here flowing about North and South but only for a short
distance, its course being extremely sinuous. Crossed river, passed
down its right bank about 3/4 of a mile and camped. Camp is hidden
from observation of Apaches except from West. Weather extremely
mild.

Distance to-day   about 4 1/2 miles.

We have all told, 220 fighting men

Friday Dec 27th Rem[aine]d. In camp expecting return of
Esquimisquin. All are confident of finding Delt-chay in the stronghold and, if so, we will make the biggest killing of the campaign. It is
rather disappointing to know that our efforts have not been as
successful as those of Randall and the others farther North, but we
hope to meet with such good fortune during the present week as
shall be a fitting recompense for all our past troubles & exertions.
12.40 P.M. Left camp, going back on our trail (north) for about 300
yds, then due West (nearly) going up very steep and strong grade
and through pass on Mountain Range that lay to West of camp of
26th (See profile of same). Halted at top of pass to let packs close
up.   two miles

We are now South of West about 5°, from High Mountain we
descended on Xmas. Country in this vicinity very badly broken.
On left hand side of this pass, Mountains are topped by a precipitous
ledge of forks, hundreds of feet high. Upon the highest peak a
solitary mescal stalk keeps watch like a sentinel upon the valleys

& cañons below. Passed down the mountain on other sides, going South West, trail very bad with loose rocks. Went about one mile and half, turned to West. Cañon going South West. Went over a hill about 300 yards and then turned North West, climbed up to top of very high Mountain, one mile. Rio Salado to South flowing West South West through an extraordinarily deep cañon. Mountain we are now on is very narrow. Passed down other side, we about half mile. Halted (going South West). Trail to-day very bad in every sense of the word, we have not only had to climb steep mountains, but had an unusual amount of climbing to do and the trails being filled with loose sharp stones, our animals with difficulty picked their way.

A mule died this morning from the effects of eating the insect called Compa-mucho and "Mayo" Weather fine. The peak we called Weaver's Needle is on the left bank of Rio Salado (apparently.) Went down through cañon to West, about 3/4 miles left hand side a precipice with an isolated peak jutting out at Western extremity. Getting anxious about Esquimisquin who has now been about (3) days. Marched South West and West, about one mile or perhaps a little more, grade very steep. Cañons precipitous on left hand side, descended into a cañon, with water running South into Rio Salado. Just before reaching camp, saw foot-prints of a squaw who had been watching us descend the Mountains and had just run down the cañon. Saw also a fresh pony track. We are now in sight of the high mesa mountain on the summit of which Delt-chay has his stronghold, so we are compelled to exercise great caution in our movements. No fires are allowed, the horses and mules are strictly guarded in order that they may not climb up on any of hills commanded by Delt-chay's Mountains. All singing, &c, is strictly forbidden and indeed no precaution is omitted tending to secure the secrecy of our movements. In the meantime every preparation is being made for a night march on foot. Each man looks to his weapons, sees that his cartridge belt is full, inspects his clothing, rejecting all that is not absolutely essential to protect him from the cold, provides himself with rations to do for a day or two, and a few matches which are of importance at every moment. Many of us have had our Apache allies make mocassins which are just the thing in which to climb mountains without giving warning to our foes.

Profile of a ridge of Sᵗ Supersticion, to N.W. of camp
Dec 26ᵗʰ 1872. Rio Salado at Base.

Profile of Mtn top near "Camp Pinal"
seen from S.W.

Profile of Sᵗ Pinal, as seen from N.W.
Camp of March 2ᵈ 1873.

The sky has become overspread with clouds. Maj Brown has accordingly allowed the Indians to strip the mule which died today, and whose remains the noble red man brought along.[19] We are to start when a certain star, known to the Indian, rises to its position in our meridian.

8 P.M., our Indians moved out in front, then Byrnes's [Burns's] Co, then Almy, Taylor and finally the Pimas under their old chief Antonio; after marching nearly due West almost 3 miles, passing two prominent sandstone buttes of considerable altitude on our right, our trail wound to the left and our general direction became more Southerly—after about 1 1/2 miles' march we came to a steep mountain, up the side of which we toiled, using great care to make no noise which might alarm the Enemy. About 12.05 the next morning we were at the summit—a distance as near as I can estimate of about (5) or (6) miles from Camp. The men rested for nearly an hour every man closing up to his proper position in the ranks and then lying prone to the ground. Apache scouts were soon sent ahead, who soon returned with the information of fires being discovered in the cañon below. The men advanced one man at a time until we reached the edge of a gloomy abyss, how deep it was I could not then discover, and upon this edge we waited in the cold piercing night air without blankets or overcoats until the morning rose[20] beamed upon the surrounding hills. We had then an opportunity to examine the locality, so much dreaded by the Pimas, used as a stronghold of the Apache-Mojaves and Tontos. Situated upon the crest of a very elevated range, it was difficult of access to large parties from all sides except that upon which we had come and even here the character of the soil was such that a footstep, unless made in the most cautious manner, could be heard for miles.

Granting that an attack could be made, the Apaches could escape unharmed under cover of immense boulders which served as a natural Chemin de Ronde.[21] Looking down into this place, no evidences of recent occupancy could be detected, a disappointment all the more bitter from its contrast to our own recent enthusiastic hopes for success.

---

19. Brown permitted the Apaches to butcher and cook the mule because the overcast would obscure their fires. See Bourke, *On the Border*, 189.

20. Bourke is equating the sun to a rose.

21. Literally a round or circular path, i.e. a switchback.

Most of the Command being fatigued sat down to rest but Joe
Felmer and a few others started down the trail towards the Rio Salado
not with any expectation of finding hostile Indians but rather from
a disposition to examine into the nature of the country. About 300
yds from where they left us, in a secluded spot, was found a recently
abandoned rancheria of (3) or (4) huts. Passing on rapidly upon
descending the mountain somewhat farther, a drove of fifteen horses
and mules was encountered and almost immediately afterwards a
rancheria was seen in an almost impregnable position, which I shall
in a few moments proceed to describe. This handful of our comrades,
with a gallantry that cannot be too highly extolled at once charged
the Indians, killing (6) and driving the remainder into the cave at
whose entrance the rancheria was situated. Word having in the
meantime reached Maj Brown, the main body was pushed forward
as fast as our tired legs would permit, the enthusiasm of the men
rising again at the prospect of a fight. To avoid verbose details, let
me say the rancheria was thus situated—In a small, elliptical nook,
upon the crest of the bluffs which here enclose the Rio Salado was
a small cave or depression in the rocks, which overhung the nook
by at least 500'—the bluff, first mentioned, being 1000 or 1200'
above the Rio Salado. In front of the cave, a natural rampart of
sandstone 10' high affords ample protection to the Indians, altho
the great number of boulders scattered in every direction screened
our men in turn from the fire of the besieged. Our policy was
obvious—the incorrigible Apaches, at least a portion of them, were
now entrapped beyond possibility of escape and in justice to our
men whose lives should not be rashly imperilled, orders were given
to make no charge upon the works, to pick off every Indian showing
his head, to spare every woman and child, but to kill every man.
Twice the besieged were asked to surrender their families, promises
were given that no harm should befall them, but, confident in their
ability to repel us, their only answers were yells of defiance. These
shouts of scorn were soon changed into groans of despair as our
shots began to fall with deadly accuracy upon them, reckless
attempts at escape being made but in each case resulting in the
death of those who tried to run our gauntlet of fire. One splendid
looking Indian over 6 feet, most beautifully proportioned, but with
a very savage countenance, did indeed succeed in breaking through
our front line and making his way down the arroyo, full of large

rocks, upon one of which he sprang with a yell of defiance, bravado or joy. I cannot say which. Twelve of us, concealed at this point, levelled our rifles and fired. Every shot must have hit him as he fell dead riddled from head to foot. This particular instance is mentioned to show the deadly nature of the fire we opened upon them, both as to accuracy and quantity. A volley was now directed upon the mouth of the cave, & for (3) minutes every man in the command opened and closed the breech block of his carbine as rapidly as his hands could move. Never have I seen such a hellish spot as was the narrow little space in which the hostile Indians were now crowded. To borrow the expression employed by a brother officer, the bullets striking against the mouth of the cave seemed like drops of rain pattering upon the surface of a lake. I must not omit to state that Capt. Byrnes, Co. G, 5th Cav, had succeeded in gaining a position upon the crest of the overhanging bluff, where they discharged deadly volleys upon the wretches fighting below. Not content with the deadly efficacy of bullets, they resorted to projecting large masses of rock which thundered down the precipice mangling and destroying whatsoever they encountered. A charge was now ordered and the men rushed forward; upon entering the enclosure a horrible spectacle was disclosed to view—in one corner, Eleven dead bodies were huddled, in another four and in different crevices they were piled, to the extent of the little cave and to the total number[*] of Fifty-seven, (20) women and children were taken prisoners, the spoils, very considerable in quantity, were destroyed. We found mescal baskets, seeds, hides, skins and the material usually composing the outfit of these savage nomads.

Our captives were nearly all wounded, more or less severely, but by good fortune we succeeded in bringing them off in safety. One of our Pima allies was killed, but, with this exception, no losses occurred. Thus ended the most signal blow ever received by the Apaches in Arizona. Not alone did we destroy an entire band, but a band actively engaged in depredating upon the Gila settlements, one that spurned every offer of the Govt to make peace. Nanni-Chaddi, the chief had been in to McDowell, last year talking with that spawn of hell, Vincent Colyer, from whom he received presents of blankets and other necessaries, promising in return to comply with the demands of the lawful Government and obey its orders.

[*] (Seventy Six altogether were killed in this fight.)

He had also visited Grant where in conversation with Col Royall, he boasted that no troops ever had found his retreat and none ever would.[22]

Taking a general Northerly direction, we travelled [*illegible*] miles across high hills untill we reached a running stream upon which we found our pack train encamped, having moved there early in the morning.

Supper was eagerly devoured by men who had eaten nothing for (26) hours and had been worn out by climbing steep mountains and the excitement of fighting for (5) hours.

Our captives were well taken care of and, excepting the guard placed over them, appeared as if in their own homes.

Sunday, Dec 29—Moved North West about one mile, West about one mile North North West one mile, then West and West by a little South for 15 miles or 18 miles, going parallel to the creek known as the Sycamore, until we reached the Rio Verde, part of the time marching in the bed of the stream (Sycamore,) dry at this part of its course—turned South, went about 4 or 5 miles to Camp McDowell, crossing Rio Verde in front of post.

Distance marched	
night of Dec 27th	8 miles
Dec 28th	10 @ 12 miles
or perhaps	15 miles
Dec 29th	25 miles
Character of country	The worst I ever saw.

Dec 28th and 27th
Weather; mild and genial
Dec 28th Our camp was on [*illegible*] of four peaks to South West of the most South one of the four.
Dec 29th Rained all night
Dec 30th Rainy, Rem[aine]d at Camp McDowell, attending to wounded and refitting &c
Express sent to Genl Crook
Dec 31st Rained all day, except at short intervals; remained at McDowell. Capt Hamilton & Lieut Keyes returned from scout, reported having found rancheria on East side of Tonto Creek & some

22. Thirty-four years later a cowboy named Jeff Adams rediscovered the cave, now full of bones of the Apache casualties. It has since become known as the Skeleton Cave Massacre. See Thrapp, *Conquest of Apacheria*, 130 n.16.

Vertical Section of cañon of the
Rio Salado, at locality where we
destroyed Nannu Chiddi's
Band, Dec 29th 1872

A B = 500 feet (Estimated)

distance beyond. Destroyed it. Captured & Brought back three children. Found four descriptive lists issued at Camp Apache and signed—one by Mr. Soule and (3) by A.J. Dallas.

Reported having met Captain Randalls Com'd Dec 25th near the Tonto Creek. The Maricopas, who accompanied this command from McDowell, behaved so badly that Capt Hamilton deprived them of their arms & sent them home, early on the trip, hence, being without Indian trackers, his success was not as great as it would have been had his earnest efforts been properly seconded.

Both Pimas & Maricopas have shown themselves to be a great fraud.

Chapter 2

❖

❖

❖

❖

❖

Meeting Cochise

January 1st 1873. New Year's. Remained in Camp McDowell
January 2d, 3d, 4th, 5th, D[itt]o.
Genl. Crook arrived January 2d. Remained until January 5th when
he returned to Grant. He was accompanied by Mason McCoy, his
chief of scouts for Southern Arizona.
January 3d Adam and Montgomery came in with their commands
and were ordered, January 4th to report to Maj Brown for duty.
January 5th Indian captives sent to Grant.
January 6th An expedition under command of Maj Brown, left
McDowell at 4 P.M.
Consisting of

Maj W.H. Brown	5th Cav.
"C" 5th Cav	Capt Adams
"B" 5th Cav	" Montgomery
"H" 5th Cav	" Hamilton
"L" 5th Cav	" Taylor
"G" 5th Cav	" Burns
"M" 5th Cav	1st Lieut Almy

1st Lieut C.H. Rockwell with Co "L"
2 Lieut W.S. Schuyler with Co "B"

2 Lieut E.L. Keys with Co. "C"
2 Lieut W.J. Ross, A.D.C.
2 Lieut John G. Bourke, A.D.C.
James Dailey
went as Volunteer Bacon Chawers.
A. McIntosh   Guide
Jos. Felmer   Guide
Antonio Besias   Interpreter
30 Apache Indians under Esqui-mas-quin or "Bocon."
Messers Bartlett, Frank Monach and Chenowith in charge of pack-trains.
Assist Surgeon J.B. Girard U.S.A. Surgeon
twenty days' Rations. Left Camp McDowell, A.T., Monday, January 6th 1873 travelled South South East x South for 2 miles, South South East x East for half a mile, crossed Rio Verde, flowing at this point South South East, passed down the river and camped on its right bank in an open flat. Country passed through to-day was an open plain, covered with brush. We brought with us some Indian captives to act as guides.
Weather charming.
Distance   3 1/2 miles
Captain Montgomery of the Rear Guard brought in news that the Eastern papers contain an account of the death of Capt F. Stanwood, 3rd Cavalry.
Thursday Jan 7th 1873. Broke Camp 8.30 a.m. Marched South East 1 1/2 mile, passing at end of one mile the South East corner post of the U.S. Mil. Reservation of McDowell.
Rio Verde still running South South East.
Weather fine. Sky cloudless.
Turned South, marched 5 miles, crossed the Rio Salado, here flowing East North East and West South West, turned East North East moving along left Bank of River 2 miles and camped.
Distance to day   8 or 9 miles.
The Command stretches along over a great distance, being 46 minutes passing a given point.
Location of camp, a bottom land, with rolling country in close proximity.
Wednesday, January 8th 1873. Broke camp 7.45 Marched East South East 2 miles, marched [in a] South East/North East [line] 1/2 mile.

Entered an arroyo, which we followed going about due South (East about 5° or 6°) for 2 miles, sides growing higher, turned East about 3/4 miles. Marched around high Peak on our left turned South East again & went about 2 or 3 miles with a little if any inclination to East South East. Made a total distance of about 10 miles or perhaps 11 miles, the last mile being over rolling grass land (the arroyo having terminated). Halted to allow packs to close up. Passed some tanks in rock, about 8 miles from last night's camp. Weather fine.

Marched North North East about 3 miles and in a general northerly direction about as many more. Came down into a little arroyo, surrounded by high hills, with a feeble stream of water flowing North. Camped. Wood, water and Grass. Distance to day about

15 miles

Two men deserted early this morning taking with them arms & horses.

Thursday, January 9th 1873. Broke camp 9 am, march down cañon, going north one and half-mile, came to junction of another cañon flowing from South East. Water in tanks at Junction. Went South East about 300 yds then East, over a little divide, one mile turned North, country now quite rugged. [W]ent in the new direction 2 miles, [k]eeping to right of a little red sandstone butte. Marched across little mountain, turn East, went one mile turned North, went about half mile, then a nearly East course (by North) for a distance of 2 miles. Halted on a bend of Rio Salado, which here flows South and makes an abrupt turn to North North West.

Distance marched to day about 8 or 9 miles

Weather mild—sky clear.

Our present Camp within 600 or 800 yds of the scene of slaughter, Dec 28th 1872.[1]

Friday January 10th 1873. Broke camp 7.45. Marched East by South up cañon creek for about 3 miles turned North North East by East up one of its tributaries for 1 1/2 miles, then a due East course for 4 1/2 or 5 miles more, finding water 10 am. 10 35 am, 11.05 am, and in tanks at many points: went about 3 miles more in a general East direction. Country very bad. Went down a steep descent into a cañon which ran to from [sic] South South East about

13 miles

1. Bourke is referring to the fight discussed in Chapter 1.

Went along this cañon about SouthEast for one mile, then turned abruptly East and made camp in a cove well sheltered from observation on the South or East. Distance to day   15 miles. Weather mild. Windy in the morning.

Saturday January 11th 1873. Remained in Camp all day 2 P.M. Capt Burns with his Command & Lieut Almy's Co, moved out with the Indian scouts on foot to scour the country to the South East. The main body having agreed upon a rendezvous, at which to meet Captain Burn's [sic] party, moved at 430 P.M. going North until we arrived on top of big mountain, then we turned East going about 3 miles, then South about 1 1/2 miles, then up a cañon, going North East a few hundred yards, then South East going across high mountain, keeping to Left of Weever's Needle making a total distance of 7 or 8 miles.

Descending into a place where a number of little cañons joined, we made camp; water in small quantities being found in tanks in the rocks. Wood scarce. Grass plenty. Saw large signal fire on top of the peak to the west. Saw water in a cañon about half way.

                                                             7 or 8 miles

Sunday Jan 12 1873. Remained in Camp expecting return of Captain Burn's [sic] party until 3.15 P.M., when we started South West going between one & one & half miles. Cañon during latter part of our march ran more in a due North & South course.

Found water & made camp. Rejoined by Capt Burn's [sic] command, which had scouted the Mountains to South and found an extremely large rancheria, lately abandoned. Trails were all running in the direction of Cave Creek.

Weather to-day calm & genial.

Total Distance   1 or 1 1/2 miles.

Monday, Jany 13th 1873. Broke Camp 215 PM. Marched North half mile. East by a little North about one mile, keeping between hills, then East North East for half a mile and East South East for same [k]eeping on South side of high mountain. Gila Valley to Right about 20 miles from us in a direct line. Turned North, went about 3/4 mile, climbing over high mountain well grassed, High Mountains on all sides. Weather cool. Sky hazy, Went about half mile to North, turned East, went about 1/2 mile and made camp in a beautiful spot, secluded from the observation of all Indians except those who may be on extreme top of Four Peaks. Water very plenty and of great purity. Grass ditto. Wood abundant, Cedar, Juniper, Oak.

We had a good view to-day of the Rio Gila, Rio Salado, Four Peaks[,] Sierra Santa Catarina, Sierra Tortolita, and the settlements at Florence & Phoenix, also the Picacho between Tucson & Sacato North

Total distance to-day about   5 miles.

Tuesday Janry 14th 1873. Broke camp about 145 P.M. March East North East for nearly half a mile going up very steep hill. Marched North North East for about one mile going down mountain and entering ravine in which we soon found running water. Followed general course of stream North East by a little North. Saw spring and a little stream on Left (3 miles). Kept on down stream until we came to its Junction with another smaller one from the left. Marched among lofty hills. Water plenty and good; wood & grass D[itt]o. Weather genial sky clear.

Distance   3 1/2 miles

Not finding a good location for a camp, the command moved in the general direction (North East) of the cañon for two miles, the trail leading along crest of a high Mountain. Made Camp at Junction of this cañon with another running from South.

Total distance about   5 1/2 miles.

Wednesday, January 15th 1873. Day opened very cold. High wind. Rem[aine]d in Camp until midday, when the entire command started on foot from camp, leaving the pack trains and horses behind in charge of Capt E Adam 5th Cavalry. Our movement was made with the greatest caution and very slowly. We marched North about half a mile. East 1/4 mile over very high mountain. Halted until night. Moved North East for about 3 miles, reaching a rancheria just about break of day. The occupants rushed from their jacales,[2] just as our men were about in position, or a little sooner, so that we did not meet with the success anticipated. We captured thirteen women and children and Killed three. We also captured the old Chief of the Band. These people were very poor, possessing but little besides what had been given them at Grant and McDowell when they made peace. A descriptive list signed by Royal E Whitman[3] dated May 2nd 1872, was found in this Camp.

Thursday, January 16th 1873. Marched West South West about 4 or

---

2. *jacal* (Spanish), a picket-built cabin or shelter.
3. See Appendix 1 (Military).

5 miles to a point in the same cañon as yesterday's camp, but about 2 miles below, where we found pack-trains & led horses[4] had moved. Water here flowing East. Made Camp. Wood, Water, & Grass plenty. Distance to day (in an air line about 3 miles)
4 1/2 miles
Friday, January 17 1873. Broke Camp 9 a.m. Marched South East and East South going up a steep Mountain crest, about one mile. Weather fine.
Last night was quite cold. Sky is clear. Pinal Mountain. East by 5° South.
Went about half mile East North East two miles South East.
Went one mile East and South about 1/2 to 3/4 miles. Camped. Wood, Water, & Grass plenty. We passed a small creek this a.m. just after leaving camp on Right. The stream upon which we camped runs from South to North. Just South of camp, there is another stream from the South East. Distance to-day   8 miles
Found that this camp was below junction of Pinto and Pappoose Creeks, at the point where we destroyed some fields of corn, in the month of July 1870.
Saturday, January 18th 1873, Broke camp 9.05. Marched South about 1000 yds, then East, going up a high mountain, after marching about one mile, halted the column on side of hill and sent out Indian scouts to capture or Kill some Apaches (hostile) who were seen on hill to our Left heard halloing at us. After a short time, an Apache boy came down the Mountain side and joined us. Maj Brown told him to go back up and bring in his band, a pass was given him to ensure his safety. These people report from being very much frightened at the sight of such great numbers of troops in their country. Moved South East through the mountain pass, found quantity of water flowing North West, going about 3 miles; halted on top of hill, alongside of the big white rocks which are to north of the site of old Camp Pinal.[5] Passed on through Mason's Valley East about 2 miles and South and South South East about 4 miles more. Descended a very steep hill, entered cañon of Mineral Creek, here flowing South, dry in a great part of its course. Weather genial, sky clear.

4. Spare horses.
5. Camp Pinal was located in Mason's Valley in the Pinal Mountains. It was established in 1870 to replace the first Camp Grant, but was abandoned a year later, after Crook assumed command of the department and revised the troop disposition. It was redesignated "Infantry Camp" before being abandoned. Altshuler, *Starting with Defiance*, 48.

Distance to day   10 or 12 miles.

Sunday, January 19th 1873. Broke camp 9 am. Marched South, one mile, then East South for about one and quarter miles, going up Shady Run. [H]alted and made camp. Water, in spring, about sufficient for cooking purposes, water for animals, one quarter mile flow. Wood and Grass plenty. Weather delightful. Sky clear.

Indians in this section of country are now begging for peace, which they say they will ask for on their Knees.

The campaign against the hostile Indians on this side of the Rio Salado may be considered at an end.

To-morrow four companies leave us to go to the new camp at Mount Graham[6]—Burn's [sic], Hamilton's, Adam's, and Montgomery's— Burns at Eureka springs and the others to take station at Kennedy's Wells. [Company] "F" 5th Cav. under Lt W. P. Hall, is already at Mt. Graham.

Monday, January 20th 1873, Commands separated at 8 A.M, one detachment going East for about 1 mile then South East, for 2, getting upon a rolling mesa land, covered with grass, then in a general South East course for 8 m. more[,] going into a cañon, with spring of water. South half a mile, West, about the same, then general South course for 4 miles to Rio Gila.

Weather Fine, Sky clouded

Distance to-day   16 @ 18 miles

(Killed 11 or 12 deer to-day & last night)

The night was very cold.

Tuesday January 21st 1873: Broke camp 8 a.m. Marched South East 7 miles, Keeping Rio Gila on our Right. High Mt Peak on the other side, and high hills on our side of the river. Turned more to the East and marched 3 miles, crossed to Left Bank of Rio Gila. Day fine, Sky clear.

Saw the Saddle Mt, to East North East, and to the East. Marched East by a little South for another mile and then South South East by South for 5 miles, going up Rio San Pedro halting within 5 miles of Camp Grant. Distance to day about 18 miles, Camp on Right Bank of River.

January 22d Continued march to Camp Grant. Distance about
                        6 miles

Courier sent to Genl Crook with dispatches from Capt. Nickerson.

6. The new location for Grant.

January 23d Rem[aine]d in Grant, conference held with Indians Friday. Rem[aine]d at Grant, Twenty six new recruits obtained for Genl Crook. DeLord [sic][7] arrived to-day bringing statement that the Territorial Legislature had in contemplation the adoption of resolutions reflecting upon the policy of Genl Crook and especially in reference to the attack made upon the Apache Mojaves at Camp Date Creek, last September or August.[8] Also a rumor to the effect that Genl Crook's warlike policy was to be discontinued.

Arrangements are now completed for sending Taylor with three companies to M[ount] Graham, where he will find Randall with 3 companies and (46) Apache scouts, Adams with four Companies, Hall with one all of Cavalry and Thompson with one of Infantry. Perhaps Sumner's and Bendire's companies will also receive orders to report to Genl Crook at Graham, making a grand total of thirteen Co's of Cav and one of Infantry to watch Cocheis'[9] Camp.

Brown and myself start to-morrow for Cocheis' camp via the San Pedro middle crossing.

Saturday, January 25th 1873

Left Camp at 11 AM, Going up San Pedro River. Weather genial. Sky clear. Marched about due South for 3 m, passing the Indian Agency and turning a little E went about one mile and half. Camped on San Pedro. Distance to day about (4 1/2) four and a half miles.

Sunday, Jan'y 26th 1873. Maj Brown having been prostrated by an acute attack of dysentery, the command was delayed in its march to-day until 9 a.m. when we broke camp & marched South East. along Right Bank Rio San Pedro for 15 miles. Made camp. Rec[eive]d important dispatches from Genl Crook, also dispatches from Captain Furey.

Monday, January 27th Maj Brown somewhat better, but still very weak. Command moved at 9 am, marched in a general South East course up valley of San Pedro for 28 or 30 miles. Camped. Passed

---

7. Bourke apparently means Sidney R. DeLong. See Appendix 1 (Civilians).

8. Bourke is referring to a conspiracy by the Yavapais at the Date Creek reservation to assassinate Crook during a council at the agency on September 8, 1872. Crook had learned several of the Indians recently had participated in the attack on a stagecoach, as well as the Wickenburg stage massacre, and he intended to arrest them. The assassination plot was discovered, and when the Indians made their move, the soldiers were ready. About seven Indians were killed or wounded. The Yavapais blamed the Mojaves. The delay between the Wickenburg massacre and Crook's attempt to arrest the perpetrators was caused by General Howard's inspection and the resultant adjustments of policy. See Robinson, *General Crook*, 117-18, 125-26.

9. Bourke's spelling of Cochise's name is erratic.

wagon train of six wagons going to Camp Grant. Weather fine, Sky clear. Strong breeze blowing to-day

28 miles

Tuesday, January 28th 1873, Broke camp 8.24 a.m. Moved in a general South East by a little South course to Tres Alamos in which village we made camp. Just after leaving camp met a train (empty) going to Grant. Passed a low range of hills on other side of river (not the Sierra Santa Catarina). Met Lt Hall & his Co at Tres Alamos, also saw Don Estevan Ochoa.

Distance to day   20 miles.

Sky clear weather cold. Windy

Wednesday Jan'y 29th 1873. Marched on road to middle crossing of Rio San Pedro & thence on G.S.O.M road to Sulphur Springs.[10] Rec[eive]d dispatches from Genl. Crook.

Day very cold. High wind. Sky clear. Night bitterly cold.

Thursday. January 30th 1873 Remained at Sulphur Springs. Yesterday a note was sent to Agent Jefferds, requesting an interview with Cochies and to-day quite a large band of squaws and children have come over to our camp but Cocheis was not with them. Mr Jefferds shortly after appeared and had a conversation with Maj Brown with whom he made arrangements for a meeting with Cochies. Express sent to General Crook

Friday January 31st 1873 Went to Camp Bowie.[11] Made trip in 4h. 35 minutes

Saturday, February 2nd 1873. Remained at Bowie.

Sunday, February 2nd 1873. Returned to Sulphur Spring's where we found a courier from General Crook. Made trip in 4h 5 minutes

Monday Feb. 3, 1873. Marched South West across Sulphur Sp[ring]'s Valley, 10 or 12 miles to the 2n[d] cañon in Dragoon Mts. where we found Cocheis and his family with a few young warriors.[12] Cocheis is a fine looking Indian of about (50) winters, straight as a rush, six

10. Great Southern Overland Mail Road. The Great Southern Overland Mail was a colloquial name for the Butterfield Overland Mail Company. Kim Frontz, Arizona Historical Society, to Charles M. Robinson III, December 12, 2001.

11. Camp Bowie was established in 1862 in the Chiricahua Mountains to guard the eastern approaches to Apache Pass. The pass and the springs located there were a key transit point for travelers and mail carriers on the road between Tucson and Mesilla, New Mexico, and a favorite ambush spot for the Indians. In 1868, it was relocated to a nearby hill overlooking the pass, and eleven years later permanently upgraded to a fort. Fort Bowie was abandoned in 1894, and is now a national historic site. Frazer, *Forts of the West*, 4; Utley, *A Clash of Cultures: Fort Bowie and the Chiricahua Apaches*.

12. For record of this meeting see Appendix 12.

ft in stature, deep chested, roman nosed, black eyes, firm mouth, and kindly and even somewhat melancholy expression tempering the determined look of his countenance. He seemed much more neat than the other wild Indians I have seen and his manners were very gentle. There was neither in speech or action any of the bluster characteristic of his race. His reception of us was courteous, altho' he said but little in the way of compliment. He expressed his own earnest desire for peace, said that in the treaty made with Howard, it was understood that soldiers could pass over the roads on his Reservation, but could not live upon it, nor were citizens to settle there. In reference to the Mex[ica]n, he said he considered them as being on one side in this matter, while the Americans were on another. The former had not asked him for peace as the latter had done. He did not deny that his boys were in the habit of raiding on Mexico, but this he could not prevent as it was no more than was done from all the Reservations. Our interview was quite brief and at its conclusion, we returned to our camp at Sulphur Sp[ring]s. I was very much astonished by the great number of children in the Indian Camp.

Distance to-day   22 or 24 miles
Tuesday, Feb 4th 1873 Marched to Kennedy's Wells, going first North West and then North North East.
Distance   30 or 32 miles
Weather fine, sky clear.
Wednesday, Feb 5th 1873 North x East a few deg[rees]. East to the new post at Mt Graham. Found Genl C.
Weather good   12 miles
Thursday Feb. 6th, Genl. Crook left for Grant. Co 'E['] & Co 'K' 5th Cav. came in under Price (with Parkhurst) and Michler. The former had Killed five; the latter (16)Bucks.[13]
Friday Feb 7th 73 Rem[aine]d at Graham
Sat'y Feb 8th 73   d[itt]o   d[itt]o
9th, 10th, 11th 12th , 13th, 14th d[itt]o   d[itt]o
Saturday 15th Moved in comd. of "L" Troop 1st Cav (Randall's Battalion) West out of cañon about 1 mile, then North West for 3 miles, then about due West for 15 more. When about 10 miles out from camp, passed down between a range of Mountains into a flat. Reached Eureka Sp[rings] about 13 miles from camp.

13. Bourke is referring to a deer hunt.

Total distance to-day 19 miles

Weather cold. Windy sky clear

Sunday Feb 16th Moved West x North about 7 miles. Just before reaching camp found the country on fire, great volumes of smoke obscured the sky and retarded our advance. This camp, like that of last night, is on the Aravaipa Creek.

Monday Feb 17. 73 West by North (5°) to Ojo Aravaypa 7 miles.

Tuesday Feb 18th Moved in a general North course for 14 miles, trail very sinuous, country rocky, passed water flowing West came down into cañon Gabilau and made camp in front of [dentation?]. Day fine. Sky clear

Total distance 14 miles

Wednesday, Feb 19. Moved in a general North direction down the cañon Gabilau, crossed divide into cañon Ventana and then down to Rio Gila (This trail I have already mapped out several times) Day clear and warm. Distance 15 miles

Thursday, February 20th Remained in Camp

Friday, February 21st. Moved up the Rio Gila about 1 1/2 miles North East. 1 1/2 miles

Weather fair, sky cloudy

Bad news came to-day from Grant, to the effect that Bocon[14] has played us false & gone again on the war-path.

Saturday, Feb 22d Birthday of Washington. Moved up Rio Gila going East for 2 miles, then 2 miles North up Rio San Carlos, making Camp on Right Bank. 4 miles

Same night Lieut Almy with Lt Watts and Co "M" 5th Cavl and Lt Bourke with Co "L" 1st Cav, Jose as interpreter and 12 Indians making a total of about 75 men moved to cut off Bocon who had now taken the war-path, armed with the munitions of war dealt out to him while in our service. Started from camp at 5 P.M. moving back on our trail to the camp of Feb 19th & 20th and thence West along Gila for about 2 miles further, making 8 miles.

Sunday Feb 23. Sky cloudy, signs of snow. Moved 3 West (along Gila) 1 1/2 miles & turned West (Gila[)] South West & North went 1/2 mile; North up arroyo 1 1/2 mile, turned up arroyo to West, marched 3 miles up arroyo and then up East side of Sierra Mescal, the top of the range being reached at 12 miles. Passed down on other side, came to little arroyo with water (flowing North), a little

14. Esquimasquin.

stream formed it from the West and then flowed on North to combine
with the West fork of the Rio San Carlos   10 miles
Rained at intervals all day.
Rained heavily all night.
Monday Feb 24th. Moved North West across spur of the Sierra Mescal
(three miles) and then down an arroyo running north of West, after
going about 6 1/2 miles from camp found water in this arroyo which
soon joined a stream flowing South North. Upon this we camped
near a quantity of young cottonwoods and in front of a low hill
crested with a black ledge of rocks, (probably basalt)   8
miles
Day clear and bright. Some few clouds.
Tuesday Feb 25th Heavy rain and cold bitter wind. Moved up high
Mountain, going North of West, went in this direction about 1 1/2
miles then West South West and South West & South for 3 miles
more, passed a stream on our Right, flowing into that on which we
camped last night, also saw a trib[utar]'y coming in on its L. Halted
in a little cañon with water flowing East x West, joining creek of our
camp last night. Halt was made under Sierra Pinal. Marched North
of West passing up this arroyo for about 2 miles, then turning South,
we crossed a small divide and entered Head waters of
[D]isappointment Creek, going 3 miles and made camp at same
place where we had camped Dec 18th. Rained and hailed furiously.
Keen wind.
Distance about   9 miles
Since first halt to day passed thro' scrub oak and scrub pine timber.
Rain ceased about sun-down.

Wed Feby 26th Marched South South West about 6 miles; first
ascending a high hill and then having down grade until we struck
Disappointment Creek at the point where it begins to flow East South
East. Halted and prospected for water, Lt Almy & (10) men went to
Rio Gila to look for the cartridges buried by Bocon. Found no water
and com[man]d. moved down Disappmt Creek to near its junction
with Gila, where we camped, making essentially the same march as
that of Dec 13th 1872. . . .
                              14 miles
(Did not get the cartridges) Day fine.

Chapter 3

❖

❖

❖

❖

❖

Mopping Up

Thursday Feb 27th. Moved back on our trail, going West North West for (12) miles, when we halted for a few moments at entrance of a little cañon on left, which had water. This day we marched up West branch of Disappt Creek. Arroyo now turned rather more to North, went about 2 miles struck trail coming in on our Left (running from South South East, our trail of Jan 22) Mountains on Left all day. Low hills on Right. Went 3 miles West keeping up this branch of Disapt Creek then crossing hills going more to North West for 4 miles more going down little cañon to Shady Run. Camped. Wood, Water, & Grass.

Day fine; sky cloudy   21 miles
Two of our Indians ret[urne]d to Grant (sick)

Friday Feb 28th Rained all night. Moved West about one mile & North about another, going over our trail of Dec 18th. Passed camp of Dec 17th in Mineral Creek; great quantities of water gushing out of the rocks on the right. Went North about one mile up cañon of Mineral Creek; went up grade of very steep hill about two miles. Minl Creek (now dry) divided into 2 cañons; one from North other from North North West. Minl. Creek flows just South South West then South South East and South South West to Rio Gila. Passed down grade on other side, going North North West, passed a little tributary of Minl. Creek flowing South South West & South South East. Day bright. Crossed over a white stone (granite) ridge and down little arroyo going West & North for 3 miles, finding running water (rain) about half-way down. Came to old Camp Pinal and camped. Distance about 7 miles.

Saturday March 1st Moved in a North direction out of Mason's Valley about 1000 yds, crossing a low divide and then following an arroyo (North) full of water running with a heavy current (1 mile). Water flows into Rio Prieto. Day fine. Sky clear.

Stream ran North & West for about 2 miles when we followed it, our trail then ran North while stream turned West, going up grade one mile North then after getting to top of high hill, turned West, going for a total distance of seven miles from camp of last night, which is South East of us: passed our old camp of Dec 17th and a little to North of it saw stream coming in to Rio Prieto from West. [A]ll the cañons are now full of water.

Sunday March 2 1873. Marched North down Rio Prieto for 1/2 mile, saw stream coming in on Left, rising from Mountains in close vicinity; passed on North a little West for 2 miles more, saw West fork coming in and crossed it; still going North North West & North for about one mile over hills, came down into an arroyo flowing into Rio Prieto and marched up this to West for about 1 mile; then North West and West North West for 2 miles and North West for 1 mile East, cañon getting quite rocky & rough. Camped at an old deserted Indian village, at junction of this cañon with one from North Location of the rancheria taken Jan 15th due W of us and across a mountain ridge. Day fine

Sky clear.   Distance   8 miles

Monday Mar. 3d Moved West by North about 1/2 mile, then North West over a little hill, continued in a West by North course for 1 1/2 mile, coming down again into cañon, which ran to South East. Country hilly and well grassed. Oak groves. Water in small springs at frequent intervals. Day fine. Sky clear. Passed on West going over little divide, and coming down into a little arroyo which joined the fork of the Rio Prieto up which we came Dec 23. . . . Passing across a little hill ascended arroyo South & West (with steep hills), finding excellent water in springs and tanks. Halted on top of a Mountain at 12.45, after being out 4 3/4 hrs, making a march of about 8 or 10 miles. Arrived at a point on trail of night of Dec 15th near the Indian village we attacked at that time. Saw to the South of us (flowing North East), the cañon upon which we had then camped.

Pinal Mountains now to East of us

10 miles

Tuesday Mar 4th Inauguration day[1]

Broke camp, moving South; going up very high mountain; saw to South South West a high butte with sandstone crest. Looking back saw the conical butte of yesterday to North of us. All the cañons about us are filled with water, melted snow or rain. Day fine. Sky cloudless. After going about 500 or 800 yds turned West and, passing over Mountain came down into our Camp of January 12th. Found an abundance of water, grass and wood. No Indian signs as yet with the exception of a [macho?] track yesterday with those of (4) men having American shoes. Indian boys say there are no hostile Indians this side of the head of Tonto Creek.

Wednesday, March 5 Day fine, Sky cloudless South through a gap in Mountains 1 1/2 m water flowing South from a spring. Turned West, going along between high Hills for about 1 mile then North West for nearly 3 reaching one of our old camps. [F]ound water running South West and then South. Rocky peak to West North West (Weaver's Needle). Turned North, going to top of High Mountain (on trail of night of Jan'y 11th). Reached summit of pass after marching over very rough country then turned W, going down grade, finding water flowing West about 1/2 mile and then North West (joining Cañon Creek[)] water of last night's camp flows into Rio Salado in the big Cañon. Weather very Hot. Birds singing on all sides. Green grass has been sprouting for some days, marched North West through mountain country, for about 1 mile then West & North for 3 more, passing a creek flowing West & North and then down a long hill to a point West of camp of Jan 9th. Total Dist (about 13 miles)

Spring from the South comes out in front of Camp.

Thursday March 6th Lt Bourke with a small party, mounted, started from camp North East through a Mountain pass and down into Cañon Creek at its junction with little stream we passed yesterday before getting into camp. Passed up Cañon Creek one mile going East.

---

1. President U.S. Grant's second term. At that time, the president was inaugurated on March 4. On October 15, 1933, Inauguration Day was moved to January 20 by the Twentieth Amendment, to reduce the "lame duck" period between election and inauguration.

Cañon very bad, walls very high[,] abundance of water. Returned to starting point in cañon and then North North West for about one mile; being unable to go any farther on acc[oun]t of huge boulders and deep pools of water, returned to last nights camp thence followed main command which had gone in a general North West direction 8 miles on trail of January 10 & 11th.

Friday March 7 Moved in a general West course to Rio Salado, at its junction with cañon in which we had camped. Rio Salado flowing East North East and West South West with a heavy current, cañon during to-day's march very rocky. Day fine, sky clear. Temperature about 75° @ 80° F: Yesterday the command bathed in the open air, something which in Penna. or N.Y. could not have been done in May. . . . . .4 miles

Sat'y March 8th, Moved across Rio Salado to Left bank, going West by North, came down again, (by turning North) to Rio over which we again crossed at a place where it is very deep 2 miles, Marched West about one mile further, when we left the river and turned North East and East x North, for about 3 miles or farther, getting down into a cañon, the mouth of which we had crossed at its junction with Rio Salado, this a.m. Found water in a side cañon to Right (some of the packers think we were encamped upon this stream, Dec 28th). Day fine, but excessively warm. Thermometer about 90°F. in shade. Sky blue and cloudless. Day's march about. . . . . . .7 miles.

Sunday, Mar. 9th. Broke camp 8 am. North up cañon about 2 1/2 m, passing hidden spring in conglomerate rock on Right. [C]rossed Brown's trail of Dec 28th [18]72. going West found water on this trail at junction of two little cañons with that which we ascended. Turned West North West & North going up arroyo, after a total march of 4 miles turned North, going over hills about 2 miles descended into an arroyo running North West, Dry, where we struck it. After two hours, found water in a little arroyo on left. Further down at junction of this water with Sycamore Creek. (North to South) camped. Wood, Water and Grass. Day lovely. No new signs. Many deer tracks. The Apache trail we saw yesterday was about two months old. Distance

12 @ 13 miles

Monday March 10th. Moved down Sycamore Creek West South West. about 5 miles. Cañon all the way. Plenty of water in stream. L[ieutenant]. Watts left the command and went on to McDowell. At crossing of the Reno road saw great numbers of tracks and three or four apparently distinct trails, horses and mules as well as foot-tracks all going toward Camp McDowell. Either the pack trains of the rest of the command or, perhaps the whole command itself, has gone to the post for rations. Day fine. Sky blue.

Distance 5 miles

Tuesday March 11th. Broke camp 3 am West South West. for about 10 miles to Camp McDowell crossing Rio Verde in front of post. Maj Brown with Taylor, Rockwell, Babcock, Michler & Brodie at post, also Price, Parkhurst, Hay, Dr OBrien, and Lt. Thomas. Dispatch rec[eive]d from General Crook saying that Epizootic has broken out among Govt. [horse] herd at Prescott. News that Spain has become a republic. You cannot make a silk purse out of a sow's ear.[2] Brown and Command left with 20 days rations to scout to East of Sierra Matizal. We remain here (4) days and then sc[o]ur to West of same range and rejoin main body at Webber Creek. Horse bitten by rattlesnake last night and recovered after application of poultice of "golondrina" weed.[3] Day fine. Thermometer about 95° in shade. Sky blue. 10 miles

Wednesday March 12th Rem[aine]d at McDowell.

Thursday, March 13th Rem[aine]d at McDowell. Randall arrived, no Indians.

Weather extremely warm.

Friday, Mar 14th. News arrived that a large body of Indians had crossed mail road South of Wickenburg, killed two men and stolen three horses, Almy and myself determined to strike across country to see if we could not find their trail. Horses at Prescott are all sick and Price has no transportation.

Marched North West 4 miles. West 4 miles to Prescott road. North North West 8 miles going between 2 Buttes. 4 miles North West, passing around corner of Mountain on left 4 miles West North West to Cave Creek camped. Wood, Water, & Grass. 25 miles

Saturday Mar 15. Broke camp by moon light, going along Prescott trail North about 1/2 mile West about 1/2 mile, crossing branch of Cave Creek; North about 1/2 mile going around point of high mesa. South 1/4 m West about 6 miles, leaving flat hill on Right and (3)

2. Bourke is referring to the short-lived Carlist uprising in Spain, and apparently anticipated its failure.

3. "Golondrina" is Spanish for the swallow bird. Apparently this was a local name for a plant that I have been unable to identify.

Buttes on Left. North North West about 2 miles, North West 2 miles, West North West about 1 mile, North West and North North West about 3 miles. Camped on New River, which we reached 2 am (17th March) Distance 15 miles. Day very hot. Night cool.

Sunday Mar 16th Rem[aine]d. in camp during day. Sent out the Indian boys who found an Indian trail made by a great party of Indians—Apache Mojaves—men, women and children, going toward a spur of the Bradshaw Mountains. or else those between the Verde and Agua fria Rivers. Bread for 2 days was broken and preparations made for a night march. At rising of the moon marched North East 2 1/2 miles, keeping in the cañon of new river; made camp in a portrero [sic]: no fires allowed. Utmost silence enjoined

    2 1/2 [miles]

Monday March 17th [Saint] Patricks day. After sunrise small fires were built and coffee made. Indians sent out to examine trail, which now looks as if great numbers had recently passed over it. Moses [Indian scout] returned at mid-day with request for command to move further up cañon. Accordingly, at 2 Pm, moved up stream North East one mile East half a mile North East one mile. Camped in a potrero, Passed a little butte on Right and saw a double headed butte due North of last Camp. Day hazy. Temperature about 75° F. Grass excellent. Water in about as great quantities as I have ever found upon such a stream in any part of the Territory.

    2 1/2 miles:

We have to-day been out after Indians (4) continuous months. Rained violently nearly all night.

Tuesday, March 18th Broke camp at 8.30 a.m. Marched up new river about 6 or 7 miles, North East. Cañon all way. Rained heavily this morning. Many of the arroyos are filled with water. Camped at junction of 2 two cañons. Water plenty. Wood rather scarce, grass excellent, and abundant. Day cloudy.

    Distance 6 @ 7 miles

Made a night march, 45 men (15 from my co) 3 officers, 4 apaches and the Interpreter Lopez. Started at night-fall, marched North East about 1/2 mile up cañon, turned East up tributary going about 5 miles and reaching top of a divide. Halted for moon. Rained a little. Mounted on top Mountain for 3 miles, then down Mountain; head of Cave Creek. here running South. no fires. Indian trail now very much scattered. Great difficulty in finding it: Wednesday March

19th Kept on East for 3 miles, then East x South for 3 miles more going down very steep and long grade to Red Creek flowing South (just below this point it turned East x South and flowed into the Rio Verde about 2 1/2 Miles) Camped and sent messenger for pack-trains, at this spot, from a deserted rancheria of (23) jacales and a corn field; jacales recently deserted. Very large timbers, cut with axes, have been used in the construction of these dwellings. (Sent outside scouts, one to East, another to North. Both returned with information that Indians have all gone across Verde. One party found Woodson in camp just across, the Verde and from him we rec[eive]d a note saying that Randall and Hamilton were following the trail of the Indians we have been following since the 15th inst.[)]

Distance from last camp   16 miles

Thursday mar 20th Packs arrived. Rem[aine]d in camp.

Friday Mar 21st Moved east over the mountain to Rio Verde. Saw Lt Woodsons' command to North of us (about 2 miles) going up stream. Upon discovering us, they halted and waved signals to which we responded. Rice (the Guide) sent to communicate with Lt W. Kept on East going over grassy plateau for 6 miles when we descended into a box cañon on Right and made camp. This cañon was full of running water, an abundance of excellent green grass, and had a sufficiency of wood. It empties into Rio Verde about a half a mile above junction of Red Creek (Last night our Indian boys discovered a fresh trail which they followed South across the Mountains bordering the Verde until they came to a recently abandoned rancheria, from which they brought back a basket.[)] Reported seeing a fire on Sierra Metitzal to East. To-day just after crossing the Verde, we came to the ruins of an old fortification of greater magnitude than any we have yet encountered. Being in a completely ruined condition, we could only conjecture its previous configuration, size and purpose, but everything seemed to indicate that in the center had been a vast rectangular two or three storied pile with well defended entrances and loop-holed walls, while the exterior-line of work represented a parapet behind which the animals could find a temporary shelter.[4] The entire work was of limestone,

---

4. Frazer (*Forts of the West*, 3ff.) does not mention a Spanish defense work in this part of Arizona. Very likely Bourke saw the ruins of Pueblo Grande, a pre-Columbian Hohokam Indian settlement, near Camp McDowell and the Rio Verde in what is now Phoenix. Pueblo Grande had a multistory principal structure surrounded by a wall, much as he described and sketched in the diary. At the time of Bourke's early writings, the ruins of indigenous cultures

laid in an adobe cement, the *vigas*[5] being of cottonwood, but so much decayed that we could only find little pieces of them in the walls. 500 or more men could be accommodated within the lines which however seemed from the number of partition walls to have been intended for storehouses. One of the corners is still more than 20 feet high—perhaps 25. Almy suggests that perhaps the structure had been erected by Coronado as a base of supplies and the suggestion is certainly a good one. If this be so, what a field for contemplation is afforded by these ruins. Our minds are carried back, to the time when Charles Vth was King of Spain and the Indies, when the Spaniards were first among nations in politeness[,] learning, wealth and enterprise. When the order of Jesuits was first established (a little handfull of seven seven men), from which order such wonderful results should come.

Coronado started in 1541 to rescue from the Moquis,[6] seven missionaries who had gone to labor among them. It was alleged that some of these clergymen had been killed or maltreated and to secure their delivery the Spanish Govn. sent an imposing expedition under command of one of the ablest men at that time in this part of America.

The expedition was gone 3 years, subjugated the Moquis, Zunies and some of the Navajoes[,] found that one missionary had been put to death and (5) others died under various circumstances, leaving alone the survivor, who had adopted the Indian customs and language, to enable him to carry on his ministry. When brought to Coronado he had nearly forgotten his native language. This is only one instance of the self-sacrificing zeal & devotion with which the Catholic missionaries to America signalized their career. Planting the tree of life amid unknown deserts and mountains and among unknown tribes, watering it with their blood and all for the sake of a principle which the world may call fanaticism, but which perhaps God may call Faith.[7] Shall we never hear the last of Elliot [sic] the

---

in the American Southwest were only dimly understood, being attributed variously to Aztecs or Spaniards. Serious archaeological investigation did not begin until the 1880s. Meanwhile, the multistory structure was razed to use as fill for agricultural lands. See Noble, *Ancient Ruins of the Southwest*, 36–37.

5. Main roof beams.

6. Hopis.

7. As Bourke himself admits at the end of this paragraph, he is not sure of the details of this expedition, and here he seems to have blended several unrelated—or only marginally related—events into a single episode. Aside from an expedition of Franciscan missionaries led by Fray Marcos de Niza in 1539, which essentially was a reconnaissance, there was no

Indian missionary who only ventured once beyond the town limits of Boston? And whose famous Bible was written in a comfortable studio?[8] All honor to him, but greater praise to these greater men the Spanish priests. The above acc[oun]t, altho garbled maybe, is true in this much. The date of Cs [Coronado's] departure & the time of his absence. About the remainder, there are several conflicting stories. 1st as to the number of padres and secondly as to the tribes among whom they labored.

To-day's march   10 @ 11 miles.

Rice ret[urne]d without having been able to overtake Woodson's command.

Saturday, May 22d Marched North East across mesa passing tributary of creek on which we camped[;] another creek itself (here flowing from North to South[)] passed across confluent from East (2 miles). Day cloudy. Temperature 60° F. Fine Grass every-where. Marched up the cañon (North) for 6 or 7 miles, finding a spring upon the Mountain side to the Right and another upon the left, the first about 2 or 3 miles up the cañon; the second at end of journey. Camped in a beautiful little cove. Excellent green grass, plenty of wood and water. We are now getting well into the bosom of the Sierra Matitzal. One of our Mexn. packers has been very sick for several days. Last night he became demented. He will most probably die within a few days.   7 or 8 ms

Sunday, Mar 23d Marched East North East up cañon about 4 miles. A few hund[re]d. yds from our camp saw where Randall had camped two days ago. His train turned to Left going North one mile from camp saw little creek coming in on Right, also saw a mounstruous [sic] quartz ledge. Mountains becoming very elevated. Sky cloudy. Weather warm but mild. Mexican very sick. Went due North up cañon one mile, Plenty of water. Trail very bad. Had to make camp on acc[oun]t of the precarious condition of the Mexican who, I am afraid, will die to-night. Distance 5 m.

---

serious effort to contact the Indians of Arizona prior to Francisco Vásquez de Coronado. The Coronado expedition, which followed up Fray Marcos's journey, was an *entrada*, a military campaign to conquer the local inhabitants and exploit resources. The American Southwest, however, did not offer the wealth that the Spaniards had come to expect following the conquests of Mexico and Peru. See Fontana, *Entrada*, 21-22, 25-31.

8. Here Bourke's Roman Catholic bias is evident. John Eliot (1604-90), Puritan preacher, evangelized the Massachusetts Indians, frequently visiting their villages in what then was wilderness. He learned their language, and translated the Bible into Algonquin. Eliot's efforts won the loyalty of many New England Indians during King Philip's War, the first great Indian uprising in New England. See Russell, "Apostle to the Indians."

Ruins of old Spanish fort on the Verde —
If this was erected by Coronado
to store his supplies, its date is 1541.

A   B

Ruins of the
Building, used as
Keep

C   D

ABCD = Rampart

Scale not given at proper time, but I think now
(February 28th 1861) that it was one block to square of 100 yds
on a side — or one of these red spaces to 100 yds. in length.
corners were paricoupé.

Monday Mar 24th The sick Mexican Presiliano Mongo,[9] died this morning at one o'clock. We buried him shortly after sun-rise and erected over his grave [a] small cross bearing his name and date of his death. To day the weather was especially charming, the whistling of birds was heard on every side and the balmy air made us forget that any part of Arizona is a desert. March[e]d North North East up cañon, going along skirt of mountain. Passed two spring's, in front of our camp on Left side of arroyo, about half mile from camp, stream divides into 2 parts, one from South South East, the other North North East shortly afterwards 2nd stream received a confluent from our Left. Mountains still very high. Kept on in a general North North East course still following the cañon passed a little stream coming in on our Right. Entered a deserted Indian rancheria—12 houses— passed through a grove of robles (scrub-oak) (3 1/2 miles total). Kept on up cañon now getting very steep, waterfall on Left, crossed stream for last time, going to its Right. Marched now due West. Getting to top of hill, saw the creek again below us. Passed through another rancheria. Found belt of pine timber on top of range (5 miles).

North one mile going down into a valley, timbered with pine, oak and manzanita; some snow on ground, water in every little arroyo. Made camp on a little stream, flowing from N to South and South West. Saw Bradshaw and Mogollon ranges in distance former to West, latter to North. To-day we have wood, water, grass in abundance. Every indications [sic] goes to prove that the Indians have been in the cañon of the past few day's march for months; we have seen more than a hundred large sized jacales, freshly abandoned.

Tuesday Mar 25 Moved North about 300 yds, then down a grade 6 miles. Saw two little Mountain streams on our Left. [C]ame down into a cañon just below their junction and near the confluence of a 3d from the Right. Beautiful waterfall on Left. (1 mile). Day fine. Hills timbered with pine & oak.

Kept on down stream until we came to East Fork Rio Verde, where we found remains of a large camp of soldiers, (3) or (4) days old at the farthest. Passed a little stream on Right. Also several Indian rancherias (deserted) 9 miles.

9. In *On the Border With Crook* (211-12), Bourke corrected the spelling to "Monje," and described the packer as "a very amiable man, who had made friends of all our party." He died of pneumonia, resulting from an untreated cold caught in the mountains.

Wednesday March 26th: Moved North North East about 500 yds, then East, about same distance along East Fr [Fork] Verde. Crossed it and moved East for a total distance 1 1/2 miles. Moved North North East for about 5 miles, again crossing East Fork at bend (East North East to West South West.). Country very hilly and well grassed. Day fine. Moved in a general North North East course for a total distance of more than 15 miles, going up East fork. Country Hilly. Just before getting into camp, came upon a heavy trail fresh following our course.   16 miles

Thursday Mar 27th. Moved North about 1/2 mile until we reached Webber Creek (flowing East South East.) Turned up that stream West North West; North North West, North, West and North for a total march of about 5 miles. Day cool, but mild. Sky clear. Passed Brown's camp about 1 mile out from our camp of yesterday. Saw some few pappoose tracks on his trail.

        5 miles

(Much oak & some little pine on Webber Creek.)

Friday Mar 28th. Moved West about 3 miles crossing very soon after leaving camp a small tributary of Webber Creek (flowing South). Country very beautiful Finely timbered with oak & some pine, well watered and abundantly grassed (Black Mesa on our Right about 2 miles) Day fine. Kept up our West course for a total distance of 7 1/2 miles. Sierra Mogollon just in front and to Right of us. Pine woods all the way. Came to Krome's Creek (here flowing about North to South.[)] Scenery beautiful. Devin's jump-off to North West

(Distance about 3 or 4 miles)

Sat'y Mar 29th: A Fresh trail of Apache-Mojaves, (men, women and children) was discovered last night leading along under the South edge of Black Mesa & going in an East direction. This morning, the Com[man]d moved to intercept the band if possible. Moved East parallel to yesterday's course for about 3/4 mile, going up gentle grade. Turned North East grade getting more severe, until we reached crest of Black Mesa 1 3/4 miles. Day fine. Sky cloudless. The ascent of the mesa was made without difficulty. East about 1/2 mile, then in a Northerly course for 2 miles, [k]eeping Webber Cañon on our Right. Pine forest the whole way. Kept along edge of the mesa for nearly [one] mile. Further, first going North East 2 miles, until we came to Head waters of Webber Creek; the other 2 miles North, Camped on the mesa Wood. Water. and Grass. Snow in patches.

Scenery beautiful. To the West, we could see Squaw Peak for 9 miles. This morning one of our Indian boys was reported as deserted he having been absent since yesterday. To-night a small party was sent on ahead to examine country and look for Indian signs. Returning, they reported having found where the Apache-Mojaves. . .had climbed up on the mesa, that they followed their trail which was about five day's old and bore evidence of having been made by a very large band of men, women & children. We have only six or seven day's rations.

Sunday Mar 30th Broke camp at 9 a.m. Moved North East for about 3 or 4 miles. Pine timber on every side. Day fine. Snow to be seen in patches at intervals. Went in same direction about 1/2 m. reaching the edge of the mesa, at the head of Webber Creek. Turned East (South) went nearly a mile and found trail which we had been hunting; trail going due East. Went one and half miles. (East) finding the place where the Indians had gone down from the mesa and also their camp (26) fires, representing an aggregate of at least two hundred. As we had no rations with which to make an energetic pursuit we were obliged to return. No doubt the Indians have gone to the Colorado Chiquito. . . . . .7 miles

Stream upon which we camped joins Webber Creek.

Monday, Mar 31st. Moved back on yesterdays trail about 4 miles. Ground very muddy from melting snow. Day fine, but rather cool. Struck the Devin's trail and marched upon it North for about one mile, passing over a little brook flowing South South West & South. Kept on North, crossing another brook (tributary of former) going some little distance (say two miles) and heading a number of small streams flowing West. We now could catch, at intervals, glimpses of the Mountains on West of Rio Verde—Squaw Peak and others. Kept on North, until the march was about (10) miles when we halted in a little arroyo (flowing North) and made camp. Wood and Water, good and plenty. Grass poor & scarce. [T]his creek flows North x East for 2/3 mile and then joins Clear Creek or Fossil Creek when flowing due West (just above Clear Creek Cañon). East Fork joins the Verde proper about 30 miles below Camp Verde—Fossil Creek runs in a mile or two above East Fork. Clear Creek joins Rio Verde 5 miles below post. Beaver Creek about opposite to post. Distance to day. . . . . . .19 miles

Tuesday April 1st. Day dawned bright and cold. Turned West, 2 miles over very hilly and timbered crossing general small confluents of

Clear & Fossil Creeks. Turning South we ascended a little stream with great quantity of water one mile, crossed it about its junction with a tributary from the South West and halted on summit of a high hill (3 miles). Country is to day broke up by a great number of gullies, all full of running water, and the elevation is perceptibly less than that of day before yesterday. Marched 3 1/2 miles South West & South crossing another little stream flowing West. Marched this last distance upon an old trail which ran in from East South East, one mile and a half South along a broad divide having creeks on each side flowing West, two miles South coming down into what the guide calls Hardscrabble Creek. Saw trail of Cavalry from South East, probably made by Burns and Hall. . . . . . 10 @ 12 miles

Wednesday, April 2d: Day clear and mild. Moved West down Hardscrabble Creek; about 1 mile out creek turns South West; our trail kept on due West. Burns trail turned South about 500 yds beyond the creek. Bill Williams Mountain[10] in distance to Right Bradshaw Mountain in the distance to West. Turned North West 3/4 mile North 1/2 miles, descended a steep mountain (40 minutes being req[uire]d to move down the declivity). Struck Fossil Creek at mouth of its cañon at a point where it turns West by South (This creek, as we saw it, was flowing from North East then North and South then West, then South West, then South— Its general course being North East to South West) Moved West one mile up high Mountains. Moved in a North course for 4 or 5 miles over an undulating, grassy mesa of lava. Came to tanks near a grove of cedar and pine (Muddy Tanks) Camped. Wood. Water and Grass. Baker's Butte due East about 12 miles.

10 miles

Thursday, April 3d. Day bright and beautiful. Marched West to Cedar Tanks 3 miles, passing cavalry trail leading North. Squaw Peak about 10 miles West 20° South. Much cedar in vicinity of these tanks, (arroyo from these tanks leads South West to Verde). Marched West & South West. 2 miles, South 2 miles West North West North North

---

10. Bill Williams Mountain (or Mountains), mentioned frequently in Bourke's Arizona texts, is named for William Sherley (Old Bill) Williams (1787-1849). A North Carolinian who moved with his family to Missouri as a child, Williams went to live among the Osages in his midteens. He worked variously as a scout, trapper, trader, and interpreter. In the 1830s, Williams explored much of Arizona, resulting not only in the mountain being named for him, but also the Bill Williams Fork of the Colorado River. He also participated in Capt. John Charles Frémont's 1848-49 Rocky Mountain expedition and was killed by Indians while trying to recover expedition property. Thrapp, *Encyclopedia of Frontier Biography*, 3:1573-72.

West and West for a total day's march of twelve miles, coming down into Clear Creek four miles above junction with Verde. Wood, water and grass plenty, and good. Passed to Right of butte, six miles before reaching camp, Trail bad. Day exceedingly warm   12 miles

Friday, April 4th. Moved down Clear Creek North North West 2 miles, turning to left and moving West North West, 3 miles to Camp Verde, crossing Rio Verde in front of post. Indian runners sent out to bring in such of the hostile Indians as may be inclined to sue for peace.

        5 miles

Found Genl Crook, Dr Bendell[,] Genl Small, Mr Marion, Dr Williams, Colonel Coppinger and all the officers of his post & of Maj Brown's Command. All well. Our comrades had killed one hundred and ten.

Saturday, April 5th. Rem[aine]d at Verde. Made a trip to Montezuma's Wells. Found the well to be the crater of an extinct volcano, situated at head of Beaver Creek nine miles North North West from Verde. The descent to the surface of water was about (150) feet in length; the depth of the well in the middle not known—near the shore seventy feet. Diameter about (100) yds, one hundred yards.

We found houses of stone and cement built by a nation of whom no traces now remain and a deep cave, also occupied as a habitation, in the centre of which rose a fine spring which shortly disappeared in the sands and then bursting through a crevice in the lava, found its way into Beaver Creek.

Returned same night to Verde.   20 miles

Sunday, April 6th. Chis-le-pun a big chief of the Apaches came in to offer his submission. He had with him about (300) people. He said he could not fight with General Crook because the General had too many copper cartridges, too many soldiers and in every way too powerful to be contended against.[11]

At night, rode on horseback to Prescott reaching there Monday, April 7.

Weather bitter cold.   45 miles

Thus terminated the first and only successful campaign against the Apaches since the acquisition of the Gadsden Purchase. The orders

11. In his autobiography, Crook quotes Cha-lipun (which Bourke spelled "Chis-le-pun") as telling him, "You see, we're nearly dead from want of food and exposure—the copper cartridge has done the business for us. I am glad of the opportunity to surrender, but I do it not because I love you, but because I am afraid of General." Schmitt, *General George Crook*, 179.

announcing the conclusion of hostilities, particularlizing the officers most distinguished for gallantry, giving instructions for the treatment of Indians upon reservations and assigning troops to stations now follow. [See Appendix 2]

The results may be summed up as follows;

By Brown's Command

Indians killed..500

by each separate detachment

Miles travelled about...........................1200

Days..142

Chapter 4

✦

✦

✦

✦

✦

Reservation and Ruins

On October 29, 1873, Lt. Col. Crook was jumped two grades
and appointed to the active rank of brigadier general, at the behest of President Grant. Up until this time, he had held command
by his Union Army brevet of major general, but with the active
rank of lieutenant colonel of the 23rd Infantry. The appointment
created hard feelings in the army because a large number of full
colonels senior to him were passed over in what obviously was a
case of presidential favoritism. Nevertheless, congress confirmed
it. In later years, this would be used against Crook and, because
of his association with Crook, would also work against Bourke.
While it did not necessarily hinder Crook, in the long run Bourke's
career would suffer.[1]

Crook's appointment is not mentioned in Bourke's diaries because there is a gap of almost eighteen months from April 1873
until September 1874. Presumably Bourke continued his journals
during that interval, but if so they are among the lost volumes.
The extant narrative resumes on September 22, 1874, when Crook
and Bourke embarked on an inspection tour of the military posts
and reservations at Camp Verde, San Carlos, and Camp Apache.

1. Robinson, *General Crook*, 137-38; Porter, *Paper Medicine Man*, 301.

*After leaving Camp Apache, they continued on to the pueblos of
the Hopis, who at that time were called Moquis. This, as Bourke's
biographer, Joseph Porter, has pointed out, represented his first
ethnographic notes of people other than Apaches.*[2]

*Bourke's description of the Hopis shows them to be a commer-
cially-minded people who, although they did not understand the
value of paper money, nevertheless managed a trade network
reaching as far as Santa Fe, New Mexico, and to various other
tribes in the region including Apaches. In fact, Apache prisoners
admitted they had obtained the bulk of their arms and ammunition from the Hopis who, in turn, had purchased them from Mormons and Utes. General Crook intended to end the trade.*[3]

*The expedition left Camp Verde on September 22, 1874, travel-
ing to the pueblos via San Carlos and Camp Apache. En route to
San Carlos, they passed the various prehistoric ruins between
what is now Tonto National Monument and Besh Ba Gowah Archaeological Park in modern Globe. These ruins were left by the
Hohokam and Salado cultures. Early Spanish explorers, however,
assumed that they and other prehistoric structures of Arizona and
New Mexico were built by the Aztecs, a belief that persisted in
Bourke's time. Consequently, his initial diary entry declared the
ruins to be Aztec, although he later revised that to "so-called Aztec." Among their guides was one who called himself Mickey Free,
who was, in fact, the same Felix Ward whose kidnapping by
Apaches fourteen years earlier had ignited the Cochise War.*[4]

*Bourke's brief, but enthusiastic entry on the San Carlos Reser-
vation is especially significant. This represented the first concerted
attempt to "Americanize" the Apaches by instituting a wage-labor
system. Beginning with the employement of Apache scouts by the
army, wage-labor expanded into other areas. Although rations
continued to be issued for the next twenty-five years, the government instituted agricultural programs to convert the Indians to
farming. Likewise, construction and maintenance of the agency
buildings and development of the reservation infrastructure pro-*

2. Porter, ibid., 24

3.Discussing the Hopi trade in guns and ammunition, Crook wrote, "I became satisfied
that they had such a traffic, but the fright we gave them put an end to it." Schmitt, *General
George Crook*, 183.

4. Bourke, Diaries, 2:5, "so-called Aztec," 2:97. This series of ruins is discussed in Noble,
Ancient Ruins of the Southwest, 167-70. The Spanish impression that the ruins were Aztec
is discussed in various places in Fontana, *Entrada*.

vided more or less steady employment, as did the military post attached to the reservation, although closure of the post later created some unemployment.[5] Elaborating in On the Border With Crook, Bourke wrote:

> [T]he enlistment of a force of scouts who were paid the same salary as white soldiers, and at the same periods with them, introduced among the Apaches a small, but efficient working capital. . . .[Crook explained] that by investing their money in California horses and sheep, they would be gaining more money all the time they slept, and by the time their children had attained maturity the hills would be dotted with herds of horses and flocks of sheep. Then they would be rich like the white men. . . they would not be dependent upon the Great Father for supplies, but would have for themselves and their families all the food they could eat, and would have much to sell.[6]

The inspections of the reservations completed, the column departed Camp Apache on October 7, arriving at the first Hopi pueblos five days later. Bourke's record of the march is a monotonous series of notes primarily of interest to people who would travel along the trail on horseback. It includes observations on terrain, grass, water, and bearings of particular landmarks, but little else. Once the column reached the pueblos, however, Bourke is at his best. Despite the disdain that pervades this and other early volumes of the diary, he demonstrates the healthy curiosity for Indian culture that in later years would change his attitude to one of profound respect. Very little escaped his attention—local crops and handicrafts, household furnishings, modes of dress, and even women's hairstyles all found their way into his notes. Although he described Hopi art as "rude" he thought it worth reproducing in his notes. In an extraneous note separate from the main narrative, he wrote:

Country of Moquis visited by Genl. Crook, U.S.A.
Oct. 1874

5. Adams, "The Development of San Carlos Apache Wage Labor to 1954," 118.
6. Bourke, On the Border, 221-22.

Villages.
Oraybe.
Teǵua.
Hualpai.   Oct. 14th 1874
Moqui.
Su-powa-levy.
Su-mo-pavy.
Muschang-nevy.
These people do not irrigate land, Do not all speak the same
language. Were first visited by Roman Catholic missionaries
in 1536; then by expedition of Coronado in 1541.[7]

*On modern maps, these villages appear as Oraibi, Hano, Walpi,
Sichomovi, Shipaulovi, Shongopavi, and Mishongnovi, respectively. They are built on three adjacent mesas, with Walpi,
Sichomovi and Hano on First Mesa; Shongopavi, Shipaulovi, and
Mishongnovi on Second Mesa; and Oraibi on Third Mesa. Bourke
is correct about the language differences, because the people of
Hano speak a Tanoan language from the New Mexico area, while
the others speak Hopi. He is less accurate concerning early Spanish contact. His observation that Roman Catholic missionaries
visited in 1536 apparently refers to the reconnaissance led by Fray
Marcos de Niza that actually occurred in 1539, and may or may
not have reached the Hopi pueblos. It is known that a scouting
party, headed by Pedro de Tovar, from the Coronado expedition,
did reach some of the Hopi towns in 1540, although this did not
include Hano, which was founded more than a century later.[8]*

*Today, the Hopi continue much of their ancient tradition, in
part because the establishment of schools at the pueblos assures a
year-round population of young people to learn the principles and
ethics of Hopi life. They also participate in the ritual and ceremo-
nial activities that sustain them as a people. The Hopi Foundation, consisting of professionals and lay persons from the tribe,
works to integrate them into the modern world, while at the same
time preserves the best of the old values.[9]*

7. Bourke, Diaries, 2:66.
8. Fontana, *Entrada*, 21-22, 26; Cordell, *Ancient Pueblo Peoples*, 14.
9. Hoxie, *Encyclopedia of North American Indians*, 253-55. For a description of
contemporary Hopi ceremonies having their origins in ancient times, see Ortiz, "Farmers
and Raiders," 177-80.

Mules died yesterday 21st.

Det[a]ch[ment] at Camp Verde 15, men

Water wheel 16 feet cost $36.00

Post in excellent condition

[October] 12th Borrowed from Sergeant Icar [?] 1.60, Green, 1.25. Cahill .25 Cahill $3.00, Scott $15

Oct 13th, General Crook borrowed of Hawes, $20 of Cahill $5; and of Mr Lewis $2, and of Lt. Bourke 10, and of Scott $5.00

Oct 16th, Camp on Colorado Chiquito, paid Cahill $5—$3[.]25 being for himself and $1[.]60 for the men of the escort—Money borrowed Oct 12th. This was done with the knowledge and consent of the Sergeant of the escort.

Oct. 19th Camp on West slope of San Francisco Mountain, paid Mr. Scott $10 (ten dollars) borrowed from him Oct 12th

General Crook desired me to note he had borrowed $4 from Mr. Lewis Oct. 14th 1874.

At end of this book will be found a printed copy of the monograph published in the Daily Alta California of Dec. 14th 1874.

Also photographs of the Moqui Villages[10]

Sept. 22d. Left Camp Verde, 8. A.M., travelling 20 miles to lower crossing Fossil Creek. Day pleasant. Trail fair. Feasted on the finest water melons and wild grapes ever eaten in Arizona. Melons from ranches on Clear Creek and grapes from vines on trail. Fossil Creek flowing with a great head of water, between very high mountains.

Sept 23. Wednesday, Broke camp at Daybreak. Generally East course for about 22 or 23 miles to East Fork of Verde river and below mouth of Webber Creek. crossing Krause's(?) Creek.

23= Country very mountainous; & trail rough. Our camp to night in front of North Peak and Massissal Mountains.[11] Day very warm.

Sept 24th (Thursday) Broke camp at day-break. General course South down Wild-Rye Creek to within a few hundred yards of its junction with Tonto Creek. (here bending from an East & West to a North and South course around North West end of the Sierra Ancha.)

10.The "monograph," published in the *Alta California* under the heading of "The Moquis of Arizona: a Brief Description of their Towns, Their Manners and Customs," is Bourke's earliest known published work. Despite his reference to it as a monograph, no copy has been located other than that published in the newspaper. The clipping and photographs, if indeed they ever were included, apparently were removed at some point. See Bloom, "Bourke on the Southwest," Vol. 8, no. 1:12, and Vol. 10, no. 1:5.

11. Mazatzal

for about 3 miles over high hills, crossing two affluents of Tonto
Creek and the creek itself on South side of which we camped. 21
miles. Day very warm. Sky clear. trail good.

Sept 25th. Friday. Moved South, by a trifle East down Tonto Creek,
until within 3 miles of its junction with S[a]lado when we inclined
more to the East, crossed Salado, turning due East, about 3 miles
and camped at a boiling spring Mesquite Springs. Water good. Day
very warm. Sky blue. Marched 27 miles. Had Matitzal Mountains on
our Left and Sierra Ancha on our Right all day. Trail very good.
Passed Old Camp Reno on our Right to-day, also saw two little
streams flowing into Tonto Creek from West. Passed a number of
old Aztec ruins to-day. Examined one and found it to be the remains of a temple,[12] an outer wall of rock had enclosed a house,
having a court-yard, in centre of which could still be discerned a
three-terraced teocalli, with foundation of an altar(?) on top: an
entrance through the house discovered signs of an attempt at making arches.

Sept 26th. 15 miles East x South making camp on Wheat fields of
Pinal creek about 8 miles from last night's camp, passed a fine spring.
March of to-day rough. Weather torrid.

Sept 27 South South East and South East 50 miles w[ith] 50 miles
crossing up through East fork of Pinal Creek, then into Mescal Mountains to Jesus' Spring, thence 14 miles nearly due East down Mountains to San Carlos. Weather very warm, Indians had a big dance to
night.

San Carlos to top of Mt Trumbull 120° San Carlos to Green's Peak
152° 30'

Pass in Mescal Mountains 275°

East x North of Mt. Trumbull near Goodwin 110°

1st Peak San Carlos 15° 2nd peak 10° 3rd peak 5°

The condition of Indian affairs on the San Carlos we found astonishing and gratifying. Indians present numbered 875. All living in
villages with regular streets, houses of brush 12' high, bunks elevated ten feet above the ground. Every morning at 7 O'c[lock].
their villages are policed with the greatest care and every Sunday

12. Above "temple" Bourke wrote "teocalli?" the Nahuatl word for "temple." This probably
was Besh Ba Gowah, much of which was bulldozed, first by the Corps of Engineers to provide
a Boy Scout Jamboree campground in 1948, and later by the City of Globe to expand
recreational facilities. The remnants are now a city archaeological park. See Noble, *Ancient
Ruins of the Southwest*, 168-70.

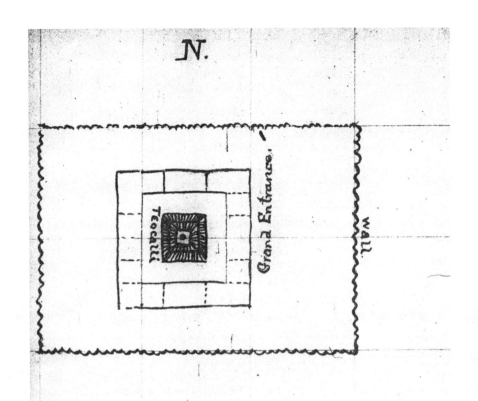

Aztec ruin, "Tonto Creek, Sept 25th 1874.

(Aztec arch.)

an inspection is made to see that no garbage has been allowed to accumulate around their quarters, and that beds and blankets are clean. Indians are detailed each morning to work in fields, to make adobes and other employments for which they make good laborers. Average 100 adobes daily to the hand. Are very happy and seem well fed. Scarcely any sickness. Under best of discipline. Governed with firmness and justice. Are very well behaved. Not at all insolent. Always uncover the head when saluting a stranger. Credit for all this is due to Maj. Randall, Babcock and Ward, also Lt London. Indian Agent Clum just arrived and has quietly adopted all the military rules of management. Seems a good man. Indians had a dance last night in honor of arrival of Genl Crook, with whom they held a long conference to-day. Santos, Juan-clishe and El Cal being the speakers. Said they were now thoroughly whipped and under General C's orders. What he said, they would do &c &c &c. Would work like white people and hoped they would have plenty of work, so they could get money to buy blankets. Wanted to live there always and if any Indians came there from other Reserves without passes, would make them go to the guard-house or would kill them as they had the other bad ones. Thought the bad ones were all dead now. At least all among them were: (Found all at S[an]. C[arlos]. pleasant, affable gentlemen)

Sept 28th, Monday Marched North up San Carlos river for 15 or 18 miles camping in sand upstream. Location very fine, Wood, Water and Grass plentiful and of good quality. Day warm.

Sept. 29th Move up San Carlos about 1 1/2 to 2 miles, climbed to top of high mesa, marched over this rough high mesa, keeping this tributary of San Carlos on our Right, for 8 miles, entered a cañon of Apache Mountains, followed this cañon 4 miles, turned East for about 1 mile, striking another affluent of S.C., which joined the first; followed up this last for nearly 6 miles, our trail being more to the East of North say North 10° East, struck a beautiful spring (Brodie's) of ice-cold water, bubbling out from under a natural cliff of rock at base of main range. Ascended the mountain, trail very rough, pine trees now being met with. Kept along mountain about 3 1/2 or 4 miles then commenced heavy down grade for 3 miles more to the Black River, where we camped. Wood, water and grass abundant and excellent. Scenery beautiful. Lofty mountains on either bank screen this lovely stream from view until you stand on the crest of the hills immediately above it. From (Brodie's) spring to Black river is eight miles. The cañon in Apache Mountains is studded with juniper and scrub oak. March of to-day is from 28 or 30 miles[.]

Archie McIntosh's squaw joined us at San Carlos and is en route to Camp Apache with the command.

Weather to-day pleasant. Good Breeze—Sky cloudy.

Summit of Butte to left of camp and on Right bank of river bears from camp 345°. River flows on our Left 292°. Directly in front of Camp flows due North (0°).

Sept. 30th Marched North East 8 miles reaching summit of the high mesa six miles from Camp Apache; thence six miles to Camp Apache where we remain. Found at post, Majors Randall and Babcock, Capts. Montgomery, Reilly, Lieuts Rice, Dodge[13] and Pratt.

A general count of the Indians took place to-day; over 1760 are present on the Reserve. A mild form of calenture prevails among this tribe during the present season. Indians all seem orderly and well-disciplined. Post in fine order. Scenery is beautiful. Maj. Babcock relieved from the Department to-day. News received by courier of our Indians from Camp Verde, under guide Zeiber [Sieber], having killed 13 renegades, 3 of our Indians killed in the fight.

Kelly's Peak bears 248°

Pass (of yesterday.) 225°.

Middle of point of pass (to New Mex[ic]o) 10°

The Apaches here appreciate to a considerable degree the importance of a circulating medium[14] and also show themselves in other respects to be keen traders. In two instances, they have entered into contracts with Mexicans to have the latter transport their crops to the post for sale to the Q.M.D.[15]

Tom, one of them, yesterday, wished Major Randall to accept as a gift the money he had saved in the last few months saying that R would undoubtedly need it in making a trip to Washington as the East is called. The amount so tendered was $35.

They seem to put a high estimate on the telegraph line, without, of course, understanding its modes of operation. Last fall, while Pitone, Alchisay and Uclenny were in Prescott, I sent a telegram from them to their friends on the Reserve, having it carried by courier from

13. Frederick Leighton Dodge, not to be confused with Lt. Col. Richard Irving Dodge, who figures prominently in later chapters of this volume.

14. I.e. money.

15.Quarter Master's Department.

Tucson to this place. Greatly to their surprise, a party of their friends met them on the mountains outside of the post, anxious to see what truth there was in the mysterious message so quickly conveyed. Pitone and Alchisay, this summer, desiring to visit Washington, quietly left the Reservation, hired themselves as drivers in an am[erican]. train and succeeded in reaching by slow marches the settlements in New Mexico where they regretfully learned that ($12) their joint capital was an inadequate sum for the defrayment of their expenses to Washington and back. The treatment received from Mexicans and Americans gratified them very much, making them feel how much superior a condition of peace with us was to that of their former Ishmaelitish warfare against all mankind. Lt. and Mrs. Rice leave here next week for Omaha, via Santa Fe and Denver.

Ogilby's and Worth's Companies of the 8th Inf. may be with us tomorrow, in which case the General and myself will depart for Prescott by Tuesday. Ramsdale's Company leaving on same day.*

2-, 3- and 4th of Oct. In showers of considerable force, the volume of water in the Sierra Blanca river being appreciably augmented. General Crook, anticipating the arrival of the officers of the 8th Inf. made arrangements for a general conference of the Indian chiefs, to whom he purposes giving instructions relative to their future conduct and also present their new commander. The conferences will be held to-morrow, Oct. 5th., To-day, Oct 4th is the feast of Saint Francis which I spent, with so much interest and amusement, last year, at Magdalena, in Sonora, Mexico.

Two Apaches are confined in guard-house for attempting to cut off their wives' noses—the punishment among this tribe for conjugal infidelity. Major Randall is determined to put an end to this and other cruel and inhuman customs of the Apache nation. Many sincere friends of these Indians regret that the philanthropy supposed to actuate those interested with their charge is not superior to the mercenary influences of trade.

The shrewdness and discernment of the savage are known to be great, for every departure from an established rule, their curiosity demands an explanation. Noticing that every seventh day, the store

---

* *[Bourke inserted the following on a blank page, facing page 31:]* Oct. 2nd 3d, and 4th, rained heavily at Apache, morning of 4th, just before daybreak violent storm of hail, lasting one hour. Hail stones of large size. *[Bourke's narrative for the above dates begins at the bottom of page 35, after the comment about Ramsdale's company]*

at the military post was closed they learned that the day was "Domingo" or Sunday and an opportunity was improved of informing them this cessation of business was in obedience to the Almighty's command, and in His honor. But while such an interpretation was of itself comprehensible enough, a collateral circumstance threw a shade of suspicion upon the integrity of the translation. The establishment at the Indian Agency, under the supervision and control of the Agent himself, was and is still kept open for business every day without distinction, to the no small wonder of the aborigines incapable of often appreciating the religious conversation of men whose actions assure the world filthy lucre alone is the object of their coming to Arizona.

Major Ogilby, Major Worth and Lieut Charles Baily, 8th Infantry, arrived at Apache October 5th.

Lt Ward, 5th Cav. arrived from San Carlos on the 6th Oct. Also Mr. S.R. DeLong reported that Indian inspector, Daniels had arrived at San Carlos. Lt Babcock left for [Camp] Bowie on 4th. Road between here and [t]he Gila very bad. A train has been stopped this side of Rio Prieto, and is now 25 days out from Goodwin.[16]

Genl Crook held a long conference with the Indians to-day. They asked for another agent, saying Mr. Roberts was a liar while Major Randall always spoke truth. Were glad to see Genl Crook and sorry to have Majr Randall leave. Hoped Major Ogilby would prove as good a commandant. Been busy all day laying in supplies for our trip to the Moqui pueblos and the Grand Cañon of the Colorado.

Oct. 7th. Lieut Ward, 5th Cav., returned to San Carlos.

Oct. 7th 1874 (Wednesday.) Left Camp Apache at 930 A.M, accompanied by three Indian guides, Mickey Free, Santos and Hero & moved North, crossing Sierra Blanca river; one mile out, met Mrs Bailey[17] and Mrs Summerhayes,[18] 8th Infty; two miles passed red

---

16. Camp Goodwin was established 1864 as a base of operations against Apaches, and abandoned by the military in 1871. At this time, the post buildings served a subagency for the San Carlos Reservation. The military reservation was transferred to the Department of the Interior in 1884. Altshuler, *Starting with Defiance*, 27-28; Frazer, *Forts of the West*, 8-9.

17. Ella Wilkins Baily, wife of Lt. Charles Meigs Baily, died in childbirth on October 28, 1875. Bourke sometimes spelled the name "Bailey." Altshuler, *Cavalry Yellow & Infantry Blue*, 17.

18. Martha Summerhayes (1846-1911) was the wife of Lt. John Wyer Summerhayes, Eighth Infantry. In her classic memoir, *Vanished Arizona*, she recorded (page 79) what may have been the same incident noted by Bourke:

> One day a party of horseman tore past us at a gallop. Some of them raised their hats to us as they rushed past, and our officers recognized General Crook, but we could not, in the cloud of dust, distinguish officers from scouts. All wore the flannel shirt, handkerchief tied about the neck, and broad campaign hat.

sandstone butte on our right and again crossed North Fork Sierra Blanca river, 3 miles entered gap in mountains. Sierra Blanca river on our Right, 5 miles met 2 cos of 8th Inf. under Lieut Craig; 6 miles met baggage wagons under Lieut Summerhayes; [e]ntered Pine forest and are now at considerable elevation above post. Day fair, and bright, weather mild. 12 miles, passed a Mexican train in camp. 17 miles passed the camp where Infantry had been last night. 18 miles came to forks of road. Right hand branch, North North East to New Mexico. Up to this time our course had been North with a few degrees of Easting. Now turned North West, going between 3 and 4 miles, country very undulating, pine and white oak forest all the way. General Crook shot a number of squirrels in the woods. Our supper to-night was a treat[.] Game in plenty, cantaloups [sic] and tomatoes given by our kind friend Mrs. Montgomery, and the usual components of a mountain cuisine[.] Mickey Free says to-morrow we shall camp on Shevelon's Fork, called by the Apaches Sin Lin; on Friday the Colorado Chiquito will be reached and on Sunday the Moqui village of Oraybe.

Distance to day 23 miles

Time seven hours.

Our camp was made in a beautiful little swale in the Sierra Blanca range, (which we had on our Right all day) around us gently rise hills covered to the summit with lofty pines, while nearer camp are groves of stately live-oak. In the near distance the main ridge of the Sierra Blanca, black with timber, protects us from chilling winds. The water in the spring is cold and sweet, thus giving us all the creature comforts to be desired in a bivouac, while our animals surfeit themselves upon the rich grasses of the hill-side.

Oct 8th, Thursday. Moved North and North West 3 miles, climbing to top of hill to North of Camp, which we broke at 6.30 A.M. Passed sign "Water," found little stream running South and East and apparently a branch of Shevelon's Fork, 300 yds to Right of road. Pine forest. Ground covered with blocks of lava. 7 miles out passed a high butte on our Right distant about 3 or 4 miles. Country open for a mile or mile and half—Grass very coarse. 9 miles out commenced going down grade.

Pine forest again very dense and grass improving in quality. About 10 miles, turned nearly due North, came down into Shevelon's fork of the Colorado Chiquito about one mile South of Cooley and Clarke's ranch. A large flock of wild turkeys ran across road directly in front of us. General Crook, Mr. Scott, and a number of soldiers started after them and killed Eleven, some of them weighing 20 pounds and all very plump and tender. At Cooley's ranch, established last year, found good, comfortable adobe houses, and outbuildings and corrals of pine fencing, crop this year consisted of 90,000 lbs Barley, Stock numbered between 230 and 250 head.

Went West for 3 miles, going to top of a gentle grade; had Shevelon's fork on our Right. Country rather more open, especially on Right. Some Juniper trees now seen. As far as the Eye can reach, a dense growth of timber darkens the mountain ranges on all sides of us. We are to make camp to night at foot of a mound 340° from us. Butte passed this morning is nearly due East of where we now are. Road still West. Our trail turns North North West. Sky now commenced to show signs of snow, fleecy clouds accumulating in North and North East.

Marched North North West and North for five miles, crossing two dry arroyos inclining towards Shevlon's Fork, here separated from us by a long high hill, running North and South, parallel to general direction of stream. Country open, well grassed and with an abundance of Juniper in clumps and pine in scattered belts along trail. Cross Shevlon's Fork flowing West, passed along a grassy mesa for 3 miles with the stream on our Left: on west of stream, hills are heavily covered with pine and Juniper but our line of march is through an open country: again crossed the Fork, flowing East; passed through a series of arroyos for a mile and half, having a basalt bluff on our Right: Saw numerous cattle trails and are now probably near Ewing's ranch. Move North East for 5 @ 6 miles, country rolling and bare, grass fair, struck Shevelon's fork (flowing West) at Ewing's ranch. Camped. About one mile from camp crossed dry bed of a little stream joining the Fork from the West.

Distance to-day—about 30 miles.

Butte of to day 145°

Pass in Sierra Blanca 132°

Banks of Shevlon's Fork are clay[.] [A]n excellent road; to connect the new and old roads to Prescott, could be built along the line of to-day's march without costing more than one hundred dollars worth of labor by troops.

Saw eight large tarantulas on trail to-day.

Night extremely cold; heavy dew fell.

Oct 9th Friday. Broke camp 6 A.M. (day break.) General Crook shot some ducks in the stream. Moved North (by about 5° West) for 2 miles then West for 1 mile, passed a red sandstone butte about 2 M. on our left then North West one mile; road passed through a little sand-stone arroyo, turning North East about 1/4 mile, then our course lay North for another mile and West for still another. Our route to-day will be a generally North West one. Road so far generally and in places quite rocky. First two miles out heavy sand. Juniper trees all this morning so far, but to the North East the country is open, and in all places undulating. (6 m. From this point Red Sandstone butte before mentioned 190°) Small conical butte about 15 m. distant 360° Kept a due north course, 9 miles from Camp, left the Juniper belt and passed through a rolling, grass country. 12 miles out, passed between two red sand-stone buttes, from between which Butte of this morning bears 180°. Line of travel is 0°. Pass in the Sierra Blanca is 145°. Country for the last six miles is sandy; mixed with red clay (about 6 miles out from this morning's camp, Shevlon's fork approaches within 800 yds of the road.)

The pass between these two buttes is about 1/2 mile long from North to South. From North end of pass a conical black butte, about 5 miles distant bears 5°. Line of march 330° for 16 miles. At 17 1/2 miles from camp passes black butte about 5 miles to North East. Country now getting bad; red clay, mixed with sand and gravel stones. Grass scanty. 21 miles, passed low sand-stone mesa, about half a mile off. Ends 25° and 35°. Trail now turned to 290° for a few hundred yards. Small red sand-stone butte to our left (not visible for any great distance[)] is 300° (about a mile away.) ten for fifteen miles to right another, saddle shaped, has for centre of depression 55°.

Went one mile, turning around head of a little sand-stone arroyo, evidently an affluent of the Colorado Chiquito; resumed our former direction of 330°, gaining summit of pass. Halting place just left is 130° from top of pass is 55° (15 centre of saddle.) Before us spreads the valley of the Colorado Chiquito running here from East to West. A Flat top mesa of small size on Right, about 25 miles away is (22°); another to left of it, saddle shaped is, to centre of saddle, ten degrees, and still another to the extreme left of the same plateau on other side of Colorado Chiquito is 318°. On this side of stream, near to-night's camp, is a small rough, yellow sandstone hill, rather low which from my present position is 340° to its centre; trail to camp goes to left of that. San Francisco Mountain, (one peak can be seen at 282° and a second at 285°[)].

Oct 10th Saturday. Broke camp at daybreak, 6 A.M. Moved down the Colorado Chiquito following the Camp Apache and Prescott road for 13 miles, when we made camp on the Right bank of stream in a clump of cottonwoods. Road to day has been very tortuous but our general direction from last night's camp was toward high peak of San Francisco Mountain. (282° a[nd] 290°.)

(About 4 miles out, passed a dry wash, with cottonwood.) joining Col. Chiquito from North East. Evidently water in this wash, a short distance above. For nine miles, mesa comes down within half a mile of stream on Right bank; on left bank the descent is by a gentle slope. Noticed a peculiar outcropping of sandstone boulders. Trees along steam show the rapid approach of water; golden yellow and bright green struggles for the mastery. The banks of Colorado Chiquito all day have been steep, clay walls. The water itself is heavily loaded with alluvial matter in suspension and although not unpleasant to taste is decidedly alkaline. Country open and arid. Grass poor. Cottonwoods and willows the only trees. We saw to-day on the road where a great flock of sheep had been grazing, probably some large band from the Rio Grande or North West part of New Mexico. Much alkali in the soil on this march; our bill of fare since leaving Apache has been varied and agreeable. Without antelope or deer meat, our larder has yet been so well supplied with different species of small game, rabbit, squirrel, hare, wild duck and wild turkey, that the absence of the first name article of diet has not been felt. When we get to the Moqui villages, as our Indians assured us we shall do early day after to-morrow morning, hopes are entertained of our being able to trade with the Moquis for fresh vegetables, fruit and mutton, all of which are raised by them in quantities; Peaches especially will be relished as an unlooked for luxury in this wilderness. A heavy rain storm has prevailed over this part of Arizona within the last fortnight. All the arroyos contain pools of water. The storm was evidently the same one which lasted for three days after our arrival at Camp Apache.

Night warm.

Oct 11th Sunday. Arose at 3.30. Moved out North West at 5 A.M. 2 1/2 miles passed a range of buttes inclining from South East to North

West about 2 3/4 passed an arroyo coming into Colorado Chiquito from 45°. Longest Butte now seems to be between 120° and 130. Centre of flat topped one of day before yesterday -3°=357°. Country sandy and barren, covered with weeds. 4 miles out, passed low sand hills on Right hand, close to trail, 4 1/2 miles, climbed to top of low white earth mesa and kept along over undulating ground for one mile in a 305° direction. San Francisco Mtns 273°. The Buttes to South of Sunset Crossing which indicate road to Verde and Prescott lie 1st (216°) and 2nd (end respectively) 232° and 236°. 5 miles out, trail turned 325°. Ground sandy and clayey—marching very bad. On Right of to-day's travel, the country is hilly, on left gently undulating.

Before us is a small rounded peak, near which our Indians say we are to camp to night, its bearing is 345°.

7 miles out, trail 317°, passed an arroyo, lined with willow and having a few green cottonwoods. Arroyo was muddy and some water lay in pools, probably from late rains. Arroyo joined Col. Chiquito and ran from 45 to 245°. Highest peak San Francisco Mtn. 272°. Buttes on Right of trail and about 5 to 6 miles distant are 45° 35° 26 1/2, flat top butte (ends) 23° and 17°. Peak [of] to night[']s camp 347°. Heavy sand on trail.

9 miles out, trail 325°. Buttes on Left Bank of the Colorado Chiquito. (on Verde road.) one 213° and the other (222°·and 226°.) San Francisco Mtn. 268 1/2° Flat-top Butte (center) 22° and the others 33°, 37°, 43° & 57° respectively. Peak of to night's camp 350°.

12 miles out, up grade all the way, ground red sand, vegetation somewhat better; grama grass mixed with various weeds. Trail 345°. Trail 345°. Flat-top Butte (centre) 43°, ends [(]42° and 46°) Butte 33° [(]last to view) other Buttes on to-day's march 53° 68° and 71°. Peak of to-night[']s camp 355°, S.F Mtn 265°. Buttes on Left Bank of Colorado Chiquito 203° and (206-212°). Crossed a wide arroyo, and then passed along it nearly due North for 6 miles. At first we passed through a little sacaton grass, but bareness and desolation soon prevailed. 14 miles, passed a stunted Juniper tree, 15 miles another, 15 1/2 a cottonwood, 16 miles arroyo narrowed from a mile and half in width to about one hundred yards; a number of tributaries joined it, some having stunted juniper and others, palo verde. Ground became less sandy, climbed to top of a mesa, about 80' high, and saw plentiful indications of the presence of limestone, also ferrugi-

nous [*sic*] earth which indeed had betrayed itself along the sides of
the arroyos for the past two miles. Country now was extremely arid,
scarcely any species of vegetation; 18 miles, camp upon an elevated
grassy plain with gravel soil. I find I was mistaken in the peak near

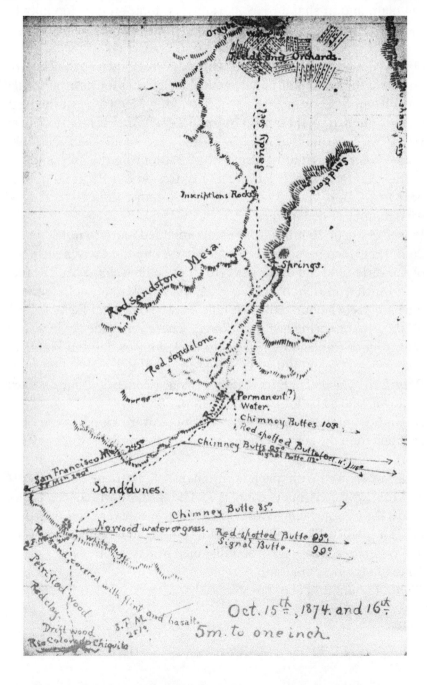

which we are to camp to night. It is to the left of the one hitherto referred to in my notes. Trail over the plain now ran 325°. Peak alongside of which we are to bivouac to-night has a white spot on face seen from the South, is only a few hundred feet above level of the plain and in shape   at foot, on left side may be

observed a large deposit of a bright red ferreginous earth. The line on which this peak is situated at extreme left, has for its other peaks the following bearings: 331°, 334, 335° 342°, 359° (the last the peak already alluded to[)] Flat-top Butte (85°-94°) Another flat-top mesa is (54°-65°); still another is (29°-44°) and a red-spotted, small chunky butte directly in front of last is 30° S.F. Mountain is 263° and the Verde road Buttes xx [?]and (212°) Buttes on our Right do not appear to be more than 5 or 6 miles distant and seem to be fringed with juniper or cedar trees.

Passed Butte at 20 miles from camp, inclined more to north and at 26 miles gained pass between two buttes, one the extreme left one of the series and the other next [to] it of conical shape. At 27 miles found spring on right of trail: spring very small, water cold but tasting of reeds [?], course the last mile or two somewhat East of North = 10°. Saw, at spring last mentioned, where renegade Apaches, on their way to the Moquis villages to trade for powder and blankets, had camped. Signal Butte, 148° Red streaked Butte 186° Left-hand Butte 215°. Conical to Spring 180° S.F. Mts. (Concealed) Butte where Spring is said to be for to-night's camp. 355°.

A Band of antelopes seen to-day but none were killed as they had scented the command long before they themselves were discovered.

SF Mtn 245°. Bill Williams [Mountains] 260°. Butte just passed 210° and 198°. Butte in front of camp is 7°. The spring at which we camped is in a little gorge facing West North West. Water very scarce. Grass inferior quality. Wood not to be had. Command is using wormwood and other weeds for fuel. Total distance to-day 36 miles.

Time of March 12 hours.

Night pleasant and cool but not cold.

Chapter 5

⟡

⟡

⟡

⟡

⟡

The Hopi Villages

Monday, October 12th, 1874. Camp aroused before dawn, but as two of our pack mules had wandered off during night, search for them retarded our departure until after day break. Left camp about 5.45 a.m. Trail 347°. After marching two miles had San Francisco Mtn. on our Left 247°, Spring Butte on our Right had a yellow mark on face, and bears 56° [Button-top] High Chimney peak butte to our rear which is a prominent landmark for reaching Moquis country has for its two points 200° 209°. Small mesa on Verde road on Left bank of Colorado Chiquito. 225° Day pleasant but cloudy & signs of snow. Country barren, soil pulverized red clay mixed with sand. Trail for the first ten miles nearly due North (347° @ 357°) Country sandy. 3 miles out, passed a second butte on Right with yellow mark on face, but this one had a flat top. 6 miles out trail passed between two buttes, over the nose of one on Right hand. Country now open on all sides. S.F. Mountain 240°. Saw where renegade Apaches had made a second camp on their way to trade buckskins for blankets with the Moquis. Killed two rattlesnakes on the trail this morning and one yesterday.

12 miles out, country still barren but interesting in a mineralogical point of view; passed a belt of white and yellow sandstone boul-

ders[;] saw a stratum of white, compact friable stone which upon examination proved to be a mixture of sulphate and carbonate of lime, cut readily with a knife and effervescing slowly under action of Colorado Chiquito water which is highly alkaline. Half a mile farther on, found a belt of white clay and black liquet, the black band exposed to view being 5' thick; the whole stratum very pure, only an occasional speck of schist being discernable. Our march of to-day was 18 miles in the general direction of the morning; about mid-day, we entered a large extent of ground planted in maize, with frequent patches of water[melons] and musk-melons. Near the trail our Indian guides stumbled upon a large pile of melons drying in the sun; to these they were helping themselves with a generous hand when a Moqui Indian, one of the number we afterwards found had been laboring in the fields, approached us and very kindly invited the whole party, numbering nearly 20, to an appreciable refection of fresh melon. Journeying a little further, we encountered other members of the tribe who addressed us kindly after the usual manner of these Indians to strangers entering one of their villages. On all sides of us now stretched a broad expanse of cultivated land, whose content was at least 2500 Acres. Soon we came upon groves of peach trees, the fruit from which had already been gathered. Perched like old feudal castles upon the very apex of a precipitous sandstone acclivity, rising hundreds of feet above us, would be seen three of the pueblos or villages of this singular people. At foot of the precipice we found a spring or tank of turbid, green water, kept for the use of their animals. Here our stock was watered and afterwards the command, under guidance of a Moqui, pushed on a few hundred yards to a small ravine full pf peach trees, where was found a small spring of water which our guide informed us was reserved for drinking purposes for the villages, the large tank just mentioned being used by animals only. Both tank and spring were walled in with masonry and had been excavated to a considerable depth; to approach the tank a ramp had been made of easy grade. We saw many flocks of sheep and goats, as well as some horses and burros, but no horned cattle—.

No sooner had we made camp than a number of men presented themselves, one announcing with a great flourish that he was an "intelplete" (interpreter), and had been to Santa Fe. A few moment's laborious colloquy with this individual, satisfied me he

was an egregarious imposter who made up for his ignorance of
Spanish by glib discourse and arrant impudence. However, after
some painful efforts and attention, I fixed the significance of many
of his words making keystones and [roussoirs?] of them to construct an arch of language to bridge the chasm of misunderstand-
ing separating us. He said he had been to Santa Fe, also had worked
for the Momo-nee. Perhaps we were Mo-mo-nee? (Mormons) Ah!
No. then perhaps we were travelling to the country of the Navajoes.
He had often been to the country of the Navajoes and was going to
the land of the Mo-mo-nee some time. He was interpreter here
and had to stay here since the Americans, living with them, had
gone away[.] The Americans, as near as could be learned, were
named Palmer, Waller, Charlie and one other a Mormon who had
removed to a ranch between them and the Navajo country. Regarding the question of corn for our animals, he was decidedly
non-committal; they had plenty of course, but it was all up in their
villages, locked up in a big stone house and their Pata (Agent)
Palmer had gone to Washington with the key; he left when the last
moon was very little; would be back in three moons more. Their
Captain had gone off with a large band of their young men to gather
acorns from the cañons in the mountains to the South East and
corn from grounds they had planted over there; the party would
also hunt for venison on the way. If we wanted corn how much
would we pay for it? He had a box, as big as his foot each way and
for one dollar he would fill it with old corn in the ear; new corn he
did not want to sell (The box would probably hold six ears of their
blue corn).

The General penetrated this old fellow's object, which beyond mis-
chance was to extort from the necessities of ourselves and animals
an exorbitant price for all we could be forced to buy. General Crook
wishing to communicate with the people in the village sent me to
open some kind of correspondence with such of the head men as
could be found in their towns. Accordingly, Mr. Scott and I proceeded up the trail to the crest of the mesa. A graded road-way,
built up with masonry, led along the side of the precipice for some
hundreds of yards speaking in very glowing terms of the industry
and patience of this people. Once in their first village (Tegua), we
saw houses built of sand-stone and cement, quite comfortable in
appearance, and having all the conveniences of the lower class of

Mexican abodes. Altho' situated at least 500 feet above the surrounding plain, their dwellings were not cold by any means. The roofs
were made of cottonwood rafters, covered with reeds and over that
a coating of cement. Some little time was consumed in hunting up
the residence of the principal man, but at last our efforts were rewarded by an encounter with one whose supply of corn seemed
large and whose bump of covetousness augured favorably for our
being able to make some sort of a trade. Giving a dollar bill for an
amount of corn worth about ten cents we prevailed upon this red-
skinned representative of Chatham Street to carry the load down
to our Camp, where the news that we had money and really intended to spend it, had drawn a concourse of greedy Indians among
whom soon appeared the so called interpreter who found himself
the recipient of a few carefully selected remarks productive of the
desired effect. He was informed that General Crook was no poor
prospector, begging his way through the country, but the big chief
of all the Americans in this country. He was the man who had
whipped into submission the Apaches, Apache-Mojaves, Tontos and
Haulpais. He had not only all the American soldiers he wanted but
more Apache and Hualpai soldiers than he knew what to do with.
The Apaches they saw with us were some of his soldiers, brought
from the Sierra Blanca. If he wanted to take their corn and melons
he could say to the soldiers now with him "to take it" and the Moquis
couldn't prevent them. But he had come here with the intention of
being their friend and hence he was anxious to pay for all the grain
and melons and peaches the men and animals could eat. All they
could bring down before sun-set would be purchased, but he was
tired of so much talking. This assured the Moquis that further delay
would be injurious to their commercial interests, & within an hour,
a long train of young men, carrying blankets filled with blue corn,
appeared in our camp and trade, to use the journalistic expression,
"showed an upward tendency." These Indians we shortly learned,
call every piece of paper money a "peso" (dollar), small fractional
currency was at once in demand and every hope was entertained
that a supply in sufficient quantity could be had,[1] but through some
misapprehension only a few notes could be procured from the en-

1. At that time the United States issued paper money in denominations of less than a
dollar, ranging from three to fifty cents. Bourke apparently meant that, since the Indians
could not distinguish between the denominations, Crook hoped to pass off fractional notes
as dollars and obtain the corn at a cheaper rate.

listed men and packers; with these, however, we managed to secure about enough forage to give all our tired animals a feed for night and morning. This night it rained for a little while.

Tuesday October 13th 1874.

Remained in camp. Sky cloudy, some rain at intervals; during day, visited mesa on which we had been yesterday. Here there are three stone pueblos. Tegua, Hualpi and Moqui,—the last having houses four stories high. The others are called Su-mo-pah-ove, Oraybe, Ma-sanga-nevy and Su-powah-levy. The mesa upon which the first three are situated is at least 500 feet in elevation above the plain, across which any column approaching in any direction can be seen for nearly twenty miles. The formation is a friable sandstone in strata from three to forty and fifty feet thick; on top the total width in places is not more than ten feet and at maximum not much over two hundred yards. The top is perfectly level, with trails worn in the solid rock six and eight inches. The men appear not so noble as the Apaches and certainly have not the same fierce and warlike countenances. The women from living inside houses, and in a fine, mild atmosphere are the handsomest and best formed as well as whitest Indians in this Territory. They possess and practice many industrial, domestic arts unknown to the Apaches and other nations on the south and west. They make a bread, in form of a blue corn paste, very sweet to the taste and undoubtedly very nutritious. They likewise lay by in one of the rooms of their houses, reserved for the purpose, ample stores of dried water-melons, musk mellons [sic], cantelopes, dried peaches, dried venison, mutton and goat's flesh, besides having onions, toma-toes, beets and an abundance of corn in the ear hung on strings, chili is also one of their vegetables and we saw strings of what appeared to be beans hanging to the rafters. Acorns are laid up in great abun-dance and are much in favor as an article of diet. The rations for daily use are placed in bins of wood and stone laid in cement, one of the stones being scooped out as a "metate," on which are ground corn, acorns and other grains.

The flocks of sheep and goats sheltered in stone corrals built in the sides of the precipice yield a large amount of wool and hair, used by the women in weaving blankets of an extra fine texture and great thickness. Coverlids or mattresses are also made of a warp of woolen strands into which they work in a peculiar way the skins of rabbits, squirrels, beavers and coyotes. The men dress in cotton shirts and drawers and buckskin moccasins wearing also one of their home made blankets of a striped pattern in blue, white and black.

The children dress in the garden of paradise costume. The women, coy and timid, eluded us as much as possible keeping to the upper stories of the houses. However, we managed to obtain a close look at a few of the young maidens who have good figures and comely refined faces; they walk with a decidedly ungainly waddle detracting much from the superiority of their figures. For dress they wear a dark blue hand made blanket reaching from shoulder to knee exposing very shapely limbs; this garment extends over the right shoulder and breast, but the upper half of the left breast is exposed. [A]bout six inches below the top and one foot above the bottom edge, run lines of yellow border work while at the waist, a girdle of red worsted confines the dress and discloses the figure. The hair is arranged a la chinoise, in three puffs; one at back of crown, and one on each side above the ears thus:

About neck are worn bands of blue and white beads. The squaws keep the interior of their houses creditably clean but the streets are rather squalid filled with garbage and emitting a perfume of putrid vegetation, drying meat, goats, sheep, donkeys, manure, dogs, chickens, and other smells for which no name can be assigned; Coleridge might have come to the Moquis villages before stigmatizing the smells of Cologne.[2]

Moqui itself is cleaner than the other two pueblos; because here the houses border upon the edge of the precipice over which the inmates throw their refuse and filth. Under each house are Kennels for dogs in which the place abounds and places for chickens, to be seen in numbers. Furnaces are also to be seen, cylindrical holes one foot in diameter and 2 feet deep, lined with cement, and used as ovens for baking corn. Halfway up the precipice at junction of two roads was

2. Bourke is referring to Samuel Taylor Coleridge's 1828 poem, "Cologne," which says, in part:
   In Köhln, a town of monks and bones,
   And pavements fang'd with murderous stones,
   And rags, and hags, and hideous wenches;
   I counted two and seventy stenches
   All well defined, and several stinks!

found a shrine of masonry containing two upright stones before which had been deposited votive offerings of petrified wood, stone and other rubbish. Of the religion of the people we learned nothing altho' we saw in nearly every house painted pieces of wood marked with rude representations of the human figure, probably idols.

The Moquis make fine baskets of various forms and pottery of delicate workmanship, similar to the fragments found in the so-called Aztec ruins of the Territory.

The chimneys of their houses are constructed of "ollas"[3] superimposed one above the other and serving their purpose very well as none of the rooms show signs of smoke notwithstanding the fact that many of their buildings have been inhabited hundreds of years. With much dickering and much annoying talk, now offering one thing, now another, we succeeded in securing from them a few "ollas" and a few of their blankets; of the value of our money they could scarcely be made to understand an idea—they know well that with it in Santa Fe, Salt Lake City, and Prescott, could be bought muslins and calicoes and powder, but of the worth to be assigned each note it was a matter of the greatest difficulty to make them believe anything. A bargain just concluded with them, often was broken through their being displeased with some figure in the engraving [on the currency]. When a woman's figure formed part of the picture, success most frequently attached to our bargains. In trade they showed themselves more keen, and we would have had no trouble in disposing of a lot of bright red flannel shirts at almost any valuation.

[O]ne of the hardest duties a young officer can be called upon to perform is to purchase grain after dark from a set of rapacious, ignorant one sixteenth civilized savages and have to do this without the necessary small change while the Indians insolently ridicule as spurious any estimate of a greenback greater than a dollar. Mickey Free, our Apache sergeant, proved equal as a trickster to any of his adversaries and to hear him expatiate with unblushing effrontery upon the almost priceless value of the paper money in his possession, one would think the Knaves were not all dead yet. For two dollars, he purchased better blankets than we could get for them and, more than the Moquis seemed to live under lasting obligations to the young imp[.]

---

3. "Jars," i.e. ceramic pipe cemented together to run up from the fireplace, which was probably also a jug-shaped piece of pottery. A similar style is used in Mexico, and currently (2001-02) is fashionable for interior decorating in Texas and the Southwest.

To-day, General Crook had a long talk with the Moquis telling them they must cease commerce with all Apaches not on the Reserves, which they promised to do. Besides, they agreed to let us have 1000 pounds of shelled corn at 4¢ a pound in sacks; a very liberal deduction from the outrageous impositions of yesterday. They are also to give us a guide hence to Oraybe their main village and, if the General wishes, from there to the Colorado Cañon[.]

To-night, Moquis came down and sold us about $30 worth of shelled corn, giving an abundant feed for our pack animals and horses as well as a good supply to take with us on the march. After dark we could hear these Indians chanting some sort of a chorus lasting nearly an hour.

Wednesday October 14th, Camp awakened at 3.30 A.M. With the first streak of dawn the Moquis again shouted some sort of a chant from the summit of the mesa and the ravines beneath. Moquis gave us a guide to conduct the column to their principal village, Oraybe which they say, we shall reach by mid-day. Our Apache guides left us today to return to the Sierra Blanca. During our stay here, [I] succeeded in securing by trade 3 very good Moquis blankets and some specimens of curious pottery. Learned yesterday that these Indians gather a variety of wild honey considered by them a rare delicacy and jealously cared for in earthen jars. Also have miscal, traded for with the Apaches, and sun-flower seeds of unusually large size. Notice the squaws baking bread; over the fire of live coals is secured a thin sheet of iron, tin or stone which they rub with fat every few moments. A paste, the consistency of thin gruel, made of ground corn, is applied with the hand and almost immediately is baked through; this is then rolled up much like we would a sheet of tissue paper the resemblance to which is very striking. Large quantities are baked at a time and put aside for consumption when needed.

Four Navajo Indians were in the pueblos yesterday on a trading excursion. A small band is camped in the plain three or four miles South East of us, and their fire could be seen until late last night. Our course after being out 7 miles this morning, was 240°. Moqui lay behind us 98°. Saw 5 miles from Moqui a planting ground where, besides corn and melons, sun flowers had been sown some of which were of enourmous size the disk of the flower being 8" to 10" in diameter filled with large nutritious seeds.

After seven miles entered a recess in the sandstone mesa and followed along this arroyo for a mile leaving it on our left and climbing
to top of mesa, whence San Francisco Mountain 227°. On this mesa
much stunted cedar. Passed a bean patch shortly before leaving
arroyo. Moqui from here 92°. After a total march of 15 miles, passing through and along fields of corn, melons and beans we arrived
at Oraybe, situated as the other pueblos, on a bold mesa of sandstone fronting to the south and east. A peculiar formation of sandstone was noticeable this morning; a base with nodules of a
homogeneous nature but entirely disconnected from the base which
being disintegrated by the action of the elements left these nodules,
in places for hundreds of yards, scattered over the ground. Saw San
Francisco Mountain capped with snow this morning. Our trail led
us up the mesa and past Oraybe and into Camp near a deep reser-
voir of crude masonry containing plenty of water. The sandstone of
the Oraybe mesa is very soft and friable presenting in some parts
broad surfaces perfectly flat, on which some half developed Moqui
artist had rudely figured representations of birds, beasts, men,
women, and sometimes, fanciful and grotesque outlines. Discernable
among these were a jackass, antelope, dog, man, woman, and a representation probably intended for the Roman Catholic Church at
Santa Fe where these Indians trade. Where the human form was
delineated, the artist did not seem to be restrained by too great a
sense of delicacy in executing his task. The village of Oraybe is now
in a condition of decadence and not perhaps as populous as the
three visited yesterday, but the buildings were at one time more
numerous, more compact and better constructed than in the other
pueblos; many houses are in total ruins, others rapidly approaching the same mournful condition.
The supply of water is more ample and the soil seemingly more
generous; in every direction, look where you will are forests of peach
trees, the limbs of not a few breaking down under their burden of
the delicious fruit upon which our hungry soldiers are now delight-
edly feasting. Not even in New Jersey, Maryland, Tennessee[,] Michigan or California, famed for their posological productions, can be
found fruits of better size for the table, more juicy or more grateful
flavor than those lying on the ground about us in hundreds of bush-
els and which the squaws, in clusters of half a dozen are engaged in
drying on the sand-stone benches on the southern side of the mesa.

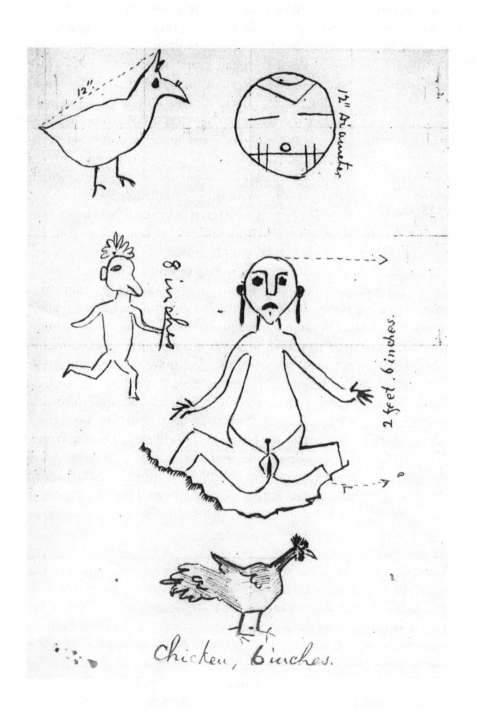

Chicken, 6 inches.

3 feet

Olla.

Gourd.
(used as drinking vessel.)

Moqui villages, Arizona
Oct, 14, 74

2 feet.

3 feet.

12 inches

Bassorelievo
12 inches.

4 feet

Deer or Elk

Burro

2 feet

5 feet.

Moqui villages, Arizona,
Soldier with shield..
Oct 14th 1874

12 inches

6 inches

12 inches.

Horse-head.

4 inches.

5 inches.
Woman's face,
(Young girl.)

Probably thousands of pounds are this moment exposed within a radius of three miles from camp. The Moquis matrons wear their hair in a manner different from that of the young maidens: it is parted in the middle from forehead to collar and gathered into two bands, one over each ear and plaited with woolen yarn.

Some of our men found an Albino among the Moquis this afternoon: they say he was perfectly white, hair between red and flaxen, and a sullen expression of countenance; would not let them see his eyes. He was averse to conversation and said in tolerable English "Go away" when addressed. Travellers, prospectors and scouting parties had evidently given him a great deal of annoyance by undue curiosity.

The Indians here say there is a Mormon settlement on the line of tomorrow[']s march.

From here, Chimney Butte bears 153°.

San Francisco Mtn. 225°.

All the rocks in vicinity of Oraybe are covered with rudely carved pictures and hieroglyphics; some so old and weather beaten as to render desciphering [sic] an impossibility. A number of these carvings are rudely reproduced in these pages. Mr Scott carved the name of our party on a large flat faced sandstone boulder, near the initials, monograms, and names of officers and soldiers of the 1st. New Mexican Volunteers, who encamped here in 1864. One of the names is "S. Baca, Capitan, 1st. NM Vol. May 12, 1864," and another, "I Mohr 1st NM. Vol. May 1864"

Mr. Scott's inscription reads;

Brig Genl. George Crook

Lieut: JG Bourke

W.G. Scott

Oct: 14, 1874

Thursday Oct 15, 1874

Camp aroused at 4 A.M. Moquis made a fearful din ringing bells from the summits of the mesa and immediately afterwards all hands turned out to labor in the fields[.] During the night, they had stripped every peach from the trees in the orchard nearest our camp; a trick we disregarded as our boxes and hampers had been fully packed yesterday afternoon. Moved out at 5:30 A.M. Not being able to obtain a guide at Oraybe, General Crook was reluctantly compelled to return towards Prescott and we moved nearly due south for 14 miles (at 9 miles passing close under a sandstone bluff on our right covered with inscriptions and Indian tracings) when reached a mesa on Left extending North and South and having a number of ravines, small in size but holding water. The one at which our animals drank contained more than all the tanks seen at the Moqui villages. Oraybe from here is 357°. San Francisco Mtn. 202° Butte (small) s. col[orado] chiquito 208°. Day pleasant[.] First five miles heavy sand dune now in red adobe clay mixed with white sand. From this point General Crook struck out across country, hoping to reach the Rio Colorado Chiquito by night. Moved for 7 miles 215° climbing to top of mesa on our right and after a mile descending it on south side and turning nearly East for a mile, to camp with running water and green grass, in the arroyo followed the morning. Our position is about 200° from springs in ravine of to-day. Country passed through to-day, red sandstone bluffs and red sand. About a mile to west of camp great quantities of broken pottery and some low crumbling adobe walls attest to the fact of the Moquis or some kindred nation having at one time had a village on this ground. Saw this morning the first Albino in Arizona.[4] The command encountered him while marching through corn fields a mile or two south of Oraybe. A person unacquainted with the existence of such a race among the wild tribes of Arizona would have addressed him in English, confident he was some poverty stricken, drunken Irish or Scotch beggar. His hair in color between a flaxen and auburn hung in long masses over his shoulders; complexion very light with red cheeks; eyes of a grayish hazel; skin much tanned. To our greetings, he returned a cheerful reply but made away with himself and load of water melons as fast and as soon as he could.

Distance to-day   24 miles
Time   8 hs. 10 m.

At this season of the year numbers of the Moquis are hunting; in Oraybe we saw many rabbits drying on rafters in the houses. Their flesh is eaten and the fur saved to make fur coverlids and mattresses. The old squaws devote much time to chasing game in the children's heads [i.e., picking out and eating the lice in the children's hair]; woe to the too corpulent pedicules unable to escape their clutches.

---

4. For some inexplicable reason, Bourke had completely forgotten the albino mentioned only a day earlier, unless he meant that he had personally seen this albino, whereas the one of the previous day had been noted by "some of our men" rather than by personal encounter.

Before he can emit one despairing howl of agony, their toothless jaws and leathery lips have done their work and the poor parasite is gone from our gaze forever.

During our stay at their villages, and perhaps as a consequence thereof, men women and children equally labored in the fields and orchards, carrying to the roofs of their houses all the fruits and vegetables approaching maturity; not so soon but that our men had plenty of melons obtained whence none could say.

These Indians although more thrifty, do not inspire the respect commanded by the Apaches who in every manly trait and virtue are far superior to the effeminate Moqui. *[For more observations on Hopi life, see Appendix 14.]*

Friday Oct: 16th 1874 Moved at dawn 5.30 after marching 2 1/2 miles, with red sandstone bluffs within 300 yards of trail on right; we came to a small cottonwood tree from which a back-sight read 49° and a foresight 235°. Day fair and bright. Ground barren and heavy red sand. Bluffs cut into all imaginable fantastic shapes by long continued action of Elements. Chimney Peaks 103°. Peak to right of them 115°. San Francisco Mtns 245°.

5 miles, country still barren; soil heavy, red sand. Bluffs on our right present the appearance of old Gothic Cathedrals, Castles, with buttresses bastions and towers complete. Little minarets 5' to 10' high not over a foot thick stand out in places; now and then one is met looking for all the world like a complete statue of man or woman. Signal Buttes 112° Chimney Butte 95° San Francisco Mts. 236 and 240° (Peaks) Mesa of San Francisco Mtn. 299° to 255°.

After moving out in same general direction for 11 miles had Chimney Butte 85° one to right of it (red spotted one of Oct 11th) 85° Signal Butte 99°. San Francisco Mountain 240°[.] Saw a band of cottonwood foliage in the distance on our left, indicated course of Rio Colorado Chiquito[.] Moved down from mesa and on towards the river which we afterwards found was nearly seven miles distant. For four miles country was fine red sand strewn with fragments of basalt, flint, and a variety of porphyry, base flint and crystals of red jasper small size. Petrified wood could be seen in profusion so nearly resembling fuel that had camp been made old soldiers would have been misled into raising it from the ground. At times the petrified chips, splinters, and blocks reminded us of the floor of a carpenter's shop. Trees petrified in the stump with stone branches lying near to parent stem were also passed, but no silicified twigs were met with. For the next four miles soil heavy red adobe clay showing traces of the extent to which the Colorado Chiquito in winter overflows its banks[;] drift cottonwood and cedar could be seen for miles, while on this clay plain, mirages sported with our confiding senses. Here came sparkling in the sun a little stream flowing to join to Colorado Chiquito. Its course could be traced for miles and at one of its bends we were not more than fifty yards from its channel when presto! it vanished whence it came into air[.] Found an easy ford over the river a very fortunate circumstance impassable cañons being according to current report on both sides of and but a short distance from camp. General Crook and Mr. Scott shot a number of wild ducks to-day, just in good time to replenish our meat larder, nearly as bare as Mother Hubbard's cupboard.

Distance to-day between 18 and 20 miles.

Time   Seven hours

San Francisco Mtn. From Camp 249° 251°.

Judging from looks of the country, this river is passable for 15 or 20 miles further down from our present camp, which has a crossing better at least at this season than either that at Sunset or Cotton-wood[.] So closes out the record of our brief stay in the country of the Moquis—a nation interesting in main points as being one of the two or three maintaining the same domain today as they did when Cortez landed at Vera Cruz; and possessing all the industrial arts which can be acquired by a people unacquainted with the working of metals; while we have made the journey not without some profit and great interest to ourselves, it is not one to be repeated with advantage.

Inhospitality, Mendaciousness, rapacity and filth are not the qualities to contemplate which one cares to travel for 80 miles across a desert without wood or grass and with only one watering place of importance and that one the stream on which we have made camp to-night with current so turbid and sedimentary that after bathing in it our faces and hands are encrusted with red clay and sands. Every one in our the party rejoices at being once more across the line separating us from "Gods country" where once at least each day can be found a pleasant spot for a bivouac alongside some purling stream or near some crystal spring[.] Regret is felt that our trip could not this time include the grand cañon of the Colorado River and, if properly equipped and rationed we could think easily from this point march North North West across foothills of San Francisco Mountain (thereby avoiding the cañon of cat[a]ract creek we would encounter farther north) to the country north of Bill Williams Mountains; from which a deflection of North North West ought to bring us to the main depth of the Great Cañon to the East of the junction of Diamond river.

Our absence from Prescott has been for all that replete with much of interest and importance; the operations of the Military posts and Indian reservations at Camps Verde, Apache and San Carlos have been inspected; the strange towns of the strange Moquis visited and much scenery, good, bad and indifferent, plain, mountain, fruitful field and arid desert, bubbling spring of crystal freshness and stagnant pool of slime and alkali, seen and experienced with varying sensations of pleasure or discomfort but all alike laid away in the recesses of memory as episodes in one of the most pleasant trips of our military career.

Saturday Oct. 17th 1874. Camp awakened at 4 A.M. moved at 5.27. 215° one mile country covered with fragments of sandstone schist. Chimney Peaks 82° 30' Signal Butte 84° 30' San Francisco Mtn. 251° course of march 182°. One mile in this new direction turned to Right crossed a sandstone walled arroyo about 100 feet deep and walls nearly vertical, course now about 236°, four miles out; line of lava bluffs on our left about 250 yards off; some few sandstone shale mounds scattered over the plain which was rather well grassed with gramma, 5 miles out reached summit of a small lava flat topped mesa, with talus of comminuted black lava at base. Chimney Butte 68°.

Signal Butte 81°. San Francisco Mtn. 255°.

Course of trail 230°

Camp of Oct. 15th 42°

Nine to ten miles out, passed between a line of lava knolls 3 in number, perpendicular to our trail, two small rounded ones on our Left and one larger conical one on Right. All three covered with white grass. Soil for last four miles finely Broken black lava covered with coarse white grass. Outcropping of black lava on Left.

Chimney Butte 65°

Day fine. Weather fair. Slight breeze from South. After a mile over this mesa course 225°. Ground elevated and undulating. In another half mile saw for probably last time Chimney Butte 66°. Red-spot-

ted Butte 72° 30' Signal Butte 77°. Trail now ran 210°[.] Passed into
a country of low rounded knolls of no great height covered with
white grass; on our Right not more than two or three miles away
stretched out from San Francisco Mtn a long line of low hills covered with pine, oak, juniper and piñon, on our trail were encountered successively scrub juniper, juniper, piñon and juniper and
then at 14 miles we entered a dense pine forest. Deer and Bear sign
plenty. At sixteen miles still in forest—trail running over lava pebble
soil. Made a total march to day of 27 miles, the last half being in a
forest of pine trees. No material deviation from the direction of 210°
except for the last mile when we marched nearly due south. Came
into a granite formation four miles from camp which is at Southern
end of the high mesa projecting from Southern end of San Francisco Mtn. Wood and grass plenty, sufficient water for command
found in springs in rocks. Saw some Mountain Mahogony this afternoon near camp. Rained constantly since mid-day.
Cleared off at night, but remained chill and damp until next morning.
Sunday Octr. 18th Morning foggy, 9 miles
One mile out spring on Left 2 miles on Right 3 1/2 miles track road
overgrown with grass followed it finding a spring where we watered
animals at 9 miles from camp. Lava and granite all day[.] [W]eather
foggy and damp. Kept nearly West and West North West for 22 miles
from last camp. The day has been so dark[,] foggy and at intervals
rainy that no observation with prismatic compass could be made.
Moved entirely around Southern mesa prolongation of the San Francisco Mountain; country one black stretch of pine trees; road very
winding; at 22 miles road crossed another. Water in springs at convenient distances on either side of the road, has been plenty all day.
Wood[,] water and grass abundant and of good quality at this camp.
Many antelope seen on the march but none near enough to kill.
At night sky cleared off and a violent wind prevailed shifting to all
points of the compass. Rained a little during night and at early morn-
ing turned very cold.
Monday Oct 19th. Moved out at day—dawn. country more open.
After going five miles back sight read 135°. High conical Mountain
Either, Sitgreaves or Kendrick 67°.
After another mile and a half of open country with wooded rills on
either side close to trail struck Law's spring; road now going 270°.

This spring is on Beales trail. Before us stretches an elevated flat country, cut up by ravines and valleys. Turned 180° over low pine hills 10 miles out country open and well grassed. Bill Williams Mtn 185° San Francisco 83°. High Mtn. Of this morning 75°. Trail running 168° after fifteen miles came upon a great many antelopes but unable to kill any. Country of same general character.

San Francisco Mtn 65°[.] After marching 20 miles trail nearly due South entered a belt of pine timber. Country to-day full of small knots covered with pine and juniper. After 30 miles struck Prescott road and followed it for 3 miles about 300° road then turned nearly West. Road bad full of lava boulders steep down grade. Squaw Peak Mtn. Bill Williams 340°.

Made a total march of 35 miles, camping at Bear Springs. Saw Chino Valley in the distance to the West. Numerous herds of deer and antelope darted across our path to-day some of them were badly wounded by marksmen of the command, but unfortunately none were killed.

General Crook and Private Green and Mr. Scott have been absent all day in the mountains hunting; signal fires have been lit to guide them to our position but as yet 6 P.M. they have not arrived.

At 6.20 P.M. General Crook and Private Green reached camp but nothing could be learned of Mr. Scott who remained absent all night. Large fires consuming whole pine trees were kept blazing until a late hour and signal guns at intervals of five minutes each were fired until nearly ten o'clock.

Tuesday October 20th. General Crook sent me on ahead to Prescott, while he remained at Bear Springs to continue the search for Mr. Scott. Volumes of smoke were sent up from the top of the rocky bluffs overlooking our camp and several parties well provided with necessaries were detailed to scour the country. One to proceed on the Prescott and New Mexico road to the North East another to go North to the foot of the highest point of Bill Williams Mountains and a third to strike across the hills to the trail of yesterday. Meantime I am to scan closely the road between here and the Chino Valley settlements in case our missing companion may have turned West and come out near the ranchos.

Left camp at 8; followed road going 234° to 180° for 7 1/2 miles, road filled with boulders of basalt and very badly worn; the end of the Squaw Peak range not more than 20 miles away lay 157°. Before leaving camp General Crook sent out pack mules to carry in the venison killed by him yesterday.

At end of 7 1/2 miles came to two cañons one running alongside road from E and N.E. the other coming in from West. Saw Squaw Peak 155°. Wild Cherry Creek Mtn. 160°. Bill Williams Mtn. 350°. North end of Squaw Peak range 168°. After 10 miles Granite Mtn. 187°. After 12 miles, course turned 250° and at 14 or 15 m. crossed a steep cañon without water coming in from North North West and bending to 70°. Red rocks seen in part at 75° Bill Williams 8°.

Travelled first 12 miles to-day down grade and in cedar forest. After 12 miles, road somewhat better grade easy and undulating and timber much scattered[.] Think the cañon just passed may be Hell Cañon. Has walls of red sandstone, and summit edged with black basalt.

Since crossing Hell Cañon, road turned first to 220° and gradually to 180° formation of ground changing from basaltic to rich earth full of small stones of lava[,] sandstone and occasionally granite. Country well grassed. About 21 miles from Bear Springs the following observations were made: Bill Williams Mountain 20° San Francisco Mountain 40°. Northern end of Squaw Peak Mountains (or Black hills) 92°[.] Direction of trail sighted on mountain believed to be back of the settlements in Chino Valley 185°. Pass in the Juniper Mountains west of old Camp Hualpai 262°. Rested here as we did at Rattlesnake and Hell Cañons a few moments on account of the horses and ourselves[.] Kept on down due south (180° to 185°) for a distance of 12 miles from Hell Cañon and a total day's march of between 28 and 30 miles reaching the ranch of Mr George Banghart in Chino Valley, where we were most cordially welcomed by the family, forage provided for our horses and a smoking hot meal of fried chicken, sweet butter, rich cream coffee and biscuits temptingly arrayed on a snowy white table cloth for our own refreshment. It is worth while to pass over Arizona's deserts and wander through Arizona's forests and mountains to appreciate the gratefulness of Arizona hospitality[.] To-morrow two or three hours before day we start on our last march for "Home" Fort Whipple,[5] twenty miles to the south of this place.

5. Fort Whipple was established December 23, 1863, in the Chino Valley, about twenty-four miles north of Prescott, and relocated to Prescott five months later. The first telegraph linking Arizona to the outside world was established between Whipple and San Diego in 1873. In 1879, Fort Whipple was consolidated with Prescott Barracks to become Whipple

From this point the bearing of Prescott is 175°. Pass in Juniper Mountains West of old Camp Haulpai 270°. Bill Williams Mountain 25°.

Wednesday Oct 20th. Left Banghart's ranch at 4.45 A.M, moving south to Prescott (Fort Whipple) 23 miles when within eight miles of Prescott taking the trail up Granite Creek and through the Granite rocks to the post, which we reached at 10.15 A.M.

Upon the San Carlos reservation we had a fine opportunity of witnessing the Apache mode of dancing and some peculiarities of their social etiquette.

Women are never invited to dance, but assume the initiative and select their own partners from the opposite sex: that is to say, one woman selects for every two, the fortunate or unfortunate masculine upon whom their choice may fall being apprised of his fate by a gentle tug at the elbow which he is not permitted to disregard.

The young woman now runs away followed leisurely by the warrior to a place where the set is being formed, in a manner somewhat the same as an American quadrille. Two men, placed about 15 feet apart, face each other, each having upon his arms two women with their backs turned to those of the pair opposite. At a given signal, all strike up a monotonous dirge or chant to whose time they advance and when the men are within touching distance, they suddenly turn their backs to each other, while the women all face those on the other side; in this new arrangement receding to the starting point. Having repeated this manuoevre two or three times, all join hands and circle around. This salutary enjoyment, if enjoyment it be, is persisted in all night, the singers as they become exhausted giving way to others of equally stentorian lungs, who continue the exercises until the sun's early rays warn them the night is ended.

It is not permitted to refuse any invitation extended by a squaw; a mark of respect to the sex not easily accounted for among Apaches usually so unmindful of the kindnesses due to the weak and delicate.

Barracks. It served as departmental headquarters until 1887, when Brig. Gen. Nelson A. Miles moved headquarters to Los Angeles. Deactivated in 1922, it is now used by the Veterans Administration as a hospital. Altshuler, *Starting with Defiance*, 63-67; Frazer, *Forts of the West*, 14-15.*f*

Part 2

Department of the Platte
1875–1876

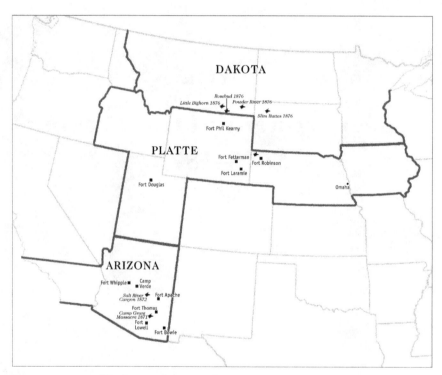

Departments of Dakota, Platte and Arizona

Background

In March 1875, General Crook was ordered to relieve Brig. Gen. E.O.C. Ord as commander of the Department of the Platte.[1] The department was headquartered at Omaha Barracks, Nebraska, and included that state, Iowa, Wyoming, Utah, and southern Idaho, and was one of four departments within the Military Division of the Missouri, a vast jurisdiction composed more or less of the central two-thirds of the United States. The division was commanded by Lt. Gen. Philip H. Sheridan, whose headquarters was in Chicago. In addition to the Platte, the departments included Texas, commanded by Brig. Gen. Christopher C. Augur in San Antonio; the Missouri, under Brig. Gen. John Pope, Fort Leavenworth, Kansas; and Dakota, under Brig. Gen. Alfred H. Terry in St. Paul, Minnesota.

Bourke's description of the trip from Arizona to Omaha, via San Francisco, is an excellent account of Southern California in its early days of development, and of Utah as it was undergoing the painful transition from Mormon theocracy to integral part of the United States. It is significant because it contains some of Bourke's most malevolent prose, directed not at Indians or government contrac-

1. Robinson, *General Crook*, 161.

tors, but at the Mormons. Brigham Young is portrayed as a sensu-
ous charlatan, his wives are called "harlots" and "concubines," and
the Mormon leadership is depicted as a sort of religious Mafia, exercising total spiritual and secular power over its followers. Bourke
contended that Mormonism could survive only in ignorance and
isolation. Thus, he believed, the transcontinental railroad through
Utah ultimately would mean the end of the sect. These passages
reflect less Bourke's own Roman Catholic views than the general
popular hatred for Mormonism that existed throughout the United
States in the nineteenth century, and which drove the Mormons
out into the wilderness in the first place.[2] In *On the Border With
Crook*, however, he devoted only one page to the entire journey
from Whipple to Omaha, and kept his opinions of the Mormons to
himself.[3]

As the new commander in the Platte, Crook assumed a jurisdiction that essentially was a powder keg waiting to explode. The trouble
went back nine years, to the Red Cloud War, when the Lakota Sioux
and their allies, the Cheyenne and Arapaho, had fought the government to a standstill. In response, a federal commission met with
the Indians at Fort Laramie, Wyoming, and negotiated what officially was known as the "Treaty with the Sioux—Brulé, Oglala, Two
Kettle, Sans Arcs, and Santee—and Arapaho, 1868," but commonly
called the Fort Laramie Treaty. Under its terms, the government
ceded to the Sioux a reservation comprised of what is now the entire state of South Dakota west of the Missouri River, as well as a
triangle of land in modern North Dakota. The government also agreed
to close the Bozeman Trail between Fort Laramie and the Montana
gold fields, as well as the three forts—Reno, Phil Kearny, and C.F.
Smith—that defended the trail. The reservation itself was declared
off-limits to all unauthorized persons. In return for these concessions, the Indians agreed to allow roads, railroads, mail stations,
and other forms of transportation and communication deemed necessary, and not to restrict travel on those routes. The government
also acknowledged that a large section of northeastern Wyoming
and southeastern Montana would be considered "unceded Indian
territory," again off-limits to all unauthorized persons. In order to

2. For a more modern, balanced view of Utah and Mormonism during the Brigham Young
era, see Bigler, *Forgotten Kingdom*.
3. Bourke, *On the Border*, 240.

encourage the Sioux to settle, learn vocations, and become (by the white definition) "productive," they received an annual federal annuity worth $1.25 million.[4]

The treaty was unworkable because of the many divergent interests of the government and settlers on one side, and the Indians on the other. The Indians already considered themselves "productive" by the standards of their culture. They hunted, raised horses, and did other things that were useful by the standards of a nomadic, hunting people; there was no need to adopt the "white man's road" of a sedentary life of farming, trades, and schools. By the same token, it was difficult for an Easterner living in a crowded city, possibly in a squalid tenement, to understand why bands of Indians needed so much land in which to practice their nomadic lifestyle. Thus, there is no question that eventually, the treaty would have broken down, resulting in a war, and the opening of the Indian lands for white settlement. Even so, the inevitable probably was accelerated by something that neither side had foreseen. When Crook was ordered to the Platte, the nation already was eighteen months into a severe depression. Known as the Panic of 1873, it was precipitated by the collapse of the New York banking firm of Jay Cooke & Company, which controlled the Northern Pacific railroad, then under construction across the northern part of Dakota Territory. Cooke's went bankrupt on September 18, 1873, and two days later the New York Stock Exchange suspended trading. In the six-year depression that followed, wages dropped twenty-five percent, while the cost of food only fell by five percent. More than a million people lost their jobs in a nation with a total population of only forty million. Many took to the roads, and sought new opportunities in the West. The impact of this migration would become especially evident later in Bourke's narrative for 1876.[5]

With an economic crisis gripping the nation, congress and the public increasingly grudged the Sioux annuity payment. Many citizens also looked to the Black Hills, in the western part of the Sioux reservation, as offering new opportunities. Although historians often have stated that the Black Hills were sacred to the Indians, the region's actual significance is ambiguous. Some Indians appeared

4. Robinson, *General Crook*, 159-60, and *A Good Year to Die*, 21-23; Gray, *Centennial Campaign*, 12-15; Lazarus, *Black Hills/White Justice*, 45-49.

5. Gray, *Centennial Campaign*, 15; Robinson, *General Crook*, 160; McFeely, *Grant, A Biography*, 392-93.

to believe that the hills were haunted by malevolent spirits, or at the very least, were of no practical value. Chiefs like Red Cloud and Spotted Tail indicated that they would have no objections to selling the hills to the government.[6] Whatever the case with the Indians, from the white perspective, the Black Hills had been rumored for more than a decade to contain large deposits of gold, which the nation needed to stabilize the economy. In 1874, the depression reached the point that these rumors no longer could be ignored, and Lt. Col. George Armstrong Custer, 7th Cavalry, was ordered to lead a reconnaissance into the region. Although ostensibly to select a possible site for military posts, the expedition confirmed the presence of gold, and the Black Hills shortly were flooded with gold seekers in violation of the Fort Laramie Treaty. The government was pledged to evict them, and in March 1875, a detachment under command of Capt. John Mix, Second Cavalry, brought out one group that had settled on French Creek. Despite these efforts, the rush for Black Hills gold was such that the prospectors and small miners soon had to share the region with large, well-funded mining corporations. Faced with the inevitable, the government began seeking ways to evict the Indians. It was at this juncture that Crook was assigned to the Department of the Platte.[7]

The boundaries of the Platte illustrated how the four departments in the Military Division of the Missouri were scattered haphazardly across the plains in a manner that, for administrative purposes, was illogical and unwieldy.The Department of Texas encompassed that state below the Canadian River. Immediately north and west of Texas was Pope's Department of the Missouri, including Missouri, Kansas, Oklahoma and the Indian Territory, Colorado, and New Mexico. North of that, the Platte was strung out from Iowa to Utah. The northernmost department, Dakota under Terry, included Minnesota, Dakota Territory (the modern states of North and South Dakota), and Montana. The only railroad across the Division of the Missouri was the Union Pacific, which ran entirely within Crook's jurisdiction. This meant that he was the only gen-

    6. McDermott, "Military Problem," 17-18.
    7. Robinson, *A Good Year to Die*, 33ff.; Utley, *Cavalier in Buckskin*, 133ff.; Bourke, Diaries, 2b:6-11; Kime, *Black Hills Journals*, 4; U.S. Department of War, RG 393, Special File, Military Division of the Missouri, "Citizens Expeditions" to the Black Hills. Custer's Expedition is discussed in detail in Jackson, *Custer's Gold*, and Krause and Olson, *Prelude to Glory.*

eral who could move large numbers of troops, supplies, and equipment over long distances rapidly. It also meant that the southwestern portions of Terry's jurisdiction (i.e., the Black Hills and Great Sioux Reservation) actually were more conveniently located to Crook's troops in Nebraska and Wyoming. Consequently, Crook routinely found himself handling situations that, theoretically, were Terry's responsibility, and, from time to time, also had to send troops into Pope's jurisdiction in Colorado.

A case in point was the Black Hills Expedition to which Bourke was assigned soon after arriving. Terry's nearest forces were hundreds of miles away on the upper Missouri River in what is now North Dakota. Crook's troops in Wyoming, on the other hand, were within easy marching distance of the hills, and had a major supply depot at Cheyenne on the Union Pacific. Thus, when the government needed troops to enforce the Fort Laramie Treaty on white interlopers in the hills, or to conduct a survey of the region, the onus fell on Crook. Likewise, he more or less was responsible for evicting miners, who entered the hills through his department for the same reason soldiers did—ease of access.

The Black Hills Expedition, headed by Professor Horace P. Jenney[8] of the Columbia School of Mines in New York, was assigned to evaluate mineral resources, and determine a fair value for trade to obtain the region from the Indians. To ensure safety, and allow Jenney adequate time for a thorough investigation, the War Department agreed to provide a military escort. On May 1, 1875, Crook ordered six companies of cavalry and two companies of infantry with adequate provisions to assemble at Fort Laramie under command of Lt. Col. Richard Irving Dodge, Twenty-third Infantry.

The expedition left Fort Laramie on May 25, and returned on October 13 after an absence of almost five months.[9] Bourke's final entry, however, is June 22, and in *On the Border With Crook*, he gave the entire expedition one half of one paragraph.[10] We therefore must assume that the remaining four months are among the volumes that were lost in the period of 1877-78. The extant account is relatively straightforward, and requires little explanation. It does, however, shed more light on the workings of the army and

8. Bourke consistently misspelled the name.
9. Kime, *Black Hills Journals*, 6-8, 23.
10. Bourke, *On the Border*, 242-43.

the attitudes of the period. Up to this point, Bourke's description of military activities concerned itself with light mobile assault units, cavalry organized to cover large areas of country in short time. With the Black Hills Expedition, we see, for the first time, a major field operation of the frontier army, and experience all the preparations necessary for maintaining large units of infantry and cavalry away from supply for extended periods.[11]

One of the problems was the inability of "American" horses (i.e. government-issue horses sent from the East) to adapt to life on the plains. This was a common complaint of the frontier army—that on long marches or chases, the government horses wore out, while the Indian ponies kept on. The reason is that the Indian mounts had had more than a century to adapt to the environment; they could live off the land and endure hard use and privation. The government horses, on the other hand, required grain, and could not be pushed beyond a certain limit without breaking down. This leads to a second problem frequently mentioned, that expeditions required massive amounts of grain—in wagons and packed on mules—for the cavalry mounts, and once the grain supply was exhausted, the horses began to die. Like many other frontier officers, Bourke believed horses should be obtained from the Western territories (his own preference was California Broncos)[12] but nothing was ever done, and the problem persisted until the end of the Indian Wars.

Bourke's writings during this period contain some of his most jingoistic comments. When the Black Hills Expedition set out, he was only a few weeks short of his twenty-ninth birthday. Like many of his generation, he had developed a sense of nationhood as a Union soldier, and thus felt a proprietary interest in the nation's future. Despite his contact with the Indians of Arizona, he still viewed the Indian cultures in their most negative aspects. The government had not yet adopted a policy of complete destruction of the Indian ways of life; neither he nor his contemporaries could envision the suffering this would entail, and which ultimately would cause him to com-

11. Besides writing in his diary, Bourke also sent dispatches of the expedition to the *San Francisco Alta California*. Other soldier journalists included Capt. Andrew S. Burt, 9th Infantry, *New York Tribune*, and Acting Assistant Surgeon J.R. Lane, *Chicago Tribune*. The expedition also was accompanied by two professional correspondents, Reuben B. Davenport, *New York Herald*, and Thomas C. MacMillan, *Chicago Inter-Ocean*. Davenport and MacMillan also would accompany Crook's Big Horn and Yellowstone Expedition in 1876. Kime, *Black Hills Journals*, 8 n13.

12. Bourke, Diaries, 2b:6.

pletely reverse his beliefs. Thus, he could describe the Black Hills
in a paragraph that was almost a summary of the entire concept of
Manifest Destiny:

> The smooth ringing sod, the various, green grass, the pretty
> little flowerets modestly peering above the sward, the spar-
> kling rivulet coursing down the ravine with little confluents
> joining it on either hand, the springs of pure, sweet, frigid
> water, the rich black soil, 6 and 8 feet deep, the compact
> belts of excellent timber and inexhaustible quarries of build-
> ing stone—all these without an indication of habitancy—
> evoked the question; why have these Black Hills, greater in
> area than several of the New England states, and which have
> never been of any value to the nomads who claim them as
> their own, and are never visited even save at rare intervals
> to obtain lodge-poles for the Sioux and Cheyenne camps—
> why have these lovely vales and hills been sequestered from
> the national domain, already too much curtailed by the set-
> ting aside of extravagant areas for Indian reservations, and
> too small in its arable acreage West of the Missouri to afford
> fit accomodations [sic] to the swarms of emigrants and pio-
> neers pushing forward each year farther into what was but
> yesterday the Western frontier?[13]

Yet, there is an odd sort of justice in his comments. In the almost 130 years since the Great Sioux War, much has been made
about the Lakota claims to the Black Hills, but they were just as
much conquerors as the government. Bourke noted in his diary
that the hills had once belonged to the Crows, who were chased
from their own homeland into central Montana by the Sioux, Cheyenne, and other more powerful tribes. After the Crows came the
Kiowas, who had been completely evicted by the Sioux by the end
of the second decade of the nineteenth century.[14]

Regardless of who had the best title to the region, Bourke could
foresee, as so often soldiers did, that the government's policies would
be ineffective in preventing a general Indian war. The settlers would

---

13. Ibid., 2b:65.
14. Ibid., Diaries, 2b:27-28; Lazarus, *Black Hills/White Justice*, 7; Robinson, *A Good Year to Die*, 5-7.

settle, the miners would mine, and the Indians would resist, regard-less of what the government might try to do to prevent it. And then the soldiers would be called in to clean up the mess. In considering how the war would be fought, he wrote:

> The probable method of procedure will be the establish-ment of a few large depots of supplies in the heart of the Enemy's country, from which as foci can radiate forth col-umns of cavalry and Infantry, carrying supplies by pack-trains, to the most hidden recesses of the Indian territory. A winter campaign may become a necessity, but in such a case the troops by following up the streams, can effect two ob-jects: one, the avoiding of much rigorous cold; the other, the assault of the enemy's villages near the streams and their expulsion to the frigid plains where they will soon freeze to death if they do not promptly submit.[15]

These words proved prophetic almost to the point of clairvoy-ance. But while Bourke envisioned General Crook as the man who could do it, Crook ultimately would demonstrate that he was not equal to the task. The government would have to look to the South-ern Plains to find officers who were.

15. Bourke, Diaries, 2b:41.

Chapter 6

❖

❖

❖

❖

❖

Farewell to Arizona

March 12th, 1875.

General Crook received telegraphic notification from Adjutant General Townsend,[1] of his assignment to duty as Commanding General of the Department of the Platte, with Headquarters at Omaha: also congratulatore [sic] telegrams from Maj. G. M. Randall, Colonel Coppinger and other officers of his old Regiment, the 23d Infantry. Colonel A.V. Kautz, 8th Infantry, assigned to take command of the Department of Arizona, with his brevet grade of Major General. The above information, altho' anticipated for some time, caused no little excitement when officially conveyed to our little community of Fort Whipple. No one can doubt the affection entertained for Genl. Crook by the officers and soldiers of his command and by their families, and altho, with pleasure he accepts the new condition of things, he and his staff will leave with many deep and unfeigned regrets the refined and hospitable circle of Fort Whipple and cherish with unalloyed affection reminiscences of the joyful days passed there.

Mrs Kautz, Mrs and Miss Lynch and Mrs. Thomas immediately concerted the necessary preliminaries for a complimentary Ball and supper to be tendered to the General and staff prior to their departure.

1. Brig. Gen. Edward Davis Townsend.

Nearly six years have dragged their sluggish course along since first I crossed the Rio Grande with a fresh commission and eager aspirations for glory: dear comrades have died, friends have come and gone, posts have been established and discontinued, yet still I have staid, apparently a fixture of the soil. But few other officers have had the good fortune to witness the operations carried on against the hostile Apaches, from their inception to their close and not one perhaps had the same opportunity of forming an acquaintance with this Territory and its people. Now to new scenes and to new acquaintances, the hand of Destiny carries us; may they be as bright and as noble as those we leave behind!

March 13th, Sunday. Telegrams of regret received from Ewing, Collingwood, Nelson,[2] Rockwell and other friends. Messages sent to Major Ogleby, 8th Infantry, acquainting him with the fact of the General's release from duty in this Dep't. Busily engaged all this day and the 14th in necessary preparations for our departure which will probably take place on or about the 25th inst. Honorable Coles Bashford, Secy of State for Arizona, transmitted by telegraph the resolution of thanks to Genl. Crook, his officers and men for the noble services performed by them in Arizona, passed by the Territorial Legislature.

March 15th. The General Crook club rooms at Fort Whipple are being elegantly decorated for the Ball of next Tuesday [*Bourke's insert:* Weds.] evening: festoons of evergreens hang from the walls, while the ceilings are adorned with stars and wreaths of the same material. Over each window, hang guidons and sabres[,] and the regimental standards of the 8th Infantry, bearing the fecund record of noble service, occupy the corners.

Whether judged by the number of guests invited to participate, or the elaborate nature of the preparations made for the occasion, there is no reason to doubt that it will be one of the finest affairs ever known on the Pacific coast.

A committee of prominent citizens of Prescott called upon Genl Crook this morning, presenting a letter from a convention held last night at the Court House, asking that Genl Crook hold a farewell reception to afford the great throng of his admirers an opportunity

---

2. First Lt. Evarts Stinson Ewing, 16th Infantry. Nelson probably is First Lt. William Henry Nelson, 7th Infantry. Collingwood cannot be identified. Heitman, *Historical Register*, 1:411, 743.

of manifesting their deep sense of his integrity, valor and ability as a true gentleman and soldier.

As the hour of our departure approaches, the scenery around Fort Whipple seems to grow more lovely, coquettishly adding new graces to the beauties we have known so long. Old Thumb Butte lifts his scraggy had above the general contour of the Sierra Prieta, which white with snow bounds our vista on the West and South; to the North, San Francisco Mountain wrapped in a mantle of virgin white, pure as the Saint whose name it bears, looms up into a cloudless sky, a noble landmark, one which will long hold a fond place in our memory. Even the pine trees on the hill-sides grow more majestic as if they sought to entice us to stay.

A sky of immaculate blue, a temperature serene as that of Italy and an atmosphere unruffled save by the softest Zephyrs, combine to make our last days at Whipple the most charming of those we have spent here.

March 19th. The ground this morning is covered with a light drapery of snow and a bracing North East wind assures us that Winter has as yet no intention of relinquishing his Dominion over Northern Arizona. General Kautz's staff as thus far known will consist of 1 Lieut. Thomas Wilhelm, 8th Inf., A.D.C. and Adjutant Genl and 1 Lieut E.D. Thomas, 5th Cav., A.D.C. and Engineer Officer. Invitations for the Farewell Ball, of Wednesday evening next are now issued. . . .

A list of invited guests. . .[:]

Mr. [*illegible*]

Mr and Mrs. Jake Marks

Col. C.P. Head.

Dr and Mrs. McCandless.

Dr. Kendall.

Mr. Bashford.

Mr. S.C. Miller.

Mr and Mrs Beach.

Mr and Mrs. L. Bashford.

Mr and Mrs Burmeister.

Mr and Mrs Gray Foster

Mr Burt Foster

Mr William Foster

Genl. J.G. (*heavy ink blot*)tler (Editor "Arizona Miner.")[3]

Mr and Mrs Merrick.

Miss Jennie Banghart.

Mr and Mrs Ed. Wells.

Mr and Mrs Jewell.

Mr Hugo Richards

3. Bourke apparently means T. J. Butler, who edited the *Miner* briefly in 1875. J.H. Marion served as editor both before and after Butler. The "Genl." appears to be honorific, as no record of a T. J. Butler can be found in Heitman's *Historical Register*. Kim Frontz, Arizona Historical Society, to Charles M. Robinson III, December 13, 2001.

Mr George Bowers   Major McDaniel
Mr and Mrs Ed Bowers   Mr Clark Wilson
Mr and Mrs N. Bowers.   Mr Thomas Moore.
Mr and Mrs Buffum.   Judge and Mrs Brookes.
Miss Evans   Mr George Curtis.
Mr Parker.

March 20th Turned over Engineering property to my successor, 1 Lieut. E.D. Thomas, 5th Cav.

March 22d General Crook relinquished command of the Department this morning in orders, General and Special, hereto appended *(See Appendix 15).*

General Kautz assumed control issuing General Orders, No 8, in which his staff is announced.

Many invited guests arrived to-day, which fact added to the bustle incident to the transfer of the Head-Qrs., imparted an air of decided activity to Fort Whipple. Lieutenants Powell, Loshe, Pitcher, (8th) Carter, 6th Cav, Captain Porter, 8th Inf., Colonel Nelson, U.S.A., Colonel and Mrs Mason, 5th Cav., Major and Mrs. Brayton, 8th Inf. were among those reaching HdQrs on this date.

March 23rd. The complimentary reception tendered General Crook by the citizens of Prescott in the name of the people of Arizona, took place to-night at 7 O'Clock, in the new brick building known as Katz's Restaurant. All the officers and ladies stationed at and visiting Fort Whipple were conveyed to town in ambulances belonging to the Q.M. Depot, and for a short time the hum and rattle of wheels bore a faint resemblance to Broadway. Upon coming to town, the party was received by a delegation from the main committee on reception and headed by the 8th Inf. band proceeded to the place of convention. Here upon an elevated, carpeted dais were seats for Generals Crook and Kautz and their respective staff, nearest the stage, rows of arm-chairs were devoted to the use of the great number of ladies present whose bright toilettes were admirably set off by the dark clothing of the surging mass of male humanity behind them.

Behind the platform and above it a canopy formed of the national standard made a simple and becoming decoration to screen the hero of the occasion.

Above the arm-chair in which General Crook took his place, hung his portrait embowered in evergreen and enclosed in the words,

"Firm, Just, Brave, True."

Mayor Luke, chairman then addressed the General as follows: "In the name of the people of Prescott, I welcome you, General Crook, the hero of Arizona". and afterwards presented to the audience Hon. John A. Rush who, in a telling speech, expressed the sentiment of regret of the people of Arizona to learn of Genl Crook's assignment to new fields of duty. The reply made by the General was terse, emphatic, full of feeling and productive of round after round of applause. In succession, remarks were then made by General Kautz, Captain Nickerson, Lieut Bourke and others, those of Nickerson being especially good and finely received.

Telegrams were read to the audience expressing a sympathy of views and a coincidence of regrets on the part of the towns of Tucson, Yuma, Phoenix &c. The entire audience, numbering considerably over 300, now came forward in single file, to shake the hands of General Crook and his staff; it was certainly a deeply suggestive scene this spectacle of merchant, miner, citizen, farmer and laborer, struggling forward to bid God-speed to the man they had learned to love as their Savior and Deliverer. Probably never in the history of our Union has such a spontaneous ebbulition of feeling been witnessed on the frontier. Everything about the affair betokened the earnestness with which the citizens had entered into it, all seeming to feel they were saying Farewell to one who had been not merely a soldier executing orders but a friend truly devoted to their welf[a]r[e].

An abundance of champagne distributed among the guests exhilarated them for the enjoyment of dancing and to the notes of the fine band many couples were soon whirling in the mixes of Lancers and Waltzes. About 10.30 P.M., General Crook, General Kautz and their staffs with the guests from Whipple withdrew.

March 24th. The farewell hop of this night was one of the grandest successes I ever knew. Whether the decorations, the arrangements of the room, the good order of the dances, the excellence of the music, the elaborate toilettes of the ladies and the fine uniforms of the officers, or, finally, the perfection of the supper—in all re[s]pects, the affair was beyond criticism and beyond description. More citizens attended this entertainment than any other given at Whipple during my residence.

A separation did not taken place until 2 A.M., of the 25th. Upon the walls were inscribed complimentary expressions of good-will towards

General Crook and the members of his personal staff departing with him. The supper, comprehending every article of diet to be procured for love, labor or money, would have done honor to Delmonico's, while the savory dishes became ten fold more appetizing when presented with so much affectionate good-will.

March 25th. A sad day of parting, perhaps to meet no more until the Earth and the Sea shall give up their dead.

By invitation, I breakfasted with General Kautz, Mrs Kautz, and General Crook. The other guests were Miss Kitty Hitchcock and Captain Porter, 8th Infantry. After breakfast, escorted by a numerous and dazzling retinue of ladies, officers and citizens in vehicles and on horseback, General Crook, Captain Nickerson and family and myself left Fort Whipple at 9 O'Clock, and took the road to Fort Mojave.[4] Miss Carrie E. Wilkins very courteously drove me in her phaeton to the rendezvous (near the Burnt Ranch about five miles from Prescott.) appointed for the final exercises of Farewell. A sky of immaculate blue, mountain scenery sweet beyond compare, a temperature of celestial serenity were the auxiliaries giving additional brightness and beauty to the gala array of carriages, horses and people drawn up on the summit of a little flat knoll in the centre of which the departing guests took station. Champagne and other stimulants were soon in generous circulation and after a few moments desultory conversation, General Kauts [sic] called the assembly to order and in a speech replete with wit and good points, bade an affectionate farewell to the late Department Commander and staff and wished them new honors in their new field of duty.

Shaking hands for the last time now followed and amid the sobs of the ladies and the tears of the sternest men this melancholy duty was at last accomplished. Over 125 people were on the ground, among them:

General [and] Mrs Kautz	Col. and Mrs Mason
Lieut-Col. and Mrs Wilkins.	Maj. Van Horn.
Miss Carrie Wilkins.	Maj. and Mrs Wilhelm
Col. Evans	Maj. and Mrs Brayton.
Col. Nelson	Lieut Loshe.

---

4. Fort Mojave was established in 1859 on the Colorado River opposite the present city of Needles, California, It was abandoned in 1890, and became an Indian school. The school was closed in 1935, and the post buildings were demolished seven years later. Frazer, *Forts of the West*, 11-12.

Lieut. Powell.

Lieut. Pilcher.

Lieut. Carter

Captain Porter.

Lieut. & Mrs. Aldrich

Mrs Small.

Surgeon & Mrs. Magruder

Miss Kitty Hitchcock

Lieut. And Mrs Lynch & dau.

Chaplain Gilmore

Lieut. Bishop

Mr Garrett.

Mr Moore

Mr Dawes

Mr Preshau,

Mr Higgins

Mr W.W. Johnson

Mr Pratt

M Kearney

Col. Head.

Col. Butler

Mr & Mrs Marion

Mr Ochoa

Mrs Bashford

Mr Foster

Mr C. Foster

and many, many others.

A runaway team of horses broke the elegant carriage of Major Wilhelm, but, fortunately only a slight fright was experienced.

Old San Francisco reared his snowy head above the scene looking majestic as an ancient king; one last fond look at the snowy crowned monarch of the Sierras, one last fonder, more lingering look at our beloved friends and amid uproarious cheers for General Crook, Captain Nickerson and Lieut Bourke, we shook from our feet the dust of the AZ terr and commenced our journey to the land of the Dacotahs. Another star gleams in the horizon of the future.[5]

Camped at old Camp Hualpai.	37 miles.
March 26th Moved to Willow Springs	45 miles
March 27th Moved to Beale's Springs	40 miles
March 28th Moved to Mojave (Fort.)	36 miles

These days' marches were without any special incident; on the 26th, we met at Anvil Rock, General Morgan and Lieut Savage returning from General Court Martial duty at Mojave. Received a letter from

5. Bourke was being overly optimistic. While Crook's jump to brigadier general over the heads of more than forty colonels might stir resentment within the army, it was not likely to create severe repercussions. Once he had his star, however, congress would have balked at any further unorthodox advancement. As the juniormost brigadier general, he was last in a long line of brigadiers awaiting advancement, and any such advancement would only come when a vacancy occurred among the very few major generals. Many of the more senior brigadiers were, themselves, national heroes with large public and congressional followings. Consequently, Crook would have to slowly move up the ladder of seniority, and indeed, was not appointed major general until 1888.

Captain Byrne, 12th Infan. As we approached Mojave, the weather grew very warm and our faces were badly burned in the sun. The banks of the Colorado were fringed with cottonwood and willow trees in full bloom and far as the eye could reach the sinuous course of the turbid stream which connects our new Department with the old could be traced.[6]

At the fort an old time hospitality awaited us, Capt. and Mrs Thompson, Lieut Allen, Dr and Mrs Lawrence, Mr Ben. Spear, Mr Paul Breon, Mr. Charles Schroeder and some others had assembled to greet us on our arrival. The Battery belched forth its salute of thirteen guns, after which an elegant dinner was served at the residence of Capt. Thompson, the post commander. To-morrow, Easter Monday, March 29th, we are to cross the Colorado river, ascend the mountain known as Pi-Ute Hill and begin our journey across the desert of Southern California.

Easter Monday, March 29th. Transferred our heavy wagons across the Colorado river at day-break; partook of an elegant breakfast with the Thompson's and received the farewell greetings of a number of friends with whom we exchanged pledges in champagne. About 9.30, started for the Ferry and were soon being pulled across the river by the sturdy arms of Mojave Charons; when on the Nevada side, one of our mules becoming frightened made a rush overboard and in doing so impaled himself upon one of the heavy iron bolts on the side of the vessel, tearing a gash in his breast about two inches in diameter and six in depth. This accident occasioned some delay but we were soon climbing slowly up the steep grade of the Eastern slope of the Pi-Ute Mountains: twelve miles out from Camp Mojave, passed the boundary monument between Nevada and California[.] Descending this mountain range on the other side, our course lay across a barren, rocky and sandy plain for nearly 12 miles when we reached Pi-Ute Springs a beautiful little jet of water in the rift of barren hills. The stone buildings and corrals here were constructed as a picket station by the 9th Infantry in bygone days.

Water is forced from its bed by a small hydraulic [seine?], in fine working order. Through the courteous consideration of Capt. Thompson, we were overtaken shortly before getting to this point by a courier with a copy of the latest number of the *Arizona Weekly Miner*, with an account of the ceremonies incident to the General's

6. The Colorado River begins in Utah which was in the Department of the Platte.

departure. . . . Heard last night and to-day that the Companies of
the 12th Inf. now in Arizona are to the removed and the posts on
the river now occupied by them garrisoned by companies from the
interior of Arizona.

To-day, the wind blew bitter cold from the North-West.

Tuesday, March 30th. A long, uninteresting drive of (40) miles to
Marl Springs, through a country barren and devoid of picturesque
adornment, with no vegetation save the wild date, cactus, Spanish
bayonet,[7] soap weed[8] and artemesia; with rugged masses of Basalt,
piled like Ossa upon Pelion[9] in grand relief with the arid desert
below. Lunched midway on the journey at Rock Springs. Found
Marl Spring station a little dug-out, excavated in the side of a mountain of marl; the joints, supporting the roof were generally branches
of the stunted mountain cedar peculiar to this section; the thatch-
ing was formed of the leaves of the wild datepalm and limbs of various species of cactus.

The thorny plants indigenous to Southern California and Arizona
had been brought into requisition to constitute railings and fences
for the corrals and other appointments of the house.

In the dug-out proper, a small den, in dimensions—15 by 20 feet,
served as a sitting room, generally sleeping apartment and bar-room.
On one side some sacks of barley were piled up and ready for issue
and sale to passing teams, in the other, a counter, provided with a
small, decrepit pair of Fairbanks' scales, was the only ornament.
Behind this, arranged on a set of weak-minded shelves, were a few
cases of peaches, tomatoes and pears; yeast-powders, sardines,
candles, heavy shirts, pickets, matches, cigars, and tobacco, in promiscuous confusion and perhaps not aggregating in value $200.

Dismal as this place was, it yet parodied the functions of a Mecca to
weary prospectors who hied from the adjacent hills to learn at the
station, the latest news or what passed for news with these poor people.
Who had "struck it rich" in the Greenwood, whose drift had "got in
on" the "pay streak", what Scotty Smith's ore was probably worth
to the ton; were "things lively" down to Arbat, who was running the
station at "Body",[10] why Wallace "got shot" and how—in lazy conti-

7. *Yucca carnerosana.*
8. *Sapindaceae.*
9. Mount Ossa is an extinct volcanic peak jutting up from the ridge of Pelion in Thessaly.
According to mythology, Ossa was piled upon Pelion by giants attempting to besiege Zeus on
nearby Mount Olympus. Bourke makes this analogy again in Chapter 18.
10. I.e., Bodie, Calif.

nuity, the talk drifted slowly along from meridian until far after sunset.

The raiment of the miners was as monotonous as their conversation; cow-skin boots, old, patched, pants, coarse woolen shirt and hat which had a look of having been born second-hand. Yet to these hardy prospectors, our nation is largely indebted for much of its material development and prosperity on the Pacific coast; the mines of Washoe, Arizona, Pike's Peak, Bode and Panamint[11] own their discovery to the very class of men whose colloquy and appearance are referred to in these pages; seldom do any of the poor wretches make money, like draws on the wave of a fast-advancing civilization they float along helplessly until they strand for ever, on some barren shore and become an example and a mockery to the children growing up in mining towns. Sometimes, one more fortunate than his comrades, will manage to sell at a fair figure mineral ledges he has "prospected" and "located"; and then for a brief carnival, the dissolute and depraved run riot with his hard-earned gains; when the last dollar has gone, with no companion save a pack-mule and dog, no fortune except a pannier or two of provisions, a pick, shovel and horn-spoon, away from the glittering lamps and squeaky music of the faro-banks which stand to him as the semblance of an alluring civilization, away to the desolate plains and rugged mountains, descending gloomy cañons or slowly climbing dizzy precipices, away restless as the Wandering Jew, until the sharp twang of the Apache's bow brings rest to the weary feet or until, worse fate, old age shall surprise him with decrepit and almost imbecile, despised as a supplicant by the same gin-mills which could trace their first prosperity to his old-time prodigality.

March 31st The character of country remained unchanged, except that during the forepart of the day, wild datepalms were much more numerous than at any other time on the trip. The last six or seven miles of the thirty-six passed over to-day led us across the dry bed of a dry lake, known as Soda Lake, about seven miles in average width and nearly thirty in length. The painful, sunny whiteness of this vast mineral deposit, unrelieved by a single stem of vegetation,

11. The Washoe strike was on the western slope of the Sierra Nevada, in Nevada. Bodie, California, was the center of a gold rush that yielded $100 million during the 1870s and 1880s. The ghost town is now a state historic park. Panamint, California, grew up in a silver and copper boom that began in 1872. The town was wiped out by a flood in 1876. Lamar, *New Encyclopedia*, 112, 842.

prepares the mind for the information that from this point northward, runs Death Valley, where no living creature exists, and where
not infrequently prospectors and travellers have perished for want
of food and water. According to Lieut. Wheeler's (U.S.A.) calculations this station of Soda Lake is 200 feet below sea level. A bubbling spring of crystal water springs to the surface near the door of
the house; experienced travellers avoid its use as being impregnated
with soda; it has the effect of a drastic purgative. As a defensive
nothing can be imagined better, altho' if slightly corrosive to the
skin.

This station consists of (2) good adobe houses with shingle roofs
and a stone kitchen.

At this station, we found a very curious and entertaining record
book of the arrivals at the station; the following will better serve to
convey an idea of the scope and character of the volume than a
more extended description;

"Tuesday, Mar 5th, Drunken Irishman, Two Mexicans, broncos,
Dutchman same who was here last week; Judge Discon, Doctor Sawyer, a teacher, two miners unknown, Saml. Patterson."

April 1st. Marched through very deep sand to Camp Cady,[12] 36 miles,
requiring 14 hours for the journey; observed along route how the
sand blasts had carved and fashioned the hardest rocks into fantastic shapes. Lunched at "the caves", in a low, narrow box cañon of
the Mojave river. Deep gashes and cracks in the rocks [lying round]
about indicate the action of earthquakes. Country very barren;
nearly destitute of wood, water and grass. Found Camp Cady an old
government post of adobe, rather dilapidated and rapidly going to
ruin.

April 2nd Make a rapid march of 40 miles over an improved country to the Cottonwood, where, finding the road to Bakersfield im-
practicable for heavy wagons, Genl. C. changed intention and
determined to move direct to Spadra, the terminus of the R.R.
Lunched this A.M. at the Fish-ponds, 20 miles out, the character of
our food on this trip has been excellent. The liberality of our kind-
hearted friends at Prescott and Fort Whipple has kept us supplied
with Champagne, claret, Whiskey, Brandy, turkey, chicken, cake
and other delicacies grateful to the weary and hungry traveller.

12. "On the Mojave River, 145 miles northeast of Los Angeles," Heitman, *Historical
Register*, 2:485.

Slept this night under the ramada; had a feline concert I cannot soon forget; an old tom-cat, whose body beyond a doubt contained the soul of a Rossini or Mendelsohn set up a most infernal squalling at foot of my bed and at end of each piece would retire behind a cottonwood pillar evidently to compose some new symphony as we could hear him run through the gamut of all the Cat music since the days of George Washington. My sleep for this reason was slightly impaired.

Chapter 7

✦
✦
✦
✦
✦

Southern California
and the Mormon Zion

Saturday, April 3d, 1875. Moved to Freer's Ranch, 38 miles; for first 20 miles, line of travel lay through a forest of date palms, afterwards bitts of scrub juniper. Progressing Los Angelesward, the houses and farm buildings improved greatly in appearance with each mile of way.

Sunday, April 4th. When we awoke this A.M., a heavy sea-fog overspread the whole face of the country, obscuring the Cucamongo and San Bernardino Mountains nearby which we saw yesterday covered with snow. The pass in which this ranch is situated is called Cajon Pass and through it the R.R. to Arizona is to be built. Passed along through a territory, gorgeous in emerald green tapestry, variegated with countless wild flowers. The adjacent fields covered with green and russet were lighted up by the rays of the morning sun, struggling through the now fast dissipating clouds. Farmhouses on every side, showing every evidence of thrift and comfort, vineyard with thousands upon thousands of vines; orange, apple, peach, English walnut and olive trees and bee hives by the hundred were to be viewed on either hand. At 10 A.M. passed the Cucamongo ranch renowned for the fine grade of wine there manufactured. The road was most excellent and our vehicles thundered along with the velocity of a R.R. train. At 12.30 P.M. reached Spadra, the terminus of the R.R. running East from Los Angeles[.] Found it a collection of hastily constructed houses, grog-shops &c, tenanted by R.R. employees and evincing signs of life, greatly different from the quiet apathy to which we had become accustomed in Arizona.

That evening, General Crook and staff and small party of friends dined at Ruebrittonis[?].

Monday, April 5th. A short ride on the R.R. brought us to Los Angeles, and carried us through the heart of semi-tropical California. The egotism and inclination to boasting of the Californians now seemed pardonable and justifiable as we were called upon to contemplate the magnificent vista of fields, gleaming in purple, green and gold with a back-ground of snow upon the deeply-scarred banks of the mountain ridges. Vineyards, alternating with orange groves and bordered by fields of alfalfa which stretched to the limit of vision, well constructed ranchos, great herds of cattle and droves of sheep, spoke in praise of the substantial wealth of the country, while the noble old mission church of San Gabriel, reaching its buttresses to within 50 yards of the iron rail appealed to men to devote some little care to the accumulation of Treasure not of this world.

The rich haciendas of Shorb, Wilson, Stoneman[1] and others lined the way and prepared us in some measure for the bright little city of the Angels, in whose streets to-day mad speculation and legitimate business distract the attention and almost banish the recollection of the fact that its foundation in 1781, by the Spaniards, was for the extension of the Catholic religion among the neighboring tribes of aborigines. The hospitality of the greeting of Los Angeles is already proverbial; in their treatment of Genl. Crook's party, the old reputation of the community was fully sustained.

The same evening, we started by rail, 31 miles to San Fernando, 31 miles [sic]; thence by stage to the town of Bakersfield; the San Fernando cut, 156 feet deep, 400 yards long, through a ridge or

---

1. Col. George Stoneman, Crook's predecessor as commander of the Department of Arizona, maintained a home in Los Angeles. James De Barth Shorb was the son-in-law of Benjamin Davis Wilson, first mayor of Los Angeles and owner of a large estate called Lake Vineyard. Wilson gave a section of Lake Vineyard to Shorb, who named it San Marino Ranch. In 1903, following Shorb's death, San Marino Ranch was purchased by real estate magnate and railroad heir Henry Edwards Huntington. Huntington dismantled the Shorb house and replaced it with an Italianate mansion, now part of the Huntington Library and Art Gallery, with its great botanical gardens. Houk, *The Botanical Gardens at the Huntington*, 15-19; Bancroft, *Register of Pioneer Inhabitants*, 777.

stratum of indurated clay and sand is a dangerous pass, just admitting one team at a time and is a favorite resort of the robbers lurking throughout Southern California. Old Fort Tejon, now known as Beale's Springs[2] is a situation deserving a more general reputation for beauty, salubrity, and value. Nesting in among lofty snow and pine clad mountains, many little bubbling brooks find their way from the rocky fastness across the grassy turf and among the clumps of oak trees which almost hide the buildings. As our vehicle slowly drove through its limits, ourselves and companions forgot in the enjoyment of the moment the bitter cold of the night previous and the petty discomforts inseparable from all stage travelling.

Taking cars at Bakersfield, a journey of 18 very pleasant hours terminated in San Francisco, where we found excellent quarters in the Lock House, famous the world over for its beautiful dining room, decorated elaborately with scenic illustrations of the Mountains, Lakes and Coast of the state of California[.] A run of visitors now commenced, leaving General Crook no time to do anything but receive calls from the prominent businessmen, politicians and army officers of the city of San Francisco as well as a goodly representation of those from the whole Pacific coast. Invitations to dinners, receptions, parties and other entertainment came in such numbers than [sic] an acceptance of them all would have prolonged our stay to weeks instead of days. At the residence of A. E. Head, we were the recipients of a complimentary dinner, more gorgeous in its appointments than any at a private mansion I have ever seen. The officers of the U.S.A., stationed at Angel Island,[3] invited us to a matinee, memorable from the throng of beautiful and refined young ladies there found assembled. Visits to the Opera ("Girofle-Girofla".) To the Theatre and Minstrels, and dinner parties with various friends made our evenings pass like a summer cloud. During the day, scores of old friends and scores of new came flocking in to congratulate the General on his new assignment and express earnest wishes for his complete success in his new field of service.

2. Fort Tejon was established in 1854 to guard the Tejon Indian Reservation. It was abandoned in 1864 when the reservation was abolished, and became part of a ranch established by Lt. Edward F. Beale, U.S.N., who served as superintendent of Indian affairs in California. Part of the post, located near the present town of Lebec, is now a state historical site. Frazer, *Forts of the West*, 32-33.

3. Angel Island was established in 1863 as part of the defenses of San Francisco Bay. It was redesignated Fort McDowell in 1900, and discontinued in 1946. It is now a state park. Ibid., 25-26.

General Lagrange, one of General Crook's subordinates during the war, and now the Superintendent of the U.S. Mint at San Francisco, invited the Genl and his staff to inspect the workings of that Institution, which was done on Monday the 12th of April. Carriages furnished by the courtesy of Genl Lagrange brought us to the mint where were passed some hours in an exhaustive examination of the processes of smelting, refining and sorting bullion, preparatory to coining into trade dollars.[4]

On this same evening, occurred one of the grandest outpourings of the people ever seen in San Francisco. . . .With vivid recollection of the ovation tendered the General by his numerous warm friends on the Pacific Coast and escorted by a delegation of admirers, our transcontinental journey began at Oakland at 6. A.M. of the 13th April.

Governor Pacheco of California met the General at Sacramento, in a very hearty and kindly manner, presenting some prominent gentlemen who had accompanied him to the depot. One of them, Major George B. Sayer, 1st Cavalry, U.S.A.

At Ogden, Utah, the disagreeable news was borne across the wires of the break in the U.P.R.R.[5] near Green river, caused by the unexpected floods which the melting of last winter's heavy snows had occasioned.

We now turned South on the Utah R.R., going to Salt Lake where General J. E. Smith and his officers were awaiting General Crook at the R.R. depot, and conducted himself and staff to the Walker House, one of the two prominent hotels where quarters had been prepared for them. After dinner, we were driven to the post of Camp Douglas,[6] 3 miles from town and 700 feet above it. Here we found the garrison of 6 companies and Hdqrs of the 14th Infantry, pleasantly situated in regard to everything except officer's quarters which were very inferior and very old. General Crook was called upon by all the officers and their families and was also honored by a salute accord-

4. Trade dollars were produced by the United States from 1873 to 1885 for circulation in the Orient to compete with the Spanish and Mexican eight-real pieces, the latter of which were the standard by which Chinese merchants reckoned the value of currency. It is not uncommon to see U.S. trade dollars, and Spanish and Mexican eight reales stamped with "chop marks," cartouches of Chinese assayers attesting to their value. See Willem, *The United States Trade Dollar.*

5. Union Pacific Railroad.

6. Camp Douglas was established in 1862 east of Salt Lake City, to protect the Overland Mail and telegraph, control the Indians of the region, and watch over the Mormons, whose loyalty was suspect. It was upgraded to a fort in 1878. Frazer, *Forts of the West,* 166.

ing to his brevet rank:[7] after witnessing dress-parade, we returned to our hotel in town.

Salt Lake has been so much written about and so greatly studied that perhaps it is better understood than any of our cities on the frontier and a diffuse description of it is not necessary in this place. We found it a community of some 20.000 people, mostly professing with more or less fervor, the polygamic sect of the Church of Later-day Saints of Jesus Christ, called generally Mormons. The situation of the town in contiguity to the Great Salt Lake and on a barren alkali flat is most unpromising but the patience and skill of the religious fanatics making the first settlements have overcome many almost insuperable obstacles and made the desert truly to bloom as a rose. The streets are 80 feet wide, with canals full of running water on either side and shade and fruit trees in abundance around all the dwellings and in front of them. The manufactories of the vicinity are yet feeble, but promise very valuable results in time: salt can be obtained from the lake water in the wonderful ratio of 1 to 4! (One to four.) Woolen goods of very excellent texture are produced in quantities sufficient for all domestic demands. Two fine hotels, the Townsend House and the Walker House, the first a Mormon, the second a Gentile establishment, afford accomodations of no mean order to weary travellers. The Walker House is provided with hot and cold baths, electric bells, gas, first class Billiard rooms, new carpets and furniture and all the modern conveniences.

April (15th[)]. General Clauson,[8] son-in-law of Brigham Young, Colonel [William H.] Hooper, formerly delegate to Congress, and other representative men of the Mormon community paid their respects to General Crook and gave him a message from President Young, asking him to visit the head of the Mormon Church at his residence, the Lion House; Mr Young offered as an apology for not first calling upon General Crook the increasing burden of his years and the remembrance of a gross insult offered him when last at the Walker House. Accordingly, under escort of the gentlemen mentioned, General Crook and staff proceeded to the Lion or Bee House, a structure irregular in plan, but vast in size, built of stone and surrounded by a close of

7. I.e., a salute for a major general rather than a brigadier general. Because Utah was in the Department of the Platte, this marked Crook's first visit to a post in his capacity as commanding general of the department. As such, he received the courtesies due the office, including the formal salute and dress parade mentioned by Bourke.

8. Apparently Hiram B. Clawson, Brigham Young's business manager.

considerable area; [t]he wall, bounding the precincts is of concrete, defended by buttresses of the same material. Over the main entrance, a lion couchant is seen and on the very apex of the building, a golden bee-hive, emblem of intelligent industry, adopted by the Mormons as one of their symbols, attracts the notice of the passer by. This building serves among other purposes, as the residence of many of Brigham Young's wives or concubines, but his favorite harlots have special domiciles allotted for their use. Amelia's house, inhabited by the youngest and prettiest of his harem, is built according to the latest Chicago touch, with Mansard roof, bay windows and projecting balconies. A portion of the Lion house is laid off for use as Offices of various kinds and in one of these, the main reception room, Brigham Young awaited General Crook's approach, surrounded by the General Council, the Apostles, Elders and other dignitaries of his sect. The meeting was cordial and interesting and endured long enough to afford me an opportunity of noting what was important or valuable for future reference. Portraits of the long line of Mormon bishops ranged about the walls gave the room the semblance of a cheap picture gallery; the artistic execution of these paintings was very inferior and spoke very forcibly of the artist's want of talent in his art or the homely traits of the dead and gone rulers of Zion; in general, the shrewd, penetrating, sensual and cold-blooded looks of these believers in the text of Moroni[9] infused the observer with repugnance and disgust; the same grasping ambition combined with some share of practical business tact can be discerned in the faces of Brigham Young and his living associates.

Brigham Young in age is 75, corpulent of body, massive in frame and yet very bright intellectually. Animal passions strongly marked in countenance and evidently a man of no common character, but, as I think, has not faith in the creed he inculcates as the only means of salvation. All the Mormon leaders are in manners plausible and in conversation insinuating; their courtesy to officers of the army stationed among them is very marked; from motives of policy, they avoid a conflict with the military forces, not perceiving apparently that a more insidious and more deadly agent than War has already seized upon the threat of their power and is quietly but surely and rapidly suffocating it. The Pacific R.R. has effected a greater revolu-

---

9. The angel Moroni, who Mormons believe delivered the text of the Book of Mormon to their prophet, Joseph Smith.

tion in Utah than 100.000 soldiers could have done in the time elapsed since its completion. Mormonism with its salient feature, polygamy, can exist only in the isolation of our Great Western solitude and this seclusion once rudely broken in upon by the iron messengers of a noble civilization and more exalted religion, the disciples of [Joseph] Smith and Young, unable to find new deserts, unacquainted with more secluded fastnesses must submit to a destiny of dispersion and extinction. If in twenty years, the vast edifices erected by this singular religion yet stand, it will be among an assemblage of unsympathizing and cynical antagonists jealous of the presence in their midst of the smallest vestige of the creed that but lately ruled the valleys of Utah.

The Mormons profess a belief in the Holy Bible and in the text of a supplementary book written or engraved on sheets of copper by one Moroni, represented as an angel of God; yet neither of these volumes command the respect accorded the "revelations", dictated by God to his chosen people by mouths of his duly designated Apostles. These "revelations" are varied and comprehensive in character, ranging from a decision upon questions of dogma to counsels in the matters of business; Grace and Green Groceries, Religious regeneration and Railway, management, Architecture and Growth in Holiness curiously mingle and alternate in the Fanatical enunciations with which Brigham Young regularly edifies the devout and regales the skeptical. The Mormons adopting the keystone of Catholic teaching—submission to authority—carry the doctrine of Blind Obedience from Religion to Politics and Commerce; the church prescribes and proscribes what article of Faith shall be believed and what article of merchandize shall be patronized come equally within the jurisdiction of the Bishops, where domination now somewhat impaired is yet of great potency.

Every street corner has its store bearing aloft the sign of a human eye, surrounded by a cabalistic symbol;

Z.C.M.I=Zion's Co-Operative Mercantile Institute.

To these establishments, the pious Mormons wend their way, buying and selling one to the other that Trade may as far as possible be kept from the hands of the Gentiles.

Nevertheless some of the mercantile firms of strongest standing, are conducted not alone by Gentiles but by seceders from their own Faith. The House of Walker Bro's, doing an annual business of millions, bears the name of young men who have openly defied the authority of Brigham and the Church.

Little can by said of polygamy except reprobation and scorn; the women who knowingly submit to a condition of concubinage in a Christian country would maybe have become prostitutes, in the absence of such a religious dispensation; yet there are among the Mormon women examples of keenness and intelligence and in my own conversation with them I was not favored with any confidential outbreak against the degrading, soul-destroying influences of polygamy such as enliven the pages and chapters of books and treatises by travellers generally.

The Mormons claim, and the claim must be allowed, that by their unaided energy they have overcome obstacles such as no other settlers in our midst have ever had to encounter, making what once was the most frightful solitude of the Great American Desert blossom as the rose. Their city is a glorious exponent of the powers of man and ranks high in the list of corporations to be noted for careful drainage, good ventilation, abundance of foliage, well-managed gardens and common-sense dwelling houses. The equability of the climate, the chain of the majestic mountain scenery near by, the abundance and cheapness of fruit, vegetables and all articles of diet and the present accessibility by R.R. promise a bright and happy future for the valley of the Great Salt Lake when the objectionable religious feature shall have been eliminated.

The noble ranges, snow clad from January to December, known as the Wahsatch and Oquirrh Mountains hem in the Valley on Right and Left and from their ore-seamed flanks have already commenced to yield rich returns in silver, iron and copper, a bright harbinger of the metallic harvest Utah will furnish the world after better development.

Salt Lake City has but few buildings of note and none of much beauty: All tourists are expected to visit the Tabernacle, as the cathedral of the Mormons is called; here courteous attendants will always be found to escort and inform visitors. Its ground plan is an allipse [sic] with Transverse and conjugate diameter of 250 and 125 feet. 40 feet above the floorings, the red sandstone walls give support to the trusses and studs bearing the ellipsidal wooden roof, 68 feet from the upper extremity of its vertical conjugate axis to the planking below and 77 feet from the wooden shingles on the exterior to the same point. Any flowing anticipation of architectural elegance is brusquely dissipated upon seeing this enormous stone mud-turtle, for such it resembles; the builders sacrificed all aspirations after a beautiful idea to the more important demands of ventilation, acoustics and capacity.

15,000 can be placed within its walls, most of the audience can be seated and in case of fire the broad doors, placed not more than 25 feet apart insure the safety of the vast multitude worshipping there on solemn occasions. The peculiar mathematical configuration of the buildings causes every note of the organ, every sentence of the preacher and the words of the singers to be heard with a refreshing and unusual distinctness in all parts of the edifice.

The organ, claimed to be the 2n largest in the U.S., and the 4th or 5th largest in the world is 48 feet from the pedestal to crest of pipes, of which it now has 2300, with the intention on the part of the Mormon authorities to augment this number to 3200 as soon as possible: it will then be worked by hydraulic power.

During our visit, workmen were *inside* the organ, busy in its repair; one of the elders of the church courteously invited us to go inside the vast instrument and for a few minutes we moved about amid immense pipes of all sizes and tones. This instrument's especial merit is the mellowness and depth of its tone and simple beauty of its external appearance. The Mormons declare themselves very proud of a production from their own resources, erected by their own people.

Upon gala days, this tabernacle is adorned in great profusion and not always in good taste with flags, banners, standards, evergreen wreaths and festoons; this occasions an odd architectural innovation in the hundreds of holes bored in the ceiling and walls the use of which is a problem of difficult solution until the guide explains that through them ropes and cables are passed to sustain the scaffolding the workmen must use in getting the necessary decorations into position.

On the spandles of the arches supporting the galleries were affixed mottoes, some of which I write from actual transcript:

"Obedience is better than Sacrifice."

"Suffer Little children to come unto me."

"We thank thee, O God, for a prophet!"

"Keep your armor bright."

"God Bless our Teachers."

"The Kingdom of God or nothing."

"Honor Thy father and mother."

"Praise the Lord, Hallelujah."

"Glory to God in the Highest."

"The Pioneers of 1847."

"Be temperate in all things."

"Utah's best crop, children."

&c &c &c &c.

This building, first commenced in 1864, was completed in 1867; an average of 300 workmen being employed on it from that time.

Near the tabernacle, a temple of very imposing character is in the course of erection in granite of fine crystallization brought from near the Emma Mine. In elevation it is almost a reproduction of Westminster Abbey.

The Mormons say all this labor has been on sequence of plans submitted to Brigham in a "revelation" by an angel: the celestial visitant's knowledge of architecture is worthy of much commendation.

The Hotels of Salt Lake, the Walker and Townsend Houses, already mentioned, are very carefully constructed, and rarely fail to give satisfaction to all who may visit them. During our stay, the "brak" on the R.R. caused many passengers, anxious to escape the inconveniences of an enforced detention at Ogden to imitate our example and seek the more pleasant accomodations of the Mormon capital. Each hotel was crowded to its utmost and in a spirit of rivalry which pervades every principle of their management, the respective proprietors gave a number of very enjoyable little hops, participated in by a majority of the guests from each establishment. The Townsend House is supported by Mormon capital, its rival representing the moneyed interest of the Gentile population. At the former house were met many young ladies belonging to the principal families of Brigham Young's church: one of them, I was informed, was the 28th daughter in a family. Very little social intercourse is maintained between the conflicting religious elements peopling the valley of Deseret; both parties seem anxious to conciliate the good-will of the military authorities, who in turn are very careful not to incline, in their official relations, toward either side. The great evening drive of Salt Lake is to the military post of Camp Douglass [sic], at the hour for band practice and dress-parade. The level, hard-beaten drive of 3 miles from town to the post is fairly lined with vehicles, filled with ladies, gentlemen and children. Around the parade-ground, at the time of our second visit to the Camp, between one hundred and two hundred conveyances of every character were ranged, the occupants listening with appreciation to the band's rendition of operatic airs. The animation of this regular evening scene is a very marked and agreeable incident in the daily routine of garrison life at Camp Douglass. After band practice, followed dress-parade of the 6 companies stationed at the post. Major [Montgomery] Bryant, 14th Inf., conducted the manoeuvers. In a pleasant evening breeze, blowing from the Lake, the spectators rapidly sought their way back to their homes in town.

Salt Lake claims one of the most elegant and complete buildings for banking purposes in the United States; unfortunately, the bankruptcy of Jay Cooke & Co., involved those concerned in the Western Enterprise and caused a suspension of business in this concern, a very handsome edifice, arranged interiorly with what looked to me more like attention to the comfort of the Bank directors than to the security of deposits to them confided.
Tesselated pavements, counters of rich black and white marble, surmounted by a railing of bronze and walnut, with windows of cut glass; heavy chandeliers of bronze, lofty ceilings very handsomely frescoed—a directors' room, furnished in red morocco and oiled oak, carpeted without consideration of cost—this grandeur and luxury will now make a poor recompense to depositors whose hard earned moneys will be withheld from them forever or at best during the whole tedious process of liquidation.

From Salt Lake to Ogden and from Ogden to Omaha, our travels were one succession of delays due to the unprecedented snows of last winter having been very suddenly melted by the great heat of an early spring; in places, for 200 miles, the track of the U.P.R.R. was washed away or had sunk in the soft yellow clay lining the banks of Green River and its affluents. Much trouble was experienced in providing sleeping car accomodations for the pent up humanity, anxious to escape from confinement; finally, our train started with its load and after a journey of five instead of two days reached our destination. Our passengers determined to make the best of a bad bargain; as we had all been previously acquainted with each other or with common friends of long standing, we became sociable more rapidly even than is the rule on the Overland road.

Our party comprised

General George Crook, U.S. Army.

Captain A.H. Nickerson, U.S.A., A.D.C.

Mrs. A.H. Nickerson and little daughter,
                Florence.

Cutler McAllister, Esq. San Francisco.

Mrs. J.G. McAllister   "   "

Chico. Forster, Esq., Los Angeles, Cal.

W.B. Hellman, Esq., and family, "   "

Thomas Mott, Esq.   "   "

Archibald Colquhoun, Esq. London, Engd.

W.B. Lyon, Esq., Los Angeles, Cal.

Mrs Keeney, San Francisco, Cal.

Albert Morrow, Esq., San Francisco

J.C. Stubbs, Esq., San Francisco.

Mrs. Stubbs   d[itt]o

and the writer.

At Laramie city, General I. S. Palmer, U.S.A., [sic] Colonel 2n Cavalry, Comdg the post of Fort Sanders,[10] met General Crook on the train and as we slowly passed the post, the band, drawn up in line, played a few complimentary strains, acknowledged as best we could by waving of handkerchiefs to the officers (Clarke and Fowler.) in charge.

At Cheyenne, Genl. Reynolds, Colonel of the 3d Cavalry, awaited General Crook's coming. Among the officers with him, we saw many old familiar faces and found our hands warmly grasped by friends we had known in the troublous days in Arizona.

The next day April 25th, our congenial party broke up, the Genl

10. Fort Sanders was established three miles from Laramie in 1866, to protect emigrant routes, the Denver-Salt Lake stage route, and Union Pacific construction crews. It was abandoned and transferred to the Interior Department in 1882. Not to be confused with Fort Laramie, which is in extreme east-central Wyoming near the Nebraska line. Frazer, *Forts of the West*, 185.

and staff remaining in Omaha, the others going by various lines East and South East to New York and Saint Louis. Scarcely had we been shown to our rooms in the Grand Central Hotel when the notes of the "General Crook March", played by the band of his old regiment, the 23d. Infantry, broke upon the air and a long line of officers, most of whom had served under General Crook from British America to Mexico, filed up the main stairway headed by the soldierly figure of Colonel R.I. Dodge. Our long journey fittingly and delightfully terminated in a warm welcome from old comrades whose bread and blankets we had so often shared on crag and in cañon, across mountain and desert in the glorious days of the long ago.

Lieut-Col. R.I. Dodge, Lieut. and Adjutant, Charles Bird, Lieut. and R.Q.M. W. F. Price [sic], Lieut F. Dodge. Capt. O.W. Pollock, Captain Charles Wheaton, Lieut P. Brodrick, Lieutenant O.L. Wieting, and Lieut. Lockwood were among those of former Arizona acquaintances who at this early opportunity paid their devoirs to the new Commander of the Dept. General Brisbin, 2n Cav., Captains Egan and Wells, Lieuts Allison and Sibley of the same regiment were among the new friends met at this time. . . .

The next morning, General Crook assumed command of the Department of the Platte and announced the members of his staff:[11] nothing of importance in the Department could well be transacted until after consultation with Lt. Genl. P.H. Sheridan, to see whom Genl Crook went, May 1st, to Chicago, taking me with him.[12]

11. See Appendix 15.
12. While in Chicago, Crook and Bourke attended the wedding of General Sheridan and Irene Rucker, on June 3, 1875. Robinson, *General Crook*, 161.

Chapter 8

❖

❖

❖

❖

A Scientific Expedition

HEADQUARTERS DEPARTMENT OF THE PLATTE,*

Omaha, Nebraska, May 12, 1875

SPECIAL ORDERS,
No. 57

(*Extract.*)

※   ※   ※   ※   ※

3. Second Lieutenant *John G. Bourke*, 3d Cavalry, A.D.C., will report, in person, at Fort Laramie, to Lieutenant Colonel *Richard I. Dodge*, 23d Infantry, to accompany the Geological Expedition to the Black Hills, under special instructions from the Department Commander.

The Quartermaster's Department will furnish the necessary transportation.

※   ※   ※   ※   ※

BY COMMAND OF BRIGADIER-GENERAL CROOK:
[Signed]
George D. Ruggles
Assistant Adjutant-General

---

* *This order, pasted into the diary, introduces this section of Bourke's narrative—ed.*

Thursday, May 13th, Left Omaha at midday, in the Pullman car "Wyoming", with the following party bound for Cheyenne: General Crook, Captain Nickerson, General Perry and Lieutenant Stevens. Mr Chico Forster also was one of the party. Reached Cheyenne, the next day at 1.30 P.M. and proceeded to Fort Russell,[1] about 3 miles out from town, where we passed the afternoon very agreeably in visiting the families of officers there stationed. General Reynolds, post commander pointed out many points of interest especially the "Burnt district," comprising ground that had been covered by six double sets of q[uarte]rs, swept away in a moment[']s time, in the conflagration of last December. This fire took place at 4 A.M., compelling feeble and delicate women and children to start terror-stricken from their beds, insufficiently clad, to withstand a temperature which nearly solidified mercury. Between the post and town, stands Russel [sic] depot, known as Camp Carlin from which the greater portion of supplies needed by the troops and posts in Northern Wyoming are drawn. Fort Russel [sic] stands upon a stratum of reddish gravel, which has been found in the course of excavations made in boring an Artesian well, to be over 1000 feet in depth. Crow creek furnishes an ample supply of pure water to the post and the salubrity of the climate is unrivalled. The great elevation, over 6000 feet, and the exposed situation upon a bleak and treeless plain across which the North wind frequently blows with the force of a tornado, sufficiently explain the frigidity of the atmosphere in the winter. South of the post about sixty miles off, can be seen the snow-clad crest of the ridge known as Long's Peak, of the Rocky Mountains.

Cheyenne we found to be a small R.R. town at the junction of the Kansas and Union Pacific R.R. The dining room at the Hotel at which we stayed over night was fantastically decorated with the heads of the mountain sheep, elk, black and white-tailed deer, and buffalo.

Leaving Cheyenne in a Government ambulance, our route lay for 45 miles in a generally North Course to the Chug, passing over

---

1. Fort D.A. Russell was established in 1867 to protect workers constructing the Union Pacific. Because the fort became an important supply base, an adjacent subpost was established, officially designated Cheyenne Depot, but often referred to as Camp Carlin or Russell Depot. Cheyenne Depot was discontinued in 1890. In 1930, Fort D.A. Russell was renamed Fort Francis E. Warren. It later was transferred to the Department of the Air Force, and is now Warren Air Force Base. Frazer, *Forts of the West*, 184-85.

the Lodge Pole and Little Bear creeks. At the Chug creek, obtained accomodations for the night at the ranch of Portuguese Philip[s], who exerted himself for our entertainment with much success. The meals spread before us, although perfectly unostentatious, were eaten with much relish; rich cream, golden home made butter, aerated biscuits, amber coffee, good ham and preserves tempted appetites already ravenous from long fasting.

The next day, May 16th a drive of 40 miles brought us to Fort Laramie,[2] on the Laramie river, half a mile or so from its confluence with the North Platte. The country passed over since leaving Cheyenne, is an undulating plain, well watered but bare of trees. The grass seems very thin and to be a species of the gramma of Arizona. The settlements between Cheyenne & Fort Laramie are increasing steadily in strength, and are to all appearances composed of a superior class of people.

At Fort Laramie, we found General Bradley, the District commander, and Colonel R.I. Dodge, 23rd Infy, who is to command the escort to the Geological survey of the Black Hills; the troops here stationed represent the 2n and 3d, Cavalry, 9th and 4th Infantry. The detachment forming the expedition, will be alluded to in detail a few pages further on; it is to consist of 4 companies of 3d Cavalry, 2 of the 2n, and 2 of the 9th Infantry. About 70 wagons will be needed for the transportation of supplies and a 12 p[oun]d[e]r Howitzer and Gatling gun are to be used in the protection of the train.

Somewhere near Harney's Peak of the Black Hills, in South West Dacotah, Colonel Dodge intends forming a depot, surrounded by a stockade, and guarded by one company of Infantry, the other being employed in escorting the wagon train to and from Laramie. No positive apprehension is felt as to the attitude the Sioux may assume towards the expedition; prudence commands vigilance and thorough preparedness, to frustrate the attempts of the Minneconjous, (Sioux), believed to be none too friendly.[3]

2. Fort Laramie was established as an American Fur Company trading post in 1834. In 1849, it was purchased by the federal government and garrisoned as a military post until 1890, when it was abandoned. Much of the post has been preserved or restored, and it is now a national historic site. Ibid., 181-82.

3. In fact, the Miniconjous were one of the lesser of the seven tribes of the Lakota (Western Sioux). The three great tribes were (in order of population) the Oglala, the Brulé, and the Hunkpapa. Besides the Miniconjous, the lesser tribes were Blackfeet, Sans Arcs, and Two Kettles.

Colonel Dodge, our commander, is a graduate of the Military Academy, (class of 1848.) experienced in Indian warfare and of great natural sagacity in matters military and otherwise.

While at Laramie, I was gratefully surprised by Captain [John] Mix, 2n Cavalry, with a present of a petrified land tortoise of unusual dimensions, being nearly 12 inches in diameter; I shall present it with other accumulations of the trip to the Museum of the Mily. Acady.

The expedition sent from here to intercept a band of raiding Indians returned to-day, after unsuccessful pursuit; the command came upon the redskins while crossing the Platte, but were unable to intercept or delay their retreat. American horses do not seem best adapted to cope with the hardy ponies of the aborigines and should be superseded by the California Broncos, which can well endure every hardship this country has to present. Accustomed from birth to pasturage alone, less grain would be needed to preserve them in good condition, a great point in favor of the change suggested.

The movement these little notes attempt to chronicle is, as had already been intimated, a military escort to the party of scientists, selected by the President to visit, examine and report upon the geological, mineralogical, and other features of the section of country known as the Black Hills, being a range of mountains situated in South West Dacotah, known to the Sioux as "Sha-sa-pa". These hills have long been reported rich in valuable minerals, tempting to prospectors as much from their remoteness from civilized neighborhoods and the vague and incoherent history known of them, as from the intrinsic value accorded in the markets of the world.

But, when in 1874, organizations of magnitude commenced to concentrate at Sioux City and Cheyenne, the attention of the general Gov't was called by the jealous remonstrances of the Sioux Indians to the fact that the hills, spoken of[,] lay in their reservation and could not be visited by white men except in direct and open violation of the treaty by which these lands had been ceded them. About the same time the command of Genl. George A. Custer, Lieut-Colonel of the 7th U.S. Cavalry, returned from a summer excursion to the vicinity of Harney's Peak, bringing back rumors of rich places seen and prospected while en route; much acrimonious discussion was awakened in the public prints, some writers affecting to doubt the credibility of the witness, others hotly contesting the motives influencing his antagonists. From his original position as taken in his official report, General Custer could not be drawn and from the archives of memory and dim tradition, men commenced exhuming stories related by French Canadian voyageurs, trappers and traders, and by Roman Catholic priests, missionaries among the Sioux, Flatheads, and Blackfeet; which narrations, it may be safely asserted, lost nothing in repetition;—finally, in the month of December, 1874, word was sent to the Commanding Officer Fort Laramie that a small band of prospectors, ignoring alike the prohibition of the authorities and the danger of attacks from hostile Indians, had penetrated to the arcanum of the Black Hills and that, upon the complaint and demand of the Secretary of the Interior ([Columbus] Delano.) the Secy. Of War, ([William W.] Belknap.) ordered them driven out. Captain Guy V. Henry's Company "D", of the 3d Cavalry was detailed to perform the designated duty, which in the terrible state of the weather then prevailing and the absence of any urgent necessity for precipitate action in the premises, seems to-day inhumane. The command was absent about a fortnight, with the thermometer indicating a temperature, at the comparatively comfortable garrisons from which they started, of from 25° to 40°, below zero (-25° @ -40° F.) No trace could be found of the intruders and the only tangible results of the Expedition were the frozen lines of famished men and horses; out of an effective strength of 50 men, the incredible number of 45 was sent sick to hospital for medical treatment. [A]mputated toes and dwarfed hands and fingers are the only evidences now in existence to attest that in the Interior Depart, "some one had blundered".

Again, in the month of March, 1875, Captain John Mix's company "M", of the 2n Cavalry, was ordered to repeat the effort to find the invading force of miners, a duty successfully accomplished after encountering inclement weather and rigorous obstacles second only to those forming the Nova Zembla[4] experience of the first command. The miners brought in numbered 48 in all, including one woman and one boy. . . .

A change of Generals commanding the Department of the Platte had occurred while these last mentioned movements were transpiring: General E.O.C. Ord, the former commander had been superseded by Brigadier General George Crook, whose achievements

4. Nova Zemlya, an archipelago in the Arctic Ocean.

on the Pacific Coast had brought him before the whole country and the whole world as the most successful Indian fighter and the only successful Indian manager the United States had ever known. Immediately after assuming control of his new military province (April 27th.,) Gen. Crook left his Hdqrs (at Omaha, Neb.,) for Chicago where he remained in consultation with Lieutenant General Philip H. Sheridan, the commander of the Mil. Div. Of the Missiouri.

Returning to his own Department, he had once set out as already stated, for [Fort] Laramie, having previously dispatched thereto Colonel Dodge, with instructions to command the expedition.

The following expresses corrected the constitution and organization of the military forces, as well as of the savan[t]s.

23d Inf.,

Col. R.I. Dodge, Commanding
1st Lieut. M.C. Foot[e], 9th Inf., Adjutant.
1st Lieut. John F. Trout, 23d Inf., A.A.Q.M.
A.A. Surgeon Lane.
2n Lieut. John G. Bourke, 3d Cav., A.D.C. to the Department Commander, accompanied the expedition under special instructions from General Crook, and acted as Engineer Officer of the Expedition.

Cavalry, 2n & 3d Regt.

2n Regiment.
Company

Spaulding E.J.	Captain
Gregg (absent.)	1st Lieut.
Coale, John H.	2n Lieut.

Company

Noyes (absent.)	Captain
Hall C.T.	1st Lieut.
Kingsbury, F.W.	2n Lieut.
Company "A"	3d Regt.
Hawley Wm.	Captain
Lawson	1st Lieut.
Morton, Charles	2n Lieut.

Company.

(absent.) Curtis,	Captain.
King, A.D.	1 Lieutenant
Foster; James E.H.	2 Lieutenant

Company

Russell, Gerald	Captain
[Lawson, Joseph crossed out]	1st Lieut.
(Russell.) absent.)	2n Lieut.
Company	
Wessels, H.W. Jr.	Captain.
Whitman R.E.	1 Lieut.
(Robinson.) absent.)	2 Lieut.
	9th Infantry
Company.	
Burt, Andrew S.	Captain
(Adjutant.)	1st Lieut.
Craig, Louis A.	2n Lieut.
Company	
Munson, Samuel	Captain
Capron T.H. (absent.)	1st Lieut.
Delaney, Hayden	2n Lieut

Artillery: 12 pdr Howr and one Gatling Gun, with 20,000 rds ammn.
Extra for entire command.

Guides   Jos Marrivale.

Train of 75 wagons, under
     1st Lieut. John F. Trout
          9th Infantry.

Corps of Scientists

H.P. Janny [sic], Geologist & Chief
     [Henry] Newton, Minerologist
     [Horace P.] Tuttle. Astronomer
     [Valentine T.] Macgillicuddy. Tpogl Engineer
     Patrick. Student.
     [William H.] Root, Miner.
     —[J.S.] Newberry, ornithologist and
     taxidermist. (resigned.)
          Photographer, sick,
     did not join

(Colonel Dodge's son, Richard Paulding Dodge, a young boy of (14),
also of the party. Under the name of Paulding, he has since won
some consideration as a member of the theol[og]ical[?] association. J.G.B.)

While at Fort Laramie, I noticed how much more comfortable troops
can be made in moderately cold than in moderately warm climates;

water, the great requisite is here found in great abundance furnish-
ing means of cultivation and adornment, while stone cellars filled
with ice from the same source of supply afford to fatigued and thirsty
troops in the heat of summer a refreshment not within their reach
in more torrid latitudes.

Not many yards outside the line officers' quarters may still be
found the boxes or coffins containing the mouldering remains of two
Indian girls; one, the daughter of Spotted Tail, the head chief of the
Brulé Sioux (and considered by many to be the smartest man and
most astute politician in his nation.) died, so tradition says, of unre-
quited love entertained by her for a young army officer at that time
on duty at the post. The coffins were placed upon upright pine stan-
chions about 15 feet high and the corpses suffered gradually to de-
compose, such being the mode of sepulture (?) In vogue among these
people. To the scaffolding is nailed the tail of the horse, whose ghost
carried the young maiden's spirit to the land of the Great Hereafter.
As the question of the Black Hills, Survey will gain some additional
interest from a knowledge of the metes and bounds of the district, it
is given below:

Commencing at the intersection of 46° North Lat. with the East
Bank of the Missouri river, south down said bank to North Boundary line of the state of Nebraska (43° Par. North Lat), West along
said parallel to the 104° Long. West from Greenwich, North, following said meridian to the 46° North Lat. and then East along this
parallel to the Initial point. Estimated area, about 26.000.000 acres.

Possession of the reserve already ceded on the East of the Missouri river was confirmed and all the Territory East of the summit
of the Big Horn Mtns declared unceded Indian Territory and ingress
of whites pretermitted. Permission to lease reservation to hunt for
buffalo along the North Platte and the Republican Fork of the Smokey
Hill rivers was conceded and it was further stipulated that when by
actual survey it should be found that there was less than 160 acres
of arable land for each person permitted by treaty to reside upon
the Reserve, the metes and bounds should be so much farther enlarged as to include the amount of soil needed.

The convention was framed at Fort Laramie, (then in Dacotah, now in
Wyoming Territory,) between W. T. Sherman, W. F. Harney, C. C. Augur, A. H. Terry, John B. Sanborn, Nath. Taylor, Commissioners on the
part of the U.S., and Red Cloud and 176 other chiefs and headmen of

the Brulé, Sans Arcs, Blackfeet, Yanctonnais, Uncpapas, Ogallalahs, Minnieconjous, Cutheads, Two Kettles and Santee Sioux and some of the Arapahoes. The treaty was signed April 24th et seq. 1868 and ratified by President [Andrew] Johnson, February 24th 1869.

The general misconduct and obliquity of the present management of Indian affairs induces the insertion of the following editorial from the "Tribune", New York, May 7th, 1875.

MARS AND MERCURY ON THE FRONTIER

We all admit that war is barbarous, and our familiarity with scenes of slaughter must offend some of the finer sensibilities of men [illegible] there must be something far more [illegible] than war in the service of our Indian Department, or we should not see the contrast which is daily and hourly presented on the frontier between the behavior of the army and that of the Indian agents of the Government, in their dealings with the aborigines and the pioneers in the Western wilderness. It should be remembered that the army has little to do with the Indians, except to keep them in bounds and to punish them when they transgress. The soldier's aspect to them is always stern and serious; while on the other hand, [the concept of] the trader and the agent are gentle and gracious ideas; from them come flour and beef and whisky, bibles and right soft greetings, and gunpowder, candy and compliments—everything calculated to make the Indian good and happy. But in spite of all this, the Indians trust the soldier as implicitly as they fear him, and they regard the civilians with whom they deal, from whom they get everything they want to gratify their vices or to support life, who form their only medium of communication with the Great Father at Washington, with an intensity of hatred and contempt which are but dimly expressed in those occasional outbursts of savage eloquence with which Red Cloud, and Spotted Tail, and others have from time to time startled the readers of newspapers.

The simple explanation of the matter is that the army is well nigh the only refuge of mere decent honesty on the frontier. Though almost his sole duty is to kill Indians, or be killed by them, the word of an officer of the army is worth more to any savage chieftain than the oath of any civilian representative of the Government. It requires no especial subtlety to see why this is so. There is a tradition of honor and honesty among the officers of the regular service which nothing but malice will deny. You may explain it in any way you choose, but it cannot be explained away. Many of them are far from saintly in various aspects, but you will scarcely ever find one of them who is not as safe as a piece of machinery in the Mint in all matters affecting the public money. One reason of this undoubtedly is that the service is so rigidly systemized that stealing is very difficult, and generation after generation of soldiers, recognizing this fact, have grown up honest, and go through no struggle of temptation when intrusted with large amounts of funds. In this they have an immense advantage over the unfortunate dependents of the Indian Ring. They hold their places from thieves; they are known to have india-rubber consciences; they work in a system which affords only encouragement to gross knavery. We have recently shown in these columns how easy it is for the agents and traders to steal about half of what they pretend to issue. We have no right to be astonished at the results. The Commissioner of Indian Affairs plaintively admitted the other day that he could not get honest and capable Indian Agents for $1,500 a year. But the Government gets officers for very little more, who are both honest and capable, because they serve with traditions of honor behind them, and under circumstances where it would be infinitely harder to commit frauds without detection than do their duty without reward.

The soldier has another useful instinct which the civilian official lacks; he is accustomed to obey orders whether they are pleasant or not. When Col. Henry was ordered last Winter to comb the Black Hills for miners, he made no question, but started off into the arctic desolation to do what he was told, paying the penalty in horrible suffering and loss of life and limb among his command. This Spring the order was renewed to Capt. Mix, and he, more fortunate, rode a month or so through trackless, snowy wastes, found the miners' stockade, and brought every man into camp. Sup-

pose Mr. Delano had been instructed with this business—
how would it have been done? A Ring would have formed by
instantaneous nebular development, "my son John"[5] and
his friends would have arranged matters among themselves,
the local rings of Wyoming would have been conciliated,
and before the expedition ended, which of course would not
have been until pleasant weather, the title to the choicest
bits of land in the territory would have been held in itching
palms, and not an order emanating from the Government
would have been executed. When the soldier receives an
order, his first and last thought is to execute it. When one of
the Indian Ring receives an order, he begins nimbly to cal-
culate what there is in it, and whether he can make more
money by disregarding it altogether than he can by pretend-
ing to obey it. If the soldier fails, he is court-martialed and
ruined. If the Ring man is caught and denounced, he is too
often vindicated by his chief; and if he is not, he is allowed
to keep all he has stolen.

The crossing of the beefherd of the command over the Laramie and
North Platte rivers was effected to-day under the superintendence of
Lieut. John F. Trout, A.A.Q.M.: ten cavalrymen surrounded the beeves
and after concentrating them in a circle, forced by threats and yells
their entrance into the river; once there, the only difficulty to overcome in their swimming the current was the tendency of the animals
to huddle together. Sticks and stones were thrown to cause their dispersion and the passage of the river was soon readily effected, only two
heads being left behind. Forage and other stores for the use of the
command were also ferried across to-day, the 21st May. Took an observation on Laramie Peak this morning and found its bearing to be 81°
(exactly West) (plat with 0° South, reading to West.)
May 22nd. Surgeon [John Field] Randolph, Colonel [Thaddeus]
Stanton, A.P.M., and clerk,* Lieut. [William Wallace] Rogers, 9th
Inf., Lieut [Henry] Seton, Capt. [Alexander] Sutorious, 3d Cav.,
arrived at Fort Laramie from Red Cloud agency and other points.
Took an observation to-day with the aneroid barometer, by which
* M.T. Challé.

5. A not-too-veiled reference to Secretary of the Interior Columbus Delano's son, John,
who extorted payoffs from surveyors in exchange for government contracts. See the
introduction to Part 3.

the height of Fort Laramie above sea level was shown to be 4750 feet; Mercury 25.25 inches.

May 23d. The officers above mentioned left post this morning for Cheyenne.

To-morrow, command will march across to North side of North Platte, and go into camp; there the wagon train and Co's of Cavalry have been since yesterday.

May 24th Col. Dodge moved the command into camp on the North Side of the North Platte river, where were found wood, water and grass in plenty and of excellent quality. Three officers of the post who were not to form part of the expedition, now presented themselves to say good bye to their comrades and receive parting message of the description usual upon such occasions. Old and almost forgotten war times were vividly recalled by the long streets of white canvass sheltering officers and soldiers, by the long train of 75 wagons laden with a three month supply of provisions & by the thousands of rounds of extra ammunition supplied in case of need against hostile Sioux. In the cavalry companies and in the Q.M. train, long lines of animals were groomed and rubbed preparatory to the long march of the morrow; our efficient Quartermaster, Trout, ran from point to point, inspecting and examining to see that every essential had been supplied and jotting down at intervals memoranda of mistakes to be rectified and omissions to be made good. The Infantry soldiers were drilled in the school of Skirmisher and exercised in the evolutions of the company formation; bustle pervaded on all sides, indicative of the earnestness with which all concerned regarded the duty to which assigned (and which they felt the country required should be done) thoroughly and well. By 9 P.M. the bugle call of taps lulled the tired and weary to rest to be broken at 4 A.M. next day when we commenced our march in a general North North East course to Raw Hide creek, over a heavy sand road, sparsely covered with coarse Buffalo and bunch grass, and interspersed occasionally with sage-brush. A journey of 18 miles brought us into camp on the Right bank of this little stream (a confluent of the North Platte) found fringed with small cottonwood and willow trees. Nothing worthy of mention occurred on this day nor on the next when our course followed up the valley of the stream to the West for some 7 or 8 miles, camping on the Raw Hide, with the great essentials of army movements in abundance and of excellent character[.] Country to-day much scored by trails of the buffalo, which of late years has not ventured so far north. Soil Sandy; at end of march, found a small ravine with walls of a very friable, argillaceous[6] sandstone, easily broken by the action of wind or water. Ascended a bluff, (directly in front of Raw Hide Peak,) and found the (barometrical.) altitude, to be 5500 feet. Saw Raw Hide peak above 1200 feet higher than our camp, covered with a heavy growth of pine and juniper. This morning, no small trouble and bother were occasioned in the passage of the Raw Hide and its affluents, where considerable work with shovel and pick and in bridge construction was demanded and performed. Observation on the aneroid barometer showed that present camp is 750 feet above Fort Laramie. Yesterday morning, noticed a very heavy dew on grass in our camp on the Platte; an atmospheric anomaly in this country. Saw to-day, pappoose [sic] slung up in her grave clothes in a cottonwood tree on the banks of the Raw Hide. Mail arrived in camp this afternoon from Fort Laramie, the last we shall have for a month. Thunderstorm of half hour's duration this afternoon.

The advent of May 27th was announced by tempestuous winds and a reduction of the mercury in the thermometer to 49°; all camp turned out at 4 A.M. uniformly equipped with army overcoats and frozen noses. These Northers, as these winds are styled, are not merely inconvenient and unfortunate, but frequently highly dangerous to the traveller's health and life. Few people in New York could be made to understand that at points not many miles North of their own latitude, the genial warmth of a buffalo robe and a pair of blankets should be acceptable and necessary by night in the very end of May; [t]he month of flowers. This day we left the waters of the Raw Hide, marching first North West until the foot of the elevation, laid down on the maps as Raw Hide Peak, was attained. Our aneroid barometers here indicated 5450, and Professor Janney who ascended the mountain to its apex, examining into its geological character, told me its altitude was 900 feet above where we had been, making a total elevation above sea-level of 6300 feet; Mount Washington [New Hampshire] has about equal height. The mineralogical formation was now distinctly different from that of yesterday; Raw Hide Peak being mainly granitic in character; then saw much gneiss, red, black and white and gray; also what I took to be a trap dyke; and a vein of white quartz, six inches

6. Compact metamorphic.

wide, in a belt of red gneiss or granite. The quartz did not show any auriferous indications to my eye. Once past the divide of the Raw Hide Peak, (which may here be said to consist of two distinct buttes, one about a mile long trending North East to South West; the other, smaller in size, running nearly due North and South. Between these two, [t]here seems to be a feasible pass, and to the Extreme North, there is a mesa, about half as high as the main peak which juts out for some four or five miles from the parent ridge.) a march, as nearly due North as the configuration of the country would allow, brought us to the Niobrara, or Running Water, at the point of its first appearance above ground. This little streak of water was not more than 3 feet broad, six inches in depth and of no great velocity. Grass in this camp inferior in quality. No wood to be had except what we had picked up on the road and carried in our wagons. In front of camp was a butte (196 feet high.) of granite or gneiss, composed mainly of mica, of exaggerated crystals and imperfect cohesion. Persons who climbed to the summit told me of some Indian fortifications there found; from their descriptions, these structures of rude piles of stone not over 3 feet high, probably served once as rifle pits or trenches to defend the Crow Indians, originally the possessors of this region, against the Dacotahs or Sioux, the present occupants. The summit has no positive evidence to sustain it, and neither the fortifications nor the conjecture were deserving of further attention.

May 28th   Thermometer at reveille indicated 31° and a heavy frost clad the hills and vallies [sic] in a robe of crystal and white. Our progress to-day was slow but very satisfactory considering the nature of the country to be dealt with. "The plains", so called are an immense plateau, rising from 4000 to 8000 feet above the Atlantic Ocean. The general undulation of these immense fields is not unlike the gentle roll of the sea in a time of calm; but by the erosive action of the numerous streams and their tributaries which course this region, gulches, ravines and crevices without number and in bewildering entanglement so add to the difficulties of passage that all this may in one word be designated a Mountain country. The above explanation should be borne in mind to account for what would otherwise be considered the short marches of our expedition. A feeling akin to loneliness seizes upon the observer who contemplates an immense area of country with scarcely a tree to give shelter against the cutting edge of the wintry "Norther", or the fervid rays of the noonday sun. Our table of distances thus far is, Laramie to Rendezvous Camp, 2 1/4 miles. Rendezvous to Camp No 2. (Rawhide)   18 1/4 miles.

Camp No 2 to No 3, Raw Hide   7 1/2 miles.

   "   "   3 to "   4, Niobrara   19 1/5 miles.

   "   "   4 to "   5, Old Woman's Fork   14 miles.

This stream is one of the affluents of the South Cheyenne, drains a considerable area of country, is very sinuous, very narrow and [as] to its current[,] is full of a white sediment, the detritus of the vicinity. To the taste, it is savory and palatable.

May 29th 1875. By hard work and after vexatious delays, a distance of a little more than 14 miles was accomplished down the Old Woman's Fork, crossed eight times since first its waters were struck yesterday. Our camp this day (No 6.) was to the East of the little butte, called the Old Woman's Mountain, upon whose summit at night the spirit of some mysterious old Indian hag enjoys the recreation of tripping the light fantastic.

An Indian medicine rag was found this evening by Lt. [Albert Douglas] King, 3d Cav., as he was engaged in posting pickets for the protection of our bivouac; in form like a banner or marker, about 14 inches by 25, attached at one end to a twig for a staff, it had emblazoned in black upon one side the representation of over 75 horse shoes; on the other a rude profile of a human head. A piece of tobacco was served up in one corner: the article was of white cotton cloth.

May 30th. South Cheyenne river, 17 1/8 miles

May 31st. Broke camp at 5.30 A.M., crossed two bends of the South Cheyenne within 1500 yards of Camp and then passed a tributary holding considerable water: our trip to-day has had no items of peculiar interest to record; our route followed down for 13 1/4 miles the line of the South Cheyenne, three of whose tributaries, the West Cheyenne, Sage Creek, and another, nameless, joined it from various directions to-day. The West Cheyenne, so Professor Janney informed me, has much of interest to the geologist and mineralogist: nodules of reniform Iron ore (oxide.) were discernible in the water and on the banks in various directions and Professor Newton discovered the veins of black lignite, the coming white population of the Black Hills may yet consume as fuel. Throughout this section are to be found the same fossil bivalves (brachyopods I think they are.) of which we observed such great quantities yesterday and the day before. In general, this country may be denominated a grassy plain; but great tracts occur where the tuna cactus[7] and sagebrush dispute the supremacy of the buffalo and bunch grass. A beautiful blue flower, probably a phlox, was to be seen with great frequency and relieved what would in its absence have been the monotony of the country. The short, thick-set growth of the tuna demonstrated with what force the winds of winter must sweep from the North across these plains. The South Cheyenne and its confluents, as seen to-day, are certainly much better timbered and with trees too of a heavier growth than the streams observed yesterday and previously. The West Cheyenne has a rich alluvial bottom, from 1000 yards to one mile wide, which, if it extend for any great distance from our point of crossing, right soon to be occupied by thrifty farmers.

A grateful feature of the march, whatever our line touched near the banks of the stream has been the sweet, shrill shirping [sic] of the bobalinks as they flit from bush to bush: now and then we intrude upon a village of prairie dogs who first watch our movements with curiosity and then, becoming indignant at the impertinence of the invasion, angrily squeak their bark of defiance and fling their little tails in the air [and] hurriedly seek refuge within their burrows.

An alarm of camp last night, occasioned by a sentinel firing his piece, under the belief that Indians were engaged in abstracting some of our horses, affords an occasion for inserting a summary description of the manner of conducting the daily march, encamping and moving out.

Of the six companies of cavalry forming the mounted portion of the command, one is detailed in proper turn to act as advance guard; in the morning, reveille is sounded at 4 A.M., following which at once come roll call, stables and breakfast. The "General" is then sounded as a signal to strike tents, then "boots and saddles", to saddle and bridle, and last of all "Assembly", when companies fall into line under arms. The advance company now moves out with the pioneer wagon, containing axes, hatchets, spades, shovels, nails, rope, timber and other requisites for bridge construction, corduroy road making, or excavating and embanking.

Arrived at a point where it is needful to guard against the miring of teams or horses, detailed men move out with axes, fell suitable cotton-

7. *Opuntia phaeacantha* or prickly pear. "Tuna" refers specifically to the fruit. Loughmiller, *Texas Wildflowers*, 33.

wood trees, which another party strip of their branches and cut into lengths suitable for stretchers and cross-pieces. Stretchers are dispe[n]sed across the stream, two feet apart, while the cross pieces cover these closely at right angles. Smaller branches fill in any gaps that may occur while a uniform, hard-packed covering of earth makes the road-bed. The Bluffs, edging the stream are now cut down to make a convenient ramp and wagons and horses are crossing almost before the written description is completed. The Company of Cavalry in advance becomes rear-guard to-morrow, marching one mile or so behind the wagon train, which is escorted by the Infantry Cos and artillery. Arrived in Camp, wagons are packed, tents pitched in streets, animals unhitched to graze, and pickets, mounted, established by the advance guard upon all the circumjacent bluffs. These videttes remain on post after night fall closer to camp, until the forward movement of the next morning and it is the duty of the officers of the Company to which they pertain to visit them at least once after midnight to see they are vigilant and ready for emergencies. The water of the South Cheyenne, turbid and alkaline, is scarcely drinkable on acc't of the great amount of argillaceous and other sedimentary matter held in suspension: a plant, plentiful in this country called the nopal, or Tuna cactus, plate cactus or Indian fig, is employed with success to clarify the water for drinking purposes. Cut into strips of an inch square and immerse in the fluid, its juices appear to act like the white of egg in coffee.[8] The fluid becomes clean and refreshing as a beverage thanks to a much despised and poorly understood vegetable, whose other virtues are so many additional arguments in favor of the beneficence of the Almighty; no more potent anti-scorbutic can be found; its powers in this regard have been tested and witnessed again and again by Army officers from Dacotah to Texas and Arizona. It should be roasted on ashes and served with salt and vinegar. Another vegetable, the wild onion, readily found on these plains, serves the same great purpose.

This night it rained for some time and blew with great force.

8. Hunting or camping, I have used both the cactus in water, and the egg in coffee. When no strainer is available and the coffee grounds are boiled with the water, the egg settles them to the bottom. However, I have always boiled the egg shell with membrane rather than the white (it gives the coffee a slightly acidic taste which is not unpleasant to the confirmed coffee drinker). In the case of water (which should be boiled or treated with iodine before consumption), the nopal pad is diced as Bourke described, and the pieces are floated. Apparently there is some sort of chemical component of both egg and nopal that lowers the density of the water so that the sediment sinks to the bottom of the container. It should also be noted that Hispanics often boil the diced nopal pads in water with ground meat, tomato bits, onion, and chile to make *nopalito*, a very good soup. The *tuna*, or fruit of the nopal, generally served sliced and slightly chilled, has a taste very similar to kiwi fruit.

Chapter 9

✦

✦

✦

✦

✦

Into the Black Hills

June 1st. Opened cold and damp with dark clouds obscuring the sky. A short journey of 9 1/4 miles, over ground demanding little or no labor in road making, brought us to the Beaver Creek, a stream about 30 feet wide, of turbid water, one half sediment, besides being so salty and alkaline as to almost occasion nausea. Grass good on the hill-sides and timber accessible on the banks of the stream. Grounds of Camp covered with prickly pear cactus.

Early in the morning, a field of wild onions was noticed, the odor being very much the same as that of garlic.

Fossil shells were found in abundance by some of Professor Janney's party on the flanks of the trail; bracyopods and ammonites: these I did not see, but from the deposits coming under my personal observation yesterday, I can without difficulty concede the truth of all I hear. The Black Hills proper are now in full view; exactly magnetic north of us to the most prominent peak of the range. In a little ravine, on to-day's line of march, the walls were composed of decomposed shale, stained black with iron, and having interspersed through the mass, crystals of selenite, (gypsum). To the right were extensive deposits of the Black, siliceous carbonate of Iron, very pure and easily worked. Major Burt, 9th Infantry, brought in a mass of crystals of selenite, very beautiful and very perfect; formed in a stratum of gypsum about 2 m west of our line of direction. Mr Root, one of the Janney party, told me he had seen what he thought must be the Muriate of [Baryta?],[1] to-day.

To-day, we have had a sharp, decidedly cool and disagreeable April shower of rain and hail: every day, we have been so favored, the result being that the march is not dusty, as in drier season it might be.

Young grass-hoppers in very considerable numbers have been visible at various points, evidently preparing, like the unconquered Sioux, to resume their depredations upon the feeble settlements of Wyoming.

The hunters of Lieut. Hall's company of the 2nd Cavalry killed four elk this afternoon; Lt. King, 3d Cav., killed a black-tailed deer and a party of Burt's company, 9th Infantry, killed and brought to camp a cinnamon bear. Upon the confines and within the limits of the Black Hills Reserve, the reflection arises what good does the present expedition do except to witness to the words that our Govt. is not desirous of depriving the Sioux of any treaty rights until after careful consideration of the subject involved, and maybe a feeble scientific light thrown upon the topography of the country and the true astronomical position of a few magnificent peaks and streams? Professor Janney has a great responsibility to bear and an unenviable position to occupy. Granting his report admits the existence of gold, has that not been known already? Or supposing no auriferous indications meet his eye, will a non-committal or a flat denial avail to slay the influx of adventurous men now congregating at Cheyenne, Sioux City and other points, fully satisfied of the existence of valuable treasures in the Sioux country, which they are all the more determined to seize because on forbidden ground?

Our phase of the business, do what our Govt. can to prevent it, will be a Sioux and Cheyenne war in which those tribes will be doomed to receive the castigation so long merited. The probable method of procedure will be the establishment of a few large depots of supplies in the heart of the Enemy's country, from which as foci can radiate forth columns of cavalry and Infantry, carrying supplies by pack-trains, to the most hidden recesses of the Indian territory. A winter campaign may become a necessity, but in such a case the

1. If Bourke means "barytes" it is a form of barite.

troops by following up the streams, can effect two objects: one, the avoiding of much rigorous cold; the other, the assault of the enemy's villages near the streams and their expulsion to the frigid plains where they will soon freeze to death if they do not promptly submit. A change in this policy from the poor and vacillating one prevailing before General Crook's arrival may bring to light the worthlessness of many officers who have no desire to serve the Army and the country, except at Sybaritic stations or in soft places. But, under General Crook, the subjcation [*sic*] of all hostile Indians within the limits of his Department may be accepted as a forgone conclusion.

Our dinner to-day was a most palatable one, a couple of the principal dishes were furnished by the country.

Roast Elk meat and boiled lamb's quarter,[2] prepared as greens with bacon. With appetites whetted by a day's travel in the teeth of a bracing breeze, the mess would in any event have rendered some tribute of justice of the viands set before them; in this case, the fresh beef of the Elk was a very savory and toothsome morsel which claimed and received our fullest attention.

June 3d. Our movements of to-day and yesterday have been through country of the same general character as noticed in preceeding pages. For some reason best known to himself Mr. Janney was determined to establish his party on the 104th Meridian and thence explore the region to the East and North-East. He seemed unable to appreciate the fact that a mile or two to the East or West of the Boundary would make little difference to the nation which is concerned not in regard to the precise longitude of the Black Hills but in regard to the alleged metalliferous deposits of South West Dacotah. The Military however had been detailed to act as escort to the Geologists and had nothing to do but acquiesce in the whims of a very inexperienced young man, who has not apparently succeeded in making a striking impression upon any who have been thrown in contact with him.[3] The subordinates of Janney's party generally conduct themselves as men of superior qualifications and extended experience. Captain Tuttle, the astronomer, Doctor MacGillicuddy, the topogra-

---

2. *Chenopodium album.*

3. Jenney distrusted the soldiers and correspondents, and kept his plans to himself. This hindered Dodge's ability to coordinate support. He also tended to work apart from the column, which frequently forced the soldiers to extricate him from some sort of difficulty. Kime, *Black Hills Journals*, 15-16.

pher, Mr Newton minerologist, and Mr Root, the practical miner, are beyond a doubt valuable auxiliaries to the expedition, if they do not constitute the sum total of its scientific strength.

The weather has remained petulant and variable; the sky is nearly all morning and afternoon covered with gloomy rain-bearing clouds; towards sun-set, a few rays force their way in upon camp and refresh the scene with their golden light; night brings back the clouds and high winds then set in, blowing with the fury of a tempest until morning. Some rain has fallen but not enough to cause more than a mere reference to it. The plains are by no means monotonous to the sight; the gentle undulation of the ground is frequently broken by the elevation of long lines of bluffs, some not more than fifty, others as much as 300 feet in height: here, there and everywhere, prominent buttes can be seen and occasionally a peak of prominence obtrudes itself upon the vision to attract notice and admiration. Laramie Peak, Injan-Kara[?], Harney's Peak, Raw-Hide Peak and others have been visible, more or less distinctly, since our journey commenced. These were, at some remote geological epoch, islands in the midst of a vast sea of which the low undulating rounds at their bases formed the bed. Our trail has led us through the bottom of this vast sea and for the past two or three days, we might say our path has been through marine fossils; lodges of indurated mud have presented themselves and in these have been masses of ammonites, brachyopods, baculites, and other sea animals whose names I cannot give. My own collection[,] the poorest perhaps in the expedition, already embraces all the varieties mentioned besides clams, muscles [sic] and other specimens. Professor Janny found the tooth of a fossil horse, estimated to have been eight feet high. Colonel Dodge has in his possession a piece of silicified wood, or rather half petrified wood, one half being stone, the other still retaining its ligneous fibre and condition. The streams which have their source in the plains themselves leach out the saline and alkaline matters predominating in the soil and as might be anticipated, are unfit for use, either in cooking or washing or for drinking. On the other hand, those whose spring-heads are found in the sandstone or granite formations of the more elevated sections are exceedingly palatable, although their hardness impairs their detersive qualities somewhat. Among the minerals discovered within the last 24 hours has been a bed of pure white gypsum, 4 or 5 feet thick. As yet, there are are [*sic*] no indications of our being in a gold country. Raw Hide Peak might prove a good place for prospectors, but the other portions of the ground traversed have generally been clay, gypsum, sand and limestone. But within 3 miles more, the geological character of the country may change completely, bringing about a complete substitution of minerals.

On June 2nd, the distance traversed, by odometer measurement, was 10 1/2 miles and on the 3rd, 13 21/25 miles, bringing the command to a very beautiful camp on the headwaters of one of the numerous branches of Beaver Creek, under the shadow of the renown Black Hills, with plenty of good water, grass and timber and in the presence of animating scenery. The little stream, fringed with willow and box elder, flowing in front of our tents, rises in the hills north of us about two miles and about half a mile below camp receives the salty, disagreeable washings of a little brook running out from the breaks to the West of it.

In this portion, Colonel Dodge has decided to place his first permanent base of supplies and the work of cutting the necessary timbers for a stockade and storehouse has already begun in earnest. The position of the camp proper will not be much changed, but an important addition will be made in the erection of a little palisade work on the crest of a little hill completely commanding the situation and from which our artillery can be enabled to play with deadly effect upon any party of Indians that may have the temerity to attack us. The Infantry companies are to leave on the 6th June with the wagon train for Fort Laramie, returning in 20 days with an additional two months' supply of rations and also such mail as may be awaiting them at that post. Meantime, parties of cavalry will be kept out with the Geological and surveying detachments, exploring the ground and mapping out its principal features, East as far as Harney's Butte, or Peak.

The absence of Indians means something, in my opinion; none have come near us thus far, altho' it is evident we are now in a part of their country often visited if not permanently occupied by them. Great trails have been seen, broad and well travelled and the indications of a great camp having been here not many months ago can be found in all directions. That this Black Hills District merits much of the eulogistic commendation of General Custer, I am inclined to believe; the mountains proper now rear their lofty head above us,

crowned with pine and cedar forests from summit to base; the air is cool and bracing, water excellent and game signs becoming more plenty. What the country may become as we advance farther into its secret recesses we should not leave to conjecture but determine by actual experiment and observation when the proper time comes.
June 4th 1875
Yesterday (June 3d.), a number of rattlesnakes were killed in camp; one had coiled up ready to attack me while I was engaged in taking topographical notes of the country.
The total distance of this camp from Fort Laramie is as follows:

Camp No 1	2 1/4	miles	Platte
" " 2	18 2/3	"	Raw Hide
" " 3	7 1/2	"	d[itt]o
" " 4	19 1/5	"	@. Niobrara
" " 5	14.	"	Old Woman's Fork
" " 6	14 1/2	"	do
" " 7	17 1/2	"	South Cheyenne
" " 8	12 1/4	"	S. Cheyenne
" " 9	8 2/3	"	Beaver
" " 10	10 1/2	"	Beaver E. Fork
" " 11.	<u>14</u>	"	Beaver water of E. Fork
	138 4/5	"	= 140 miles.

Call it in round numbers 140 miles.
A slight amount of rain fell to-day.
June 5th. Major [Andrew] Burt, Capt. Munson, Lieuts. [Hayden] Delaney & Craig, 9th Inf., with their Companies started back at Reveille this morning for Fort Laramie to replenish the supply train. They are expected back by the 23d to 25th and will bring with them any mail matter that may have accumulated for officers and men of the Expedition.
Indian signs continue to be reported and Indians themselves are seen each day, but none have presented themselves in camp up to the present writing[.] Five were seen yesterday by our hunters and a fresh trail of fifteen who camped last night 8 miles above us on the Creek was reported by Professor Janney, who made a trip into the first range back of us and is now all aglow in his enthusiasm over the country. He says it rivals the Blue Grass regions of Kentucky. General Custer's report upon the wonderfully beautiful aspect of

the parks he visited and the great adaptability of the Hills, in their entirety to pastoral uses will, I feel pretty sure, be substantiated by the cumulative testimony of Janney and all connected with the survey. An elk and seven black-tailed deer were brought into camp this evening, our fresh meat ought to hold out well now, supplemented by the incessant requisitions made upon the game preserves of the Dacotahs & Cheyennes.

June 5th.[4] A sharp, biting wind and the mercury not much above freezing point made overcoats this morning essential; the climate of the Black Hills is, to say the least, peculiar. At this season of the year, the nights are as cold as in the Eastern states they would be in November; as day advances, the sun's rays make the temperature much more agreeable, and as night approaches, it again becomes necessary to assume heavy coverings and seek the warmth of great wood fires. In Lieut. Hall's tent yesterday afternoon the officers gathered about a little camp stove glad to receive the warmth it afforded. In despite of these disadvantages, the air is so pure and bracing that perhaps no more salubrious locality can be found in the U.S. for persons whose constitutions are not so much impaired as to demand indoor nursing or residence in semi-tropical latitudes.

Game in abundance and great variety is to be found in every ravine and upon every acclivity. Our men are busy hunting and much meat rewards their Exertions: elk and black-tail deer have been killed in sufficient numbers to supply messes of both men and officers. The arrangements of camp are now perfected, tents laid out in long, parallel streets, those of the Commanding Officer and Staff being in a pleasant little clump of box-elder trees, and so furnished with paulins for floor covering and tables made out of Q.M. and Commissary boxes as to be most comfortable. In our present position, there is not much work to do and under the insidious influences of our surroundings, sloth has seized upon our faculties and rendered hard study disagreeable. The routine of the day is, Bkft [Breakfast] immediately after Reveille, then read until about noon when most of the messes spread lunch: after meridian, many indulge in sleep until dinner which winds up the day. Evening finds us congregated about some camp-fire, discussing army matters or those pertaining to the scientific objects of the trip: many curious things have been noted in the way of minerals or vegetation and Mr Newton, who seems a

4. Bourke apparently means June 6.

very intelligent student in his specialty, very kindly places the resources of his knowledge at our disposal. The above partition of our
time, with that involved in the performance of necessary duties of
camp, brings us down to 10 O'clock at night, when we mix a social
toddy and then saunter off to our tents to turn in for rest.

June 7th. A beautiful day in every sense of the word; a cloudless
sky, warm but not too [fervid?] sun, pleasant breeze and spring-
like temperatures are all the more to be appreciated after the cool
winds and rain-laiden clouds of yesterday and the week preceeding.
The strip of country we are now camped in should be thrown open
to settlement at an early day; to Wyoming and Dacotah it may yet
act as a centre of attraction for a valuable pastoral and perhaps
manufacturing community.

It is impossible to form an opinion of the Black Hills as a whole
until after having had an opportunity for a more careful examination and I am determined, even at the risk of making my Diary read
as dry as a Patent Office Report to insert no item which I have not
had time or occasion to verify in person or for which I cannot name
the best available authority; and not to expatiate in the language of
enthusiasm upon beautiful scenery, pellucid streams, dense forests
and precious ledges of gold and silver but to ennumerate simply
what the country contains, and when, where and in what quantities observed. In vicinity of our location, the rocks are of the two
general classes of sandstone and limestone; the limestone of exceptional purity. Gypsum, pure white, and rose tinged, and in the crys-
talline forms of selenite occurs with such frequency and in such
quantity that I refer to its presence more as a duty than to attract
attention to it. The carbonate of Iron, (Black.) already noticed on
the journey, is again found on this stream a few hundred feet from
the line of tents: red clay deposits are visible in the line of hills to
our front, the crests of which are sandstone crags, 1050 and 1650
above the thread of the stream. Much of the limestone is very compact shells of a little animal called by Profr Janney, the "productus",
being interspersed throughout the mass. The water is wholesome,
even if a trifle "hard" with sulphate of lime; the knolls upon which
grow a small closely matted species of nutritive grass would afford
sustenance to great herds of sheep, requiring no protection from
the weather other than that afforded by the elevated cordillera a
mile north of us. I am almost ready to assert my conviction that

this valley will never be very warm in summer nor cold in winter. There are no indications, at least I neither saw nor heard of any, that great overflows occur: the valley is very clean and has no dead trees or other driftwood to mark a former elevation of its waters. The timber question may as well be accepted as a matter of fact; The main ridge, is black with it and scrut[eniz]ing through the powerful glass on the theodelite of the topographers discloses unvarying excellence in its quality from base to crest. The palisading for the block-houses now erected has been under my charge, as assistant to Colonel Dodge; the trees used were selected for two considerations;—to get them from pineries as close to camp as possible to avoid unnecessary labor and trouble in their subsequent transportation and to have them of a uniform diameter not greater than 12 inches. Those I have inspected do not therefore fairly represent the superior grades, but no one can complain of the excellence of the timber of these mountains taking these even as inferior samples.

Hoping that the photographer of the expedition might soon be with us, no previous mention of any objects or passages in the scenery has been made, preferring to let the sun-portraits speak for themselves. The delay of the artist in joining us is a matter of deep regret now that we are at the entrance gate of the "parks" and in the face of scenery which merits in the fullest degree the epithet, "picturesque". No prettier sight can be imagined than our camp with its long rows of immaculate white tents nesting in the shade and foliage of the box-elder; in sinuous folds the babbling waters of the Beaver flow over their rocky bed past our camp to their junction miles below with the current of the South Cheyenne; beyond us, to the North can be traced the valley through which it courses and the range from which it rises. Grassy slopes and wooded declivities, not precipitous, although abrupt in their elevation, hem in the valley on either hand and terminate the vista. Above, a sky, without stain, completes the picture and give[s] exalted hopes of the country prospected by Profr Janney yesterday and before and over whose beauty and fascination he went into such ecstacies that language failed him.

June 8th. Soldiers of the log-cutting detachment brought in from the pinery this morning a canteen filled with water tasting like writing ink; Mr Newton says it contains in solution both alum and sulphuric acid. A piece of the rock cropping out near the spring was handed me; it is a clay shale, black with decomposed iron pyrites and yielding by a double decomposition, under the influence of air and water, alum and dilute sulphuric acid. Dr. Lane and Lieut. Morton rejoined camp from three days' hunting excursion to Harney's Peak and the South West corner of the Black Hills; the minerals brought back with them were what looked to me like Binary granite and Tourmaline in quartz. According to their report, the country visited is heavily timbered and very mountainous with wide grassy plains and glades surrounding the rocky elevations which must have considerable altitude as a snow-bank was passed on their route. Custer's trail was followed for 6 or 8 miles. Berries of different varieties, strawberries, June berries &c were noticed in blossom. The timber is pine, quaking asp[en], cottonwood and birch. Water in great frequency, collected in great pools or lakelets on the flat table summits, fed by the slowly melting drifts of snow, last winter's legacy. The palisade redoubts to defend camp against surprise have been completed to-day, ready for the reception of the artillery. To-morrow, we move on in the direction of Harney's Peak then to establish another camp at which the companies left behind at this point will join us with those escorting back from Laramie our train of supplies. Weather to-day, quite pleasant and genial; not too warm and no cold wind.

June 9th 1875. Colonel Dodge, with Spalding's and Hall's Companies of the 2n and Wessell's Co. of the 3d Cavalry, moved out as an escort to the scientific party this morning, leaving Col. Hawley with 3 companies of the 3d Cavalry to await at Camp Jenney (No 11.) the return of the wagon train from Laramie. Our route North up the valley of Spalding's Fork of Beaver Creek commenced at Camp Jenney and winding close to the red sandstone bounding valley on R. after causing some delay to construct a passage-way of rocks across an abrupt bend of stream where it ran in upon its vertical walls, brought us into a series of small valleys of no special feature, one being an exact type of all the others, to wit. Through the centre flowed the stream without any great tributaries except dry arroyos which cut up the ground with frequency. Surrounding these vales or basins were low bluffs of even height of strata of gypsum upon red clay. Rarely have I seen sulphate of lime in a condition of as great plenty and the deposits in extent were simply fabulous. These bluffs on the summit were ordinarily bare of all herbage, except weeds, and, at very distant intervals, small clumps of scrub pine and cedar. Back of these bluffs, a mile or two on each side rise two parallel ridges of the Black Hills, upon which could be seen excellent timber growing almost as thick as grass. The ground work of the little basins as well as the soil close up to the rim of the gypsum hills was matted thick with a carpeting of rich, blue-green grass, a fit setting to the many springs that sparkled like jewels upon the brown of the plain. The geological formation of the day was very plainly defined; red sandstone, gypsum, red clay and limestone forming in due order the framework of the lofty ranges on our Right and Left. At one point where the limestone strata had been tilted upwards at an angle of 50° from the Horizontal the earth seemed honeycombed with springs: walking my horse slowly, I passed by five in twenty minutes, leaving numerous others unnoticed. The water gushing out from them was not good and in one of two cases gave decided taste of alum. Many of them were depositing travertine upon their margins and all were hard from the presence in solution of various lime-salts, either sulphates or carbonates. Around these sources, grew luxuriantly clumps of wild plum, cherry, currant and gooseberry bushes. Wild roses were also in profusion and strawberries in blooms have been reported. About noon stream ran dry for awhile, but we followed along parallel to its dry bed until 2 P.M., when we found ourselves in a "park country", where the scenery was most enchanting and exhilarating. The same geological formation continued but the mountains and gypsum bluffs receded for 2 or 3 miles, leaving a wide stretch of luxuriant grass-covered country, with not a bush to interrupt the vista of green sward to the Right and Left, the front and rear of Pine forests now reached down from the higher reaches and capped the summits of the lower hills; outcroppings of snowy gypsum or crimson red clay rendered more conspicuous by contrast the emerald tint of the herbage. Look where we might, turn where we would, new beauties obtruded their claims upon our bewildered attention, each demanding, each in turn receiving the palm of superiority. While the clouds lowered, the majestic mountains on our flanks looked gloomy and grand; nothing could be added to the charm of the scene; but where the sun's ray's lit up cañon and crag with a farewell gleam and cast a generous glow over hillock and plain, the plaintive picturesqueness of only an hour ago was almost forgotten in the greater charm of the present moment.

In one of these lawn-like parks, the stream again rose above ground, this time in a cañon with almost vertical walls, nestling confidingly under the protecting shadow of the highest pinnacles of the Main Range. Near a pleasant-looking spring whose water sought a junction with those in the cañon, our tents were pitched and as if to teach us there must be something to dull the edge of every mundane enjoyment, something to recall us from the poetic exaltation inspired by the scene, the water of the spring altho' ice-cold and sweet to the taste was so hard with CaO,SO3[5] that when we washed or rather when we attempted our ablutions, an insoluble lime-soap formed upon our hands and left them actually dirtier than before. This afternoon, a violent thunder storm set in, which lasted with but slight intermission, all night.

June 10th. Make a North line of 12 3/8 miles, climbing slowly to summit of an elevated table land, where the Barometrical indications were 7800 to 7850 feet. Followed along narrow crest of summit, passing around the heads of scores of little feeders of Spalding's Fork of Beaver Creek and enjoying an undescribably beautiful view of the country to North West, and north to Beaver Lodge Butte and Terrill's Peak (?) looming up grandly in foreground. Water[s] to Left of trail flowed to West North West and evidently find their way either directly or through affluents to the Belle Fourche.

For a few miles, pine was almost replaced by the "quaking aspen", the pine and other coniferal [trees] reappearing as we began descending the declivity; at one heavy grade, the trail ran down 300 feet vertically in three furlongs; fortunately, no wagons suffered and after pushing on rapidly through a blinding rain, hail and snow storm, we reached a beautiful little vale, answering in every sense to the appellation, "Floral Valley", given it by Custer whose trail we struck at foot of Mountain and followed for one mile. While going to Spalding's Fork this morning, we halted for an hour on the brink of its gloomy cañon, 650 to 750 feet deep, with a solid cushion of stately pine trees almost hiding its rugged limestone cliffs and concealing entirely from view the rushing stream below whose murmur we distinctly heard three icy-cold springs gushed out from the rocks under our feet and added the tribute of their strength to the current singing over the rocks beneath. We had now attained and passed the highest point of the Black Hills on the South West; no auriferous[6] indications were to be detected,

5. Calcite and sulfate, i.e. gypsum.

the geological formation forbidding the idea of precious metalliferous[7] deposits existing. The strata were almost uniformly coarse sandstone, with limestone also in great quantity. On this side, the Black Hills are to all intents and purposes an elevated table-land, covered with dense forests of pine and having its flanks scarred by countless ravines which flow, with scarcely an exception, into Spalding's Fork of Beaver Creek. Our camp this evening, made as it was in the midst of a disagreeable storm, which was not calculated to improve our tempers or excite enthusiasm over any prospect except that of a warm fire and a good cup of hot coffee, spread before us in such a delightful little glade that the most stolid gave way to their feelings in expressions of admiration and keen enjoyment: The glen, in its greatest breadth could not have been more than 300 yards, but there were so many little lateral glades and gulches that its dimensions were to first appearances, considerably augmented. Noble spruce pines, straight and graceful, shut in the horizon on all sides; now in clumps upon the grassy knolls, now alone like sentinels upon picket, or breaking away into little openings in which the quaking aspen found foothold or standing in dense, compact masses which laughed to scorn the penetrating rays of the sun. Not many flowers were seen, the season perhaps not being sufficiently advanced, but upon the velvety turf, rose three peerless little springs whose water, from every deleterious trait, shows by actual test, the icy temperature of 39° F. In this fairy glen our troops reposed until midday of June 11th 1875, when command passed down Custer's trail in a generally East and South East direction for twelve and three eighths miles, moving up creek on which last night's camp was placed and crossing divide into narrow ravine of Castle Creek, flowing East South East in a narrow gulch, bounded by crags of calcarous sandstone, fringed with pine forests. A feature of this day's march has been the number of fine springs bursting out from the ground in bewildering confusion; one was chal[y]beate of considerable strength. Beaver dams occurred in great frequency and in consequence bridges had to be constructed at every crossing of the creek. Willow thickets lined its course from its source to the site of our camp. Formation now changing. Quartz rock, slate with quartz and quartz in taleose schist seen near trail.

6. Gold bearing.
7. Ore producing.

Crags hemmed in the little valley on Right and Left: one of those, under which camp was placed, being 950' above level of the stream. The whole of the country, as seen from the summit of one of these crags was a lovely alternation of gently rising hills and sloping dales; the lower portions of emerald green with a thickly matted grass eaten greedily by our animals; pine woods hemmed in the landscape in every point of sight. In these forests, rich grass grew everywhere, the almost total absence of underbrush giving a tone to the scene reminding one of the well-kept lawns and parks of some private mansion. In no part of America can be found a more pleasing belt of territory, or one promising more munificent returns in dairy products when a hardy, intelligent population shall have been given liberty to make their homes therein. The smooth ringing sod, the various, green grass, the pretty little flowerets modestly peering above the sward, the sparkling rivulet coursing down the ravine with little confluents joining it on either hand, the springs of pure, sweet, frigid water, the rich black soil, 6 and 8 feet deep, the compact belts of excellent timber and inexhaustible quarries of building stone—all these without an indication of habitancy—evoked the question; why have these Black Hills, greater in area than several of the New England states, and which have never been of any value to the nomads who claim them as their own, and are never visited even save at rare intervals to obtain lodge-poles for the Sioux and Cheyenne camps—why have these lovely vales and hills been sequestered from the national domain, already too much curtailed by the setting aside of extravagant areas for Indian reservations, and too small in its arable acreage West of the Missouri to afford fit accomodations to the swarms of emigrants and pioneers pushing forward each year farther into what was but yesterday the Western frontier?   Setting aside the existence of gold, Wyoming and Dacotah and North West Nebraska, have much reason to believe that before many months, the markets of the East and West shall be supplied with meat, butter, cheese, hides, horns and wool from the herds and dairies of the Sha-pa-pa.

June 12th 1875.

One of nature's sweetest days; a stainless sky, a genial sun, brought out with superb effect every minute detail of the picture stretched in front of and around us. Our progress to-day has been extremely slow; into the soft, black loam of the valley bed, the wheels of the wagons sank to the hubs and one wagon broke down completely, so only a fraction more than four and a half miles of advance was made when we found ourselves in Custer's Camp of July 28th, having gone first South East then East, and latterly North East through a district whose geological formation was markedly different from yesterday's; now the flanks of the ravines are immense slate ledges, with leads of iron-stained quartz, attracting attention every moment: this slate is siliceous and must extend a considerable distance to Right and Left, since several tributaries whose course we examined ran through the same formation for miles. Our camp tonight was placed on the Left bank of a little tributary, coming in from South East and in picturesque beauty of situation and abundance and excellence of the great essentials, wood, water and grass, the rival, perhaps the superior of the one we left. Interest in the mineralogy of the country was keenly excited by the discovery of a fleck of gold in some dirt panned by one of Profr. Jenney's servants on the bank of the rivulet. Professor Jenney now determined to remain and this creek to pursue geological inquiring to the utmost; Colonel Dodge, therefore, left Wessell's Company of the 3d Cavy. to protect the scientists in their labors, while he with the other companies pushed on closer to Harney's Peak there to establish the permanent depot and focus of operations.

June 13th, 1875. Moved South East 10 2/3 miles, through a country of same characteristic features as those noted yesterday; left the waters of Castle Creek and made camp in a little cañon, with slate walls, through which ran a bright, cool spring rivulet which we took to be Spring Creek. About 2 miles above camp, we left Custer's trail, hoping to improve on it by making a cut-off; the rugged walls of slate, hemming in our camp, convinced us of our mistake, not to our disappointment, however, since it afforded us an opportunity for making a bivouac in a little glen whose beauty pen cannot well portray. The same fascinating scenery, the same cold, pure water and our now accustomed alternations of timbered crests, grassy slopes and spring-watered, shady glades. In this camp, the "color" of gold was again found by one of the command—Mr Long, a citizen.

June 14th, 1875. Our march to-day was 16 1/3 miles, in a direction; for first ten miles South East; and last six miles very sinuous, but bearing generally East South East. Retracing our steps for 2000 yards, we resumed Custer's trail, following it over the divide separating Spring from French creeks, and halting on the latter at Custer's Camp of July 29th, 1874. Here we have to the North West, some five or six miles from us, the now famous Harney's Peak, a comparatively insignificant and decidedly pug-nosed butte, of granite rock, barren of timber, and which looks ashamed of its own pretensions in presence of people who have traversed the loftier ridges beyond it. Not a voice dissents from the verdict that General Custer's report is fully sustained by facts; we have now attained the gold country, and find after dispassionate scrutiny of every statement made by Custer and Forsyth[8] that this region is far more beautiful and valuable than they claimed it to be and that the most glowing description a vivid fancy and facile pen can give will fall short of the merits of the case. On the crest of the last divide crossed, again the geological formation varied, mica schist first appearing then ledges of vesicular, honey-comb, iron, stained quartz, and a poorly crystallized granite or gneiss, with large fragments of quartz, feldspar, tourmaline and mica, feebly holding together. Another sign of importance has been that all the streams have quartz gravel beds, altho' no black sand is visible. Many garnets, small and inferior, sparkle in the sun-light from the stream bed; the soil around us is a rich, deep black loam topped with green sod. Within 100 rods of Head-quarters is the stockade of the miners whom Mix took out from here in April last—an important measure on the part of the Gov't, because these streams are now full of miners, whose fires send up volumes of smoke from the glens to the South, South East, and South West of us.

Mr Bratton, Colonel Dodge and others have visited their camps five miles away and saw them pan out floss gold from the gravel in which they were working; it averages 5 c[arats]. to the pan, from the grass roots down, improving with every foot of descent. No bedrock has yet been reached, nor has great work been done in excavation, the poor devils being nearly starved, their sole diet for the past fifteen days having been venison and spring water. Parties have been sent back to Cheyenne for supplies, bearing with them dust from the placers: their advent, with the proofs of rich diggings, will cause Cheyenne, Omaha, Sidney and Sioux city to hum like a swarm of angry bees. Our men have been washing the mud from near the brook bank, finding "color" in most unlikely localities. The gold, which I have

8. Major George Alexander (Sandy) Forsyth, Ninth Cavalry, who explored the region in 1868.

seen, at a rough guess, is worth 18.50 to 19.50 per oz: is clear, bright orange yellow and in pieces from the size of pinhead to pinpoint. The miners claim that with ground and box sluicing, they will make from $5 to $75 per diem to the hand, but say, and say justly, work cannot be done without food, for which they are now waiting.

June 15th. Men put at work, building corral for the cattle herds. Lieut. Trout and wagon train started for Camp Jenney. In company with Mr Bratton, I visited miners' camp and verified, if verification were needed, Colonel Dodge's report. The miners say they are having a hard struggle against hunger, are destitute in every sense, know they are on forbidden ground and expect the Military will receive orders to drive them out; but if expelled, they propose returning and facing every obstacle, knowing a fortune awaits them with the developments of these bottoms: the quartz ledges, they have not thoroughly examined, not having any mercury, but have crushed the rock with mortar and pestle and found "color" in horn-spoon. One party was working a small box sluice and in the gravel found, besides gold, many fine topazes so called, one as big as an English walnut; another had laid out a garden patch, planting a little corn, some melons, peas, beans, turnips, squashes and other garden truck, which has made an appearance above ground and promises finely. While the indications are very fine, an additional advantage possessed by this district over others longer known is the great mass of fine timber crowding down close to the streams, the purity and plenty of the water, the accumulations of building materials, the richness of the grasses, and above all the proximity to the Pacific R.R's and the facility of ingress. By next year, the Black Hills should be filled with a self-supporting population of 10.000 fighting men.

June 17th. Professor Jenney arrived in camp, evidently greatly chagrined and crest-fallen; he cannot ignore the presence of gold, and plenty of it; but affects to deprecate the value of the mines; instancing the obstacles the miners must overcome before their claims will pay. All this I told him the miners understood as well as he did; that the existence of gold was all they asked to learn; subsequent developments must take care of themselves. Finally, Professor, they will not wait longer for your report; because messengers bearing specimens of gold are by this time near [Fort] Laramie and the moment their mission is known in Cheyenne nothing can restrain the miners from invading those precincts. This seemed to disquiet him

greatly and no doubt he felt his duties here were ended.
(Slight fall of rain to-night[)].

June 17th. [*sic*] Have been busy writing until 1 A.M. and also since
6.30 this morning; mail party sent in to cut across Beaver Creek
bridge some 15 miles below Camp Jenney. Spalding is to make a
road and Trout brings back the wagon train, as soon as Burt's command can be intercepted. Mail matter may reach here by 23d inst.
Weather delightful but warm.

June 18th. Morning very sultry: afternoon a heavy thunder and rain
storm prevailed lasting until late in the night.

June 19th. Made topographical survey of the line from camp to the
miner's box sluice. 4 1/4 miles.
Day charming.

June 20th. Examined country to North West of camp, about 9 or 10
miles, climbing up on the rugged granite walls of a promontory in
the range of Harney's Peak. Since half dozen pinnacles of granite,
almost equal in size, made it a matter of difficulty to distinguish
which was entitled to the designation; so, perforce our investigation proved unsuccessful.

June 21st Suffered from a violent attack of neuralgia in the right
eye, which nearly blinded me and rendered abortive any attempts
at topography.

June 22nd. Captain Spalding arrived in camp with a heavy mail,
my portion contained 30 letters and a large package of newspapers.
Letter from Genl. J.McE. Dye, of the army of Egypt, to General Crook,
offering me the position of Major on the Military staff of the Khedive.
Also note from Captain Nickerson, advising acceptance and saying
I had better run in at once to Omaha.[9] Letters from Mr Hittell and
many other friends.

Saw in the papers the editorials appended and also a notice of the
death by suicide in New York of Captain W.H. Brown, 5th Cavalry,
one of Genl. Crook's soldiers in the campaign against the Apaches
in Arizona.

---

9. In the 1870s, Egypt theoretically was a dominion of the Ottoman Empire, governed by
a khedive, or viceroy, appointed by the sultan and functioning in his name. In reality, the
khevidal government was virtually independent of Constantinople, and the khedives were
hereditary princes who increasingly were becoming clients of Great Britain. Because of growing
nationalism and pressure for reform among their own officers, the khedives preferred foreigners
for key military and civil positions. The majority were British, although Germans, Austrians,
and the occasional American could be found in Egyptian service. Such an appointment was a
virtual guarantee of wealth, power, and prestige. See Moorehead, *White Nile*.

Part 3
The Great Sioux War
1876–1877

Introduction

The remaining Bourke manuscripts in this volume deal with the Great Sioux War of 1876-77, a brutal conflict most famous for the destruction of Lt. Col. George Armstrong Custer and five companies of the 7th Cavalry at the Little Bighorn on June 25, 1876. The war was an outgrowth of many factors. The Indians were increasingly disillusioned with reservation life, and those who had never gone on the reservations were contemptuous of those who had. As more abandoned the reservation for the free, nomadic life, the center of resistance shifted from Red Cloud, who had more or less come to terms with the government, to the Hunkpapa Sioux chief Sitting Bull, who advocated breaking all connections with the whites, including the acceptance of government rations.[1]

The great sore point was, of course, the Black Hills, which, regardless of what the Indians might have thought of them as a geographical feature, were increasingly becoming a point of honor. Although Red Cloud, Spotted Tail, and other agency chiefs indicated a possible cession of the Black Hills to the government, leaders of the northern, non-agency bands of Lakotas and Cheyennes an-

1. Robinson, *Good Year to Die*, 29-31.

nounced that they would go to war first. To emphasize their position, in the spring of 1875 the Indians closed the two roads leading into the Black Hills from Nebraska. Settlers and prospectors were killed, and livestock run off. Soon raiding extended into Wyoming.

The situation presented a golden opportunity for the army command. With the end of the Civil War, the American public had resumed its traditional disdain for professional soldiers, and viewed the army as a tool of the increasingly unpopular Radical Reconstruction of the South. With the election of General Grant, however, army officers believed they had finally found an advocate for their views, particularly on westward expansion and the nagging "Indian Question." Given Sheridan's enthusiasm for expansion in general, and the writings and opinions of officers such as Custer, Dodge, Maj. James S. Brisbin, and Maj. George A. Forsyth, the soldiers attempted to sway public and congressional opinion toward the army as an instrument of national development. Thus President Grant faced growing pressure to annex the Black Hills away from the Indians.[2]

In the fall of 1875, a commission consisting of General Terry, Sen. W. B. Allison, S. D. Hinman, G. P. Beauvais, and several Easterners met with the Indians at the Red Cloud Agency, in northwestern Nebraska, in an effort to convince them to cede the region. The meeting was a fiasco, and the temper of the Indians was such that the commissioners were lucky to emerge alive. It became obvious the government would have to take by force what it could not gain by negotiation. On December 6, Commissioner of Indian Affairs Edward P. Smith, acting on instructions from Secretary of the Interior Zachariah Chandler, instructed the agents in the Dakotas and Nebraska to notify the various bands that they would have to be within the reservations on or before January 31, 1876. The timing was poor. Because of the winter, many Indians would not even get the word until well after the deadline. It made no difference. On February 1, 1876, the Interior Department gave the War Department responsibility for all non-agency Sioux.

The immediate task fell to General Sheridan, the division commander. He envisioned a winter campaign of three converging columns, a tactic which had been used with success on the Southern Plains, most recently during the Red River War of 1874-75. Crook

2. McDermott, "Military Problem," 18-19, 25-26.

would move up from the south, Col. John Gibbon would move east from his bases in western Montana, and Custer would move west from Dakota. They would batter the Indians back and forth until they submitted.[3]

Although Bourke pointed out that Crook had "the prestige of complete success in every campaign hitherto undertaken," he was overly optimistic in saying that the general was "by all odds the worst foe the Sioux have ever yet had to meet."[4] In fact, this war probably was the low point of Crook's career. While he understood the economic and cultural differences between the northern tribes and the Apaches, he did not understand the region. Crook's earlier assignments, Arizona and the Pacific Northwest, were small in comparison to the Platte, and the terrain was more familiar. Those areas also were more heavily settled, and the soldiers were never more than a few days from supply and support. In the western part of the Platte, by comparison, there was little white settlement north of the Union Pacific line, and large portions of Terry's department were equally vacant. The northernmost post in Crook's department was Fort Fetterman, Wyoming, and the nearest posts in the Department of Dakota were hundreds of miles away. The Indians in this area reigned supreme, and many were hostile. This situation hindered Crook at every turn, and whatever success he enjoyed was almost entirely through the efforts of subordinate officers.[5]

Amid the preparations for war, the government found itself rocked by scandal. Personally honest, President Grant nevertheless was a poor judge of character, and often appointed men to high positions who were not as honest as he. Secretary of War William W. Belknap resigned under allegations of influence peddling in the appointment of traderships at military posts. Resignation notwithstanding, he subsequently was impeached. Presidential advisor Orville Babcock was involved in the "Whiskey Ring," a group of distillers and distributors who bribed treasury employees to accept falsified measurements and supply tax stamps beyond the amount paid. Another casualty was Interior Secretary Columbus Delano, forced to resign after it was learned he had obtained substantial government surveying contracts for his son, John, who in turn shook down trained

3. Robinson, *Good Year to Die*, 37ff.; Gray, *Centennial Campaign*, 21ff.
4. Bourke, Diaries, 3:96
5. Robinson, *General Crook*, 166-67.

surveyors for payment in order to obtain work. Grant's image was further tarnished because he stubbornly remained loyal to his associates long after common sense dictated that he should have abandoned them to their fates. Even Orvil Grant, the president's brother, was implicated in payoff schemes, although Orvil, a perennial survivor, managed to weather the storm.[6]

Orvil Grant's problems went so far as to affect the organization of the campaign against the Indians. Custer, who had been openly critical of corruption among government officials on the upper Missouri River, was summoned to testify before congress. Much of his testimony was simply rumor and speculation, but he did implicate Belknap and Orvil Grant. While President Grant did not particularly care for his brother, Orvil nevertheless was family, and the president was unwilling to tolerate an attack on him by a lieutenant colonel. Custer was removed from command of the Dakota Column in the coming campaign, and only General Terry's intercession allowed him to accompany the expedition at all—as a cavalry commander subordinate to Terry, who would lead the column.[7]

General Sheridan, however, faced another problem. Although the winter campaign of converging columns was proven in the south, the climate of Montana and Dakota was substantially different from that of Texas and Oklahoma. Only Crook, coming up from Wyoming, would be able to enter the field on schedule. The Montana and Dakota Columns were still snowbound. To make matters worse, Terry, a wealthy attorney who had gained his Regular Army general's star because of his tenacious and successful assault on Fort Fisher, North Carolina, did not make any serious effort to have them ready to march as soon as the weather allowed.

Bourke frequently mentioned Sitting Bull and the Oglala chief Crazy Horse. In doing so, he inadvertently contributed to the great body of mythology that has emerged around these two chiefs. Much of the myth was developed to fit the white concept of monolithic leadership, whereas in reality, no one single person had tangible authority in Plains Indian society. Except in rare cases, a chief's role essentially was symbolic. This appears to have been understood by Lt. W. Philo Clark, who prepared an overall assessment of the war for General Crook, after most of the hostilities had ceased.

6. McFeely, *Grant, A Biography*, 405-7, 427-29, 430-33.
7. Ibid., 431-32; Utley, *Cavalier in Buckskin*, 158-63.

He wrote:

> Great prominence has been given Crazy Horse and Sitting
> Bull in this war, the good fighting strategy and subsequent
> muster by retreats being attributed to them, whereas they
> are really not entitled to more credit or censure than many
> others so far as plans and orders were concerned, but they
> headed two of the worst bands on the plains, and were the
> two fiercest leaders the Sioux nation has produced for
> years.[8]

Nevertheless, the legend refuses to die, and has been accepted
and passed on by the Indians themselves.

With this section, Bourke began a format he would use with few
exceptions throughout the remainder of his life: a bound notebook,
written on both sides of each page. Additionally, he usually began
numbering the pages of each subsequent volume in sequence, picking up the pages of each subsequent volume with the number of the
final page of the preceding one. He began with preparations for what
was designated the Big Horn Expedition. This was the opening campaign of the war.

This period also shows the copious attention to detail that would
characterize the diaries throughout the remainder of Bourke's life.
Although it follows a daily sequence of events, it is less a diary than
a memoir, and is one of the best contemporary accounts of the organization of an Indian campaign, and of the routine followed by
Indian War soldiers in the field. The flow of the narrative is complete, abbreviation is rare, and sentence structure and punctuation
are a vast improvement over earlier volumes. It also shows evidence
of careful rereading and some editing. In several cases, Bourke inserted later corrections in the margins or on the bottom of the page.
Another indication is his entry for March 13, which states his ink
had frozen and burst the bottle so that the remainder of that particular volume would be in pencil.[9] As the extant copy is entirely in
ink, however, one must surmise that he copied it over, and probably expanded the original as he went along.

8. Clark to AG, Platte, September 14, 1877, U.S. Department of War, RG 393, Special
File, Military Division of the Missouri, Sioux War, herafter referred to as Special File—Sioux.
9. Bourke, Diaries, 3:85-86.

He begins with an account of the Big Horn Expedition, the first of Sheridan's converging columns to get into the field. Theoretically the expedition was commanded by Col. Joseph J. Reynolds, who, despite an admirable record in the Union Army, did not inspire confidence from his superiors or subordinates. In the Department of Texas, which Reynolds commanded from 1870 to 1872, Col. Ranald S. Mackenzie accused him of corruption regarding civilian supply contracts. By 1876, in an era when the army was rife with petty jealousies, Reynolds' own regiment, the 3rd Cavalry, was particularly notorious for its factionalism. Although General Crook's official position was that of an observer, it soon became clear that he was de facto commanding officer. His reasons for usurping the command are obscure. In his official report, he stated that he "accompanied" the expedition to personally observe the feasibility of winter campaigns. However, he also implied there were other reasons, which may have indicated that he shared the lack of confidence in Reynolds. While Crook's active and continual interference did not initially create problems, it appears to have undermined Reynolds' position as the march progressed, and undoubtedly contributed to the lackluster outcome of the expedition.[10]

In his description of the soldiers' morale along the march, Bourke acknowledged the difference between the Union Army volunteer who marched into battle "with banners flying, drums beating and the pulse beating high with the promptings of honorable ambition and enthusiasms, in unison with the roar of artillery," and the professional soldier of the Indian Wars, who encountered "a foe whose habits of warfare are repugnant to every principle of humanity and whose presence can be determined solely by the flash of the rifle . . . or the whoop and yell."[11]

The Union soldier, as historians Don Rickey, Jr., and Robert Utley have pointed out, generally belonged to a volunteer unit connected with a specific locale that the soldier could call home. He had community support, and was identified with a regular vocation or profession that was temporarily suspended for the duration of the war. The regular soldier, on the other hand, was seen as having no roots, a shiftless drifter who opted for the army because he was "too lazy

10. U.S. Department of War, *Annual Report*, 1:502; Robinson, *Bad Hand*, 52-53, and *General Crook*, 167.
11. Bourke, Diaries, 3:79-80.

to work." A large percentage of the troops came from the ranks of the urban poor, with some skilled artisans interspersed. Many were foreign. An ill-informed Eastern press also tended to connect the regular soldier with atrocities against the Indians, much as the conscript soldier in Vietnam a century later was seen as a "baby killer." Ironically, many of the atrocities were perpetrated not by the regulars, who merely executed the policy of the political government, but by volunteer troops from the local frontier population who had personal scores to settle with Indians.[12]

Keenly aware of the attitude toward soldiers, Bourke remarked that the troops "are sent into the field, endure great hardships and suffer untold discomforts; if victorious, they are railed at by the 'religious' press of the country as unbridled butchers; if defeated, as all expeditions must expect to be, ridicule and contumely are poured out upon them."[13] For the first time, Bourke allowed himself a veiled criticism of General Crook, by referring to "an almost inexcusable oversight in the organization of our column" and "our objectionable method of marching."[14] Although inserted in the entry for March 16, when Reynolds led the cavalry independently of Crook, the description itself can only apply to the expedition as a whole, in which Crook had a direct—and heavy—hand.

The march culminated in a fight on the Powder River of Montana on March 17, 1876, known variously as the Powder River Fight, the Reynolds Fight, or the Crazy Horse Fight, because the soldiers came to presume that they had destroyed the camp of the Oglala chief Crazy Horse. In fact, Crazy Horse was not even present and, from a military point of view, the fight was a debacle. The column attacked a village that was predominately Cheyenne, a tribe that had considered itself neutral up to this point. This particular band was on its way to Fort Laramie, in compliance with the government edict. The attack and destruction of the village threw the Cheyennes firmly into the hostile camp.[15]

Neither Bourke nor Crook ever admitted the mistake, despite all evidence that they had attacked a non-hostile village. Three months

12. Rickey, *Forty Miles a Day*, 26-27; Utley, *Frontier Regulars*, 22-23.
13. Bourke, Diaries, 4:253.
14. Ibid., 3:103-4.
15. Three Cheyenne accounts of the fight are found in Greene, *Lakota and Cheyenne*. The first official indication that Reynolds hit the wrong village is contained in a letter from Lt. George Ruhlen to General Terry, April 19, 1876, with endorsements, Special File–Sioux.

later, Bourke referred to a telegram received in camp "that the Crazy Horse fight was an attack upon a band of peaceable Indians travelling back to their Reservations. . . .a lie, so ridiculous that we can afford to laugh at everything except its malignity."[16]

There is no question that Reynolds completely mismanaged the fight. Aside from hitting the wrong camp, he had allowed his horses to become exhausted, did not scout the terrain, and ultimately, allowed dead and living wounded to fall into the hands of the Indians. Two company commanders likewise did not live up to expectations. Captain Alexander Moore, who previously had bungled an expedition in Arizona, found that the terrain did not allow him to fulfill his assignment, and held his men back, allowing other companies to carry the brunt of the fighting. Captain Henry E. Noyes, on the other hand, was overly concerned about carrying out his assignment of securing the pony herd, when common sense dictated supporting the companies that were actively engaged. Upon return to Cheyenne, Crook ordered all three court-martialed.

Bourke is venomous about what he termed Reynolds' "imbecility" and went so far as to call Moore a "coward." He also dwells to some degree on their impending courts-martial. The trial of Captain Noyes was held almost immediately upon returning to Fort D. A. Russell, because charges against him, primarily involving poor judgment, were the most easily dispatched. He received an administrative reprimand. The charges and specifications against Reynolds and Moore were far more severe, and their careers were on the line. After several postponements that severely damaged morale in the 3rd Cavalry, they ultimately were tried and convicted in January 1877. Reynolds was suspended from rank and command for one year, and Moore was suspended from command and ordered confined to the limits of his post for six months.[17]

Crook, meanwhile, went to the Red Cloud Agency, where he hoped to repeat his Arizona tactic of playing factions within a tribe against each other, this time with the Sioux. He met with Red Cloud, and several other Oglala chiefs, including one named Sitting Bull (designated as "Sitting Bull of the South" to distinguish him from the great Sitting Bull, who was Hunkpapa). Bourke transcribed the interviews into his diary, giving much insight into the Indian view

16. Bourke, Diaries, 5:439.
17. Robinson, General Crook, 171-72, 209-10.

of things. Although the chiefs appeared interested, the intervention of their agent, James S. Hastings, ended any ideas they might have had for cooperation.[18]

Meddling by the agents was a recurring theme throughout the Great Sioux War, as they attempted to keep their Indian charges from participating in a war against other Indians, even those tribes who traditionally had been their enemies. This, in turn, opened old wounds between the Interior and War Departments. For the first fifty years after the Constitution was adopted, the Indians were the responsibility of the War Department. This mainly was because most of the Eastern tribes had sided with the British during the Revolutionary War and therefore were potential enemies. In 1849, however, the newly created Department of the Interior was placed in charge of Indian matters, although the soldiers continued to be summoned to handle outbreaks. Initially, the War Department had no objections to the change, because it was one less administrative responsibility. But as the nation expanded, Indian outbreaks became so common that the generals were convinced that the Interior Department was incapable of handling the situation. Congress, which should have intervened in the dispute, was itself divided between the Senate, which had the actual power to make treaties with Indians, and the House of Representatives, which sought to assert itself by including Indian legislation in its bills. Consequently, federal policy was confused, contradictory, and erratic, and the frontier soldiers were left on their own to sort things out. The continuing strife, together with allegations of corruption in both departments, led to the Peace Policy, whereby administration of the Indian agencies was turned over to religious groups in an effort to "civilize" the Indians and end corruption. While the corruption was substantially reduced (despite military accusations to the contrary) religious groups and their representatives had preconceived notions of Indians that had very little to do with reality.[19]

As Bourke's transcripts show, the Indians themselves found the government's position frustratingly erratic. The chiefs pointedly told

18. Hastings was infuriated by Crook's absurd claim that Reynolds' troops had found the so-called "Crazy Horse" camp attacked on March 17 to have been well stocked with ammunition and other supplies provided through the agency. Having talked with the expedition's Indian scouts, he had a better grasp of the facts than Crook would admit, and was determined not to assist the general in any way. See Hyde, *Red Cloud's Folk*, 259 n.5.

19. Prucha, *Great Father*, 111-12; Priest, *Uncle Sam's Stepchildren*, Chapter 2; Robinson, *General Crook*, 102.

Crook that, during visits to Washington, the president had instructed them to refrain from any kind of war, and their agents were reinforcing that edict. Yet the army, traditionally viewed as the enemy, now was seeking their help against other bands of their own people.

While Crook contended with problems in the Platte, the two northern columns—the Montana Column under Gibbon, and the Dakota Column under Terry with Custer in tow—finally got underway. Now, it was Crook's turn to delay, and his new Big Horn and Yellowstone Expedition, once in the field, assumed the safari atmosphere that would characterize it through much of the first half of the summer of 1876. The officers—not the least of whom was Crook himself—hunted and fished, while the ordinary soldiers fished, bathed in the mountain streams, and busied themselves with what appear to be the absolute minimal duties necessary. Bourke, who spent much of his time reading, writing, and napping, admitted that it was "nothing but a picnic without exploit and without advantage."[20]

In Crook's defense, it must be pointed out that during the first part of June, he was awaiting the arrival of Indian scouts, without whom he could not effectively operate. Nevertheless, the lethargy continued. The only real excitement occurred on the evening of June 9, when a group of Indians that Bourke's Diaries identify only as "a mounted party of Sioux warriors" fired into the camp. The entire affair was summed up in only a couple of paragraphs.[21] Yet when Bourke recalled the incident fourteen years later in *On the Border With Crook*, he said the attack was made "in a most energetic manner by the Sioux and Cheyennes," adding:

> This attack was only a bluff on the part of "Crazy Horse" to keep his word to Crook that he would begin to fight the latter just as soon as he touched the waters of the Tongue River; we had scoffed at the message at first, believing it to have been an invention of some of the agency half-breeds, but there were many who now believed in its authenticity.[22]

Interestingly enough, the diary contains no reference to any such "message" from Crazy Horse, nor is there any indication that, at

20. Bourke, Diaries, 4:379.
21. Ibid., 4: 368–70.
22. Bourke, *On the Border*, 296.

this point in the war, Crazy Horse was even aware of Crook's existence. In fact, the first mention of Crazy Horse in the extant Bourke writings was an offhand, generic comment concerning non-reservation chiefs. The statement goes to show how much the specter of Crazy Horse had grown in Crook's—and by extension, Bourke's—minds during and after the war.

Soon after this attack, the Indian scouts arrived, and Crook finally began moving into Montana on June 16.

Chapter 10

✦

✦

✦

✦

The Big Horn Expedition

Left Omaha, Neb., February 17th [1876] for Cheyenne, Wyoming, in company with Gen. Crook, Col. Stanton, Col. Van Vliet, 3 Cav. and Ben. Clarke, of Indian Territory, whose services Gen. Crook has secured as a guide.

Reached Cheyenne on the 18th and put up at the Inter Ocean Hotel. During the day and evening, the officers stationed at Fort D.A. Russell and Camp Carlin improved the occasion of calling upon the Genl. to pay their respects.

Found the pack-train of the Expedn. ready to take the field, and well equipped under the experienced management of Tom. Moore. The proposed expedition is to consist of ten (10) companies of Cavalry, five of 2d and five of the 3d under the command of Gen. J.J. Reynolds, Colonel of the 3d Cavalry. Those to start from Fort Russell comprised

Co. "E", 2d Cav. Lt. Rowelle [sic] & Lt. Sibley.

Co. "B", 2d Cav. Capt. Peale & Lt. [Frank Upham] Robinson.

Co. "A" 3d Cav. Capt. Hawley and Lt. Lawson

Co. "E" 3d Cav. Lt. J.B. Johnson, Adjt.

Co. "F" 3d Cav. Capt. Moore & Lt. Reynolds.

Gen. Reynolds has appointed Lieut. Charles Morton, Adjutant, and

Lieut Drew, A.A.Q.M. of the Command. It is the intention to move in the lightest marching order possible, hence everything not absolutely needed in the way of clothing, and mess equipage and bedding is to be rejected.

Saturday, the 19th, and Sunday, the 20th, remained in Cheyenne, working up the details of the organization. The two companies of the 2d Cav. got off early on Sunday morning. Gen. Palmer, of the 2d Cav. came down from Fort Sanders on Saturday to consult with Gen. Crook. He returned on Sunday. Col. Roger Jones passed through from San Francisco on Saturday, going to New York.

Capt. Nickerson, A.D.C., arrived back from the Indian agencies at Red Cloud and Spotted Tail,[1] where he had gone to secure guides and trailers from among the half-breeds, and also to note passing events. We are now on the eve of the bitterest Indian war the Government has ever been called upon to wage: a war with a tribe that has waxed fat and insolent on Gov't bounty, and has been armed and equipped with the most improved weapons by the connivance or carelessness of the Indian Agents. Of this, more hereafter.[2]

In Cheyenne, we could see and hear nothing but "Black Hills." Every store advertises its inducements as an outfitting agency, every wagon is chartered to convea [sic] freight to the new Pactolus.[3] The Q.M. Dept. experiences grave difficulty in finding the transportation needed by the Army at the different camps. Everything is bound for the Black Hills. Cheyenne is full of people and her merchants and saloon keepers are doing a rushing business. Great numbers of new buildings, mostly brick, have been erected during the past six months, giving the town a bustle and activity as well as an appearance of advancement in favorable contrast with Omaha, Denver and Salt Lake.

1. The Red Cloud and Spotted Tail Agencies were in northwestern Nebraska near the present city of Chadron. The Red Cloud Agency served the Oglalas and was guarded by Camp (later Fort) Robinson. Spotted Tail, which served the Brulés, was guarded by Camp Sheridan. Both these agencies were named after the most prominent chiefs of their respective tribes, and both figured conspicuously in the coming war.

2. This assertion is questionable, as Bourke admitted in his later writings. In fact, many of the reservation Indians were on the verge of starvation because government rations often were late, and when they did arrive, were inadequate. Agents often found it necessary to pad their rolls to avoid famine. The most prosperous Indians, ironically, were those who eschewed the reservation and government rations, in favor of the unceded lands of Wyoming and Montana. See Robinson, *A Good Year to Die*, 43-44, 260.

3. In *On the Border*, Bourke used almost exactly the same sentence, except that he said "the new El Dorado" (248).

Monday, Feby. 21st. Capt. Nickerson, A.D.C. left for Omaha at 2 O'Clock this A.M. Five companies of 3d Cavalry, including besides those already mentioned, Co. "D", 3d Cav. Lt. [William Wallace] Robinson, and Co. "M", Capt. [Anson] Mills and 1st Lt. A.C. Paul, left for Fort Fetterman[4] at 6 O'Clock

Feby. 22d. Left Cheyenne for Fort Laramie, passing through Camp Carlin 1 1/2 miles from Cheyenne and Fort D.A. Russell, 3 miles distant: 18 miles from Cheyenne is Lodge Pole Creek which joins the South Platte near Sydney [Nebraska] and 10 miles beyond that the Horse Ck. an affluent of the North Platte; the divide between these two small streams must therefore be some 7000 feet above sea level, as Cheyenne is about 6100. Stopped the first night at Portuguese Phillips', a frontiersman of great experience especially among the Sioux Indians. His conversation was full of reminiscences of the Fort Phil. Kearney massacre which he witnessed.[5]

Arrived at Fort Laramie in the afternoon of the 23rd the distance being about 90 miles from Cheyenne. At the post, there was much excitement and bustle attendant upon the departure of Capt. Egan and Capt. Noyes and Lieut Hall of the 2d Cavalry, whose companies are to form the Expedition.

Doctor Munn, who is to be Surgeon of the Command, was occupied in preparing the field medicine chest and other details pertaining to his Department.

In the evening witnessed a theatrical entertainment given by the ladies and officers of the post; the pieces "Faint Heart never won Fair Lady" and "A Regular Fix" were capitally interpreted, the best performance being, in my opinion Maj. Burt, 9th Inf[antry], Miss L. Dewey, Miss Lucy Townsend, Mrs. L.P. Bradley, and Mr. Ford.

From this point and on the road, I saw many adventurers journeying to the Black Hills; their wagons and animals looked new and good as a general thing and the supplies carried ample in quantity.

4. Fort Fetterman was established in 1867. It was abandoned in 1882, and turned over to the Interior Department two years later. The post buildings became a tough cow town that served as the model for the town of Drybone in Owen Wister's *The Virginian*. It is now a Wyoming state historic site. Frazer, *Forts of the West*, 180-81.

5. On December 21, 1866, a large band of Indians attacked a wood train carrying lumber to Fort Phil Kearny from the post sawmill a few miles away. A detachment of eighty men under Capt. William J. Fetterman, 18th Infantry, was ordered to drive away the Indians and bring in the train. Fetterman, however, disobeyed orders and chased the Indians, allowing himself to be drawn into a trap. The entire command was wiped out. Bourke consistently misspelled the name of the fort as "Kearney," but there is no second "e." Fort Fetterman, which Crook used as a base, was named in memory of William Fetterman. See Brown, *The Fetterman Massacre*.

However, there were many on foot and without adequate sustenance and some begging their way from ranch to ranch along the trail. What they hope to gain by going at this time to the Black Hills where the thermometer is reported to be -23° F., creeks frozen up and all placer mining frustrated is one of those things no one can find out.

It is strongly suggestive of the want and misery of the Eastern states that so many people should rush upon slight stimulus towards the new El Dorado.

The reason the Cheyenne route is preferred is the new iron bridge across the North Platte river, constructed under the supervision of Captain Stanton of the Engineer Corps, U.S.A, which gives secure passage not found on the other trails leading out from Sydney, North Platte, and elsewhere.[6]

Indications of bad weather approaching are now discernible in the sky: hopes are entertained that if a storm comes up the Sioux may be compelled to keep under shelter and thus give our columns a chance to creep undetected into the Yellowstone and Tongue river country, where their villages are. General Crook was busy all day, the 25th, in examining guides and scouts and studying maps of the country in which we are to operate. Wrote to Captain Nickerson and to sister.

February 27th. Arrived at Fort Fetterman last evening in company with Gen. Crook, Gen. Reynolds, Lieut. Crew, Lieut. Morton. Our journey of two days' duration took us over some 80 miles of country, barren of vegetation, lying along the Right bank of the North Platte and watered by its tributaries from the Laramie [river.] Black Hills on our Left. The scenery was of most monotonous character, destitute of herbage, except buffalo grass and sagebrush. An occasional buffalo-head, bleaching in the sun, gave a still more ghastly aspect to the landscape. From time to time, the prairie-dog protruded his little head above the entrance of his domicile and barked at our cortege passing by. That night (25th) we camped with Egan's and Noyes' companies of 2d Cavalry at the Buyll Bend of the North Platte, about 32 miles from Fort Laramie, in a very pleasant grove of cottonwood trees.

---

6. The iron bridge still spans the North Platte River at Fort Laramie. It allowed travelers to avoid the slow and sometimes dangerous crossings by river ferries on the other routes. See Bourke, *On the Border With Crook*, 248.

In spots, the soil was arable in the event of water being applied. Its general character bore out Gen. Hazen's aspersion against the "Great American Desert."

Boulders of Gneiss, Greystone, Porphyry, and other rocks from the Laramie Peak lined the bottom and sides of the different dry arroyos passed on this march. On the 26th, we passed the Twin Springs, a pair of pretty little sources of water, then Horse-shoe creek, Cave springs; Elk Horn creek, La Tone creek, Wagon-Hound creek,[7] Bed tick creek and Whisky Gulch. The last is 3 miles from Fort Fetterman and is the place of concealment of all the vile intoxicating drinks smuggled in for the use of the enlisted men of the command.

Red clay, evidently gypsifurous, and of same general type as that to be encountered going into the Black Hills of Dacotah formed the road bed. Stunted pine and cedar were growing in all the crevices and gulches of the little hills near by.

At Fort Fetterman found [Capt. Samuel Peter] Ferris', [Capt. Edwin Mortimer] Coates' and [First Lt. John Wilson] Bubb's companies of 4th Infantry, and [Capt. Thomas Bull] Dewees of the 2d Cavalry. This post, commanded by Major Alex. Chambers of the 4th Infantry, is [illegible] the most northern of those protecting our settlements from the incursions of the Sioux, Cheyennes and Arapahoes. At the time of our arrival, Black Coal, an Arapaho chief of not much prominence* was at the post with his small band. He reported Sitting Bull and the Minneconjous,[8] living on the Powder river, below old Fort Reno,[9] some 100 miles from Fetterman.

On the 27th, Captain Peale with Lt. F.U. Robinson, Lt. W.C. Rawolle and Lt. Sibley, all of the 2nd Cavalry, arrived with 2 companies of their regiment. Paymaster Stanton also reached the post in the afternoon, bringing with him Mr. Strahorn, special correspondent of the *Rocky Mountain News*. My old classmate, Lt. D.S. Pearson, of the 2d, insisted upon taking care of Lt. Morton and myself during our stay at the post. Made the acquaintance of his charming young

* This is a mistake: I should have said that Black Coal ranked with Sharp Nose in influence, but at the time mentioned, he only had a few lodges under his immediate command.

7. A wagon hound is the "V" shaped brace that reinforces the tongue against the "sand" or forward bolster.

8. At this time, Bourke appears to have believed that Sitting Bull was a Miniconjou chief, and that the Miniconjous were the center of resistance. In fact, Sitting Bull was Hunkpapa, and the Hunkpapas, as a group, led the free-moving Lakotas in defiance of the government.

9. Fort Reno was established by General Patrick Connor in 1865 and abandoned under the terms of the Fort Laramie Treaty of 1868. Its site is just east of the present town of Kaycee, Wyoming. Frazer, *Forts of the West*, 183-84.

wife and received during this day calls from all those stationed at the post, among whom were quite a number of old friends. Telegraphed to Nickerson to-day.

Quite an amount of business was transacted to-day, by the various officers connected with the proposed expedition of which Genl. Reynolds to-day formally assumed command. I may now say without much impudence that Gen. Crook hopes to be able to strike such bands of ill-disposed Minneconjous as he may encounter in the Powder, Tongue and Big Horn rivers, between the old Montana road[10] and the confluence of the above named streams with the Yellowstone. Gen. Crook telegraphed to-day to Gen. Custer, in reply to a telegram from the latter, that Gen. Reynolds would leave in a few days for the Big Horn country with ten companies of cavalry and two of infantry, but could communicate no plan of operations as that would have to be determined after arrival in that country. If we should drive the Sioux into Custer's hands, no doubt he would make short work of them, but their line of retreat would more probably be towards the Reservations.

Gen. Bradley, 9th Inf, commanding at Fort Laramie was this day ordered by telegraph to furnish all escorts needed to Fort Fetterman; also to keep telegraph line in repair. This to last until return of Gen. Reynolds' Expedition.

The various detachments of the 2d and 3d Cavalrys reached the post this P.M. in good order and condition.

Also the pack trains to form so valuable a feature of the coming season of operations. It may not be amiss here to give a brief description of the manner in which these trains are organized and managed as they form a new departure in the transportation employed in the Dept. of the Platte.

First, in the selection of the animals themselves, care is taken to exclude those of unsuitable age—from 4 to 8 years is the best age to commence with, altho' mules of much more advanced years can be found in all trains. A mouth which has become bridle-worn, unfits the animal for pack train service, because it cannot drink from a stream, as the water will run through the corners of its mouth; it must have a large belly to feed upon the grass of the hills, ofttimes its only sustenance; it should not slope down to the withers, because the load would then press more heavily upon its fore-shoul-

10. The Bozeman Trail.

ders and stave the animal up. Its back must be strong, free from scald, blemish or sore; its disposition ought to be gentle and kind. In organizing the train, bell-mares, called by the Mexicans "senceros", are provided; these are most preferably white mares* having bells hung around their necks. The mules speedily learn the sound of their proper bell and rarely fail to heed its warning. The bell-mare is ridden by the cook, an important personage in every sphere of life, but notably an officer of dignity and trust in a pack-train.

The load to be carried should be evenly divided, so as to balance well: for army packs, 250 to 325 pounds, exclusive of the weight of the aparejo (60 lbs.,) is the most the animals should average, dependent upon conditions of climate and food.

First, the mule must be blindfolded with "tapojos",[11] then the "suedero" or sweat cloth is placed upon the withers, followed by two saddle-blankets and the "sobrenjaluca", which supports the aparejo, made of stout canvass, faced with leather, and of the following dimensions and length, 76 inch. width 32 in; thickness 3 in. This is made to double in the middle of its length and secured to the animal by a "cincha", or belt of canvass, passing around the girth. Covering the aparejo, comes the "corona," a gorgeously ornamented covering of frieze or blanket, often wrought with odd and fantastic designs cut out of scarlet or azure cloth. Finally comes the "cargo", as the pack is technically called, securely held in its place by two ropes[:] the "reatas" and the lasso,† worked into a peculiar knot called the diamond hitch. The animal's eyes are now freed and altho' it may display a desire to extricate itself from its burden, it soon learns to comport itself as a well-bred pack-mule and follows docilely the lead of the bell-mare. The packers themselves are robust, hard-working and good-natured fellows, great eaters and generally good story tellers. One man to every five mules is the allowance in a well-regulated train. The above is a very barren outline of what a pack-train consists of, and is only interpolated to give an idea of the means taken to get our supplies over the ground as fast as a Cav'l. Command can move.

---

* Mules manifest a great liking for *white* horses or mares and in one case that I remember, in Arizona, they nearly crushed a little white colt to death, in the pack-train with Genl. Crook's Expedition against the hostile Apaches in 1871.

† Or "guante" rope.

11. Blinders.

Hitherto, for a large command to surprise mounted savages has been a rarity and in all cases, the Indians evaded full punishment by leaving the heavily laden wagons of the soldiers far in their rear. The same wise system of logistics which did so much to shatter the power of the hostile Apaches in Arizona is now to be brought into play to conquer the haughty Sioux. But we have not the same knowledge of country which proved so invaluable in that campaign, nor the same unerring Indian auxiliaries who led us into the dens and fastnesses of the enemy with clock-like accuracy. To compensate for this the enemy now operated against is comparatively luxurious, and is well provided with animals, of course so much the more easy to trail. Then too he has good reason to believe our Gov't to be afraid of him and Indians like [him] will repose confidence in his numerical superiority and venture to attack us in situations where the more wily Apache would prefer to retreat.[12]

General Reynolds to-day (Feb. 28th) issued General Orders, No. 1 and No. 2, announcing the organization of the Big Horn Expedition. In No. 1, Lieut. Charles Morton, 3d Cav., is announced as adjutant, Lieut. Drew, A/A/Q.M. and Mr. Thomas Moore as Master of Transportation of the Expedition. In No. 2, the command was divided into Battalions, composed and commanded as follows:

1st. Cos. "M" & "E",   3 Cav.,   Capt. Anson Mills, 3 Cav. Comg.
2d. "   "A" & "D"   "   "   Wm. Hawley "   "   "
3d. "   "I" & "K"   2d "   "   H.E. Noyes, 2d "   "
4th "   "A" & "B"   2d "   "   T.B. Dewees,2d "   "
5th "   "F" 3d & "E" 2d "   "   A. Moore,   3d "   "
6th "   "C" and "I" 4th Infantry" E.M. Coates, 4th Inft. "

The pack trains were assigned as follows.
Mr. McAuliff's to 1st Battalion.
"   Closter's   " 2d   "
"   Foster's   " 3d   "
"   Young's   " 4th "
"   DeLaney's " 5th   "

February 29th. Early in morning troops comprising the garrison of

12. Again, Bourke at this point knew little of Northern Plains Indians who, like most other Western Indians, preferred to avoid open and direct confrontation. With the single exception of the Rosebud, every major action during the Great Sioux War was initiated by the army. Despite Bourke's remarks about "numerical superiority," the Western Sioux and Cheyenne realized that the government could easily replace military casualties, while they, a nomadic tribal people with only a limited number of fighting men, could not sustain heavy losses.

Fort Fetterman were mustered out by Colonel Chambers, the Commanding Officer.

Weather is now changing & sky cloudy and leaden in appearance. Wind chilly and damp. Indications of a snow storm approaching. Command is all encamped (with exception of the 2 Infantry companies,) on the banks of the North Platte river, with system and order rapidly asserting themselves. We expect to get off early to-morrow morning, March 1st, and as our line of March will probably be for a long time along the road to old Fort C.F. Smith, Montana,[13] I append the itinerary of Major E. R. Wells, 2d Cavalry, for which I am indebted to Lieut. W. P. Clarke, Regl. Adjutant of the 2d Cavalry.

Leaving Fort Fetterman, W[yoming].T[erritory]., the road crosses the North Platte and runs in a northerly (North by West) direction:

Ponds of Left of Road	(Brackish water.)	5 miles
Head of Sage Creek.	(")	15 "
Brown's Springs.	(Water.)	29 "
South Cheyenne	(Water and Wood.)	33 "
Humphreyville's Creek	(Water.)	42 "
Middle Cheyenne	(Water.)	47 "
Wind River	(Water and Wood.)	53 "
N. Fork Wind River	(Water.)	55 "
Curtis' Spring, one half mile to Right of Road. (Water.)		61 m.
Head of Dry Fork Powder River (Water & Wood.)		73 "
Buffalo Spgs. (In Dry Fork Powder River(]), (Water Brackish. Wood)		77 "
Fort Reno on Powder River (Water & Wood)		88 "

Distance from Fetterman.

Fort Reno to Dry Creek, (Water at times.)		96 "
Crazy Woman		Wood. 111
Clark's Springs		Wood. 118
Conner's Springs		——— 127
Clear Fork	Good Water at all seasons.	Wood. 132
Rock Creek		Wood. 135
De Smet Lake		Wood. 141
1/2 mile. To Right		

---

13. Fort C.F. Smith was established in 1866 as the northernmost of three posts designed to protect the Bozeman Trail, the others being Fort Phil Kearny and Fort Reno, in Wyoming. All three were abandoned under terms of the Fort Laramie Treaty of 1868.

Shell Creek		Wood. 146
Fort Phil Kearney		Wood. 149
(on Turkey Creek(])		
Fort Phil. Kearney to.		
Little Piney	(Water and Wood.)	155
Big Piney	(" " ")	160
Last crossing B.P.	(" " ")	167
Goose Creek	(" " ")	170
To Wolf Creek Crossing	(Water and Wood.)	172
Dry Creek	(Water at times)	179
Middle fork Tongue River	(Water & Wood.)	183
North fork " "	(Water & Wood.)	185
Dry Creek	(Water at times)	192
Trout Creek (Snow June 8th '72) Water & Wood.		200
Box Elder creek	(Water.)	201
Little Horn	(Water & Wood.)	205
Grass Lodge Creek	(Water & Wood.)	212
Muddy Creek	(Water & Wood.)	220
Rotten Grass	(Water & Wood.)	228
Fort C.F. Smith on Big Horn,	(Water & Wd)	240

Recapitulation

Fort Laramie to Fort Fetterman	80 m.
Fort Fetterman to Fort Reno	88 m.
Fort Reno to Fort Phil Kearney	61 m.
Fort Kearney to Fort C.F. Smith	91 m.
Total	321 m.

Distances Estimated.

Chapter 11

✦

✦

✦

✦

✦

The March North

March 1st. The command moved off in fine style this morning, officers and men in good spirits and horses champing on their bits as if eager for the journey. The snow storm of last night has ceased and upon the serene sky not a trace of cloud could be seen. The weather promised to be all we could desire; perhaps if it were a little bit more severe our purpose would be better served. Last night, Genl. Crook and General Reynolds had a council with the company commanders and gave them to understand what would be required of them. Much enthusiasm is manifested especially among the younger officers, partly from the hope of distinction that may be gained, partly from a desire to explore unknown country and perhaps a desire to escape from the restraints of Garrison life. The chief obstacle to campaigning at this season of the year in Northern Wyoming is the absence of forage; in the valleys and river bottoms when snow has not fallen, nutritious grasses may be found the whole year round. On the hills, prairie fires burn it off, cold winds deaden it or snow and ice cover it up from the horses. Consequently, our 80 wagons are given up to carrying grain, even the ambulances being heavily laden with it and the pack mules likewise carry it as their principal burden. Whenever good grazing can be found, no grain will be issued; at most only half to three quarters rations will be fed.

Next in importance comes the apparel of officers and men; when it is understood that during the storms of Polar wind which howl across these plains, the mercury congeals in the bulb and frequently remains solidified for weeks at a time, while the minimum thermometer indicates -25° F., -40° F, and even, as I was assured, on one occasion at Fort Sanders last winter -51° F, the precautions taken to guard against such Hyperborean vicissitudes will not be considered Sybaritic.

For cavalry, great care is demanded to protect feet, knees, wrists and ears. Commencing with the feet, first a pair of close fitting lamb's-wool socks is put on, then one of same size as those worn by women, so as to come over the knees. Indian moccasins of buckskin reaching well up the leg are preferable to boots, being warmer and lighter. Cork soles should be used with them. Then comes the overboot, of buffalo-skin, hair side inward, reaching well up the thigh, and opening down the side and fastened by buckles or brass buttons like a pair of Mexican breeches. They should be soled, heeled and boxed with good leather, well tanned. Some prefer to wear leggings to buffalo skin, legs separate, strapped to pistol belt, and to use the clumsy buffalo overshoe of the Q.M. Department. This is a mode of attire more readily taken off during the warm parts of the day, and for that reason, worthy of recommendation, but open to the objections that difficulty is generally experienced in getting the clumsy, awkward shoe into the stirrup. All people agree in denouncing as pernicious the practice of wearing tight foot-gear which by impeding the circulation assures the freezing of the lower extremities. For under clothing, first put on a good suit of lamb's wool or merino, then one of buckskin perforated to permit the escape of exhalations. Over this a heavy suit, the heavier the better. Finally a loose dark overshirt of thick texture or a heavy blanket blouse, made of a mission blanket, double-breasted; large buttons, well sewed on. If cold winds prevail, nothing will afford the body complete protection except a coat of beaver or buffalo skin, reaching to the knees or below and made loose at the elbows. For the head, a cap, loosely fitting over the cranium, of dark cloth, with leather visor to protect the eyes, and a border two inches to three in breadth, of beaver fur to turn down, when required, over the ears. Fur collars are provided for the throat and may be of any good skin; a very good one, I bought in Omaha, is of plucked beaver, lined with brown silk, about 5 to 6 inches in breadth and fastened in front with a button and loop. It has the advantages of being cheap, warm, elegant and durable.

"Pulse warmers" about six inches long will preserve the wrists and fur gloves or gauntlets extending well toward the elbow and worn in wet weather over tightly fitting woolen gloves, are the only adequate safeguard for the hands and fingers. An India rubber covering, formed of two of the U.S.A. ponchos sewed together, will very effectively shield both rider and horse from rain and snow. I regard it as unnecessary and would not recommend it, when the other garments specified are at hand, but it will always come in play to exclude the dampness of the night, coming either from ground or sky.

Buffalo robes form the best bedding. A small mattress of chopped cork, not more than one half inch to an inch thick, on the under side covered with thin leather and quilted in parallel lines transversely to allow of its being rolled into a very small compass would be a valuable addition to the outfit of every officer employed on this frontier duty.

For a pillow, I had made of canvass [sic] bound with leather, a small cylinder, 6 inches in diameter and long enough to reach nearly across the bed. Inside, can be kept a couple of changes of underclothing, an extra thick shirt or vest and a sufficiency of handkerchiefs, socks [illegible], besides a toilet case. In the event of a sudden march, in light marching order, this can be rolled up in the blanket bundle, to which it gives shape and an officer has the satisfaction of knowing his baggage is in *one* bundle, light and easy to pack or unpack. A small hair pillow, with colored chintz case, is no great addition to weight and is a decided augmentation to one's comfort.

Blankets should be dark-colored, large in size, and of best fabric. A good comforter is better perhaps, but I cannot speak from my own knowledge.*

A robe of wolf, coyote, bear or beaver skin *lined*, is of much use.

An officer should finally supply himself with canvas covering to enwrap his bedding and good long leather straps for buckling it up. His outfit will now consist of:

---

* After careful trial, I strongly recommend cotton comforters and buffalo robes as best bedding for winter campaigning in Wyo. and Montana.

One canvass [sic] wrapper,
One pair heavy blankets, best
One comforter (best)
One pair Buffalo robes
One large wolf or beaver robe.
One *rollable* mattress.
One pillow.
One Canvass [sic] pillow-valise.
One India-rubber poncho, large.
With the above, any temperature almost may be defied.

If tentage should be brought along, one "A" tent ought to do for three persons. The poles should be cut and bolted, to admit of the whole affair being done up in the smallest compass for carriage on pack-mules.

General Crook and myself remained back at Fetterman for the day, awaiting the mail which came in from Medicine Bow, on the U.P.R.R.[1] about 10 a.m. Busy all morning replying to various communications, including some from home and from my friends Egan, Clarke (2d Cav.) Byrne (12th Inf.) Thomas and Price, 5th Cavl & Surgeon Dennis.

Gen. Crook was notified by telegraph from Red Cloud ([via] Laramie.) That some three hundred lodges of Northern Indians had arrived at that point;[2] also that the subsistence supplies of the Indian Bureau are almost exhausted and will not last many days and that no replenishment can be expected until Congress shall make the necessary appropriation.

Weather delightful, Sky serene, temperature about 30° F. No winds.

Mar. 2d. General Crook escorted by a detachment of Co. "F", 3d Cavalry, under command of Capt. Alex. Moore, 3d Cav. marched across the country to the 2d camp of the Expedition.[3] The distance, though my estimate differs from those of other officers, is about 33 miles, and the line of march presented no features of interest in a country, sandy, barren and treeless; not even the feeble merit of poor grazing can be asserted in favor of this wretched tract; some few bluffs, of no great altitude, scattered to Right, to left and every-

1. Union Pacific Railroad.
2. As a general rule, a Lakota lodge averaged about seven persons, and a Northern Cheyenne lodge, eight. Therefore three hundred lodges would have been about 2,100 to 2,400 people. Gray, *Centennial Campaign*, 313.
3. Moore had already earned Crook's wrath by botching a movement against Apaches in Arizona in 1871. He would do far worse on this campaign. Robinson, *General Crook*, 110.

where, by giving an undulatious contour to the soil, relieve in part
the monotony of the aspect; of which I can find not one word further to say.

Fifteen miles out from Fetterman, we came to Sage Creek, a petty
stream one half mud, the other half alkali. Twenty-nine miles brought
us to Brown's Springs at the head of the South Cheyenne, which we
followed down for some three or four miles untill we came to Camp
No. 2, where we found our comrades, snugly in tents.

During the course of the night, a small band of Sioux Indians, boldly
entered our camp, wounded the beef-herder and stampeded the
forty-five head of cattle upon which we had placed our main depen-
dence for fresh meat during our absence. Captain Moore and Lieut.
Reynolds of the 3d Cavalry were detailed to follow the missing herd
which they did for six miles, until assured that it had returned all
the way to Fetterman and that it had not fallen into the hands of
the enemy. The herder, altho' shot with a rifle bullet through the
lungs did not appear to be in a precarious condition and was carried along with us in an ambulance. He says that two Indians approached him, when he shouted to alarm camp, but before assistance could be rendered they had inflicted the wound and decamped.
This incident had an excellent effect upon officers and men by im-
pressing upon all hands the need of unceasing vigilance if we would
not have exertions come to naught.

March 3d. Moved out in advance of the Main Body with Colonel
Stanton's detachment of scouts—as sweet a lot of cutthroats as ever
scuttled a ship. Half-Breeds, Squaw-men, bounty-jumpers, thieves
and desperadoes of different grades from the various Indian Agencies composed the outfit. I do not mean to reflect upon Colonel
Stanton for the personnel of his corps d'elite, most of which was
recruited before his assignment to its command, and besides some
of these, the minority it is true, but a respectable minority, were
men of a high type of character, of great previous experience and
likely to come of inestimable use in any sudden emergency.

Among them might be mentioned Ben Clarke, Frank Grouard,
Louis Richaud and others, names unknown.

Ben Clarke has been on many scouts and campaigns against the
hostile Indians of Texas, Indian Territory, Kansas and Colorado,
attracting the favorable attention of such distinguished officers as
General Sheridan. He is not acquainted with the Big Horn country,

displayed in looking after the train betokened the discipline of veteran soldiery.

Indications of the close proximity of hostile Indians continued all day. Lodge pole trails were about as numerous as yesterday and pony tracks approaching to and receding from our camp of last night proved our foe were watching our movements with zealous interest. About six or seven miles out discerned two young bucks mounted on fleet ponies who awaited until the head of our column had approached within one thousand yards when they scampered rapidly over the hills and were soon lost to sight. Yesterday afternoon a signal smoke was observed on the apex of a high hill to our front, and in consequent of all these signs our movements have been very circumspect, but very rapid.

General Crook will not allow any pursuit of these Indian videttes; to catch them would break down at least (20) of our animals and result in no good. And thereby letting them fancy from our cautiousness we are in fear of them, they will become emboldened to approach more closely and even in large bands, perhaps to make an attack upon us.

General Crook's plan of operations is now pretty well established. From this point, a small party of picked scouts, mounted on Indian ponies, is to set out by tonight's moon and push down the Powder river as far as they reasonably dare. Being mounted on Indian ponies and few in number, their tracks will not excite suspicion from any strolling parties of Sioux or Cheyennes now in this vicinity. Within three days they ought to be able to be able to [sic] thoroughly prospect the Powder River Valley down below the mouth of the Crazy Woman. If the hostile Indians are found in force our men will have to conceal themselves until our advance; but it is more than likely they will be fortunate enough to seize a few families living on the outskirts of some of the villages and escape with them to the appointed rendezvous. From these captives much valuable information can be extracted and the General's plans changed or persisted in according to circumstances.

Fifteen days' rations are to be packed to-night with the mule-train. To-morrow, we start for the Crazy Woman's Fork of the Powder river, going into camp at its intersection of the old Montana road. There we are to remain at that camp all to-morrow night and all day the 7th. The night of the 7th., our wagons will be left in camp under care of the Infantry, while the mounted forces move down the Crazy Woman to its junction with the Powder or until meeting the scouts coming back from their reconnaisance.

Every one in the command evinces a commendable eagerness to encounter the enemy and a confidence of success which is half the victory. If we can find the Indians there will be another Black Kettle affair to impress upon them the folly of waging war upon the whites.[4] If we do not have success in finding them there an all summer's campaign will have to be inaugurated to break the back-bone of avowed hostility and squelch the covertly ill-disposed on the Reservations who might seek to foment trouble when the Government comes to carry out its determination to remove all the Indians to the Missouri river, in order that the country East of the Big Horn Mountains may become available for settlement.[5]

One exception must be made when speaking of the good spirits of all the expedition—the exception I am sorry to say is our colored cook, Jeff,[6] whose culinary efforts have earned a praise which cannot be shared by his patriotism or valor. What fear nature first placed in his breast has been greatly developed under the arduous instruction of Col. Stanton and other friends of the freedmen, along with us: at this time, the very name of an Indian stops the circulation of his blood and at night his terror is almost laughable. The stories told him are frightful enough, but lack the element of probability and veracity. Of him, more hereafter.

Made a march to-day of 15 miles. Storm dissipated as we were making camp and before night the sky had resumed its former pleasing serenity: the temperature, however, by its coldness, showed traces of the storm.

Scarcely had the sun disappeared behind the lofty buttresses of the Big Horn Mountains when pickets were posted about 300 yards in

4. By the time Bourke wrote this, there had been two "affairs" involving the Cheyenne peace chief Black Kettle. The first was at Sand Creek, Colorado, on November 28, 1864, when a group of Colorado territorial volunteers, whose hundred-day enlistments were about to expire without having seen any action, attacked Black Kettle's village. Although the Indians were under a government amnesty and Black Kettle had raised the U.S. flag above his lodge, more than a hundred Indians were killed, the majority of whom were women and children. Black Kettle himself escaped. The second incident occurred in southwestern Oklahoma on November 27, 1868, one day short of four years after Sand Creek. On that occasion, troops of the Seventh U.S. Cavalry, under Lt. Col. George Armstrong Custer, attacked a chain of Indian villages along the Washita River as the Indians slept in the early morning. This time, Black Kettle was killed. See Hoig, *The Battle of the Washita.*

5. This country had been guaranteed to the Indians under the Fort Laramie Treaty.

6. Jefferson Clark.

front of camp to detect the approach of any prowling Indians and frustrate their attempts to steal stock. Captain Coates, 4th Infantry, had just left his men in position when they discovered a small party of Indians stealthily creeping up through the grove of cottonwood trees near our camp. Fire was at once opened by our men and returned by the enemy, whose plan was then comprehensible. The little party referred to was to make an entrance, if possible, into our bivouac from the Fort Reno [i.e., north] side and by shouting, shaking buffalo robes and shooting, cause a stampede among our mules and horses. With many hundreds of animals wild with terror rushing through and over our tents and picket lines, it would require every exertion to save our own lives, or at most catch a few horses and mules. In the confusion the bold intruders could easily escape to their confederates posted on the other side of the camp, whose duty it would be to seize upon the herd and decamp, leaving us in the middle of a terrible desert, without an animal to bring us back to Fort Fetterman.

Such in general terms was the plan sought to be pursued by the small gang of Indians who had dogged our footsteps all day, and its complete defeat is worthy of especial praise as evincing the vigilance of our videttes and the care taken in tying up our animals at night instead of letting them run loose around the camp.

Finding their scheme a failure, the Indians adopted a vexatious kind of tactics and for some thirty or forty minutes kept up a brisk fusillade upon our campfires which had not yet been extinguished. Their shots came with provoking deliberation and accuracy; our men were soon in line but did not answer the fire of the enemy as their position could only be ascertained by the flash of their rifles. Nevertheless some occasional shots were fired where the foe exhibited rather too much boldness. Our fires were at once put out, but the enemy having obtained range, maintained their fusillade for some little time longer.

Considering it was the first time many of the command had ever been exposed to an attack (the majority being recruits, many of them as yet imperfectly drilled.) the coolness and precision with which they obeyed orders were remarkable. Only one of our men, Corporal Slavey, of Major Coates' Company,[7] 4th. Infantry, was wounded, (slightly in the cheek.) but many close calls were made.

7. Bourke is now using Coates' Union Army brevet.

After remaining under arms about half an hour our line was withdrawn, leaving strong picket posts at suitable points about 300 yards to our front.

These little night attacks are excellent things and serve to turn the raw recruit into a veteran with great celerity. They impress upon the mind of young soldiers the necessity and value of the discipline and subordination they so frequently ignore and also make them acquainted with each other's merits in moments of trial and danger.

The best school of instruction is the school of war, where officers not seldom find they have as much to learn as the men they command.

The party of picked scouts sent out this evening, had advanced along the road five or six miles when a halt was made to consider fully what course they should pursue, as well as to give their animals a few moments' rest.

Happening to look back, one of them discovered the light of the rifles and shrewdly surmised that some of the Indians were engaged in an attack upon our camp. It was then decided best to return as the Sioux might in following after come upon their trail and perhaps render their expedition abortive. And again, they had some hopes of getting in rear of those who were annoying us and killing a few of them. When the scouts had re-entered camp, (somewhere near midnight.) General Crook expressed his satisfaction with their behavior. In such expeditions as they were engaged in, all depends upon the secrecy attending the actions of those engaged; their business is to bring in information without arousing the suspicions of the enemy.

The night passed quietly. Before reveille, the line of videttes was again established, but no sound of hostility disturbed the slumbers of those in camp.

I was much amused by the coolness and imperturbability of General Crook, who had retired to rest shortly before the firing began; he seemed to divine the ideas and position of the Sioux from the very moment the first shot was fired, and explained to me all they would do and all they could do: after inquiring how General Reynolds had posted our videttes; with which he was entirely satisfied, he turned over and went to sleep. In all relating to what is called Indian warfare I am each day, more and more convinced General

Crook is a complete master; Those officers and men who knew him in California, Oregon, Washington Territory, Nevada and Arizona, expect equally great things from him in the Department of the Platte and their confidence is shared by those who have only made his acquaintance during the past year. Would to God that the wretched imbecility and vacillation of the Government's management of Indian affairs in this part of the country may now terminate.

Mar. 6th. Everybody awoke at a very early hour. Our cook, Jeff, had not entirely recovered from the fright last night's events had occasioned him and for that reason we were willing to accept in patience and with charitable good will many shortcomings in the culinary arrangements of the morning. To our surprise, however, our generosity had no occasion to manifest itself; in truth, the breakfast to-day excelled any we had seated ourselves to on the whole trip. The cold, bracing air, sweeping down from the mountains exhilarated us wonderfully and was eagerly used as an excuse for the ravenous appetites which consumed fabulous quantities of biscuits, butter, meat, potatoes, eggs and stewed dried apples, washed down by copious draughts of excellent, hot and strong, coffee. We soon crossed the ice and water of the Powder river, a stream unworthy of much consideration. Observed the banks were composed of an argillaceous sand, very adhesive and very quagmiring in rainy weather. The bed of the stream is mainly quicksand and has the reputation of impassability, except at the ford which we used. Upon climbing the opposite bank our advance entered the ruins of old Fort Reno. Nothing now remains but a little of the stockade formerly surrounding the post, part of the bake-oven, the chimneys of the trader's store and one or two of those belonging to the officers quarters. The whole aspect is most dreary, the face of the country grassless, and destitute of any redeeming feature. Yet in this miserable spot, a garrison of the U.S. Army, maintained a place for two years (1866 and 1867.) to protect, in conjunction with Fort Kearny[8] 61 miles to the West near the head-waters of the Tongue river and Fort C.F. Smith, at the big bend of the Big Horn river, the overland line of travel to Montana, then a most promising field of adventurous gold hunters. The "Fetterman" and "Fort Kearney" massacre, as it is indifferently entitled, proved the rancor of the Sioux and the

---

8. In all cases, Bourke is referring to Fort Phil Kearny, Wyoming, rather than Fort Kearny, Nebraska.

treaty of Fort Laramie, made in the winter of '67 and '68, yielding up to hostile Indians an immense belt of country, abandoning the most practicable route to a new and promising territory and dismantling all military posts north of the North Platte river was a striking illustration of the amount of tomfoolery that can be transacted under the name of a treaty. Every concession demanded by the Indians was granted by our Govt. [N]ot one concession was made by the red-skins unless we include promises, thin and fleeting as air, in such a category. Richelieu[9] is credited with the axiom— "the pen is mightier than the sword"—and the axiom in the main is true, but much depends on who holds the sword and who guides the pen. The general interpretation of this apothegm would appear to falsely argue that any red-headed, scrofulous lawyer's clerk slinging ink over legal cap paper was a more dextrous diplomat than the General whose armies were to save the destinies of their country. This is not so. History shows that the most skilled in statecraft have been the minds that had been trained in the rough lessons of the skirmish and bivouac.

From the crest of the bluffs overlooking the Powder, a magnificent view was obtained of the Big Horn range. Piercing far above the superincumbent clouds, the snow-capped emminences seemed so many sentinels guarding the country at their base.

Heavy belts of black pine and juniper brought into bold contrast the glaring white of the summits and marked more plainly the line of separation from the yellow grassy plains beneath. Prominent foothills, themselves mountains of great elevation, extended out as flying buttresses from the main crest. The sky of faultless blue revealed in perfection the rugged profile while the effect of light and shade was most striking. Here the sun's rays lit upon some bold peak, the eye rested with pleasure, but sated with such beauties turned with satisfaction to the relief afforded in the gloom of the deep gorges and cañons, through which noble little streams find their way to the currents of the Big Horn, Powder, Tongue and Rosebud.

The altitude of the highest peaks is, I have been informed, 13.500 feet.

All day long we pursued our way over a very good road, without rocks or breaks to impede the progress of the trains.

---

9. Armand Jean du Plessis, Cardinal Duke of Richelieu, chief minister of France in the early seventeenth century.

The immediate scenery was most uninviting, no grass, except at rare intervals & no grass within rifle-shot. . .Two or three of our guides went off on each flank and by afternoon were successful in bringing down three nice fat antelope which will help to vary the bill of fare most pleasantly.

The temperature at noon was almost like summer, making our heavy winter-clothing oppressive; in the shade, it was quite chilly and on the banks of the Crazy Woman's Fork, which we descended to between 3 and 4 P.M., the ice was found thick enough to bear the weight of a horse and his rider. Here we made Camp, finding the first really good water since leaving Fetterman. For fuel, we had plenty of dry cottonwood, but there was no grass for our animals which had to get along as best they could on the scanty ration of forage (grain.) issued from the wagon-train. Distance to-day has been about 25 miles. A vein of an apparently good quality of lignite protruded from the banks of the stream immediately in front of our camp, but did not have time to examine it before night came on. Coal is probably abundant in this section of Wyoming: since starting, have noticed its outcroppings in several placers on the South Cheyenne and Wind Rivers.

Indian signal smokes were to be seen all day away off on our Right, and once or twice our guides noticed signals flashed across country. These signals are made by the reflection of the sun from the small round looking glasses, Indians wear about their necks, and are flashed according to some pre-arranged system, which I have not yet been able to learn.

A great column of dust to our Left and rear was seen, and was undoubtedly made by a village of Sioux or Cheyennes moving down Powder river to get out of danger.

Fresh buffalo tracks seen on road and the animal itself seen in the distance by one of the guides.

All the officers connected with the Expedition were summoned to General Crook's tent at sun-down to receive their final instructions. In a few clear, well-considered sentences, General Crook enunciated his ideas upon the very important topic of baggage. He directed that officers should examine the bundles made up by their men for carriage by the pack-mules and see that each has one buffalo-robe, or two blankets and no more. The clothing upon their backs was all that should be carried. No tentage to be allowed, but every man might take a piece of shelter tent and every two officers, one tent fly. Officers to be governed in regard to clothing and bedding by the same rules as the men.

No messing arrangements to be taken along for officers: company officers to mess with their companies and those of the staff or unattended to eat with the pack-trains. Rations for 15 days, to consist of hard-bread, half-bacon, coffee and sugar. Each officer to be provided with one tin cup and one tin plate.

One hundred rounds of ammunition to be carried on the person and an equal amount to go with the pack-train.

Upon the suggestion of General Reynolds, it was decided to send the Infantry companies with the wagon-train back to Reno. They will attract the attention of the enemy and help to bewilder them in regard to our movements, which must be inexplicable to the Sioux, as we have made no pursuit of them when seen in our front, and at same time our precautions against surprise and stampeding are unusually stringent.

The General's instructions were received with the careful attention that remarks of such an astute Indian campaigner are entitled to, and I am very much mistaken if he find[s] any cause of complaint for want of enthusiasm or zeal against a single officer of the command during the trip.

I was directed to act as Engineer Officer, a thankless position, as with night-marching it is almost an impossibility to take topographical notes in an enemy's country.

During the night, no attack was made, but a few shots were fired, as it afterwards turned out, against one of our own men, who ventured too near the line of videttes.

Chapter 12

❖

❖

❖

❖

❖

The Soldier's Routine

March 7th. Day Blustering.

Remained in Camp all day, busy in writing up notes and making the necessary preparations for our movement. At night, about 7 O'clock, by the light of a very fine three quarters moon, commenced our march, which lay to the West for two miles and then moved towards the North star for the remainder of the distance which summed up thirty-five miles.

At first the country had the undulating contour of that near old Fort Reno, already visited, but soon the prairie swells were superseded by bluffs of bolder and bolder character until as we came to the summit of the divide where Clear Fork heads we found ourselves in a region deserving the title mountainous. In the bright light of the moon and stars, our little column of cavalry wound its way up the steep hill-side like an enormous snake whose scales were glittering revolvers and carbines. The view was certainly very exhilarating backed as it was by the majestic landscape of moonlight on the big [*sic*] Horn Mountains.

Cynthia's silvery beams never lit up a mass of mountain crests more worthy of commemoration upon the artist's canvas. Above the frozen summit of Cloud Peak, the evening star, cast its declining rays.

Other prominences rivalling in altitude this one boldly thrust themselves out against the midnight sky. Exclamations of admiration and surprise were entoned from the most stolid as our column made its way rapidly from bluff to bluff, pausing at times long enough to give every one an opportunity to study some of nature's noble handiwork.

Finally, even the gorgeous vistas I have so feebly attempted to portray failed to assuage the cold and pain in our limbs or to drive away the drowsiness Sleep was placing upon our exhausted eyelids. With no small degree of satisfaction we noticed the signal which at five O'clock in the morning bade us make camp on the Clear Fork of Powder River.

The site was deary enough; scarcely any timber in sight, plenty of water but frozen solid, and only a bare picking of grass for our tired animals. However, what we most needed was sleep and that we sought as soon as horses had ben unsaddled and mules unpacked. Wrapped up in our heavy overcoats and furs, we threw ourselves on the bleak and frozen ground and were deep in slumber.

It will give a faint idea of the climatic vicissitudes to which campaigning exposes a soldier in Northern Wyoming when I say that after going to sleep under the bright, calm and cheerful moonlight of this morning, we were awakened about 8 O'clock by a bitter, pelting storm of snow which blew in our teeth whichever way we turned and almost extinguished the petty fires near which our cooks were trying to arrange our breakfasts, if we can dignify by such a lofty title the frozen bacon, frozen beans and frozen coffee which constituted the repast. It is no part of a soldier's business to repine, but if there are circumstances to justify complaint, they are the absence of warmth and good food after a wearisome night march and during the prevalence of a cold winter storm.

After breakfast, General Crook moved the command down Clear Fork, five or six miles in a North North West direction to a pleasant cove, where we remained all this day.

(March 8th, 1876.) Our situation was not enviable; it is true, we experienced nothing we could call privation or hardship, but we had to endure much positive discomfort. The storm continued all day, the wind blowing with keenness and at intervals with much power. As we were without tents, we had nothing to do but grin and bear it; some officers stretched blankets to the branches of trees, others found a questionable shelter under the bluffs, one or two constructed non-descript habitations of twigs and grass, while Genl Crook and Col. Stanton seized upon the abandoned den of a family of beavers which sudden change in the bed of the stream had deprived of their home.

To obtain water, holes of suitable dimensions were cut in the ice, here found to be eighteen inches thick, clear in color and vitreous in texture.

We hugged the fires as closely as we dared, ashes and cinders with every turn of the breeze being cast into our faces. The narrow thread of the stream, with its opaque and glassy surface of ice covered with snow, here drifted into little masses, here again carried away before the gale, looked the picture of all that could be imagined cheerless and dreary. We tried hard to find some pleasure in watching the troubles of our fellow-soldiers, obliged for any reason to attempt a crossing of the treacherous surface the ice presented[.] Commencing with an air of boldness and confidence, with some even of indifference, a few steps forward would generally serve to intimidate the unfortunate wayfarer, doubly timid now that he found himself the butt of our gibes and jeers. Now one foot slips, now another, but still he struggles manfully on and has almost gained the opposite bank when—slap! bang! both feet go from under him and a dent in the solid ice commemorates his inglorious fall. In this way, we tried to dispel the weariness of the day. Every one welcomed the advent of night which enabled us to seek such rest as we could find and, clad, as last night, in the garments of the day, officers and men, wrapped up in blankets from the pack-train, found rest but not much repose. Our men shared with their animals their own scanty allowance of blankets, as the bad weather and poor rations had made our animals look gaunt and travel-worn.

Snowed all night.

March 9th. In the teeth of a blustering wind and very disagreeable snow, pushed this morning in a course, bearing nearly due North, across high mountain ridge, probably a spur of what is laid down on the maps as Panther Mountains, to a little affluent of Tongue River, called by our guides Prairie Dog creek. On the way about five miles out from last night's camp crossed the last tributary of Powder river, the Big Piney, a small stream upon which old fort Phil. Kearney was situated.

The snow continued all day long and the bitter North wind blowing in our faces made us imagine old Boreas to be in league with Sitting Bull, to prevent our occupancy of the country: Moustaches and beard coated with pendent icicles several inches long and bodies swathed in raiment of furs and hides made this expedition of Cavalry look like a long column of Santa Clauses on their way to the Polar regions to lay in a new supply of Christmas gifts.

Saw fresh buffalo manure, also very recent Indian signs. Scouts were pushed ahead to scan the country, while the command was put in camp in a secluded ravine which besides affording a sufficiency of cold, sweet water, cottonwood fuel and good grass, shielded us from the observation of roving Indians, altho' with bad weather as now prevails it is improbable that very many Indians are unnecessarily braving the inclemencies of the winter.

This afternoon, the thermometer indicated -6° F. All night long the snow continued, but our men awakened in the morning very cheerful and our animals in very good condition. Much better than we had any right to expect. Some protection was afforded them by the sides of the ravine where the wind had not as great a sweep as it had on the more open ground of yesterday's camp.

March 10th snowed all day. Our sleep last night was very comfortable in spite of wind and snow. Had a good breakfast this morning or to speak more distinctly had a breakfast whose every dish was seasoned by a keen appetite. Hard tack, bacon, coffee, beans and stewed apples disappeared in quantities comprehensible only to persons who have campaigned with soldiers and mule-drivers in the mountains in winter.

While standing by the cook-fire, heard one of our recruits, an Italian,[1] soliloquising thus: "Och, then, boi Jaysus, shure foi didn't Oi inlist in to Fut. Bee Mee sowl, they hev nothing to do but march with the wagons and mar-r-rch back home again. Shure the cavalry dus be mar-r-rching all the toime! They takes uz across the mountins all noint, in a sthar-rum of sch-now, widout a boite of gr-r-rub, bee God, and this, General Crook, will say, "[']now bois make yerssilves as comfartibble as yiz can—Throw yirsilves down on yer picket-pins[2] for a math-thrass and cover yirsilves wid yir lar-rhiat roapes[']."

1. Bourke is being facetious; the bulk of the foreign contingent was Irish, as this trooper obviously was.
2. The picket pin was a long metal stake driven into the ground. The horse was tethered by a sixteen-foot lariat, giving it freedom of movement while keeping it from wandering.

The poor fellow had such good grounds for complaint that I could only laugh at his lamentations and move to one side.

After a twenty-two mile march down Prairie Dog Creek to a point near its junction with Tongue river, (line of direction nearly due North all day.) made a good camp with an abundance of the three great essentials to a soldier's comfort,—wood, water and grass. Camp well screened from observation. Prairie Dog creek, at first flows down a rather narrow gorge which soon widens into a flat valley, full of the borrows of the little animals from which it takes its name. During a temporary lull in the storm, these could be seen running around in the snow to and from their holes and marking the snow in every direction with their tracks. This dispels any idea I used to have that these little creatures hybernated.

Ground was extremely slippery and icy to-day, men and horses slipping and falling constantly, especially in crossing the abrupt arroyos cutting across the trail every two or three hundred yards. Fortunately, only one man, a corporal in: Lieut. W.W. Robinson's, company, "D", 3d Cav. was hurt, but he so seriously that it is feared he will not recover. His horse slipped down and fell upon him, causing great injury to the spine or kidneys. Doctor had a trail-stretcher made to carry him, dragged behind a mule, the most comfortable arrangement that could be devised.

Our guides returned this evening and reported having come across a very recently deserted Indian village of sixty "tepis", or lodges, and every indication of a long habitancy. The Indians belonging thereto had plenty of buffalo and deer or elk meat, some of which they left behind upon their departure. A young puppy, strangled to death, was found suspended to a tree by a piece of rope. This is one of the greatest delicacies of a Sioux feast—choked pup—and its abandonment betokens that these savages have been apprised of our coming and left in haste.

Guides brought us in some fine venison—a good dish, roasted in hot ashes.

Night extremely cold. Moon shining at intervals and again yielding to the snow storm.

March 11th (Saturday.) Thermometer at 8 O'clock this morning showed between -22° F and -39° F. (N.B.[)] Our instrument is not graduated below -22° F, and the mercury had shrunk low down into bulb, altho' it did not congeal. Wind ceased to-day and snow gradually gave way, leaving cloudy sky.

Marched North down Tongue river, between 8 and 9 miles, crossing stream 5 or 6 times. This is a fine stream between 30 and 40 yards wide, banks thickly fringed with box-elder, cottonwood, ash and willow. Gramma grass abundant, along foot-hills. This was finest camp of the expedition.

This morning shone out bright and clear, frost glistening like diamonds on the grass and snow. Our poor horses were coated with a white covering of ice and snow.

Our guides explored as far West as the Rosebud river, but no Indian signs were to be seen to-day.

March 12th Last night, the sky cleared off, giving us a fine moonlight but letting the mercury run down in the bulb so low that it has been difficult to decide whether it congealed or not. Fortunately, no one was frozen and the casualties from cold up to date amount to a frosted ear and finger, but cases very slight.

Doctor Munn, our Surgeon, has been very vigilant and is well supplied with all the materia medica recommend[ed] for the treatment of frozen limbs. The exemption of the command from frost-bite is not more remarkable than the scarcity of complaints of the pneumonitic type, there is not an instance of pneumonia, influenza or even bad cold in the whole camp. We must ascribe this in part to the precautions taken by all concerned, but with this qualification, great as it may be, the claims of the climate of Montana to be looked to as a sanitarium for invalids afflicted with lung disorders not of an aggravated nature and not too deeply seated, cannot be too highly extolled.

One of our outlying pickets fired at another last night, mistaking him for an Indian, but did not hit him.

During the existing Hyperborean temperature, the genial good humor and cheerfulness of the command are deserving of honorable mention: nothing tries the spirit and temper of the old veteran, not to mention the young recruit as does campaigning in despite of unusual climatic vicissitudes, at a time when no trace of the enemy can be seen. To march into battle with banners flying, drums beating and the pulse beating high with the promptings of honorable ambition and enthusiasm in unison with the roar of artillery, does not call for half the nerve and determination that must be daily exercised to pursue mile after mile in such terrible weather, over asporous mountains[3] and through unknown cañons, a foe whose habits of warfare are repugnant to every principle of humanity and whose presence can be determined solely by the flash of the rifle which lays some poor sentry low or the whoop and yell that stampede our stock from their grazing grounds.

The life of a soldier in time of war has scarcely a compensating feature; but he ordinarily expects palatable food wherever obtainable and good warm quarters during the winter season. In campaigning against Indians, if anxious to gain success, he must throw to one side every idea of good food and comfortable lodgings, & make up his mind to undergo with alacrity privations from which other soldiers would shrink back dismayed. His sole object should be to strike the enemy and strike him hard and this accomplished no smaller gains should compensate him. With all these disadvantages the system of Indian warfare is a grand school for the cavalrymen of the future, teaching them fortitude, endurance, vigilance, self-reliance and dexterity, besides that instruction in handling, marching, feeding and fighting troops no school can impart in text books.

This is the way in which I have tried to moralize over our marches and their accompanying cheerless meals and other discomforts; the attempt is not on every occasion as successful as I should wish, notably at breakfast time which burlesque upon a good square meal occurs with the first ray of day-light. Our cook must first chop with an axe the bacon which over night has frozen solid as marble: then if he has made any soft bread, i.e. flour bread baked in a frying pan, he has to place that in front of a strong fire for a few minutes to thaw it so it can be eaten. Breakfast is apt to be no meal at all unless the eater display great adroitness and agility. First, the cook spreads down a long piece of canvass for a table-cloth arranging upon it tin cups, plates, knives and forks in proportion to the number in the mess. A huge mess-pan of boiled or baked beans, flanked by pepper and salt bottles and several platters of hard tack, or if the cook has had time to make it, soft bread baked in a frying pan, is placed upon the canvass, followed by hot coffee, crisply fried bacon, and generally, stewed dried apples.

To the inspiring war cries of "Grub pile", "Yar's yer has", "Suppah-h" &c. &c. The wolfy appetites of the packers press forward to

---

3. Indicating porosity, in that the mountains had cracks, fissures, and other openings through which water could flow.

the festive board. Old hands, experienced old seeds who know what cold weather is now seize their plates and give them a twirl or two in front of the fire: in like manner, knives, forks and spoons are heated* and the work of carnage commences. This is not the proper place to specify the quantities of solid foods consumed at each meal by a hard-working packer; the amount would almost certainly do a small family for a day.

The conversation is not of a pronouncedly intellectual type, yet it should not be presumed packers, as a class, are ignorant. On the contrary, they are generally sharp observers, men who have accumulated considerable experience of a peculiar kind it is true, during their roaming over the Western country. They are proverbially hospitable, good-natured and hard-workers. Their habits are not bad and only a few of those I have known have been heavy drinkers.

Our march to-day, 7 hours in duration, brought us 20 miles down the Tongue river which we crossed eighteen times. Its valley gradually narrowed down to a little gorge bordered by bluffs of red and yellow sandstone, between 150 and 200 feet high, in some places much higher, well fringed with scrub pine and juniper and having coal measures, of a quality we did not determine definitely, cropping out in several points along trail.

We now found ourselves well across the Southern boundary of Montana, in a region well grassed with gramma and the black sage, a plant almost as nutritious as oats. It is hard to say if much of the land is arable, but I should answer in the affirmative for the river bottoms.

Our scouts crossed over to the Rosebud where they saw no Indians signs but killed an old buffalo bull, whose meat was brought to camp and roasted in the ashes. Another buffalo was killed at head of column: an enormous old fellow, whose flesh though very tough was eaten thankfully.

Camp well supplied with wood, water and grass all of best quality.

Our hopes of being able to catch trout in this river have not yet been realized: the fish will not bite in this cold weather.

March 13th (Morning[)] Last night was very warm in comparison with its immediate predecessor. Growing careless about covering, we were reminded by rheumatic twinges in the back and shoulders

---

* Forks and spoons heated in ashes to keep them from freezing skin of the lips and tongue.

that our early youth and vigor no longer remained with us. This morning sky was overcast with snow-clouds with all the premonitions of a snow-storm, but notwithstanding they lowered over us all day we have had no storm. It is hard to predict the weather in this country. We go to bed with a bright moon beaming over us and awaken in the midst of a violent snow-storm or if we retire to rest with a storm blowing we are apt to find the sun shining upon our breakfast.

We are beginning to feel disappointed in not finding Indians. Our rations are now about one half out and we may be obliged to return unsuccessful. Were there a post at the mouth of the Big Horn, the question of Sioux subjugation would be much simplified. Ink frozen hard on this trip. About this time, to my great annoyance, the little bottle of ink, brought along with so much care from Omaha, burst from the freezing of its contents; hence the remainder of these notes will be taken in pencil. Our march to-day was twelve and three eighths miles through a country not in any essential different from the other parts of the Tongue river valley. The weather all day has been decidedly unsatisfactory, but we comfort ourselves as much as we can by reflecting the Sioux must suffer exactly as we, perhaps worse and that they cannot know as accurately of our whereabouts as they would in finer weather.

Passed an affluent coming in on the Right: took it to be Hang woman creek, a mule track crossed our trail about ten miles out from camp. General Crook had it followed up for a short distance when our guides returned with a fine animal, a young mule, an estray from an Indian village in close proximity. Saw several Indian graves this morning. The corpse is not interred in the ground, as with other nations, but wrapped in the cerements of death and then firmly fastened to the stout branches of some lofty tree. After decomposition has done its work with the flesh, the bones are incinerated.* If my memory deceive me not, Herodotus mentions a similar custom as prevalent among the ancient Scythians.

Noticed a number of deserted Indian villages, the uprights supporting the cross-pieces upon which these savages dry their winter's supply of buffalo meat were still standing; also the corrals where their ponies had been enclosed. It was remarkable to observe the quantities of cottonwood timber they had felled to the ground for

---

* This is a mistake.

no other purpose than to feed their stock upon the bark of the tender young shoots and branches.

Coal was again seen near trail to-day, and the bluffs as yet are mainly ferriginous [sic] sandstone. The timber on the Tongue river is unrivalled in size. Dozens of cottonwood trees can been seen on each march of four feet, five feet and six in diameter.

Another buffalo shot to-day and the meat is now served up on every mess canvass. We find it tough, fibrous and lean, but an excellent substitute for no meat at all.

Guides sent in advance again to-day with instructions to scout down to the Yellowstone river and rejoin us in two days, farther downstream.

The weather has now moderated so much that little fear of any one freezing to death is felt; the present temperature (20° F.) Twenty degrees above zero would be considered cold in any civilized community when taken in conjunction with a deep wind and disagreeable snow; to us, accustomed to much more rigorous temperatures, there seems to be nothing to complain of.

Sleeping on the cold ground without tent has been reduced to a science by General Crook and a few others in the command who have given the subject considerable attention. The way they do [it] is this; having selected as sheltered a spot as can be found, they build upon it two or three moderate sized fires, the ashes from which being swept away, dry grass is spread to the depth of an inch or two over the surface and the blankets then unrolled. The warmth imparted by the heated ground is astonishing. To protect from the wind, saddles, overcoats, any kind of impediments in fact, are piled up in the desired direction, or twigs are stuck in the earth and a rough wattle-work made to support canvass or other suitable material.

We are gradually beginning to see that campaigning in this latitude can be made much more comfortable in winter than in spring when the early thaws having made the trails slippery, horses can with difficulty force their way and the men will find it impossible to keep their feet dry and warm, the great sine quo non [sic] for a healthy command.

Still, he errs greatly who supposes our animals have an easy time in winter. They do very well on level ground, dry or snow-covered; but the passage of every little gulch or piece of ground where ice may be looked for is a period of anxiety to every company commander and to every train-master.

In this respect, our mules average much better than our horses. Many a hearty laugh has been excited by seeing the caution and deliberation of their approach to the edge or crest of a ravine and then, having considered the situation, notice them fold their hind legs under themselves, stiffen their fore legs and slide to the bottom like a boy coasting down hill.

They do this with much agility and some grace. Only one accident has, up to present writing, happened. A mule broke his back descending an icy ravine leading down to Clear Fork of Powder River.

Not much time is now lost after getting into camp until everything is in what sailors call "ship shape". Companies take the positions assigned them by the Officer of the Day, mounted videttes are at once thrown out on the neighboring bluffs, horses are unsaddled and led to the grazing ground, mules are unpacked and follow after, wood and water are brought in great quantities for the cooks whose enormous pots of coffee and kettles of beans even now are exhaling a tempting aroma.

The afternoon meal is ready without appreciable delay; hunger gives place to satiety and for a brief interval we gather around the fires to narrate the occurrences of the march or exchange the song and story.

Well has the Spaniard observed
    "Barriga llena",
    "Corazon contento",
that is "A full belly,
    "Makes contented heart."

The sky is becoming darker than usual, I was going to say the sun has set; but it is not correct to use such a term as the God of Day has not shown himself much to speak of this week.

Mules and horses are now brought back and fastened up inside of camp; sentinels and videttes are inspected, everything made sure, and we now retire to rest within the little square corral formed of the mules' aparejos and sleep undisturbed save by an occasional inquisitive animal walking over us or nibbling at our blankets for long forage.

Our packers, I have already spoken of; our pack master, Kloster, is an old, white-haired and white-bearded man, snugly wrapped up in an Ulster blouse, made of green blanket [material], fur cap and heavy boots. His beard is almost always smeared with tobacco juice and his kindly countenance marked by a pleasant smile.

Our cook is not much to brag of; he is a native of the town of Nieu Dieppe in Holland, but left his native country at so early an age he never imbibed those notions of cleanliness distinguishing the Hollanders above their neighbors and so very desirable in a culinary artist.[4] His professional attainments are limited to a very feeble and hazy parody upon the achievements of M. Soyer; a deficiency, the more to be regretted, because his constituency embraces some of the most appreciative and omnivorous appetites every chronicled. Justice forces me to say that, to the limit of his knowledge, our cook exerts himself conscientiously to satisfy the appetites and escape the criticism of his patrons. His boiled beans au naturel and his fricandean of old buffalo bull meat are unique in their way, but demand a most liberal seasoning with the sauce of appetite to make them palatable. The most captious would have to allow that our cook has the one great virtue of promptness, and with this concession to his virtues and abilities we can leave him to his fate.

While describing these members of our mess, it may not be amiss to allude in a few words to the personal appearance of General Crook, differing as it does from that of any other officer of high ranks I have ever seen in the U.S. Army. The general's boots are of the Government patterns, no[.] 7's; pantaloons of brown corduroy, badly burned at the ends, shirt of brown, heavy woolen; blouse an old army style; hat brown Kossuth of felt,[5] ventilated at top. An old Army overcoat, lined with red flannel, and provided with an enormous wolf-skin collar, completes his costume, except a leather belt of forty or fifty compartments for copper cartridges. This belt is held up, suspended by a couple of leather bands passing over the shoulders. His horse and saddle are alike good and with his rifle well cared for. The General, in size is about six feet even, weight one hundred and seventy pounds, built very spare and straight, limbs straight, long and sinewy: complexion, nervo-sanguine; hair,

4. Bourke does not explain when Jeff Clarke was replaced by the man from Dieppe.
5. A high crowned hat, generally with one side of the brim turned up and sporting a plume, made popular by the Hungarian resistance leader Kossuth Lajos in 1848, and adopted by U.S. officers because of its dashing appearance. An almost identical hat, called the Hardee, was issued to U.S. officers in the 1850s. Photographs of Crook, however, show that he apparently discarded the plume and wore the brim flat.

light-brown; cheeks, ruddy without being florid; features, delicately and firmly chiseled, eyes blue-gray; nose, a pronounced Roman, and quite large; mouth, mildly chiseled, but showing with the chin much resolution and tenacity of purpose. His general expression is placid, kind and good-humored. Unaffected and very accessible in his general demeanor, there is a latent "noli me tangere" look of dignity about him repelling undue familiarity. His powers of endurance are extraordinary and his fortitude remarkable. A graceful rider, a noted hunter, and a dead-shot, skilled in all the secrets of wood-craft and Indian warfare, having the prestige of complete success in every campaign hitherto undertaken, he is by all odds the worst foe the Sioux have ever yet had to meet.

On one occasion during our march, a small covey of pin tailed grouse flew across our path. General Crook with seven shots from his Army rifle laid six of them low; all, but one, were shot in the neck or head. This shooting was very good, considering the rapidity with which it had to be done and the fact that the General's hands were tired and numbed from riding in the cold.[6]

March 14th. Moved down Tongue River about nine or ten miles, camping opposite mouth of Pumpkin Creek where the scouts had agreed to meet us on their return.

Nothing unusual to report in the topographical features of the country. Weather unpleasant: dark gray clouds hanging over us all day and snow dropping in fitful gusts. Keen wind blowing in our faces from the North.

Bluffs along river banks much higher than they were yesterday; one or two of them as much as 750 feet above us: juniper and pine trees covering them pretty thickly.

A small band of four or five old buffalo bulls seen this morning and fired upon by our advances. General Crook badly wounded one under the fore-shoulder but the old bull escaped.

All along trail to-day, marks of recent Indian occupancy very frequent. Our train has now very little to carry and the mules press close upon the heels of the Cavalry companies.

---

6. This kind of shooting with a rifle or carbine is conceivable, depending on the choice of weapon and skill of the marksman. If Crook, indeed, used a military weapon with a solid slug, it almost had to be an old, seven-shot Spencer repeating carbine, because the Springfield that was standard issue at the time of this incident had to be reloaded after each shot. One can only imagine the effect on the grouse; the Spencer fired a .50-caliber bullet that would have all but blown away the head or neck.

Our camp to-night is on the Left bank of the Tongue river opposite mouth of Pumpkin creek; we have a bountiful supply of pellucid water, good grass and enough fuel to last us for months, thanks to the Sioux Indians who had a large village just below us where wood, dry and ready for use, can be found piled up by the dozens of cords. On the soft inner bark of the cottonwood trees, rude, obscene pictures have been scrawled by the young Indians in a number of places. In execution they are as feeble as in design they are disgusting.

Surrounding us is a forest of cottonwood trees many of which are at least six feet in diameter across the butt; the largest I have ever seen.

A human arm, belonging to an Indian, and still in a fair state of preservation, was picked up in the abandoned Indian village to-day; it has been amputated at the elbow-joint, two of the fingers had been shot off and (5) buckshot wounds were in it.

March 15th. Awakened this morning to be gladdened at the sight of a glorious sun-rise. Air was very keen and cold but there was no wind and the sky was cloudless.

Our breakfast this morning had an important addition in a grouse stew made from the birds General Crook shot on the march.

Remained all day in camp expecting return of our guides. Boiled a pot of corn with cottonwood ashes to make hominy for our supper. Thermometer at 7 O'clock this morning indicated (-10° F.); at 10.00 A.M. (24° F.) and at 3 P.M. (32° F.) Day remained bright and fair, comparatively. About 4 P.M. guides returned from their reconnaissance to our front; reported having found no villages and no Indians, but saw in their ride of 25 miles down the river that all the trails led across the hills to the Powder river. General Crook determined to remain here until morning and then march to the East by North to Otter Creek.

Some venison brought into camp by our guides who killed six deer—five white-tail and (1) black-tail.

Chapter 13

✦

✦

✦

✦

✦

The Powder River Fight

March 16th. Nothing eventful last night.

Slept very comfortably[.] Our animals enjoyed very superior graz-ing on the foot-hills overlooking camp. Breakfasted at 5 a.m. this morning under a clear bright sky filled with bright stars. Mercury standing at 7 a.m. at (-8° F.) Broke camp at 8 a.m., moving East-wardly, up valley of Pumpkin Creek, a little stream which from hasty inspection, I should say is finely adapted for agricultural and pasto-ral purposes. Fine grasses covered the lower hills, leaving the higher elevations to the possession of juniper and pine forests: country this morning reminded me somewhat of the Black Hills of Dacotah. After a march of 18 miles came down into valley of Otter Creek, a tributary of Tongue River.

Guides saw and pursued two mounted Indians who escaped. Gen-eral Crook halted command, made coffee, issued one day's rations to men and a feed of grain to horses and ordered (6) companies, three of each Regiment, to follow train under General Reynolds: and to await the approach of remainder of command on Powder river. Day has been very blustering and chilly: keen freeze blowing and snow clouds lowering over us. About 5.20 P.M., commenced our march following train up branch of Otter or Pumpkin Creek to its head and then across [the] divide into valley of Big Powder river, which we could discern about 2.30 or 3 a.m. This night was especially severe in temperature, wind blowing keenly all the time and snow falling spasmodically. Frank Gruard, our Kanaka[1] guide discovered wonderful discernment in his calling, leading the column with the accuracy of a bird, and following like a hound the tracks of the two young Indians our guides had come upon so suddenly in the morning. Accustomed as I have been to the powerful keen[n]ess of vision and capacity as trailers of the Apache Indians of Arizona, there was nothing remarkable in Gruard's success, except the development of such wonderful knowledge of country in one not native to it and who had been obliged to familiarize himself with its topography when travelling through it as a prisoner in the hands of the Sioux.

About this time, we had advanced so far and the night was so nearly spent, (it was about 2.30 a.m.) it was thought best to conceal ourselves in some convenient ravine and let Frank Gruard and one or two picked men scour the country for any trails leading to villages. General Crook is convinced that Sitting Bull and the other hostile chiefs will be found encamped somewhere about the confluence of the Big and Little Powder; hence our cautiousness.

A dry ravine was soon reached and in this we took our places in line, enduring great suffering from the intense frigidity of the atmosphere, and the impossibility of taking adequate exercise to restore the circulation in our benumbed limbs. (Men in this ravine became drowsy from excessive cold: officers had to kick and shake them to keep them awake and save them from freezing to death—Interpolated April 22d. 1878) Our poor horses were more patient than we, but had to undergo much suffering, not only from the cold but also from straining themselves in climbing up and sliding down the glassy acclivities and declivities on our line of travel. Little gulches, insignificant crevices in the surface, even when not more than 3 or 4 feet deep, stopped our march for several minutes until an examination would reveal where a passage was feasible without incurring the risk of breaking our animals' necks.

An almost inexcusable oversight in the organization of our column is the absence of anything like a corps of pioneers: if the men

1. Native Polynesian.

of the advanced guard were provided with hatchets, suspended from saddle-bow, a few moment's work would suffice to reduce grades, clear away ice from steep trails or cut ramps down river banks to let our horses reach the water conveniently. It may be well to remark here that one of the most grievous privations of our stock has been the great dearth of water; the Ice King has set his seal upon the rivers and we cannot remove it. Many places on Tongue River have ice between two and three feet thick.

It may also be proper to criticize our objectionable method of marching: battalions are allowed to leave camp in the morning as soon as they are ready, instead of being obliged to observe an hour designated for the whole command. Troops are not kept closed up and halts at suitable intervals are not made as they should be to have stragglers regain positions, let saddles be readjusted and other matters of sound character be attended to. In going into camp, too, we manifest a reprehensible carelessness' our bivouac is not sufficiently compact, by this, throwing an unnecessary increase of responsibility upon sentinels.

To atone in a great measure for this laxity our videttes are extremely wakeful and attentive to duty.

This night was so dark, could not make any comprehensive or intelligent observation of the country near us, but saw enough to assure me the general lay of the land was what we used to call in Arizona "rolling mesa", the Northern exposures of the hills around us and the little ravines passed on march being well studded with pine and juniper timber and the slopes fairly grassed, in many places gramma being the predominating variety. Sandstone cropped out in every direction, but could make out no other species of rock, altho' there must have been many different classes of minerals at the head-waters of Pumpkin Creek, on the summit. Once or twice had a chance to see the [Big] Dipper which told us our path lay nearly due East.

Frank [Grouard] soon found that the Indians we had followed belonged to a small hunting party of 30 or 40 Indians, mounted, whose trail disclosed itself plainly to our view. As the light was stronger, we advanced upon this trail with considerable rapidity until a dense volume of smoke arising from a point in the valley of the Powder admonished us to be more circumspect. Our hopes that this smoke pertained to a large village were shortly dispelled by learning some coal measures[2] were on fire and from them the dense masses of smoke proceeded. As we were resting for a few minutes, discussing casual topics, our indefatigable and invaluable scout, Frank, galloped back among us in great glee and announced to General Reynolds that right down in the valley beneath us, in one word, directly under our feet, lay a village of more than a hundred lodges, with great herds of ponies grazing on the rich pasturage of the river bottoms.

It is a difficult task to describe graphically the excitement, enthusiasm and intense interest this announcement created. While some eagerly questioned Frank to ascertain with more precision the situation and apparent strength of the enemy's lodges, others beckoned impatiently to our tardy comrades to accelerate their progress, and others still examined with minute attention the state of their weapons and fastenings of their saddle-girths. We could hardly realize we had at last come upon the Sioux in their chosen retreat, but each one anticipated that any conflict we might engage in would prove bloody, protracted and desperate. Our Government has been so vacillating in its deportment towards these Indians, our Commissioners and other representatives have frequently been so inexperienced, imbecile or treacherous to the interests confided to them, and our soldiery has been so badly handled, especially during the time General Ord was in command of the Department of the Platte, that the Sioux proverbially insolent, have grown bolder and more haughty, imagining our people subsidiary to them.

I speak now of those on the Reservations:—the sentiments entertained by chiefs like Sitting Bull of the North,[3] Crazy Horse, and Little Big Man, who have never gone on a Reserve, and refused all offers of Peace, scorned all concessions and particularly adhered to a career of spoliation and murder, would not be exaggerated by any flight of rhetoric.

The clouds and mists began slowly to separate, and the sun that so short a time ago we had cursed for his dilatoriness, climbed with a terrifying rapidity upon his course for the day. Some other Phaeton, undeterred by the fate of ambitious predecessors, had evi-

---

2. Fissures of coal often found in eastern Wyoming, and extended deep into the ground. At the lower levels they sometimes ignite from spontaneous combustion, and the smoke works its way up to the surface.

3. Bourke uses this to distinguish the great Sitting Bull from a lesser chief of the same name, who was called Sitting Bull of the South.

dently stolen Phoebus' chariot and was driving it madly across the heavens;[4] every moment of darkness was precious to us, so much depends upon the suddenness and unexpectedness of the attack in all conflicts with American savages.

It was long after sun-rise when our final preparations were completed: looking over the crest of a steep ridge, the young Indian bucks could be seen in the valley below, moving about in the valley among the tipis, while their horses and mules grazed quietly on the banks of the river nearby.

General Reynolds detailed Major Noyes'[5] battalion to move to the Right, descend to the riverbank and charge the village, while Moore's Battalion dismounted, was to occupy the crests of the ridge overlooking the village, and make it lively for the Indians after the first attack had been made. This part of the programme was arrayed with the concurrence of Frank Gruard who understood the situation of the Indians and warmly urged by Captain Moore who expressed great anxiety to get an opportunity to crawl in close to the enemy, give them what he called a "blizzard" and get a "bucket-full of blood." He made many remarks of similar purport, forgetting that a true soldier in the hour of trial conducts himself with modesty and gentle quietness of manner.

General Reynolds said to me, "I am sending Noyes' Battalion to charge the village, because we can give them, (the Indians,) Egan's pistols," and "when they start from the village Moore will catch them from the top of the ridge."

As the village was strongly situated in a copse of cottonwood with a thick undergrowth of wild-plum bushes, Mills' Battalion was to follow closely upon the charging column, occupy the underbrush, possess themselves of the tipis and destroy them.

This plan did not work as satisfactorily as it should have done for reasons hereafter to be explained.

In accordance with our orders, Noyes' Battalion, composed of Company "I", 2n Cavalry, (Capt. H.E. Noyes and 1st Lieut. C.T. Hall.) And Co. "K", 2n Cavalry, (Captain Egan,) with Lieutenant Bourke, A.D.C., and Mr. Strahorn, [(]as volunteers,) moved rapidly to the Right. Unfortunately, the gently undulating surface over which we

4. In Greek mythology, Phaeton was the son of Phoebus (Apollo), the sun god. Phaeton lost control of Phoebus's sun chariot and nearly destroyed the earth by fire before falling to his death.

5. Bourke uses Noyes's brevet rank.

had travelled during the night, gave way rapidly to an extremely asporous and rugged series of brakes, ravines and gulches, where the passage of Infantry, much less Cavalry, was but little less than an impossibility. But, with superhuman exertions, we forced our way down for 1 1/2 or 2 1/2 miles, to a point giving us concealment and yet affording a fine view of the grassy plateau in the immediate vicinity of the village where some of the young Indian boys were by this time driving their herds to water. (See Map.)

It was a great tax upon our patience, at this moment, to remain quiet, but Major Noyes was very firm in his determination not to attempt any charge before ascertaining the nature of the surface to be traversed. Within a few moments, Ba[p]tist Pourier, "Big Bat.", one of our best guides, had completed his examination and reported that after we should have advanced, the Indians could not escape in any way on our side.

Major Noyes then moved us up in position, Egan in front and we started out as follows: we moved in column of twos, Egan at the head of his Company, until we had emerged from the gulches when the command—"Left Front into Line"—was given and the little company of forty-seven men formed a beautiful line in less time than it takes to narrate the movement.

Egan ordered us to keep at a walk until we had entered the village or been discovered by the enemy; then to charge at a slow trot, (our animals being too tired and cold to do more) and upon approaching closely to fire our pistols and storm the village, or, failing in that, too wheel around and charge back. Moving in this order, we were soon in among the herds of ponies, which trotted off to the Right and Left at our approach.*

The village soon appeared on our Left, not so much in our front as we had thought it would be, but situated somewhat as in the diagram, the arrowhead showing line of direction of charge. I omitted to say that at edge of village we unexpectedly had to cross a steep ravine, 10 or 12 feet high and 40 or 50 wide, in places wider still. The lodges were sheltered in little coves and nooks among the rocks and finely protected in front by a little clump of cottonwood and a dense undergrowth of the wild-plum. Running out of their lodges by

---

* An Indian boy, herding his ponies, was standing within ten ft. of me. I covered him with my revolver & could have killed him: Egan said "let him alone John." The youngster betrayed great stoicism, maintaining silence until we had passed and then shouting the war-whoop to alarm the village.

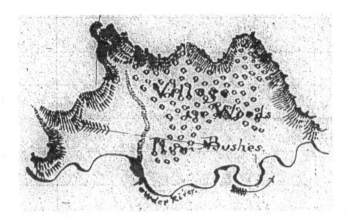

dozens, the Indians who at first were greatly frightened now threw themselves behind the brush and opened upon us in a lively fire which was returned with apparently good effect from our pistols as the Indians abandoned the first line of trees and took refuge farther to the rear. During the 3 or 4 minutes this little affair lasted, our command, (Egan's) behaved very gallantly.

Our casualties* were; three men wounded; one in lower part of lungs, one in elbow-joint and one in collar-bone. Some time after this, a very brave soldier, Private Schneider, was killed. Six horses were killed and two wounded, not including Captain Egan's horse which was also wounded once in neck. My bridle-rein was cut in two by a bullet and a number of the men were shot through the clothing.

The Indians, seeing the paucity of our numbers, regained confidence and rushed forward to cut us off, but we dismounted and formed line on foot as rapidly in the undergrowth, whence we opened up upon them such an unpleasant fire from our carbines that the Sioux were only too glad to retire and leave us in possession of that end of the village.

The side attack by Moore's command was not made as promptly as was promised, partly because the Indians did not leave the village as quickly as we had expected and partly on account of mistakes which might have been anticipated by a more energetic administration.

Noyes moved up very promptly in our rear and wheeling suddenly to the Right pounced upon the enemy's animals. These were, after the engagement, found to number over 700 and included horses, mules and brood-mares, many with American brands. Noyes was assisted in this manoeuvre by our small detachment of half-breed guides.

* Up to this time, in Egan's Company alone.

Had Noyes, instead of making this evolution, charged in echelon on our Left flank, many Indians would have been captured and great numbered killed: but he only carried out his instructions, which he did very well.* After half a hour's delay, Moore opened fire from the cliffs, but not from the position he had been ordered to occupy; in truth, his stand-point was to our Left and rear, so far out of range that a few of his bullets fell among our men moving into the village: the Sioux were not slow to perceive this mistake which gave them a loop-hole not of escape alone but of shelter from our bullets which otherwise would have slain them by he scores. From their impregnable position, they opened a deliberate and telling fusillade that inflicted upon us in the next hour much damage.

Mills, to our great good luck, came up as fast as his men could get in on foot and passing through the village, with Egan on his Right, but not joined, gained the woods to our front and held them, while details in the rear set fire to the one hundred and five, or thereabouts, lodges forming the village.

After Egan had dismounted us and the village had been taken, to my great surprise, I found the right great toe and the adjoining one so badly frozen I could not walk: I sat down in the middle of the village and noted many points of interest and value.

Their tipis were large, conical tents, of canvass obtained at the Agencies and elk and buffalo skins, procured by the chase. They support them on a number of ash and fir poles, meeting in a point a top and radiating out at bottom until the floor has a diameter of 18 to 25 feet. An aperture at the apex allows egress to the smoke ascending from the fire in center of floor. The entrance is by a small trap-door of skin, at the side.

These Indians, the band of the villainous old rascal Crazy Horse, a noted desperado, had grown so rich from the plunder of the white settlements in Montana and Wyoming and bold from their long-continued immunity from punishment that they never dreamed of an attack being made upon them in the depth of winter upon their village which we found surprisingly rich in everything a savage would consider comfortable and much that would be agreeable in a white man's house.

---

* In truth, the most effective help received was from Stanton & Sibley, who, without orders, moved up with their half-breeds to our assistance.

There was no great quantity of baled furs, no doubt they had disposed of all their surplus, but there was a great deal of (loose) Buffalo robes, beaver skins and bear-skins, many of extra-fine quality. Some of the Buffalo robes were wonderously embroidered with porcupine quills, paint and trimmings; an elk-skin was found as large as two and a half army blankets, placed together. It was nicely trimmed and ornamented. The couches in every lodge were made of these valuable furs.

Every squaw and every buck was provided with a good-sized valise-trunk, of tanned buffalo, deer, elk or horse hide, painted in gaudy colors and filled with fine clothes, those of the squaws deeply embroidered with bead-work. I found the chemise of a young woman and it was assuredly a fine piece of work, bead in very pretty patterns being sewed on back, breast and shoulders to a depth of six inches.

Each family had similar trunks for carrying kitchen utensils and the different varieties of herbs that savages prize as highly.

We discovered war-bonnets strikingly beautiful in general appearance, formed of a band of red cloth encircling the head and stretching down to the heels, adorned with eagle-tail feathers, bells, ribbons and other gew-gaws. They were the most elegant things of the kind I had every beheld. In each lodge, knives and forks, spoons, tin-cups, platters, mess-pans, frying-pans, pots and kettles of all kinds, axes, hatchets, hunting knives, water-kegs, blankets, pillows and every imaginable kind of truck was seen in profusion.

Of the weight of dried and fresh buffalo meat and venison, no adequate idea can be given; in 3 or 4 lodges, I estimated there were not less than 1000 pounds. Ammunition, in abundance; pig-lead, metallic cartridges and percussion caps enough for a regiment. One hundred and fifty saddles were burnt in the flames of the tipis, which each exploded with a puff! as its little magazine of powder ignited.

Much bad management was displayed about this time: General Reynolds ordered everything to be destroyed and with a command undergoing every hardship, suffering from intense cold and hunger, tons of first-class meat and provisions were destroyed and many things of positive necessity to the men wantonly burned up. I regret to mention this proof of gross ignorance on the part of our commanding officer who seems incapable of learning the first principles of Indian warfare. In like manner, with 700 captured ponies and scores of useless Indian saddles and lariats, we abandoned, to our shame be it said, the corpses of our gallant dead, 3 or 4 in number and one poor wretch, shot in arm and thigh, fell alive into the hands of the enemy and was scalped before the eyes of a comrade.

These errors, the errors of General Reynolds' imbecility, cannot reflect upon the reputation of the brave officers and men who essayed so hard to do their whole duty, and it should not be forgotten that we had attacked in open day an enemy that had never been whipped; that scorned the Government that has been cringing to them for years:—an enemy, better supplied than we with the essentials of warfare and better skilled than many of our recruits in their use and who had a position from which, under better discipline fifteen hundred men could not have driven them.

Captain Egan, 2n Cavalry, during the whole affair, was under fire, displaying distinguished gallantry, coolness and fine soldierly qualities;* all our officers, that I observed did well; General Reynolds was very cool under fire, discharging duties, at least as far as he understood them, efficiently and cooly.

Colonel Stanton was very early in the rancheria and acted as well as the best: altho' without any positive command during the Expedition, he has, while in command of our scouts and guides, rendered invaluable services.

Mr. Strahorn acted like a veteran and was of great use to Capt. Egan during the fight.

After burning up the village, we started out, driving away over seven hundred head of stock and having our rear protected by a strong skirmish line which exchanged a few, desultory shots with Indian bushwhackers in the hills. I heard, after quitting the ground, that when our men were leaving the burned village on one side, the Sioux were entering on the other; but I did not see this.

We marched South South West up Powder river for twenty miles, to the mouth of Lodge-Pole creek, where we camped to await the coming of General Crook with the pack-train and the other four companies. Did not reach this locality until some time after sun-set.

Had plenty of water, or ice, a sufficiency of wood, but very little grass for our large herd of animals.

---

* Note, April 22nd, 1878[:] It should be observed that I was there speaking of officers I observed: i.e. Egan, Stanton, Mills, Paul, Sibley and Johnston and Mr. Strahorn. Capt. Moore kept to the rear and I did not see him. Capt. Noyes went off after the Indian herd, a commendable action in some points, but censurable under general features.

Officers and men were very uncomfortable from want of adequate clothing, altho' to-day has been much warmer than yesterday. Have no rations, not even for our poor wounded men.

Occasionally, an officer will be found with a small quantity of cracker-crumbs in his saddle-pouches, another one has carried away a small quantity of buffalo meat from the rancheria and a third, mayhap, has a spoonful of tea or coffee. We make a miserable apology for supper; a piece or two of buffalo meat, roasted in the ashes, goes around among five or six, each getting a mouthful only; and a cup of coffee is sipped like the Pipe of Peace at an Indian Council.

Our slumbers are sound, despite the cold, as we have marched between 68 and 75 miles since yesterday morning, besides fighting five hours to-day.

Our men are, of course, very tired: guard duty is done by running tours of the whole company, but we feel almost satisfied with our day's work which has been praiseworthy and brilliant enough when we take into regard the disadvantages we had to contend against to gain any success at all.*

The men name this Camp Inhospitality a name well deserved and will bestowed. Doctor Munn came up to the fire near which I was lying and from him I learned that our casualties in men, consisted of four killed and five or six wounded, two of them seriously.

Heard also that when some of our half-breed guides reached into the village they found an old Indian woman stretched on a couch, sick. They questioned her and learned that the head chief of the village was Crazy Horse, who had with him Little Big Man. The Indians represented were Ogallallah Sioux, Minneconjou Sioux and Northern Cheyennes. One or two lodges of Sitting Bulls band were there and about same number of Indians from Red Cloud Agency, who had come in that morning to trade.

Those of our men who were on the skirmish line under Mills saw an Indian chief in full war costume, riding and running up and down among his men on the cliffs, haranguing them and animating their valor. We conjectured this to be Crazy Horse, whose every interest demanded our expulsion from the village: as superstitious [as] are Indians generally that a chief who meets with any great misfortune

---

* Note, April 22d 1878[:] I here allude in a cautious way to the disadvantages under which we labored: i.e. the inefficiency of Genl. Reynolds and the cowardice of his trusted counsellor, Captain Moore. These notes were written very guardedly to prevent any trouble in case they should fall into the hands of soldiers or others of the Command.

in war has great difficulty in holding together the remnants of his people who delay not to show a preference for a captain whose "medicine" is less unlucky.

We could form no estimate of the number of savages slain; when wounded, they will always display more coolness and better judgment than white men in same circumstances, and will resort to various artifices to deprive an enemy of the satisfaction of knowing he has inflicted damage upon their people. For all that we captured no bodies, we had excellent reasons for believing we had killed and wounded many in the enemy's ranks—a conviction softening in a slight degree the grief felt at the sudden death of our own gallant comrades.

March 18th. Awakened at sunrise; it would be more exact to say arose at sun-rise, since the cold had awakened many a poor fellow earlier in the night. Mr. Strahorn and I had made a couch out of a worn out saddle-blanket, covering ourselves with a large, untanned buffalo robe I had brought out of the village; it was so stiff, we might just as well have employed a board for a blanket. Had my frozen toes painted with the Tincture of Iodine for a second time, (they were first painted on the field yesterday.) The Doctors tell one that if applied as soon as the injury is done, or about the time a reaction has set in that this remedy is a positive specific. A great number of cases of frosted and frozen feet, noses and fingers reported among the enlisted men.

Our Doctor, Munn, is commendably assiduous in his attentions to the wounded men and those suffering from the effects of the weather, among whom are to-day numbered two poor devils unable to walk from inflammatory rheumatism. The Hospital Steward, O'Brien, who had his horse shot from under him yesterday is a great assistance to his superior officer in the execution of duties devolving upon him.

Our herd of ponies that had not been guarded last night; strayed some little distance from camp this morning and were driven off by a small squad of Indians who had doubtlessly been long watching for so fair an opportunity.

The theft was promptly reported to General Reynolds and one of our guides told him the animals were still in plain sight, going over the ridge nearest camp, three or four miles distant. To the surprise of all, General Reynolds declined sending any detachment to attempt their recapture. Great dissatisfaction now arose among all: several of the officers vented their ill-feeling in splenetic criticism and openly charged Reynolds with incapacity.

This exhibition of incompetency was the last link needed to fastening the chain of popular obloquy to the reputation of our Commanding Officer. It was remembered that no guard had been placed over the cattle-herd the Sioux had stampeded near Fort Fetterman[,] that our vidette system had been neglected until General Crook had interfered and caused it to be instituted; that in yesterday's fight our troops had been badly handled, the heights overlooking the enemy's position not seized upon as a single glance of the eye would have suggested; that our men were now suffering for food and covering, while everything they could desire had been consumed before their eyes in the village, and worst shame and disgrace of all, our dead and dying had been abandoned like carrion to the torture and mutilation of the Indian's scalping knife. The favorable impression General Reynolds' affable manners had made upon his subordinates has been very rudely and completely effaced. I cannot use a better term than to say we look upon him as a sort of General Braddock,[6] good enough to follow out instructions in a plan of battle conducted according to stereotyped rules, but having nothing of that originality of thought, fertility of conception and promptness of execution which is the characteristic of great military men. Reynolds' imbecility is a very painful revelation to many of us. All in camp look forward to General Crook's arrival with feelings of impatience and anxious expectancy. We lay in camp all morning, while couriers went to hurry him up. Day bright and pleasant, the only really good one had since leaving our wagons.

General Crook rejoined us near mid-day: was much pleased to learn of our having encountered the Sioux and taken their village; he seemed annoyed and chagrined upon being told we had left our dead upon the ground and that our ponies had been recaptured through our own carelessness; but he said nothing, keeping within his own breast the thoughts that moved him. His party retook fifty of the herd which the Indians were attempting to drive past them

6. Major General Edward Braddock led a British force against French-held Fort Duquesne, Pennsylvania, in 1755. Trained in the linear tactics of European warfare, he was unable to adjust to the wilderness fighting of North America. The column was attacked by a large French force with Indian auxiliaries, and thrown back with heavy losses. Braddock was killed in the fight. See Marston, *The Seven Years' War*, 10-11.

and the General himself got a very good sight on a savage upon whom he fired. The pony, saddle, buffalo-robe and blankets of the buck fell into our hands, but he was carried off by his retreating comrades.

Moved our camp eight miles South up Powder river to a point where we could have Wood, Water and Grass for our animals. Had a good, warm supper and a drink of brandy from one of our doctors. Commenced snowing at sun-down, Very cold to-night. Slept very soundly and with great refreshment, except during the short time the Indians were firing into camp: this time their attack lacked spirit, very decidedly and our videttes had no trouble in assuring the Indians they had awakened the wrong passengers. Crook was in camp and his presence was equal to a force of a thousand men: so our men felt.

Struck in the head with axes and killed forty or fifty of our captured ponies, which seemed too young or too feeble to keep up with our march. Many of our men, all of our guides and a few officers cut off steaks and choice pieces from the young ponies and ate them for food. Their verdict an emphatic endorsement of hippophagy.

March 19th. Breakfasted by light of the stars, between 3 and 4 a.m. Night extremely cold. Shot forty Indian colts and brood-mares this morning. Moved rapidly South South West up Powder River to the mouth of the Crazy Woman's fork, twenty-five miles. Our rations are getting very slim. In such cold weather and with arduous service, the amount allowed by Government for the daily ration is too small; the increase should be to such an extent as to make the individual apportionment of Hard bread (20) ounces, bacon, one pound, beans and sugar, double what they are at present and have some variety of dried fruit, or in lieu of this, citric acid, made a component.

This was a very good camping ground. Wood and Water were abundant and in close proximity to use and good grass was accessible in sufficient quantity.

March 20th, Last night snowed all night. Had no bother from Indians. Snowing this morning. South wind. Snow hanging very heavily on our clothing and on our horses' backs. Trail decidedly muddy.

Moved South and South South West up Powder river for twenty miles. Saw much cottonwood timber in river bottom, but no timber on the bluffs overhanging stream. Coal seams protruding from the bluffs in great frequency. Found good camp; no cause to complain of deficiency or quality in Wood, Grass or Water. Ice in stream getting weak. Alkaline ice is treacherous. It will barely support our horses. Sent messengers in advance to Fort Reno, to our wagon-train.

Mar. 21st (Vernal Equinox.) Marched up Powder, South, for thirty miles, a toilsome stretch with our weary horses and pack-mules. Day murky. Ground plastic, with a viscuous mud oozing out from the track made by the horses' feet. Country very dreary, no timber at all on bluffs and a greatly diminished quantity along stream. Ice growing weaker: find it vastly thinner than it was on Tongue river, where it cut from (2 1/2) to three feet in thickness. Horses and mules are now beginning to play out, chiefly among the condemned stock brought along. Reached our Infantry camp near old Fort Reno, at 4 P.M. Major Coates, Major Ferris and Lieutenant [Charles Winder] Mason made us heartily welcome. Our animals were fed on grain and carefully tended. Our men enjoyed a good square meal, the first for many days.

March 22d Lay in camp all day. Rained a cold drizzle in morning, but cleared off cold towards afternoon. General Crook sent mounted party in advance to Fort Fetterman, with dispatches, among them the following to General Sheridan, U.S. Army, Chicago.

["]Cut loose from wagon-train on 7th. Inst., scouted Tongue and Rosebud rivers, until satisfied there were no Indians upon them, then struck across country toward Powder river.

General Reynolds with a part of command, was pushed forward on a trail leading to the village of Crazy Horse, near mouth of Little Powder river.

This he attacked and destroyed on the morning of the 17th, finding it a perfect magazine of ammunition, war material and general supplies. Crazy Horse had with him the Northern Cheyennes and some of the Minneconjous, probably in all one half the Indians off the Reservations.[7]

Every evidence was found to prove these Indians to be in copartnership with those at the Red Cloud and Spotted Tail Agencies and that the proceeds of their raids upon the settlements have been

---

7. This statement is patently absurd. The camp held at most about 735 people, of which only 210 were warriors. On the other hand, several thousand Indians were off the reservations with more leaving as summer approached. Gray, *Centennial Campaign*, 55, 321ff.

taken in to the Agencies and supplies brought out in return. In this connection, I would again urgently recommend the immediate transfer of the Indians on those Agencies to the Missouri river.

Am satisfied if Sitting Bull is on this side of the Yellowstone, that he is camped at mouth of Powder river, but did not go there for reasons to be given by letter.

Had terribly severe weather during absence from wagon-train, snowed every day but one and the mercurial thermometer on several occasions failed to register. Will be at Fetterman, 26th inst, so if you desire me to move the Indians, please have instructions for me there by that date, or close[.] I shall return Cavalry to Rail Road at once for recuperation.

    (Signed.) *Crook*

        Brigadier General.["]

March 23d, Took up line of march to return to Fort Fetterman, moved fifteen miles along to head of Dry Fork of Powder river. Nothing to note to-day. Our wounded have been taken off the traveaux[8] and placed in the ambulances. Our pack-mules are unloaded and our cavalry has put everything possible in the wagons to ease the horse's loads. Day rather cool, but pleasant. Command in fine spirits.

March 24th. Rained at intervals during night. Day opened cool and damp. Rained from time to time during the day. Road soft and sticky. Marched along the Fort Fetterman road 21 miles to the head of the Wind River. Made camp. Water and grass sufficient, but no wood in vicinity: had to carry what was needed for fuel from last night's camp. The work of recording the events of this march has now become monotonous enough; there is nothing to narrate but the diurnal progress of the column and the variations of climate. We are very much astonished at the great change for the better in climate since quitting Tongue river.

Mar. 25th. Marched 20 miles along road to South Cheyenne river. Day Gloomy and dark. Some snow fell. A considerable quantity covered ground last night. Wagon road obliterated and animals "balling" terribly.[9] Found an Indian pony and rifle. Two antelope killed by our scouts—also one sage hen.

8. Correctly spelled "travaux," it is technically the plural form of "travois" although the latter generally is used for both the singular and the plural.

9. By "balling," Bourke means the mud was sticking to their hooves, packing around their feet in a sort of ball. If left untended, permanent injury could result.

March 26th. Made a tedious tramp of 27 miles through snow to Fort
Fetterman where we were gratefully received by Col. Chambers and
his officers about noon. Wagon train and mules reached post between 3 and 4 P.M. A great quantity of letters, telegrams and newspapers were here for Genl. Crook and their contents were perused
with much eagerness. Learned of the fall of Secretary of War Belknap,
detected in peculation and wrong-doing in regard to post-traderships:
also of the moral conviction of Babcock, Secretary to President
Grant.

Our sick and wounded, hauled on sledges to Fort Reno, 100 miles,
thence 90 miles by wagon to Fetterman, were placed in the post
hospital and seemed to enjoy the change.

Genl. Sheridan telegraphed Genl. Crook to make what dispositions
he found needful to recuperate the command's horses and then resume campaign against hostile Indians.

Genl. Crook, having maturely revolved in his own mind the evidence bearing upon the management of our attack upon the Indian
village has concluded that General Reynolds must be held responsible especially in view of his neglect to investigate the behavior of
Captain Alex. Moore, 3d Cav., believed by most of the officers to be
guilty of cowardice. He has drawn up against General Reynolds
Charges and Specifications which will be inserted in their proper
place.

Mar. 27th. Genl. Reynolds expressed intense mortification at the
Charges and Specifications preferred against him and came to Gen.
Crook to solicit a withdrawal of them, claiming he had attempted to
enforce in good faith all orders and instructions received during
campaign.

Gen. Crook declined acceding to this request, saying the behavior
of every one in the action of the [1]7th must be examined into and
the responsibility for the neglects charged placed upon the proper
person.

Gen. Reynolds had an interview with me, asked what I remembered of the circumstances of the affair and after he had learned
my views, in a subsequent interview asserted upon the authority of
Gen. Crook that I had told him, Crook, [that] he, Reynolds, intended abandoning him.

This I strenuously repelled and Gen. Crook denied having made such
a statement, upon which Gen. Reynolds acknowledged his error[.]

Lieut. Morton, 3d Cav. [Reynolds's adjutant], in my opinion, has done much to embroil and precipitate matters by ill-judged criticisms upon Mr. Strahorn, the correspondent of the *Denver [Rocky Mountain] News*, who is with us, and who boldly avers he is going to publish the truth in spite of all the Reynolds and Mortons in the Army. Gen. Crook has no other remedy left but to probe the matter to the quick by a General Court Martial.

Distributed the captured ponies to-day among scouts who had conducted themselves with gallantry, and the soldiers of the ten Cavalry Co's.

Capt. Egan, 2d Cav., preferred a series of Charges and Specifications against General Reynolds, for abandoning his dead and dying on the field of Battle.

Telegraphed Nickerson to-day and made arrangements to leave, to-morrow for Omaha, where we are to remain until May 1st. when active work will be resumed.

March 28th. Left for Cheyenne, by way of the cut-off, which crosses the Laramie river at the mouth of the Chug[water River]. Ascending the latter, we stopped at Portuguese Phillip's for dinner, and then drove on to Fagan's Ranch, on Horse Creek. Made the journey to Cheyenne, 155 miles, in four days, experiencing snowy and rainy weather the whole or nearly the whole time. Along the road, between Cheyenne and Fort Laramie, passed squad of people en route to the Black Hills. They were in general well provided with supplies, but ignorant of the dangers and trials in store for them.

At Philips, were informed that sixty eight, of these adventurers had sat down to supper in one day, while at Fagan's during the snow-storm of March 26th or 27th, two hundred and fifty had slept in the kitchen, stables and out-houses. . . .

Chapter 14

A Trip to the Indian Agencies

The following orders were promulgated by Colonel Reynolds upon our arrival at Fort Fetterman.

> Hd. Qrs. Big Horn Expedition,
> Fort Fetterman, Wyo. Territory,
> March 27th, 1876

General Orders
No. 3

I. By direction of the Department Commander, the Big Horn Expedition organized by General Orders, No. 1. Fort Fetterman, W[yoming].T[erritory]., February 27th, 1876, is hereby dissolved. The companies comprising the expedition will return to their posts, by easy marches, under their respective Company commanders.

II. The thanks of the Department Commander and of the immediate commander of the troops are hereby returned to the members of this command for the cheerfulness and fortitude with which they have performed every duty devolving upon them throughout a campaign, of twenty-six days in an inclement season of the year, including temperatures (26) degrees below zero, with the slightest possible shelter and sometimes short rations. And especially for

the cold night march of thirty five miles resulting in the surprise
and destruction of a large Indian village.

The march to and consequent upon this engagement of three hours'
duration was fifty-five miles in twenty-five consecutive hours.

By order of Colonel Reynolds,

(sig.) Charles Morton,

2 Lieut., 3d Cavalry

Adjutant.

By May 10th, the various preparations needed for a reopening of
the campaign were so far completed that Genl. Crook found himself able to run up to the Indian Agencies to sound the Indians at
Red Cloud and Spotted Tail and know just what people were left in
our rear and also what assistance might be looked for. In starting
out from the Rail Road with the greater part of the cavalry in the
Department, but little protection is taken from the settlers; the inefficiency of the cavalry has become a public scandal: people cannot learn that the scattering of troops diminishes their efficiency
and that it is only by concentrating our forces and moving in converging lines into the enemy's own country and making him feel
the hand of War fall heavily upon him that we can hope to end the
systematized spoliation of the little hamlets along and adjacent to
the U.P.R.R. With the co-operation of the columns commanded by
General Terry and Colonel Gibbon, we may expect to corral some
of the hostile bands and inflict severe punishment upon them.

To relieve the Cavalry from their stations, companies of the 23d
Infantry were sent out from Omaha Barracks: Randall's & [Otis
Wheeler] Pollock's to Sydney Barracks,[1] [Charles] Wheaton's to Fort
McPherson,[2] and [Patrick Thomas] Broderick's to Fort Hartsuff.[3]
Lieut C.H. Heyl, of the 23d infantry, has just added to the laurels
gained in Arizona by another feat of gallantry and efficiency against
a small raiding party of Sioux Indians in the Loup Valley near Fort
Hartsuff. With a small party of Infantry mounted on mules from the
Q.M. corral, he pursued and caught up with the hostile Indians,

1. Sidney Barracks (which Bourke tended to spell as "Sydney"), at the present town of
Sidney, Nebraska, was established in 1867 as a outpost of Fort Sedgwick, Colorado. It became
a separate post in 1879, and was redesignated Fort Sidney. It was abandoned and transferred
to the Interior Department in 1894. Frazer, *Forts of the West*, 90.

2. Fort McPherson was established in 1863 on the South Platte River, eight miles above
its confluence with the North Platte. It was abandoned in 1880, and transferred to the Interior
Department in 1887. The post cemetery is a national cemetery. Ibid., 88.

3. Fort Hartsuff was established in 1874 near the present town of Burwell, Nebraska. It
was abandoned in 1881, and transferred to the Interior Department in 1884. Ibid., 86-87.

surrounding them on a little hill where they should all have been captured had the citizens who were along acted in any way gallantly. Heyl had one Sergeant, Dougherty, killed, and it is believed, killed one Indian. General Crook referred to the matter in appropriate orders.

Much regret was felt by all the officers interested in keeping the honor of the army pure and bright to think that the trial of General Reynolds for misbehavior in presence of the enemy and of Captain Moore for cowardice (both during the Crazy Horse engagement,) could not be hurried through with before the commencement of the present movement; the moral effect of a General Court Martial in their cases would have been most salutary.

Left Omaha on the 9th May and reached Cheyenne next day without especial incident; met Cols. Gilliss, Mills and Brady, and Lieuts. Robinson, (W.H.) Paul,[4] [Samuel Austin] Cherry and Bolling;[5] also Mr. Tom. Moore.

Impending Indian troubles were the theme of excited conversation in Cheyenne. The attacks upon consignment trains going to and returning from the Black Hills had done much to exhibit the bad temper of the Indians, who had now crossed the North Platte and driven off thirty-two head of horses from Hunton's ranch on the Chug, on the Cheyenne and Laramie road. Mr. Hunton was killed by the party and when the body was found it had eleven wounds, three from arrows. Lieut. [James Nicholas] Allison, of the 2d Cavalry, followed the trail in the direction of Red Cloud Agency until it was obliterated by a severe snow storm.

The troops of the 3d Cavalry and some of the 2d, engaged in the recent expedition are very badly demoralized and many are deserting from Rowelle's (Well's.) Co of the 2d; eleven have deserted, saying they would not fight under men who would leave their dead and dying to fall into the hands of a savage foe. The officers, many of them at least, [who] act as if they thought the remembrance of recent misconduct would be effaced from the public mind by persistent silence and by their behavior towards gentlemen suspected of knowing anything to the discredit of Moore and Reynolds[,] are really guilty of an intimidation of witnesses. Such behavior will react upon themselves; it has already done so. It makes no difference

4. Bourke probably means Augustus Choteau Paul. Heitman's *Historical Register* does not list a W. H. Paul.
5. Bolling cannot be identified.

what verdict the Court Martial may find, the private soldiers have already passed sentence.

May 12th. A Raw and Bleak day. Moved 50 miles to Portuguese Philip's ranch on the Chug; were kindly cared for by the warm-hearted proprietor whose reputation for hospitality is well known among army people. Saw unmistakable signs of an abatement in the Black Hills' fever: the tide is now turning back. The ignorant wretches who pressed in there in the depth of winter, unable to wash gold out of the frozen earth and destitute of subsistence have become very badly scared by Indian attacks and bring back most despondent accounts from Custer city and other towns in the auriferous district. Their stories are no doubt much exaggerated and intended to account for their failure upon some other theory than that of ignorance, laziness and want of proper working facilities. Yet these tenderfooted pilgrims bring back with them tangible proofs that the precious metal may be found in quantities to pay well, altho' as a gulch mining country the Black Hills will never attain great prominence[. O]ne very handsome coarse nugget that I saw weighed [at a value of] $6.20; and I learned of another from Deadwood creek worth $120.54.

From the Chug to Fort Laramie, 45 miles, our ride was uninteresting, but the undulating country to the Right and Left had assumed its new spring dress of green and so saved us from what without would have been a monotonous day.

At Laramie, found the same officers almost seen there last February: Maj. [Edwin Franklin] Townsend of the 9th Infantry in command. Was entertained very hospitably by Capt. and Mrs. Munson. Heard from W. B. Hayes whom we met on the Chug, that my old friend Mr. W.G. Scott, with whom and General Crook, I made a trip to the Moqui villages in 1874, had commenced to lecture in Elmira, N.Y., taking as his text our mutual experiences in the South-West. (See note-book on Moquis) [Chapter 5--ed.]

From Fort Laramie to Red Cloud the road runs in a North of East direction for 77 miles, crossing the North Platte river a short distance from Fort Laramie, over the fine new iron bridge not long since completed under the direction of Captain Stanton, of the Corps of Engineers, U.S.A., (This bridge is very finely built and provided with ice-breakers on the side next the current.) For 21 miles to Raw Hide creek and 24 miles to the Niobrara the road is much obstructed by sand and passes through a very desolate and treeless waste. A good camp may be found on the Raw Hide, a small, swift, clear stream with hard bottom, mostly sand & gravel, and having some trees growing along its banks. The Niobrara, the next stream, on the contrary, is hard to cross, chiefly by reason of the abruptness of its banks, has a clayey bottom, no timber of any kind available and a general air of desolation. From the Niobrara crossing, (which occurs at the junction of the main stream with a little marshy brook, coming in from the north, and just West of a reed-covered pond or lake half a mile in diameter,) to the head of White Earth river is 14 miles; the road still very sandy follows down the valley of the White Earth, hemmed in by bluffs of the argillaceous sediment giving the stream its name. The scenery is very pretty but rather of the placid order; the road crosses the stream rather too frequently for comfort but finally reaches Camp Robinson,[6] on the Left Bank and about one mile or more from the agency of Red Cloud's band of Indians. Found accommodations here in the Post Hospital, a very neat and orderly structure under the care of the Post Surgeon, Munn, our chief medical officer on the last Expedition.

At Camp Robinson, met Major [William] Jordan, Captain [Frederick] Mears, [Michael John] Fitzgerald and Lieuts. [Thomas Sidney] McCaleb, [William Barrett] Pease, [William] Hoffman & [Jesse Matlock] Lee.

Also Col. [Elisha Harrison] Ludington, Inspector General, Col. [Thaddeus] Stanton, Paymaster and Mr. Strahorn, on their way back from Spotted Tail Agency.

At that place, Colonel Stanton had an interview with the Indian chief Spotted Tail and after some desultory verbal skirmishing, reference was made to our Crazy Horse fight. Stanton remarked we were soon going out again whereupon the crafty old Indian observed sarcastically; "if you don't do better than you did the last time, you had better put on squaws clothes and stay at home." General Crook now made arrangements for a conference with Red Cloud and his Indians, to take place in front of Major Jordan's quarters at noon on Monday, May 16th. Mr. Hastings, the agent at Red Cloud, the suc-

6. Camp Robinson was established in 1874 to control the Indians of the Red Cloud and Pine Ridge Agencies. It was redesignated as Fort Robinson in January 1878. During the Second World War, it was used as a dog training center for the K-9 Corps. It was abandoned in 1948 and now is a Nebraska state park. Buecker, *Fort Robinson and the American West*; Schubert, *Outpost of the Sioux Wars*.

cessor of Mr. Howard (removed last year upon the recommendation of the Congressional Investigating Committee for inefficiency and peculation,)[7] was absent at Spotted Tail Agency, leaving his own duties to be discharged by a subordinate named McCavanaugh, who imagined his dignity outraged by any conference which did not include himself as a star of the first magnitude. For this, he exerted what influence he had to keep Young Man Afraid of his Horses and others from calling upon General Crook to learn what he had to say. But in spite of his malevolent interposition Sitting Bull, (of the South.), Three Bears and Rocky Bear, three chiefs ranking next to Red Cloud in power and influence came into the post about eleven in the morning and were conducted by our guide, Louis Richaud, to the Adjutant's Office, where General Crook, Colonel T.H. Stanton, Major Jordan, 9th Infantry, Lieutenant John G. Bourke, 3d Cavalry, A.D.C., and Frank Gruard, guide were already seated.

After necessary preliminaries, of hand-shaking and "How! Cola," (How are you, friend,) had ben concluded, the conversation commenced, Louis Richaud acting as interpreter.

General Crook. Have they heard anything about going out?

Sitting Bull. We have heard about some of our people being wanted to form part of the next expedition against the Indians up north: we would like to have the agent and Red Cloud here so we can have a talk all together and make up our minds.

General Crook. Tell them the troops are now marching to Fort Fetterman and I cannot stay here over to-morrow. I want to find out their minds before I go and I do not think I can wait until the agent comes back.

Sitting Bull. The agent promised us he would be back to-day.

General Crook. I do not care about getting their opinion just to-day, but merely mention this matter for their consideration. We are going out now and the President has said all these Indians must go on their Reservations and we must stay out after them until they do. There is only one thing to bring us back and that is if the President changes his mind which is not likely to happen.

7. Bourke is mistaken. E. A. Howard was agent at Spotted Tail. The Red Cloud agent, Dr. J.J. Saville, was the target of allegations by Red Cloud himself that he was issuing substandard food. The Board of Indian Commissioners, a quasi-governmental citizen's group established to oversee Indian affairs, set up a special committee that investigated the allegations for five months before finally acquitting Saville. Nevertheless, Saville resigned, although he was said to have been the rare instance of an agent leaving office poorer than when he went in. He successor was James S. Hastings. Larson, *Red Cloud*, 165-67, 198.

Last winter we were out and had the Indians up North in our grasp, but misconduct on the part of certain persons, defeated our plans. This will not happen again. I don't want Indians along to do the fighting, but to follow along with the soldiers, point out where the villages are and gobble up the ponies and things of that kind.

The Crows have sent word they wanted to come along with us. I would prefer to have the Sioux from the Reservation, but if they won't come, I'll telegraph for the Crows to come. A great many people tell us not to bring the Sioux along with us for fear they would not be true, but I trust them and will take them in preference to the Crows if they will come of their own free will. I want to tell them all about it now as they can talk it over among themselves.

He (Sitting Bull,) has been to Washington and has seen how many people we have; how we are pushing out across the rivers and mountains on all sides of them. It is only a short time since the Sioux owned all the country to the Mississippi river, now their country is getting smaller and they are being crowded more and more every day. The Buffalo is getting scarcer. Soon the Indians must all come to live on the Reservations set out for them or be killed off. The bad Indians up north have many ponies which they have stolen. It is better for the Indians here to get those ponies than to let other people get them. We are bound to get them and to stay out until we do.

If all the soldiers now in the country were to be killed off, others would come to take their places. I talk as their (the Sioux') friend, anxious to do them good. They know that in a few years they must submit and they may as well be our friends and help us as be our enemies. They might just as well get those ponies as let anyone else get them, and when they come back the soldiers will protect them in keeping those ponies and also against any attack the Northern Sioux may try to make.

I want them to think over this to-day and let me know by to-night or as soon as they can.

Sitting Bull. For my part, I always listen to the whites: when I take a notion to do anything I always try to do it. I have seen my Great Father: my Great Father has told me to keep friendly with the whites; I have done it: I have done it here and at the agency. I don't sleep at night but stand guard over my friends here and at the agency. I have always listened to my Great Father. Last winter, the Crows and Rees killed a great many of us and we had made up our minds to get revenge, but our Great Father told us to stay here at the agency. For my part, I am willing to go alone and to go into any village ("of the hostiles", understood,) you want me to go into. I have always listened to the Whites. In the fight on the other side of the South Platte river, during the Indian war,* I had a son killed. I have some sons out there, (on the Yellowstone) and I have sent them word to come in. They have the guns the Great Father gave me. I had to make up my mind to go out after my own sons and to take away their horses. We have all got our own ideas of war and our own ways to fight, when *we* see our enemies we want to kill them. Your Great Father has sent you out to kill those Indians and has given you fast horses to do it. We want to see you do it first.

General Crook. They will have no fault to find about that.

Sitting Bull. We are here in the centre of our land with the agency on it. In our fighting, we use the arms and the bow and always whip. When you go to fight the Minneconjous, take a fast horse and kill them with a club:—they are not brave. In winter, they are very poor in stock and can't get away: in summer, you can't catch them. They are on the watch every night. They get up every night and listen to hear if the soldiers are coming. I have as great a number of children out there (on the Yellowstone,) and one wife; but if you kill them it won't change my mind toward you. My heart is good. I started last Fall to bring them in and told them if they won't come in to bring my guns in anyhow.

General Crook. I will loan them guns and give them plenty of ammunition if they will go out. Two band guns.[8]

Sitting Bull. Are you going back from here or going to Spotted Tail Agency?

General Crook. I am going back.

Sitting Bull. You should have talked with Spotted Tail first. He is the oldest Indian and he might want to go along.

General Crook. That makes no difference. If Spotted Tail goes, he shall have the ponies: if not, you shall have them. You know very well, the biggest Indian is the one who has the most ponies.

* (1866-67-68)

8. By "Two band guns," Crook apparantly meant the caliber .45-70 Springfield infantry rifle, sometimes called a "Long Tom," which secured the barrel to the forestock with two steel bands.

The Indians now withdrew to confer with their people. Sitting Bull in the conversation said to General Crook. ["]We have our way of fighting. We will run in and count 'coo,' (corruption of the French 'coup'=blow or stroke.) And the soldiers can do the fighting." This refers to a custom prevalent among these people of a young war chief anxious to signalize himself, rushing in at the head of his band and striking one of the hostile party with his lance, medicine bow or arrow, at the same time crying out "coup" or ["]coo." His bravery is then considered beyond dispute.

Towards evening, Agent Hastings returned to Red Cloud and word was transmitted to Genl. Crook who drove over to the agent's quarters, reaching there shortly before sun-down. In the same room with us were Agent Hastings and his son, General [William] Vandever,[9] Inspector of Indian Affairs, Colonel Stanton, U.S.A., Major Jordan, U.S.A., Mr. R.E. Strahorn and Mr. D. J. McCann, contractor for Indian supplies.*

Mr. Hastings the agent in conversation with General Crook, said he should interpose no objection to any Indians accompanying the Expedition that the General might persuade to go, but that he should not recommend any to go.

That the Indians had been tampered with was evident to one from the start and a slight item of suspicious behavior I may say that the Agent before sending for the Indians with whom General Crook wished to confer, called General Vandever into a back room and held an earnest conversation with him with closed doors.

Shortly, the chiefs sent for arrived; at first only those the agent designated; afterwards, one or two of those General Crook wanted. Young Man Afraid of his Horses was reported to have gone home, but his father, the Old Man d[itt]o. was present. The Chiefs were seven in number, namely Red Cloud, Old Man Afraid of his Horses, Blue Horse, American Horse, Little Wound, Sitting Bull (of the South[)], and one not known to me. (Rocky Bear?)

General Crook asked Sitting Bull if he had told as yet to Red Cloud and the other Indians the substance of the conversation had between them this morning.

Sitting Bull said he had not, but would do so now and then pro-

---

* In November, 1878, Mr. McCann was convicted by a Wyoming Court of fraud as contractor for Red Cloud Agency & sent to the Penitentiary.

9. In subsequent volumes, Bourke sometimes spelled the name "Vandeveer."

ceeded to converse with the other chiefs in a low tone in his own language: when he had concluded,

Red Cloud asked General Crook if it was the President or the Secretary (of the Interior.) [who] had sent him after those Northern Indians.

General Crook. Both.

Red Cloud. They didn't do it right. This is a peaceful house. They ought not to do that way. This is the place for you to go around. The Great Spirit is first in our eyes but the President takes the Great Spirit's place. We do what he says. The Utes and Snakes[10] and Crows were our enemies; the Great Father said we must not go out there (in their country.) and we are now here as he ordered with our young men.

Some of our young men went out there but the Crows killed them. We wanted to go out there then, but the Great Father said No!, so we didn't go out. Here is the Commanding Officer, (Major Jordan, 9th Infantry,) who has been here a long time. He has a good head and good sense. He knows us and never has any trouble with us. Here is our agent. Spotted Tail has another. This man treats us well. That is the reason we have him with us. I suppose you came here for something, but I don't want you to say anything but go right in to wherever you are going, and say nothing to us. The Government sent ten commissioners here to hold a council with us on the White Earth river below here. The Sioux have been thinking of that Black Hills Council all winter. Since they left we had no trouble. But an expedition went out and whipped some Cheyennes[11] and now we have trouble and here is the man who has made all this trouble.

General Crook. Is that all he has to say?

Red Cloud. Yes.

General Crook. I came to give him an opportunity to express himself definitely, so I might learn his views. I don't care whether he goes or not.

General Crook now asked Agent Hastings if he had seen the correspondence relating to this expedition and the authority for it.

Hastings. Oh. Yes. I understand all about this.

General Crook then mentioned that Secy. Chandler, Ass't Secy. Cowan, Commissioner Smith and Secy. Belknap were present at the Council when President Grant decided the Northern Sioux

10. Shoshones
11. Red Cloud was referring—accurately—to the Reynolds fight on the Powder River.

should go upon their proper reserves or be whipped.[12] If these Sioux (from Red Cloud Agency) went out with the expedition, they could have the captured ponies, otherwise somebody else would.

Red Cloud. I am here raising young children. The Great Father told us to stay here. I don't want to go anywhere.

Little Wound. You have told us the President and Secretary sent you out. We don't believe it. I have been twice to Washington. The Great Father told me not to go to War anymore; not to fight enemies anymore:

General Crook. I have nothing more to say.

Little Wound. I have heard of a war and heard of a fight (in former times) with the Great Father.[13] But both parties were out a good deal and had nothing to gain. I told the Agent once I didn't want to have any trouble. I am glad you came to talk—

General Crook. I have nothing else to talk about but their going out. I have nothing else to say.

Red Cloud. When do you start?

General Crook. When I get ready.

Red Cloud: They (the Northern Indians.) have stolen some of our horses: a party of our young men have gone out after them and have been gone several days.*

General Crook and party now left: Mr. Wm. Dear, the post trader invited us into his quarters and treated our party (which was joined by Genl. Vandever, Mr. Hastings and, Mr. McCann) to a glass of cool champagne. We then drove back to the post.

A comparison of the two conventions above recorded will show without much delay there was something wrong: in the morning, we find the representative men of the tribe anxious to go out with the troops. In the evening, these same men are kept in the back-ground to let Red Cloud and Little Wound re-echo the sentiments of the Agent and Genl. Vandever. Last week, the Hay scales at Red Cloud Agency were burned by the Indians who behaved so very ugly that the Agent sent

* Agent Hastings wanted Gen. Crook to ask Red Cloud what he thought of the campaign made recently against Crazy Horse, but Inspector Vandever objected, saying it was no use to open up discussion upon that point. Agent Hastings then stated that Red Cloud had expressed himself as pleased to hear the troops had gone after Crazy Horse and Sitting Bull.

12. Crook refers to a meeting in November 1875, between himself, President Grant, General Sherman, Secretary of War Belknap, Interior Secretary Zachariah Chandler, Assistant Interior Secretary B.R. Cowan, and Commissioner of Indian Affairs Edward B. Smith. Robinson, *A Good Year to Die*, 40-41.

13. Little Wound could have been referring to any of several conflicts in the late 1850s and early to mid-1860s.

Mrs Yates, wife of the post trader to Camp Robinson, where she now
is for protection. The agency herd of ponies (seven.) was this morning run off from Red Cloud and yesterday from Spotted Tail.

General Vandever remarked this evening that the Indians at both
these agencies were in a very good frame of mind and anxious to
sell the Black Hills to Government for a fair figure. This means that
somebody is organizing a gigantic raid on our depleted Treasury.
We shall see what we shall see.

In the personal adornment of the Sioux chiefs nothing peculiar
was to be observed: all wore pantaloons, loose in cut, of dark blue
cloth; moccasins of buck or buffalo skin, covered with bead work;
Mackinaw blankets dark blue or black in color, closely enveloping
the frame, (some of these blankets variegated by a transverse band
of bright red cloth worked over with beads;) strings of beads, shells
and brass rings encircling the neck, while underneath the blankets
coarse dark woolen shirts were discernible. The hair was worn long
but plain, parted in the middle and the line of parting painted with
vermillion or red ochre. An unusual thing with Indians as far as I
can say, their faces were not marked with paint of any kind.

Pipes were smoked made of the red pipe-stone from the quarries in the Upper Missouri, above Standing Rock. (This pipe-stone
is either a steatite or else an indurated ochreous clay, the latter,
judging from the weight, being the more probable assumption.)
Only the bowl is of stone but this is inlaid very skillfully with silver; the stem is of a hollow or flat reed, the arrow wood, burned
through; devices wrought in feathers, beads and paint give con-
spicuousness and barbarous beauty to the instrument. The bowl
is prolonged at the lower extremity to allow the oil of tobacco to
collect there. Each Indian takes 3 or 4 whiffs and then passes the
pipe along to his neighbor on the Left. A rough representation of a
Sioux pipe is given. . . .

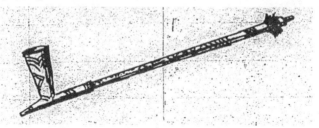

Sioux Pipe. (Red Cloud Agency, Neb. 1876)

Frank Gruard obtained information verifying our suspicions that these Indians had been tampered with by the Agent before General Crook's arrival. Rocky Bear, Three Bears and Sitting Bull told Frank that altho' the agent in person did not say anything to them, (he was too cunning for that.) his clerk, McCavanaugh and Interpreter, Billy Hunter, had spoken with them and told them the agent said they must not go on the Expedition with the troops and in many other ways antagonized the President's policy. Sitting Bull was taken severely to task for having presumed to speak with General Crook until after consultation with the Agent. These three Indians, however, told Frank to say to General Crook they would try to raise a small party at the agency, of about 20 or 30, and start out to overtake the Expedition near Fetterman. By thus frustrating General Crook's plans of bringing with his column a force of young Indians from Red Cloud's people, General Vandever and Agent Hastings have thrown themselves in direct opposition to the early pacification of the recalcitrant Sioux. Had General Crook obtained a few hundred warriors, the U.P.R.R. would have been safer to just that extent; in the absence of cavalry from the line of posts guarding that road, the temptation to rob and murder would be too great for the unruly young Indians to resist, hence in withdrawing that number of young warriors from the agency we reduced the number likely to prey upon the ranches of Wyoming and Nebraska, besides having hostages for the good behavior of those not under our immediate surveillance. This would [be] the most important feature of the contemplated arrangement, but as soon as our column should have penetrated to the Yellowstone country, as trailers, guides and scouts, our Sioux auxiliaries would have been worth their weight in gold and saved our soldiers and horses from many hours of weary toil and marching. By broadly defining the line of separation between the good Indians and the bad, this alliance would have been shown to the intractable Uncapapa Sioux that their line of communication with the agencies was cut off and that when this present force of men and supplies was destroyed or reduced, there would be no alternative but an unconditional surrender. An Indian is precisely like a white man in that he will fight as long as he thinks himself certain of victory: but he is never like the white man in dying on the field of battle rather than see his country enslaved. The ordinary course of our Indian wars has been first a long series of petty quarrels and fights between the advance guard of pioneers, trappers and settlers and the red man: small detachments of troops are next sent out to give "protection" to the settler. They are as feeble in numbers and so inexperienced in training, that the establishment of military posts is very frequently rather an encouragement to the savage than an intimidation. To exemplify my meaning, let one cite the case of the various Reservations and public lands ceded to the Sioux; the total area, inclusive of the Big Horn country, cannot be less than 60.000.000 A[cres]. and as the Regular Army, all told, is by law restricted to 25.000 aggregate enlisted men and never at one time muster more than 23.000, it can be seen at a glance that every private soldier, supposing the whole Regular Army to be detailed to watch over this one tribe, would have something like four square miles of territory to stand guard over. Surrounding the vast belt of country now occupied by the Sioux or Dacotah Indians are the reservations of other tribes, who have shown themselves more amenable to the influence of civilization: among these, rank first the Absaraka or Crow Indians, owners of the country comprehended between Laramie Peak and the Big Horn Mountains. They are now confined to the extreme Western rim of their proper country through fear of their hereditary enemies whom our Commissioners by the Treaty of 1868, made at Fort Laramie, seemed to recognize as owners of the soil.

It seems not to be generally known that the Dacotah tribes until within the last generation were residents of the belt of territory contiguous to and immediately West of the Great Lakes, along which the Ojibways or Chippeways and other branches of the great Algonquin race dwelt. (Parkman who is good authority, claims the Dacotahs as limbs of that great ethnic trunk. vide "The Jesuits in North America".)

Sometime very early in the present century, the small-pox swept like a scourge among the tribes along the Right bank of the Missouri river, reducing all in strength and completely decimating and demoralizing some of the most powerful as the Mandans and, perhaps, the Arapahoes.

Synchronously with this dire visitation, the Dacotahs, then stretching from the headwaters of the Mississippi to where the village of Yankton now stands on the Missouri, crossed the latter stream at the mouth of White Earth river probably on the ice in winter.

The invaders found hospitality and assistance among the Sheyennes or Cheyennes, a powerful tribe, roaming over the plains from the big bend of the Missouri to the Arkansas.

From the Mandans, Pawnees, Poncas, Otoes and Crows, nothing but resistance was offered; the invading columns separated the band now styled the "Big Bellies" or Gros Ventres from the Arapahoes and the Rees from the Pawnees: the Mandans were subdued by disease as also no doubt the Poncas and Otoes had been. But be that as it may, the advent of the Sioux marked the commencement of an era of hostility which has never abated between them and the tribes above named as well as the Utes of Colorado and the Sho-sho-nees or Snakes of Idaho and Wyoming.

When the Missouri was first crossed the Dacotahs were "foot" Indians and to this day the Hohe Dacotahs or, as they are known to us, the Assiniboines, whom domestic feuds similar to the wars of the Romans & Sabines drove away to the North to the confines of British America, are "foot" Indians, having no horses but using dog sledges for the transportation of their movables while the Uncapapas, Brulés, Minneconjous, Ogallallahs and other bands of the Sioux (or "cutthroat") Indians are owners of immense herds of ponies whose ancestors they obtained by trade from their confederates, the Cheyennes, and they in time from the Kiowas and Commaches [sic] who stole them from the Mexicans. The Sioux have constantly improved the advantages first gained; they have been the scourge of the neighboring tribes among whom civilization and Christianity will make no progress until a feeling of security is imparted by a thorough reduction of the disturbers of their repose: no later than 1874, the Sioux sent out a war-party which surprised a village of Pawnees on the Republican River at a time when all its male members were absent a short distance hunting the buffalo. They attacked the helpless old women and children and did not suffer one to escape to breathe the dreadful tale.

Yet they had promised to keep the peace with these Indians whose advancement in any of the arts of domestic life cannot be looked forward to with much hope until they are assured of the fullest protection from our Government. Of the obligations entered into by the Sioux at the treaty made at Fort Laramie in 1867 and 1868 and ratified soon after, not one has been kept. They have not refrained from war with Pawnees, Crows, Utes, Mandans, Rees or Shoshones;

they have persisted in stealing stock and other property from the whites. The value of the animals thus carried off within the past year alone runs up into hundreds and thousands of dollars. They have killed numbers of our fellow citizens whose blood still stains the soil of Wyoming & Nebraska[;] their promise [sic] to become self supporting within four years after the signing of the treaty have been completely ignored and to quote from the Report of the Red Cloud Investigating Committee made last autumn, "$5000 would certainly cover the value of all the produce raised by all the bands of Sioux since the signing of the Treaty". (Our Government meantime has spent between $13.000.000 and $15.000.000 upon these gentlemen beggars, who are too proud to work and too robust to go hungry.) Their children have never been sent to school and in no manner have they been faithful to that convention except in drawing rations.

On its side, our Government has been faithful to its obligations; has broken up at astounding cost posts on the north side of the Platte and kept all soldiers to the South of that stream until the cold-blooded murder of Lieut. Robinson of the 14th Infantry in 1874, aroused the country to a sense of what was due to its own dignity. It remains now to point out some of the causes which have led to this state of affairs and to suggest the remedy which must be applied to secure a better state of things on our frontier.

It has already been noted that when troubles between the various tribes and the Whites or among the Indians peaceably disposed and those persistently hostile are in their incipiency, our policy has been to send small detachments of soldiery among the savages who soon learn to despise a Government as feebly represented [as ours]. It is as much as the soldiers can do to protect the agent's own person and the supplies shipped for consumption by the Indians. The Indians finding themselves under no control hatch out in their reservations plans of raids and marauding expeditions against the settlements and being very quick in their movements and thoroughly acquainted with country find it easy to elude the feeble detachments of troops sent out after them and escape back to the Reserves where this prowess gives them prestige among their fellows and excites an emulation to do likewise. Finally, an Indian war does come; the troops are sent into the field, endure great hardships and suffer untold discomforts; if victorious, they are railed at by the "religious" press of the country as unbridled butchers; if defeated, as all expeditions must expect to be, ridicule and contumely are poured out upon them.

In their privations they feel they must expect no commiseration; in their sufferings and dangers, no sympathy.

It generally happens that the Indians are promptly subdued and then the acme of the farce of American Indian management is reached. A reservation is laid out for them, if one be not already established and an "agent," nominated by some of the religious denominations, is appointed to look after them. Admitting the savage aborigine to be guileless as a child, plastic as clay in the hands of the potter, it may be seen at a glance that the qualities an Agent must possess are honesty, singleness of purpose, great administrative and executive capacity, and impartial firmness. To suppose that any man gifted with these qualities will sacrifice himself for the miserable stipend of $1500 per annum and a precarious tenure of office is to suppose we are living in Utopia. The denominational selections are consequently of a lower average than the political dead beats who managed the Indians from 1849 to 1857. They may be divided into two general classes—incompetent or fanatical imbeciles and sanctimonious rascals; the first class includes good and well-meaning old men who have failed in every business enterprise ever undertaken by them but whose religious fervor and general probity of character must be admitted by everybody. This class is "nuts" for the contractors and other cormorants hanging around the agency. By catering to the various weaknesses and especially to the religious prejudices of the incumbents of the respective agencies, contractors soon have things all their own way and make fabulous sums of money. It is amusing to note the Theological variations of character among those contractors who have several agencies to look after; at one, they will be found unctiously Evangelical; a day or two finds them Low Church Episcopalians[;] another, they are Ritualistic and before the week is over [Saint] Dominic himself, the author of the Inquisition, could not have such a horror of heresy and schism.

The other class of agents are those "who steal the livery of heaven to serve the devil in"—The most sanctimonious of the whole congregation they are most anxious to go out among the Indians for the mere pleasure of evangelizing them; this category is not in general terms looked upon with favor by the contractors who find the lion's share of the spoils stolen from the Indian appropriation claimed by the pious fraud who has wriggled his way into his position by the influences and under the patronage of some Christian church.

This set of agents is very readily known—they are decidedly "on the make" and rarely let the grass grow under their feet. The list of agency people, under their supervision, is something like this.

Zorababel Sleek, Agent.

Mrs. Z. Sleek. Chief Clerk.

Z. Sleek Jr. Ass't Clerk.

Aninidal Sleek. Interpreter.

Enoch Chadband (cousin.) Head farmer

and so on through the family list.

By and Bye, there arises a murmur of discontent from the contractors who are kept out of their share of the spoils: and "pressure" as it is called, is brought to bear; an investigation follows: Agent Sleek's proceedings are characterized as "irregular" and his appointment is revoked and he superceded by the fervid and zealous Christian, Luther Honeyman, who is just the man the contractors have been looking for.

That this is no overdrawn picture of the general current of Indian affairs in the West every honest and experienced person must, however, reluctantly, confess, and that some radical change should at once be made no disinterested man or woman will fail to admit. Under the present personnel of the Indian Department, a great improvement has been effected, but the Indian Bureau is an Augean Stable[14] which cannot be cleaned until the stream of journalistic criticism is turned full upon it.

The late Commissioner of Indian Affairs, the Revd. E. P. Smith did much to bring the Peace Policy into disrepute. Such men as Mr. Wm. Welch of Philad[elphi]a and Professor [Othniel C.] Marsh of Yale College openly charged him with corruption and after vainly essaying to stem the tide without refuting the evidence Smith retired from office and sank into deserved obscurity.

As a remedy for these chronic evils, it has been proposed and the proposition meets with cordial acceptance from all classes who have disinterested[ly] studied the Indian question, to transfer the Indian

14. Bourke refers to one of the labors of Heracles in mythology, in which the hero is required by King Augeas to clean a year's accumulation of dung from the royal stables in only a day.

Bureau in toto to the Department of War and have the agencies managed by Army officers of experience, under the control of the Secy. of War. Such a transfer it is contended would result in immense savings, first in the salaries of the Agents and Inspectors, because Army officers would discharge their new functions without increased remuneration, thus saving about half a million yearly and, secondly in the increased efficiency of administration the War Department could bring to bear in the adoption of its greatly superior methods of accounts and checks upon disbursements. In the year 1849, the last year the Military had control of Indian affairs, the total expenses of the Indian Bureau was $850.000. In the present year, the same Bureau asks for $7.000.000 and a deficiency of some $450.000.

Secondly, in the Honesty of officials, because an army officer holds his position by a life or good-conduct tenure; has a recognized place of prominence in society; the hope of promotion and distinction as a reward of faithful service and feels besides that the pettiest act of peculation is certain to be traced to him through the rigid system of accounts he must conform to and the jealous scrutiny of his associates who however lenient they may be in other respects, show no mercy toward the cowardly or dishonest.

The Commissioner of Indian Affairs in his last annual report makes the sorry confession that after twenty six years of experience and untrammelled administration, the Indian Bureau has no system of accounts which will prevent speculation and asks Congress to turn over the purchase and distribution of supplies to the appropriate Staff Bureaus in the War Department!

An army officer must not only not commit fraud against the Government himself, but by the Articles of War he is forbidden association with those convicted of it. How different the rule of conduct in the Indian Bureau. The other day Inspector Vandever and Agent Hastings might be seen in a confidential brotherly check by jowl conference with Mr. D. J. McCann! Not the formal intercourse of official duty but a long ride from Red Cloud (45 miles) to Spotted Tail and Back. This Mr. D.J. McCann is the contractor the Red Cloud commission last year found guilty of putting up 100 lbs of flour in an 88# sack, and of charging the Government for 210 miles of transportation over a road which only measured 156 miles. Then [to] see such an individual travelling as the guest and boon companion

of trusted Government officials, gives rise to grave suspicions of the
sentinels supposed to be on the watch over public interest. Vandever
is the last of the appoint[ment]s secured through the influence of
the now disgraced Secretary Belknap: perhaps a close scrutiny into
his character and integrity might disclose something of interest to
those people who are as earnestly working for a purification of the
Civil Service.

An argument against the transfer, the one which seems to be a
favorite with those people who derive influence or emolument from
the present system, is an augmentum ad hominem, an appeal to
the prejudices of the American people. It commences by conceding
all that is claimed for the transfer proposed, but tacks on to this
logical prothesis the apodosis that the Indian will degrade rapidly
under the influences military association will surround him with.
This argument takes very well and is constantly employed either
by those pecuniarily concerned in the perpetuation of the present
system or by the credulous and unsuspecting religious portions of
our communities whom rascals find it so much to their profit to
deceive.

Let us examine this argument by the light of facts: every agency is
now protected on the frontier by detachments of troops more or
less strong. Either these officers and soldiers debauch the female
Indians or they do not. If they do, let the country hear of it. Let
Agents come out and denounce the unprincipled scoundrels who
perpetrate or permit such crimes. If they do not do this now, it is
difficult for the average American to see how the mere transfer of
papers from Agent to Army officer is going to secure unrestrained
gratification of his passions, if so disposed. If the Indians themselves were questioned a different phase might be placed upon this
controversy—one which if not implicating the Agents personally
would at least convict many of them of neglect or indifference to
the moral surroundings of their wards by allowing the residence
upon the Reserves of so many squaw men, the lowest, vilest set of
rascals that has ever been pawned upon the world. These are the
fellows who fringe the Agency buildings with their own hovels and
tepis, who are at the bottom of all the rascality at the Agency, who
incite the Indians to nearly every ebullition of malevolence they
are guilty of. It was through the instrumentality of such tools that
the Indian Ring last year tuned up the Indians to demand

$70.000.000 from the United States as the price of the Black Hills
and it may not be amiss to note here a word of caution[:] just such
another job is now being hatched out at Red Cloud and Spotted Tail
Agencies by men whom the people suppose are devoted to the public weal. It is hardly possible the tax-paying part of the community
will quietly and without indignant protest agree to pay $70.000.000
to these savages or rather to the rings that live upon their appro-
priations and at the same time listen unconcerned to the wailing
and lamentations of the women and children in other large manufacturing cities in the East go supperless to bed because husbands
and fathers are destitute of work.

One word more and this subject is dropped. Delicacy forbids an
expatiation upon so disgusting a theme, but those who are known
to be posted insist upon it that much of the diseases of a syphilitic
or Hemorrhaging type that work such havoc among our Indians are
spread among the tribes of those members who have been taken to
Washington where it is asserted the practice has been to provide
the chiefs with prostitutes at the public expense! This is a grave
charge—one that should be carefully examined by people acquainted
with the facts,—but it should be examined nevertheless. It might
be well in this connection to look up the reasons why Red Cloud
and his party were so dissatisfied with their treatment during their
last visit, to Washington as compared with former ones.

Chapter 15

✦

✦

✦

✦

✦

The Big Horn and
Yellowstone Expedition

May 16th Left Red Cloud Agency in company with Col. Stanton,
Colonel Ludington, Lieut. Griffith, 9th Infantry and a few citizens,
guides, discharged soldiers &c. Our united escorts numbered about
65 men, too many for any small party of Indians to think of attacking.

As we left the Post, a few curling wreaths of smoke showed the
signals were being made, but for what purpose we could not conjecture. As we approached the head of White Earth river the mail driver,
going to Red Cloud Agency, passed us.

We camped by the springs on White Earth shortly after passing the
mail wagon and remained long enough to partake of a cold lunch;
had our sense of hearing been a little more acute, we might have
heard the death cry of the poor mail driver. That night we reached
the ranch on the Niobrara. It surprises me to think that the Agent
would suffer these ranches to be constructed on the Niobrara and
the Raw Hide, as those places lie within the limits of the Sioux
Reservation.

About midnight, a courier reached us from Major Jordan, 9th Inf.,
Comdg Camp Robinson with a dispatch reading as follows:

HdQrs. Camp Robinson, Neb.,
May 16th, 1876

2 Lieut. John G. Bourke,
3d Cavalry, Aide de Camp,
Lieutenant.

I have the honor to report for the information of the Commanding General of the Department that about 2 P.M to-day a white man, named Joe Roots, reported to me that the mail carrier (a man named Clark) while en route from Fort Laramie to the Agency was killed by a small party of Indians about noon to-day in the White (Earth.) River cañon at a point about ten miles from here.

Mr. Roots was with two other men who were taking oxen to the ranches on Running Water (Niobrara,) when they heard several shots fired, saw the mail carrier lying dead in the wagon immediately afterwards and saw the Indians—four in number—drive off the two horses that were attached to the wagon.

About 2.45 P.M., the two Mr. Dears started with a party of about twenty friendly Indians to try and capture the Indians that committed the outrage.

Soon after the report reached me, I sent Lieut. McCaleb, 9th Infantry, with two enlisted men in an army wagon to bring in the body of the murdered man, the mail (which was not molested) and the mail wagon.

I am Lieutenant, Very Resp. &c.
(Sig.) Wm. H. Jordan
Captain, 9th Inf. Comd Post

I have inserted the above that it may speak for itself: it proves that while the Agent has been busy representing the peaceable attitude of his Indians, they have murdered men almost under his nose.

And additional cause for the opposition of Mr. Hastings to the enlistment of a contingent of auxiliaries from among the Red Cloud Indians lies in the fact that if by any means the hostile Indians of the North shall be subdued, there will be no difficulty in transferring the Red Cloud and Spotted Tail Bands to the Missouri where, being congregated in one large Reservation, the Sioux Indians can do without the present force of Agents and interpreters and be made to work for their own support. It appears to be the settled purpose of these Agents to keep the savages in a condition of vagabondage, because, if they should once be placed on the highway to improvement, agents would simply be an impediment in their path.

Reached Fort Fetterman on the [1]7th and remained there overnight. Munson's, Burt's and Burrough's companies of the 9th Infantry were preparing to start with the expedition. Genl. Crook received a telegram from General Sheridan saying General Terry's column had left Fort Abraham Lincoln,[1] on the 16th. Also one saying General Sherman had decided upon the detail for the Court to try General Reynolds, and that it would convene July 15th.

Moved out, May 18th, with Colonel Stanton, toward Fort Fetterman. Road passes along Right bank of the North Platte for the first 13 miles within sight of the river, road very sandy to Warm Springs, up grade: road then becomes fairly good to Cottonwood Creek 22 miles: then it winds over the Bull Bend Mountains and for 4 or 5 miles is very rocky and difficult. Again comes in sight of the river and goes down grade, good travelling to Twin Springs, (31 miles) a pair of springs with perennial and pellucid water. From Twin Springs to Horse Shoe creek (36 miles) road is very good. Country thus far is rolling and well adapted for grazing. Some little cedar and scrub juniper with here and there a stunted pine tree on adjacent hill tops. Between Cottonwood Creek and Horse Shoe Creek the North Platte winds through a cañon, with rocky walls. During this day, the weather was very beautiful, but as evening approached, heavy storm clouds gathered over us and a few drops of rain fell.

The next day, May 18th [*sic*], the road for 9 miles to Elkhorn creek (45 miles) was very bad, much cut up by heavy trains coming in on the cut-off road from the Chug. Crossed the Elkhorn and went 13 miles to the La Bonté (58 miles) which we found very high, about 2 1/2 feet deep, 60 feet wide and current quite swift. Crossing very good.

All the creeks mentioned here at least at this time of year, a good flow of water, & rapid currents, but are safe to cross. The La Bonté is much the largest. From the Horse Shoe to the La Bonté the geo-

---

1. Fort Abraham Lincoln was located at the confluence of the Heart and Missouri Rivers across from present-day Bismarck, North Dakota. It was established as Fort McKean on June 14, 1872, but on November 19 of the same year was redesignated as Fort Abraham Lincoln. The post was abandoned in 1891, and the structures were dismantled by area residents in search of building materials. The partially reconstructed post is now a North Dakota state park. Frazer, *Forts of the West*, 111-12.

logical character of the country is red clay and sandstone; and gypsiferous earths. From the La Bonté to Fort Fetterman on the Right Bank of the North Platte, and the mouth of La Prele (Rush.) Creek, the country is more or less sandy, with some indications of lime or gypsum in the soil. The streams crossed, the Wagon Hound and Bed Tick are insignificant except during the rainy season.

Remained at Fort Fetterman, Sunday Monday and Tuesday, the General busy in transporting supplies across the ferry. A sand bar had formed about 15 feet out from the South shore of the Platte and before any great amount of stores could be taken across, a wing dam of boards, old planks and gunny-sacks filled with stones and gravel had to be built to deflect the current and a platform constructed to give greater depth and to serve as a wharf. Then it was found the pulleys running along the guy-rope had too small grooves and that the tiller ropes were fastened too high up on the ferry boat's side. Iron rods were made to run from side to side and the rope fastenings were placed at the water line. New pulleys were fixed to the guy ropes and everything done to make the boat run more smoothly and easily. 30.000 lbs of stores were taken across the first day and over 60.000 pounds the next. A small detachment was thrown across to guard the piles of property heaped up on the opposite bank.

Our day at the Post was made as pleasant as possible by the officers and their families. My own comforts were carefully looked after by Dr and Mrs. [Joseph Ruff] Gibson, who kindly made me their guest during our whole stay; but for all this attention and the courtesies of others stationed at the post, it was difficult at times to banish ennui; after giving up as much time as I could to writing letters, reading and visiting, I was sensible each day of the oppressiveness of waiting at a frontier post for the arrival of the slowly moving columns and supplies coming up from Fort Laramie and from Medicine Bow. (On the U.P.R.R.) Frank Gruard and a picked body of soldiers was sent to explore a way for our wagon train to Powder River to the Left of the old Fort Reno road, which crosses that river at a very muddy and dangerous ford. They were discovered and nearly cut off by hostile Indians, who followed them almost back to the Platte.

Col. Chambers, 4th Infantry, and Mr. Wasson, the correspondent of the *"Alta California"* arrived on the 22d. . . .

Wednesday, May 24th, 1876. The telegraph line was repaired today. It has been down since the storm of Saturday night. One of the

first communications sent over was one from General Sheridan to
Gen. Crook, announcing that Captain [Thomas Lee] Brent of the
3d Cavalry had been retired; this vacancy promotes 1 Lieut [Peter
D.] Vroom to be Captain and the writer to be 1 Lieut of "L." Company, 3d Cavalry. General Sherman telegraphed (through the Lieut.
General [Sheridan]) that, after reading the official reports of the
recent expedition to Montana and the attack upon the village of
Crazy Horse, he was satisfied that Gen. Reynolds' trial should take
place immediately after the return of the Expedition. General Crook
received information also that Col. Royall's column of the 3d and
2d Cavalry and 9th Infantry had not left Laramie before Tuesday
morning, April 26th, owing to bad weather and heavy roads. Colonel [Andrew Wallace] Evans' column from Medicine Bow, on the
U.P.R.R. came within sight of post this afternoon and next morning.
Thursday, May 25th, [Evans' column] Marched into Fort Fetterman
and immediately commenced crossing the North Platte river by the
Ferry and also by swimming the horses and mules. This latter operation was only partially successful; only a small number of ani-
mals could be made to swim this river, the remainder stampeding
in large herds rather than make the venture. Col. Evans had with
his command Captain A.H. Nickerson, A.D.C.[,] Maj. J.V. Furey,
A.Q.M.[,] Maj. G.M. Randall, chief of scouts, Captain [William]
Stanton, Engineer Officer, Asst. Surgeon [Julius] Patzki, and the
following companies.
"B", 3d Cav. Capt. [Charles] Meinhold & 2nd Lt. [James F.] Simpson.
"C", 3d Cav.—[Frederick] Van Vliet & 1 Lt.[Adolphus] Von
Leuttewitz.
"G". 3d Cav.—1 Lt. E. Crawford.
"I", 3d Cav. Capt. [William H.] Andrews. & 2d Lt. E.H. Foster.
"L" 3d Cav. Capt. P.D. Vroom & Lt. [George F.] Chase
"D" 2d Cav. 1st Lt. [Samuel M.] Swigert, 2d Lt. [Henry D.] Huntington
and "D", 4th Inf. Capt. A.D. Cain & 1 Lt. H. Seton.
May 26th. The hawser of the ferry broke this morning about 11
O'clock. Not much trouble was made because most of the supplies
and nearly all the troops had already crossed. By hauling the slack
of the rope across the stream the break was repaired in a few hours.
One of our teamsters, Dill by name, a driver of one of the HdQrs.
Teams was drowned in swimming the Platte this afternoon. The
first company, Munson's, 9th Inf., of Royall's command arrived on

the other side toward evening, bringing mail. A courier party, including Mr. Strahorn and Louis Richaud came in from Fort Laramie with dispatches for Genl. Crook.

The orders for the organization of the Expedition were promulgated to-day,* reading as follows:

HdQrs. Big Horn and Yellowstone Expedn.

Fort Fetterman,

W[yoming].T[erritory]., May 28th 1876.

General Orders,

No 1.

I The undersigned assumes command of the troops comprising the Big Horn and Yellowstone Expedition.

II. Lieut. Col. W.B. Royall, 3d Cav., will command the Cavalry of the Expedition.

III Major Alex. Chambers, 4th Inf., will command the Battalion, composed of companies of the 4th and 9th Infantry.

IV. Maj. A.H. Evans, 3d Cavalry, is assigned to the command of the Battalion composed of companies of the 3d Cavalry, reporting to Colonel Royall.

V. Capt. H.E. Noyes, 2d Cavalry, is assigned to the command of the companies of the 2d Cav., reporting to Colonel Royall.

VI. The following named officers will compose the staff of the Expedition:

Captain A.H. Nickerson, 23d Inf. A.D.C. & A.A.G.

Lieut. John G. Bourke, 3d Cav., A.D.C.

Capt. Geo. M. Randall, 23d Inf., Chief of Scouts.

Capt. W.S. Stanton, Engr. Corps, Chief Engr. Officer.

Capt. J.V. Furey, A.Q.M., Chief Q.M.

1 Lieut. J.W. Bubb, 4th Inf. Actg. Comy. Subsist.

Ass't Surgn. Albert Hartsuff, Medl. Director.

(Signed.) George Crook

Brigadier General

Comdg. Expeditn.

Official

John G. Bourke,

Aide de Camp.

May 28th. Bustle and activity prevailing in camp: officers, orderlies and detachments of men passing constantly to and from the Garrison;

* Promulgated on 28th.

the ferry, repaired during the past night found no respite all day. Wagon loads of grain, ammunition, subsistence and other stores crossed the Platte to the camp on the other side which spread out in a picturesque panorama along the level meadow, surrounded by a bend of the stream. The long rows of shelter tents, herds of animals grazing or running about, trains of wagons and mules passing from point to point, made up a scene of great animation and spirit. The allowance of baggage for the present expedition has been placed at the lowest limit; shelter tents for the men and "A" tents for the officers. All trunks and heavy packages ordered to be left at this point. An allowance of twenty-five wagons for the fifteen companies of Cavalry and six for the five of Infy. Necessitated the leaving behind of every article not needed absolutely for the welfare of the command. The number of wagons loaded with forage was *[no number given]*, and those holding subsistence stores and ammunition *[no number given]* and *[no number given]* respectively. *

The ferry worked constantly during the day, transporting quantities of stores so that by night-fall but little was left on the Fetterman side. Between 8 and 9 O'clock in the evening, the cable, the new one ordered up from Laramie, snapped in twain, letting the boat swing loose in the current. It was soon recovered and the toilsome work resumed of splicing the ruptured hawser. Our ferrymen were well-nigh exhausted and with much difficulty exerted themselves to restore communications.

Early in the morning, Captain Egan, 2d Cavalry, telegraphed from Fort Laramie the result of his scout from that post, just completed. He found on Sage Creek nearly one hundred lodges, mostly of warriors who numbered, according to his estimate, 600. All he could do was to drive them away from the wagon trains they were attacking. He also reported that many lodges had left the agencies going North and that the Arapahoe and Cheyenne villages (at Red Cloud.) were deserted. . . .(To protect the Black Hills road, we have only Egan's and Russell's companies of Cavalry and three of Infantry, one from Omaha Barracks and two from Fort Bridger.)[2]

---

* A total of one hundred Three.

2. Omaha Barracks was established in 1868 on the right bank of the Missouri River within the present city limits of Omaha, Nebraska. It was designated Fort Omaha in 1878. The post was replaced by Fort Crook in 1895, but has been reactivated several times, and the government has retained the military reservation. Fort Bridger, in southwestern Wyoming, was established as a trading post by Jim Bridger and Luis Vasquez in 1842, and leased to the government in 1857. It was permanently abandoned and transferred to the Department of the Interior in 1890. Ibid., 89, 178.

May 29th. Left Fort Fetterman at one o'clock and joined Colonel Royall's column which was then slowly defiling out from its camp on the Left bank of the Platte: The long black line of mounted men stretched for more than a mile with nothing to break the sobreness of color save the flashing of the sun's rays back from the arms of the men. A long, moving streak of white told us our wagons were already well under way and a puff of dust just in front indicated the line of march of the Infantry Battalion. After moving North West for eleven or twelve miles, camp was made on Sage Creek. Nothing to note to-day. The road was rather dusty and without interesting scenery. Its characteristic features have already been noticed in the description of our winter campaign. Where then we heard only the howling of the fierce North Wind, the twittering of silvery-voiced meadow-larks assured us balmy summer now held sway.

At a late hour, we secured supper and then gave some time to an examination of the mail which had overtaken us from the post.

The following is a correct list of the companies and officers serving with the expedition:

For Staff &c. see G.O. No 1

Company "A", 3 Cav.	Lt. Morton.
"B",	Capt. Meinhold, Lt. Simpson.
Company "C", 3 Cav.	Capt. Van Vliet, Lt. v. Leuttewitz [sic].
"D",	Capt. Henry[,] Lt. Robinson.
"E"	Capt. Sutorious
"F"	Lt. B. Reynolds
"G"	Lt. Crawford
"I"	Capt. Andrews, Lt. Foster, Lt. A.K. King
"L"	Capt. L.D. Vroom[,] Lt. Chase
"M"	Capt. Anson Mills, Lt. A. S. Paul[,] Lt. Schwatka
"A" 2nd Cav.	Dewes, Lt. Peirson
"B"	Rowell (Lt.)
"E"	Capt. Wells, Lt. Sibley.
"I"	Capt. Noyes,
"G" 2nd Cav.	Lieut. Huntington
Compy. "C" 9th. Inf.	Capt. Sam Munnson, 1Lt. Capron.
"H"	Capt. A.H. Burt, 2Lt. Robertson.
"G"	Capt. T.B. Burroughs, 1Lt. W.L. Carpenter.
"D" 4th Inf.	Capt. A.B. Cain, 1Lt. Henry Seton.
F	Capt. Ger[h]ard Luhn.

Surgeons. Patski [Charles R.] Stevens (McGillicuddy) & [Junius I.] Powell.

Charles Russell & Thomas Moore Masters of Transportation

Frank Gruard, Louis Richaud, and Big Bat. [Pourier] guides.

Joseph Wasson, R.E. Strahorn, J. Finerty, W.C. McMillan [sic] and R.B. Davenport, Reporters for public Press.

May 30th. The companies of Cavalry under Captain Meinhold, 3d Cavalry, [were] sent forward this morning to find a better road and a better ford across Powder river than the one followed by last Expedition. Frank Gruard, our guide, accompanied them.

Command moved 20 miles to the South Cheyenne river a shriveled stream of muddy and alkaline water, standing in pools. Current sluggish, about four to six inches deep and 15 feet wide. Banks gently sloping—bed of the stream clayey and muddy. In high water, passage is difficult. Wood in sufficiency for the command. This camp was not agreeable. High cold wind all night and sky cloudy.

May 31st. Moved 20 miles North West to North Fork of Wind river, a confluent of the South Cheyenne, passing Humphreyville Creek and the Middle Fork of the South Cheyenne, during day. This day's march was very monotonous; day very cold and bleak. All the officers and men wrapped in overcoats. A man was brought in from Meinhold's command accidentally wounded in thigh (gunshot.) Found in this camp a sufficiency of cottonwood and water, the latter of poor quality. Grass good and plenty.

June 1st. A cold miserable day; heavy clouds laden with rain hanging over us; snow and sleet falling during the morning. Road pursued to-day follows along a back-bone between ravines and gulches, running down toward the Dry fork of Powder river. Country very broken and destitute of timber, except in the brakes where a few scrub juniper trees can be found secreted. Distance marched to-day 21 1/2 miles, in a direction generally North West, but extremely tortuous. Grass improving in quality. Passed to the South and West of the Pumpkin Buttes four in number, some 15 or 20 miles distant. They lie nearly East and West, are insignificant in elevation, but form a very important water-shed, inasmuch as they divide the waters flowing into the Belle Fourche on East from those reaching the Little Powder on the North, the Dry Fork on South and the main Powder river on the West. Elk, I am informed, resort to the vicinity of these buttes in large herds. Major Burt pointed out to me, a rare bird, the Missouri sky-lark, not often found this far to the West. Noticed a great scarcity of game along road; numbers of antelope tracks were seen, but only one killed. At this camp found wood, water and grass in plenty and were rejoined by Meinhold's command returning unsuccessful from a search after a new road to Reno. A party of (65) miners, travelling from Montana to the Deadwood district in the Black Hills, left an inscription on a board stating they had camped here on the 27th. Van Vliet's command had been here on the 29th. The two notices were examined and read with something of the curious interest mariners evince when a piece of a wreck is found floating at sea. No sooner had we got our tents pitched than we were compelled to kindle fires to keep in any way warm: water froze in the buckets and a cold wind blowing from the ice-covered domes of the Big Horns warned us not to trust too much to the assertion of the Almanac that June 1st is the first day of Summer. We are now in a country of the geological tertiary period; all the bluffs through which the streams have eroded their channels are formed of strata of indurated yellow clay and light-yellow sandstone superimposed conformably upon beds of lignite from six inches to four feet thick. The lignite is not exposed in all cases, but when I had a chance to examine it, appeared of fair quality, friable in texture and some indications of the presence of sulphur. When the stream of emigration sets in towards the Big Horn country, these deposits will beyond a peradventure prove of consequence.

June 2nd. Road followed down the Dry Fork of Powder river, 7 1/2 miles to old Fort Reno, and was generally good and of easy downgrade. Found Powder river very low, not more than two feet deep and (100)[†] feet wide. Had no trouble in crossing, but am convinced of the accuracy of the statement that it is impassable in time of high water. The bottom is a deep, heavy mud. Met Van Vliet's command in camp. The Crow Indian scouts had not joined as partly expected. This river bottom is well timbered (cottonwood.) and has a rich, black, loamy soil. Camp this night was on the site of old Reno, a post abandoned to the Sioux Indians by the stipulations of the hasty and ill-digested treaty of Fort Laramie.

Our three guides Frank Gruard, Big Bat, and Louis Richaud, were

† [inserted above line:] (112.6).

sent out in advance this evening with instructions to penetrate as far West as they might find necessary for the purpose of bringing in the Crow Indians, whose assistance will be equal to that of an additional Regiment.

This afternoon, in company with Mr. Davenport of the *N.Y. Herald* and Mr. Jos. Wasson of the *N.Y. Tribune* and *Alta California*, visited the ruins of old Fort Reno. We first wended our way to the cemetery, a lonesome spot on the brow of a squatty bluff overlooking the valley of the Powder. It would be hard to compress, within the limits of a note-book, an adequate description of the utter desolation now prevailing in the Sacred Field, or to analyze the emotions to which the sight gave rise. Not a head-board remained in place, not a paling of the fence which once surrounded the tombs was now in position: a rude cenotaph of brick masonry, erected by the loving hands of the former garrison to commemorate comrades who had fallen in the war with the Sioux lay dismantled, a heap of rubbish at the entrance. Directly in front of it, a line of graves covered with rough boulders held the remains of the braves who in the dark days of 1866 and 67 gave their lives to protect the emigrants and freighters, travelling to Montana. A few feet beyond these, a promiscuous heap of boards held inscribed the names of some at least whom the graves had sheltered. Curiosity impelled me to attempt a transcription from those upon which the inscriptions were still legible:

No. 12

Private C. Slagle, Co. F. 27th Inf. Killed May 30th '67

	8	No 10.
Clure	C. Riley	L.T. Morner
Killed	[2]7th Inf	27th Inf
Mar 27.	Killed by	Mar. 31st
67	[I]ndians	'67
	[March?] 27. '67	

Passing into the enclosure of the post, in the kitchen of the roofless and dilapidated building, formerly the Commanding Officer's Quarters, a dead and dessicated wolf hung suspended by the heels from a hook in the chimney well. Probably the trophy of a soldier's prowess, displayed there to gratify his own and his comrade's eyes and forgotten in the disgraceful hurry in which our Gov't abandoned this outpost. From the beams, stones, bricks and old iron of the ruins, the party of Montana miners who passed here a few days ago, had hastily improvised a number of lunettes and redoubts to check any attack the Sioux might make: As we looked down from this desolate solitude where the wary pickets secreted behind the tombs and chimneys afforded the only sign of animation, we can see out-spread before us the well-ordered camp of the command and the bustling air of readiness visible in everything: the thought would rise in my mind that perhaps the year 1876 would witness the re-venge of the horrible scenes of 1866 and '67 and the humiliation of the savages who had participated in the slaughter of our feeble gar-risons. Frank Gruard has an account from the Indians engaged, of the Fetterman Massacre in which three officers, [William J.] Fetterman, [Frederick H.] Brown and [George W.] Grummond, three citizens, names unknown,[3] and seventy-five soldiers were enticed out from the post of old fort Kearney by a band of Indians ostensibly attacking a train of wagons belonging to the post. The troops followed in hot pursuit of the Indians who retreated for about (3) miles, when suddenly the soldiers found themselves surrounded by thousands of Indians and after a desperate fight and the loss of their last cartridge were slaughtered to a man. The Indians claim, according to Frank's narration, to have had eight thousand warriors in the fight and to have lost one hundred eighty-five killed and wounded.[4]

June 3d, Last night was very cold for the season; sheet-ice one eighth of an inch thick covered the water-buckets. The Infantry column moved off at 4 A.M., under a blue and cloudless sky. Road some-what winding but very firm and good. Its direction was a little North of West, going towards Cloud Peak in the Big Horn Mountains of which a magnificent view was presented.

The massy domes of Cloud Peak and the neighboring prominences towered high in the sky, white with their mantles of snow; here and there a dark streak betrayed the attempt of the tall pine trees on the summit to penetrate to the open air above them. Heavy belts of forest covered the sides of the range below the snowline and ex-tended along the skirts of the foot-hills well out into the plains be-low.

3. Only two civilians, James Wheatley and Isaac Fisher, were killed in the massacre. Their companion, Portugee Phillips, was not present. Brown, *Fetterman Massacre*, 175.

4. The total number of Indians involved is reckoned at about two thousand, consisting primarily of Lakotas, Cheyennes, and Arapahos. The best estimate of Indian losses is about sixty killed in battle, and three hundred wounded, of whom about one hundred later died. Ibid., 178, 183.

Were this noble range more widely known, its bounties would not lack appreciative criticism as one of the grandest and most rugged spurs of the Rocky Mountains.

The singing of meadow-larks and the chirping of thousands of grass-hoppers enlivened the morning air and save these no sound broke the stillness except the rumbling of our wagons slowly creeping along the road. Soil becoming gypsiferous; found sulphate of lime in the form of flakes of selenite to the right of the road; also small patches of red clay. Captain Nickerson shot five Missouri sky-larks which Gen. Crook preserved as specimens. Gen. Crook found under a small sage-brush, a nest of the white-ringed black-bird, with six small turquois[e]-blue eggs; the ordinary complement is five. Indications of the close proximity of Indians observed to-day: fresh pony-tracks close to the road and off in the distance, pillars of smoke signalling our approach. A few Indians, probably pickets watching us, were seen scampering off as our column moved on. After marching twenty-seven miles, reached our former camp on the Crazy Woman creek, a branch of the Powder river. Here we found a stream 18 in. deep, 50 feet wide, current of eight miles. Banks generally sloping and bottom, hard clay. Cottonwood plenty and grass good. Camping ground overgrown with cactus and sage-brush.

June 4 (Sunday.) A serene atmosphere, balmy breeze and cloudless sky were our assurances this morning that summer had come at last and as if anxious to repair past negligences was about to favor us with all its charms. Marched at 5 a.m., over rolling country, well covered with fine grasses just heading into seed, but without any timber at all except upon the spurs of the Big Horn Mtn's to our Left, where dark dense belts of pine, juniper and oak(?) were visible.

The only eminences to be seen were the Pumpkin Buttes fast fading out of view in the dim distance behind us. The monotonous swell of the country extended well up to the Big Horn Range, rising in rank over rank to our Left and with sides seamed and gashed with numbers of deep cañons and gulches whence issue waters to feed the Tongue and Powder rivers. The geological and mineralogical features of the country remain almost unchanged since leaving the North Platte; brown and gray arenaceous[5] clays, friable yellow sandstone, gray and yellow marls, clay shales, lignite and an argillo-cal-

5. Sandy, from the Latin *arena* (sand).

careous[6] sandstone rapidly disintegrating when exposed to natural agencies, alternate with varying sequence, but constant appearance. The lignite beds thus far seen are generally of no commercial value, the same being of inferior quality and very small thickness. This lignite is frequently colored with iron and habitually contains sulphur. One lump found by a soldier was silicified at one extremity; at the other the appearance was that of fresh charcoal. The bluffs along the side of the road were capped with a deposit of modified drift which was also the bed of the different streams, after leaving Reno.

First buffalo tracks seen this morning.

Much difficulty was given the transportation by a shallow wash out, with vertical sides. A half hour's work with spade and pick cut away the escarpment and filled up the ravine well enough to let the wagons pass safely. This suggested to one the advantage to accrue from having with every large train, a pioneer and repair division to prevent delay and offset accidents. One of the first wagons should be loaded with a sufficient number of axes, hatchets, picks, spades, shovels, coils of rope &c. and immediately upon reaching a ravine, quicksand, rugged passage or miry river bottoms, the designated detail would spring to work, excavate and embank, corduroy or bridge as the exigencies of the case might require. The last wagon of each train should be loaded with extra poles, couplings, open links, and such parts of harness as may most frequently need replacement or repair. When an accident happened, the teamster could await the approach of the repair wagon and the forge accompanying it and under the protection of the rear-guard be placed in good travelling condition.

After travelling 25+ miles, our camp was made in an inviting bend of the Clear Fork (of Powder river,), at its junction with a small tributary. Three or four miles to the Eastward of this camp, passed Conner's Springs, pools of clear water, rocky bottoms, on either hand of road. Clear Creek is 50 feet wide, bottom of gravel, banks gently sloping, channel 18 in. to two feet deep and flowing with a current of eight miles an hour. Water sweet and cold, being melted snow from the Big Horn Ranges. Antelope and deer killed in small numbers by our hunters. General Crook killed a number of sucker fish with his rifle. The way to do [it] is to fire immediately under the fish which rises

6. Metamorphic carbonate.

to the surface stunned by the concussion. In this camp had an abundance of fine grass and pure water, but wood was rather scarce. A dense column of smoke arose on our Right during the afternoon and was at first taken for an Indian signal: after sun-set two miners came in and said the smoke came from burning prairies, accidentally ignited by their party of sixty-five miners, journeying from the Black Hills to the Big Horns on a prospecting tour. Their camp was now on Crazy Woman's fork, where they intended to commence an examination of the country. Had seen no Indians but great numbers of signs going North. (Saw no lodge pole tracks.)

This means that the Sioux warriors are joining the hostile bands and leaving their families at the Agencies for protection and subsistence. June 5th. Last night was clear and bright. No demonstration from Indians, a thing we must now look forward to at any and every moment. Colonel Royall, Colonel Chambers, Col. Evans and Maj. Noyes have been very careful regarding the manner of posting pickets around our camps. Nightly, the wagons are corralled to serve the double purpose of barricades and obstructions. Mounted parties are thrown out on the highest bluffs, there to remain until after sun-down when they are withdrawn to more sheltered positions nearer camp. One of our picket parties was last night stationed in a little gulch where all were to sleep except the one on post who crawled to a foothold in the wall of the ravine giving him an easy view along the ground above. Only his head protruded above the edge of the ravine and his instructions were to pull a rope attached to the Sergeant's leg whenever he needed help or wanted to attract attention. The Sergt. was then to awaken his party, move them stealthily up to the side of their comrade and give any hostile Indians wandering around camp a bloody welcome.

Day dawned bright and beautiful: cirrhus [sic] clouds relieved the intensity of the sun's rays. Broke camp at 5 A.M. our course lay North West close alongside of the Big Horn range and in among the outermost line of its foot-hills. Fine grass grazing everywhere. Crossed three or four little streams breaking out from the cañons; beds generally hard-pan and gravel. Water cold and sweet, but hard, with carbonate of lime, I think. Width of streams from 10 feet to 30 feet. Current 6 to 9 miles an hour.

Eight miles from Fort Kearney to the East is Lake de Smet named after the celebrated Catholic missionary, who passed his life among the Sioux, Crows and Blackfeet Indians.[7] The view of this body of water from the roadside is very beautiful. In length it is nearly 3 miles; in breadth, not quite a mile. The water is clear and cold but alkaline and disagreeable. No timber is to be found along its border, a peculiarity of the little streams already spoken of, which have only a few dead cottonwood trees scattered at extruded intervals along their banks. Sedge grass, coarse and thick, obstructs their channels and indicates their course.

Geese and ducks resort in great quantities to Lake de Smet, and fish, (a variety of pickerel), can be found there with ease at all times. Came to old Fort Kearney early in the day; distance from last camp, 15 2/3 miles: ruins of this old post are situate[d] on the Left Bank of the Piney creek, a branch of the Clear fork. This little creek travels along over a rocky bottom at a rate of nearly 10 miles an hour. Rapids and beaver dams obstruct its progress: very little wood in proximity. Grass is good and plenty and scenery beautiful but of rather a placid type. Broken pug-mills stand near the banks and a kiln of bright colored bricks looms up like a monument. The grave-yard in which were interred the bodies of Maj. Fetterman and the other gallant dead of the Kearney Massacre is without stone or board to mark the place of their last repose. The pallisading once sur-rounding the garrison has long since disappeared and ere many more years shall have lapsed the side of this historic spot will have become doubtful.[8]

Our men this afternoon trapped a young beaver; a few curlews (sickle-bills.) and pin-tailed grouse and one sage-cock were killed. The Sage-cock weighed 5 lbs. and the curlew 1 1/4 lb. Each. A re-port reached us to-night that a herd of buffalo was in close vicinity of camp. Gen. Crook, Capt. Nickerson and others started in pur-suit, but were unable to verify the report. They saw a great way off a few elk and some antelope. Capt. Nickerson killed an elk and brought the meat to camp: we pronounced it tough, coarse, and not agreeable. Colonel Chambers showed me a small fragment of rock found in a spur of the Big Horn Mountains: it was remarkably light. S[pecific]. G[raviy] not more than 1 or 1.25; vesicular, rough, quite hard and in color, reddish brown. It was no doubt, pumice stone or lava of some kind.

7. Pierre Jean de Smet.
8. Fort Phil Kearny is now a Wyoming state historic site.

Chapter 16

✦
✦
✦
✦
✦

Camp Life

June 6th. Our camp to-night is on a tributary of Goose Creek,* one of the head waters of the Tongue river, 17 3/4 miles from the site of last night's bivouac. Owing to the sultriness of the day and the bad road running over steep grades, this march has told upon both men and animals. Country during morning was extremely well-grassed, the herbage resembling growing wheat. The latter part of the march, the vegetation tho' still good was of coarser quantity. My judgment is that the foot-hills of the Big Horns will one day be one of the finest stock ranges in the world. The seasons are evidently clement, cold winds being warded off by the high ranges of hills, and the supply of water is constant and well distributed. On our trail, crossed many little tributaries of the sources of Powder and Tongue rivers; these little brawling brooks are not more than two or three feet wide, 8 inches to a foot deep and a rapidly-flowing current. Wood for fuel is not very thick along streams, but inexhaustable quantities are obtainable from the whole range of mountains directly in front. Intermingled with the cottonwood, observed box-elder and elm trees. Killed a rattlesnake this morning: a young fellow with nine rattles and a button. Several

---

* We afterwards discovered that we had reached Prairie Dog creek at its junction with Tongue River.

others were killed yesterday. Passed Massacre Hill, the scene of the lamentable Fetterman Massacre, alluded to in preceeding pages. Soon after came down into the valley of our present camp: skirted the bank of the stream for six or seven miles. The valley is not over a mile broad and is hemmed in by bluffs, of red sandstone, but well coated with grass. One formation of sandstone, exhibited traces of having been exposed to igneous action. Pebbles in streams along trail, granitic in character. Our camp is well supplied with water from the creek flowing in its front which is about 25 feet broad, 2 feet deep, moderate current 4 or 5 miles, its sluggishness being due apparently to beaver dams, bottom drift rock and quartz pebbles, banks clayey but crossing good.

Our first buffalo was killed this morning by a man from the pack-train. Musquitoes [sic] were very troublesome near the stream. Prairie dog villages lay scattered under the bluffs wherever a sandy soil afforded easy digging. The last hour or two of this march was very unpleasant; the heat of the sun almost unbearable. Dense masses of clouds moved sluggishly up from the West and North while light flaky feathers of vapor flitted across the sky, coquetting with the breeze, now obscuring the sun, now revealing his fierce rays. Low rumbling thunder sullenly sounded across the horizon and with the first flash of lightning changed into an almost continuous roar. The nearest peaks of the Big Horn were hid from our gaze. The heavy arch of clouds now supported itself upon the crests of the bluffs enclosing the valley of our camp.

It was a pretty picture: the parks of wagons and pack-mules, the bright rows of tentage and the moving animals and men gave enough animation to relieve the otherwise too sombre view of the elements at War. This night, the soldier of Captain Meinhold's company, (who was accidentally wounded on Wind river by the falling of his own revolver while he was cutting wood,) died.

Six buffaloes killed to-day.

June 7th Early in the morning, Capt. H. E. Noyes, 2d Cav. (who had been benighted while trout-fishing on Goose Creek, 6 miles to our West) returned to camp.

A dense fog obscured sky: cold rain slowly falling until meridian. Grass of different variety appearing along line of march; rather coarse, but dark green and succulent. Bluffs reaching from immediate vicinity of stream; valley is by this time two miles wide in some places. A high ridge of sandstone extended down the valley for some distance on the Right. Stream increasing in size, swelled by the tribute of several subsidiary rivulets. Water very good and cool. Timber very scarce excepting a narrow fringe upon the banks. Found in a box-elder bush a nest, formed of interlaced twigs, of an old crow hen which flew away upon our arrival. This nest contained four pea-green eggs, mottled in brown and black, the greater part of the marks on the butt end. In shape they were probate spheroids and in size, A=1 1/3 in., B= 3/8 in.

Game is becoming more frequent at our mess-table. Grouse (pintail.) Sage cocks and Sickle-bill curlew are the fowl thus far met with; white-tail deer, elk and buffalo, the kinds of meat. Capt. Andrews, 3d Cav., in command of pioneers, had much difficulty this morning to prepare a suitable road for the wagon-train to follow; the amount of excavating and embanking, corduroying and grading required was rather unusual and most laborious.
General Crook and the writer had the pleasure of killing their first buffalo this afternoon.
After sighting the herd in the distance, we advanced rapidly, mounted, until within convenient distance and then commenced to stalk our game on foot. When we reached the edge of a little bluff, overlooking a small valley joining that of Tongue river, the herd of eight bulls was come upon directly under us. They were grazing quietly like domestic cattle and except for the heavy goat-beard and mane might have been taken for such. One old bull gazed intently and curiously at me for a moment: as luck would have it, the wind was blowing from the herd and my hat was slate colored like the shale rocks amid which we stood. The antiquated patriarch resumed his browsing. Genl. Crook took careful sight along the barrel of his rifle, fired and struck the bull under the fore shoulder on the near side. The herd now started on a loose-jointed shambling lope, making every excellent time. Our horses could not catch up with them, and soon fell well to the rear. General Crook's bull dropped on his knees, after going one hundred yards and one or two others dropped behind their comrades, badly wounded by our bullets. We found the wounded bull quietly nibbling grass in a little cove in the

bluffs. Gen. Crook gave me a first shot at him, which struck his side among the big ribs: two others aimed at him did not harm him at all, one being too high, the other too low. The General then fired and broke the animal's neck. Still his vitality was so excessive, that he was able to plunge his head about in an alarming degree: two more shots finished him. We left the carcass on the ground, noting its location; two pack-mules brought in the meat.

When reaching camp 15 1/2 miles, ascertained that the creek we have followed the past two days is not Goose Creek, but Prairie Dog creek, the same marched down in February. Our permanent camp is at its confluence with Tongue river and presents the essentials of abundant pure water, gramma and other grasses, cottonwood and other timber, seclusion from observation and charming scenery. After retreat this evening, occurred the interesting ceremony of interring the remains of Private Timan, of Co. "B" 3d Cavalry,[1] accidentally killed. Besides the funeral escort of non-com[missione]d officers and twelve men prescribed by regulations, all officers and men and employees, not engaged on duty, joined the procession which acquired magnificent proportions, fully 600 persons being present. Capt. Henry, 3d Cavalry, commanding Battalion, read the funeral services in a very impressive manner. The cavalry bugles sounded "taps", sod was thrown upon the rude coffin, the grave was rapidly filled up, the companies at quick step returned to their camps and the rites were completed.[2]

This night, long after our camp was wrapped in slumber, a party of Indians halloed at our pickets and tried to open up conversation. We had no one with us understanding any of the aboriginal dialects. The interviewing party then withdrew. Some of our men claimed they had heard them ask something about a Crow camp. This may

1. Private Francis Tierney, who went by the name of Doyle. Finerty, *War-Path and Bivouac*, 87.

2. John Finerty, of the Chicago *Times*, described the funeral in more detail in his book, *War-Path and Bivouac* (88). Tierney, he wrote,

> was buried during the afternoon with military honors. Every officer and soldier not on duty attended the funeral, and the burial service was impressively read by Col. Guy V[.] Henry over the grave, which was dug in a lonely spot among the low hills surrounding the place. The body was wrapped in an overcoat and blanket, and Captain Meinhold shoveled the first spadeful of clay on the cold remains. A rough granite boulder was rolled upon the grave and the young soldier was shut out forever from the living world. Three volleys, the warrior's requiem, pealed above his tomb, and we left him to his ever-enduring sleep. Except, perhaps for the burial of a human being in mid-ocean, the interment of a soldier in the great American wilderness of that epoch was about the gloomiest of funeral experiences. It was, indeed a sad destiny that led this young man to die, accidentally, it is true, by his own hand, the first of Crook's brigade to lay his bones in the terra incognita of Wyoming.

have been a wild freak of imagination.[3] We are yet, June 8th, in doubt as to whether they were friendly Indians from Gibbon's or Terry's command or hostile Sioux. The burden of opinion inclines to the latter presumption.

Our camp remained at this point, awaiting the return of our guides from the Crow country. The monotony of camp life was broken in upon by an interchange of friendly visits among the officers who gather in the evening about the various Hd.Qrs. To indulge in a social cup of toddy and to exchange the gossip of the day.

Some pass the day in reading, some in writing journals of the trip: in places, little squads may be seen indulging in games of cards, or discussing with animation the probabilities of our success. Fishing allures the lovers of the sport to the banks of the river, there to catch chub and soft-shell tortoise, which has appeared at our mess-table in the form of a most savory stew. After lunch, drowsy Morpheus has many votaries. There are no newspapers to act as firebrands by scattering information of Exciting topics into the midst of our little world, and the requirements of routine duty are so slight, we might as well be inmates of a monastery for all the exercise our mental powers are called upon to perform. A courier entered the camp before sunrise on the 9th, with official dispatches to Gen. Crook that One hundred and twenty Snake Indians would be at Fort Kearney about the 8th to join our column. Learned also that the great mass of the Indians at Red Cloud Agency had gone away to join the hostiles, that eight companies of the 5th Cavalry, that excellent regiment which achieved a fine reputation under General Crook in Arizona, were en-route to Red Cloud to take station and that General Sheridan had determined that no Indians should be allowed to return to Red Cloud until whipped. This good news gratified us all exceedingly.

Found a disabled pony last evening, the property of one of the prowling bands hovering about our columns for some days past. Two miners joined us from the camp of their main body on Crazy Woman's Creek. Rained during the morning of the 9th. Passed the time reading from Hayden's[,] Reynold's[,] Warrens[,] and Forsyth's[,] and Jones' reports of explorations in this Region.

3. Ben Arnold, who was serving as a messenger, recalled the incident:
The first night we camped on this stream a Crow Indian came to the farther bank and tried to talk with us. We could make nothing out of what he said. If it had been daytime I could have talked with him in the Chinook sign language. As it was, we did not get the message he evidently wished to give us. Crawford, *Exploits of Ben Arnold*, 242-43.

The monotony of camp life was agreeably broken in upon the evening of June 9th by an attack upon our camp by a mounted party of Sioux warriors. Our mess had only risen from dinner when our pickets on the East side commenced firing at the approaching enemy. The Sioux moved rapidly along the bluff on the North side separated from us by the waters of Tongue river and from a safe position behind the crest fired annoyingly into our wagon trains and cavalry horses. Colonel Chambers was instructed to send out three companies of the 9th Inf. Burroughs, Burt's and Munson's to occupy the heights on the Right, while Mills with four companies, his own, Sutorious', Andrews' and Morton's of the 3d Cavalry, from Royall's command, pushed across the river, climbed the steep bluffs on the opposite bank and drove the enemy to flight. Our casualties were two men wounded; one in the leg, one in the arm, both by spent balls and wounded of no consequence—and three horses and one mule wounded—all badly. Bullets passed through canvass, [sic] tent-poles, stove-pipes and wagons and struck the ground amidst our troops, but no further casualties received.

It is to be hoped the Indians may make attacks of this kind every night: no greater advantage can accrue to young troops than to keep them constantly under fire; they learn the importance of implicit obedience to authority, of keeping constantly in readiness for instant attack or defense and above all things of saving their ammunition. Pickets and sentinels display more vigilance: officers become more zealous and energetic. Loose ends are gathered up; animals are herded with care and wakefulness and a general air of soldierly discipline is infused. Then when real work is required and fighting has to be done, young recruits are found to have insensibly changed into veterans and perform their duties with a thoroughness not frequently to be hoped for otherwise. It was reported that some of Captain Noyes' pickets had killed one of the Indians, but the report was not verified; I give it merely as it passed current in camp.

One of the horses wounded and afterwards killed was the personal property of Capt. Burt, 9th Infantry, who prized him very highly. The little animal was very fleet for short distances. It had won two races that very afternoon; scrub races, hastily improvised, run for a can of corn, or tomatoes. Lieut. Robertson's horse was also shot. Besides the horse races mentioned, our packers organized a foot race of one hundred yards, to which a large concourse proceeded. As a race the less said the better; as an incident, as a piece of driftwood in our ocean of monotony, it is worthy of notice. Lieutenant Lemly, 3d Cav., was somewhat surprised the other evening when about to retire, to find a rattlesnake coiled up in his blankets. Being somewhat exclusive in his notions, Lemly had the intruder banished from his bed and killed.

A cold shower commenced after sunset, June 9th, and lasted, spasmodically, through the night.

Sunday, June 11th. Finding grass getting scarce, Gen. Crook determined to remove camp to a location nearer the mountains. This brought us to a very pleasant spot at the confluence of the two forks of Goose Creek seventeen miles and a half from our position on Tongue River. The situation has many advantages: excellent pasturage is secured from the hilly slopes adjacent, water in profusion, clear, sweet and icy-cold with a gentle murmur and the swiftness of a mill-race through the channels on each side of us. Fire-wood in sufficiency can be gathered along the stream-banks. Where we crossed it, Goose Creek has an average width of 20 yds, with a uniform depth of three feet, but greatly swollen by recent rains and melted snow. We were visited during the march by a succession of brief storms of hail and rain, which we at first thought was the sequence of last night's storm; as we neared our camping ground, clouds gathered, black and deep-bellied, thunder commenced to growl among the peaks nearest us and in a very few minutes, the command was exposed to all the unpleasantness of a summer-storm in the Rocky Mountains. Tents were erected as hastily as possible affording much desired shelter. Scarcely had our preparations been completed than the rain issued, the rays of the sun reappeared for a short interval and a very lovely rainbow spanned the sky. Little knots of officers soon congregated at HdQrs, discussing the storm, the non-appearances of our promised Snake and Crow allies and the probabilities of the campaign. A very curious variety of owl was caught in a rotten log at this camp; the little bird, when perched, measured not more than 5 or 6 inches in height; had a white blaze on face between eyes which were large, yellow orbs with black irises. Head very large, covered with thick growth of seal-brown feathers. Breast, yellowish-brown. Back, wings & tail, whitish brown. Bill, black and curvated. Claws, long and pointed. In disposition, this little bird showed dignity, cour-

age and good nature: would freely allow itself to be handled, but
would peck and strike with both beak and claws when teased. Our
amateur fishermen turned out in squads after the rain to try their
luck with trout; only two, young ones, were caught, the failure
being due to the muddiness of the current. Mr. Harrison, who
brought mail to the command from Fort Fetterman returned to
that post to-night, (Sunday, June 11th 1876.) carrying official dispatches, private letters and journalistic correspondence. His business is of an extra-hazardous character: one that demands a
peculiar gift of caution, daring, keen judgment and topographical
knowledge. By travelling at night only and hiding during day-light
in out of the way places, he will have some points in his favor;
confess however that while all hope and expect to hear of his safe
arrival back on the Platte, no one will be at all taken aback to
learn of his capture and murder by prowling Indians. Heap of letters and little packages of manuscript accumulated in Nickerson's
tent in the course of the evening: secure, compact packages were
made of these and strapped on the pack-animal. With the darkness, Harrison sallied out on his perilous task accompanied by the
corporate who was his associate on the way out from Fetterman.
The command now settled down in the somnolent apathy of permanent camp life, looking for our Crow friends. Frank Gruard, Louis
Richaud and Big Bat have been absent about ten or twelve days. It
seems very likely that their duty has called them up into the ranges
of the Indians they were seeking, far beyond the Big Horn range.
Their delay is thus easily accounted for but is none the less vexatious. We are compelled to fritter away much valuable time: instead
of hunting the Sioux and engaging in action with them, we have
only routine duties to occupy our attention. The weather has assumed a most charming phase; the gently undulating prairie, upon
whose bosom camp reposes, is decked with the greenest and most
nutritious grasses. Our animals lazily nibble along the hill-skirts or
deep in the genial light of the sun. The two little mountain brooks
joining below our camp are lined with a fringe of box elder and
willow bushes in whose shade throngs of sweet-voiced meadow larks
sing all day. At rare moments, the chirping of grass-hoppers may be
distinguished in the herbage; in front of our line of tents; a cook is
burning or browning coffee—it is just as often one as the other—an
idle recruit watches the process with a semi-attentive stupification.

The report of a carbine aimed and fired by an exasperated teamster at another attracts general notice; the teamster has just now been put in confinement; a languid discussion of the merits of the case floats in ripples through our camp. It soon dies away and each resumes his favorite panacea for ennui and its kindred ills. A few officers are in Gen. Crook's tent, playing whist. At noon, Captain Stanton takes his astronomical observations. A minimum of books had [been] surreptitiously kept with us on the march: a copy of Shakespeare, one of Macaulay's Essays, the works of Stowe and others not now remembered. These are perused by appreciative critics as also are the official reports of the explorations of this region made years ago by Reynolds, Maynardier, Hayden, Warren, Forsyth and others.

Colonel Royall, gave us an interesting account of his early days in Mexico, California and other places, and his experience on the plains of Texas and Kansas in fights with the Comanches and other wild tribes. The narrative was replete with interest aside from the attention deserved as the personal history of a gallant and distinguished old soldier. Squads of officers and soldiers have been out on little hunting and fishing parties. Colonel Mills' squad killed a cinnamon bear on the 12th and the same day numbers of Rocky Mountain trout were caught by Noyes' and other detachments. Lieut. Carpenter and Maj. Burt, 9th Infantry, have been assiduous collectors of ornithological specimens and what with Gen. Crook's accumulations in the same line, the feathered residents of the Big Horn foot-hills are well-represented. Lieut. Foster, 3d Cavy. has made a series of creditable, rough pencil sketches of points of interest along the route: it is his intention to send them to *Harper's Weekly* for publication.

Fearing a sudden dash from the Sioux and a general stampede of our herd, Gen. Crook has insisted upon extraordinary precautions being taken to prevent surprise. The ordinary line of pickets is established as usual upon the summits of buttes and bluffs, commanding camp: in addition to this, outlying detachments are maintained during the day [at] a great distance beyond the pasture-grounds. They are powerful enough to gobble up any small party of Indians having designs upon camp, or to hold large bodies in check until after the herds have been driven in and the various battalions saddled up and formed in line of battle. In this way, Capt. Henry's entire company was sent to take station up one branch of Goose Creek, while at same time, Reynolds with his company advanced up the other and a strong detail from Meinhold's and Vroom's companies occupied a high bluff on the Left Bank of the main stream. The horses of these companies are saddled but not bridled unless for a half-dozen or so of the guard on observation. All the men are within grasp of their animals, carbines in hands & ammunition ready for instant service.

A small patch of ripe strawberries was found to-day by Col. Mills' 3d Cavalry. The fruit was very small but of delicious flavor and aroma. June 13th (Tuesday.) Still in camp. Day Balmy. Temperature in tents 88° F. Sky faultlessly blue. Day passed without incident of consequence. A number of very fine, fat trout brought to camp. Major Burt, 9th Infantry, Mr. Strahorn and a party of miners left camp early in the morning to prospect the gulches close in to the flanks of the mountains. It has long been supposed that gold exists throughout the entire Big Horn and Wind River ranges: if a demonstration can be made that such is the case, miners and settlers will soon crowd in, strong towns arise and a very heavy blow struck from this mere fact against savage supremacy in the North-West. Major Wells, 2d Cav. caught eighteen trout to-day and Major Noyes, of same regiment, six; all very fine specimens. In company with Col Royall, visited pickets this morning: could not find Henry's company which had evidently advanced very far up the Left fork of Goose creek.

June 14th Early this morning, sometime before day-break an alarm was occasioned by the premature discharge of the carbine of a sentinel about to go on post. The reason being ascertained, quiet was restored. Officers and men by this time are always on alert, prompted to move out to repel attack from any quarter and at any time. Firing of arms of any kind has been prohibited within picket lines; hence any discharge of gun or pistol, especially about night-fall or just before dawn is regarded with suspicion, and herders are ready to drive in all their stock to prevent a stampede. Anxiety for the early return of our guides is expressed by all and a few go so far as to imagine that evil may have befallen them. This is not probable however, as each of them has had extraordinary experience in wood and mountain craft and is well versed in all the wiles and strategems of the savages. Yet it would be a relief from doubt and anxiety to have them back that we might commence in dead earnest the work of the campaign, which up to this time has been nothing but a picnic without exploit and without advantage. Our hunters to-day killed (2) elk and one buffalo bull. Major Burt's party returned from prospecting tour up the valley of Tongue river without discovering any traces of precious metal.

Great joy was diffused through camp when Frank Gruard and Louis Richaud came back this afternoon, bringing with them an old Crow Indian. They reported to General Crook that they had proceeded on their journey as far as the site of old Fort C.F. Smith, on the Big Horn river. On the other side, discovered a camp of many lodges, but were not assured of identity as Sioux or Crows. Rested at that point a short while, making dinner and giving feed to animals. The smoke from their fire probably attracted the attention of the Indians who galloped out in great numbers across the broad plain stretching along the other side of the river, boldly swam its torrent and charged up the acclivity after our messengers, one of whom narrowly escaped a bullet from one of the Crows, before mutual recognitions were made and satisfactory greetings exchanged.

Our men followed the Crows to their town, found to consist of two hundred and odd lodges. At the beginning, difficulty was experienced in persuading the Crows' to let a detachment of their young warriors go join General Crook: their chiefs alleged many reasons. Their families were starving and they wanted to get them meat. The buffalo was in vicinity and they could not lose the opportunity of a big hunt. They were afraid we wouldn't stay out to fight the Sioux or that we might remain out longer than the summer. Much palavering followed, our guides neglecting no persuasion to induce them to agree to come.

They appeared suspicious of some plot at first, but finally consented to send a band of One Hundred and seventy-five picked warriors to aid us as scouts and spies. They said that General Gibbon's command was in camp on Left bank of the Yellowstone, opposite the mouth of the Rosebud, unable to cross. The Sioux were watching the troops from the other shore. An attempt made by Gibbon to throw his command across had resulted in the drowning of one company's horses. The Sioux had alas, in some unexplained way, succeeded in running off the ponies belonging to thirty Crow scouts with his command, and word had been sent for a remount. The main body of the hostile Sioux were on the Tongue river, at mouth of Otter creek, and below. The Crows further reported that they

had heard a war party of Snakes had started out, or intended to
start out to participate in the campaign. When Frank and Louis
crossed Tongue river, near onto [our] old camp, much discontent
was manifested by the Indians because they misunderstood our
march back to a new camp for grass as an indication of the abandonment of the campaign. They forgot that 1800 or 1900 mules
and horses consume immense quantities of grass daily and need a
frequent removal of pasturage. Under this misapprehension, the
great majority declined to follow further, so Frank and Louis pushed
ahead bringing with them one chief, leaving Big Bat to come along
more leisurely with 15 or 16 of the Crows who remained. A good,
palatable meal of hot coffee, sugar, biscuits, butter, venison, jam
and stewed apples was spread before them; having consumed this
with hearty zest and smoked a pipe-full of tobacco, the old chief
was ready for business. His name cannot at present be given, as the
North American Indian never will answer when questioned upon
this head. After a brief conference, General Crook directed the
chief, Louis Richaud and Major Burt, 9th Inf., to return and en-
deavor to bring the Crows back to the command. A curious feature
in this conference was the medium of communication employed.
The sign language is the [channel?] of correspondence between and
among the different aboriginal tribes roaming from the Saskatchewan
to the Rio Grande.

A mute language, it is ideographic and not literal in its elements.
Every word, every idea to be conveyed has its characteristic symbol. The rapidity of transmission is almost telegraphic, and frequently the sign language is employed preferentially by members
of the same tribe, on account of its ease, accuracy and promptness.
At some future time, I hope to collect and insert herein a more
valuable and elaborate account of this singular vehicle of interpretation. We were enlightened by this chief as to the nature of the
colloquy carried on with our sentinels some nights since by Indians
supposed at the time to be Sioux. He says they were a war-party of
five Crows, who wished to converse with us but were scared away
by being questioned in the Sioux language, as was the fact.

The mission of Major Burt was a perfect success. Before dusk he
was with us again, this time riding at the head of a long retinue of
savage retainers, whose grotesque head-dresses, variegated colored
garments, wild little ponies and warlike accoutrements, made up a

quaint and curious spectacle. While the main column halted just inside our camp, the three chiefs, [O]ld Crow, Medicine Crow, and Good Heart, were presented to Genl. Crook and made the recipients of some little attentions in the way of refreshments. Our newly-arrived allies bivouacked in our midst, sending their herd of ponies out to graze alongside of our own horses. The entire band numbered one hundred and seventy six, as near as we could ascertain. Each Indian had two ponies. The first thing to be done was to erect their war lodges of saplings covered over with blankets and shreds of canvass. Fires were next built and a feast made ready of the supplies of coffee, sugar and hard-tack, dealt out from our Commissary train. These are the prime luxuries of an Indian's life. A curious crowd of lookers-on, officers, soldiers and teamsters, congregated around the little squads of Crows, watching with eager attention their every movement. The Indians seemed proud of the distinguished positions they occupied in popular estimation and were soon on terms of easy familiarity with our soldiers, some of whom can talk a few words of Crow and others a little of the sign language. In stature, complexion, dress and general demeanor, a marked contrast was observable [be]tween our friends and the Sioux Indians, a contrast decidedly to the advantage of the former.

The Absaraka,[4] or Crow Indians, perhaps as a consequence of their residency among the elevated banks and cool, fresh mountain ranges between the Big Horn River and the Yellowstone, are somewhat fairer than the other Indians about them. They are all above medium height, not a few being quite tall and many have a noble expression of countenance. The dress of the members of this tribe consists of shirt of flannel, cotton or buckskin; breech-clout, leggings of blanket, moccasins of deer, elk or buffalo hide, coat of bright-colored blanket, made with sleeves and hood and a head-dress, fashioned in divers shapes, but most frequently formed from an old black Army hat, with top cut out and sides bound round with feathers, fur and scarlet cloth. Their arms were all breech-loaders, throwing metallic cartridges, most of them Calibre .50, with an occasional .45. Lances, medicine poles and tomahawks figured in the procession. The tomahawks, made of long knives, inserted in shafts or handles of wood or horn, were most murderous weapons. Accompanying these Indians were a few little boys, none of them over 15

4. I.e., "Bird People."

years old: their business will be to hold horses and other unimportant work while their elders conduct the dangerous operations of the campaign. A sentiment of contentment, pleasure, satisfaction and security diffused itself throughout the entire expedition; with our Indian auxiliaries to follow the trails of the hostile Sioux and discover their villages, our men will be spared the onerous duty of scouting in advance and enter into any contest that may occur fresh, vigorous and hopeful. No one now doubts we shall be victorious; the only discrepancy of opinion is in regard to the numbers we may find. The sanguine nature and enthusiasm of some cause them to make extravagant estimates, but all are confident, all determined.

Retreat having sounded, the officers commanding Battalions were directed to repair to the open space in front of General Crook's tent, where the Commanding Officer of the Expedition was in waiting. His remarks were characteristically terse and soldierly. The command would cut loose from wagon and pack-train on the morning of the 16th, taking four day's rations in the saddle-bags. One blanket to each man and officer, either the saddle blanket of ordinary issue or a bed blanket, to be used as such. No extra clothing whatever for officers or men. One hundred rounds of ammunition to each person with the expedition, to be carried in the saddle-bags. Lariats and side-lines, but no extra shoes and no picket ropes for horses. The wagons were to be parked and mules to be corralled in a defensible position up the valley of the Tongue, there to be guarded by a detachment left for the purpose. All the available force that could be mounted and equipped to accompany the General. Men from the Infantry companies who could ride and shoot and who so desired to be detailed; the same rule to be applied to volunteers from among the teamsters and packers, mounts to be obtained from extra cavalry horses, team and pack mules; saddles from the wagons and in case of deficiency, blankets and surcingles to be used.

It was evident the General meant business. It we strike the Indian village on Tongue river, rations can be reserved from their accumulations of buffalo and other meat, or we can push down to the Yellowstone and draw supplies from Gibbon or Terry.

Scarcely had this conference been ordered, when a long line of glittering lances and brightly-polished weapons of fire announced the anxiously expected advent of our other allies, the Sho-sho-nees, or Snakes, who to the number of eighty-six came galloping rapidly up to

HdQrs. and came Left Front into Line in splendid style. No trained soldiers ever executed the evolution more prettily. Exclamations of praise and wonder greeted the barbaric array of these fierce warriors, warmly welcomed by their former enemies but present strong friends, the Crows. General Crook came out to review their line of battle, resplendent in all the fantastic adornments of feathers, beads, brass buttons, bells, scarlet cloth and flashing lances. The Shoshonees were not slow to perceive the favorable impression made and when time came for them to file off by the right, moved with the precision of clock-work and the pride of veterans.[5] A general council was the next feature of the evening's entertainment. Without undertaking the difficult task of preserving an exact picture of this interesting scene, which abler pens have attempted to describe, a record of the salient features may be of some interest and some value. Around a huge fire of crackling boughs, the officers of the command ranged themselves in two rows, the interest and curiosity depicted upon their countenances acting as a foil to the stolid and imperturbable calmness of the Indians squatted upon the ground on the other side. The breeze blowing the smoke aside would occasionally enable the flames to bring out in bold and sudden relief from the intense blackness of the night, the sepulchral whiteness of the tents and wagon-sheets, the blue coats of the officers and soldiers, (who thronged among the wagons behind their superiors,) the red, white, yellow and black-banded blankets of the savages, whose aquiline features and glittering eyes had become still more aquiline and still more glittering, and the small group in the centre of the circle, composed of General Crook, Captain Nickerson, the interpreters, Frank, Louis and Bat, and the Indian chiefs. One quadrant was reserved for the Sho-sho-nees, and one for the Crows. Each tribe selected one spokesman who repeated aloud to his people the words of the General as they were made known to him by the interpreter. Ejaculations of Ugh! Ugh! from the lips of the chiefs was the only sign of interest betrayed upon their faces, tho' it was easy enough to see nothing was lost that was addressed to them. Pipes, of same kind as those the Sioux have, were kept in industrious circulation. I did not succeed in keeping a verbatim account of the council, which was of same general purport as those

5. The Shoshone proficiency in drill was due to the influence of Tom Cosgrove, who served in a Texas cavalry unit during the Civil War, lived among the Shoshones, and apparently taught them the Confederate cavalry drill. Bourke explains this farther on.

already reported. The Crows and Snakes showed great eagerness to commence the campaign which they hoped would break the spirit of their hereditary and cruel enemies, the Sioux. They asked however the privilege of scouting in their own way, a privilege General Crook very willingly conceded, confident that nothing would be lost in so doing. Good Heart, a young chief, (by the way the name of the one who came in advance to-day was Mountain Feather.) said he wanted nothing but Sioux. The Sioux had robbed and killed the Crows and now the Crows wanted to get even. The Crows and the Snakes would go ahead of the soldiers, discover the Sioux' camp and run off their horses. When the Sioux had no horses their village would have to stay there, and the soldiers could readily destroy it and the Crows and Snakes would help them do it. He wanted to make the Sioux' women and children work for the Crows, and divide the Sioux' ponies among his people. His heart was good towards the whites: he would go wherever General Crook said. The council ended at 10.20 P.M., General Crook shaking hands with the more prominent chiefs as they passed. The supposition was these tired Indians would without delay retire to rest. Their day's ride had been over 60 miles in length and the night was already far advanced. The erroneousness of this assumption was disclosed very speedily. A long series of monotonous howls, shrieks, groans and nasal yells, emphasized by a perfectly ear piercing succession of thumps upon drums improvised from "parfleche", (dried buffalo skin) attracted nearly all our soldiers and many of our officers not on duty to the allied camp. Peeping into the different tipis was much like peeping through the key-hole of Hell. Crouched around little fires, not affording as much light as an ordinary tallow-candle, the swarthy figures of naked and half-naked Indians were visible, mooing and chanting in unison with some leader. No words were distinguishable; the ceremony partook of the nature of an abominable incantation and as far as I could judge had a semi-religious character. One of the Indians, mounted on a pony and stripped almost naked passed along from tepi to tepi, stopping in front of each and calling upon the Great Spirit, (so our interpreter said,) to send them down plenty of scalps, a big Sioux village and lots of ponies. The inmates would respond with, if possible, increased vehemence and the old saying about making night hideous acquired a new significance. With this wild requiem ringing in his ears, one of our soldiers, a patient in hospital, Private Wm. Nelson, Co "L." 3d

Cavalry, breathed his last. Our herd of beef-cattle, now reduced to six, became so frightened that they tore away from the control of those caring for them and broke madly for the hills. A continuous drizzle pattered down upon our tents all night. The Crows now with us boast some distinguished warriors. One of them, a very young man, performed last winter the achievement of entering a Sioux village alone and stealing a valuable horse which he tied to a tree nearby. Returning to the village, he lifted the flap-door of one of the tents and fired his rifle inside, killing one of the Sioux. He made his escape without accident, riding the captured animal.

June 15th A very fine day, highly appreciated by the busy officers whose exertions to equip and mount their different commands were untiring. Colonel Chambers had to mount all his Infantry Battalion on pack-mules and gave every moment of the day to inspecting and choosing pack-mules and hunting up saddles and bridles from the little extra in that line [that] the Cavalry had with them. Amusing incidents there were in plenty and many scenes of grand and lofty tumbling occurred when the improvised dragoons attempted for the first time to mount their charges. Perseverantia vincit omnia.[6] Col. Chambers was bound to go and his gallant subalterns and men equally so. When night fell, 175 mounted riflemen were ready for the field. In like manner, Tom Moore, our chief of pack-train, organized from among his packers a small force of twenty wiry, hardy, horny-handed veterans, every one a fine rider and as near being a dead-shot as men generally get to be on the frontier.

Sick men had to be examined and sent to Hospital, but it is remarkable to note that they went under protest. The conviction is widespread that now or never are the haughty Sioux to be humbled and that Crook is the only man to do it. Maj. Randall has not had too much leisure to-day; his new honors are bringing in a heavy harvest of new responsibilities. He is equal to the occasion and enters into his task with all the vim and intelligent animation that gained him in Arizona the reputation of being one of the best Indian fighters in the Army.

In the packtrains, racks made of willow branches supported loads of wild meat, drying in the sun. Deer and antelope venison, buffalo, elk and grizzly bear meat, the last two killed by a hunting party from the pack-train yesterday. The preparations our savage allies

6. Perseverance conquers all.

were making were no less noticeable. In both Snake and Crow camps, could be seen squads of young warriors, looking after their rifles, which by the way among the Snakes are all the latest models, Cal. 45, and kept with scrupulous care in regular guard-racks; sharpening lances or adorning them with feathers and paint; making coup sticks, which are long willow branches, about 12 feet from end to end, stripped of leaves & bark and having each some distinctive mark in the way of feathers, bells, paint or fur or bright col[ore]d. cloth or flannel. These serve a singular purpose; the great object of the Crows and Snakes in making war is to set the enemy afoot. This done his destruction is rendered more easy if not more certain. Ponies also are the wealth of the conquerors; hence in dividing the spoil, each man claims the animal first struck by his coup stick.

With the Snakes were three white men, [Tom] Cosgrove, [Nelson] Yarnell and [Bob] Eckles, all Texans, and one French Canadian half-breed named Luisant. Cosgrove, the leading spirit, was during the rebellion a captain in the 32d Texas (C.S.A.) Cavalry, and shows he has not forgotten the lessons of the war by the appearances of discipline and good order evinced by his command, who in this respect are somewhat ahead of the Crows. We were informed that on the march across from Wind River, the Snakes in one afternoon killed one hundred and seventy-five buffaloes, on the East side of the Owl Creek mountains.

The Crows had a foot-race this afternoon for twenty cartridges a side. The running was quite good for the distance of 150 yards, or thereabouts.

The funeral obsequies of Private Wm. Nelson, Co. "L", 3d Cav. occurred this evening and were attended by all the command, or an important element of it. The salute over the grave made the Crows and Snakes think the Sioux were making an attack upon our camp; up they came charging close to the lines of the funeral cortege where they remained gazing upon the proceedings, feathers nodding in the breeze and lances gleaming in the sun. Some of them had as many as four earrings in one ear, the rim of the whole cartilage being perforated from apex to base. Their pantaloons fit the leg very tightly, but have a tuck, nearly six inches wide, down the outer seam: see diagram.

Chapter 17

✦

✦

✦

✦

✦

The Battle of the Rosebud

The Battle of the Rosebud in Montana, on June 17, 1876, has always been a controversial fight, but most students of the war generally agree that despite his claims to the contrary, Crook was defeated.[1]

The tribal hatreds rampant among Plains Indians, that long predated white contact, are evident. The Crows and Shoshones, ancient enemies of the Lakota, served as scouts, and were active

---

1. Although Crook never openly admitted defeat, privately he must have realized it because the Rosebud remained a sensitive topic. True to character, he looked for scapegoats. In August 1886, shortly after the tenth anniversary of the fight, he confronted Colonel Royall, who had commanded the cavalry, in the presence of Colonel Guy V. Henry, another Rosebud veteran. "For ten years," he told Royall:

> I have suffered silently the obloquy of having made a bad fight at the Rosebud, when the fault was in yourself and Nickerson. There was a good chance to make a charge, but it couldn't be done because of the condition of the cavalry. I sent word for you to come in, and waited two hours, nearer three, before you obeyed. I sent Nickerson three times at least. Couriers passed constantly between the points where we were respectively. I had the choice of assuming the responsibility myself for the failure of my plans, or of court-martialling you and Nickerson. I chose to bear the responsibility myself. The failure of my plan was due to your conduct.

Royall countered that Nickerson had only come to him once, and that he had responded immediately. Henry verified it, and Crook eventually backed down. Given his personality, and considering how quickly he had acted against Reynolds, Moore, and Noyes after the Powder River fight, he doubtless would have court-martialed Royall and Nickerson if there had been the slightest grounds for doing so. Kennon, Diary, entry for August 7, 1886, pasted on back board; Robinson, *General Crook*, 287-88.

319

and ruthless participants in the battle. These Indians were useful, but exasperating. They knew the country, and they knew the enemy. Often, however, they appeared to be more interested in hunting buffalo, and reciting past grievances against the Lakota, than actually going out and scouting for them. Nevertheless, it was a chance encounter between these scouts and a hunting party of Lakotas and Cheyennes that set the battle into motion.[2]

Bourke's narrative jumps from the order to move out of camp to the fight itself, and offers no account of the three hours or so in between. In fact, Crook had ordered a halt in the valley of the Rosebud, to rest men and animals still tired from a thirty-five mile march the previous day. The cavalry unsaddled and grazed their horses, some men prepared coffee, and others caught a nap. The Indian scouts patrolled the hills beyond. Crook and several of his officers were engaged in a game of whist when the scouts came charging back down from the hills, with the hostiles hard on their heels. Infantry skirmishers were sent to hold off the attackers while animals were saddled and efforts were made to deploy.[3]

Bourke continually remarked about the failure of the hostiles to show themselves, at one point calling them "cowardly devils."[4] Indeed, it almost seems as though he expected them to confront Crook in standard line-of-battle according to the West Point drill manual. Indians, however, tended to avoid direct confrontation whenever possible, because as a tribal, nomadic people, they could not afford heavy losses. Bourke himself acknowledged this, even as he accused them of cowardice, by writing, "Every one of their dead, is one whom they cannot replace, while each wounded man requires at least two attendants."[5]

It is nothing short of incredible that Bourke, given his previous experience with Indians, could have so completely misunderstood the situation. Describing the fight, he wrote, "we drove them from hill to hill, ravine to ravine."[6] He failed, as indeed every officer did that day, to realize the Indians were following their proven tactics of scattering, dividing the troops into small units, drawing them away from support, then turning on them in force and defeating

2. Mangum, *Battle of the Rosebud*, 53.
3. Ibid., 52-55; Robinson, *General Crook*, 182.
4. Bourke, Diaries, 5:409.
5. Ibid., 5:431.
6. Ibid., 5:410. Years later, in *On the Border*, Bourke reevaluated the fight, saying, "In one word, the battle of the Rosebud was a trap. . . ." (311)

them piecemeal. Disaster was averted only because the troops pulled back and regrouped, turning it into a protracted fight that began to run up Indian casualties. This ultimately prompted the hostiles to withdraw and end the battle.[7]

Although the troops were stalemated, and forced to withdraw into Wyoming, Bourke persisted in his hagiography, acclaiming the Rosebud as a victory that once again proved Crook was the man who would end the nation's Indian problems. "[T]o subjugate the hostile Indians," he wrote, "nothing is needed but courage, energy, fortitude and skill—qualities rare enough in themselves, still more rare in combination, but undeniably concentrated in a remarkable degree in our Commanding General"[8]. *Yet on the day Bourke wrote this—June 26—Crook's men were organizing a mule race, while Custer and five companies of the 7th Cavalry were lying dead in the Montana sun less than seventy miles to the north. This, more than any other factor, disputes the notions held by Bourke, Crook, and company, that the Rosebud was a victory. As Bourke himself later admitted, both Crook and then Custer fought the same vast Indian village within a span of eight days.*[9] *Having defeated Crook on June 17, the Indians were surprised by Custer's attack on June 25, but confident of the outcome; the army neither frightened nor impressed them.*

The officers who participated in the battle of the Rosebud, at least those who were writing while it was still fresh on their minds, were cautious in their comments. Three days after the fight, Lt. Henry Rowan Lemly, 3rd Cavalry, wrote that it was "still the all-absorbing topic of conversation, and some of its incidents are rather severely commented upon. . . .[Crook's] enemies say that he was outgeneraled. That his success was incomplete, must be admitted, but his timely caution may have prevented a greater catastrophe."[10] *Lt. Thaddeus Capron, 9th Infantry, was equally noncommittal, noting in his diary, "The result of [the] fight is in our favor but we did not do as much as could have been done."*[11]

7. The battle of the Rosebud is described in many works, among which are Neil Mangum, *Battle of the Rosebud: Prelude to the Little Bighorn*; J.W. Vaughn, *With Crook at the Rosebud*; two books by Jerome Greene, *Battles and Skirmishes of the Great Sioux War* and *Lakota and Cheyenne*; John S. Gray, *Centennial Campaign*; and two books by Charles M. Robinson III, *A Good Year to Die* and *General Crook and the Western Frontier*.

8. Bourke, Diaries, 5:439.

9. Ibid., 6:591.

10. Lemly, "Fight on the Rosebud," 17.

11. Capron, Diary, 33.

Anson Mills, however, was less charitable, but considerably more accurate. In his memoirs, written more than forty years later, Mills summed up the Rosebud in a single sentence: "I do not think that General Crook knew where [the hostile Indians] were, and I do not think our friendly Indians knew where they were, and no one conceived we would find them in the great force we did."[12]

Even Bourke, despite his pro-Crook posture, began to realize that something had gone terribly wrong. By July 10, after receiving news of the Custer debacle and looking back on the Rosebud fight, he grudgingly commented, "Since our Rosebud fight, my opinion has changed to an advocacy of the Fabian policy. We must remain here now until winter, worrying the enemy as best we can. When frost comes, and not till then can we hope to strike a decisive blow."[13]

June 16th Day warm but heavy clouds in sky.

Moved North at 5 A.M. Crossed Tongue river, ford good but banks on one side muddy. Bottom of firm gravel. Channel 25 yds wide, 4 feet deep and current of eight miles. Tongue river as seen from the bluffs among which we marched, presented a very beautiful valley, green with rich grass and dark with a heavy fringe of cottonwood and willow. Its sinuosities enclose many park-like areas of meadow land which are bounded on the land-side by deep bluffs of drift and other deposits near the Tertiary. Our course soon turned North West and afterwards to nearly West. As we emerged from our permanent camp, a motley column of Indians defiled alongside of us and took the lead. It was easy to see they had come for war to the death upon the Sioux; everything was in readiness for active work on a second's warning: horses and Indians alike.

A medicine man of the Crows kept up a piteous chant, reciting the cruelties of their enemies and stimulating their young men to war-like valor. In everything possible these Indians reminded one of the recounts given of the Arabian Bedouins. The grass was at first starting up very good: Five or six miles out from camp, we crossed an important tributary of Tongue river, evincing in[to the valley] with great force from a cañon in the Big Horn range. (Just before reaching this had come back into valley of Tongue for a short distance.)

12. Mills, *My Story*, 398.

13. Bourke, Diaries, 6:578. Fabian tactics were developed by Quintus Fabius Maximus against Hannibal in the Second Punic War, and call for avoiding a direct confrontation, in hopes of wearing out the enemy so that a decisive blow can be struck.

The creek spoken of is about same cross-section and same velocity as the one upon which our permanent camp is located. Our trail has gradually bent more and more North West From top of a small bluff hereabouts, an observation made with a prismatic compass (0° South) showed a B[ack]. S[ight].[14] along column of 300°. (560° S.W.) Two miles after (7 miles from camp) the B.S. was 11°: South 11° West. High snow-clad peak in Big Horn 9° Cloud Peak (?) 355°. The rate of travel became very fast. Save very short halts for grazing, the column kept right along for 27 miles. 12 miles out passed small spring and half a mile farther, crossed a little creek, about hidden by willow and box-elder. After this country became poor & grass thin and coarse: some prairie-dog towns on either hand. Mineralogical features, argillo-calcareous sandstone cropping out with frequency, clay shale, and burnt-out lignite beds. Also streak of sandstones burnt out by decomposition of iron pyrite. Scrub pine in sheltered recesses near summits. 20 miles out crossed little stream with dead cottonwood on the banks. Water rather scarce. Banks muddy and plastic[,] Rocky Bottom: about two yards wide, one foot deep, and slow current. Tongue river five miles in distance to Right behind high bluffs. A small divide intervened between the creek just crossed and one of its tributaries, which we ascended, turning nearly due West. Country becoming very broken: grass giving way in many places to cactus (nopal) and artemisia (worm-wood and sage-brush.). 25 miles out pasturage improving. Buffalo signs very thick. Trails cut into ground in every direction and grass nipped off close as if cut with a scythe. Buffalo seen in droves, in distance. Halted for a long time near the head of this creek. Scouts came running in with report the Sioux must be in vicinity: signs had been seen.

The cavalry dismounted and unsaddled to await the results of the Examination to be made by a picked party of Crows and Snakes. The other Indians joined in a wild, strange war dance, the younger warriors almost becoming frenzied before the exercise terminated. The young men who had gone out to spy the country, neared us on a full run from the top of the hill overlooking our bivouac[;] they yelled like wolves, the conventional signal that they had seen their enemy. Excitement among the Indians at least, was at fever heat. To meet the advancing couriers, many spurred out and escorted

14. A rod reading on a point of known elevation.

them back like a guard of honor. The old chiefs held their bridles whilst they dismounted and the less prominent warriors deferentially formed in a circle to listen to their narrative. It did not convey much information to my mind, unaccustomed to the indications, so familiar to them. It simply amounted to this[:] that the buffalo herds were very thick a little ahead of us and were running away from a Sioux hunting party. Knowing the unfaltering accuracy of an Indian's judgment in matters of this kind, General Crook told the chiefs to arrange the plan of march according to their own ideas. While this was going on, the Indians were charging about on their hardy little ponies, to put them out of breath so that when they regained their wind, they would not fail to sustain a whole day's battle. A little herb is carried along to be given to the ponies in such emergencies, but what virtues are attributed to this "medicine", I was unable to ascertain. Much solemnity is attached to the "medicine arrows" of the medicine man who seems to posses [sic] the powers of arbitrarily stopping a march at almost any moment.* Noon had passed. The march was resumed to gain the Rosebud, a tributary of the Yellowstone; we marched along through an elevated undulating table-land, mantled with emerald green grass eagerly nibbled by our horses and mules. Without possessing any decided beauty, its picturesqueness was very marked and pleasing. Every few rods, a little brook coursed down to pay its tribute to the Deje-Agis, as the Crows call the Tongue river. No timber, except an occasional small cottonwood or willow, could be seen along the banks, but wild-roses by the thousand laid their delicate beauties at our feet:[15] a species of blue-flower, I think a phlox, was there in profusion also; and in the bushes, multitudes of joyous-voiced singing birds piped their welcome as the troops filed by. Yet this beautiful country is given up to the domination of the thriftless savage, the buffalo and the rattlesnake. We could see the latter winding along through the tall grass, rattling defiance as they sneaked away. Buffalo crowded the country in every point, in squads of ten and twelve and droves of sixty and seventy; these were not rejected old bulls, but fine fat cows with their calves following close behind them. One young bull calf trotted close down to the column, his eyes beaming with curiosity and wonder. He was allowed to approach within a

*Here Bourke inserts "Buffalo Head," apparently the name of the medicine man.

15. These wild roses give the Rosebud its name.

few feet, when our prosaic Crow guides took his life as the penalty
of his temerity. Thirty buffalo were killed this afternoon, and the
choice pieces, hump, tenderloin, tongue and heart packed on our
horses. The flesh was roasted in the ashes, salt sprinkled over it and
a very savory and juicy addition made to our scanty supplies. We
made bivouac on the extreme head-waters of the Rosebud, here a
feeble rivulet of snow-water, sweet and palatable enough when the
muddy ooze is not stirred up from the bottom. Wood was found in
plenty for the slight wants of the command, which made very small
fires for a few moments to boil coffee, while our animals pretty well
tired out after the day's march of 35 or 40 miles, rolled and rolled
again in the matted bunches of succulent herbage, growing at their
feet. Our lines were drawn up in hollow square, animals inside, and
each man sleeping with saddle kit for pillow and arms by his side.
Pickets were posted on the bluffs near camp, and after making what
collation we could, sleep was song [but?] at that same moment the
black clouds above us had begun to patter down rain. A party of our
scouts returned late at night and stated they had come across a
small gulch, where a little band of Sioux hunters had been secreted
and that the enemy had left so hurriedly as to abandon meat cooking on the fire and an India-rubber blanket. We are now right in
among the hostiles and may strike or be struck at any hour. Mr.
Finerty's pistol was accidentally discharged to-day, burning and
breaking his saddle and very nearly wounding him.
June 17th Marched at daylight down Rosebud river. (4 mile) The
preceding line had not been completed when a couple of Crow scouts
came at full speed into the head of the column, crying Sioux! Sioux!
and shot after shot on our Left was heard. The line of sentinel's on
that side was very strong, and was immediately increased by a respectable detail of skirmishers to cover the companies busily at
work saddling up their horses. From the crest of the little ridge
immediately West of our bivouac, the long line of advancing Sioux
could be seen moving towards us seemingly confident they had but
to attack to succeed. Our Indian allies showed courage and skill;
they advanced hand in hand with the troops [and] where opportunity occurred charged with gallantry. The Sioux had, it seemed almost conclusive, made up their minds to seize our stock first and
with this end in view had pushed down two little ravines, coming in
from the West. Their attempts in this were frustrated by the vigi-

lance of our pickets and the rapidity with which the troops saddled up and took their positions. An advance at once took place to repel the demonstration of the enemy. Our men behaved with decision and coolness, the errors, if any, made being due to want of judgment and not to deficiency of courage. A detachment of Co. "I" 2d Cavalry, being without an officer, the men consented to follow my leadership and very gallantly stormed a rock-breasted, steep bluff, on whose summit the Sioux had taken post firing from behind little piles of stone. The cowardly whelps would not give us a show at close quarters, but whenever our lines came within 300 yards of theirs, would make for the next ridge with pusillanimous haste. Our people were mostly on foot, hence the slowness of our advance. Once at the crest of the bluff, my men were ordered to rest and take breath previous to charging for the other hill where our enemies now were. For a few minutes a very lively fire was poured in upon us and Sergeant Maher (Co. "I", 2d Cav.) was badly wounded in Right arm at or near the elbow.

The Snakes had now formed ready to charge and as it looked to me the best and speediest way to solve the question of who was to control that position, I determined to accompany them. Mounting my good-natured little pony and placing myself in line on their Right, it was not very long before I found myself on the summit of the ridge, in a place commanding an excellent view of the whole field. From the immediate front of our little party, the Sioux were flying in dismay, to the number of fifty or thereabouts. Mention should be made here of the gallantry of two enlisted men, who shared the perils of the charge. Private Leonard, Co "A", 3d Cavalry and Bugler Snow, co. "M", same regiment. Major Randall here came up to one and suggested falling back from that point to one more sheltered, in the rear. The Shoshonees, as is their wont, executed the order at a gallop, leaving Bugler Snow and the writer alone upon the ridge, unsuspicious of danger. Scarcely had I mounted my horse and mechanically loaded my carbine, than I called out to Bugler Snow to mount at once as Sioux were charging up the ravine on Left of Hill. Sure enough they came to the number of thirty or more, poor Snow being still on the ground. I gave them the contents of my carbine, at not more than 30 yds. at the same time yelled to make them believe there were still many of us there. Whether my purpose answered or that their ponies were winded with climbing up the steep hill-side, I don't presume to say: I only know they halted for one brief space, long enough however to let Snow and myself put spurs to our horses and rush after our comrades, nearly 400 yards away. My usual good fortune attended me, but poor Snow got back to our lines badly shot through both arms, near the wrists.* General Crook was at this point with the greater portions of Chambers', and Evans' battalions. He ordered Tom Moore to take his packers and form a line among the sandstone rocks directly in front of our standing-point. It is nothing but waste of pen, ink & paper to say Tom Moore and his party performed their allotted duty cheerfully and well. The Sioux made a rush out to charge them, thinking from the paucity of numbers, our men could easily be driven. There must have been a mistake somewhere, as the Sioux now know to their cost. The interview lasting only a moment, but cost them two or three dead warriors, the same in wounded and a few ponies. Moore and his party are nearly all fine shots, cool men and old Indian fighters. Colonel Royall had advanced on the extreme Left: his numbers did not exceed one hundred all told. The Sioux attempted to cut them off from the rest of our troops. Five Hundred well-armed but cowardly devils kept up a spiteful fire upon them which our brave fellows could not return with much effect. The Sioux rarely exposed themselves. Our loss at this point was heaviest, (Captain Guy V. Henry, 3d Cavalry, was shot through both cheeks, at the intersection of the jaws.[16] Colonel Royall, his adjutant, Lieut[.] Lemly and Lieuts. [James E.H.] Foster and [Bainbridge] Reynolds—all had narrow escapes.) General Crook here ordered a forward movement at a trot with heavy lines of skirmishers in front. The Sioux could not be prevailed upon to stay, but took to their heels every time we came within 5 or 6 yds. of them. We followed them seven miles, chasing them from position to position. It is proper to state that the Sioux had made every preparation to capture and destroy or at any rate to drive us back horseless to the Platte. They had the advantages of numbers, fresh horses, attack and acquaintance with the lay of the land. But we drove them from hill to hill, ravine to ravine. (Of our own losses we can speak authoritatively;

---

*Snow was helplessly crippled, discharged [from] the service and pensioned to fullest extent allowed by Law. He is now, May, 1878, a resident of Athol, Massachusetts.

16. Guy Henry recovered from his wound, returned to service, and served with distinction in the Spanish-American War. He was a brigadier general at the time of his death on October 27, 1899. Heitman, *Historical Register*, 1:523.

of the enemy, of course, not so much is known: We had ten killed
and nearly 25 wounded, soldiers and Indians.) The hostile numbers were estimated by such veteran experts as Col. Royall, and
others at not less than 1500, maybe more. Every time one of their
comrades was shot, they would run him off to the rear on his pony.
We only got (eleven)* scalps, but my impression is not less than
fifty of our enemies were killed and wounded. The ponies wounded
and killed were not counted.

This engagement gives us the morale over the boastful Dacotahs. (It
is the prelude to the campaign in which we hope to destroy every
village they have. Our soldiers, white and red, did splendidly. The
manner of fighting adopted by them the Snakes and Crows is peculiar and yet excellently well suited to circumstances. To attack, they
charge with impetuous velocity, running for fifty to one hundred yards,
then suddenly halting and circling about, the riders meantime lean-
ing from side to side to derange the enemy's aim.) The command was
concentrated late in the afternoon, and returned to camp, on Rosebud, at same place where we had halted in the morning.

Dead and wounded were brought back, the former for burial, the
latter for treatment. Our Snakes, who had had one of their band
killed right in our camp, (his mutilated corpse lies on the bank of
the stream just below where I sit.) commenced an infernal
caterwhaul as soon as they came in sight of his corpse. Having discharged this sad rite of bereavement, they went to the corpses of
two Sioux, lying nearby and most systematically cut and shot them
to pieces. (General Crook's horse was shot in the leg during the day,
but not mortally hurt.) A conference was held with both Crows and
Snakes toward sun-down, to learn their ideas relative to the prosecution of operations. I have no intention of throwing praise indis-
criminately; justice compels me to say officers and men behaved
with pronounced gallantry: to this rule, I know of no exceptions.
There was no leaving of dead and dying and no Alex. Moore skulk-
ing, this trip. Our coward was left at Fort Russell. Shortly after getting into camp, horses and mules were turned out to graze, pickets
established and a small, rude structure made with willow boughs,
rushes and blankets. Our badly wounded were placed under this
and examined by the attending surgeons. The appliances at hand
for surgical or other treatment are so slim, it is a matter of con-

*thirteen taken.

gratulations to know that there are few, if any, cases requiring immediate amputation.

The number of casualties of all kinds reported is fifty-seven, including (10) killed outright, (4) mortally wounded, and many of no significance. Doctors Hartsuff, Patzki and Stevens assisted by Lieut.
[Frederick] Schwatka, who has a slight knowledge of therapeutics,
have been and are doing all that is possible to ameliorate the condition of the unfortunates under their care. Nature in such cases generally comes to the assistance of the physician. When I visited the
Hospital in the evening, the patients were doing very nicely, with
one or two exceptions.

June 18th An immaculate sky this morning overhead and a heavy
frost under foot: turned out of our rude beds at 3 O'clock. Made a
hasty breakfast of coffee, hard-tack and bacon. Surgeon Hartsuff
informed me that the condition of the wounded was all that could
be hoped for; all had passed a good night. Our jaded animals are
much recuperated. God knows what they would have done had pasturage not been good and plenty and the weather pleasantly cool. A
large ration of them would have broken completely down. Travaux
for the transportation of the severely wounded have been made, of
poles from the trees in the streams, bound together with thongs of
hide and pieces of rope. With such mean & rude methods of transportation, we carried our brave comrades over a rough trail, some
twenty miles long, from last night's camp to a compact, readily defended little grassy nook watered by a feeble and nameless affluent
of the Tongue river. We struck out well to the South of our in-going
track; that the wounded might not have to be dragged across several deep tributaries of the Tongue which gush out from the foot-
hills in this vicinity. But in avoiding Scylla, we struck upon
Charybdis;[17] our sick-list was spared the discomfort and annoyance
of being dragged through swift-flowing waters, but the asperities of
the mountain sides were productive of almost as much inconve-
nience. Each sick man had six enlisted men detailed to attend his
litter; on steep grades the ends of the poles were carried by the
attendants who performed their duty with alacrity and without a

17. In *The Odyssey*, two sea monsters dwelling on either side of what are presumed to be
the Straits of Messina, between Italy and Sicily. Scylla had six heads with vicious teeth and
would snatch sailors off their ships and devour them. Charybdis would suck the water down
in a giant whirlpool. Ships trying to avoid the one invariably would fall afoul of the other.
There is, in fact, a whirlpool in the straits known as Charybdis.

murmur, notwithstanding its onerous nature. Sergeant Warfield, of Co. "F", 3d Cavalry, an old Arizona veteran, was charged with the superintendence of the detail. His discharge of his functions called forth warm eulogies from all observers. Tom Moore, our chief-packer and all his command were very efficient assistants in this delicate and important work. Leaving camp, our Crows came upon the body of a Sioux, wounded or killed yesterday. They said life was not yet extinct and the Sioux was moving when they came up. He was not moving much when they left. My informant told me they cut off the legs at the knees, the arms at the elbows, broke open the skull and scattered the brains on the ground. This is the manner of treatment all Indians pursue towards their enemy.[18]

During my interviews with various tribes of the American aborigine, I have not seen enough nobleness of mind among them all to make a man as good as an ordinary Bowery rough. The sooner the manifest destiny of the [white] race shall be accomplished and the Indian as an Indian cease to exist, the better.[19] After contact with civilization of nearly 300 years, the American tribes have never voluntarily learned anything but its vices. The exceptional instances have been among the natives of Spanish America. Among them the system of "repartimiento", objectionable as it undoubtedly was as being slavery disguised under a high-sounding name, did more for the compulsory advancement and christianization of the savage than all the methods elsewhere adopted.

The purely missionary efforts of such missionaries as the French Catholic priests Jogues, Garnier, Colusnotte, Breboeuf, in 1638 and the next decade were sublime labor, but they were the labors of Sisyphus[,] and had the same amount of self-negation, simple-

18. Richard Irving Dodge, who spent much of his career studying Plains Indians, explained the reasons behind mutilation. After noting that scalping "annihilates" the soul's existence, he wrote:

   A warrior killed in battle and not mutilated, shows, in the future life, no sign of wound; but if the soul be not annihilated by scalping, every mutilation inflicted on the body after death also mutilates the soul. If the head, or hands, or feet are cut off, or the body ripped open after death, the soul will so appear and exist in the Happy Hunting Grounds. Some believe that if the dead body is transfixed with arrows and left to decay, the soul must always wear and suffer from the phantasms of those arrows. This accounts for this habit, quite common, especially with the Sioux, and for the great apparent waste of arrows. If a body so found, pierced with many arrows, is unscalped, it was for the vindictive purpose of the murderers forever to torment the soul. If the head was scalped, the shooting was in mere bravado and cruel wantonness. Dodge, *Our Wild Indians*, 180-81.

   19. By this, Bourke means the imposition of white culture on the Indians, at that time generally seen as the only alternative to total extermination.

minded faith and undaunted resolution been displayed in an attempt for the regeneration of their own country, France would to-day be a community of saints.[20]

But to return to the Indians of the present day: the Crows were undoubtedly actuated to their worst by the conduct of the Sioux yesterday who took the greatest pains to mutilate and butcher the two bodies that fell into their hands. One of these was a Snake warrior (already spoken of.) whom they scalped from the back of his head to the crown. His bare skull presented a ghastly sight when we found him. Another was one of our soldiers, a recruit, Private Bennett, Co. "L", 3d Cavalry, who was badly wounded and lay hid in the rocks as the Sioux charged by. When they retreated under the fire of our advancing line, this poor wretch mistook them for the friendly Crows and came out from his hiding place. They cut him to pieces with their long-handled (eight foot) tomahawks and lances. They tried to scalp him and another soldier. This compelled them to dismount. Before they could execute their hellish project, our men were upon them and the red fiends scampered off. Last night, a deep trench was dug in the muddy banks of the Rosebud, near the water-line, our brave dead ranged therein, mud and earth packed down, a large fire built over the spot and every other means taken to conceal from the enemy the extent of our losses.[21] We were not fired into during the night an almost conclusive presumption of the heavy blow given Sitting Bull's band in the fight. This morning as we were breaking into column of march, our Crow guides called out there were Sioux in sight and sure enough, two or three miles off to the Left, coming over the crest of the ridge, [that] Randall and the writer had taken at the head of the Snakes yesterday three mounted Sioux might be seen moving along the battle-ground looking for their dead. They showed no sign of intending to molest us and most certainly had enough fighting yesterday to last them until we come back. We are going back to permanent camp on Tongue river for a number of cogent reasons; the medical staff has many wounded to look after and has no supplies to do it with. Several brave fellows, badly hurt, are riding with the column to diminish

---

20. Bourke refers to the Jesuit missionaries to the Hurons of French Canada, chief among whom was Jean de Breboeuf, who suffered a hideous martyrdom at the hands of the Iroquois. See Parkman, *The Jesuits in North America*.

21. Despite these precautions, the Indians discovered and plundered the grave. Robinson, *A Good Year to Die*, 152.

the labors of the Doctors and give the more seriously disabled a greater share of attention.[22]

We struck out at first on our back trail, following it nearly due South to the head of the Rosebud. This little stream has muddy bottom as far as I saw it (that is to say from its extreme head to a point into cañon seven miles below the point where the Sioux made their attack.) It has but little timber except in the sandstone crags which draw near its current. Here quite a supply of good pine fuel can be obtained. Thick sedge grass and a variety almost identical with that known to the Mexicans as "Sacaton" obstruct its channel. Striking closer to the mountains, this morning we entered a knolly country where the resources of pasturage are practically unlimited. The summit of the divide between the Rosebud and the Rotten Grass, (an affluent of the Little Big Horn[)] is marked by a small conoidal hill, studded with pine trees. This is the site of a sanguinary engagement had in times gone by between the Crows and Blackfeet Sioux. The latter were surrounded and badly whipped. The column halted for a short interval to give the rear-guard time to close up with the wounded. This opportunity our horses devoted to grazing and the Crows to a scalp dance. This was another exhibition of the power of the average Indian to howl as much like a Devil and make himself as disagreeable as possible. In this exercise the hirsute adornments of our defunct enemies were borne aloft on tall poles, shouted at and derided. A volley of musketry terminated the performance. Looking down from this high point to the drainage of the Little Big Horn on the West and South, the passages of landscape were very fine. Long, narrow ravines opened down into the valley of the Rotten Grass and framed in the scenery in a way at once beautiful and unusual. The high peaks of the Big Horn mountains, still snow-capt, screened the horizon in our front, extending to Right and Left as far as eye could reach. Intervening, the valleys of the Little Big Horn and Rotten Grass, filled all the middle-ground, the ridge dividing them standing out dimly in the haze. There were enough clouds in the sky to bring out some pleasing effects of light and shade and dark pine trees to prevent the grassy slopes of the hill-sides from becoming monotonous. The numerous small bluffs and back-bones,

22. Besides the wounded, Crook had just enough food to get back to Goose Creek, and his ammunition had been reduced to fifty rounds per man. Consequently, he had no option other than to withdraw to his base. Ibid., 149.

separating the rivulets forming the Rosebud and Tongue from those paying tribute to the Little Big Horn are numerous enough in themselves to impart a charming diversity to the country. Their rounded contours are frequently broken in upon abruptly by protruding ledges of sandstone which likewise, in places, caps their crests. In this delightful region, elk, deer and buffalo, roam at pleasure, sharing the country with the savage nomad. Our line of march to-day followed deep-cut buffalo trails, as conspicuous as a wagon road. Skeletons and carcasses line the train on either side; and in the near distance, droves of the living animals, scared at the sight of us, hurried off to remoter recesses. Our hunters secured some fresh meat as we were coming down the narrow divide between Ash Creek, one of the forks of the Little Big Horn, and the head of Tongue river. The Crow Indians left for their homes this evening, as is the custom of all the Indians, after an engagement with an enemy. They promised they would be back within fifteen days, or that at any rate their nation would be largely represented during succeeding movements. Whether moving with the soldiery or in independent columns, it is now almost a certainty these friendly Indians will strike many a blow against the Sioux before snow falls. The Nez Perces will also come down from the North-West.

June 19th. Last night was very cold—one of the coldest for a summer night I ever experienced. Frost covered the ground and our sleep was interrupted by the intense cold. An alarm of the pickets brought all to their feet about one o'clock, but after careful examination it was found to be groundless. We broke into column at daybreak, striking straight across the hills to the forks of Goose Creek or Tongue river, winding up and down steep hill-sides where vegetation was more sparse than at any time during our four days' absence. Cactus and artemisia appeared with undesirable frequency, but water becoming better and more plentiful as we came down into the sources of Tongue River. No Indians made their appearance, but buffalo were discovered early in the day and three of them killed. We passed the North Fork of Tongue river without accident or trouble to our wounded. A total march of (25) miles brought us to Major Furey's corral, 2 1/2 miles above (South.) the place where we left it. He reported no molestation from hostile Indians but had taken every possible precaution against surprise. His wagon-train had been packed in a grassy bend of the stream, affording water on all sides and much protection through a heavy line of willow trees and underbrush. From wagon to wagon, along the line of wheels, ropes were stretched and at every eligible spot, breastworks of earth and logs had been thrown up[,] from behind which sharpshooters would have made it lively for any antagonist.

(Hunters from his train had killed that day six buffaloes and three elk.) General Crook pushed the command onto a new camp, 2 1/4 miles to secure green forage. Our pickets were at once posted in strength on the bluffs commanding camp, animals unsaddled and turned out to graze and drink, details of men set to work putting up the hospital tents and our wounded kindly cared for. A few of the officers had lemons left in their satchels or valises—these were brought out—there were not half a dozen in all, but enough to make a pleasant glass of lemonade for each patient. The eagerness of their drinking was a most welcome token of their gratitude and their improving condition. This evening, Genl. Crook sent a courier in to Fort Fetterman with the following telegram to General Sheridan.

Camp on South Fork, Tongue River, Wy.

June 19th 1876

Lieut. General Sheridan
Chicago, Illinois:

Returned to camp to-day having marched as indicated in my last telegram. When about forty miles from here on Rosebud Creek, Montana, morning 17th instant[,] scouts reported Indians in vicinity and within a few minutes we were attacked in force, the fight lasting several hours. We were near the mouth of a deep canyon through which the creek ran. The sides were very steep covered with pine and apparently impregnable, the village supposed to be at the other end about eight miles off. They displayed strong force at all points, occupying so many and such covered places that it is impossible to correctly estimate their numbers; the attack, however, showed that they anticipated that they were strong enough to thoroughly defeat the command.

During the engagement, I tried to throw a strong force through the canyon, but I was obliged to use it elsewhere before it had gotten to the supposed location of the village.[23] The command finally drove

---

23. This refers to a detachment under Capt. Anson Mills, that was sent up the canyon, then recalled. The village was not located where Crook supposed it to be, but was northwest of the Rosebud, on the Little Bighorn side of the divide. Mangum, *Battle of Rosebud*, 48.

the Indians back in confusion, following them several miles[,] the scouts killing a good many during the retreat. Our casualties were nine men killed and fifteen wounded of 3d Cavalry, (2) wounded, Second Cavalry, three men wounded 4th Infantry and Captain Guy V. Henry, 3d Cavalry, severely wounded in the face. It is impossible to correctly estimate the loss of the Indians, many being killed in the rocks, others being gotten off before we got to that part of the village, (13) dead being left.

We remained on the field that night and having nothing but what each man carried himself, we were obliged to return to the train to properly care for the wounded who were transported here on mule litters and are now comfortable. All doing well.

I expect to find those Indians in rough places all the time and so have ordered five additional companies of Infantry and shall not probably make any extended movement till they arrive.

Officers and men behaved with marked gallantry during the engagement.

(Signed) George Crook,
Brigadier General

Chapter 18

❖

❖

❖

❖

❖

Hunting and Fishing
on the Tongue

This chapter is the chronicle of a camping trip. Indeed, it hardly seemed like a war zone, and if there was any concern over the possibility of Indian attack, Bourke did not mention it. The reader might well wonder how they felt they could spend this time in the mountains with their attentions devoted almost entirely to hunting, fishing, camping, and prospecting. The answer was overconfidence. Having convinced themselves that their defeat at the Rosebud was a great victory, they felt the Indians were on the run, and would not dare attack. On July 6, Bourke commented, "The absence of hostile demonstrations since our fight of June 17th speaks very plainly of the severe handling the Sioux received that day. Were they victorious or had the day been even undecided, our camp would long since have been beleaguered by the sharpshooters."[1] As yet, they were unaware that these same Indians had annihilated Custer only eight days after the Rosebud.

One is struck by the amount of wildlife that existed in the region before it was developed for settlement and ranching. Bourke wrote that in one stream:

1. Bourke, Diaries, 6:561.

> *Many trout were abstracted from its cool and shady re-*
> *cesses almost as soon as the command to unsaddle had*
> *been executed. I have abandoned any attempt at comput-*
> *ing the number; certainly, not less than 10.000 have been*
> *cooked and eaten, and the grand total may reach as high*
> *as 15.000! This number may seem incredible; let it be borne*
> *in mind, we have not less than fifteen hundred and fifty*
> *officers, soldiers, teamsters and Indians subsisting on this*
> *delicate fish and that they have been eating them freely for*
> *more than three weeks. Then the aggregate will be accepted*
> *without a murmur.*[2]

Bourke was not alone in his enthusiams. Lieutenant Lemly wrote:

> *In close promixity to our camp, there are many ponds,*
> *formed by beaver dams and filled with fine salmon or rain-*
> *bow trout. Already the soldiers are making nets of com-*
> *missary twin. Just fancy seining for trout!*[3]

It should be borne in mind, however, that the camp was constantly
on the move, to avoid exhausting forage and resources, and the
trout were taken from various streams over an area of at least
twenty or thirty square miles.

More disturbing is the wastage of wildlife that would cause
any modern hunter/conservationist to recoil in disgust. Record-
ing a hunting trip by Louis Richaud and several companions,
Bourke wrote that they found the country "filled with Rocky Mtn
sheep, of which they secured six or seven out of a great number
killed. They had taken station on a precipice two hundred feet
high, shooting down from the top. Many wounded lambs and ewes
escaped to die elsewhere. Our mess was presented with a supply
of fresh, tender mutton, acknowledged with gratitude."[4] *Appar-*
ently he gave no thought to the sheep that seem to have been wan-
tonly killed or wounded to provide the fresh mutton.

With time on his hands, Bourke devoted much attention to camp
routine. He described the plan and operation of Indian Wars-era

2. Ibid., 6:627.
3. Lemly, "Fight on the Rosebud," 18.
4. Bourke, Diaries, 6:624.

*military camps during extended periods on the field, and consid-
ered ways that organization and equipment could be improved.
As Indian auxiliaries often were present, he had ample opportunity to observe them, and develop respect for their ability to adapt
to a situation. He also realized, as many of his contemporaries
failed to do, that the West Point manual had no place in Indian
fighting. Comparing their performance with that of the soldiers,
he commented, "We have much to learn from the savage in the
matter of Cavalry training; the trouble is our prejudices of education are so deeply rooted, common sense and observation have no
permission to assert themselves."[5]*

*Bourke also vented his spleen against the Indian agents, ac-
cusing them of lining their pockets at government expense and
virtual complicity with the hostiles. Referring specifically to the
Red Cloud Agency, he wrote, "The damnable frauds perpetrated
at that sink of iniquity daily call to Heaven for redress."[6] This was
hardly fair to the agents. To some degree, the effort to end fraud at
the agencies was successful by 1875, despite continuing military
allegations to the contrary. The army resented the transfer of control over Indians to the Department of the Interior, and the notion
of corruption by the civilians in charge was, as historian John S.
Gray has pointed out, practically dogma among the soldiers. The
facts, however, do not bear this out. Indians often made a game of
relocating from one area to another, in order to inflate the agent's
count, and this normal state of affairs had been exacerbated in
1875 by large-scale movement among the Indians. Additionally,
government rations were woefully inadequate for the large number of people they were expected to feed, and simple humanity
often prompted the agents to pad their censuses to obtain sufficient food to avoid widespread hunger and suffering.[7]*

*Crook was out on yet another hunting and fishing trip when
news arrived of the Custer disaster, which had a sobering effect
on the men in camp. Bourke, who was one of those men in camp,
now took another look at the situation, and commented, "The General has set an example of recklessness that cannot too strongly
be condemned: this rashness must be foregone in the future. Else*

5. Ibid., 6:597.
6. Ibid., 6:595.
7. Gray, *Centennial Campaign*, 309-310; Robinson, *A Good Year to Die*, 260.
8. Bourke, Diaries, 6:579.

some day his mutilated corpse will be found. . . ."[8] *Yet the good fairy that seemed always to have watched over Crook was working overtime, as she would continue to do for the remaining fourteen years of the general's life.*

June 20th. Under a bright genial sun, pushed up Tongue River, seven miles, and made our camp on the banks of a prattling brook, some 30 feet wide, 2 or 4 feet deep, current of great velocity and shady banks. Bottom of large boulders, forming gloomy pools under the alluvial banks. Every indication of a trout stream. After wounded comrades and tired animals had been cared for, and camp laid out, great numbers of officers and men sought refreshment in the sparking waters, and when bathed came back to camp to do what might be required of each for sending wagon-train back to Fetterman for ammunition and supplies.

Heat was very great throughout the day; at 3 P.m., the thermometer indicated 103° F. in the shade. The result is that the grass about us is drying up rapidly and if we do not have rain within a few days, our animals will suffer.

June 21st At 4 O'Clock in the morning, our wounded were placed in the wagons, upon couches of fresh clean grass and moved off to Fetterman under the escort of Col. Chambers who had under him Munson's and Luhn's Companies of the 9th and 4th Infy. The following officers accompanied him:

Captain Nickerson, (with his orderly, Reynolds)

Captain J.V. Furey, A.Q.M

Captain W.S. Stanton, Engineer Officer, (with his draughtsman, Mr. Koehneman, and party.)

Captain Guy V. Henry, (wounded) and Captains Munson and Luhn and Lieuts. Capron and Seton.

Also Mr. M[a]cMillan, correspondent of the *Chicago Inter-Ocean.*[9] I was very glad to see poor Nickerson go away; his health has been wretched upon the trip, and only his indomitable energy could have sustained him.[10] His gallantry and coolness during the engagement

9. MacMillan's health had deteriorated to the point that the medical officers recommended he leave. Bourke later wrote that MacMillan "had shown that he had as much pluck as any officer or soldier in the column, but his strength was not equal to the hard marching and climbing, coupled with the violent alternations of heat and cold, rain and shine, to which we were subjected." Knight, *Following the Indian Wars*, 193; quote from Bourke, *On the Border*, 193.

10. Nickerson had received a near-fatal chest wound during the Civil War, and still suffered severely from the aftereffects. Robinson, *General Crook*, 85

have been warmly eulogized by all who saw him, but have not occasioned astonishment in the minds of those who know him. As the newspaper reports of the affair promise to be very complete and exhaustive, it is labor thrown away to refer too much in extreme to the recent action, but before I forget to mention it, I will refer here to the magnificent appearance presented by one of our savage allies—a Snake chief. His head-dress of feathers was a gorgeous piece of work and his whole appearance, as mounted on a fiery little pony he charged along the slopes, circling, wheeling and charging at the head of his wild squadron, decidedly majestic. Medicine Crow, the Absaraka Chief looked like a devil; his head-gear was of fur, plumage and buffalo horn.

Our Snakes left to-day with the wagons going to their homes on the West side of this range. Five of them remained with the command, a pure prognostication that Mr. Cosgrove's efforts to bring the others back will be successful after they get through with their scalp dance and other ceremonies in their village. As things now look, we shall within fifteen days, be reinforced by five additional companies of Infantry, armed with long range rifles, one company of Cavalry, a body of half-breed scouts, rations and supplies for sixty days, and 300 to 400 rounds of ammunition. Any numbers from 300 to 500 friendly Indian scouts will be with us or around and near us—Crows, Snakes, Nez Perces, Utes and maybe Pawnees, who assured of our intentions to crush the Sioux, will flock in to plunder and exterminate their enemy. Terry and Gibbon ought to be in communication with us by that time and a combined onward movement determined upon for breaking the enemy's power to pieces. The Sioux must divide up to hunt the buffalo and thus place themselves in our power, remain in one body and be hacked to pieces or go in upon the Reservations, whipped. Every cartridge lost by them now is lost forever. Every one of their dead, is one whom they cannot replace, while each wounded man requires at least two attendants. On our side, we must remember our ignorance of the country, the fact we have to carry everything upon our horses' back, whereas the Sioux can leave much behind in their villages and ride bareback, the great ratio of recruits in the command and worst of all the demoralization brought about by the cowardice of Capt. Alex. Moore, 3d Cavalry, in the Crazy Horse fight. The company "F" 3d Cavalry, that did so little under the braggart and coward, Moore, did excellently well under that brave youngster, Reynolds on the present occasion.

This day and yesterday more than fifty* fine trout were caught in the little mountain brook just in front of our line of tents; more could have been taken, I think, were it not for the plashing of men bathing and animals drinking in the water which must have frightened the timid little fish. The thermometer must have shown a very high temperature to-day; everybody suffered more than yesterday. Swarms of large green and black flies tormented us all day. Luckily, the nights are so very cold, sleep is not disturbed at all and every one is refreshed and rested during the night.

June 22nd. We were not favored last night with the storms the clouds promised; a few drops of rain fell and a violent wind prevailed for nearly half an hour, threatening much damage, but doing none except to rip up the hospital tent fly. The heat has slightly moderated, with indications of rain and electrical disturbance. General Crook, Col. Van Vliet[,] Major Burt and a small party started up the mountain to hunt and fish. Colonel Royall left in command of camp. Within the picket lines, squads of men are devoting their leisure hours to bathing and trout-catching. Our breakfast comprised some delicious fried trout—one of the greatest luxuries imaginable.

June 23d. Breakfast had hardly been finished when a courier rode up in front of my tent with a packet of dispatches for General Crook; he stated that he had started from Fetterman with Lieut. Schuyler, A.D.C., and that the latter would be with us in a few moments. The dispatches embraced a telegram from Lieut-Gen. Sheridan, at Red Cloud, giving notice that Lieut-Col. E.A. Carr, with eight cos. of the 5th Cavalry, had started out from that point with six wks' supplies to scout the country down the Little Powder to about where Terry was supposed to be.

This movement will help us somewhat, and if Genl. Crook will now order into the field Spalding's,[11] Mize's and [Capt. Henry] Wessells' companies of the 2d and 3d Cavalry, the Sioux will be crushed ere the Summer solstice. The presence of these companies is not essential to the successful prosecution of the campaign, but very desirable that all the Cavalry and most of the Infantry of the Department of the Platte may have the opportunity to share in the glory of the good work. Schuyler was warmly greeted by old friends and new who pressed eagerly about him to extract the latest news.

*(Altogether about 90 to 95.)

11. Captain Edward James Spaulding, Second Cavalry.

[Rutherford B.] Hayes (of Ohio) and [William A.] Wheeler (of N.Y.) were the Republican nominees for President and Vice President. The former is a friend of General Crook's—a man, if not previously eminent as a politician, at least unsullied in his record as a soldier and public man. Wheeler is cousin to Lieut. Foster, of our command.

General Emory had been retired, the promotions following being Merritt as Colonel 5th Cav., Dudley as Lt.-Col. 10th Cav.[12] and [George Bliss] Sanford, Major 1st Cavalry. This puts Mason 5th Cav., at head of list of Cav[alr]y. Captains.[13] Some 1800 young warriors had left Red Cloud Agency to take the war-path. A fight with Terry's command was reported at the agencies—one with heavy loss on both sides but indecisive in results. This is the Indian story, very probably, a lie out of whole cloth.[14] It was rumored in camp that five Government Commissioners were coming out to treat with the Sioux Indians, to learn the terms upon which they would agree to peace. This is a stupid piece of tom-foolery, as stupid indeed as scarcely to deserve mention. Schuyler's little party of three had made the ride from Fetterman in four days, travelling by sun and by dark. A very perilous proceeding which cannot be too severely condemned. On the other side of old Fort Reno, they came suddenly upon the hour-old trail of a small war party of Sioux and lay hid in the rocks all day. When night came, they galloped forty-five miles without halting. Our supply trains were met at the crossing of Clear Creek, thirty odd miles to the East of us. Nickerson examined the mail and conversed with the party which then recommenced the long ride of the night terminating a few hours after sun-rise in the camp of the Expedition at this point.

June 24th My journal is lacking in interest to-day. Camp was moved this morning three or four miles up Tongue river. We found a broad flat plain, carpeted with grass and flowers, bounded on the East by a row of small hills, jutting out from the first great rampart of the Big Horn. The Tongue river flows out from a deep, dark cañon in

12. This is an error. Nathan Augustus Monroe Dudley was promoted from major of the 3rd Cavalry to succeed Merritt as lieutenant colonel of the 9th Cavalry. Heitman, *Historical Register*, 1:386.

13. Julius Wilmot Mason, with whom Bourke had served in Arizona, was promoted to major with this shuffle. Ibid., 1:695.

14. The report was erroneous, but prophetic. Two days later, on June 25th, Custer and five companies of the 7th Cavalry, part of Terry's command, would be annihilated at the Little Bighorn.

this rampart and at the foot of the small row of grassy hillocks spoken of a branch meanders near the plain a mile or more away from us and joins the stream below camp. Rapids and deep pools of icy-cold water, shaded by a heavy growth of willow trees, give a home to multitudes of mountain trout which have been heavily assessed all day to give the officers and men a delicate meal. The total no. caught was not estimated, Lieut. Lemly caught twenty and Major Noyes forty. As our wagons, with one exception, had gone back with Major Furey, some trouble was given to pack baggage from one camp to another, the pack-mules doing, as usual, heavy work. Tents were carried, rolled and slung to the running gear of the ambulances and wagon: subsistence and forage on pack-mules and mess-chests and other cumbrous property in the army wagon. The Infantry remained in old camp all night. Nearly all my terms of praise have been exhausted in speaking of the beauty of the Big Horn Mountains: the present camp, probably the best we have had, must be passed over with a mere reference to its beauties. Had a photographer accompanied us, his camera would have constantly been occupied in reproducing scenes of picturesque and noble beauty.

June 25th Colonel Mills brought in this afternoon one hundred trout caught by himself and assistants. Other parties were equally successful. What was so lately a luxury, is now becoming a component of the daily ration. Squads of men and officers constantly pass HdQrs en route to the cañon a couple of miles above. There the river is broken into numerous little falls and rapids, trout are caught there every moment, and some little game of other kinds is shot, coming down to drink.[15]

June 26th The long-looked for and anxiously expected courier trotted into camp, very early this morning—before some of the command had breakfasted. The mail delivered included personal correspondence for nearly every one and newspapers and a few magazines for General Crook and myself principally, but thanks to the attending remembrance of those at HdQrs [in Omaha], we had such an excess of reading matter that all could come and help themselves. General Crook's dispatches were rather meagre, containing no definite advices regarding Terry or his movements. Our newspaper files were very complete, representing prominent New York,

---

15. On this particular afternoon, less than seventy miles to the north, the 7th Cavalry was being cut to pieces at the Little Bighorn.

Philadelphia, San Francisco, Washington, Chicago, Omaha and Cheyenne publications. They contained many allusions to the present Expedition. . . much concerning the Presidential nomination and considerable in regard to the deposition and suicide of Abdul Asiz, the Sultan of Turkey and the portentous aspect of European affairs, foreboding a general War.

In domestic affairs, the Centennial Exposition is occupying the place of prominence in public consideration. Next comes the Sioux trouble and its collateral issues. It would be unwise to disguise the powerful and vindictive opposition General Crook must stem before the Sioux can be struck; to subjugate the hostile Indians nothing is needed but courage, energy, fortitude and skill—qualities rare enough in themselves, still more rare in combination, but undeniably concentrated in a remarkable degree in our Commanding General. To fight the enemy in the rear, to rebut and refute the averments and malicious slanders of the strikers and hangers-on of the Indian ring, is a task more difficult and more dangerous, simply because that foe is more insidious, and more cowardly, but more desperate. General Vandeveer's telegram that the Crazy Horse fight was an attack upon a band of peaceable Indians travelling back to their Reservations. . .is a lie, so ridiculous that we can afford to laugh at everything except its malignity: this astute, cold-blooded old specimen of double-dealing is now near the end of his rope. To use a coarse, but emphatic, *Western* expression, the time has come "to bust him wide open."

Our packers organized a mule-race this evening, over a 200 yard track: if the distance was small, the enthusiasm was great. The aggregate of the stakes was ten dollars, betting to that total being very active in sums of five, ten and twenty cents. The victorious mule, a bright little black beauty, was warmly caressed and admired. Our cavalry horses are saddled up twice daily and exercised at a walk, trot, (principally) and gallop. This besides accustoming our recruits to the manage, hardens and toughens the animals and improves their wind. Rain fell in a desultory way during the afternoon, turning into a sharp shower which lasted well through the night.

June 27th Morning Cloudy, damp and cold. General Crook went up the cañon to hunt and fish, but at night-fall upon his return, had only slight success to report. His party killed a cinnamon bear.

June 28th. Bright and clear. Day rather warm. Camp is about equally divided in occupation: one fourth reading, one fishing, one hunting and one on picket. (It is estimated that fully 500 five hundred trout have been brought into camp to-day. Colonel Mills and squad caught one hundred and forty-six. The HdQrs. twenty, and nearly all who persistently tried their luck were rewarded with from fifteen to fifty apiece. Most of them were small "pan" trout, but very toothsome.) A courier started to-night with mail for Fort Fetterman.

June 29th. Hot and Cloudy. A heavy storm is approaching. Camp struck at noon and moved a short distance, about one mile, up the river, to the mouth of the cañon. . . .

Rained heavily this afternoon and continuously during the night. Buffalo and elk killed for meat in the evening and very many trout caught, (fifty-five by Lieut. Bubb alone.)

June 30th. Cloudy all day with occasional storms of rain. Very disagreeable, murky weather.

It should have been stated that Frank Gruard went out last night (28th) [sic] to examine the country near our command. Smokes had been observed and even small bodies of Indians reported. Frank's tour failed to confirm such impressions. In all camps wild rumors sporadically become prevalent: ours is no exception to the rule. An old citizen, following in our train, reports that he went out a day or so since to look for a stray horse. Having wandered some distance, he lay down to rest in the shade of some trees by a brook-side. The noise of a rifle or pistol awakened him in time to see two Indian boys scampering off; a small hole in the saddle-cantle, he asserts, was made by the bullet they fired at him.

Thirty Montana miners joined us yesterday and to-day. This being the last day of the second monthly review, muster and inspection of the troops were held at 7 A.M. Col. Evans mustered 3d Cavalry, Capt. Noyes 2d Cavy. and Maj. Burt the Infantry and the hospital.

July 1st. A serene atmosphere and spotless sky. General Crook, with a small party of officers and civilians started to-day to examine Big Horn range. Big Bat, the guide, started this morning for the Crow Agency: At 10 a.m., our party assembled to the number of ten or fifteen and the preliminaries of saddling and packing our mules were promptly completed. Each member carried four days' rations of bacon, sugar, coffee and hard-tack in saddle-bags, together with rifle or shot-gun and necessary ammunition, while the pack-mules were loaded with a scant supply of blankets and buffalo robes and one or two kettles and pans for boiling coffee and frying meat. Our personnel comprised General Crook, Lieut. Bourke and Lieut. Schuyler of his staff, Colonel Royall and Lieut. Lemly, Major Burt and Lieut[.] Carpenter, Messers Wasson, Strahorn, Finerty and Davenport and five or six experienced packers, under guidance of Mr. Young. Our sober-sided mules behaved with a decorum becoming the occasion; they had all been picked out with especial reference to strength, gentleness and tameness under saddle.

For three miles, trail was extremely steep compelling momentary halts every short distance to give ourselves and animals a breathing spell. When the summit of the "cover-face" of the Big Horn was attained it was noticed with gladness by all that a level, or gently rolling, surface spread before us. Turning about, an extensive landscape was visible to Right and Left, repaying amply the toil of gaining the point of sight. The grassy foot-hills, surrounding camp, lay directly beneath, the different branchlets of the Tongue river, coursing among them. Apparently at our very feet, the long lines of white tents showed the locations of the different battalions. Beyond these, the country opened out as far North & West as the valley of the Little Big Horn (?), while the limit of vision in front was the line of sharp bluffs at the mouth of the Tongue river cañon: to the West and South, on our trail we saw the frozen precipices of Cloud Peak and its sister promontories, down on whose flanks huge patches of snow slowly yielded to the assaults of a summer sun. Every few hundred yards, little gurgling rivulets and spring brooks leaped out from the protecting shade of pine and juniper groves and sped down to join the Tongue which warned us of its own near presence in a cañon on the Left by the murmur of its waters passing swiftly from basin to basin down a success of tiny falls. Exuberant Nature had carpeted the hills and dells with a grateful matting of grasses and flowers. Along the brook-sides, wild rose-buds peeped out, harebells, wild flax, forget-me-nots, astragalus and innumerable varieties not determined, disputed with their more gaudy companions, the sunflowers, possession of the soil. The grass was not as rich as that growing on the lower levels; still, our animals plucked at it with zest. None of our public parks that I have seen displayed a greater variety of picturesque scenery. Toward the summit of this first ridge, imperfectly crystallized granite begins to displace the siliceous limestones and red clays and sandstone representing the geological types nearer the valley. Much pine and fir timber was encountered: at first, in small copses, then in more considerable bodies; finally in dense forests. The quality of the pine was in general below the average, but how much of that inferiority is attributable to the absence of protection against the devastation of fire and hurricanes[16] is difficult to tell.

A very curious variety of juniper makes its appearance near here. It is very stunted, grows prone to the ground and until approached very close might be mistaken for a bed of moss. Our party soon drew near the rim of a lakelet of pure water: judging from its rocky bottom, its supply was perennial and fed partly by melting snow and partly by springs. Upon its glassy surface, a duck swam gracefully, admiring its own reflection in the pellucid water.

Six miles of hard marching through, between, over and amidst fallen timber, swept down by the tempestuous blast from the mountain tops or seared and charred by the lightning's fell stroke, brought us to the banks of a tributary of Tongue or Goose creek, where we made camp for the night. We saw to-day piles of fir trees cut by the Indians to make lodge-poles. The exterior bark and coating are stripped off, the heart preserved. This from its elasticity and strength is much prized for the purpose designated. We had hoped to attain the divide of the snowy range, but its peaks still lay a mile or two away from us. We found consolation in admiring their beauty as we prepared our frugal supper. Piling up dry wood took but a moment and in another a blazing fire awaited our coffee and bacon. The former was readily made in a tin canister; the latter, sliced then placed upon a willow twig, soon frizzled to a palatable crispness. Our appetites, aggravated by the keen mountain air and the climb of twelve miles, condoned the frugality of the repast. Epicures might not envy our food; they certainly would have sighed in vain for the pleasure with which it was devoured. After supper, each officer and man took his mule to the stream to drink and then staked him out to graze for the night. Game tracks marked the ground on all sides, but strange to say no game could be seen; neither would any of the agile trout darting about in the rocky pools regard the tempting bait of grasshoppers and flies held out to entice them. A black-tailed deer was shot near night-fall. General Crook, who went out hunting amid the hills near bivouac told us when he came back that the

16. I.e. high wind storms.

summits of the many knolls and hills close by were studded with lakelets of silver water; their great depth, size, limpidness and coldness of water, gravelly bottoms and lily pads growing above the surface are proofs of their permanency and the important part they assume in the water supply of Tongue, Goose, Clear and Big Horn rivers. This bivouac presented us with an abundance of the purest water, good fuel and sufficient grass for our stock and was besides so sheltered that we slept with much comfort during the night unannoyed by musquitoe or cold, the twin annoyances of these great elevations.

July 2d After an early breakfast, took up the trail of yesterday, which was made by our Sho-sho-nee allies on their way back to their homes in the Wind River country. The grandeur of the scenery encountered on this day's march is worthy of portraiture by abler pens than mine, nor would I assume the task were we not the first Americans to penetrate the arcana of its beauties. We first passed across one or two openings in the forest of considerable area and to all appearances suitable for the growth of cereals; then the cañon suddenly became very restricted in breadth and the path very rugged. Our sturdy mules climbed over fallen timbers, slipped down granite boulders, threaded their way with firm steps across the swift-rushing stream which coursed down the bed of the cañon, or forced a path between dense pine, juniper and fir timber with almost impenetrable undergrowth.

All geological formations had by this time yielded undisputed sway to the nuclear granite which on every hand, above us, below and in front, lay in Titanic masses, like Ossa upon Pelion piled, or frowned down as precipices hundreds of feet high, along whose vertical faces the scattered pine and juniper with difficulty maintained a foothold. The decomposition of the fibre of these conifers has filled the narrow pass with a peaty mould that covers the deposits of drift and large masses of rock, accumulated near the stream bed. Wherever springs oozed out from this peaty soil or tributaries divided it, to cross was almost impossible. Our individual difficulties were to some extent alleviated by the reflection that personal misery did not lack company. Mr. Finerty, especially would have been pitied, had not the ridiculousness of his discomfort banished all sense of pity from our breasts. He lost his hat, his carbine, his seat in the saddle and his temper all at once. His ejaculations of "Oh, By Jesus Christ" were more profane than elegant, but so emphatic there was no mistaking his meaning.

We grew tired counting the springs bubbling up from the rock,—in fact, the whole valley had become a sponge, yielding water, fresh, cold and pure from every pore. We had long before this got well into the snow-banks; frozen heaps surrounded us, in color often pinkish. The stream had dwindled much in breadth but its volume was unimpaired as its velocity had almost trebled. We could see clear up to what we took to be the head of the pass, cascade after cascade, separated from each other by not more than ten or twenty feet of horizontal distance; none of these water-falls was of great height but so choked up with large fragments of granite that the current lashed into fury, foamed like milk. The sun's rays were much obscured by the interlacing branches of the majestic spruce and fir trees, blocking our path and the rocky escarpments looming above the timber line. We could still see the little rivulets dancing along and hear it singing its song of the icy granite peaks, the frozen lakes and piney solitudes that watched its birth. The divide, we began to congratulate ourselves, could not be far off. Already the pine trees had begun to thin out and the straggling ones, still lining our trail, were dwarfed and stunted. Our pretty friend, the mountain brook, like a dying swan, charmed most in its last moments. We saw it issue from some icy spring in the vertical ledges above the timber line and bade it farewell to plunge and flounder through the deep snow drifts lining the crest. In this last effort, ourselves and animals were sorely tested. From the divide was seen a little lake not over 500 to 800 yards in diameter, with cakes and floes of ice resting upon its bosom. Many of these, nearest the shore, were more than a foot thick, black and solid looking, covered with a superficial crust of snow and regelated ice. This little volume of water, surrounded by bald hills, without a tree near it, seemed bleak enough. On one side, its waters escaped to the North to find their way into Shell Creek or some other affluent of the Big Horn. We had hoped to find a suitable camping place hereabouts. Granite and Granite alone could be seen:—in many crags, timberless and barren of any trace of vegetation, towering to the clouds; in bold-faced ledges, the home of the mountain sheep and in Cyclopean blocks, covering acres upon acres of surface. Maintaining our Westerly course, we pressed over another snow clad ridge, not much higher than the one we had been on, and from its apex saw distinctly the white ridges of the Wind River Range, 130 miles distant. Breaking through them was a dark line, I took to be the course of the Big Horn river.

With some difficulty a way was made for three miles down the asporous declivities of the cañons of No Wood creek, commencing exactly at our point of crossing the Range, and after being sated with the monotonous beauties of precipices, milky cascades, gloomy forests and glassy springs, the welcome command was given to make camp. The total number of miles to-day must have been fifteen; the extreme altitude reached over 12.000 feet, as we had been far above the timber line and in the region of perennial snows. Still at that elevation, a few pleasant-faced little blue and white flowers, principally forget-me-nots, kept us company to the very verge of the snow-beds. The snow-banks near camp were slowly melting away. At their edges, I plucked a nosegay of pretty blossoms and at same moment was graciously tormented by musquitoes and flies! This bivouac was very charmingly situated. The cañon had widened to a breadth of 600 yards, the crags forming its sides were liberally coated with spruce pine, (we had descended so rapidly that the timber belt once more was about us.), the grass was green, juicy and rich, and the water, excepting its coldness, most palatable. The Eastern horizon was shut in by the naked escarpments of the Big Horn Range; but for a Western outlook, the more gentle declination of our valley permitted a view several miles in extent of rounded knolls, black with spruce and fir forests, or green with newly springing grasses.

Our party had no implements for mining: not even a pick, pan and shovel; consequently, observations upon the metalliferous resources of this section of the Big Horn Range must be very scanty. No gold or silver indications were discernible on yesterday's line of march: to-day we saw (on Eastern slope principally,) quartz, vesiculas and vitreous, as float rock and running in ledges through the granite, and deep gravel beds and black sand near the streams;—these are all favorable indiciae of the existence of the precious metal.

Buffalo signs were found in plenty in this cañon and up on the summit of the barren divide, animated nature is not densely represented in these gloomy, impenetrable recesses. Besides the Buffalo, the only living creatures above the timber were mountain sheep, tit larks, butterflies and grasshoppers (rare.) flies, (scarce.) and musquitoes in swarms. The denudation of the higher protuberances has rendered vegetation there an impossibility; consequently, animal life is also curtailed. In the upper parts of the streams, at and near their point of issuance from the crests, trout and other fishes cannot be found; lower down in the forests, they are plentiful in all the pools. Undoubtedly the iciness of the water has something to do with their absence, but the first reason is the main one.

General Crook and Lieut. Schuyler, killed two of the Rocky Mountain sheep, indigenous to this region. These animals resemble a deer, sheep and mule. The head is that of a sheep surmounted by a ponderous pair of horns, convoluted. The Body in a slight degree resembles that of a mule, but is much more graceful, while the legs closely imitate a deer's limbs, but are more chunky. The tail is short, slender and furnished with a brush at the extremity. Hair is not long and is chocolate gray in color. The stories told by trappers, guides and hunters of the saltatory agility of these animals smack of the fabulous. Having heard them from Mexicans and Indian[s] in Arizona and from trustworthy guides in Wyoming, I must withhold a partial assent to their credibility. It is asserted that these strong and dexterous animals, living constantly among crags and rocky pinnacles, will, when pursued by hunters or frightened from any cause, make their escape by jumping down precipices of marvellous height, alighting on their horns, turning a somersault and regaining their feet. I have never seen them do this and only tell the story as I heard it, but it is in my belief, true to a certain extent. The horns are massive appendages, designed for strength. Those I have seen, have been battered against rocks or other hard substance. The sun by this time had gone down; our hunters had brought in their game.

Supper was eaten by fire-light. It was in truth an enjoyable meal, made as good as possible by contributing each one's stories to a common stock, we had tea, coffee, ham, bacon, mountain sheep, soft bread and hard-tack. To make this soft bread, a dough is first kneaded from flour, water and brown sugar. This turns sour and serves as a leaven for the mass of sweet dough, the loaves are to be made of. An oven is formed by placing one mess pan under another inverted; a trough is dug, filled with hot cinders, with which the bread-oven when placed in position is also covered, and a palatable, nourishing article of food is soon ready for the mess. The rim of the under pan should, if necessary, be cut down an inch. Sometimes, it is prudent to first heat the trench very thoroughly; then place therein the bake-pan, covered with earth to prevent steaming and upon this earth-covering to build a strong fire.

Mountain sheep mutton is very juicy and tender; the fat, especially of the bucks, is apt to have a "bucky" taste, unpleasant to new beginners. It makes a very toothsome dish, if fried before a fire, by being stuck on a twig with slices of bacon interlarded. Or it may be stewed in mess-pans or fried in the ordinary pan. When boiled it is also an agreeable article of food. Elk-heart boiled is a true bonne-bouche, sheep heart also.

For dessert, we had a can of preserved peaches, the juice put to one side to make a toddy which closed the evening's conversation. As we sat around the fire, talking and drinking, Mr. Wasson remarked that the gap through the mountains traversed by us to-day reminded him in all the details of its scenery of the Saint Gothard Pass in the Alps.

Couches of cedar boughs, covered with blankets and buffalo robes invited us to sleep and pleasant dreams. Our rest was not to be unbroken; in the middle of the night, a smart pattering of rain awakened us, interfering seriously with rest. The storm did not last long but dissipated very soon and gave way for a cold wind lasting until day-dawn.

July 3d Remained in camp during morning while a detachment went down stream to prospect for gold. One or two miles below here, commences a chain of beautiful lakes, embowered in spruce pine groves. The limpidness of their water and that of every spring and stream observed on this trip is something to wonder at. Holes five to ten feet deep have water so clear that every grain of sand at the bottom is as clear and distinct as if magnified. Many of these fine water sources burst out from the solid stone.

Gen'l. Crook, Lt. Schuyler, Maj. Burt, Lt. Carpenter, Mr. Strahorn and the writer remained in camp, busied in preparing the hides and heads of the Rocky Mt'n sheep killed yesterday, for transportation and preservation. The fat and flesh was removed thoroughly and a strong solution of common salt applied to the inside of the head which was then spread out in the shade to let it dry slowly.

At twelve, the packers returned. They had proceeded six or eight miles down stream, washed sand in frying pan and found "color". This fixes the existence of gold in this cañon; the great head and

volume of water and the timber and building stone so readily accessible will make the cost of collecting it very small. Colonel Mills and
Mr Finerty, who advanced down the valley to a point more than
half-way to the Big Horn river found the general topography of the
country a corroboration of the Army maps. They also confirmed
the first impression that last night's camp was on No Wood creek.
Mr Finerty killed his first buffalo and brought the tongue back on
his saddle.

We broke camp at mid-day, climbed the slippery granite sides of
the Ridge separating Shell and No Wood creeks, going nearly due
North. For the first time in my life, I followed water straight across
a mountain; the tributaries of Shell and No Wood creek are both fed
from the same snowbank; this we floundered across, seeing running water every step and then down a steep mountain grade to a
narrow valley whose surface was covered by a deep lake. A herd of
18 or 20 elk was grazing by the water side: we could not get near
enough to kill any. Ground hogs, (wood-chucks.) as large as a small
poodle dog and of a yellowish red color are plentiful on the flanks of
the mountain.

The clear sky and warm sun of to-day have been playing havoc with
the snow: I would conjecture that it all disappears by July 15th,
except on the topmost cliffs where it lodges the whole year round.
The ground became so miry we feared to go back to Tongue river on
our incoming line of march. General Crook accordingly struck out
on this new trail, leading over rough granite ledges to avoid the
interminable springs and rivulets this country is cut up with. A buffalo trail was found leading in the right direction: we kept upon this
for some time until he had gone about 5 or six miles from last camp
(no 2.)[.]

Here we bivouacked, the water in the creek being so cold that it
pained my hands and face when I made my ablutions. This night
was very cold.

July 4th On awakening, saw frost covering the ground and ice formed
upon the water. As we wanted to take our Centennial Fourth of July
dinner with our comrades in permanent camp, we determined to
start early and make camp Cloud Peak by sun-down if we could.
Gen'l. Crook, whose wonderful abilities as a woodman all conceded,
thought he could pilot us across country and save a great deal of bad
and unnecessary travelling. We had great confidence in our Com-

mander, but feared he over-rated his powers, as he had never been in the Big Horn range before. We climbed to top of a low sag, picking our steps among granite slabs and knobs. Upon the top there was nothing except the pretty forget-me-not. The Wind River Range was very distinctly traceable from this position. We also contemplated a wide expanse of territory to the North and East. No elevated points could be discerned above the general level; hence any hopes of taking good observations with the Prismatic Compass were not realized.

Descending this grade was the worst feature in the day's march and nearly as bad a piece of work as anything offered us on [the] second day's travel. The task was a vexatious and dangerous one. At last it was over and we stood in the valley where we had bivouacked the first night. To give our animals a little rest and pasturage we stayed at this place an hour. Twenty-six Montana miners, under Captain Graves, passed us going up the creek to examine the rock at its head. They reported everything quiet at Camp Cloud Peak. We had now a downgrade of twelve miles; the mules shared in our anxiety to end the day's march at an early hour in the afternoon and trotted along quite freely. On top of one of the peaks overlooking camp, a flock of Rocky Mountain sheep were quietly grazing: they looked at us with a wondering air. Two of them were killed by General Crook and others. At one o'clock, camp was reached. Here we found all well. The heat was the only thing unsatisfactory. It seemed intolerable, after the cold breezes of the mountain ranges. A courier had arrived in the morning from Fetterman bearing dispatches for General Crook from General Sheridan, in acknowledgment of his report of the Rosebud fight. Sheridan's instructions were to "hit them again and hit them hard". Colonel Merritt had assumed command of the 5th Cavalry, rendezvousing at the Black Hills crossing of the South Cheyenne [river].

One of Colonel Mills' company, a recruit, brought in some shot gold discovered in the little gulch fronting camp. The announcement created a stir and maybe the prelude to more important findings.

Major Burt secured two fine specimens of the tit-lark, a rare bird, living above timber line, and two of a small gray-bird, the size of a martin, with short black beak and bright yellow patches on throat, neck and shoulders.

Frank Gruard and Big Bat were in camp; they attempted to get through to the Crow Agency: they had got out to the Little Big Horn where suddenly a small band of Indians appeared. Our guides could not make out for certain who they were, but feared they were a war party of Sioux and galloped back in hot haste.

The Section of Big Horn Range on other page is not exact: it is estimated as carefully as means would permit. No aneroid barometer was on hand to give altitude. The snow line is placed somewhat higher than it was where we crossed. The deepest drift I saw must have been between 50 and 75 feet high. The heavy timber commences with formation No 4, the nucleary granite.

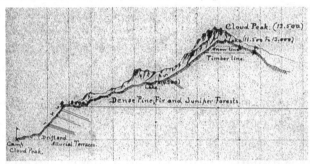

It is much to be regretted that a corps of scientists does not form part of the Expedition; there is such a vast area unexplored in the Big Horn Mountains, undoubtedly fruitful in interest and value: and at this time of uneasiness among frontiersmen, it would be well to determine exactly whether the mountains are rich in treasure of the precious metals, in timber, pasturage and pure water or not.

July 5th

Waiting for our returning supply train is a monotonous and tedious piece of business; we have such poor facilities for killing time. Books and newspapers are not to be had: hunting involves great labor and much time; yet we have many devotees of the chase. Trout fishing retains its place in the good opinions of the majority: our command boasts of very accomplished fishermen whose hauls are something unusual. Gen'l. Crook has caught seventy in one day and expresses his determination to make the number an even hundred. Lieut. Bubb brought in eighty on July 4th. The greater part however are content with taking just enough for one meal, say from twelve to twenty or thirty. Each bank of the stream has its enthusiastic amateurs, nestling in the shade of some overhanging tree, armed with a rod cut out from the limb of a willow sapling. For bait, grasshoppers and flies are esteemed most highly. The places most frequented by the game are the dark, cool pools under the shadow of a rock and in the swirl below a rapid. Those fishermen who are willing to be more venture-some and wade about in the thread of the current are rewarded by the most liberal returns. Nothing can be more palatable or more digestible than a nicely fried or broiled trout, served with Nature's sauce. Our enlisted men feast as much, if not more on this food than the officers. Sickness is almost unknown in the command, a condition resulting from the fine climate perhaps fully as much as from the good food. One of the first duties upon laying out our camps has been the constructions of sinks[17] for officers and men: these are placed as far away from running water as possible and in a ravine when one is conveniently near. Shades of willow or pine branches are provided and the deposits carefully covered with sand or earth morning and evening.

July 6th. Moved up valley one mile, going into camp in another beautiful situation bountifully replete with every desideratum of pioneer life. The movements are of use in many ways: they supply our animals with fresh pasturage, altho' that is scarcely needed be-cause the grass is so thick and rich in all these valleys it might be harvested with a mowing machine; and they break the troops in to all the details of quickly taking down and putting up tents, packing and unpacking wagons, saddling and unsaddling horses, laying out camps, building sinks, moving into column and other things that can only be learned by constant practice.

A little rain fell this morning—only a few drops.

Frank Gruard, Lieut. Sibley, Mr. Finerty and twenty men started at noon to reconnoiter toward the Little Big Horn river and ascertain, if they can, what the enemy are doing. The absence of hostile dem-onstrations since our fight of June 17th speaks very plainly of the severe handling the Sioux received that day. Were they victorious or had the day been even undecided, our camp would long since have been beleaguered by the sharpshooters.

17. Latrine pits.

Chapter 19

✦

✦

✦

✦

✦

The War Resumes

July 7th. Gen'l Crook, accompanied by Lieut. Schuyler, Maj. Burt. Col. Van Vliet, Major Wells and others started for the summit to hunt, expecting to be absent four days. Major Randall, Lieut. Bubb, Mr. Stevens and self arranged a fishing excursion. The site selected was not much over a mile from camp. There we found all that fishermen could desire: shady pools, cool water, little cascades and delightful country. I didn't catch any trout, being ignorant of the peculiarities of the bright little fish. Lieut. Bubb, who is an expert caught eight in a very few minutes and lost three, making eleven in all. Major Randall and Mr. Stevens had no luck. There was in [the] middle of the current a large, high, flat block of granite with the water rushing around it on both sides and a dark, glassy pool below. Upon this block, I took my station stripping off all clothing in order to reach it. The trout could be seen darting about by twos and threes, but so satiated with food or so scared by the throng of fishermen whipping the stream ever since we first camped on it three weeks ago that my baits did not excite them as much as I had hoped they would. A dark brown fly General Crook gave me wasn't noticed, but the grasshoppers placed on my second hook were freely bitten at. Two fine specimens adhered to my hooks, but both became detached before they could be landed. There were so many men, like myself ignorant of the proper methods to pursue but eager to win the prize of a fine mess of trout that I saw it was impossible to do much in that locality, altho' the trout were very plenty [sic]. My next effort shall be well up the stream at a good distance from camp. Major Dewees who had taken station three miles up the cañon made a bag of sixty-eight fine fish. Since we came on this branch, some three weeks since, not less than three thousand trout have been cooked and eaten in the commons: this is my own estimate, based on numbers obtained from officers of the expedition; but the general calculation is very much higher and placed the total catch at an average of 400 a day for twenty-one fishing days.

This afternoon the air became very sultry; gray-blue clouds gathered along the mountain ranges and lay in heavy strata low down the valley. Little puffs of wind blew from various quarters, those coming down the cañon from the West being most severe. We finished dinner about half past five and were gathered in a little group noting the gathering storm when a sudden rush of wind from behind tore down the dining tent and scattered camp-stools, bedding, books and papers like so many leaves. The heavy dining table, with its trestles was carried more than a hundred yards down hill. All hands turned out to save the tents from destruction; the great danger in such cases is from "ballooning", that is the wind get[s] inside the tent and lifts it clear from the ground or rips it into shreds. The remedy applied was to hold the tent down firmly by putting new and staunch pins into every loop, tying the door flaps tightly together and affixing guy ropes around the whole tent, at upper extremity of both uprights and just under the ridge-pole. The flies were also taken off as they are of no use in a storm, but very frequently a detriment. This night's experience settled into conviction a suspicion flitting through my mind for a long time—the inefficiency of our Q.M.D[1] and its disinclination to adopt new ideas or to modify old ones. The strings for tying up tentage should be replaced by straps and buckles, the tent pins should be of iron, the roofs strengthened by diagonal bands of canvass and the back with a horizontal one; at the corners should be sewed leather gussets. Around the sides of the tents, pockets of canvass or light cotton cloth should be affixed, giving great convenience as receptacles for combes,

1. Quarter Master Department

brushes, books, papers &c. A flooring of canvass is a preventive of disease by keeping out earth-dampness. During the movement of the past winter, many complaints were made of the pattern of pantaloons issued the soldiers; they should be made with a flap in front to exclude extreme cold.

The violent wind lasted until after ten o'clock at night: its subsidence was the signal for an hour's long fall of rain. Lower down the valley, the storm must have raged with still greater vehemence, if any opinion could be predicated upon the black clouds gathered there and emitting bright forked lightning. We were greatly worried at the commencement of the storm to hear that Major Noyes was missing: he had gone out early in the morning to fish in the cañon and it was feared some accident had befallen him. Lieut. Kingsbury, with a detachment of two men, provided with a hound, hunted him up after dark and found him after some little search. The Major had become exhausted with severe climbing over rocks and wading through deep water; he had given instructions before leaving camp for an orderly to be waiting with his horse at a certain place. The orderly could not find the Major and had come back. Noyes had fallen asleep on the ground when awakened by the detachment looking out for him.

July 8th Morning opened cool and a trifle damp: heavy belts of clouds in sky which remained throughout day. Two soldiers passed through HdQrs to-day, carrying, suspended from a pole, one hundred and twenty trout. Learned that Major Noyes, alone, yesterday, caught one hundred and ten.

July 9th. Lieut. Sibley returned early this morning. Reported that between twelve and one o'clock on the 7th, while going trough a ravine in the foot-hills he was attacked by a party he estimated at from 300 to 400 strong, altho' the calculation of Frank Gruard, the guide, was that the enemy was in as strong force as at the Rosebud fight. One hundred of the Indians fired a volley in front, giving a chance to those on the flank to charge in which the attention of Sibley's little command was thus diverted. The whole country was covered with them. None of our men were killed or wounded, but their horses and one mule were, the latter slightly. Sibley endeavored to maintain his position in the place of attack, or near it, but found this impossible. The enemy pressed him so strongly he was obliged to abandon his animals and rations. Our men retreated home through the mountains, followed by the enemy, all of the 7th and 8th. They say that a war party of Sioux was seen coming this way. When the party reached camp early this morning, they were all completely prostrated, having marched over mountains for two nights and one day, without food or sleep. That this little reconnaisance should have terminated so unfortunately is a matter of regret; but it had to take all the chances of the situation and it has been successful at least in demonstrating the enemy's presence and power. Within a week, we may expect to have an engagement in force.

Last night, a party supposed to be white men, were fired at by the pickets of Infantry camp and about same time a horse was stolen from the pack-train, supposed to be by same parties as the animals were picketed and hobbled within one hundred yards of Mr. Moore's tent. General Crook's hunting party has so far been quite success-ful. Word has come from them that they have killed fourteen elk. A courier was dispatched to the General, bearing advices of Lieut. Sibley's reconnaisance. . . .

July 10th. Louis Richaud and Ben Arnold came into our bivouac at daylight. They brought most important telegrams and correspon-dence from General Sheridan. The first envelop[e] opened was from Major Jordan, commanding at Camp Robinson, saying that Indians there reported the fight on Rosebud was hotly contested. They ad-mitted a loss of five killed and thirty wounded, which is far below the trust, as we obtained thirteen scalps. Further, the Indians at the Agency were very generally in mourning, a fact to be taken into consideration when the ridiculous statement of their own losses is regarded. They claim that though they withdrew it was with the intention of concentrating at their village to repel the attack threat-ened by Mills' column and with the hope of annihilating it. Red Cloud's son[2] and son in law were in the fight. The former had his horse shot under him and had his pistol and knife taken from him by a Crow Indian. Louis said all the young bucks had left the Red Cloud Agency, but not many had yet gone from Spotted Tail. Gen-eral Vandeveer, the lying emissary of the Indian Ring, was at Red Cloud with instructions from Washington to the Sioux that they must either make up their minds to fight or to peacefully go to such reservations on the Missouri or elsewhere as might be selected for

2. Jack Red Cloud

them. Two wagons loaded with ammunition, arms and delicacies from Cheyenne, were abandoned by Indians leaving Red Cloud Agency, pressed by the Fifth Cavalry. General Sheridan, while at the Agency, called upon Agent Hastings to make issues according to his books: it was found that not half the Indians represented were present. The damnable frauds perpetrated at that sink of iniquity daily call to Heaven for redress. To think that Government Agencies should harbor Indian cut throats and that Government Agents should screen their misdoings is something too dreadful for contemplation. Some changes must be brought about and without delay, or the Sioux will never be subjugated. General Sheridan sent General Crook, an outline of the press accounts of the terrible disaster lately befallen Custer's command. With the hope and prayer that official intelligence may abate the grief occasioned by this journalistic dispatch, I give its contents.[3]

On June 26th* morning, Terry and Gibbon with seven companies of Infantry, and four of cavalry, advanced up the Big Horn river, while Custer with his whole Regiment, the Seventh Cavalry swung around on the Left to scout the Little Big Horn. Early next morning, a village of two thousand lodges, three miles long was discovered. Custer taking five companies, made a charge at one end, while [Maj. Marcus A.] Reno, his second in command, was to do the same at the other. All that is known is the alleged result. Terry and Gibbon, pressing forward upon hearing the noise of battle, found Reno with his command entrenched on a hill near the village which was in flames. Swarms of Indians surrounded the devoted remainder of the Seventh, but were kept back until the arrival of our reinforcements, when they took to flight. Terry, moving forward, found the ground covered with dead ponies, saddles, burnt and burning lodges and charred corpses. He soon discovered the bodies of Custer and eleven of his officers and more than three hundred dead soldiers, but no wounded. In one pile, 271, two hundred and seventy one of our dead were found and buried in one grave. Terry, after burying dead and destroying the remains of the village, fell back to the mouth of the Big Horn to refit. A regiment of Cavalry and Infantry were to be sent to him. (Whether one of each or one only, not stated.)

* At the top of the page Bourke wrote, Should be 25th.

3. As Bourke notes, this account is very preliminary, as such, it contains extensive errors. Terry's official notification to Crook is found on pp. 365–8.

Sheridan's opinion was that the Sioux had suffered very heavily and are now much hampered with their wounded, who must be very numerous.[4] He urged upon Crook to hit them the hardest blow possible while they were in this state and promised all the aid he needed either in Cavalry or Infantry, saying he could have the Fifth [Cavalry] regiment if he wanted it. Such is the meagre outline of this terrible news brought us—news which made every lip quiver and every cheek blanch with terror and dismay. Grief—Revenge, Sorrow and Fear stalked among us. We are beginning to realize that our enemies have been fostered and pampered at a terrible outlay; our skeleton army meanwhile has been so depleted and fettered that a Regiment doesn't equal a Battalion, a company cannot muster more than a squad.[5] Our men are so occupied with the extraneous duties of building posts and cantonments, no time is left for learning military evolutions. They are all willing and brave enough, but are deficient in experience and military intelligence. Since our Rosebud fight, my opinion has changed to an advocacy of the Fabian policy. We must remain here now until winter, worrying the enemy as best we can. When frost comes, and not till then can we hope to strike a decisive blow.

To feebly offset the disastrous tidings of the morning, we learned our wagon train, with seven companies of Infantry as escort, was to be at the Clear Creek to-night and with us day after to-morrow. Also that one hundred and fifty Snakes might be expected on the 10th (to-day) and two hundred Utes within a week. Last night, an attack was made on our Infantry camp, two miles below here, but without effect. The Indians set fire to the grass in the lower valley,

4. Historian Richard G. Hardoff collected and tabulated both published and unpublished accounts from Indian informants. The majority of the informants estimated the Lakota and their allies lost between thirty and forty in the fight itself, and the number of wounded may have reached into the hundreds. These were substantial numbers for a nomadic, tribal people. See Hardoff, *Hokahey!*

5. In the years immediately prior to the Great Sioux War, congress reduced the strength of the army three times, in 1869, 1870, and 1874. The ceiling was set at 25,000 soldiers of which about three or four thousand were in non-combat positions (i.e., support services, West Point, Fort Leavenworth Prison guard, and recruiting details). That, together with the fact that replacements did not keep pace with losses through attrition meant that the number of soldiers available for combat was appallingly low. In view of these circumstances, the number of privates in a company rarely reached fifty, and often was much lower. The old citizen-militia tradition was strong, because volunteer units had made up the bulk of the victorious Union Army, and the professional soldier suffered accordingly. (It should be noted that the Indian-fighting soldier was not the only one to feel the shortage. A study of the histories of the forts defending Eastern ports during this period shows that many had reduced garrisons or were occupied only by a caretaker sergeant.) Utley, *Frontier Regulars*, 15-18, 60-61.

hoping to annoy us and to diminish our pasturage. The smoke towers high in the sky, but endangers nothing except perhaps the Infantry camp. Colonel Royall has ordered the camp to concentrate, bringing the Infantry up close to his own detachments, and sending down all the pack-mules to carry away the subsistence stores yet piled there. General Crook's non-arrival this morning is the source of undisguised alarm. We all apprehend danger to himself and his party, yet no one can say definitely in what way. The General has set an example of recklessness that cannot too strongly be condemned: this rashness must be foregone in the future. Else some day his mutilated corpse will be found and this whole scheme of Sioux pacification fall to the ground.

Sky became hazy and filled with clouds, as the day advanced. In the course of the afternoon, a mounted party was discovered coming down the cañon; hope prevailed that it might by our Commanding Officer returning. It turned out to be the pack-train sent yesterday afternoon to take in the game slaughtered by his party: this game was found at the point specified by the General, but no trace of him or his companions could be detected. The packers reported that there were no Indian signs at all and that they thought Col. Mills' battalion would find the General before sun-down. This proved to be a correct surmise. At 5 O'clock, the General, with his whole party, came in safe and sound; to the exceeding relief of the many anxious hearts that welcomed them.

After night, rain, continuous and effective, fell upon the dry grass, rendering abortive the efforts of the Indians to destroy any more pasturage. My supposition is that the savages have been heavy losers in their engagements with the troops this summer and are endeavoring to put a zone of desolation between us and themselves, at least until they can repair damages. Meantime, their young warriors, in parties of fifty and sixty, can annoy our camp from time to time, run off an occasional head of stock or do a little harm of that kind. Our wagons ought to be here to-morrow: we can then sally out and pursue the policy of worrying the savages to destruction.

July 11th. After last night's rain, we find the air delightfully cool and fresh. Many clouds remain in the sky, presaging another storm. Captain Wells, with his company of the 2d Cavalry, was dispatched to meet the wagon-train and escort, and show a good road across country from old Fort Kearney. Two hundred and thirteen Snake

Indians joined us in the afternoon; with them came their old chieftain Wash-a-kie, and others of prominence. Mr. Thomas Cosgrove
said they had returned to the Agency in five days, most of the journey being made at a run. Dancing and pow-wowing consumed many
precious hours, much to the uneasiness of Cosgrove who was well
aware of Genl. Crook's impatience to have the assistance of a band
of such effective allies. Wash-a-kie's principal objection—that he
had no good horse—was overcome by an assurance that Gen'l. Crook
would make his want good; he then wanted to defer starting until
joined by the Bannocks and Shoshones from the Fort Hall (Snake
River.) Reservation [Idaho], for whom Cosgrove had telegraphed.
He was induced not to delay for them and at last determined to
start. Getting the head-chief was getting the best of the band.
Cosgrove had only hoped to get a hundred: double that number
followed him, ten of them squaws, wives of the wounded men in our
camp and of Wash-a-kie and other chiefs. Two of the party are
Bannocks, living 300 miles West of this, but familiar with the Sioux
country from having raided into it after stock. Once, these two men
entered a Sioux village, hoping to drive off a few ponies. They were
discovered. A great hubbub was raised and they in danger of capture. Passing quickly among the excited Sioux, they took refuge in
a lodge, wrapping themselves up in furs. When quiet had been restored and the Sioux were again asleep, our imitators of Dick Turpin[6]
crept out, stole two horses apiece and made their escape in the
darkness. It looks as if the flame of war were about to break out
among all the savage tribes, contiguous to the Sioux and combine
them in unity of action to harass and humble their blood-thirsty
enemy. The Snakes say the Bannocks and Utes will soon commence
a campaign, which will make our task easier.

If we can carry on warfare throughout this summer, gaining a little
prestige from our occupancy of the country and killing some of the
enemy or running away herds of stock, the hostile Sioux will lose
influence with those at the Agencies, who now supply them with
war material. When winter returns, they will be out of ammunition,
unsupplied with food, losers in horse-flesh and, if good luck attend
our exertions, in mourning for burned villages and slaughtered relatives. Before Spring, we should have killed, captured or dispersed
their last war-party.

6. A famous highwayman in eighteenth century England.

The shields of the Sioux, I was informed to-day by Frank Gruard, are made of the skin of the buffalo bull's neck, which is an inch in thickness; the squaws place a layer of earth upon this and kindle a fire above. The skin is greatly hardened but not burnt. These shields turn a lance point and repel arrows.

July 12th We had no momentous occurrences to disturb us last night. From sun-down until mid-night, the Snakes indulged in a war song. The camp after that sank to rest until the rising of the moon when the bang, banging of the rifles in the hands of our pickets alarmed us for a brief space.

This morning it was reported that one of our pickets discovered a Sioux Indian crawling down the hill-side into camp. Our picket fired. Simultaneously, the other pickets at the Left end of line opened on a small gang of eight working along that side. The Sioux exchanged a few shots and then desisted from [the] attempt to steal any of our horses. When daylight returned, Lieutenant Kingsbury, in charge of picket, found a couple of Sioux knives, dropped by our assailants. Our pickets on the night of the 10th, killed the horse of a Sioux, attempting to approach mounted. The dead animal was found three or four hundred yards outside our lines. Wash-a-kie, the Sho-sho-nee chief, explained to General Crook this morning his ideas of the position and strength of the Sioux; while he was doing this, three men dressed in army blue, faded and travel worn, trotted up to General Crook and announced themselves as bearers of advices from General Terry! We looked at the three modest heroes with a mixture of pleasure at hearing from the distinguished General and admiration for the nerve and courage sustaining them throughout their perilous trip. Each had a letter from Gen'l. Terry, written in triplicate, to lessen chances of loss. Below is the letter itself:

HdQrs. Dep't. of Dakota, In the field
Camp on North side of the Yellowstone River,
near mouth of Big Horn, July 9th, 1876

Gen'l. George Crook,
    Comdg. Department of the Platte, (In the field.)
General.

On the 25th ult. General Custer, crossing over from the valley of the Rosebud to the Little Big Horn found on the last named stream an enormous Indian village. He had with him his whole Regiment and a strong detachment of scouts. At the time of the discovery of the Indians he had but eight companies close at hand but with these he attacked in two detachments, one, under himself, of five companies; the other under Major Reno, of three companies.[7] The attacks of these two detachments were made at points nearly, if not quite, three miles apart. I greatly regret to say that Custer, and every officer and man under his immediate command, were killed. Reno was driven back to the bluffs where he was joined by the remainder of the Regiment. He was surrounded by the enemy and was obliged to entrench himself, but succeeded in maintaining himself in this position with heavy loss until the appearance of General Gibbon's column induced the Indians, on the evening of the 26th, to withdraw. Two hundred and sixty-eight officers, men and civilians were killed and there were fifty-two wounded.[8] This affair occurred about twenty miles above the junction of the Little Big Horn and the Big Horn.

While Custer's column was in motion, Gibbon[']s column of about one hundred and fifty cavalry, one hundred and sixty Infantry and three Gatling guns, was advancing to join Custer and co-operate with him in the attack upon the Indians. It was ferried across the Yellowstone at a point just below the mouth of the Big Horn, on the 24th ultimo. On the 25th, it advanced through country of extreme difficulty. The Infantry twenty two, the cavalry thirty six miles. Custer had been informed that Gibbon's column would reach the mouth of the Little Big Horn, on the evening of 26th, ultimo. Its advance was within four miles of that place at midnight of the 25th ult. Reno's position was reached by Gibbon on the morning of the 27th ult. It is estimated that not less than twenty five hundred warriors were in the fight. Besides the lodges in the village, a vast number of temporary shelters were found, showing that many Indians were present there, besides those who properly belonged to the village. A reconnaisance southward was made on the 28th ultimo and a very large train was found leading down the stream, a distinct trail from the one (a heavy one,) which Custer had followed from the Rosebud.

7. Custer had sent the remaining companies, under Capt. Frederick Benteen, up the valley to locate any other Indians who might be in the vicinity, and also to head off any who might try to escape to the south.

8. The civilians were Custer's younger brother, Boston, his nephew, Armstrong (Autie) Reed, newspaper correspondent Mark Kellogg, Scouts Charles Reynolds and Isaac Dorman, and Drs. James DeWolf and George Edwin Lord, contract surgeons. Also were killed was Bloody Knife, head of the Ree Indian scouts.

Captain [Edward] Ball, of the 2nd Cavalry, who made this reconnaisance, was of the opinion that after leaving the valley the Indians divided into two bands, one making towards the mountains and the other towards the South and East. It was a difficult task to get our wounded away, as the character of the country had not permitted ambulances to accompany the troops and mule litters had to be made. They have now been sent by boat to Fort A. Lincoln.

In view of the shattered condition of the 7th Cavalry and the damage done to our small pack-train, I have thought it best to bring the troops down to this depot to refit. I have sent for horses and mules for the dismounted men of the 7th Cavalry and for two more companies of Infantry. I have twice tried to communicate with you but my scout each time has been driven back by Indians, or rather reports that he was driven back. This morning, I received from General Sheridan a copy of your dispatch to him, giving an account of your fight of the 17th ultimo, and as it gives me information of your position at that time, I hope that the bearers of this may be able to find your train and reach you.

The great and, to me, wholly unexpected strength which the Indians have developed seems to me to make it important and indeed necessary that we should unite or at least act in close cooperation. In my ignorance of your present position and of the position of the Indians, I am unable to propose a plan for this, but if you will devise one and communicate it to me, I will follow it. The boat which took down our wounded, will, I hope, return with a supply of horses and mules with material for the repair of my saddles, &c., and with some reinforcements.

I expect her back about the 18th inst. and soon after that I hope to be able to move.

I hope that it is unnecessary for me to say that should our forces unite, even in my own Department, I shall assume nothing by reason of my seniority, but shall be prepared to co-operate with you in the most cordial and hearty manner, leaving you entirely free to pursue your own course. I am most anxious to assist you in any way that promises to bring the campaign to a favorable and speedy conclusion.

As my base of supplies is movable, (being a steamboat.) I can start out from any point on the Yellowstone, which may afford the readiest means of joining you and I think I shall be able to take with me from

15 to 20 days' rations on pack-saddles, though no forage. If, however, I should move up the Rosebud, I could take a wagon train with me. The following officers were killed on the 25th ultimo General Custer, Colonel Custer,[9] Captain [Myles] Keogh, Captain [George W.] Yates, Lieutenants [Benjamin H.] Hodgson, [Donald] McIntosh, Cook (Adjutant.);[10] A.E. Smith, Calhoun,[11] [James Ezekiel] Porter, Sturgis[12] and Riley.[13]

Lieutenant [John Jordan] Crittenden, 20th Infantry, (attached to 7th Cavalry.) Assistant Surgeon Lord, A.A. Surgeon De Wolf.

Lieutenant Harrington, missing.[14]

Also Mr. Boston Custer and Mr. [Armstrong] Reed, brother and nephew respectively of the General.

I am General,

Very truly Yours,

(signed) Alfred H. Terry,

Brigadier General.

The story was now assured; Custer had with imprudent rashness pushed ahead into the thickest of the enemy, seeking for a glory not to be eclipsed or even shared by his superiors and comrades. His fate was most horrible, above all when we regard the involution of others' lives in the same deadly conflict. The brave couriers, Evans, Stewart and Ball, all members of Captain Clifford's company of the 7th Infantry, had not much to add to the official narrative. Custer, moving up the Rosebud, had struck the same village fought by us on the 17th ult., then transferred to the Little Big Horn. To avoid any imputation of making up this record from sensational rumors or carelessly collected reports, I will refrain from writing all that was told by the couriers. They were positive in asserting that among the Sioux were many whites, (squaw men.)[15] and half-breeds from the American agencies and the Red river country[16] in British America. Two kegs of whiskey were found in the Indian camp and

9. Captain (bvt. Colonel) Thomas W. Custer, another brother.

10. William W. Cooke.

11. James Calhoun, Custer's brother-in-law.

12. Lieutenant James G. (Jack) Sturgis was the son of Col. Samuel Sturgis, the Seventh Cavalry's nominal commander. Colonel Sturgis was on more or less continual detached duty so Custer held actual field command.

13. Second Lieutenant William Van W. Reily.

14. Second Lieutenant Henry Moore Harrington later was determined to have been killed. Heitman, *Historical Register*, 1:502.

15. As seen here, the allegation of whites among the hostile Indians has been part of the Little Bighorn mythology almost from the beginning, and they may or may not have been present. White renegades often are credited with the accurate sniping at Reno Hill. Some

everything in the way of mess-equipage needed or possessed by the majority of civilized people. The loss of the savages was believed to be very severe. The trails of the litters on which their wounded were dragged away could be seen in great numbers.

General Crook sent to General Sheridan the following:

> My last information from Red Cloud Agency was that the Cheyennes had left there to re-inforce the enemy in my front. As this takes away all the disturbing element from that section, I have availed myself of the Lieutenant General's permission and ordered the eight companies of the 5th Cavalry to join me at this point.
>
> The best information I can get from my front is that the Sioux have three fighting men to my one. Altho' I have no doubt of my ability to whip them with my present force, the victory would likely be one barren of results and so have thought better to defer the attack until I can get the 5th here and then end the campaign with one crushing blow.
>
> The hostile Indians are, according to my advices, encamped on the Little Big Horn, near base of the mountains and will probably remain there until my re-inforcements come up. Received dispatch from General Terry this morning asking me to co-operate. I will do so to the best of my ability.
>
> (Signed.) George Crook.
> Brigadier General.

Instructions were by same courier transmitted to General Merritt to push forward with his command to effect a junction with General Crook's forces: further, should his line of march be through Laramie and Fetterman, he will bring at least two hundred and fifty rounds of ammunition to the men and all the spare horses, saddles and bridles to be found at those posts.

---

accounts call them squaw men, and others say they were former Confederates who hated all U.S. soldiers because of some wartime atrocity. See Hunt, *I Fought With Custer*, 104.

16. Bourke means the Red River of the North. The Canadian mixed-bloods from that region were known as Métis.

17. Camp Brown was established in 1871 on the Wind River in west central Wyoming, to protect the Shoshones. In 1878, it was renamed Fort Washakie, in honor of the paramount Shoshone chief. It was permanently abandoned in 1909, and turned over to the Interior Department to use as headquarters for the Shoshone Agency. Frazer, *Forts of the West*, 186-87.

Word was sent to the Commanding Officer of Fort Fetterman to telegraph to the Commanding Officer, Camp Brown[17] for information regarding the movements of our allies expected from among the Utes and Bannocks.

To-day was the date fixed by general consent for the wagon train's return; it did not appear, but the dust made by it and the marching escort could be traced over a long low spur shooting out into the Goose creek, three or four miles below. Flies in great numbers swarmed into camp this afternoon: "fly-blow", in great patches, was deposited on all articles of wool or fur. General Crook and Major Randall's overcoats and blankets had this "fly-blow" heaped up upon them, in clumps, quarter of an inch high, by six inches in diameter. July 13th. Contrary to general expectation, our pickets were not molested last night. While we were at breakfast, the head of the wagon train was descried making its advance up the valley. A party of officers, mounted, left camp to meet and exchange salutations with friends in the column. Among these were Lieut. Hayden Delaney, 9th Infantry, who has given up a six months' leave to share the perils and glories of the campaign. Delaney's reputation is already firmly established in the Army as a gallant young soldier: I am greatly in error if this record does not contain further allusion to him before the end of our work in the field. Lieut. Calhoun, brother of Calhoun of the 7th Cavalry and Lieut. Crittenden,[18] cousin of the lieutenant of the same name—(both of whom were massacred and horribly mutilated in the late terrible disaster under Custer;)—are with the Infantry companies brought back by Col. Chambers. A heavy mail—of letters and newspapers—was distributed to-day. Extracts from the latter as far at least as they concern our Expedition and the one under General Terry and the condition of affairs in the Black Hills, will be posted with great liberality. The letters received by General Crook, comprehended, in two cases, anxious inquiries as to the fate of certain enlisted men, reported killed or wounded in our Rosebud fight. Nickerson communicated with both General and myself, stating he had secured some fifty Ute Indians to serve as scouts and would send them up as soon as could be with the new recruits now coming out to join 3d Cavalry.

My commission as 1st Lieutenant, 3rd Cavalry came from the Department of War and same afternoon, Lieut. Schuyler, A.D.C.,

18. Second Lieutenant Frederic Sanscay Calhoun, 14th Infantry. The Crittenden cousins had the same given name, John Jordan. The Crittenden mentioned was a second lieutenant of the 22nd Infantry. Heitman, *Historical Register*, 1:338.

administered the oath of office prescribed by law.

A high wind visited the valley not long after meridian, followed by brisk thunderstorm of short duration. Snake Indians devote every evening an hour or two of their time to running their horses through the evolutions, incident to active skirmishing. They deck themselves out in feather war-hats and all the paraphernalia of war, the general effect being very impressive and exciting. To see these wild Indians rush in mad career to the shock of battle, makes a soldier think how irresistible we should be in war, were we provided with a contingent of ten thousand such cavalry. The Snakes ride bare-back during a contest; Caucasians might not be able to do the same, but there could be improvised a light riding gear of saddle-blanket, surcingle and stir-rups to cover the animal and a heavy bridle of hard rope knotted about the lower jaw. Cavalry as constituted at the present day is a mere freight train, every horse loaded down like a baggage wagon with the necessaries or supposed necessaries of the soldier. All that a soldier absolutely requires, and I am speaking of civilized warfare in one's own country, is arms, ammunition and an overcoat. This latter should be of extra heavy material, well lined, long and terminating in a hood or other head covering. A fatal mistake permeating the minds of Cavalry officers, even the most distinguished, is that mounted troops must move habitually at a walk: nothing could be farther removed from the truth. The lope is the gait conducing most to the service's best interests, to the soldier's comfort and the animal's pleasure. We have much to learn from the savage in the matter of Cavalry training; the trouble is our prejudices of education are so deeply rooted, com-mon sense and observation have no permission to assert themselves.

July 14th. Sky filled with heavy dark rain-clouds. Morning extremely damp and rather disagreeable. There was no picket-firing last night of any consequence.

In the afternoon, the Sho-sho-nees, mounted on their ponies, and in all the glory of war bonnets, scarlet cloth, bright blankets and gleaming weapons, made the circuit of camp, the cynosure of all eyes. The parade was intended partly to familiarize our newly ar-rived soldiers with the looks of our Indian allies and vice versa. To prevent any confusion in time of battle, from not being distinguished, small rectangular flags of cotton cloth are worn in the heads of the Sho-sho-nees and make a very conspicuous mark. These Indians are among the finest light cavalry in the world. My ride with them yesterday was a novel experience. I could not refrain from admiring the ease with which they rode their ponies or the admirable discipline maintained among them. We moved out in column of twos, at a fast walk, almost a trot. The young warriors sat their horses like so many statues—horses and riders moving as one. No conversation could be heard, until the voices of the leaders broke out in their war song to which the whole column at once lent the potent aid of nearly two hundred pairs of sturdy lungs. The head dresses of the more prominent warriors were gorgeous combinations. The most generally affected type was a crown of eagle tail feathers, mounted on scarlet or other cloth, as a band to encircle forehead. These were very dashing in style and gave their wearers a warlike look. In one or two, buffalo and antelope horns were fastened to the sides.

Another style had a stream of feathers and beads hanging down the horse's flanks; nearly identical with the Sioux' mode. Each feather is tipped at the extremity with a small tassel of horse-hair, stained yellow. One chief wore as an insignia a broad scarlet sash profusely ornamented with white stars. The osiflamme[19] of the tribe, the medicine pole, was borne along in the procession: the staff is about 12 feet long and decorated elaborately with feathers of the eagle.

The sultriness of the day, attending with high winds, was broken near sunset by a severe fall of rain, accompanied by thunder and lightning. The sky partially cleared for a brief spell, after rain had fallen for an hour or more, but by midnight the darkness of Erebus hung over us and the storm recommenced, lasting spasmodically until day-break. We had no trouble on the picket line this night.

19. I.e., totem.

Chapter 2 0

✦
✦
✦
✦
✦

A Case of Nerves

Much of this chapter contains copies of dispatches between Crook and other officers, and copied by Bourke into the diary. These dispatches, the originals of which can be found in the Special File, Military Division of the Missouri, Sioux War, in the National Archives, show a different Crook from the man commonly perceived as stoic in the face of adversity. Deep down, he must have known that his so-called "victory" at the Rosebud was a farce, and the Custer disaster may have unnerved him. The Indian campaign of harassment—sniping along the picket lines, and efforts to steal horses and fire grass around the camp—was beginning to tell, and Bourke's own narrative begins to show a nervous edge. In order to show the mood of the expedition and its command structure, I have included the correspondence as Bourke copied it in the manuscript.

July 15th. Sky overcast, air, moist and unpleasant. Camps presented an idea of business-like activity around the Commissary, Quartermaster and Ordnance supply trains where officers and men assembled to secure their apportioned allowances of ammunition, subsistence and clothing.

July 16th A faint sprinkling of rain last night relieved, very gratefully the oppressive sultriness of the day. This morning, laggard banks of clouds hung above us threatening another storm. Paymaster [William] Arthur began the work of paying off the troops. Camp moved from site occupied so long to a new position on a branch of same stream, three miles to the West. General Crook sent dispatches to General Sheridan, together with duplicates of three forwarded by last messenger. He also sent word to General Terry, confiding the message to a Black Hills miner named Kelly—a half-witted sort of fellow, possessed of an assorted[?] stratum of cunning and common sense his more talented fellow citizens might envy.

He took for his supplies a small bundle of matches, a meagre allowance of sugar and coffee and a sack full of hard bread. His rifle and eighty rounds of copper cartridges finished his list of supplies. No overcoat, no blanket—nothing else. His dispatches to General Terry were wrapped up with great care in a linen envelope, sealed and addressed. The General and a small circle of officers bade him good bye and God speed. The brave fellow went outside our line of tents, twenty or thirty yards. General Crook went up to him and asked what he needed. He answered that he wished a little tobacco, but would not turn back for it as he made it a point never to turn back after he had once started. He was at once handed what he needed and was in a moment more lost to sight over the hill. This man started out from Fort Fetterman to carry dispatches to the Expedition. When on the South Cheyenne his horse was shot accidentally, but he resolutely trooped along on foot, carrying the mail on his back, a distance of more than one hundred and thirty miles! General Crook's dispatches read as follows:

HdQrs. B.H. and Y.E.

Camp on Goose Ck. Wy. July 16th-76

General Sheridan,
    Chicago.

I forgot to say when I dispatched my last courier that I had sent out Lt. Sibley, on the 6th, with a small detachment of the 2d Cavalry, to escort my guide, Frank Gruard, in making a reconnaisance. When the party came, on the 7th, to a point near where the Little Big Horn debouches from the mountains they encountered the Sioux in very strong force and saw enough to convince them the main village of the hostiles is not far from that point. They succeeded in making their escape only after abandoning their animals and marching across the rugged foot-hills of the Big Horn mountains. The men were nearly exhausted when they reached camp. Lieut Sibley and Frank Gruard, the guide, are entitled to great credit for the manner in which they carried out my instructions and the coolness and judgment displayed in saving the detachment when surrounded by [a] largely superior force of enemy. Mr Finerty (John F.) Mr. Pourier and Jim Traynor (i.e. John Bechtel) accompanied Lt. Sibley, as observers and behaved well.

(signed.) George Crook,
Brigadier General.

2d Dispatch to General Sheridan, same date.

I send in courier to-day to carry in duplicates of my dispatches to General Merritt for fear the originals may not have reached their destination. I send a courier to-night to General Terry to inform him that I will co-operate with him and where to find me. Also giving what information I have in regard to the Indians. My intention is to move out after the hostiles as soon as Merritt gets here with the 5th and I shall not probably send in any other courier unless something special should occur requiring me to do so. I am getting anxious about Merritt's ability to reach me soon as the grass is getting very dry and the Indians are liable to burn it any day.

(signed.) George Crook,
Brigadier General.

3d. (Same date.)

Brig. General A.H. Terry,
Comdg. Dept. Of Dakota.
In the field.

I have the honor to acknowledge receipt of your letter of July 6th, brought into this camp on the 13th instant by Corporal Stewart and party of the 7th Inf. As the corporal told me you were about to send a duplicate of the same dispatch by the hands of some of the Crow Indians with your command, I deferred an answer until the present thinking they would certainly arrive shortly after your first party.

I have decided to wait no longer but to entrust this to a courier who will try to reach you. I had determined to attack the Indians immediately after the arrival of my supply-train, but about that time I learned that the hostiles had received reinforcements and I also learned at the same time that I could get the eight companies of the 5th Cavalry, so I concluded to defer the movement until the arrival of those companies which have now been ordered here. I expect to be joined by them about the last of the present month. On the 5th inst. I sent out a party of mounted troops under Lt. Sibley, 2d Cavalry, to escort one of my guides who was to reconnoitre the country in our front. When they reached a point near where the Little big Horn debouches from the mountains, they came upon a large party of Indians and were convinced that the village of the main body of hostiles is in that vicinity. Since then I have had nothing definite—more than seeing large smokes down Powder and Tongue rivers, but am of the opinion they are still in the locality before indicated by the reconnaisance. I am rationed up to the end of September and will share with you and your command everything I have as long as it lasts. Should the two commands come together, whether the Indians shall be found in this or your Department, if you think the interests of the service will be advanced by the combination I will most cheerfully serve under you. When the 5th arrives, I expect to have about sixteen hundred fighting men, besides some friendly Indians and it is my intention to move without any further delay.

It is also my intention to leave my wagon train on the Tongue river near where it comes out from the Big Horn Range, so should you not meet any large trail of Indians going down the River, or not receive any further information from me, it would probably be best for you to move to my supply camp. We broke camp on the South Goose this morning and are grazing gradually along the foot-hills towards the Tongue and anticipate getting as far as the North fork of the Goose about same time my reinforcements come up.

I am, General,
Very Sincerely and Truly Yours,
(signed.) George Crook.
Brigadier General

Our men were detailed in small squads this evening to burn the grass around camp; this to make abortive any attempts of the enemy to annoy or harm the camp by their infernal tricks of that kind, very frequently practised during the dry season, or rather the season when the grass has cured into hay. Kelley, the courier returned as we were almost asleep; the night was so dark he could not see before him and had severely wounded his foot by treading on cactus. (N.B. He finally started July 17th, A.M.)

July 17th Kept very busy copying dispatches and other matter into record book. Cavalry and Infantry Battalions drilling in school of the skirmisher and school of the company and exercising their horses, morning and afternoon. Shoshonee scouts prospected the country for three or four miles to our front and right. Saw no fresh Indian signs. It is reported by one of these Shoshonees that our pickets the other night killed a Sioux Indian, whose body lies outside our last camp and that the fire made in the grass burned all the hair off the Sioux' head, so the Shoshonees could not get his scalp. The story is discredited by General Crook. Wash-a-kie, the Shoshonee chief ascends the hills around camp, every morning at sun-rise and every evening before the pickets are withdrawn to the valleys, and gazes with searching glance through his field glasses over the land in all directions. He then reports to General Crook the result of his observations.

Weather for the last day or two has been extremely sultry.

July 18th. Another courier was dispatched to Fort Fetterman after dark last night. He was employed by the officers of the 14th Infantry to carry private mail and was not entrusted with official dispatches from these HdQrs. Weather continues sultry. High wind from N.W. after sun-down.

July 19th Weather much cooler this morning, as a consequence of the continuous blow of the night, which has not yet altogether abated. Orders given to move camp to-day to a little tributary a short distance across the low ridge to North West of camp where our pickets are now posted. Wind veered around to South, carrying myriads of grass-hoppers which covered the sky like a dense snow storm; our tents were hit by them like fastly dropping pellets of rain. To the undisguised satisfaction of everybody, the same wind that brought them also wafted them away. These insects are grateful diet to the trout that are now fattening upon them. The quantity of fish in these streams in something startling. A man this morning caught more than one-hundred in a very brief space of time. (Trout.) Our march to-day was very short; a difficult passage of a stream was encountered successfully by tearing away the beaver dam blocking the current. Kelly came back to-day saying he had gone as far as Rosebud without seeing Indians, but near that point had seen & been seen by the Sioux' pickets. At sun-set a courier party of four Crow Indians came in from Terry's command with duplicates of dispatches carried by Corporal Stewart *. They also had a letter transmitted from General Gibbon, dated July 16th. Two mountain sheep and a deer, killed along camp lines this evening.

July 20th Our letter-bearers, rested by the repose of the night previous were conducted to the front of General Crook's tent, where a conference was held with them through the medium of the sign language. They stated they had been in the fight with Sitting Bull:[1] none of their tribe who were with Custer had been killed but one had been wounded in the thigh, bone not broken. During the fight, the Crows had run off forty head of ponies belonging to the Sioux. The whole valley of the Little Big Horn was covered with dead and dying Sioux ponies. They [sic] Sioux got but few horses alive from Custer's men. They did get much ammunition. There were many Crow Indians with Terry under their chief Iron Bull. The Sioux had recently sent a war party to the Crow village and killed two of their young men: one of them a brother of our informant. Coming up, they had noticed two Sioux trails: one going up the Little Big Horn, the other down the Tongue. Believe the camp of the Sioux' wounded to be near the cañon of Tongue river, or else they were going in to the Agencies. Thought the main body of the hostiles would remain close to the mountains. Had seen two steamboats come up Yellowstone, just before they left, with many mules and horses and some soldiers. Had heard more soldiers were coming. Had also heard that a very large band of miners, 1000 strong, was on the way down from Montana and should now be near the Big Horn River.

To learn all this news without the exchange of a word and through an interpreter not familiar with half a dozen words of the language of

* Evans *[Bourke's marginal note, identifying one of the couriers who, together with Stewart and Ball, brought copies of the dispatches. He does not state why he mentioned Evans— ed.]*

1. Bourke errs in identifying the battle of the Little Bighorn with Sitting Bull. As usual with Indian fights, no single chief was in charge, and at the Little Bighorn, the Indians were on the defensive, each individual taking advantage of whatever opportunity to gain the upper hand over the soldiers.

the people he was talking with may well be noticed as an event of great interest. How this language could have spread, as it has spread, from tribe to tribe, differing in language and sentiments, frequently antagonistic and commonly diverse in interests, is a mystery beyond my power to solve; this wide dissemination sustains the suspicion that this channel of commercial intercourse is not of very recent growth. The Arapahoes are credited by some people with being the inventors; this tribe is the Jewish trading element of the aborigines of the plains. Having no well defined territory of their own, they are always to be found in association with other bands, and perhaps from this cause are more constantly obliged to use this language and by continual practice have become most expert in its use. The Crows are likewise quite dexterous in communicating their ideas in this way. Kelley, the courier, made his third start this morning, much encouraged by the information the Crows gave that no Indians were to be found near Terry's camp or on the trail thither. He intends getting to Tongue river to-night, thence pushing across the divide to Ash Creek which he will follow down to its junction with the Little Big Horn. There he expects to be able to make a raft of broken willow branches and cottonwood timber, down this to float rapidly to the Yellowstone, if the current be deep enough: if not, he will have to push down to the Big Horn itself which carries a volume of water all the year round great enough to float a large sized steamboat.

From the direction of Powder River, a heavy cloud of smoke has been rising since noon: a deer ran through camp this afternoon and several large bunches of heavy, good sized trout were carried to the cook fires. Weather oppressively warm all day. Temperature must have been at least 110°.

July 21st. The fervid rays of the sun to-day have made the temperature more intolerable than yesterday. Complaints are made very generally of lassitude and indisposition. A few cases of diarrhea and mild forms of calenture prevail, due as much to want of something to do as to any predisposing cause. Drilling is maintained and the cavalry horses are exercised as usual. They are now in fine condition, fat and spirited, from the rich grasses spread before them during the past month. Unheard of quantities of trout have been taken from this stream, North Goose creek, to which we moved to-day, 3 miles from yesterday's camp. The Shoshonees catch these fish with hook and line and also by driving their ponies into the current and marching them up stream. The frightened fish are thus easily driven to some riffle or shallow pool where they are caught by hand.

Many buckets have been brought to camp in this way while the quantities taken by the packers and teamsters are something wonderful. Our mess has feasted upon them for the last four or five meals, reserving our stock of bacon for the hard work of active campaigning, soon to commence. Harwood, a courier, brought us mail and dispatches from Fetterman to-day: the dispatches referred generally to the Custer massacre and to the reinforcements, if any, we might need. General Sheridan said he had ordered the remaining four companies of the 5th Cavalry from the Dep't of the Missouri to Fort Laramie, and if Gen'l Crook should need them they were to join him. The Lieutenant General seemed anxious to have Gen'l. Crook and General Terry's commands combine.

The bill for the construction of the Yellowstone posts has passed and their construction, or at least of one, would be commenced immediately.[2] There had been no recent raiding on settlements. Merritt's command helped to overtake and punish a party of 800 hostile Cheyennes, leaving the Agencies to go North to join hostiles.[3] This would, however, not delay him more than a few days. (Mrs. Crook has been injured in a R.R. accident, coming home from Little Rock, but now doing well.[)] (Much mourning was noticed among the Red Cloud Indians, due to the battles with Crook's and Custer's commands. If General Crook needed any more troops he could have them.[)] Horses and other supplies had been ordered up to come with Merritt. [Sheridan writes:] "I am entirely satisfied with what you have done and have the greatest confidence in what you will be able to do as soon as you are fully ready to go to work. I want you to communicate with me more frequently. The public is constantly being excited by erroneous and sensational rumors of engagements with Indians when any length of time elapses without hearing from you." Again he said, "I have thought you both [Crook and Terry] may have communicated and concentrated, if deemed prudent, for any other operations. If the Indians still hold together, I hope you may be able to give them a good hard blow." (Nickerson telegraphed that the Utes were anxious to come but that the agent has interposed. Authority was

2. This would refer to Fort Keogh, Mt.
3. The fight at War Bonnet Creek, on July 17, 1876.

applied for to Washington and Nickerson hoped to get them started very soon to join the expedition. . . .[)]

July 22d. Day opened a trifle cloudy. Hot wind from the South. As uninteresting a day as any to be mentioned in the whole campaign. The Sho-sho-nees whiled away the afternoon in horse racing and running matches.

July 23d Copious, genial showers refreshed the parched earth and dissipated, for a brief season at least, any lurking apprehensions we might have indulged that small bands of the enemy would make an effort to burn us out of the country. The current season has been so dry the grass would ignite almost from the rays of the sun, had not the sluice gates been opened and the waters poured down. The Crow Indian couriers were dispatched back to Terry's command this afternoon, taking with them Evans, Stewart and Ball, the brave soldiers who preceded them with messages from the same army. A heavy mail was forwarded to Fort Fetterman, including letters from the whole command and dispatches from General Crook to General Sheridan, bearing this date and station:

General Sheridan,

Chicago.

I find myself immeasurably embarrassed by the delay of Merritt's column, as the extremely hot weather of the last few days has so completely parched the grass, excepting that on the mountain tops, that it burns like tinder; besides, our delay is a source of uneasiness and dissatisfaction to our Indian allies.

On Powder, Tongue and Rosebud rivers, the whole country is on fire and filled with smoke. I am in constant dread of an attack; in their last, they set fire to the grass, but as much of it was still green, we extinguished it without difficulty; but should it be fired now, I don't see how we could stay in the country.

I am at a loss what to do: I can prevent their attack by assuming the aggressive, but as my effective strength is less than twelve hundred, exclusive of Indian allies, I could do but little beyond scattering them which would render it impossible to subdue them until the cold weather narrowed their limits; and, in the meantime, they could do an incalculable amount of damage to the settlements.

The Corporal, who came through as courier from General Terry gives a very intelligent account of what he saw on his journey; says he followed up the train reported by Capt. Ball, as going towards

Rosebud, until it reached that stream, where it again divided; the main trail, with nothing but pony tracks upon it, following up Rosebud while all travau[x] trains went Eastward. This means that the wounded were sent where they could be cared for, while the able-bodied rejoined the hostiles.

All indications are that the Sioux are in the Big Horn Mountains from which point they can see clear to the Yellowstone and discern the approach of Terry's column for a distance of at least fifty or sixty miles; this will prevent a union of our columns without their becoming aware of it.

I don't think they will fight us combined, if they know it, but will scatter: So, I have suggested to Terry that the first column which struck them should try to hold them until the other came up. Should these Indians scatter unhurt, they would have greatly the advantage over us, as we would be obliged to divide accordingly, while their thorough knowledge of the country and rapidity of movement would enable them to concentrate on and destroy our small parties.

I understood the New York Herald has published most villainous falsehoods from the correspondent with this command in regard to the Rosebud fight, of the 17th ultimo, which are intended to do the command and myself great injustice.[4] Of course the reason is very obvious. There was a correct account furnished from here to the *N.Y. Tribune* but it never reached its destination and it is supposed here that it was suppressed in the Telegraph Office at Fetterman.

(signed.) *George Crook,*
Brigadier General.

My own correspondence was very limited, embracing a few brief sentences to mother and a note to Capt. Nickerson, A.D.C. Spasmodically, during remainder of day and night rain fell in our camp; not, however, in the quantities needed and expected. Captain Sutorius, 3d Cavy. was placed in arrest during the afternoon and charges preferred against him of drunkenness on duty, while in charge of pickets. While a gambling game was going on in the camp of half-breed

---

4. Crook was referring to a dispatch by Reuben Davenport, which inspired an editorial by the *New York Herald*, both of which are reprinted in Appendix 16. Bourke was outraged, and mentioned Davenport in derogatory terms on pp 383–84. Not everyone agreed, however, and Davenport had his share of supporters. Among the latter was Lt. Col. Richard Irving Dodge, who joined the campaign later in the fall. After two weeks of observing General Crook, Dodge commented in his own diary, "I don't blame Davenport of the Herald one bit. He stated what he saw & is cordially hated for it. I cant state what I see except in this private journal." Kime, *Powder River Expedition*, 66.

scouts this night, the amount of money displayed by the bank excited the cupidity of a couple of bystanders, who at once attempted to effect a stampede by discharging their revolvers. They effectively scared the whole camp, which for a short spell imagined that a sneaking detachment of Indians was trying to scare our mule herd. Camp soon quieted down, after venting a thousand execrations upon the teamsters and guides who had occasioned the alarm. I applied myself for several hours after dark to preparing copies of the orders convening the Court, which to-morrow morning at 8 O'clock will proceed to the trial of Captain Sutorius upon the following, Charge. Drunkenness on duty in violation of the 38th Article of War.

Specification. In this that he, Captain Alexander Sutorius, 3d U.S. Cavalry, being officer in charge of the pickets of the 3d Cavalry, a portion of the Big Horn and Yellowstone Expedition, in the field, was so much under the influence of intoxicating liquors as to be unfit for the proper performance of his duty. This when an attack by hostile Indians might at any moment be expected in the camp of Big Horn and Yellowstone Expedition, on Middle Goose Ck, Wy. on or about the 22d day of July 1876.

Colonel Royall, 3d Cav., commanding Cavalry Battns, forwarded the charges requesting an immediate trial. General Crook immediately issued Special Field Orders, No 20, appointing the Court to meet at these HdQrs, on the 24th day of July, 1876, at 8 o'clock A.M. with the following

Detail.

1. Major Alex. Chambers, Fourth Infantry.
2. Major William Arthur, Pay Department.
3. Captain Anson Mills, Third Cavalry.
4. Captain Andrew S. Burt, Ninth Infantry.
5. Thos. B. Burrowes, Ninth Infantry
6. Captain W.E. Noyes, Second Cavalry.
7. Captain Wm. H. Powell, Fourth Infantry.
8. Captain Samuel Munson, Ninth Infantry.
9. Captain Fred K. Van Vliet, Third Cavalry.
10. Capt. D.W. Burke, Fourteenth Infantry
11. Captain Elijah R. Wells. Second Cavalry.

First Lieutenant Thad. H. Capron, Ninth Infantry, Judge Advocate.

Mr. Davenport, the correspondent of the *N.Y. Herald*, has been prowling about camp like a whipped cur, since the arrival of the late mail with files of his journal containing his letter upon the Rosebud fight and the editorial based thereupon. He seems to feel that everyone has detected his nefarious mission to belie Crook and elevate the unfortunate Custer as his expense. His miserable failure to do this has brought about a retribution of contempt hard to be borne even with his unusual immodest audacity. General Crook has shown a rare self command and an equally unusual foresight in declining to take any personal notice of Davenport, who he permits to remain with the command as usual, the recipient of the same privileges as the other correspondents.

July 24th Moved camp across North Goose Creek to the West bank. Court to try Captain Sutorius convened this morning. Sky very cloudy and temperature extremely sultry. Air full of electricity. As the sun climbed the heavens, the clouds became more compact and at length yielded an abundant, gentle and refreshing shower enduring until night. And far into the horns of night, the welcome storm lasted, cooling the brazen sky and moisturing the dessicated herbage so lately a cause of gloomy mistrust, for should it by accident or design have been enkindled, it would have been hard for us to foresee what result our labors to extinguish it would have.

July 25th A leaden mantle palled the sky: all morning the rains poured down, welcome as a strong ally against the Sioux. Nothing to do in camp except read and write, play whist or engage in conversation. The Court for the trial of Captain Sutorius resumed its session after a short adjournment taken yesterday to give the accused an opportunity to secure counsel and prepare his defense. A brief lull in the rainstorm was improved by our Sho-sho-nee allies in making a reconnaisance to the front as far as the South fork of Tongue river, four or five miles to the North West. There they saw and were seen by a patrol of the hostiles, numbering fifty or more. No shots were exchanged. The two parties contented themselves with signals of mutual defiance and challenge, by waving blankets. The Sho-sho-nees returned to camp on a full run. Herds were drawn in, pickets strengthened and other preparatory movements ordered. But no attack was made upon us. Yet as we are now in almost plain sight of the pickets and patrols of our foe, it does not occur to me how a conflict can be averted much longer. If the 5th Cavalry delay many days, hostilities must be commenced without them. The heavy showers of the few days just elapsed have saturated the ground with moisture [and] we need not be disturbed with fears of a conflagration: at least, not for a week and by that time, we ought to be able to assume the initiative. Some little while after dark, Louis Richaud and a few companinons who had been hunting in the craggy hills in the cañon of South Tongue river made their way back to camp. They had seen no Indians and no fresh signs during their absence, but reported those streams as filled with fine trout and the country filled with Rocky Mtn sheep, of which they secured six or seven out of a great number killed. They had taken station on a precipice two hundred feet high, shooting down from the top. Many wounded lambs and ewes escaped to die elsewhere. Our mess was presented with a supply of fresh, tender mutton, acknowledged with gratitude.

July 26th. No disturbance last night, owing, we may suppose, to the continuation of the storm. Frank Gruard, Cosgrove and a small party were sent out to follow the tracks of the Indians seen yesterday: they established the character of the hostiles as a patrol observing our movements and then returned.

Showers fell on the course of this day, preserving the beneficial effects of the heavy falls of yesterday and preceeding days. The General Court Martial in Captain Sutorius' case completed its labors to-day, but adjourned until 10 A.M., of the 28th to give the accused an opportunity to prepare his final statement. A grave accident happened this evening to a mule train crossing with an empty wagon to the other side of the creek, whose waters had increased greatly in consequence of heavy rains near the summit of the mountains. The teamster neglected to keep his animals headed up stream; one of them, frightened at an object on the bank, reared and plunged and its mates sharing its terror, speedily became unmanageable. The wagon itself caught against one of the boulders in the torrent and was almost in an instant overturned by the rushing waters and snapped in twain. Three of the miles were drowned in the harness, but the other three and the driver were rescued by a small party of Sho-sho-nees who were standing on the stream bank near the ford. Charles Russell, our master of transportation, saved the fragments of the wagon and afterwards showed the inexperienced teamsters how to manage their animals under similar circumstances. He took a wagon, loaded with a weight of 3000 lbs., to give it steadiness, attached to eight strong mules, and had a man on horseback go in front, leading the animals by a leather strap. The stream was crossed diagonally to secure the best ford and to obviate to the fullest the pressure of the water.

July 27th At day-break, struck tents and moved camp four miles North West to the Middle fork of Tongue river. It is hard to distinguish between the different branches of this stream, issuing from the Range. They are, without an exception of considerable volume, rocky beds, currents very swift, 6 to 8 miles an hour and even more, water, very cold and amply stocked with trout. This one is the smallest yet camped upon. It is not more than ten yards wide. Many trout were abstracted from its cool and shady recesses almost as soon as the command to unsaddle had been executed. I have abandoned any attempt at computing the number; certainly, not less than 10.000 have been cooked and eaten, and the grand total may reach as high as 15.000! This number may seem incredible; let it be borne in mind, we have not less than fifteen hundred and fifty officers, soldiers, teamsters and Indians subsisting on this delicate fish and that they have been eating them freely for more than three weeks. Then the aggregate will be accepted without a murmur. Clouds of grass-hoppers flew over camp this morning carried by a good strong upper current of air in a direction East South East. They fairly well darkened the rays of the sun.

Heavy smoke arose in the points of the compass where Rosebud and Little Big Horn rivers flow.

Captain Mills, of the 3d Cavalry, with a small detachment ascended the mountain summits a few miles from camp. He observed the country with much care and gave as his opinion that something unusual was going on. A large fire was burning on the Little Big Horn and signal smokes were appearing and disappearing with frequency.

July 28th. Most important news was brought to camp to-day, by courier, Fairbanks. The dispatches from General Sheridan read as follows:

Chicago, Ills., July 25, 1876.

General George Crook, &c.

I have received all your dispatches including those sent by the courier of the 15th.

General Merritt, with ten companies of his Regiment, will reach your camp, August 1st. He drove the Indians who recently attempted to join the hostiles back to the Agency, killing one.[5] It is thought they are now sufficiently frightened to remain in. I approve of your inten-

---

5. This was Yellow Hair (also known as Yellow Hand), a Cheyenne who was killed in single combat with Buffalo Bill Cody at War Bonnet Creek.

tion to form a junction with Terry and after Indians are defeated, if they make a stand, I will want Terry, and a portion of his command to build the post on the Yellowstone and will want you to continue the campaign. Terry moved his depot from the mouth of Powder river to either the mouth of Rosebud or Big Horn and expressed the greatest desire to join you. We cannot afford a reverse to either column so long as there is a chance of uniting and thus increasing our strength.The Ute Indians will be sent you to help clean up the country and the Crows have asked and received additional ammunition to take the field. The Indian Dept. has given me entire control over Indians at the Agencies and I propose not to allow any Indians in the field to return to them until they have unconditionally surrendered all arms, ponies and families. I will build both posts on the Yellowstone, if the stage of water will permit and will supply them well so that the force operating in the field in the fall and winter can draw from them. I have been pressed to call out volunteers, but have not seen as yet any necessity.

Reno writes that the 7th Cavalry could have handled the Indians on the Little Big Horn, if they had all gone in together. If you succeed in defeating the Indians I will go up the Yellowstone about August 20th to push the posts and will try and communicate with you.

Look to your base of supplies until you have heard from me definitely about supplies on the Yellowstone. As soon as Merritt joins you, I think it will be well to push out without further day.

(signed.) P.H. Sheridan,
Lieutenant General.

Red Cloud 18th July, via Ft. Laramie
19th July   10.15 A.m.

General George Crook,
Camp on Goose Ck, via Fort Fetterman.

Your dispatch of the 12th just received. By authority from the Lieutenant General, I moved from Raw Hide by forced marched to intercept eight hundred Cheyennes and a number of Sioux who were reported leaving the Agency for your front. I succeeded in cutting them off, but being informed of my presence by runners, they succeeded in escaping from the trails to the Agency. I don't think they will attempt to go North again. I will march to join you without unnecessary delay. I am sorry that my horses are much jaded but a few days' reasonable marching will make them all right. We are all anxious to be with you.

(Signed.) Merritt

General Williams telegraphed from Omaha that Surgeon Clements was on his way to join the Expedition as Medical Director of Expedn.,* and also sent the following,

Omaha, Neb., July 23d, 1876.

Major General Crook &c.

Ute Indians were prevented from joining you by Agent. Lieutenant [James Herbert] Spencer, Fourth Infantry, left Rawlins [Wy.] about five days ago with requisite authority from Interior Depart. for them and will bring them forward at the earliest moment. Cannot tell as yet how many there will be, or when they will arrive at Rail Road [in Rawlins]. Will hurry them forward as soon as possible. Merritt leaves Laramie to-morrow and hopes to join you about 1st of August. I send forward to him and you all available horses and horse equipment at Cheyenne; this, after consultation with the Lieutenant General.

There will be ample supplies of all kinds for you at Fetterman. Some depredations in neighborhood of Sydney [Nebraska] reported. All well and working well.

(signed.) R. Williams
Assist. Adjutant General.

The burden of the information conveyed in our private correspondence was the horror and agitation occasioned throughout the country by the news of the Custer massacre. Fairbanks encountered great trouble from storms of rains: floods prevailed over the country. Powder river was 12 feet deep. Crazy Woman had been fully as bad a day or two before he reached its banks. At and near Fort Fetterman, pools of water a foot in depth, covered the ground, while the beds of the dry creeks between Fort Fetterman and Fort Reno had turned into quagmires.

This day has been bright and cloudless and not too warm. Capt. Sutorius' court adjourned sine die. . . .[6]

A game of Base-Ball, Infantry Picked nine of lieuts versus Cavalry ditto,—was played this evening. Infantry Officers won the game 17 to 30.

---

* "On recommendation of the Medical Director [of the department] and by suggestion of the Surgeon General".

6. Sutorius was dismissed from the service on September 25, 1876. Heitman, *Historical Register*, 1:937.

Appendix 1

❖

❖

❖

❖

❖

Persons Mentioned in the Diary

Due to the large number of sources for the biographical sketches in this section, footnotes or endnotes would have been impractical. Consequently, I have placed the sources in parentheses at the end of each entry. In cases where the author has only one publication in the bibliography, I have used only the author's last name. In case of multiple publications by the same author, I have placed the date of publication of the edition cited.

Military

When discussing the careers of cavalrymen, the designation of units overlapping the Civil War tends to be confusing. In mid-1861, the Regular Army had six mounted regiments, viz. First and Second Dragoons, Mounted Riflemen, and First, Second and Third Cavalry. On August 3, 1861, congress reorganized these regiments, designating them all "cavalry," and renumbering them as follows:

First Dragoons to First Cavalry

Second Dragoons to Second Cavalry

Mounted Riflemen to Third Cavalry

First Cavalry to Fourth Cavalry

Second Cavalry to Fifth Cavalry

Third Cavalry to Sixth Cavalry.
After the war, additional Regular Army mounted units were authorized as needed. (Herr and Wallace, 116)

ADAM, Emil (1931-1903), which Bourke spelled "Adams," was captain in the 5th Cavalry. A native of Bavaria, he served in that country's army before settling in Illinois. He served in the Illinois infantry during the Civil War and entered the Regular Army in 1867. He was breveted to major for gallantry in action against Indians at Muchos Cañones, Arizona, on Sept. 25, 1872, but was suspended for six months in 1874, when his failure to react to an attack on a wagon train near San Carlos led to a major outbreak. He participated in Crook's Bighorn and Yellowstone Expedition in 1876, and in the Nez Percé War. He retired as a major in 1893. (Heitman, 1:151; Altshuler, 1991, 2-3)

ALDRICH, Bishop (1835-77) enlisted in the army in 1855. After serving in the Civil War he was promoted to first lieutenant in 1866. He was regimental quartermaster of the 8th Infantry, and died at Fort Whipple of heart disease. (Altshuler, 1991, 5)

ALLEN, William (1845?-82) was a Volunteer private during the Civil War, and enlisted in the Regular Army in 1865. While a sergeant in the 23rd Infantry, he participated in the fight at Turret Mountain on March 27, 1873, for which he later received the Medal of Honor. He was promoted to second lieutenant of the 12th Infantry in 1873. He died at Fort Mojave of an intestinal inflammation. (Altshuler, 1991, 7)

ALLISON, James Nicholas, entered West Point in 1867, and upon graduation was posted to the 2nd Cavalry as a second lieutenant, a position he held at the time Bourke knew him. (Heitman, 1:160)

ALMY, Jacob (1842-73) was first lieutenant in the 5th Cavalry. A Quaker from Massachusetts, he nevertheless joined a state volunteer unit during the Civil War, but was mustered out in 1862 to accept an appointment to West Point. After graduation, he served in Indian campaigns in Kansas, Nebraska, and Wyoming, before being posted to Arizona. He commanded the post at San Carlos where he was murdered during a confrontation with unruly Indians during a ration issue on May 27, 1873. See CHAN-DEISI; COCHINAY; Appendix 14. (Heitman, 1:161; Altshuler, 1991, 7-8)

ANDREWS, William Howard (d. 1880), joined the Volunteers as a captain in 1862, and was mustered out as a brevet major. He was named first lieutenant of the 12th Infantry in 1866, and assigned to the 3rd Cavalry at Camp McDowell, Arizona, in December 1870, serving as post adjutant for the next ten months. He retired in disability as captain in 1879. (Altshuler, 1991, 10; Heitman, 1:167)

ARTHUR, William, joined the Volunteer artillery as first lieutenant in 1862. He distinguished himself during the Civil War, rising to the brevet rank of lieutenant colonel. He joined the 3rd Artillery as second lieutenant in 1866. He was appointed major and paymaster on July 26, 1876, and retired in 1898. (Heitman, 1:172)

BABCOCK, John Breckinridge (1843-1909), a native of Louisiana nevertheless served in the Union Army during the Civil War, and was breveted to major for gallantry. In 1867, he was commissioned as second lieutenant of the 5th Cavalry, and promoted to first lieutenant the following year. He went to Arizona with the regiment in 1872. He was breveted to colonel for gallant service in action against Indians at Tonto Creek, on June 16, 1873, and at Four Peaks, Arizona, on January 16, 1874. He retired as a brigadier general in 1903. (Altshuler, 1991, 14-15; Heitman, 1:178)

BAILY, Charles Meigs (d. 1885), whose named Bourke sometimes spelled as "Bailey," was the son of Maj. Elisha Ingrahm Baily, medical director for the Department of Arizona. Charles Baily was second lieutenant in the 8th Infantry at Camp Apache. (Altshuler, 1991, 17)

BALL, Edward (d. 1884), joined the army under an assumed name in 1844. In 1861, he was appointed second lieutenant of the 12th Infantry, and the same year transferred to the 2nd Cavalry. He was appointed captain in 1865. Ball was major of the 7th Cavalry at the time of his retirement in 1884. (Heitman, 1:187)

BENDIRE, Charles (1836-97), a native of Darmstadt, enlisted in the U.S. Army in New York in 1854. He served in Arizona and New Mexico prior to the Civil War, and in the Regular Army during the war. He returned to Arizona in 1871, but was detached to recruiting duty the following year. His subsequent Indian campaigns were in the Northwest. Following his retirement in 1886, Bendire became a renowned ornithologist. (Altshuler, 1991, 28)

BIRD, Charles (1838-1920), was appointed first lieutenant of Volunteers in 1861, and eventually mustered out as colonel. In 1866, he was commissioned second lieutenant of the 14th Infantry, which was reorganized as part of the 23rd Infantry later that year. He was promoted to first lieutenant in 1867. He served under Crook in the Departments of the Columbia, Arizona, and the Platte, and retired as a brigadier general in 1902. (Altshuler, 1991, 33)

BISHOP, Hoel Smith (1850-1925), graduated from West Point in 1873, and was posted to Fort Whipple as second lieutenant in the 5th Cavalry. In 1876, he participated in Crook's Big Horn and Yellowstone Expedition, and in the Bannock War in Wyoming and Idaho in 1878. He retired as colonel in 1913. (Altshuler, 1991, 35)

BRADLEY, Luther Prentice (1822-1910), native of Connecticut, was appointed lieutenant colonel of a Volunteer regiment in 1861, rising to brigadier general by 1864. In 1866, he entered the Regular Army as lieutenant colonel of the 27th Infantry. He commanded Fort C.F. Smith, Montana, during the Red Cloud War. As lieutenant colonel of the 9th Infantry, he was in command of Camp Robinson, Nebraska, when Crazy Horse was killed there in 1877. Bradley was appointed colonel of the 3rd Infantry in 1879, and was commander of the Military District of New Mexico in 1881, during the Cibicue outbreak in Arizona. He took troops to reinforce Fort Apache, Arizona, and commanded a special military district created to deal with the crisis. When New Mexico was attached to the Department of Arizona during the Geronimo War, Bradley served under Crook in an effort to contain the raiding. He retired in 1886. (Thrapp, 1991, 1:157; Heitman, 1:239)

BRADY, George Keyports (d. 1899), enlisted in the Volunteers in 1861, but soon was commissioned first lieutenant of the 14th Infantry. He served with distinction in the Civil War, finishing with the brevet rank of lieutenant colonel. In 1866, he transferred to the 23rd Infantry as captain. He was lieutenant colonel of the 17th Infantry when he retired in 1894. (Heitman, 1:239)

BRAYTON, George Mitchell (1834-1911), was appointed first lieutenant of the 15th Infantry in 1861, breveted to major for gallantry in 1865. The following year, he transferred to the 8th Infantry as captain. He was named commander of Camp Verde in 1874 and participated in several scouts. Although he left Arizona with his regiment in 1878, he frequently was sent back throughout the remainder of his career. He retired in 1892 as colonel of the 3rd Infantry. (Altshuler, 1991, 42; Heitman, 1:241)

BRENT, Thomas Lee, Jr. (ca. 1846-80), entered West Point in 1861, and upon graduation was assigned to the 2nd Cavalry. In 1871, he was captain of the 3rd Cavalry in Arizona, where he served under Crook during a skirmish above the Mogollon Rim. He retired in 1876. (Thrapp, 1991, 1:165; Heitman, 1:242)

BRISBIN, James Sanks (1837-92), known as "Grasshopper Jim" for his interest in developing Western agriculture, was commissioned as second lieutenant of the lst Dragoons (renumbered 1st Cavalry) in 1861. He finished the Civil War as major general of Volunteers. In 1866, he was transferred to the 9th Cavalry, as captain, and two years later was appointed major of the 2nd Cavalry. As commander of Fort Ellis, Montana, Brisbin led a relief force to rescue forty-six citizens besieged by Indians at Fort Pease, a private stockade on the Yellowstone River. This incident, in February 1876, was one of the first actions of the Great Sioux War. He later served under Col. Nelson Miles, when Miles followed Sitting Bull as far as the Canadian border. He was colonel of the 8th Cavalry at the time of his death. Brisbin wrote several books boosting development of the West, the best known of which is *The Beef Bonanza: or, How to Get Rich on the Plains.* (Thrapp, 1991, 1:170; Heitman, 1:246)

BRODIE, Alexander Oswald (1849-1918), an 1870 graduate of West Point, was posted as second lieutenant of the 1st Cavalry at Camp Thomas (later Camp Apache), Arizona in 1871. He received commendations for actions against Apaches in 1873. He left with his company for the Pacific Coast in May 1873. He resigned in 1877, but reentered the army in 1883, serving sporadically in the Regular Army, Volunteers, and National Guard, for the next thirty years. He succeeded Theodore Roosevelt as lieutenant colonel of the Rough Riders, and after Roosevelt became president, was appointed territorial governor of Arizona. He retired as colonel in 1913. (Altshuler, 1991, 43-44)

BRODRICK, Patrick Thomas (d. 1886), native of Ireland, was an 1868 graduate of West Point. He served in the 23rd Infantry under Crook in the Departments of the Columbia and Arizona. Chronically ill, he died in New York. (Altshuler, 1991, 44).

BROWN, Frederick H. (d. 1866), native of New York, enlisted in the 18th Infantry in 1861, earning a commission later the same year. He was regimental quartermaster at Fort Phil Kearny, and died in the Fetterman Massacre on December 21, 1866. See also FETTERMAN, William Judd; GRUMMOND, George Washington. (See Brown; O'Neal, 56-57)

BROWN, William Henry (1840?-75), native of Maryland, was inspector general of the Department of Arizona under Crook. He enlisted in the army in 1861, and was made second lieutenant of the 5th Cavalry later that year. He was breveted to major in 1865 for gallantry and meritorious service at Five Forks, Virginia. Crook recommended for brevets to brigadier general for service at the Battle of the Caves in 1872, and fights in the Superstition Mountains, Sierra Ancha, and Mazatzals in 1873. He committed suicide on June 4, 1875. According to Constance Wynn Altshuler, he may have been in love with Irene Rucker, who had married Lt. Gen. Philip H. Sheridan the previous day. See also NANNI-CHADDI. (Altshuler, 1991, 46; O'Neal, 57-58; Heitman, 1:254; Bourke, Diary, 2b:73)

BRYANT, Montgomery (1831-1901), native of Kansas, joined the army as second lieutenant of the 6th Infantry in 1857. He went west with the regiment in 1859, serving at Fort Mojave, Arizona, and Fort Yuma, California, until October 1861, when the 6th was transferred east. He served with distinction in the Civil War. He was promoted to major of the 14th Infantry in 1874. He retired as colonel of the 13th Infantry in 1894. (Altshuler, 1991, 47)

BUBB, John Wilson, enlisted in the 12th Infantry in 1861, and was commissioned as lieutenant five years later. In 1869, he was assigned to the 4th Infantry as first lieutenant, serving as quartermaster from 1872 to 1875. During Crook's Big Horn and Yellowstone Expedition, he was acting commissary of subsistence, and played a significant part during the campaign. (Heitman, 1:257)

BURKE, Daniel Webster (1841-1911), native of Connecticut, enlisted in the 2nd Infantry in 1858, serving in Minnesota, Dakota, and Nebraska. He was commissioned as a second lieutenant in 1862, serving with distinction in the Civil War. In 1876, he was captain of the 14th Infantry, serving in Crook's campaigns. He commanded Camp Sheridan, Nebraska, at the Spotted Tail Agency, when Crazy Horse surrendered, and it was at his suggestion that Crazy Horse went to Camp Robinson, where he was killed. Burke, however, had no knowledge of any plans to confine Crazy Horse at Robinson. He retired in 1899 as brigadier general. See also CLARK, Walter Philo; CRAZY HORSE. (Thrapp, 1991, 1:192-93)

BURNS, James (ca.1836-74), native of Ireland, enlisted in the army in 1858. He was commissioned as second lieutenant in the 5th Cavalry in 1865, eventually rising to the rank of captain in 1872.

Crook recommended Burns for three brevets after actions resulting in the surrender of some two hundred Yavapais. Burns suffered from an unspecified pulmonary disease, and died of a lung hemorrhage on August 15, 1874. Bourke sometimes spelled it "Byrnes." (Altshuler, 1991, 50; O'Neal, 65-66; Heitman, 1:265)

BURROUGHS refers to Capt. Thomas Bredin Burrowes (d. 1885), who was appointed first lieutenant of the 18th Infantry in 1861, dismissed and reinstated. He was promoted to captain in 1864. At the time of Bourke's writing, he was captain of the 9th Infantry. He retired in 1879. (Heitman, 1:267)

BURT, Andrew Sheridan (1839-1915), native of Ohio, enlisted as a Volunteer in 1861, but almost immediately was commissioned second lieutenant of the 18th Infantry. He was promoted to the active rank of captain in 1863, and breveted to major for gallant and meritorious service during the Atlanta Campaign. After the war he was posted to Fort Bridger, Utah, and Fort C.F. Smith, Montana. With the reduction of the army he was reassigned to the 9th Infantry. Burt participated in Crook's Big Horn and Yellowstone Expedition in 1876. He retired as brigadier general in 1902. (Altshuler, 1991, 50-51; Heitman, 1:267)

BYRNE, Thomas (c. 1827-81), native of Ireland, enlisted in the 2nd Infantry in Philadelphia in 1854. He was commissioned second lieutenant in 1862, and was breveted for gallantry at Gettysburg. He was a captain at the time of his reassignment to the 12th Infantry in 1871. He died at Fort Mojave in 1881. (Altshuler, 1991, 51-52; Heitman, 1:272).

CAIN, Avery Billings (d. 1879), of Vermont, was appointed first lieutenant of the 4th Infantry in 1861, and promoted to captain in 1863. He was breveted to major for gallant and meritorious service at the North Anna River in Virginia in 1864. (Heitman, 1:273)

CAPRON, Thaddeus Hurlbut (d. 1890), enlisted in the Volunteers in 1861, and was commissioned first lieutenant in 1863. After the Civil War, he was commissioned second lieutenant of the 9th Infantry, and promoted to first lieutenant in 1871. He retired in 1887. Capron left a diary and series of letters on the Big Horn and Yellowstone Expedition. (Heitman, 1:281)

CARPENTER, William Lewis (1844-98), native of New York, enlisted in the 2nd Artillery in 1864. He was promoted to second lieutenant and assigned to the 9th Infantry in 1867, and promoted to first lieutenant in 1873. He served on survey and scientific expeditions, including to the Bighorn Mountains, and was elected a fellow of the American Association for the Advancement of Science. He later served in Arizona, where he was promoted to captain. (Altshuler, 1991, 58-59)

CARR, Camillo Casatti Cadmus (1842-1914), native of Virginia, he joined the 1st Cavalry in 1862, and was commissioned as second lieutenant the following year. He served with distinction during the Civil War. In 1866, he went to Fort McDowell, Arizona. After service elsewhere, he returned to Arizona as captain of Company I, 1st Cavalry, and was recommended for a brevet for gallantry in the 1872-73 winter campaign. He was promoted to brigadier general in 1903, and commanded the Department of Dakota until he retired in 1906. His memoirs, *A Cavalryman in Indian Country*, edited by Dan L. Thrapp, were published in 1974. (Altshuler, 1991, 59; Heitman, 1:284)

CARR, Eugene Asa (1830-1910), native of New York, was an 1850 graduate of West Point, and served on the frontier until the outbreak of the Civil War when he joined the Volunteers. He was breveted to brigadier general of Volunteers in 1862, and received the Medal of Honor for gallantry at Pea Ridge, Arkansas. After being mustered out of the Volunteers, he was appointed major of the 5th Cavalry, retroactive to 1862, and again posted to the frontier. He was appointed lieutenant colonel in 1873. After service in Arizona from 1872 to 1876, the 5th was transferred to the Department of the Platte. Carr participated in the Big Horn and Yellowstone Expedition, and led the preliminary relief force at Slim Buttes, on September 9, 1876. He was promoted to colonel of the 6th Cavalry in 1879, and retired at brigadier general in 1893. See also EMORY, William Helmsley; MERRITT, Wesley. (King; Altshuler, 1991, 60-61; O'Neal, 67-72)

CARTER, William Harding (1851-1925), native of Tennessee, served as a dispatch rider during the Civil War. He entered West Point, graduating in 1873, and was posted to the 8th Infantry at Fort D.A. Russell, Wyoming. He was sent to Camp McDowell the following year, and remained in Arizona in the 5th and 6th Cavalry Regiments for the better part of a decade. He received the Medal of Honor for gallantry at the Cibicue Creek fight. He retired as major general in 1915, although he was recalled to duty during the First

World War. Carter wrote several military histories, the best known of which is probably *From Yorktown to Santiago With the Sixth Cavalry*. (Altshuler, 1991, 62-63)

CHAMBERS, Alexander (1832-88), native of New York, was an 1853 graduate of West Point. He served in the Southwest and against the Seminoles in Florida. At the outbreak of the Civil War, he was captain of the 18th Infantry. He finished the war as a brevet colonel of the Regular Army and brevet brigadier general of Volunteers. In 1876, he was major of the 4th Infantry, in command of Fort Fetterman. In October of that year, he was promoted to lieutenant colonel of the 21st Infantry. He commanded the infantry contingent of Crook's Big Horn and Yellowstone Expedition, and led them in the fight at Slim Buttes. He was colonel of the 17th Infantry at the time of his death. (Heitman, 1:293; Thrapp, 1991, 1:248)

CHASE, George Francis (1848-1925), 1871 graduate of West Point, was assigned to the 3rd Cavalry the following year. He participated in the Big Horn and Yellowstone Expedition, and, as first lieutenant, served in Arizona. He retired as a brigadier general in 1912. (Altshuler, 1991, 67)

CHERRY, Samuel Austin, of Indiana, entered West Point in 1870, and upon graduation was appointed second lieutenant of the 23rd Infantry. He transferred to the 5th Cavalry on July 28, 1876. He was murdered by a soldier on May 11, 1881. (Heitman, 1:298)

CLARK, William Philo (1845-84), native of New York, graduated from West Point in 1868, and was appointed second lieutenant, 2nd Cavalry, at Fort D. A. Russell, Wyoming. He served on General Crook's staff in 1876 and 1877, figuring prominently in the Great Sioux War, particularly with events surrounding Crazy Horse's death. Much of the acrimony between Clark and Crazy Horse that set the event into motion appears to have stemmed from Frank Grouard's mistranslation of a remark by Crazy Horse. During the Cheyenne Outbreak of 1878-79, Clark managed to round up a large band without bloodshed. His book, *Indian Sign Language*, remains definitive. He also wrote an account of Crazy Horse's death, which was edited by Robert A. Clark, and published in *The Killing of Chief Crazy Horse*, in 1976. See also BURKE, Daniel Webster; GROUARD, Frank; CRAZY HORSE. (Thrapp, 1991, 1:278; Robinson, 1995, 337-38)

CLEMENTS, Bennett A., was assigned to departmental headquarters in Omaha. He joined the army as a first lieutenant and assistant surgeon in 1856, serving in Florida, Texas, and New Mexico. He was promoted to surgeon and major in 1863, and administered hospitals during and after the Civil War. Dr. Clements participated in General Crook's Horse Meat March, and filed a report giving the medical effects of the ordeal. He also was one of the medical officers who, in 1884, certified that Ranald Mackenzie was insane and unfit for further duty. Clements's report on the Horse Meat March is found in Greene, 1993, 97ff; and on Mackenzie in Robinson, 1993, 323-24.

CLIFFORD, Walter (d. 1883), of New York, enlisted in the 16th Infantry in 1860, and was commissioned as second lieutenant in 1863. He transferred to the 34th Infantry in 1866, and was promoted to captain a year later. In 1871, he was assigned to the 7th Infantry. (Heitman, 1:310)

COALE, John Holbrook (d. 1883), of Maryland, was commissioned as a captain of the commissary service in the Volunteers in 1862, and promoted to lieutenant colonel a year later. In 1867, he was commissioned second lieutenant of the 27th Infantry, but at the time of Bourke's writing, was serving in the 2nd Cavalry. He was a first lieutenant at the time of his death. (Heitman, 1:312)

COATES, Edwin Mortimer, was commissioned first lieutenant of the Volunteers in 1861, but resigned to accept a commission as second lieutenant of the 2nd Cavalry. At the end of the Civil War, he was captain, and at the time of Bourke's writing, was serving in the 4th Infantry. He retired in 1900 as colonel of the 7th Infantry. Bourke refers to him as "Major Coates," but no such brevet appears on his record. (Heitman, 1:312)

COPPINGER, John Joseph (1834-1909), native of Ireland, was a professional soldier. He was appointed captain of the 14th Infantry in 1861, and served with distinction during the Civil War. In 1866, he was assigned to the 23rd Infantry, serving in San Francisco and Alaska before arriving in Arizona in 1872. He commanded Camp Verde until 1874 when he was reassigned to the Department of the Platte. He was breveted to colonel for service against hostile Indians. He was confirmed as brigadier general in 1896, and commanded the Department of the Platte. He retired in 1898, after being appointed major general of Volunteers. (Altshuler, 1991, 78; Heitman, 1:327)

CRAIG, Louis Aleck (1851-1904), native of Missouri, was an 1874 graduate of West Point. In 1875, he joined the 6th Cavalry at Camp

McDowell, and spent much of the following decade in Arizona. He became senior instructor in cavalry tactics at West Point. He retired because of ill health as major of the 15th Cavalry in 1903. (Altshuler, 1991, 83)

CRAIG, Samuel, of New Jersey, enlisted in the Volunteers in 1862, and was commissioned as second lieutenant in January 1864. In 1866, he was commissioned second lieutenant of the 16th Infantry. From 1869 until he resigned in 1878, he was assigned to the 8th Infantry. (Heitman, 1:334)

CRAWFORD, Emmet (1844-86), native of Pennsylvania, enlisted as a Volunteer during the Civil War and was mustered out as first lieutenant. In 1866, he was commissioned as second lieutenant in the 27th Infantry. With the consolidation of regiments, he was assigned to the 3rd Cavalry at Camp Verde in 1871, moving with the regiment to the Platte where he served in the Big Horn and Yellowstone Expedition. Crawford was promoted to captain in 1879, and in 1882 was assigned to Camp Thomas, Arizona. Upon Crook's return to Arizona, he assigned Crawford as commander of Indian Scouts, and military superintendent at San Carlos. During the Geronimo Campaign, he was killed in a skirmish with Mexican militia. See also THREE BEARS. (Altshuler, 1991, 84-85; O'Neal, 95-96)

CREW. Bourke's mention of Lieutenant Crew probably refers to First Lt. Hanson H. Crews, 19th Infantry. (Heitman, 1:338)

DALLAS, Andrew James, military Indian agent at San Carlos, attended the U.S. Naval Academy from 1846 to 1851. In 1861, he served briefly as a private in a District of Columbia Volunteer unit, but in May of that year was commissioned as captain of the 12th Infantry. Dallas served with distinction and was breveted to major for gallant and meritorious service at Petersburg. He was promoted to major of the 23rd Infantry in 1869, and in that capacity served as agent until he was relieved by General O. O. Howard, and replaced by Dr. Milan Soulé in 1872. He retired at lieutenant colonel of the 22nd Infantry in 1880, and died four years later. See HOWARD, Oliver Otis. (Heitman, 1:351; Bancroft, 1889, 565)

DELANEY, Hayden (1845-90), native of Ohio, served as an enlisted man in the Volunteers during the Civil War. He was appointed second lieutenant of the 9th Infantry in 1867, and was breveted for service against the Paiute Indians of Oregon in 1868. He was breveted a second time for action in Col. Ranald Mackenzie's attack on the Cheyennes on November 25, 1876, during Crook's Powder River Expedition in Wyoming. He was promoted to captain in 1889, but suffered from lung hemorrhages. He died during sick leave. (Altshuler, 1991, 100; Bourke, 1980, 390-92)

DENNIS. No surgeon named Dennis is listed in Heitman.

DEWEES, Thomas Bull (d. 1886), native of Pennsylvania, enlisted in the 2nd Dragoons in 1858. When the regiment was redesignated 2nd Cavalry in 1861, he was promoted to second lieutenant, eventually attaining the rank of captain. In October 1881, he was named major of the 9th Cavalry. Bourke occasionally refers to him as "major," but no such brevet appears on his record. (Heitman, 1:370-71)

DODGE, Frederick Leighton (d. 1891), native of New Hampshire, enlisted in the Volunteers in 1862, and was appointed first lieutenant in 1865. In 1867, he was named second lieutenant of the 23rd Infantry in the Department of the Columbia. He was transferred to Fort Whipple, Arizona, in 1872, and promoted to first lieutenant a year later. His regiment transferred to the Department of the Platte in 1874. In 1889, he suffered a mental breakdown, and retired two years later. A few months after his retirement, he committed suicide. (Altshuler, 1991, 105)

DODGE, Richard Irving (1827-95), 1848 graduate of West Point, was a grand-nephew of Washington Irving who shared Irving's literary bent. Like Bourke, Dodge was a prolific diarist and observer as well as a naturalist, publishing several books on western wildlife and on Indian culture. Perhaps his best known are *The Black Hills: A Minute Description of the Routes, Scenery, Soil, Climate, Timber, Gold, Geology, Zoology, etc.* (1876), and *Our Wild Indians: Thirty Three Years' Personal Experience Among the Red Men of the Great West* (1882). He spent part of the period prior to the Civil War on the Texas frontier. Unlike many of his contemporaries, who transferred to the Volunteers to attain advancement during the war, Dodge remained in the Regular service, although he was breveted to colonel for faithful and meritorious service in the organization of the Volunteer armies. Promoted to the active rank of major in 1864, he spent much of the postwar era on the frontier. He was named lieutenant colonel of the 23rd Infantry in 1873, and promoted to colonel and aide-de-camp to General Sherman in 1882. He retired in 1891. Wayne R. Kime has edited Dodge's book, *The Plains of North America and Their Inhabitants* (1989), as well as his journals of the Black Hills Expedition, the Powder River Campaign, and service in Oklahoma. For all his work, it is remarkable that Dodge has received little mention in biographical encyclopedias. (Kime, 1997, 9; Heitman, 1:377)

DREW, George Augustus (1832-1921), native of Michigan, was appointed a captain of the volunteers in 1862, and promoted to major the following year. He was breveted for distinguished service in the Shenandoah and against Richmond. He was named second lieutenant of the 10th Infantry in 1866, and promoted to first lieutenant in 1868. A year later, he was reassigned to the 3rd Cavalry. He was transferred to Camp Bowie in 1871, and to the Department of the Platte the same year. He served as acting assistant quartermaster for the Big Horn Expedition under Reynolds in 1876. He retired as a captain in 1896, but was advanced to major in 1904. (Altshuler, 1991, 108-9)

EGAN, James (d. 1883) called Teddy by his friends, was a native of Ireland who enlisted in the 2nd Cavalry (later renumbered 5th Cavalry) in 1856. He served with distinction in the Civil War, and was named second lieutenant of the new 2nd Cavalry in 1863. He was promoted to captain in 1868, and in 1872 was among the officers assigned to the Grand Duke Tsarevich Alexis's tour of the Plains. Egan's initiative during Reynolds's Powder River fight prevented a confused, blundering situation from becoming potentially disastrous. He retired on disability in 1879, due to wounds and injuries received in the line of duty. (Thrapp, 1991, 1:454; Heitman, 1:399)

EMORY, William Helmsley, 1826 graduate of West Point, served in the Mexican War and was commissioner for the 1857 boundary survey with Mexico. During the Civil War he earned the brevet rank of major general. After the war, he spent much of his tenure as colonel of the 5th Cavalry on detached duty. Actual command of the regiment was exercised by Lt. Col. Eugene Carr. Emory retired on July 1, 1876, with a "graveyard" appointment as brigadier general. He died in 1887. See also CARR, Eugene Asa; MERRITT, Wesley. (King; Heitman, 1:405)

EVANS, Andrew Wallace (1829-1906), native of Maryland, graduated from West Point together with Crook in 1852. He served on the frontier until 1863, and was breveted for the battle of Valverde in 1862. He was named colonel of the 1st Maryland Cavalry in 1864, and was breveted for distinguished service in the Appomattox Campaign. In 1865, he was promoted to major of the 3rd Cavalry, and posted to the frontier. He went to Arizona in 1870, and served under Crook as departmental inspector general. Evans transferred to the Department of the Platte in 1876, and commanded a battalion during Crook's Big Horn and Yellowstone Expedition. He retired in 1883 as lieutenant colonel of the 7th Cavalry. (Altshuler, 1991, 123)

FERRIS, Samuel Peter, of Connecticut, entered West Point in 1857, and upon graduation was appointed second lieutenant of the 8th Infantry. He transferred to the Volunteers and served as colonel of the 28th Connecticut Infantry. In 1866, he was promoted to captain of the 30th Infantry, Regular Army, and transferred to the 23rd Infantry in 1869. He died in 1882. (Heitman, 1:417-18)

FETTERMAN, William Judd (ca. 1833-66), native of Connecticut, enlisted in the Union Army during the Civil War, and was breveted to lieutenant colonel for distinguished service. Commissioned as a captain in the 18th Infantry, he was posted to Fort Phil Kearny, Wyoming. On December 21, 1866, he led his men against a band of Indians, following a decoy party into a trap. Fetterman and his entire eighty-man command died in the fight. (O'Neal, 113-15; Brown)

FITZGERALD, Michael John, native of Ireland, served as an enlisted man first in the artillery then in the ordnance from 1856 to 1861. He served as hospital steward until 1863, when he was commissioned second lieutenant of the 9th Infantry. By 1876, he was captain. He retired in 1879. (Heitman, 1:423)

FOOTE, Morris Cooper, native of New York, enlisted in the Volunteers in 1861, and was promoted to lieutenant the following year. In 1866, he was appointed second lieutenant of the 9th Infantry, and in 1868, to first lieutenant. He was adjutant on the Dodge-Jenney Black Hills Expedition, and later served as regimental adjutant of the 9th from 1879 to 1883. He retired as brigadier general in 1903. (Heitman, 1:427)

FORSYTH, George Alexander "Sandy" (1837-1915) is best remembered for holding out with fifty men during a six-day siege by some 750 Sioux and Cheyenne warriors at Beecher's Island, Colorado, in 1867. A native of Illinois, he enlisted in the Volunteers in 1861, and was appointed first lieutenant later that year. He served as an aide to Maj. Gen. Philip H. Sheridan, and was breveted to brigadier general. In 1866, he was appointed major of the 9th Cavalry. After serving intermittently as secretary and aide to General Sheridan between 1869 and 1881, he was promoted to lieutenant colonel of the 4th Cavalry. He served in Arizona from 1884 to 1887. A year later, he was suspended for three years on half pay for financial irregularities. He retired in 1890, and wrote two books, *The Story of the Soldier* and *Thrilling Days of Army Life.* (Altshuler, 1991, 133-34; Lamar, 381; Thrapp, 1991, 1:509-10)

FOSTER, James Evans Heron (1848-83), native of Pennsylvania, enlisted in the Volunteers in 1864 and was discharged in 1865. He was commissioned second lieutenant in the 3rd Cavalry in 1873, and distinguished himself in the Rosebud Fight. He was promoted to first lieutenant in 1879, but tuberculosis forced him onto the inactive list in 1881. (Thrapp, 1991, 1:511)

FOWLER, Joshua Lounsberry (d. 1889), entered West Point in 1864, and upon graduation was commissioned second lieutenant of the 2nd Cavalry. He was promoted to first lieutenant in 1869, and served as regimental quartermaster from 1874 to 1880. He was major of the 10th Cavalry at the time of his death. (Heitman, 1:433)

FUREY, John Vincent, of New York, enlisted as a private in the Volunteers in 1861. Taking a discharge in 1862, he reentered the Volunteers two years later as quartermaster captain. He was breveted to major of the Volunteers for meritorious service in the Quarter Master Department during the Civil War. Furey was appointed captain and assistant quartermaster of the Regular Army in 1867. Although Altshuler (*Cavalry Yellow & Infantry Blue*) does not list him among the officers who served in Arizona, he was Crook's quartermaster both there and later in the Platte. He retired in 1903 as brigadier general. (Heitman, 1:441)

GIBBON, John (1827-96), known to the Indians as "No Hip Bone" or "One Who Limps" because of a crippling wound he received at Gettysburg, was an 1847 graduate of West Point. During the late 1840s and 1850s, he served in Mexico, the frontier, and in the Seminole campaigns in Florida. During the Civil War, he commanded the "Iron Brigade" at Second Manassas and in Maryland, ultimately rising to the rank of major general of Volunteers. After the war, he was appointed colonel of the 36th Infantry, and in 1869, of the 7th Infantry. With Brig. Gen. Alfred Terry, he relieved Maj. Marcus Reno at the Little Bighorn, and discovered the remains of Custer's column. He also participated in the Nez Percé War, and in 1885, was appointed brigadier general. He retired in 1891. (Warner, 171-72; Thrapp, 1991, 2:551-52)

GIBSON, Joseph Ruff, of Pennsylvania, was appointed assistant surgeon in 1862. He was breveted to captain and major for service during the Civil War, and to lieutenant colonel in 1866 for meritorious and distinguished service during a cholera outbreak at Harts Island, in New York Harbor. He was a lieutenant colonel and departmental surgeon general at the time of his retirement in 1895. (Heitman, 1:454)

GILLIS, James (d. 1898), of the District of Columbia, was appointed second lieutenant of the 5th Artillery in 1861. In 1864 he became captain and assistant quartermaster, a position he held at the time of Bourke's writing. He was colonel and assistant quartermaster general at the time of his death. (Heitman, 1:457)

GILMORE, Alexander (d. 1894), of New Jersey, was appointed chaplain in 1870, and was post chaplain at Fort Whipple at the time of Bourke's writing. He retired in 1879. (Heitman, 1:458)

GRIFFITH, George R., of Ohio, was appointed first lieutenant of the 9th Infantry in 1865. He resigned in 1877. (Heitman, 1:479)

GRUMMOND, George Washington (d. 1866), native of Michigan, entered the army as a captain of Volunteers. He was breveted to lieutenant colonel for service in the battle of Bentonville, North Carolina. In 1866, he was commissioned second lieutenant of the 18th Infantry, and posted to Fort Phil Kearny. He died in the Fetterman Massacre of December 21, 1866. See FETTERMAN, William Judd; BROWN, Frederick H. (See Brown; O'Neal, 127-29; Heitman, 1:482)

HALL, Christopher Tomkins, entered West Point in 1864, and upon graduation was appointed second lieutenant of the 2nd Cavalry. In 1869, he was promoted to first lieutenant. He resigned in 1880, and died in 1887. (Heitman, 1:488)

HAMILTON, John Morrison (1839-98), native of Ontario, enlisted as a Volunteer in New York in 1861. He attained the rank of first lieutenant with a brevet to captain during the Civil War. In 1867, he was commissioned as captain of the 39th Infantry in 1867. In 1870, he was assigned to the 5th Cavalry, and was posted to Camp McDowell, Arizona, in January 1872. He was breveted to major for gallantry in action against the Tonto Apaches in the foothills of the

Tortilla Mountains on January 16, 1873. After the 5th was reassigned to the Department of the Platte in 1876, he participated in Col. Ranald Mackenzie's roundup of Red Cloud's band at Chadron Creek, Nebraska, and the attack on the Cheyenne camp during Crook's Powder River Expedition. He was lieutenant colonel of the 9th Cavalry when he was killed in the Battle of San Juan Hill in Cuba in 1898. (Altshuler, 1991, 152-53; O'Neal, 130-31; Heitman, 1:493)

HARTSUFF, Albert, entered the service as assistant surgeon in 1861, and was promoted to major and surgeon in 1876. He was breveted to captain and major for faithful and meritorious service during the Civil War, and to lieutenant colonel in 1866, for meritorious and distinguished service during a cholera epidemic in New Orleans. He was colonel and assistant surgeon general at the time of his retirement in 1901. (Heitman, 1:507)

HAWLEY, William (1838-1914), a native of Washington, D.C., enlisted in the Volunteers in April 1861, but was commissioned first lieutenant of the 3rd Cavalry four months later. He was promoted to captain in 1864, and in 1870, was posted to Camp Verde, Arizona. He participated in Crook's campaigns in the Platte in 1876, including the notorious Horse-Meat March. This march undermined his health, and he retired for disability in 1879. His retirement was upgraded to lieutenant colonel in 1904. (Altshuler, 1991, 161)

HAY, Charles (1840-92), was first lieutenant of Company C, 23rd Infantry, at Camp McDowell, Arizona, until 1874, when his company was transferred to the Department of the Platte. He was promoted to captain in 1888. He died in Denver. (Altshuler, 1991, 161)

HAZEN, William Babcock (1830-87), an 1855 graduate of West Point, served with distinction against the Indians in California, Oregon, and Texas, and was seriously wounded in action with Comanches in 1859. This wound, aggravated by diabetes, ultimately caused his death almost thirty years later. He was breveted to major general for his service in the Civil War. In 1867, he was assigned to the Southern Military District in charge of the Indian tribes in Kansas and Oklahoma. As colonel of the 6th Infantry, he commanded Fort Buford, North Dakota, from 1872 to 1877. In 1880, he was promoted to brigadier general and chief of the Army Signal Corps. An outspoken critic and reformer of the army system, he made many enemies. (O'Neal, 142-44; Kroeker)

HENRY, Guy Vernor (1839-99), the son of an army officer, was born at Fort Smith, Arkansas. Upon graduating from West Point in 1861, he was appointed to the 1st Artillery. He distinguished himself in the Civil War, earning brevets as colonel of the Regular Army and brigadier general of the Volunteers. He rejoined the 1st Artillery as captain, and in December 1870, transferred to the 3rd Cavalry which was posted at Camp McDowell, Arizona. In July 1871, Henry led an expedition from Camp Apache to McDowell, which established the efficiency of Indian scouts in Apache campaign. During the battle of the Rosebud in 1876, he was severely wounded in the face, losing the sight in his left eye. He recovered and as major general of Volunteers, he commanded the Department of Puerto Rico following the Spanish-American War. He was promoted to brigadier general of Volunteers in 1898, and assumed that rank in the Regular Army following his discharge from the Volunteers in June 1899. He died four months later. (Altshuler, 1991, 164-66; O'Neal, 145-46)

HEYL, Charles Heath (1849-1926), native of Pennsylvania, was commissioned lieutenant of the 23rd Infantry in 1873, and posted to Camp Verde a year later. The same year, after distinguishing himself in combat, he moved with his regiment to the Platte where, with three men, he routed a party of hostile Indians near Fort Hartsuff, Nebraska. Heyl was breveted to first lieutenant for gallantry in action against Indians on the Verde River in Arizona in 1874, and against Indians near Grace Creek, Nebraska, in 1876. He was awarded the Medal of Honor for the fight near Fort Hartsuff. All awards were conferred in 1890. He retired as colonel in 1904, but was recalled to active duty in 1918-19. (Altshuler, 1991, 167; Heitman, 1:527)

HOFFMAN, William Edwin, entered the service as first lieutenant of Volunteers in 1862, and was promoted to captain a year later. In 1867, he was commissioned as second lieutenant of the 31st Infantry, and in 1870, was assigned to the 4th Infantry. He retired as captain in 1889. (Heitman, 1991, 1:527)

HOWARD, Oliver Otis (1830-1909), native of Maine, graduated from Bowdoin College and West Point, spent more than half his antebellum service at West Point. Known as "the praying general," he was a devout Congregationalist, and at one point considered resigning from the army to enter the ministry. With the outbreak of the Civil War, he resigned his commission as first lieutenant in the regular army, and became a colonel of Volunteers, and was breveted to brigadier general in September 1861. He lost his right arm in the battle of Seven Pines. He finished the war as major general of Volunteers, and brevet major general of the Regular Army with the active rank of brigadier general. He headed the Bureau of Freedmen, Refugees, and Abandoned Lands from 1865 to 1872, after which he was appointed special Indian commissioner. Among his accomplishments was negotiating an end to the Cochise War. He later served as commander of the Department of Columbia, where his high-handedness helped provoke the Nez Percé War. After a period as superintendent of West Point and commander of the Department of the Platte, he was promoted to major general in command of the Military Division of the Pacific, and subsequently the Military Division of the Atlantic. He retired in 1894. He also founded Howard University, serving as its first president. See also COCHISE; JEFFORDS, Thomas Jonathan; WHITMAN, Royal Emerson. (Warner, 237-38; Thrapp, 1991, 2:683-84)

HUNTINGTON, Henry Dunstan, entered West Point in 1871, and was commissioned second lieutenant of the 2nd Cavalry upon graduation in 1875. He was first lieutenant at the time of his death in 1886. (Heitman, 1:558)

JOHNSON, John Burgess (1847-96), native of Massachusetts, was named second lieutenant of the 6th U.S. Colored Infantry in 1863. In 1870, he joined the 3rd Cavalry as first lieutenant in Arizona, remaining there until his regiment was withdrawn in 1871. He participated in Crook's expeditions of 1876. He was a captain at the time of his death. (Altshuler, 1991, 181)

JOHNSTON, John Lloyd (1841-1922), native of Philadelphia, entered the Volunteers as a corporal in 1861. He was named first lieutenant a year later, and mustered out as captain. He was breveted for gallantry at Petersburg, Virginia. Johnston was commissioned first lieutenant of the 21st Infantry in 1866, and served as post quartermaster at Camp McDowell and later at Camp Lowell. He left Arizona with the regiment in 1872. (Altshuler, 1991, 182)

JONES, Roger, entered West Point in 1847, and upon graduation was breveted to second lieutenant of the Mounted Riflemen. After moving up through the grades, in 1861, he was appointed major and assistant inspector general, and in 1867, lieutenant colonel AIG.

At the time of his death in 1889, he was brigadier general and inspector general. (Heitman, 1:582)

JORDAN, William Henry, of Ohio, entered West Point in 1855, and upon graduation was breveted to second lieutenant of the 2nd Infantry. He was commissioned second lieutenant of the 9th Infantry in 1861, and by the end of the Civil War was major of the 8th California Infantry. In regular service he had risen to captain of the 9th Infantry, and at the time of Bourke's writing, commanded Camp Robinson. He retired in 1891 as colonel of the 19th Infantry. (Heitman, 1:584)

KAUTZ, Augustus Valentine (1828-1895) was a native of Germany brought to the United States as an infant. After serving with an Ohio infantry regiment during the Mexican War, he was appointed to West Point where he graduated with Crook in 1852. They traveled together to their first assignment in California. During the Civil War, he rose to brigadier general of Volunteers, and brevet major general in the regular army. As commander of the Department of Arizona, Kautz was the opposite of Crook. Suffering from ill-health and domestic problems, he rarely exercised decisive command. Indian depredations increased while Kautz became embroiled in disputes with the territorial government and internal controversies within his regiment. In 1878, he and his regiment were transferred to Angel Island, California. Kautz served briefly again in Arizona in a subordinate role in 1886. He retired as a brigadier general in 1892. (Altshuler, 1991, 184-87)

KEYES, Edward Livingston (1843-1917), which Bourke sometimes spelled "Keys," native of Massachusetts, joined the 5th Cavalry as a second lieutenant in 1872. During Crook's 1872-73 campaign, he was recommended twice for brevets. He later served in the Department of the Platte during the Great Sioux War. He was court-martialed and dismissed for drunkenness in 1877, studied medicine, and became a prominent surgeon. (Altshuler, 1991, 191)

KING, Albert Douglas (1844-1900), native of Ohio, enlisted in the 2nd California Cavalry in 1864. He was commissioned second lieutenant of the 3rd Cavalry in 1867, and was posted to Camp McDowell in 1871. He transferred to the Department of the Platte, and served in the Big Horn and Yellowstone Expedition. Returning to Arizona in 1882, he scouted extensively against the Apaches. He was retired for ill-health in 1891. (Altshuler, 1991, 191-92)

KINGSBURY, Frederick William (d. 1897), entered West Point in 1866, and upon graduation was commissioned second lieutenant of the 2nd Cavalry. He was promoted to first lieutenant in 1880, and was captain at the time of his death. (Heitman, 1:601)

LAWSON, Joseph (ca. 1821-81), native of Ireland, joined the Volunteers as a second lieutenant in 1862. He was commissioned as second lieutenant of the 3rd Cavalry in February 1866, and promoted to first lieutenant five months later. He was posted to Camp Date Creek from 1870 to 1871, when the 3rd transferred to the Department of the Platte. He participated in the Big Horn and Yellowstone Expedition. During the Milk River fight in Colorado in 1879, command devolved on Lawson after Maj. Thomas T. Thornburgh was killed, and he is credited with averting a massacre. (Altshuler, 1991, 198)

LEE, Jesse Matlock (1843-1926), native of Indiana, enlisted in the Volunteers in November 1861, and was commissioned second lieutenant eleven months later. He finished the Civil War as a captain, and was appointed an infantry officer. By the mid-1870s, he was first lieutenant of the 9th Infantry at Camps Sheridan and Robinson, Nebraska. He reported that he was in the Powder River fight in March 1876, but this was purely a cavalry action with no infantry involved. Bourke does not mention him until a visit to Camp Robinson, after the expedition ended. In 1877, Lee convinced Crazy Horse to accompany him to Camp Robinson. Upon arrival, however, Crazy Horse was placed under arrest over Lee's protests, and in the ensuing fight, the chief was mortally wounded. In 1879, Lee, now captain, was recorder for the board inquiring into the conduct of Maj. Marcus A. Reno during the Battle of the Little Bighorn. He retired as a major general in 1907. (Thrapp, 1991, 2:832)

LEIB, Edward Henry (ca. 1839-92), native of Pennsylvania, was commissioned second lieutenant in the 2nd Cavalry in April 1861, and promoted to first lieutenant six weeks later. He was promoted to captain in 1863, and served with distinction in the Civil War. He was assigned to Camp Grant in 1872. He also took part in the Big Horn and Yellowstone Expedition in the Department of the Platte. He was dismissed in 1877 for unspecified reasons. (Altshuler, 1991, 201-02; Heitman, 1:627)

LEMLY, Henry Rowan, of North Carolina, entered West Point in 1868, and upon graduation was appointed second lieutenant of the

2nd Cavalry. He served with Crook on the Big Horn and Yellowstone Expedition in the 3rd Cavalry, and wrote an account, "The Fight on the Rosebud," that later was included in the Papers of the Order of the Indian Wars. He was a captain of the 7th Artillery at the time of his retirement in 1899. (Heitman, 1:627)

LEUTTWITZ, Adolphus H. von (d. 1887), native of Prussia, entered the service as a private of Volunteers in 1862, and was commissioned second lieutenant the same year. He finished the Civil War as captain. In 1867, he was commissioned second lieutenant of the 3rd Cavalry. Three years later, he was cashiered as first lieutenant, but reinstated to former date of rank in 1874. Leuttwitz served in Crook's Big Horn and Yellowstone Expedition, and lost a leg in the Slim Buttes. He retired in 1879. Bourke sometimes spelled the name "Leuttewitz." (Heitman, 1:989; Robinson, 2001, 196)

LOCKWOOD, James Booth (1852-84), native of Maryland, was commissioned second lieutenant of the 23rd Infantry in 1873, and was posted to Camp McDowell briefly in 1874 before being transferred to Nebraska. He died during an expedition attempting to reach the North Pole. (Altshuler, 1991, 204)

LONDON, Robert (ca. 1850-92), native of North Carolina, was assigned as a second lieutenant of the 5th Cavalry after graduating from West Point in 1873. He was posted to Camp Lowell, and later to Camp Apache, where he was recommended twice for brevets for distinguished service during scouting expeditions. He also served at San Carlos and Camp Apache. During the Great Sioux War, he participated in the Big Horn and Yellowstone Expedition. (Altshuler, 1991, 204-05)

LOSHE, Charles Frederick (d. 1878), native of Germany, served in the enlisted ranks of the infantry from 1858 to 1863, after which he was first lieutenant of the Volunteers. He was commissioned second lieutenant of the 8th Infantry in 1865, and promoted to first lieutenant the following year. He resigned in 1875. (Heitman, 1:642)

LUDINGTON, Elisha Harrison (d. 1891), was appointed captain of the 17th Infantry in 1861, and major and assistant adjutant general in 1864. He served with distinction in the Civil War, earning brevets to major for gallantry, lieutenant colonel for meritorious service, and colonel for meritorious service in his department. He retired in 1879. (Heitman, 1:646)

LUHN, Gerhard Luke, native of Germany, enlisted in the 6th Infantry in 1853, and in 1863 was commissioned as second lieutenant of the 4th Infantry. He was promoted to first lieutenant in 1864, and captain in 1875. He wrote a diary and letters on Crook's Big Horn and Yellowstone Expedition. He retired in 1895. (Heitman, 1:646-47)

LYNCH, Edward (1831-1908), native of Ireland, enlisted in the 3rd Infantry in New York in 1858. He was appointed second lieutenant in the Veteran Reserve Corps in 1863, and served with distinction during the Civil War. After postwar service as a senior non-commissioned officer, he was commissioned second lieutenant in the 33rd Infantry, which was consolidated as the 8th Infantry in 1869. He served in Arizona from 1874 to 1878. (Altshuler, 1991, 207-08)

MC CALEB, Thomas Sidney (1853-1934), 1875 graduate of West Point, was appointed to second lieutenant of the 9th Infantry, serving in the Department of the Platte during the Great Sioux War. He later served in Arizona, the Spanish-American War, and the Philippine Insurrection, and retired as major in 1902. (Altshuler, 1991, 208)

MACKENZIE, Ranald Slidell (1840-89), called "Bad Hand" or "Three Fingers" by the Indians because of an injury received to his right hand at Petersburg, was an 1861 graduate of West Point. He served with distinction in the Civil War, rising to the brevet ranks of brigadier general of the Regular Army and major general of Volunteers. In 1867, he was appointed colonel of the 41st Infantry, and in 1870, he was transferred to the 4th Cavalry. He developed the 4th into a mobile assault force, fighting the Southern Plains Indians with their own hit-and-run tactics. During the Red River War of 1874-75, he smashed a large Indian camp in Palo Duro Canyon, Texas, destroying their lodges, food stores, and pony herds, a stratagem he would repeat under Crook in Wyoming. Nevertheless, he was mentally unbalanced, which would become increasingly evident during the Great Sioux War. Promoted to brigadier general in 1882, he was institutionalized for insanity in December 1883, and invalided out of the army the following year. (Pierce, and Robinson, 1993)

MAGRUDER, David Lynn, was appointed assistant surgeon in 1850, and in 1862 promoted to surgeon major. He was breveted to

lieutenant colonel for faithful and meritorious service during the
Civil War. He retired as a colonel in 1889. (Heitman, 1:684)

MASON, Charles Winder, was commissioned as second lieutenant in the 13th Infantry in 1875, and transferred to the 4th Infantry
later that year. (Heitman, 1:694)

MASON, Julius Wilmot (1835-82), native of Pennsylvania, was
commissioned as second lieutenant in the 2nd Cavalry (subsequently
renumbered as the 5th Cavalry), in April 1861. He earned two brevets in the Civil War, and emerged from the war with the active
rank of captain. He was posted to Camp Hualpai in 1872, and was
recommended for two additional brevets for the 1872-73 campaign.
As commander of Camp Verde, and acting agent of the reservation,
he made substantial improvements. Mason was promoted to major
of the 3rd Cavalry in the Department of the Platte in July 1876, but
remained with the 5th until the end of the Big Horn and Yellowstone
Expedition. He joined the 3rd at Camp Robinson, Nebraska, in October 1876. He returned to Arizona in 1882, as commander of Fort
Huachuca, where he died on December 19 of that year. (Altshuler,
1991, 223-24)

MEARS, Frederick, entered the service as a lieutenant colonel of
Volunteers in 1861. Later that year, he was mustered out and accepted a commission as second lieutenant of the 9th Infantry. He
was promoted to captain in 1863, and breveted to major for faithful
and meritorious service. He was lieutenant colonel of the 4th Infantry at the time of his death in 1892. (Heitman, 1:700-01)

MEINHOLD, Charles (ca. 1827-77), native of Berlin, enlisted in
the army 1851, possibly with previous military experience in Germany. He served in Texas and New Mexico until his discharge in
1862, after which he served as an officer of the 3rd Cavalry. During
the Civil War, he distinguished himself in New Mexico, and during
the Vicksburg campaign, and was promoted to captain in 1866. Sent
to Arizona in 1871, he investigated the Wickenburg Stagecoach
Massacre the following year, He also served in Crook's Big Horn and
Yellowstone Expedition in 1876. (Altshuler, 1991, 226)

MERRITT, Wesley (1834-1910), native of New York, was an 1860
graduate of West Point. He served with distinction as a cavalry leader
during the Civil War, rising to the rank of brevet major general of
Volunteers. After the war, he was appointed lieutenant colonel of
the 9th Cavalry, spending much of his time on the Texas frontier

albeit in largely administrative functions. When Merritt's promotion to colonel of the 5th Cavalry was announced, Lt. Col. Carr presumed that he would continue to exercise de facto command while Merritt, like Emory, remained on detached duty. When Merritt announced his determination to assume active command, Carr (who was yet unaware of the disaster that had befallen Custer) wrote his wife, "It seems curious that the government should find it necessary to spend huge amounts of money & some blood to teach Terry, Crook, Gibbon, Merritt & others how to fight these prairie Indians when there are Custer & myself who know how to do it and are ready & willing." Upon assuming command, however, Merritt quickly made up for his lack of actual Indian fighting experience, distinguishing himself in the Great Sioux War, the Nez Percé War and the White River Ute Uprising. During the Spanish-American War, he commanded U.S. troops in the Philippines. He retired in 1900 as a major general. See also CARR, Eugene Asa; EMORY, William Helmsley. (O'Neal, 166-67; Heitman, 1:706; quote from Carr to Mary Carr, July 3, 1876, Carr Papers)

MICHLER, Francis (1849-1901), native of New York, was assigned to the 5th Cavalry after graduating from West Point in 1870. He was posted to Camp Hualpai in 1872, and took to the field almost immediately. He was commended in departmental general orders five times, and later received brevets for gallantry at Muchos Cañones and Tonto Creek. In 1873 he was appointed aide to Maj. Gen. John M. Schofield, and later served as aide to Maj. Gen. Nelson A. Miles. He was promoted to major shortly before his death. (Altshuler, 1991, 227-28)

MILLS, Anson (1834-1924), native of Indiana, is perhaps most famous as the designer of the Mills cartridge belt, which became the standard equipment of many of the world's armies, and made him wealthy. Although a resident of Texas at the outbreak of the Civil War, Mills departed for Washington, D.C., where he was commissioned first lieutenant of the 18th Infantry. He received three brevets during the war, rising to major for gallant and meritorious service at the Battle of Chickamauga. He emerged with the active rank of captain. He transferred to the 3rd Cavalry in December 1870, and was posted to Arizona the following spring. In 1871, he and his company were transferred to the Department of the Platte, where he figured prominently in Crook's Big Horn and Yellowstone

Expedition. He later was breveted for his part in the fight at Slim Buttes on September 9, 1876. He retired in 1897 as brigadier general, and in 1918, published his memoirs, *My Story*. (Altshuler, 1991, 231-32; Heitman, 1:713; Mills)

MIX, John, of New York, enlisted in the 2nd Dragoons in 1852; with its reorganization as the 2nd Cavalry in 1861, he was commissioned second lieutenant. He was major of the 9th Cavalry at the time of his death in 1881. (Heitman, 1:718)

MONTGOMERY, Robert Hugh (1838-1905), native of Philadelphia, enlisted in the 2nd Cavalry (later renumbered to the 5th) in 1860, earning two brevets during the Civil War, and spending the last twenty months of the war as a prisoner. He was promoted to first lieutenant in 1865, and to captain in 1870. He was posted to Arizona in 1872, and served with distinction during the 1872-73 campaign, earning brevets as major for gallantry at Muchos Cañones on September 25, 1872, and during a scout through the Tonto Basin in November and December 1874. During the notorious Horse Meat March of 1876, his company lost fewer horses than any other in the 5th, largely because of his attention to training. He retired as major of the 10th Cavalry in 1891. (Altshuler, 1991, 235; Heitman, 1:720)

MOORE, Alexander (1835-1910), native of Ireland, was appointed first lieutenant of Volunteers in October 1861, and was breveted to major for service during the Civil War. In 1867, he was commissioned captain of the 38th Infantry, and posted to New Mexico, where he served on scouting expeditions. In 1870, he was assigned to the 3rd Cavalry, joining it in Arizona in early 1871. Moore aroused Crook's ire in 1871, when he moved his troops openly across a plain, spoiling the chance to surprise an Apache raiding party. His failure to act decisively during the Reynolds Fight on the Powder River in March 1876, led to his court-martial and suspension. He resigned in 1879, and became a wealthy rancher. (Altshuler, 1991, 235-36; Robinson, 2001, 110)

MORGAN, Charles Hale (1834-75), native of New York, graduated from West Point in 1857. He participated in Col. Albert Sidney Johnston's Mormon campaign of 1859. During the Civil War, he served under Maj. Gen. Winfield S. Hancock as chief of artillery and chief of staff. He finished the war as brevet brigadier general, and reverted to the active rank of captain. He later was promoted to major of the 4th Artillery, and was stationed at Fort Alcatraz, California, at the time of his death. (Warner, 331-32)

MORTON, Charles (1846-1914), native of Ohio, enlisted in the Volunteers in 1861. After the war, he entered West Point, graduating in 1869. He was appointed second lieutenant of the 3rd Cavalry, and served with distinction in Arizona in 1870 and 1871. He participated in the Big Horn and Yellowstone Expedition in 1876. He retired as brigadier general in 1910. (Altshuler, 1991, 239-40)

MUNN, Curtis Emerson, joined the Volunteers as a hospital steward in 1861, and in 1863 was appointed assistant surgeon. He was commissioned as assistant surgeon in 1868, and served in the Crook-Reynolds Big Horn Expedition. He was a surgeon major when he retired in 1900. He died in 1902. (Altshuler, 1991, 239-40)

MUNSON, Jacob Frederick, of New York, enlisted in the Volunteers in 1861, and was promoted to second lieutenant in 1863. After distinguished service in the Civil War, he was commissioned second lieutenant in the 6th Infantry, and soon promoted to first lieutenant. He retired as a captain in 1896. (Heitman, 1:736)

MUNSON, Samuel, enlisted as a sergeant in the Volunteers in 1861, but was shortly commissioned second lieutenant. Later that year he accepted a commission in the Regular Army as second lieutenant of the 9th Infantry. In 1865, he was promoted to captain. He died in 1887. (Heitman, 1:736)

NELSON, Anderson D., entered West Point in 1837, and upon graduation was breveted second lieutenant of the 6th Infantry. In 1842, he received an active appointment to the same rank. He had a distinguished career during the Civil War, finishing with a brevet as colonel. He was appointed lieutenant colonel of the 5th Infantry in 1868, and assigned to the 12th Infantry in 1870. He retired in 1879, and died in 1885. (Heitman, 1:743)

NICKERSON, Azor Howitt (1837-1910) served on General Crook's staff from 1866 to 1878. A native of Ohio, he joined the Union Army as a second lieutenant of Volunteers in 1861. He was breveted to major for gallantry at Antietam and Gettysburg, receiving a near-fatal chest wound in the latter battle. He entered the Regular Army in 1866. His wound left him in frail health and, although he tried to accompany Crook on his Indian campaigns, sometimes the surgeons would declare him unfit for field duty. He attempted to retire in 1882, but a scandal over a fraudulently obtained divorce from his second wife prompted the War Department to void his retirement. He resigned in 1883 to avoid court-martial. Nickerson later wrote an essay, "Major General George Crook and the Indians," which, although never published in its entirety, has become an integral part of the Crook hagiography. (Crook to Rutherford B. Hayes, January 4, 1872, R.B. Hayes Papers, Crook Collection; Heitman, 1:747-48; Altshuler, 1991, 244-45)

NORTON, Charles Carroll, entered West Point in 1870, and upon graduation was commissioned second lieutenant of the 1st Cavalry. He resigned in 1879. (Heitman, 1:752)

NOYES, Henry Erastus (1839-1919), native of Maine, graduated from West Point in 1861 and was commissioned second lieutenant of the 2nd Dragoons (later redesignated as 2nd Cavalry). During the Civil War, he earned two brevets, and finished the war as a captain. His failure to provide adequate support during the Reynolds fight on the Powder River in 1876 led to a reprimand. He participated in the Big Horn and Yellowstone Expedition the same year. He retired as colonel of the 2nd Cavalry in 1901, and his retirement was upgraded to brigadier general in 1904. (Altshuler, 1991, 249; Robinson, 2001, 171-72)

OGILBY, Frederick Darley (1841-77), native of New Jersey, was commissioned first lieutenant of the 15th Infantry in 1861. He earned two brevets during the Civil War, and in 1864 was promoted to captain. In 1869 he was posted to the 8th Infantry, which was sent to Arizona in 1874. He was recommended for another brevet for service in scouting expeditions. He died of pneumonia at Camp Apache. Bourke sometimes spelled the name "Ogleby."(Altshuler, 1991, 253)

ORD, Edward Otho Cresap (1818-83), 1839 graduate of West Point, served in the Seminole Wars in Florida, and in California during the Mexican War. He then served in the Pacific Northwest off and on until 1861, when he was appointed brigadier general of Volunteers and ordered East. When the war ended, he was in command of the Army of the James and the Department of North Carolina. Ord was appointed brigadier general of the Regular Army in 1866 and commanded the Department of the Platte until relieved by Crook. He retired as a major general in 1881, and died of yellow fever in Havana two years later. (Warner, 349-50)

PALMER, Innis Newton (1824-1900), native of New York, was an 1846 graduate of West Point. He was assigned to the Mounted Riflemen (later redesignated 3rd Cavalry), and served with distinction in the Mexican War. He spent much of the period between the Mexican and Civil Wars on the frontier. At the close of the Civil War he was brevet major general of Volunteers, and brevet brigadier general of the Regular Army. During the Great Sioux War, he was colonel of the 2nd Cavalry. He retired in 1879. (Thrapp, 1991, 3:1104)

PARKHURST, Charles Dyer (1849-1931), native of Massachusetts, graduated from West Point in 1872 and was posted to the 5th Cavalry at Camp Date Creek. He participated in the 1872-73 campaign, and was commended in departmental orders and recommended for a brevet. In 1875, he was transferred to Kansas, and a year later, participated in Crook's Big Horn and Yellowstone Expedition. He received a Silver Star for gallantry during the Spanish-American War. Parkhurst retired as colonel of the Coast Artillery. (Altshuler, 1991, 257-58)

PATZKI, Julius Herman, native of Prussia, enlisted as a private in the Volunteers in 1863, and was appointed assistant surgeon the following year. He was appointed assistant surgeon of the Regular Army in 1867, and retired in 1892 as surgeon major. Dr. Patzki's moment in history came in 1871 when, as post surgeon of Fort Richardson, Texas, he examined the bodies of the victims of the Warren Wagon Train Massacre. The massacre led to the trial and imprisonment of two Kiowa chiefs, and permanent divisions within the Kiowas. (Heitman, 1:776; Nye, 131)

PAUL, Augustus Chouteau (1842-1904), native of New York, was appointed captain in the Volunteers, and served with distinction in the Civil War. In 1869, he was commissioned as second lieutenant of the 3rd Cavalry, and was posted to Arizona a year later. He remained in Arizona until December 1871, when his regiment was sent to the Department of the Platte. He resigned in 1881 following court-martial. (Altshuler, 1991, 258-59)

PEALE, James Thompson, was commissioned second lieutenant in the Volunteer cavalry in 1862, and finished the Civil War as a brevet lieutenant colonel of Volunteers. He entered the 2nd Cavalry as second lieutenant in 1866, and shortly was promoted to first lieutenant. He attained captain in 1875, and was dismissed in 1880. (Heitman, 1:778)

PEARSON, Daniel Crosby, of Massachusetts, entered West Point in 1865, and upon graduation was commissioned second lieutenant of the 2nd Cavalry. (Heitman, 1:779)

PEASE, William Barrett, of Connecticut, enlisted in the Volunteers in 1862, and in 1863 was appointed second lieutenant of the 8th U.S. Colored Infantry. He was commissioned as first lieutenant of the 11th Infantry in 1867, and later assigned to the 9th Infantry. He retired as captain in 1887. (Heitman, 1:779)

PERRY, Alexander James, of Connecticut, entered West Point in 1847, and upon graduation was breveted to second lieutenant of the 2nd Artillery. The rank was made active in 1852. After the Civil War broke out, he was made captain and assistant quartermaster, and finished the war as colonel and quartermaster. He was breveted as major, lieutenant colonel, colonel, and brigadier general for faithful and meritorious service. In 1866, he was appointed quartermaster major, and lieutenant colonel and departmental quartermaster general in 1875. He retired as colonel in 1892. Perry is listed in Appendix 1 of Warner's *Generals in Blue* as "breveted as. . .brigadier general for services rendered during the Civil War, but not appointed to full rank." (Heitman, 1:785; Warner, 591)

PITCHER, William Lewis (1852-1930), native of Texas, was different from most officers in that he attended the Naval Academy for two years, rather than West Point. He was commissioned as second lieutenant of the 10th Cavalry in 1871, but transferred to the 8th Infantry in June 1872. He was posted to Arizona in October of that year, and remained there until 1877. He retired as colonel of the 27th Infantry. (Altshuler, 1991, 263-64)

POLLOCK, Otis Wheeler (1833-1916), native of Pennsylvania, was appointed first lieutenant of Volunteers in 1861, and promoted to captain the following year. In 1866, he was commissioned as lieutenant of the 14th Infantry which was later amalgamated into the 23rd. Promoted to captain, he served in Arizona in 1873-74, and then in the Department of the Platte, serving in Crook's campaigns during the Great Sioux War. He retired as a major in 1897, upgraded to lieutenant colonel in 1904. (Altshuler, 1991, 264)

PORTER, Charles (1838-1902), native of Ireland, enlisted in the 5th Infantry in 1858. Working his way up through ranks, he was first lieutenant when he transferred to the 8th Infantry in 1870. He was promoted to captain in 1872, and posted to Arizona two years later. He served with distinction in the Apache campaigns, and later was breveted. He left Arizona in 1878. He retired as lieutenant colonel of the 22nd Infantry in 1898. (Altshuler, 1991, 266)

POWELL, James W. (d. 1884), native of Ohio, enlisted in the Volunteers in 1861, and was promoted to lieutenant soon afterwards. In 1866, he was named second lieutenant of the 15th Infantry. Eventually, in 1869, he joined the 8th Infantry as first lieutenant. He was assigned to Arizona from 1874 to 1878, and was a captain at the time of his death. (Altshuler, 1991, 267)

POWELL, Junius. The only Junius Powell listed in Heitman was appointed assistant surgeon in 1878, beyond the range of this volume. This may be a typographical error on the part of Heitman, or Bourke may be referring to a contract surgeon named Junius Powell. It is also possible that Dr. Junius Powell, contract surgeon, was later commissioned as an army surgeon. (Heitman, 1:803)

POWELL, William Henry (1838-1901), native of Washington, D.C., enlisted in the District of Columbia Militia in 1861, and was commissioned as an officer of the 4th Infantry the same year. He was captain in the 4th when he served on Crook's Big Horn and Yellowstone Expedition. He retired in 1899 as colonel of the 9th Infantry. He was the author of several professional and historical works about the army. (Thrapp, 1991, 3:1169-70)

PRATT, Edward Barton (1853-1923), native of Virginia, joined the 23rd Infantry as second lieutenant in 1872, and was posted to Arizona from 1873 until 1874, when his regiment was transferred to the Department of the Platte. He served in Crook's Powder River Expedition of 1876-77. Pratt retired as brigadier general in 1909. (Altshuler, 1991, 267)

PRICE, George Frederick (1835-88), native of New York City, joined the 2nd California Cavalry as second lieutenant in 1861, and participated in several Indian campaigns over the next two years. The first reference to service in Arizona is on a reconnaissance between Salt Lake City and Fort Mojave in 1864. In 1866, he was appointed second lieutenant of the 5th Cavalry. He was posted to Camp McDowell in 1872, and soon after was promoted to captain. He was nominated for brevets twice for service in Crook's 1872-73 campaign, and was commended for moving Indians to the Rio Verde Reservation after Date Creek was closed. He also supervised construction of the military telegraph between San Diego and Tucson.

Transferring to the Department of the Platte, he participated in Crook's Big Horn and Yellowstone Expedition in 1876, and was present at the Slim Buttes Fight. In 1882, he published his memoirs, *Across the Continent with the Fifth U.S. Cavalry*. (Altshuler, 1991, 268; O'Neal, 185-86; Heitman, 1:806)

RANDALL, George Morton "Jake" (1841-1918), native of Ohio, was one of the most competent officers to serve under Crook in Arizona. He commanded Camp Apache from 1872 to 1874, during which it was considered the best administered post in the entire department. He also had the most outstanding scouting record of any infantry captain in Arizona. Randall was breveted to colonel of the regular army for gallantry at Turret Mountain and Diamond Butte in 1873, and Pinal in 1874, and for distinguished service during the Indian campaigns in Arizona. He enlisted as a private in the Volunteers in July 1861, and commissioned as 2nd lieutenant in October. By the end of the war he had been breveted to colonel of Volunteers. He was appointed brigadier general of the regular army in 1901 and retired four years later. (Heitman, 1:814; Altshuler, 1991, 272-73)

RANDOLPH, John Field (d. 1880), was appointed assistant surgeon in 1855, and promoted to surgeon major in 1862. He was breveted to lieutenant colonel for service during the Civil War. (Heitman, 1:815)

RAWOLLE, William Charles (d. 1895), native of Prussia, was commissioned as second lieutenant of the Volunteers in 1861. He distinguished himself during the Civil War, rising to the rank of lieutenant colonel. He was commissioned second lieutenant of the 2nd Cavalry in 1869, and promoted the following year. He was captain at the time of his death. Bourke spells the name variously as "Rowelle," "Rowell," and "Rawolle." (Heitman, 1:817).

REILLY, Bernard (1843-1906), native of Pennsylvania, enlisted in the volunteers in April 1861, and was commissioned second lieutenant in November. In May 1868, he was appointed second lieutenant of the 5th Cavalry. He went to Arizona as a first lieutenant in 1872, and was nominated for a brevet for leading several successful scouts. Transferred to the Department of the Platte, he participated in the Big Horn and Yellowstone Expedition. He resigned in 1878 to practice law. (Altshuler, 1991, 277)

REYNOLDS, Bainbridge (1849-1901), eldest son of Col. Joseph J. Reynolds, was born at West Point, where he graduated in 1873.

He was posted to the 3rd Cavalry, was breveted for action in the Battle of the Rosebud in 1876. He served in Arizona from 1882 to 1884. He resigned in 1891 to avoid court-martial. See also REYNOLDS, Joseph Jones. (Altshuler, 1991, 277-78)

REYNOLDS, Joseph Jones (1822-99), native of Kentucky and an 1843 graduate of West Point, initially served on the Texas frontier. Resigning to enter private business in 1857, he rejoined the army at the outbreak of the Civil War. IIis distinguished service resulted in his being breveted to major general of Volunteers. In 1870, he was named colonel of the 3rd Cavalry and, with his brevet rank, commanded the Department of Texas. During that tenure, Col. Ranald Mackenzie hinted that Reynolds was involved in corruption with supply contracts for Fort McKavett, which Mackenzie commanded. Reynolds was transferred with his regiment to the Department of the Platte in 1872. Despite the verdict and sentence handed him by Crook's court-martial following the Powder River fight, Reynolds was allowed to retire for disability in 1877. Many historians believe that Crook should have shared a heavy amount of the blame for the fiasco. (Thrapp, 1991, 3:1210; Heitman, 1:825; Robinson, 1993, 52-53)

RICE, William Fletcher (d. 1884), native of Massachusetts, enlisted in the Volunteers in 1861, and was commissioned as second lieutenant in 1863. He was commissioned second lieutenant of the 23rd Infantry in 1866, and was first lieutenant when he arrived in Arizona in 1872. During the 1872-73 campaign he served as acting company commander, and was recommended for brevets. He commanded Indian scouts at San Carlos. In 1874, he was transferred with his regiment to the Department of the Platte. He was killed when he fell from a moving railroad train. (Altshuler, 1991, 278-79)

ROBERTSON, Edgar Brooks (1852-1924), native of Massachusetts, graduated from West Point in 1874, and was assigned to the 9th Infantry at Camp Robinson, Nebraska. He participated in the Big Horn and Yellowstone Expedition, and was in the fights at the Rosebud and Slim Buttes. He later served in the Southwest, in Cuba, and in the Boxer Rebellion in China. He retired as colonel. (Altshuler, 1991, 284)

ROBINSON, Frank Upham, of New York, became second lieutenant of the 41st U.S. Colored Infantry in 1864. He was commissioned second lieutenant of the 19th Infantry in 1868. In 1869, he was assigned to the 2nd Cavalry. (Heitman, 1:838)

ROBINSON, Henry Eleazar, of Pennsylvania, entered West Point in 1867, and upon graduation was commissioned second lieutenant in the 4th Infantry. (Heitman, 1:838)

ROBINSON, William Wallace, Jr. (1846-1917), native of Ohio, graduated from West Point in 1869, and was posted to the 3rd Cavalry. He served in Arizona from 1870 to 1871, when the regiment was transferred to the Department of the Platte. After so many officers of the 7th Cavalry were killed at the Little Bighorn, he was transferred to the 7th and promoted to first lieutenant. He retired as a brigadier general in 1910. (Altshuler, 1991, 285)

ROGERS, William Wallace (d. 1890), of Pennsylvania, enlisted as a private in the Volunteers in 1861, and became second lieutenant on December 31 of that year. He distinguished himself in the Civil War and was breveted to lieutenant colonel for gallant conduct in the field. In 1866, he was commissioned first lieutenant of the 45th Infantry. At the time of Bourke's writing he was with the 9th Infantry. He retired as captain in 1889. (Heitman, 1:844)

ROSS, William J. (1846-1907), aide to General Crook from 1871 to 1875, was a native of Scotland who grew up in Connecticut. He enlisted in a Volunteer regiment, rising to the rank of major of Volunteers during the Civil War. He was commissioned as second lieutenant of the 32nd Infantry (later amalgamated into the 21st Infantry) in 1868, and sent to Arizona a year later. On September 8, 1872, at Camp Date Creek, he saved Crook's life when he kicked a would-be assassin's rifle out of the way. When Crook was transferred to the Department of the Platte in 1875, Ross resigned and settled in Arizona. (Altshuler, 1991, 288; Robinson, 2001, 126)

ROYALL, William Bedford (1825-95), native of Virginia, was commissioned as first lieutenant of a Volunteer unit in 1846, after the outbreak of the Mexican War. After two years of service in the Southwest, including a major Indian fight in 1848, he left the Volunteers. In 1855, he was commissioned first lieutenant of the 2nd Cavalry (later renumbered 5th Cavalry). He distinguished himself during the Civil War, rising to the brevet rank of brigadier general. He served in Arizona as major of the 5th from 1872 to 1875, when the regiment was transferred out. In December 1875, he was promoted to lieutenant colonel of the 3rd Cavalry, commanding Crook's cavalry

during the Big Horn and Yellowstone Expedition. He later was breveted for gallantry at the Battle of the Rosebud. In 1881, he succeeded Ranald S. Mackenzie as colonel of the 4th Cavalry. He retired
in 1887. (Heitman, 1:849; Altshuler, 1991, 288-89)

RUSSELL, Gerald (1832-1905), native of Ireland, enlisted in the
Mounted Riflemen (later redesignated as 3rd Cavalry) in 1851. In
1862, he was promoted to second lieutenant. He distinguished himself during the Civil War, and earned a brevet. He arrived in Arizona
as captain in 1870, and participated in scouting expeditions until
the 3rd was transferred to the Department of the Platte. During the
Powder River Expedition, he participated in Mackenzie's fight with
the Cheyennes in November 1876. He served in Arizona a second
time from 1882 until 1885. He retired as major in 1890, later upgraded to lieutenant colonel. (Altshuler, 1991, 290-91)

SAVAGE, Egbert Barnum, was commissioned first lieutenant of
Volunteers in 1862. Following the Civil War, he was appointed second lieutenant of the 15th Infantry. He transferred to the 8th Infantry as first lieutenant in 1869. He retired in 1899 as lieutenant colonel
of the 13th Infantry. (Heitman, 1:861)

SAYER, George B. This officer could not be located in Heitman's
under Sayer, Sawyer, Sayre, or Stayer.

SCHUYLER, Walter Scribner (1849-1932), native of New York,
was an 1870 graduate of West Point. He served in Arizona from
1872 to 1875 as a second lieutenant of the 5th Cavalry, distinguishing himself in several actions during that period. After a year's leave
in Europe, he joined Crook as aide-de-camp in Wyoming as a first
lieutenant in 1876. He resigned as aide-de-camp and returned to
his regiment the end of 1881, after a falling out with Crook over his
management of a mine in which Crook had invested heavily. He
was breveted several grades for gallantry in action in Arizona and
Wyoming. He retired in 1913 as a brigadier general. (Altshuler, 1991,
294-95; Heitman, 1:867; O'Neal, 193-94; Robinson, 2001, 249-50)

SCHWATKA, Frederick (1849-92), native of Ohio, attended West
Point and was commissioned as second lieutenant of the 3rd Cavalry in 1871. He participating in campaigns against the Yavapais
and Apaches in Arizona until 1872, when his regiment was transferred to the Platte. During Crook's Big Horn and Yellowstone Expedition, he took part in the Rosebud fight, the Horse Meat March,
and the Slim Buttes fight. Subsequently, as both soldier and civil-

ian, he became a noted explorer in the Arctic, southwestern U.S., and northwestern Mexico, lecturing and writing several popular books. He died of an overdose of laudanum (tincture of opium), which he took to relieve chronic stomach pain. (Thrapp, 1991, 3:1279-80)

SETON, Henry, of New York, was appointed captain in the Volunteers in 1864, and second lieutenant of the 4th Infantry in 1866. He was promoted to first lieutenant in 1872. Heitman lists him as still being with the 4th until 1898, when he was promoted to major of the 12th Infantry. Bourke, on the other hand, lists him as being in the 9th. He retired in 1899. (Heitman, 1:874)

SIBLEY, Frederick William (1852-1918), native of Texas, graduated from West Point in 1874, and was assigned to the 2nd Cavalry in the Department of the Platte. He participated in the Reynolds fight on the Powder River, and, during Crook's Big Horn and Yellowstone Expedition led what became known as the Sibley Scout. He and a small party of men encountered a large band of Lakotas and Cheyennes, but managed to withdraw under heavy fire without losses, and make their way back to Crook's camp on foot. It is considered one of the narrowest escapes in the Indian Wars, and Sibley was breveted for gallantry. He later served in the Far East, and in the Mexican Punitive Expedition of 1916, retiring later that year as brigadier general. (Thrapp, 1991, 3:1303-04)

SIMPSON, James Ferdinand (1841-99), native of Massachusetts, was appointed second lieutenant of Volunteers in 1862. He distinguished himself in the Civil War, and in 1867, was commissioned as an infantry officer. He transferred to the 3rd Cavalry in 1871. He served in Arizona throughout much of the period until 1884, when he was committed to a government mental institution, after which he was released on sick leave. After a second commitment in 1887, he was retired as a captain. (Altshuler, 1991, 302-03)

SMALL, Michael Peter, of Pennsylvania, entered West Point in 1851, and upon graduation, was appointed to brevet second lieutenant of the 3rd Artillery. At the outbreak of the Civil War, he was active second lieutenant of the 2nd Artillery. He was assigned to the commissary service, and was breveted to brigadier general in 1865. His active rank was captain of the commissary service until 1874, when he was promoted to major. He was lieutenant colonel at the time of his death in 1892. Small's significance to history is that, as commissary of subsistence for the Department of Texas in 1881, he noticed irregularities in the transfer of funds from Fort Davis. This led to the court-martial and dismissal of the post's acting commissary, Second Lt. Henry O. Flipper, the army's only black officer at the time. (Heitman, 1:893; Robinson, 1994, 14-15)

SMITH, John Eugene (1816-97), native of Switzerland, was brought to the United States as a child. He was secretary to Governor Richard Yates of Illinois at the outbreak of the Civil War, and became a colonel of the Volunteers. He earned brevets to major general in both Volunteers and Regular Army, and in 1866 was appointed colonel of the Infantry. He served on the frontier as commander of the 14th Infantry until his retirement in 1881. (Warner, 459)

SPAULDING, Edward James (ca. 1836-88), native of New York, enlisted in the 2nd Dragoons (later renamed 2nd Cavalry) in 1857. He was commissioned as second lieutenant in 1862, earning a brevet during the Civil War. He was promoted to captain in 1867, and transferred to the 4th Cavalry as major in 1886. He was killed in a hunting accident in Arizona. Bourke spelled the name "Spalding." (Altshuler, 1991, 313)

SPENCER, James Herbert, of Massachusetts, enlisted in the Volunteers in 1861, and was promoted to first lieutenant in 1863. He was mustered out as captain. In 1866, he was commissioned first lieutenant of the 12th Infantry. In 1869, he transferred to the 4th Infantry. He retired as captain in 1885. Five years later, he was breveted for gallant service in action against Indians near Fort Fred Steele, Wyoming, in 1869. (Heitman, 1:910)

STANTON, Thaddeus Harlan (1835-1900), native of Indiana, enlisted in the Volunteers in 1861. On October 3, 1862, he was designated paymaster, a position he held for the rest of his career. He finished the Civil War as a brevet lieutenant colonel of Volunteers. Apparently Stanton moonlighted as a correspondent for the *New York Tribune*, and in that capacity accompanied Crook and Reynolds on the Big Horn Expedition in the convenience position of chief of scouts. With no previous combat experience, he distinguished himself in the Powder River fight, and later commanded the citizens and irregulars who joined Crook on the train during the Big Horn and Yellowstone Expedition. In 1890, Stanton was breveted to lieutenant colonel of the Regular Army for the Powder

River fight, and in 1895, he was appointed paymaster general of the army with the rank of brigadier general. (Thrapp, 1991, 3:1357; Heitman, 1:916)

STANTON, William Sanford, of New York, entered West Point in 1861, and upon graduation was commissioned first lieutenant of the engineers. He was promoted to captain in 1871. (Heitman, 1:916)

STANWOOD, Frank (ca. 1842-1872), native of Maine, was commanding officer at Camp Grant at the time of the massacre of the Indians by Tucson citizens and their allies. He was on a scouting expedition with much of the garrison, however, and the fact that most of the troops were absent prompted the citizens to move against the Indians. Stanwood entered the army as a second lieutenant of the 3rd Cavalry in 1861. He finished the Civil War as a brevet lieutenant colonel, and was promoted to captain in 1866. He died of tuberculosis on December 20, 1872. Some works spell the name "Standwood," but "Stanwood" is the form on the official record, and the form used by Bourke. (Altshuler, 1991, 315; Thrapp, 1988, 85; Heitman, 1:916)

STEVENS, Lieutenant. Heitman does not list a Lieutenant Stevens on active duty during this period. The only one who would approximate is Robert Ratcliff Stevens, who entered the Military Academy in 1873, and was assigned to the 6th Infantry in 1877, which would have placed him in West Point at the time Bourke made this entry. This does not necessarily mean, however, that a Lieutenant Stevens did not exist. (Heitman, 1:922-23)

SUMMERHAYES, John Wyer (1836-1911), enlisted in the Volunteers in 1861, and was commissioned as an officer in 1863, earning two brevets during the Civil War. He was commissioned second lieutenant of the 33rd Infantry in 1867, and was transferred to the 8th Infantry two years later. He was posted to Arizona in 1874, serving there for four years. In 1900, he retired as major, later upgraded to lieutenant colonel. His wife, Martha, wrote a memoir, *Vanished Arizona*, about army life on that frontier. (Altshuler, 1991, 323-24)

SUMNER, Samuel Storrow (1842-1937), native of Pennsylvania, was commissioned second lieutenant of the 2nd Cavalry (later renumbered 5th Cavalry) in 1861. He earned several brevets during the Civil War, and emerged from the war as a captain. He was posted to Arizona from 1870 until 1876, when he joined the Big Horn and Yellowstone Expedition. He retired in 1906 as a major general.

(Altshuler, 1991, 324-25)

SUTORIOUS, Alexander (ca. 1837-1905), native of Switzerland, enlisted in the Mounted Riflemen (later redesignated 3rd Cavalry) in 1854. He was commissioned second lieutenant in 1863, and was breveted for gallantry in the Civil War. He went to Arizona in 1870 as a captain, serving until 1871, when the regiment was transferred to the Department of the Platte. He was court-martialed and dismissed for drunkenness during the Big Horn and Yellowstone Expedition. (Altshuler, 1991, 325)

SWIGERT, Samuel Miller, of Kentucky, entered West Point in 1863, and upon graduation was appointed to second lieutenant of the 2nd Cavalry. He was promoted to first lieutenant in 1869. He retired in 1903 as colonel of the 5th Cavalry. (Heitman, 1:941)

TAYLOR, Alfred Bronaugh (d. 1903), native of the District of Columbia, served briefly in the Volunteers before enlisting in the 5th Cavalry in 1862. He was commissioned second lieutenant in 1863, and was breveted for service in the Appomattox Campaign. He arrived in Arizona at a captain in 1872, and was breveted for gallantry in action in the Salt River Caves fight of December 28, 1872. (Altshuler, 1991, 327; Heitman, 1:945)

TERRY, Alfred Howe (1827-90), native of Connecticut, was an attorney rather than a trained soldier. With the outbreak of the Civil War he joined the Volunteers, ultimately rising to the rank of major general. His successful assault on Fort Fisher, North Carolina, in 1865, which hastened the end of the war, won him an appointment as brigadier general of the Regular Army. Terry commanded the Department of the Platte at the time of the Great Sioux War. In 1886, he was appointed major general, and commanded the Military Division of the Missouri until his retirement in 1888. (Warner, 197-98)

THOMAS, Earl Denison (1847-1921), native of Illinois, served in the Volunteers during the Civil War, and graduated from West Point in 1869. He joined the 5th Cavalry, and went to Arizona as a first lieutenant in 1872. He was breveted for gallantry in the Salt River Caves fight. When Kautz assumed command of the Department of Arizona, Thomas remained as his aide until 1878. He then joined his company in Wyoming. He later was appointed brigadier general, and commanded the Department of the Colorado. He retired in 1911. (Altshuler, 1991, 330; Heitman, 1:953)

THOMPSON, Edmund F. (1846-80), native of Massachusetts, enlisted in the 18th Infantry in 1864, and was commissioned as lieutenant in 1865. He was reassigned to the 27th Infantry, and in 1867 was promoted to captain. He served in Arizona from 1872 to 1875, and again from 1878 until his death at Camp Grant two years later. (Altshuler, 1991, 330-31)

TOWNSEND, Edwin Franklin, entered West Point in 1850, and upon graduation was breveted second lieutenant of the 3rd Artillery. He resigned in 1856, but reentered the army as first lieutenant of the 14th Infantry in 1861. He distinguished himself during the Civil War, and was breveted to major for gallantry at Shiloh, and to lieutenant colonel for continued and faithful service in the Ordnance Department. At the time of Bourke's writing, he was major of the 9th Infantry. He retired in 1895 as colonel of the 12th Infantry. (Heitman, 1:967)

TROUT, John Franklin (1843-1912), native of Pennsylvania, enlisted in the Volunteers in 1861, and emerged from the Civil War as a major. He was named second lieutenant of the 9th Infantry in 1866. As first lieutenant, he was dismissed under sentence of court-martial in 1869, but reinstated at previous rank a year later. He transferred to the 23rd Infantry and went to Arizona in 1872, and commanded Camp Date Creek when it was abandoned on August 25, 1873. In 1874, his company went to the Department of the Platte, and he commanded the infantry on the Dodge-Jenney Expedition to the Black Hills in 1875. He was retired on disability in 1883, after his ankle was crushed by a falling tree. His retirement was upgraded to captain in 1904. (Altshuler, 1991, 335-36)

VAN HORN, James Judson (1835-98), native of Ohio, was an 1858 graduate of West Point, and joined the 8th Infantry in Texas. When Texas seceded, Van Horn was taken prisoner, and exchanged in 1862. During his internment he was promoted to first lieutenant and captain. He earned a brevet to major at Cold Harbor, Virginia. He served at the Red Cloud Agency and Camp Robinson, Nebraska. He was posted to Arizona in 1874, and spent much of the next decade in the Southwest. He was colonel of the 8th Infantry at the time of his death at Fort D.A. Russell, Wyoming. (Altshuler, 1991, 340; Heitman, 1:982)

VAN VLIET, Frederick (1841-91), native of New York, was commissioned second lieutenant of the 3rd Cavalry in 1861. He earned brevets to lieutenant colonel during the Civil War, and was promoted to the active rank of captain in 1866. He served in Arizona from 1870 to 1871, when the regiment was transferred to the Department of the Platte. Van Vliet participated in the Big Horn and Yellowstone Expedition in 1876. As major of the 10th Cavalry, he served again in Arizona during the Geronimo Campaign. He died of injuries received in a wagon accident. (Altshuler, 1991, 341)

VROOM, Peter Dumont (1842-1926), native of New Jersey, served as an officer of Volunteers, earning several brevets during the Civil War. In February 1866, he was commissioned second lieutenant of the 3rd Cavalry, and was promoted to first lieutenant the following July. Promoted to captain in 1876, he participated in the Big Horn and Yellowstone Expedition, distinguishing himself at the Battle of the Rosebud. He served in Arizona from 1882 to 1885, when he was appointed major/inspector general. He retired as a brigadier general in 1903. (Altshuler, 1991, 346)

WARD, Edward Wilkerson (d. 1897), a native of Kentucky, was appointed first lieutenant of the Kentucky Scouts in 1861, and was mustered out of the Union Army in 1865. He was commissioned second lieutenant in the 5th Cavalry in 1869, and was posted to the Department of the Platte. He served in Arizona from 1873 to 1875, commanding Indian Scouts at Camp Apache, and serving as post commander at San Carlos. He retired as captain due to ill health in 1879. (Altshuler, 1991, 352)

WATTS, Charles Henry (1849-1917), native of New York, was an 1872 graduate of West Point, and was posted to Arizona as a second lieutenant of the 5th Cavalry. He was in the 1872-73 campaign, and was twice recommended for brevets. He departed with his regiment in 1875. During the Big Horn and Yellowstone Expedition in 1876, he suffered an accidental gunshot wound. Recovering, he participated in the Wind River Expedition of 1877. He retired as colonel of the 9th Cavalry in 1911. (Altshuler, 1991, 353)

WELLS, Elijah Revillo, of New York, enlisted in the 2nd Dragoons in 1858. After its reorganization as 2nd Cavalry, he was commissioned second lieutenant. He distinguished himself in the Civil War, earning brevets up to major. At the time of Bourke's writing, he was captain of the 2nd Cavalry. He retired in 1879, and died in 1891. (Heitman, 1:1017)

WESSELLS, Henry Walton, Jr. (1846-1929), native of New York, attended the Naval Academy for two years before enlisting in the

7th Infantry in March 1865. The following August, he received dual commissions as second and first lieutenant retroactive to July 21. He transferred to the 3rd Cavalry in 1870, joining his company in Arizona in April 1871. Eight months later, the regiment transferred to the Department of the Platte, where Wessells was promoted to captain. He commanded Fort Robinson, Nebraska, during the Cheyenne Outbreak of 1879, and was wounded in the fighting. He was retired for disability as colonel in 1901. Karl Malden's portrayal of Wessells as an alcoholic Prussian martinet with a heavy German accent, in the 1964 film *Cheyenne Autumn* is fictitious, as is the film itself. (Altshuler, 1991, 355-56)

WHEATON, Charles (1835–1913), native of Rhode Island, was commissioned as second lieutenant of Volunteers in 1861, and finished the Civil War as colonel. He was appointed captain of the 33rd Infantry in 1867, and served on Reconstruction duty before going West. He was in Arizona from 1872 to 1873, and assigned to the Department of the Platte in 1874, where he took part in Crook's Powder River Campaign. He was retired for deafness in 1889. (Altshuler, 1991, 360)

WHEELER probably refers to First Lt. George Montague Wheeler, Corps of Engineers. (Heitman, 1:1024)

WHITMAN, Royal Emerson (1833-1913), native of Maine, enlisted in the Volunteers in 1862, and finished the Civil War as a colonel. General Howard, who was related to him by marriage, helped Whitman secure a commission as second lieutenant in the 3rd Cavalry in 1867, and he was promoted to first lieutenant two years later. He went to Arizona in 1870, and was acting commander at Camp Grant at the time of the massacre. Because he sided with the Indians in the subsequent investigations, he became the most hated officer in Arizona. When Crook assumed command of the department, he ordered Whitman court-martialed for "conduct unbecoming an officer," a catch-all used to rid the army of undesirables. The court-martial board, however, threw out the charges on a technicality. Whitman's cordial relationship with General Howard, who was inspecting the department, infuriated Crook even more. Later, while serving as acting Indian agent at Camp Grant, he was again court-martialed, this time at the behest of Maj. Gen. John M. Schofield, commander of the Military Division of the Pacific, for disobedience of orders to muster Indians for a daily roll call. Although he again was found not guilty, he was accused of breaking arrest while awaiting trial, and this led to a third court-martial, in which he was found guilty and sentenced to reprimand, suspension of rank and command for six months, and confinement to post during that period. He retired in 1879. See also ESKIMINZIN; HOWARD, Oliver Otis. (Altshuler, 1991, 365-66; Thrapp, 1988, Chapters 7 and 8; Schmitt, 170-73; Robinson, 2001, Chapter 8; Heitman, 1:1030)

WIETING, Orlando Luther (1846-93), native of Pennsylvania, served as an enlisted man in the Volunteers from 1864 to 1865. After the Civil War, he entered West Point, graduating in 1870, but resigned the same year. In 1872, he re-entered the service, commissioned as a second lieutenant of the 23rd Infantry. He was post quartermaster at Fort Whipple, and later served in the Departments of the Platte, and the Missouri. He was a captain at Fort Sam Houston, Texas, at the time of his death. (Altshuler, 1991, 367-68)

WILHELM, Thomas (1838-1922), native of Pennsylvania, served in the Volunteers during the Civil War, and was mustered out as major. He was commissioned second lieutenant of the 8th Infantry in 1866, and promoted to first lieutenant the same year. He was assigned to Fort Whipple with the change of command in Arizona in 1874. He retired as a major of the 21st Infantry in 1899, and later served with the California Militia. He wrote several military histories and reference books. (Altshuler, 1991, 369)

WILKINS, John Darragh (1822-1900), of New York, was an 1846 graduate of West Point, and served with distinction in the Mexican War. During the 1850s, he was posted to Texas and New Mexico. He finished the Civil War as major with several brevets for distinguished service. In 1869, he was transferred to the 8th Infantry, becoming lieutenant colonel four years later. He arrived at Fort Whipple with the change of command of the Department of Arizona in 1874, and assumed command of the post. He retired as colonel of the 5th Infantry in 1886. (Altshuler, 1991, 369-70)

WILLIAMS, Robert (d. 1901), native of Virginia, entered West Point in 1847, and upon graduation was assigned to the 1st Dragoons (later 1st Cavalry). In 1861 he was breveted to captain and appointed assistant adjutant general, and served in the Adjutant General's Department throughout the remainder of his career. In 1865, he was breveted to brigadier general for "diligent, faithful, and meritorious service in the Adjutant General's Department during the war." He was assistant adjutant general of the Department of the Platte during Crook's administration. Williams retired in 1893 as brigadier general and adjutant general of the army. (Heitman, 1:1042)

WOODSON, Albert Emmett (1841-1903) native of Kentucky, went to Washington Territory in 1859. Three years later, he enlisted in the territorial volunteers, serving as a hospital steward until 1863 when he was commissioned a second lieutenant. In 1867, he was commissioned first lieutenant of the 36th Infantry in the Department of the Platte, and in 1870 was transferred to the 5th Cavalry. In Arizona, he participated in Crook's Apache campaigns, distinguishing himself in fights in the Tonto Basin. As a captain, he was on the Big Horn and Yellowstone Expedition, and in the Slim Buttes fight. He later served in the Nez Percé War and in the Philippines. Woodson retired as brigadier general in 1903. (Thrapp, 1991, 3:1593-94)

WORTH, William Scott (1840-1904), native of New York, was the son of Mexican War hero William Jenkins Worth. In 1861, he was commissioned second lieutenant in the 8th Infantry, his father's old regiment. He earned two brevets in the Civil War and was promoted to captain. He came to Arizona with his regiment in 1874, remaining until 1878. He returned to Arizona in 1886 during the Geronimo campaign. He was severely wounded in the Spanish-American War, prompting his retirement as brigadier general in 1898. (Altshuler, 1991, 380-81)

YOUNG may refer to Robert Hunter Young of Kentucky who, after distinguished service in the Volunteers during the Civil War, was commissioned second lieutenant of the 30th Infantry in 1867, and transferred to the 4th Infantry a year later. In 1890, he was breveted to first lieutenant for gallant service in action against Indians near Fort Fred Steele, Wyoming, in 1869. He retired in 1891. (Heitman, 1:1067)

Civilians

ARNOLD, Ben (ca. 1844-1922), was the alias adopted by Benjamin M. Conner because of chronic enlistments and desertions in the Union Army during the Civil War. A native of Ohio, Conner had already deserted twice when he enlisted under the name of Monroe in the 11th Ohio Volunteer Cavalry in 1863, and traveled with the regiment to Platte Bridge Station (now Casper), Wyoming. Here he again deserted and permanently assumed the surname of Arnold. He wandered throughout the Northern Plains, working at times as a trapper, freighter, and wolfer. He eventually settled in the Grand River country of Dakota, driving beef to Indian agencies, farming, and working as a military courier to Nebraska and Wyoming. During the Great Sioux War, he served as a dispatch rider for General Crook. Following the Rosebud fight, he moved to Deadwood, and in 1891 to Pierre. He died at Fort Pierre. (Crawford)

BARTLET or BARTLETT. Muleskinner and guide in the Department of Arizona.

BELKNAP, William Worth (1829-90), native of New York, was secretary of war during the Grant Administration. Belknap was the son of Brig. Gen. William Goldsmith Belknap, who distinguished himself in the Mexican War, and on the Texas frontier. He served as a volunteer during the Civil War, rising to the rank of brigadier general. He was appointed secretary of war in 1869, but in 1876, a congressional committee on War Department expenditures found evidence that he had accepted a bribe in the appointment of a post trader at Fort Sill, Oklahoma. It was generally believed in the army that the corruption was not limited to Fort Sill. He was impeached, but the Senate did not get the majority needed to convict, largely because many of the senators were satisfied with Belknap's resignation. He practiced law in Washington where he died. (Johnson and Malone, 2:147-48.)

BENDELL, Herman, was Indian superintendent for Arizona; in 1871-72, after which the office was abolished. (Bancroft, 1889, 544)

BESIAS, Antonio, Arizona guide and interpreter, had been kidnapped a child from his home in Sonora and raised by the Apaches. (Bourke, 1980, 19, 184; Porter, 9)

CHANDLER, Zachariah (1813-79), succeeded Columbus Delano as secretary of the interior in October 1875, and held the position until the end of the Grant Administration in March 1877. He reorganized the Interior Department, restoring some if its integretiy with large-scale dismissals for dishonesty and incompetence. Chandler was a Republican political boss in Michigan, serving as one of that state's senators from 1857 to 1874, and again for a few months prior to his death in 1879. During the Civil War, he was a member of the Joint Committee on the Conduct of the War. See DELANO, Columbus. (Johnson and Malone, 3:618)

CLARKE (or Clark), Ben, frontiersman from Oklahoma and married to a Cheyenne woman, served as a scout in Sheridan's Winter Campaign of 1868-69. He guided Custer's troops to the Indian camps along the Washita on November 27-28, 1868. For that reason, Sheridan summoned him to Nebraska to consult with Crook, although Clarke knew nothing of the region. See also BLACK KETTLE. (Hoig, 71, 123-24)

CLUM, John Philip (1851-1932), native of New York, went west in 1871 as a meteorological observer with the U.S. Signal Corps in Santa Fe. In 1874, he accepted the position of Indian agent at San Carlos, which then was under the administration of the Dutch Reformed Church as part of President Grant's Peace Policy. He left the Indian Service in 1877, eventually moving to Tombstone, where he founded the *Tombstone Epitaph*, and served as mayor and postmaster. See also ESKIMINZIN. (Thrapp, 1988, Chapter 14; Clum)

COLYER, Vincent (1824-88), native of New York City, was a prominent artist. During the Civil War, his Quaker religion notwithstanding, he organized and became colonel of a black regiment. He was appointed secretary of the Board of Indian Commissioners by President Grant. In that capacity, in 1869, he visited New Mexico and northeastern Arizona, where his views on the Apache situation earned him the enmity of the local population. Feelings against him were so bitter that when he revisited the Southwest in 1871, Arizona Gov. Anson P. K. Safford believed it necessary to provide an escort for his protection. He also visited Alaska. See also ESKIMINZIN; NANNI-CHADDI; WELSH, William. (Thrapp, 1988, 102-03; Bancroft, 1889, 560-62)

COSGROVE, Thomas, native of Texas and former Confederate cavalryman, who, together with Robert Eckles and Nelson Yarnell, lived among the Shoshones and trained their warriors in conventional cavalry tactics.

DAILEY, James, Crook's brother-in-law, sometimes accompanied expeditions as a civilian employee. He had been a Confederate guerilla fighter in West Virginia during the Civil War, and almost certainly was a member of a partisan group that captured Crook in early 1865. After the war, Crook married Dailey's sister, Mary. In calling him a "bacon chawer," Bourke probably meant that Dailey's presence had no practical purpose, and was simply a case of nepotism, not uncommon among ranking officers of the period. George Armstrong Custer likewise carried civilian relatives on the government payroll, and Lt. Gen. Philip H. Sheridan appointed his brother, Michael, as military aide. (Robinson, 2001, 72, 124)

DANIELS, Jared W., an Indian agent, and member of the 1876 commission that deannexed the Black Hills from the Great Sioux Reservation. (Robinson, 1993, 261)

DAVENPORT, Reuben Briggs (ca. 1852-1932), correspondent for the *New York Herald* during Crook's administration of the Department of the Platte. He was born in New York City, and joined the *Herald* in 1871. He accompanied Custer's Black Hills Expedition of 1874, and the Dodge-Jenney Expedition. Davenport was the prototype of the modern investigative reporter. His persistent questioning prompted many Westerners to tell him some tall tales, but his dispatches show that he generally was skeptical. Of all the correspondents, he was the least impressed with Crook, reporting the facts as he saw them. A Quaker, he nevertheless distinguished himself for valor during the Battle of the Rosebud. However, his unflattering account of the fight earned him the enmity of Crook and his inner circle. He later covered the Spanish-American War, and served as chief editorial writer for the Paris edition of the combined *New York Herald-Tribune*. He died in France. (Thrapp, 1991, 1:376-77; Knight, 172-73; Appendix 17)

DELANO, Columbus (1809-96), secretary of the interior during the Grant Administration, initially joined the administration in 1869 as commissioner of Internal Revenue. During his term, already established whiskey revenue frauds continued. The following year, he was appointed secretary of the interior, and again, a preexisting pattern of corruption in the Department of the Interior's Bureau of Indian Affairs was allowed to continue, ultimately becoming a national scandal. Under pressure from newspapers, he resigned in 1875. (Johnson and Malone, 5:217-18)

DE LONG, Sidney Randolph (1828-1914), native of New York, went to California during the Gold Rush in 1850. He went to Arizona as part of the 1st California Infantry in 1862, and was a member of the garrison that established Camp Goodwin. After the Civil War, he settled in Tucson, where he was a merchant, editor of the

Tucson *Star* and a member of the local Committee of Public Safety. He was among those indicted for the Camp Grant Massacre. He later served as mayor of Tucson and member of the territorial legislature. (Thrapp, 1991, 1:389; Altshuler, 1981, 194, and 1991, 100-1)

DE SMET, Pierre-Jean (1801-73) a Belgian-born Jesuit, ministered to the Indians of Montana, Oregon, and Idaho for more than three decades beginning in 1840. During this period, he also made nineteen trips to Europe to recruit priests and nuns to work among the Indians. He served as mediator between the Indians and whites, including at the Fort Laramie Treaty conference in 1868. (Utley, 1997, 122)

ECKLES, Robert (Texas Bob). See COSGROVE, Thomas.

FELMER, Joseph, post blacksmith at Camp Grant I, was a native of Germany. He enlisted in the California Volunteers in 1861, and served in the Southwest. He was promoted to lieutenant in 1864. After the Civil War, he remained in the Apache country, where he married an Apache woman and learned her language. (Thrapp, 1988, 66 n.9)

FINERTY, John Frederick (1846-1908), a political refugee from Ireland, became a correspondent for the *Chicago Times*, and covered more Indian war campaigns than any other professional journalist. In 1876, he covered Crook's expeditions, and his book, *War-Path and Bivouac* is one of the most complete accounts. He also covered the Ute campaign of 1879, visited Sitting Bull in exile in Canada, and covered the 1881 Apache uprising. He was a member of congress from 1883 to 1885. (Finerty; Knight, 173-74; Lamar, 369)

FORD, John W., was post telegraph operator at Fort Laramie. (Hedren, 1988, 58)

FREE, Mickey. See Ward, Felix.

GROUARD, Frank (1850?-1905) claimed that he was born in the Friendly Islands, the son of an American missionary and a Polynesian noblewoman. While this is the most generally accepted version, and most probably true, his numerous detractors disputed it, some insisting that he was mulatto, and others that he was Indian-white. Grouard was a braggart, and his own accounts cannot be considered completely reliable. Despite his assertions to the contrary, he also nursed an unexplained, but deep-seated hatred for the Oglala chief Crazy Horse, possibly resulting from several years spent in Oglala captivity. The animosity ultimately became a factor in Crazy Horse's death. Despite his faults, Grouard was a great scout and an experienced frontiersman, and his services to the government were invaluable during the Great Sioux War. In later entries, Bourke spelled the name "Gruard." See also CLARK, Walter Philo; CRAZY HORSE. (DeBarthe; Robinson, 1995)

HAYES, Rutherford Birchard (1822-1893), served under Crook as a brigadier general of Volunteers during the Civil War, and became Crook's life-long friend, supporter, and admirer, even naming one of his sons after him. Declared president after a controversial, and hotly contested election, Hayes held office from 1877 to 1881. He was determined not to be distracted by campaign considerations, and therefore did not seek a second term. Consequently, in many cases the full effect of his reforms was not apparent until after he left office. Nevertheless, he was one of the more capable presidents of the last three decades of the nineteenth century. (See Robinson, 2001, and Hoogeboom)

JEFFORDS, Thomas Jonathan. (1832-1914), which Bourke spelled "Jefferds," sometime prospector, mail contractor, and trader, became friends with Cochise in 1867, after he singlehandedly confronted the chief over the deaths of fourteen of his mail carriers. He was instrumental in bringing about peace with Cochise, and subsequently was appointed agent for Cochise's reservation in the Dragoon Mountains. See also COCHISE; HOWARD, Oliver Otis. (Sweeney, 1991; Lamar, 572)

JENNEY, Horace P. (1849-1921), was a professor at the Columbia School of Mines in New York, who was placed in charge of the surveying party in the Black Hills Expedition of 1875. His previous field experience was limited to fourteen months in west Texas and New Mexico conducting surveys for a projected railroad. He owed his position on the Black Hills Expedition to the recommendation of J. S. Newberry, the expedition's geologist. His elitist attitude alienated the officers and soldiers of the expedition. Jenney later headed the U.S. Geological Survey's Division of Zinc. (Kime, 1996, 6)

LA GRANGE, Oscar Hugh, native of New York, became a captain of a Wisconsin Volunteer unit in 1861. He was breveted to brigadier general of Volunteers in 1865 for "faithful and meritorious service." La Grange is listed in Appendix 1 of Warner's *Generals in Blue* as "breveted as. . . brigadier general for services rendered during the Civil War, but not appointed to full rank." (Warner, 588; Heitman, 1:611)

MC COY, Mason, was a scout Crook had known in Oregon. (Thrapp, 1988, 119)

MC GILLYCUDDY, Valentine T. (1849-1939), contract surgeon with General Crook, and topographer for the Dodge-Jenney expedition, was a native of Michigan. He served as post surgeon at Camp Robinson, where he tended the mortally wounded Crazy Horse. He served as agent for the Oglalas from 1879 to 1886, when he was relieved in part because of disputes with Red Cloud. McGillycuddy also was first mayor of Rapid City, South Dakota, and served as president of the South Dakota School of Mines. Bourke spelled the name "MacGillicuddy." See also CRAZY HORSE. (Thrapp, 1991, 2:905)

MC INTOSH, Archie (1832-1902), was the son of a Scots Hudson's Bay trapper and a Chippewa woman. After a period of clerking for Hudson's Bay Company in Canada, he immigrated to the United States, where in 1855 he became an Army scout in Oregon. He served under General Crook in Oregon and moved with him to Arizona. He served several years as a guide, culminating in Crook's Sierra Madre expedition of 1883. He was married to a Chiricahua woman and lived near the San Carlos Reservation until his death from cancer. His younger brother, Lt. Donald McIntosh, 7th Cavalry, died at the Little Bighorn on June 25, 1876. (Thrapp, 1991, 2:908-09; O'Neal, 164-66)

MACMILLAN, Thomas, which Bourke spelled "McMillan," a native of Scotland, reported for the *Chicago Inter-Ocean*. Although only twenty-five years old, his poor health cut short his participation in the campaigns of the summer of 1876. Like Reuben Davenport, he had accompanied the Dodge-Jenney Expedition. Dodge described him as "very gentlemanly, hard to stuff, & with excellent good sense" who won "the liking and respect of everyone." (Knight, 171-72; Kime, 1996, 57)

MARÍA, José, Arizona guide and interpreter who had been kidnapped as a child from his home in Sonora and raised by the Apaches. He and Tom Horn served as interpreters for Lt. Charles Gatewood negotiating the surrender of Geronimo in 1886. (Thrapp, 1991, 2:675; Bourke, 1980, 19, 184)

MARION, John Huguenot (ca. 1836-91), publisher of the *Miner*, was considered the ablest newspapermen in central Arizona. Bourke called him "one of God's noblemen." Little is known of his early life, although he probably was born in New Orleans, and went to California in the mid-1850s. He was in St. Louis in 1856-57, returned West and purchased the *Miner* in 1867, operating it for ten years. One of his sons was named in honor of General Crook. (Thrapp, 1991, 2:942)

MERIVALE, Joseph, whose name Bourke spelled "Marrivale," was a long-time resident of the Fort Laramie area, who had served the army as a guide on several occasions prior to the Dodge-Jenney Black Hills expedition of 1875. Nevertheless, during the expedition, Dodge determined that Merivale knew very little about the Black Hills, and instead used him as a courier and interpreter. (Kime, 1996, 12-13)

MOORE, Thomas (1832-96) was one of the preeminent mule packers of the West and, with General Crook, streamlined the military pack transportation system to a model of efficiency. A native of St. Louis, he began his Western career by traveling to California in 1850. He joined Crook as civilian chief packer in 1871, and served in virtually every major Indian campaign until 1895. He also organized transportation for hunting and camping trips by Crook and other dignitaries. His sister was Carrie Nation, temperance activist famous for smashing saloons in the Midwest. (Thrapp, 1991, 2:1011-12)

NEWBERRY, J. S., was geologist for the 1875 Dodge-Jenney Black Hills Expedition. Bourke erroneously refers to him as an ornithologist. See also JENNEY, Horace P. (Kime, 1996, 6)

O'BRIEN, M. A printed roster of acting assistant surgeons on duty in the Department of Arizona, pasted in vol. 1 facing page 149 of the diary, shows Dr. M. O'Brien as assigned to Camp McDowell. He appears to have been a civilian contract surgeon because Heitman does not list an army surgeon by that name, nor does he list contract surgeons prior to 1898.

OCHOA, Estevan (1831-88), native of Chihuahua, became involved in the trade between the Southwest and St. Louis as a boy. He was a member of the Tucson firm of Tully, Ochoa & Co., which was the largest merchandizing house in Arizona until the arrival of the railroad in 1880. (Thrapp, 1991, 2:1072)

PACHECO, Romualdo (1831-99), first native-born Californian to become governor under U.S. jurisdiction, served for nine months in 1875. As lieutenant governor, he succeeded Gov. Newton Booth, after Booth left office to accept a seat in the federal Senate. Pacheco later served two terms as a member of congress. (Bancroft, 1964, 764)

PALMER, A. D., was agent to the Hopis (Moquis) in 1869-70. Bourke appears to have been under the impression that he still held the office at the time of Crook's visit in 1874, but in fact the agent was W. S. Defrees, who was absent. (Bancroft, 1889, 548)

PHILLIPS, John "Portugee" (1832-83), was born Manoel Felipe Cardoso in the Azores. He came to California on a Portuguese ship about 1850, and became a prospector. On August 14, 1866, he and two partners, James Wheatley and Isaac Fisher, arrived at Fort Phil Kearny, where they accepted employment with the post quarter-master. When Wheatley and Fisher were killed in the Fetterman Massacre of December 21, 1866, Phillips volunteered to carry news of the disaster and a plea for assistance from the besieged garrison at Phil Kearny to Fort Laramie. He left Phil Kearny that night, making the 236-mile ride alone through blizzards in four days, arriving shortly before midnight Christmas Day in the middle of a holiday ball. He was bedridden with exhaustion and frostbite for several weeks after the ride. He appears to have received no special reward or consideration for his efforts, although in 1899, the government gave his widow $5,000 in belated gratitude. Bourke never arrived at a consistent way of spelling Phillips' name, or in using an apostrophe with the "s". See also FETTERMAN, William Judd. (Thrapp, 1991, 3:1140; Brown, 203)

POURIER, Baptiste (1841-1932), called "Big Bat" to distinguish him from another scout, Baptiste "Little Bat" Garnier, was born in St. Charles, Missouri. The descendant of a long line of French fur traders and explorers, while still in his teens he accepted employment with trader John Richaud, who later became his father-in-law. Pourier became an interpreter and guide at Fort Laramie in 1869, serving in that capacity until 1880. (Gilbert)

RICHAUD, Louis (ca. 1846-1897) was the son of fur trader John Baptiste Richaud and his wife, Mary Gardiner, who was part Oglala. He grew up along the Platte River in Wyoming, where he and his brother-in-law, Big Bat Pourier, helped operate John Baptiste

Richaud's toll bridge. Although a competent scout, his service under Crook was marked with quarrels with Frank Grouard and he was permanently discharged after the fall 1876 campaign. Thrapp spelled the name "Richard," but most works give it as Richaud, or, phonetically, "Reeshaw." (Thrapp, 1991, 3:1214-15)

SCOTT, W.G., a friend of Bourke's who accompanied the 1874 expedition to the Hopi country.

SIEBER, Albert (1844-1907), a native of the Rhineland who was brought to the United States as a child, achieved national fame as one of the leading scouts in Arizona. General Crook especially depended on him during his Apache campaigns. Sieber and Archie McIntosh, Crook's other favorite scout, disliked each other but nevertheless worked well on a professional basis. (Thrapp, 1995)

SOULÉ, Milan, served as acting agent at San Carlos from 1872 to 1873, when he was replaced by James E. Roberts. See DALLAS, Andrew James. (Bancroft, 1889, 565)

STRAHORN, Robert Edmund (1852-1944), who signed his dispatches "Alter Ego," was a native of Pennsylvania. He obtained his first newspaper job when he was fourteen. In 1870, he went to Colorado, where he worked in Central City and Black Hawk before joining the Denver *Rocky Mountain News*. In addition to his regular job with the Denver paper, he also sold dispatches to the *Chicago Tribune*, *Omaha Republican*, *Cheyenne Sun*, and *New York Times*. Strahorn later settled in Spokane, Washington, and became a land developer and railroad executive, with extensive interests throughout the Pacific Northwest. (Knight, 169-71; Thrapp, 1991, 3:1376)

VANDEVER, William (1817-93), native of Maryland, served as United States Indian inspector under the Grant Administration from 1873 until 1877, prompting Bourke (who sometimes spelled it "Vandeveer") to call him "the lying emissary of the Indian Ring." Like many of Grant's appointments, Vandever had served in the Union Army during the Civil War, and was mustered out with the brevet rank of major general. He practiced law until his appointment as Indian inspector. He had served as a congressman from Iowa from 1858 to 1871, and, after moving to California, served as a congressman from that state from 1886 to 1891. He lived in Ventura, California, at the time of his death. (Warner, 523-24)

WARD, Felix, born Felix Tellez, was the son of a Mexican woman, Jesusa Tellez, and was adopted by her husband, an Irishman named

John Ward. In 1860, he was kidnapped by Apaches, and spent much of the remainder of his childhood with them. As an adult, he called himself Mickey Free, and scouted for the U.S. Army in Arizona. (Thrapp, 1988 and 1995; Lamar, 228)

WASSON, Joseph, was one of the first newspaper correspondents who actually covered the Indian Wars from the field, joining Crook's 1867 expeditions against Indians in Idaho, Oregon, and northern California. At the time, he and his brother, John, owned the Silver City, Idaho, *Owyhee Avalanche*. The Wasson brothers later established the Tucson *Arizona Citizen*, where Joe renewed his acquaintance with Crook and came to know Bourke. He was covering the Big Horn and Yellowstone Expedition for the *New York Tribune*, *San Francisco Alta California*, and *Philadelphia Press*. (Knight, 32-33, 168-69)

WELSH, William, was first chairman of the Board of Indian Commissioners. He resigned when the board failed to gain control of Indian expenditures, but remained active in the Indian Rights movement. Bourke spelled the name "Welch." See also COLYER, Vincent. (Priest, 28ff.)

YARNELL, Nelson. See COSGROVE, Thomas.

Indians

ALCHISAY (ca.1853-1928), White Mountain Apache, enlisted as a scout on December 2, 1872, quickly rose to sergeant, and won the Medal of Honor during the 1872-73 campaign. He was discharged in 1874, although he advised Crook on his return to Arizona in 1882, and served during the Geronimo Campaign. He received a gold medal from President Cleveland in 1888, and was prominent in reservation affairs until his death. (Thrapp, 1991, 1:12-13)

AMERICAN HORSE (ca. 1840-1908), Oglala Sioux chief, sometimes confused with another Oglala chief named American Horse, who was killed at Slim Buttes in 1876. He participated in the Fetterman Massacre, but subsequently settled at the Red Cloud Agency and was not involved in the Great Sioux War. He was an associate of Red Cloud, toured with Buffalo Bill, and as a leader of the Oglalas, earned enemies by often siding with the government in controversies. He died at Pine Ridge, South Dakota. (Thrapp, 1991, 1:21-22)

BLACK COAL, Arapaho chief, who, in 1874, led his people against the government and its Shoshone allies under their powerful chief Washakie. Nevertheless, he ultimately sided with the government during the Great Sioux War. Years later, in 1891, after the Arapahos had been placed on the Shoshone Reservation at Wind River, Black Coal challenged Washakie's authority, demanding—and receiving—equal status for the Arapahos. See also WASHAKIE. (Hyde, 1975, 297; Hoxie, 676)

BLACK KETTLE (ca. 1803-1868), Southern Cheyenne, generally was peaceful with whites, and was instrumental in avoiding the massacre of Colorado troops in a fight with Cheyennes in May 1864. Nevertheless, his band was attacked and many killed in the Sand Creek Massacre of November 29, 1864. Despite this, he signed the Little Arkansas Treaty of 1865, and the Medicine Lodge Treaty of 1868. On November 28, 1868, almost four years to the day after Sand Creek, his camp was attacked by the 7th Cavalry under Lt. Col. George Armstrong Custer, and Black Kettle was killed. In writing of Black Kettle, Bourke appeared to accept the official military view that he had been hostile. (Thrapp, 1991, 1:122-23)

BOCON. See ESQUIMASQUIN.

CHAN-DEISI (d. 1874), whom Crook called "John Daisy" because of the similarity to the pronunciation, was also known as She-shet. He was a discharged scout who belonged to Cochinay's band, and was involved in the killing of Lt. Jacob Almy at San Carlos in 1873. After the murder, he fled into the wilderness, and along with Chunz, Cochinay, and Delshay, ravaged the countryside. Crook offered a bounty for his head, which was brought in to Camp Apache in June 1874. See also ALMY, Jacob; DELSHAY; CHUNZ; COCHINAY. (Thrapp, 1988, 152ff.)

CHUNZ or Chuntz (d. 1874), Tonto Apache chief, was one of the most ruthless and elusive Apache leaders of the era. He was declared an outlaw by the military after he split the head of a Mexican boy with an axe at Camp Grant in 1872. The civilian agent, however, would not permit his arrest. After the outbreak at San Carlos in 1873, his band, along with those of Delshay, Cochinay, and Chandeisi, terrorized Arizona until mid-1874. He was tracked down by a band of Apache volunteers under Desalin, who brought Chunz's head, and six others, to San Carlos, where they were lined up on the parade ground. See also DELSHAY; CHAN-DEISI; COCHINAY. (Thrapp, 1988, 148 n.11, 151, 159-61)

COCHINAY (d. 1874) was among the chiefs who broke out at San Carlos following the killing of Lt. Almy. He terrorized the countryside for a year, until a band of scouts caught him about a mile from Tucson. His severed head was taken to San Carlos for bounty. See also ALMY, Jacob; DELSHAY; CHUNZ; CHAN-DEISI. (Thrapp, 1988, 155ff.)

COCHISE (ca. 1824-1874) is one of the most famous American Indians, largely because of his efforts to maintain peace following the Cochise War. The war itself started after the incident with Lieutenant Bascom mentioned in the text, and lasted almost twelve years before Brig. Gen. Oliver O. Howard was able to negotiate a peace. At Cochise's direction, the government established a reservation centered on the Dragoon Mountains, that occupied much of the southeastern part of Arizona. It was abolished two years after his death and the Chiricahuas were concentrated at San Carlos. Cochise was the son-in-law and associate of Mangas Coloradas, who is considered perhaps the greatest of all Apache leaders. He inherited the mantle of supremacy following Mangas's death in 1863. In the nineteenth century, there was no consistent spelling of Apache names, and Bourke uses "Cochies," "Cochis," and "Cocheis," the latter of which was most common among whites. See also JEFFORDS, Thomas Jonathan; HOWARD, Oliver Otis; MANGAS COLORADAS. (Sweeney, 1991; Lamar, 228)

CRAZY HORSE (ca. 1840-1877), Oglala war chief, drew attention not only for his mysticism and introverted personality, but also because of his red hair and pale, freckled complexion. In 1865, he was designated one of the four Oglala "shirt wearers" or leading political chiefs, but lost the position five years later following an altercation involving another man's wife. He distinguished himself in the Fetterman Massacre of 1866, and subsequently during the Great Sioux War. Arrested on September 5, 1877, he was bayoneted during a scuffle at the guardhouse at Camp Robinson, Nebraska, and died about midnight. During the latter half of the twentieth century, he became a symbol of Indian political and social resistance. See also BURKE, Daniel Webster; CLARK, Walter Philo; GROUARD, Frank; LITTLE BIG MAN; MC GILLYCUDDY, Valentine T. (Utley, 1997, 109-10; Nickerson, 20; DeBarthe, 117)

DELSHAY or Delt-chay (ca. 1838-1874), Tonto Apache, was a noted raider, sometimes leading his band in concert with other raiding bands. Although he sometimes led his people onto reservations, he remained restless and could not refrain from raiding. Crook offered a bounty for Delshay's head. Two separate claims were submitted, one with a scalp and ears, and the other with the complete head. Crook paid both. See also CHAN-DEISI, CHUNZ, COCHINAY. (Thrapp, 1991, 1:389-90)

EL-CAHN, whom Bourke called "El Cal," (d. 1890) Bronco Apache, apparently undistinguished until 1889, when he and several others were sentenced to life at Yuma, Arizona, Territorial Prison for murder of a freighter. El-cahn and two others escaped. El-cahn was killed by troops and the other escapees were recovered. (Thrapp, 1991, 1:457)

ESKIMINZIN (d. 1896), Arivaipa Apache chief, was leader of the band that had been massacred at Camp Grant. His confidence in the government was restored after meeting with Vincent Colyer, and he became a scout for the army. He maintained a farm on the San Carlos Reservation. Eskiminzin established a working relationship with San Carlos Agent John Clum based on mutual trust and respect. In 1888, his association with an outlaw known as the Apache Kid led to his arrest, and internment in Florida and subsequently in Alabama. Allowed to return to San Carlos, he lived quietly until his death. See also CLUM, John Philip; COLYER, Vincent; WHITMAN, Royal Emerson. (Bourke, 1980, 183; Schmitt, 168; Lamar, 351)

ESQUIMASQUIN (d. 1873), also known as "Bocon" (Big Mouth), was an Apache scout leader. Bourke described him as "crafty, cruel, daring, and ambitious," but added he overindulged in tizwin. His tendency to become intoxicated from drink after a fast of several days led to his death a few months after the end of the 1872-73 campaign. (Bourke, 1980, 183)

LITTLE BIG MAN, Oglala "shirt wearer" or senior chief of Crazy Horse's band, initially was pegged—justifiably—as a trouble maker when he arrived at the Red Cloud Agency in 1872. His name had nothing to do with stature, but was to distinguish him from his father, also named Big Man. Little Big Man surrendered with Crazy Horse in 1877, pledging to General Crook that he would maintain the peace. During the scuffle in which Crazy Horse was killed at Camp Robinson, Little Big Man pinioned his arms. He always maintained the death was an accident. He settled at Pine Ridge where, in 1879, he became a policeman. See also CRAZY HORSE. (Hyde, 1975, 198, 243n 297-98)

LITTLE WOUND, Oglala chief, attempted to be accommodating, but government blundering drove his band to hostility in 1865. He signed the Fort Laramie Treaty of 1868. Like Red Cloud and other chiefs, however, he understood the treaty was simply to restore peace and trade, and refused to abandon his hunting grounds to the government. Nevertheless, he settled at the Red Cloud Agency, and, together with Red Cloud, probably saved Agent J. J. Saville's life from a kangaroo court organized by Little Big Man and Pretty Bear over a dispute about rations. In 1877, he combined with Red Cloud and other Oglala leaders to support General Crook against Crazy Horse. He eventually settled at Pine Ridge. See also CRAZY HORSE, LITTLE BIG MAN, RED CLOUD. (Hyde, 1975, 155, 164, 169, 209, 297)

MANGAS COLORADAS (1793?-1863), Chiricahua leader, was probably the greatest Apache chief of historic times. He first became known to the American public in the 1840s, although his relations with Americans at that time was cordial. As American settlement threatened the Apache way of life, however, he began raiding mining camps, ranches, and stagecoach stations. His ill-feelings were aggravated after he was badly beaten by a group of American miners. Mangas was badly wounded in a fight with troops in 1862. After his recovery, he attempted to negotiate a peace, but was taken prisoner, and appears to have been tortured with heated bayonets before being killed. Cochise was his son-in-law and protégé. See COCHISE. (Hoxie, 354-55)

NANNI-CHADDI, Apache leader whose band was annihilated by troops under Capt. William Henry Brown on December 28, 1872. A year earlier, he had met with Vincent Colyer, and promised to obey the government. The destruction of his band demonstrated that soldiers could penetrate Apache country, and locate and destroy hostile groups, no matter how well secluded or defended. See also BROWN, William Henry; COLYER, Vincent. (Thrapp, 1988, 127-30)

OLD MAN AFRAID OF HIS HORSES arose to leadership of the Oglalas during a power struggle in the early 1850s. Details are sketchy but he appears to have been recognized by the government as head chief during this period. In 1854, he tried unsuccessfully to head off the confrontation between troops commanded by Second Lt. J. L. Grattan and Lakotas near Fort Laramie, which resulted in the massacre of Grattan and his men, and essentially marked the beginning of the Sioux Wars. This failure led the government to designate Bad Wound as head chief. Although the government considered him a peace chief, he joined Red Cloud in refusing to sign the proposed Fort Laramie Treaty of 1866. He did, however, sign the 1868 treaty. By this time, however, his prestige had begun to wane, and Red Cloud, about five years his junior, assumed preeminence. He eventually settled at the Red Cloud Agency, and later at Pine Ridge. See also RED CLOUD; YOUNG MAN AFRAID OF HIS HORSES. (Hyde, 1975, 67-68, 73-74, 139, 164)

RED CLOUD (1822-1909), Oglala, became a powerful war chief through his own accomplishments. He appears to have taken his first scalp at sixteen, in a raid against the Pawnees. He participated in the Grattan Massacre, and was a distinguished leader against Gen. Patrick Connor's failed North Plains Expedition. During a treaty council at Fort Laramie in June 1866, Red Cloud and his followers walked out in protest of a proposal to surrender more hunting grounds to the government. This led to the Red Cloud War of 1866-68, that forced the government to abandon the Bozeman Trail and Forts Reno, Phil Kearny, and C.F. Smith. After signing the Fort Laramie Treaty of 1868, Red Cloud never again went to war, although during the Great Sioux War, his sympathies were with the hostiles. This led Crook to depose him as paramount chief of the Lakotas in favor of Spotted Tail in September 1876. Following the death of Spotted Tail in 1881, Red Cloud again emerged as paramount chief. More visionary than many of the other leaders, he saw that the survival of his people depended on adapting to government expectations. He died at Pine Ridge. See also YOUNG MAN AFRAID OF HIS HORSES; SPOTTED TAIL; THREE BEARS. Red Cloud's life is covered in Olson; Hyde, 1975; and Larson.

ROCKY BEAR, Oglala chief, together with Sitting Bull of the South, and Three Bears, persuaded young warriors of the Red Cloud Agency to enlist as scouts for General Crook, over the objections of Red Cloud and Agent James S. Hastings. See also SITTING BULL OF THE SOUTH; THREE BEARS. (Hyde, 1975, 259)

SHARP NOSE, Arapaho chief, led his tribe's contingent serving under General Crook in the summer and fall of 1876. Besides being a noted warrior and leader, soldiers praised him as one of the most outstanding guides. He was especially valuable in guiding Mackenzie's cavalry to the main Cheyenne camp on November 24-25. (Dunlay, 82)

SITTING BULL (1831?-90), Hunkpapa war chief and holy man, as a young man attained a superlative record as a warrior, and in 1857, was designated a war chief. His conflicts with whites appear to have begun when Montana-bound gold seekers came up the Missouri River. The government soon began building forts along the river, prompting Sitting Bull to lead his people in a five-year war. By this time, his interest had turned to spirituality, and he was known among all the Lakota tribes as a holy man. In his combined capacity of military and religious leader, he became the focal point of the Lakotas resisting the Fort Laramie Treaty of 1868, and the subsequent settlement on reservations. His warriors fought troops on a survey expedition into the Yellowstone Valley in 1872 and 1873. Rather than surrender during the Great Sioux War, he led a remnant of his people into Canada, where they remained until 1881, when he turned himself in at Fort Buford, North Dakota. He toured briefly with Buffalo Bill's Wild West Show, but spent most of his time on the Standing Rock Reservation, adopting white methods he deemed useful, and rejecting those he did not. As more of the Indian lands were taken, Sitting Bull became a leader of the Ghost Dance movement at Standing Rock. He was killed on December 15, 1890, in a fight that broke out when Indian Police tried to arrest him. (Utley, 1993; Hoxie, 593-95)

SITTING BULL OF THE SOUTH (1841-76) was a name that whites gave to the Oglala leader Sitting Bull to distinguish him from the great Hunkpapa chief Sitting Bull. As a young man, Sitting Bull of the South became friends with a telegrapher, who taught him to read and write, and to use the telegraph. He was fluent in English. Following the Sand Creek Massacre in Colorado in 1864, he joined a hostile faction, and participated in several fights, including the Fetterman Massacre in Wyoming. Later he settled at the Red Cloud Agency, and accompanied two delegations to Washington. He was ambushed and killed by a group of Crows while on a truce mission to Crazy Horse. See also ROCKY BEAR; THREE BEARS. (Thrapp, 1991, 3:1315)

SPOTTED TAIL (1823?-81) , was a Brulé "shirt wearer" or senior chief, and war leader. Although he was involved in the Grattan Massacre of 1855, he surrendered the following month. He was de-tained at Fort Leavenworth, Kansas, and Fort Kearny, Nebraska, for a year, during which he learned enough about the whites to realize their numbers and technology made them an irresistible force. From that point onward, he strove to maintain peace, and obtain education for his people, while preserving their ancient culture. He did, however, lead an assault against Julesburg, Colorado, in retaliation for the Sand Creek Massacre of 1864, and government restrictions on Lakota travel along the Platte River. Soon after, he permanently ceased fighting whites, signed the Fort Laramie Treaty of 1868, and took up residence on a reservation in Nebraska. In 1876, General Crook deposed Red Cloud as head chief of the Lakotas, and designated Spotted Tail in his place. Although Spotted Tail negotiated the surrender of hostile bands, he rejected the proposition that the Lakotas be relocated to Oklahoma. In 1880, a political struggle developed among the Brulés, with opposition centering around Spotted Tail's cousin, Crow Dog. On August 5, 1881, an altercation developed between the two men, and Crow Dog shot Spotted Tail. After his death, the Brulés ceased to play a significant role in Lakota affairs. See also RED CLOUD. (Hoxie, 603-05; Hyde, 1987)

THREE BEARS, Oglala, served as first sergeant of scouts during Crook's Powder River expedition of 1876. Together with Young Man Afraid of His Horses, he opposed Red Cloud's obstructionist policies. Previously, in October 1874, they had headed off a confrontation between several hundred unruly warriors at the Red Cloud Agency, saving a small detachment of troops from Camp Robinson, under Lt. Emmet Crawford, from potential massacre. After that, Crawford considered Three Bears a close friend. See also CRAWFORD, Emmet; RED CLOUD; ROCKY BEAR; YOUNG MAN AFRAID OF HIS HORSES. (Dunlay, 137, 141-42)

WASHAKIE (1804?-1900), powerful and autocratic chief of the Shoshones, spent most of his life maintaining peace with the federal government. His position was reenforced in 1863, when Col. Patrick Connor defeated and subdued Shoshone dissidents who had joined Bannocks in raiding against white emigrants. In 1868, he signed the Fort Bridger Treaty establishing a Shoshone reservation in what is now western Wyoming. In the 1870s, he led his people as scouts, first against the Arapahos, and later as part of Crook's Big Horn and Yellowstone Expedition. He opposed some government policies, including the resettlement of Arapahos on the Shoshone

Reservation. Nevertheless, he cooperated, realizing that to oppose the government would bring disaster for his people. In 1878, at General Crook's behest, the government upgraded Camp Brown, Wyoming, on the Shoshone Reservation, renaming it Fort Washakie, in his honor. See also BLACK COAL. (Hoxie, 675-76; Robinson, 2001, 221)

YOUNG MAN AFRAID OF HIS HORSES (ca. 1830-1900) was a hereditary Oglala chief through is father, Old Man Afraid Of His Horses. He was an associate of Red Cloud, and participated in various fights along the Bozeman Trail and in the Fetterman Massacre during the Red Cloud War. He was a party to the Fort Laramie Treaty of 1868, and thereafter worked as a sort of mediator between Indians and whites. Although he opposed the sale of Sioux lands to the government, he eventually was designated president of the Pine Ridge Indian Council. He also adamantly opposed the Ghost Dance religion. See also OLD MAN AFRAID OF HIS HORSES; RED CLOUD; THREE BEARS. (Thrapp, 1991, 3:1614-15)

Appendix 2

❖

❖

❖

❖

❖

Orders of particular importance to Bourke's narrative—Arizona

Crook Assumes Command of Department of Arizona
[Volume 1, Page 15] *
Headquarters Department of Arizona,
                    DRUM BARRACKS, CAL., JUNE 4, 1871
GENERAL ORDERS,
No. 12.

In obedience to paragraph II, Special Orders No. 176, Adjutant General's Office, current series, the undersigned assumes the command of the Department of Arizona.

The following named officers constitute the Department Staff:

Captain *A. H. Nickerson*, 23d Infantry, Aide-de-Camp, Acting Assistant Adjutant General.

Lieutenant-Colonel *Charles H. Tompkins*, Deputy Quartermaster General, Chief Quartermaster.

Captain *John W. Turner*, Commissary Department, Chief Commissary.

Surgeon *E. I. Baily*, Medical Director.

Major *Charles J. Sprague*, Chief Paymaster.

---

* *Volume numbers refer to the manuscript volumes as arranged in the West Point Library—ed.*

Major *James Nelson*, Paymaster.
Major *Robert Morrow*, Paymaster.

GEORGE CROOK;

Brevet Major General,

OFFICIAL:
[No signature]

Aide-de-Camp

Bourke Named Aide-de-Camp
[Volume 1, Page 18]
Headquarters Department of Arizona,

DRUM BARRACKS, CAL., SEPTEMBER 1, 1871

GENERAL ORDERS,
No. 18.

The following named officers having been directed by the War
Department to report for duty upon the personal Staff of the
Department Commander, are hereby announed as Aides-de-Camp
to the undersigned:

Second Lieutenant *William J. Ross*, 21st Infantry.
Second Lieutenant *John G. Bourke*, 3d Cavalry.

GEORGE CROOK,

Lieut.-Col., 23d Infantry,
Bvt. Major General,
Commanding.

OFFICIAL:
[signed]
John G. Bourke

Aide-de-Camp.
Cessation of Hostilities
[Volume 1, Page 186]
Headquarters Department of Arizona,

PRESCOTT: APRIL 7, 1873

GENERAL ORDERS,
No. 12.

It is with pleasure the announcement is made of the surrender
of large numbers of Indians lately hostile, against whom military
operations have been prosecuted for the past four months; and
the assurance through the chiefs and head men of these tribes of

their desire and the desire of their people to conclude a permanent peace.

These propositions are made in the midst of a campaign in which they have been severely punished, and the Department Commander, believing in their sincerity, announces and hereby declares peace with the tribes referred to.

The basis of this peace is simply that these Indians shall cease plundering and murdering, remain upon their several reservations, and comply with the regulations made by the Government, through authorized agents, for them.

So long, therefore, as they remain true to their agreement, they will be protected by the Military of this Department in the enjoyment of all their rights under the law.

After sufficient time shall have elapsed to enable the friends of any renegades still at large to bring them in upon their proper reservations, post commanders will use the troops at their command to pursue and force them in, and in case any such straggling bands continue to remain absent without proper authority, they will be forced to surrender or be destroyed.

BY COMMAND OF BREVET MAJOR-GENERAL CROOK:

A. H. NICKERSON,
Captain, Twenty-third Infantry,
A.D.C., and A.A.A. General.

OFFICIAL:
[signed]
John G. Bourke
Aide-de-Camp.

Instructions for Officers Commanding Troops
on Indian Reservations
[Volume 1, Pages 188-89]
Headquarters Department of Arizona,
PRESCOTT: APRIL 8, 1873

GENERAL ORDERS,
No. 13.

The following memorandum of instructions is hereby published for the guidance of officers commanding troops stationed on the several Indian Reservations in this Department:

I. With a view to bringing the straggling bands and families still at large upon the reservation, and to serve as a nucleus for the establishment of civil government, a small number of the Indians recently used as scouts will be retained in service under existing laws, at each of the reservations hereafter specified.

Each of these detachments will be under the command of an officer, designated by the Department Commander, who will have charge, under the supervision of the commanding officer of the post, of their clothing and accounts; but the post commander may communicate with them direct, at any and all times.

These Indians will be selected from among the best of their several tribes, and will be liable to be mustered out for misconduct towards the Indians of their own or other tribes, or other good cause, and their places filled by others duly slected. They will constitute the police force of the resrvations, and while required to attend regular musters and inspections will not only be allowed, but will be required to cultivate the soil and perform the various industries prescribed by the Indian Department, the same as other Indians.

They will be used, from time to time, upon the application of the agent, or the commanding officers' own motion, to preserve the peace, report and correct any irregularities that may occur among their own or other tribes in the vicinity.

II. Commanding officers will aid the duly authorized agents in instructing the Indians in, and establishing among them civil government in the simplest form, enabling them to settle their differences according to the usages of civilization, gradually showing them its benefits as contrasted with their own barbarous forms and customs.

To do this effectually will require different forms to suit the pecularities of different tribes, and the agents of the several reservations are requested to meet the officers commanding the military on their respective reservations and agree upon the necessary forms, being careful not to make them too complicated at first for the comprehension of the tribes to which they are to be applied, leaving them to be enlarged with their capabilities, so that when the auxiliary force an be dispensed with, they will be capable of self government and eventually become good citizens.

While they should not be judged harshly for acts which in civil codes would constitute minor offenses, care should also be taken that they do not succeed in deceiving their agents and the officers, in matters of greater import, being careful to treat them as children in *ignorance*, not in *innocence*.

Perfect harmony between the officers of the Indian and War Departments, on duty together, is absolutely necessary in treating Indians so lately hostile and so apparently incorrigible, and the Department Commander earnestly enjoins this harmony, and directs that in case of difference in the matters where the line is not plainly marked, that officers carefully avoid such differences being made known to the Indians, and that they refrain from any overt act in the matter at issue, until instructions from these Headquarters shall have been received.

BY COMMAND OF BREVET MAJOR-GENERAL CROOK:

A. H. NICKERSON,

Captain, Twenty-third Infantry,
A.D.C., and A.A.A. General.

OFFICIAL:
[No signature]

Aide-de-Camp.

Appendix 3

[Volume 1, Pages 78, 80]

Names of Indian tribes
in Arizona Department

Cocopahs	Rio Colorado	Friendly
Yumas	"	"
New River	"	"
Chimahuevis	"	"
Mojaves	"	"
Cohuallas (Uilas)	California	"
Diguneos	"	"
Pah-utes	Cal & Nevada	Dubious
Sevintz	Rio Colorado	"
Sampas	Arizona	"
Hualpais	"	Friendly
Apache-Mojaves	"	Whipped
Apache-Yumas	"	"
Apache-Tontos	"	"
Moquis	Arizona	Friendly
Zunis	Arizona and New Mexico	Friendly
Navajoes	New Mexo.	Dubious
Apaches	Arizona	Whipped
Tontos	"	"
Pimas	"	Friendly
Maricopas	"	"
Papagoes	"	"
Opatas	Sonora	"

Yaquis   "   "
Mayos.   "   "

The last three tribes come to Arizona to trade at Tucson, or to seek employment.

Appendix 4

[Volume 1, Pages 82, 84]

Names of Indian agents and agencies in Arizona

Hon. H. Bendell. (1871-72)	Superintendent, Prescott AT
Dr. R A Wilber	Papago Agency
J H Stout	Maricopas & Pimas[,] Sacaton
J A Robert	White Mountain Reservation[,] "Camp Apache"
C.F. Larrabee	San Carlos Division White Mt. Res.
Dr. J.A Tonner.	Colorado Reservation
[Thomas] J Jefferds	Chiricahua Reservation
J. Williams	Rio Verde Reservation
Capt Ths Byrne	Beales Springs Reservation

Appendix 5

[Volume 1, Page 86]

Posts in the Department of Arizona

Name	Latitude	Longitude	Altitude
Camp Apache	34 deg	109 deg. 45 m	5600
Bowie	33. deg. 40 m	109 d. 25 m 30 s	4826
Date Creek	34 deg 45 m	112 d. 18 m	3726
Beales Springs	[Not recorded]		
Grant	[Not recorded]		
Haulpa	35 deg. 10 m	113 d. 50 m	[Not recorded]
Lowell	[Not recorded]		
McDowell	33 deg. 40 m	111 d. 40 m	1800
Mojave	35 deg 24 sec.	114 d. 34 m 40 s	600
Fort Whipple	34 de. 29. m. 6 s.	112 d, 30 m 30.s	5700
Fort Yuma	32 d. 23 m 3 s	114 d. 36 m 9 s.	355

Appendix 6

❖

[Volume 1, Pages 88]

❖

❖

❖

Table of distances between Prescott and the following points

	miles
San Francisco via Los Angeles	916
Camp Apache via Tucson	481
Camp Apache via Little Colorado	268
Camp Bowie	364
Camp Date Creek	60
Prescott	259
Florence	[Not recorded]
Maricopa Wells	161
Camp Hualpai	39
Camp Beales Springs	124
Camp Mojave	165
Camp Colorado (Colorado Reservation)	236
Ehrenberg AT	190
San Diego Cal.	530
Los Angeles Cal.	430
Tubac AT	207
Guaymas Mex	610
Fort Yuma Cal.	338
Arizona City	338
Wickenburg	88
La Libertad Mexico	484
Fort Cumming NM	473

Camp Cady Cal	295
Camp Verde	39

Table of distances between Prescott and other points

Lobos, Mexico	473 miles
old Camp Reno	203 miles
Camp McDowell	170 miles
Camp Independence, Cal	716 miles
Old Camp Pinal AT	244 miles
Old Camp Crittenden A.T.	310 miles
Old Camp Goodwin AT	409 miles

Appendix 7

❖

[Volume 1, Page 118]

❖

❖

❖

Command of Maj. Brown which left Mt. Graham, February 15, 1873

Comdg. Officer

W.H. Brown, Capt 5th Cav Brevt. Maj U.S.A. A.I.G.

5th Cav [companies listed below]   1st Cav [companies listed below]

"L" Lt Bourke A.D.C.

"A" E. Woodson   &

"M" Lt Brodie 1st Cav

"F" L. W.P. Hall

"G" Capt Burns   &   commd by Captain

"H" "   Hamilton   Geo Randall, 23 Infty

"I" Lt Babcock

"L" Capt Taylor   Indian Scouts [listed below]

"M" (1st Lt Almy[)]   Grant Apach[e]   Lt Almy

2d Lt Walls   Sa. Blanca "   " Brodie

Yavapais   ———   Lt Schuyler

Volunteers   Lts Ross, Rockwell, Bourke

Surgeons   Girard, Harper, Matthews Porter

Guides   McCoy, McIntosh, Ellet, Rice, Spears, Noble, Clark

Officers   d[itt]o   17

Rationed for 30 days

Appendix 8

[Volume 1, Pages 150, 152, 154]

Tables of distances between Fort Yuma and Various Points

Tables of distances from Ft Yuma to

Camp Apache via Tucson	497 miles
Camp Bowie	380
Camp Colorado	195
Camp Crittenden	326
Camp Date Creek	278
Camp Goodwin	425
Camp Grant (old)	268
Camp Lowell (Tucson)	275
Camp McDowell	222
Camp Mojave	503
Camp Reno	263
Camp Hualpai	377
Camp Verde	377
Fort Whipple	338
Guaymas, Mex	626
La Libertad, Mex	500
Ehrenberg AT	140
Lapaz, AT	130
Lobos, Mex	489
Maricopa Wells AT	177
San Diego, Cal	192
Tubac, AT	321
Los Angeles Cal	279
Fort Cummings N.M.	494

Appendix 9

[Volume 1, Pages 156, 158]

Table of routes to posts in southern Arizona

In the following table, Bourke lists two routes to posts in southern Arizona, one overland from San Francisco, and one via the Gulf of California and up through Mexico along the Colorado River. In the 1870s, the gulf route was often favored as more convenient and sometimes safer than the rugged overland route, and soldiers coming directly to Arizona from the eastern United States routinely sailed directly from Panama to the Colorado River with stopovers in Acapulco and Guaymas.

Table of distances from San Francisco to

		miles
Camp Colorado	via the usual route	753
	" Gulf Cal	2459
Camp Lowell (Tucson)		1006
Fort Whipple (Prescott[)]		882
Fort Yuma	usual route	731
Gulf Cal		2280
Yuaymas [*sic*] Mex		1700
Ehrenberg AT.	usual route	711
Gulf Cal		2420
Mouth of Colorado		2130
San Diego Cal		585
Wilmington, Cal		427
Camp Mojave	usual road	717
	Gulf Cal	2595

Appendix 10

[Volume 1, Pages 160, 162, 164, 166]

Names of chiefs who assisted Crook in the Apache Campaign

Pah-Utes

Captain Jack
Hualpais
Sharum
Levi-Levi
"Charlie"
Allelulia
Panao.

Apache-Yumas

Jamaspie
Tom
Wabbie-Yuma

Apaches (S[ierr]a Blanca)

Miguel
Es-kel-te-se-la
Es-qui-pi-tou-cha
Pelona
Capitan Chiquito
Pedro
The Beggar
Na-va-ta-ne-a
Es-quid-ti-es
Santos

Lame chief
Ba-ba-da-dinie
Jose de Leon (Captive)

Apaches. ([Camp] Grant)

Es-qui-minzin
Santos
Es-qui-nopsus.
Es-qui-nas-quisn.
or "Bocon"=Big Mouth

Appendix 11

[Volume 1, Page 168]

Names of hostile chiefs in the Apache Campaign

Cocheis.

Delt-chay	whipped
Chlit-le-pin	(")
Clib-ba-cli	(")
Nanna-Chaddi	Killed.

Appendix 1 2

[Volume 1, Pages, 177, 179, 181, 183]

Interview between
Major W. H. Brown and Cochise

Account of the interview between Maj. W. H. Brown, 5th Cav and the Indian chief Cocheis or Cheis.   February 3d 1873.[1]

Major Brown. I have come from General Crook to this part of the country to see Cocheis: the General hears that Cocheis is at peace and he knows by (Cocheis') actions that he has kept it. The General is anxious also to keep this peace in all its integrity according to the terms of the treaty; but, in order to be able to do this, he wants to know what the terms of the treaty are. He has never been furnished with a copy of the treaty, and altho' he will receive a copy, in time, yet it is a long way to Washington and the easiest way to get these terms [is that] he has sent me to Cocheis to find out what he understands these terms to be, and, especially with reference to the movements of troops within the reservation of Cocheis—and particularly, whether troops are to be permitted to come upon the Reservation or not—and also what has been the understanding about Mexico, whether the peace applies to the people of that country or not.

Cocheis. The troops were to pass and repass by the roads in the Reservation, the same as ever, according as the emergencies of the service might require, but none were to come upon the Reservation to live, nor were citizens to do so.

1. This interview was interpreted by Agent Thomas J. Jeffords, Cochise's friend and confidant. Bourke wrote it partly in transcript and partly in paraphrase.

Brown—What stipulations, if any, were made in the treaty with regard to the people of Mexico?

Cocheis. (Endeavoring to evade the question) now said that permission had been given them by General Howard to go to Mount Graham in seed-time to gather acorns, [and] mesquite beans, but they were not to live at Mount Graham.

Maj Brown [to Jeffords]—Tell them that is all right; they can go to Mount Graham and get seeds and such things as they may want, so long as they live upon the Reservation—but, they must always tell the agent so the troops may expect their coming. Say also if they want to come and see where the new post is going to be placed, some of them can accompany me on my way back.

(Maj Brown now repeated the question about Mexico.)

Cocheis. The Mexicans are on one side in this matter and the Americans on another. There are many young people here whose parents and relatives have been killed by the Mexicans, and now these young people are liable to go down, from time to time and do a little damage to the Mexicans. I don't want to lie about this thing; they go, but I don't send them.

I made peace with the Americans, but the Mexicans did not come to ask peace from me as the Americans have done. I don't myself want to go down to Mexico and will not go but my boys may go there. I consider myself at peace with Mexico, but my young men, like those at all the other Reservations, are liable to occasionally make raids. I don't want to lie about this; I can't prevent it. There are bad people everywhere. A great many of us were one time at peace at Fronteras[2] and some of the Mexicans used to tell us to come up here and steal American horses, which are big and worth a great deal of money in Mexico. But when our people came back there with them, they killed them and took the horses and cattle away. Why don't the Americans tell us to go down and steal from the Mexicans[?]

Maj Brown. Tell them we are now at peace with Mexico and cannot do them any harm. When we make friends with a man we never to anything behind his back to hurt him. If ever we go to war with Mexico, we shall send word to the Mexicans, and tell them we are coming. If we whip them, we shall whip them fairly,

2. Fronteras, Sonora, in Mexico, due south of Cochise's stronghold in the Dragoon Mountains of Arizona.

but not by doing anything behind their backs. I have said all I have to say & when I go back I shall tell the General all about Cocheis so that he will know all about him the same as if he had come here himself.

Cocheis. It is all right. When this ground was given me it was that we might roam over it as we pleased. I don't intend to let my young men do any wrong on this ground. I like the way in which you talk. (The remainder of this sentence, not being understood by me as Maj Brown appeared to understand it, has been omitted). I am glad of the peace and my people rejoice at it.

The meeting closed, as it had begun, with a general hand-shaking.

Present Capt. W. H. Brown, Bv [i.e., Brevet] Major &

lst Lieut C.H. Rockwell, 5h Cav

2nd Lieut John G. Bourke, 3d Cav

Mr Stevens, actg agent for the San Carlos Reservation

Mr. Jefferds, Agent for Cocheis' Band

Archie McIntosh, Guide.

The interpretation was made by Mr. Jefferds.

Appendix 13

✦

✦

✦

✦

✦

Letter from Bourke regarding Lieutenant Jacob Almy's Death

Undated Clipping from the Arizona Miner
Volume 1, Page 187
[Handwritten comment by Bourke] Murdered May 27th 1873
[Clipping from newspaper]

"Readers of the MINER will be pained to learn of the murder, at the San Carlos Indian agency, on the 27th ultimo, of lst Lieut. Jacob Almy, 5th Cavalry, a young officer of prominence during the recent campaign.

From the meagre details thus far furnished, I can only state that Lieut. Almy's death occurred while endeavoring to quell a disturbance among the Indians of the San Carlos Reservation. These disturbances, growing out of rivalry and antagonism between the former and the present agent, to which the Indians became involved. The particulars of this hostility have been known to the Indian Department in this Territory for some time.

Lieut. Almy was, I believe, a native of Massachusetts and a graduate of the U.S. Military Academy at West Point, in the class of 1867. His first services were seen in the campaign of 1867-68, against the hostile Cheyennes and Arapahoes, in which he displayed the same high qualities which afterwards made him so conspicuous in General Crook's operations against the Apaches. He was present for duty during that campaign, from its first inception to its close, and such were his gallantry, coolness, sound judgment and enthusiastic desire for distinction, that although inferior in rank to many of the officers present, he was selected to command one of the columns to operate in the Tonto Basin. His arduous and valuable services were fittingly acknowledged by General Crook in the congratulatory orders issued upon the termination of hostilities, in which orders Almy's name occurred three times.

He won the esteem and regard of the Department Commander by his energy, capacity and modest demeanor; of his associate officers by his daring gallantry and noble qualities. His soldiers revered him as a man with whom failure was impossible, and our Indian allies as a soldier whose word was as inflexible as iron.

In him our Territory has sustained a loss of the gravest character; it is rare, indeed, that so much ability is united to so much worth and that the desire to place our struggling Territory upon its feet is expressed in vigorous action in place of empty words.

The grief of his family will be alleviated by the assurance that it is shared by all his brother officers and soldiers and by all classes of our citizens.

May he rest in peace."

[clipping hand signed]
John G. Bourke
3d Cav.

Appendix 14

❖

[Volume 2, Pages 116, 118, 120]

❖

❖

❖

Extraneous notes of Hopi life

At the Moqui villages, a very noticeable feature is the agility and perfect fearlessness with which little baby children run up and down the steep narrow stone steps leading to the roofs of the four story houses. These stairways are unprotected by ballustrade or railings of any kind, have a "raise" of eight inches and a "tread" of only four to six. It was with extreme caution our heavily booted soldiers climbed up the same stairways and ladders.

The rafters, beams and ladders used by the Moquis are constructed of cottonwood; a tree to which we should hereafter assign, under favorable treatment, a greater degree of durability than is at present conceded. No timber of this species can now be found in quantities, within less than 50 miles of Oraybe, and if much were needed search might have to be made for 100 miles.

Secured some seeds of peaches, corn and other vegetables to take to Prescott.

The Moquis have no doors, no window-shutters and no window panes. In very cold weather warmth is afforded by closing doorways with fur coverlids.

Moquis make a regular Mexican "puchero" or "olla padreada" of chopped mutton, chile, tomatoes, beans, corn and onions. A large basin of the stew is placed on the floor and each of the guests squatted around it darts into a dirty pan and helps himself to such "bonnes bouches" as attract his eye or taste. The men eat alone and before the women or children, who fall to on the remnants of their lord's and masters' feast.

Moquis are, according to their own account, monogamists. Women marry almost immediately upon attaining age of puberty. Families average four and five children.

Women nubile at twelve years.

Towards strangers, women of this tribe are reserved and deserve commendation for chastity; among themselves, at least until after marriage, women are at liberty to follow their own inclinations.

Referring to the Albinos among them, the people of Oraybe say they are now reduced to three; a man, a woman and a little girl. Once they were very many, but all, excepting the few now with them, have died. The other towns also have Albinos.

For travelling purposes, they make a canteen of the long-necked gourd wound around with a network of woolen yarn.

The women of the Moquis exhibit in many instances a pronounced Mongolian type of features.

Some of the old men bore on their faces the marks of small pox.

Appendix 15

[Volume 2a, Page 18]

Orders of particular importance to Bourke's narrative—Dept. of the Platte

Orders of Particular Importance to Bourke's Narrative–
The Platte
Crook Relinquishes Command of Department of Arizona
Headquarters Department of Arizona,

PRESCOTT, *March* 22d, 1875

GENERAL ORDERS,
No. 7.

Complying with the provisions of General Orders, No. 18, Adjutant General's Office, current series, the undersigned relinquishes command of this Department

GEORGE CROOK,
Brigadier-General

OFFICIAL:
[Signed]
John G. Bourke.
Aide-de-Camp.

Crook Assumes Command of Department of the Platte
[Volume 2a, Page 150]
HEADQUARTERS DEPARTMENT OF THE PLATTE,
Omaha, *Nebraska, April* 27, 1875
GENERAL ORDERS,
No. 10

I....In accordance with the provisions of Paragraph III, General Orders, No. 18, current series, from the War Department, the undersigned hereby assumes command of the Department of the Platte.

II...Captain *Azor H. Nickerson*, 23d Infantry, and Second Lieutenant *John G. Bourke*, 3d Cavalry, are hereby announced as the Aides-de-Camp of the Commanding General.

III...Captain *A. H. Nickerson*, 23d Infantry, Aide-de-Camp, is appointed Acting Assistant Adjutant-General.

IV...Captain *Henry G. Litchfield*, 2d Artillery, is assigned to special duty at these Headquarters.

V...With the additions herein before-mentioned, the Department Staff will remain as constituted.

GEORGE CROOK,
Brigadier-General,
Commanding.

OFFICIAL:
[Signed]
John G. Bourke.
Aide-de-Camp.

Appendix 16

❖

✦

◆

❖

New York Herald coverage of Crook's Big Horn and Yellowstone Expedition

Reprinted below are Reuben Davenport's account of the Battle of the Rosebud, and the New York Herald *editorial, that Bourke mentioned so derisively in his diary. The* Herald *bluntly suggested that Crook had been defeated, pointing out that he had been stalled and forced back to Goose Creek, while the Lakotas retained complete freedom of movement. Crook was furious. He expected correspondents to earn their keep by representing his views, and the contention that the Rosebud could be anything other than total victory was unforgivable. Davenport was ostracized, and the other correspondents, eager to maintain their "insider" status with Crook, took his side against their colleague.*

Davenport's dispatch on the Rosebud Fight
New York Herald, *July 6, 1876, reprinted in Jerome Green,*
Battles and Skirmishes of the Great Sioux War, 1876-1877:
The Military View, *26-40.*

Three days ago the first fight of the campaign against the Sioux in this military department took place. The fighting column marched from the camp, situated at the fork of Goose Creek, on June 16, accompanied by the 250 Indian auxiliaries who had arrived on the preceding day, and numbered about 1,300 men. The infantry were mounted upon mules borrowed from the pack trains. Twenty mounted packers were also allowed to go, and carried carbines. The friendly Indians were loaned firearms belonging to the govern-

ment and their belts filled with cartridges. Old Crow was the principal leader of the Crows, and Medicine Crow and Good Heart were
his lieutenants. Louissant, called by his tribe "Weesaw," was the
chief of the Snakes, or Soshonees [sic], who are divided into two
companies, regularly disciplined in imitation of the white soldiers.
Louissant is captain of one and Cosgrove, a white man, commands
the other. They march sometimes in column, and nearly every
Soshonee[sic], in going to war, carried a long white wand ornamented with pennants or streamers of fur, hair and red cloth. They
wear parti-colored blankets, and ride usually either white or spotted ponies, whose tails and manes they daub with red or orange
paint. Nothing could be more bright and picturesque than the whole
body of friendly Indians as they galloped by the long column of the
expedition early in the first morning of the march, as it wound
around the bases of the low foot hills called Chetish or Wolf Mountains, which were traversed in moving toward the head waters of
Rosebud Creek. Several of the Snakes still carry their ancient spears
and round shields of buffalo horn and elk hide, besides their modern firearms. Imagination did not require more than the presence
of the brown arid hills and the distant snow-capped mountains to
convert them into a cavalcade of Bedouins. After crossing the ster-
ile hills and leaving behind them stunted thorns and cedars the
column stretched like a great serpent over a green divide, whose
surface is undulating as billows of mid-ocean, and which separates
the watersheds of the Tongue River and the Rosebud Creek. The
country is beautiful. The march was silent as possible, and the column was dispersed so as to avoid causing dust, which might give
warning to the enemy. It was hoped to approach within thirty miles
of the Sioux village and then to advance on it during the night.

After a weary march of thirty-five miles the column bivouacked
at the head of the valley of the Rosebud on June 16. The soldiers
placed their blankets so that in sleeping their lines formed a hollow
square, inside of which the animals were picketed.

On the morning of June 17 the command moved at five o'clock.
The Crow scouts went in front and on the flanks, but they had omitted to send forward their spies during the night, although on the
previous day they had found indubitable signs that the Sioux were
then engaged in hunting the buffalo southward. About half-past seven
an advance of ten miles had been made, when, suddenly, the Old

Crow appeared on a hill near the stream, and gave a signal. Soon other scouts dashed into the valley. Meanwhile the Crows were catching their war ponies, stripping off their superfluous garments, and some of them had formed in line and were singing their war song. A halt had been made at the first signal of the scouts, and the order was given to unsaddle the animals, it being supposed that they had merely seen some of the Sioux, near their village upon the hills, engaged in herding their ponies. The two battalions of the Third cavalry were resting on the south side of the creek and one of the Second on the north side. Suddenly yells were heard beyond the low hill on the north, and shots were fired, which every moment were becoming more frequent. The Crows were wild with excitement, and shouted to the interpreters that their scouts were being killed and that they must go to join them. After circling on their ponies in the valley for ten minutes they dashed over the hill and disappeared. The firing became more and more rapid. The cavalry were making ready to mount, when scouts came galloping back again, hallooing that the Sioux were charging.

General Crook rode to the first crest and saw that they were coming forward to attack the whole command in the valley. Orders were given to Colonel Royall to lead the battalions of the Third cavalry across the steam, deploy his troops as skirmishers and occupy the hills in the possession of the enemy. Captain Henry's battalion of the Third cavalry, consisting of Companies D, B, L and F, advanced northward up a series of ridges occupied by the Indians, who retired before the steady charge from point to point. At last was reached the top of a ridge lying adjacent to the highest crest, but separated from it by a deep ravine. The Sioux were in front and were promptly attacked. They occupied also a palisade on the left, about 800 yards distant. Captain Andrews' company had become detached from its battalion and had advanced on the extreme left, and it was employed in checking an early flanking movement of the Indians. Colonel Royall, in advancing, had crossed and left behind him the deep hollow west of the main ridge on which the Sioux first appeared and back over which they had been driven by a line of infantry to a higher crest, stopping on its northern extremity.

The troops were going forward with an ardor and enthusiasm which found vent in cheers, and their officers were surprised to observe that they were receiving no support from the centre, which was yielding ground and permitting the enemy to turn their fire against the right flank. After checking the advance behind a friendly crest behind which his soldiers lay while pouring into the Sioux a hot answering fire, Colonel Royall was expectant of seeing the advance on his right resumed, as the latter were then apparently beginning to feel a panic. Seeing the long gallant skirmish line pause, however, they dashed forward on the right and left, and in an instant nearly every point of vantage within, in front and in the rear, and on the flank of the line, was covered with savages wildly circling their ponies and charging hither and thither, while they fired from their seats with wonderful rapidity and accuracy.

At this moment the loss to the troops commenced. They opened a severe fire upon the Indians, which was seen to have instant effect, but a cry arose that they were the Crows, and immediately it was checked. Thus was lost an excellent opportunity for punishing them severely. They screened themselves behind elevations and continued a harassing fire. Still the troops on the right did not advance, and the suspense grew terrible and the position was every moment more perilous as the Sioux appeared at intervals on the left flank, charging on their ponies and each time further toward the rear. In the meantime they swept down into the valley where the command had halted in the morning at the first alarm, directly behind the left wing, and, killing a Snake, captured a small herd of ponies which he was guarding. Lieutenant Foster, with a squad of men from Captain Andrews' company, was sent to cut off the Sioux and recapture the ponies. He dashed after them two miles and only halted when he found the enemy springing up so thickly around him that he feared it would be impossible to fight his way back. In rejoining the left wing he rode through a series of ravines, and in emerging from them at full gallop was unfortunately mistaken for a party of the enemy and three volleys were fired at him by the troops. No damage was done to his men.

As Colonel Royall was determining to make a rapid charge on the heights held by the Sioux, and by desperately dislodging them, extricating himself from his exposed position, Captain Nickerson, aide-de-camp, having made a wide circuit around the hollow lying between the General's headquarters and Colonel Royall's line, dashed down a steep side hill under a concentrated fire, the bullets making the dust fly under his horse's hoofs, and delivered the unexpected order to fall back. The line on the main ridge, backed by a mass of cavalry and infantry, still remained stationary. To retreat into the hollow on the right, which would be necessary in order to form a junction with the centre, was to risk the certain loss of nearly the whole battalion. Colonel Royall, however, obeyed his order to extend his line in that direction by sending Captain Meinhold's company of the Third cavalry around by such a route as saved it from much exposure and then slowly receded from crest to crest, keeping a strong line of skirmishers continually deployed to amuse the enemy. As the retreat progressed they obtained better range upon the troops at every moment, but the skirmishers did their utmost in firing cooly and with steady aim. It cannot be doubted that their bullets took effect among the savages crowded on the high point of the main ridge. Many were seen to fall and subsequently several dead ponies strewed the ground. The horses belonging to the dismounted cavalrymen were led first into the small ravines in the bottom of the valley.

At this juncture the soldiers felt great discouragement, but preserved their coolness, although death had just begun his work among them, a murderous enfilading fire causing them to drop every moment. Captain Vroom, Lieutenant Morton and Lieutenant Lemley [sic], of the Third cavalry, took places in the skirmish line when the enemy were within range, and used their carbines with effect. Unwilling to let slip an opportunity for helping the extrication of the left line, with which my own fate was identified by the chance of battle, I dismounted at several points during our retreat and fired with the skirmishers. At least, when the receding line reached the last ridge next the fatal hollow, it became evident that the sacrifice of a few lives was inevitable for the salvation of many more. Colonel Royall sent his adjutant, Lieutenant Lemley [sic], through the storm of bullets to ask a support of infantry to protect his retreat. About the same moment Captain Guy V. Henry, who had remained at the head of his battalion under the hottest fire, was horribly wounded in the face. He was lifted from his horse and led to the rear by two of his soldiers. The tide of retreat now grew more excited and turbulent, and I was pressed back, with the soldier attending me, over the rearward crest upon the slope, which was raked by an oblique fire from the north.

The Infantry which was expected to relieve this line was not in position soon enough to check the wild advance of the Sioux, who, observing the retiring body becoming crowded together on the edge of the gap which it must cross under fire, rushed both down and up the valley on the right while they poured their fire from the high bluff across the low elevation, rendering it utterly untenable, while they were charging at the same time to prevent its abandonment. A swarm of Sioux were within 1,000 yards of me in front and I heard their shots in the rear as they murdered the poor soldiers of the rear guard of the retreat. I was obliged either to take the chance of death then or wait to cross with the battalion, which would attract a still more fatal fire, because it would form a large mark for the aim of the enemy. The hill where the General's headquarters were and a large body of troops which had not yet been engaged was more than half a mile distant. I chose the converging ravines and rode through them a greater part of the way, but as I galloped up the slope opposite the one I had left I heard the yells of the savages close behind, and the reports of their rifles, as I emerged from the safer ground, sounded remarkably near and loud.

Looking behind I saw a dozen Sioux surrounding a group of soldiers who had straggled behind the retreat. Six were killed at one spot. A recruit surrendered his carbine to a painted warrior, who flung it to the ground, and cleft his head with a stroke of the tomahawk. William W. Allen, a brave, old soldier, who had been twenty years in the army, fought with magnificent courage, and was killed. The Sioux rode so close to their victims that they shot them in the face with their revolvers and the powder blackened the flesh. Captains Burrow's and Burt's companies of infantry by this time were firing well directed volleys from a position half way down the west side of the high bluff, and just after my escape the Snake Indians, gallantly led by their chiefs, Louissant and Cosgrove, dashed with thrilling shouts into the hollow, among the Sioux who were on the rear of the cavalry, and drove them back. Captain Henry, weak from the bleeding of his wound, had been unable to keep up with the retreat and had sunk on the ground. Louissant put himself astride the body and for five minutes kept the Sioux off, when some soldiers of his company rushed back and rescued him. About the same time a corporal of F company, of the Third cavalry, made a last charge, with three men, and captured from the enemy the bodies of their comrades, thus saving them from the scalping knife. The Snakes took two scalps from the Sioux whom they killed in the hollow, and swung them, fresh and bleeding, with gleeful triumph above their heads as they returned. The infantry under Captains Burrows and Burt executed their part admirably.

It remains to be said of the portion of the engagement which I have thus far described that it was the most important and dangerous, and that in it Captain Henry's battalion of the Third cavalry and Captain Andrews' company of the Second cavalry, with all their officers, displayed a most honorable degree of fortitude and bravery. They had a more arduous duty and suffered more severely than any other portion of the command. Colonel Royall was circumscribed by orders in every one of his movements, and the disaster attending the retreat would have been much greater had it not been so skillfully directed by him. On the left of his line was a lofty crescent-shaped palisade, toward which, early in the morning, he deployed skirmishers. Had the order to fall back been a little later this would have been occupied. It would then have been impossible for the Sioux to have circled around to the rear, and a fire could have been turned upon the last high point held by them, which would have compelled them to hide behind it, while the cavalry could have charged up the hollow and reached them before they could realize their predicament. Then the soldiers could have dismounted and fired such volleys as would have ended the fight and made a chase.

It is now time to glance at the other portions of the field, where there were three times as many troops as were on the left, and yet where there was hardly any fighting, except that done by successive lines of skirmishers, which held the southern end of the great ridge.

In the morning, after the Crows and Snakes had rushed forward to meet the Sioux, Captain Kane's[3] company of infantry was first ordered forward to the top of the nearest hill. From that point it commenced firing. The Sioux were seen in great numbers beyond, covering every summit, and were engaged with the friendly Indians in a warm fusillade. The infantry advanced toward the high ridge, resting upon each successive elevation, which they mounted to discharge volleys into the groups of the enemy occupying still higher points. Captain Noyes, in command of the battalion of the Second cavalry, composed of companies A, B, D, E and I, saw the impor-

3. Avery B. Cain.

tance of carrying a portion of the main ridge immediately before they could advance further south and attack the column in the valley, where a portion of the cavalry was not yet mounted. He, therefore, advanced before receiving any orders, passed the right flank of the infantry and took a knoll beyond them.

The friendly Indians had been carried by the impetuosity of their first charge far beyond the front of the infantry, and a party of Snakes seemed to be fighting independently on a cone-shaped mound, just visible two miles away. As the sequel showed, they killed and scalped a small party of Sioux there, and held their ground until the troops advanced beyond them. The Crows and the rest of the Snakes were between the troops and the Sioux, and it was feared that the bullets intended for the latter would strike our allies. After great shouting by the interpreters of General Crook's wishes they retired running, as if in flight. The Sioux, was well as the cavalry on the left, mistook the movements, and the former became extremely bold and advanced in swarms. It was then that Colonel Royall's line found itself too far ahead in the very midst of the enemy. Captain Mills' battalion of the Third cavalry, composed of companies A, E, I and M, which had been ordered to make the first charge, now advanced through the battalion of the Second cavalry, deployed in a skirmish line and charged the point above where the smoke of the Indian rifles was growing dense. It was carried with inspiriting shouts, and the Sioux ran back to another, still higher, apex. The hostile lines were here face to face, although each availed itself of the protection of the stony summits. Volley after volley was exchanged between them, and the Sioux lost several of their warriors. General Crook saw thirteen of them fall.

Early in the engagement a squadron of the Third cavalry, comprising companies C and G, under command of Captain Van Vliet, had occupied a steep bluff on the south side of the stream to protect the troops in the bottom while they were saddling their horses. It was withdrawn as soon as the whole command was engaged in the forward movement, and was now posted on the high ridge, dismounted and ready for action in the rear of Captain Mills' line. The Indians meanwhile were flocking to a butte northeast of this position, and had opened fire upon it.

Captain Mills received an order to wheel his battalion to the right, advance a furlong, then wheel to the left and charge the steep incline. It was executed with rapidity, and the summit carried, but not until the enemy before dispersing had delivered three heavy volleys at the advancing line. The battalion, after halting on the bluff, was ordered by General Crook to advance directly through the canyon of the stream northward, toward the supposed locality of the Sioux village. By transposition of the forces, it now formed the right of the command, and the Second cavalry battalion was ordered to follow it as a support. The General directed that the battle in progress should be ignored by this wing of the command and that it should capture and destroy the village. Frank Gruard was ordered to ride in front and select the route of march. It was expected that the tepees of the bands of Sitting Bull and Crazy Horse would be found only ten miles distant. Hardly had the first battalion moved away when Captain Noyes was sent a counter order, based upon a new report brought to General Crook by a Crow, that the village was in an exactly opposite direction. Captain Nickerson, aide and acting assistant adjutant general, was dispatched at full gallop to check Captain Mills' advance, and overtook him only after a chase of five miles, during which he was accompanied by a solitary orderly. The two battalions recalled were ordered to positions to protect the rear and command the valley where the morning halt had been made.

The Indians, after the withdrawal of Captain Mills' battalion from the long ridge, had regained the crest which he evacuated, and engaged Van Vliet's squadron at the same time that they poured a terrible fire into Colonel Royall's line on the left, compelling him, after holding his position at a disadvantage so long and with such brave retaliation, to order at last a rapid retreat across a deep defile, with the enemy charging both flanks and the rear. This was the last effort of the Sioux. The infantry and Snakes drove them steadily back from the moment that the left wing emerged from its race of the gantlet [sic].

After the firing had ceased the whole force was concentrated, and it advanced in pursuit of the Indians. It was observed, however, that the Crows remained behind on the summit of a hill, where they were holding a pow-wow. They had captured a pony from the Sioux, which they had left at home in their village and they feared lest it had been attacked during their absence. They also desired to take back two of their braves who were wounded, and to condole the squaw of the young Snake who belonged to their band and who was killed. General Crook, on learning of their disaffection, determined to return to the point where the battle began and to rest there until evening, so that the Crows might fully determine what they would do. They told him, at length, that they could not stay, but must have their war dance at home over the scalps which they had won. Believing that the Sioux village had been removed during the fight, and dreading to march forward through so rough a country after the desertion of his scouts, General Crook determined in the morning to move back toward Goose Creek. The object of the scout, which was so unsuccessful and yet not without an encouraging result, was to discover and destroy the village of the Sioux, which the guides, while half-breed and Indian, agreed in declaring to be on the Yellowstone River, between the mouths of the Rosebud and the Tongue. It proved to be nearer the base of the expedition than was believed, and General Crook's ignorance of its proximity, due to the negligence and inactivity of the Crow allies, who were intrusted with the work of scouting, is the cause of the failure of the movement. The Sioux were certainly repulsed in their bold and confident onset, and lost many of their bravest warriors, but, when they fled, could not be pursued without great danger in the rough country through which their way lay.

Had his scouts proved faithful, so that he could have been prepared to occupy the commanding positions with infantry in advance of the main column, he would have had warning of the concentration of the enemy to impede his course, and could have driven him back into his village and ended the campaign by destroying it. It will be seen that the blame of the miscarriage of the scout belongs to the Crows, whose instinct, vigilance and knowledge of their own country was relied upon to render every move of the force intelligent. On the contrary, their undisciplined frenzy and failure to discover the lodgment of the enemy in time to frustrate the meditated attack precipitated a battle which began with a stupendous advantage on his side and in a spot of his own choice naturally suitable to the success of their method of warfare. The Sioux's strength was masked, except when, emboldened by the disastrous withdrawal of the left wing of the cavalry, they made a dash from both ends of a deep hollow which lay in its way and exposed it to a murderous fire, and suddenly swarmed on the front, left and rear. Then it was that the timely fire of the infantry upon their main body, the charge of the Snakes into the hollow and rapid pursuit of them for three miles, dismayed them utterly and they fell back and disappeared. Had it not been for their occupation, unperceived by the General, of positions from which they could pour an enfilading fire upon both flanks of the body of cavalry on the left, they would not have stood in the face of the troops a moment after their first charge. The injury inflicted upon them must have been much greater than that which we suffered. Their loss of lives is estimated at about one hundred. There is no doubt that all the northern Sioux warriors were engaged in the battle, and it is believed that they have been severely crippled.

New York Herald, *June 24 1876, clipping in Bourke Diary,*
Volume 6, Pages 676-77.
The Battle in the Big Horn Country.

The first regular battle between the United States forces and the hostile Sioux has resulted in what looks very like a defeat of the soldiers. The graphic despatch [*sic*] from the HERALD correspondent accompanying the expedition; and who witnessed the fight, will be found elsewhere. From it we learn that after a rapid march from his supply camp on Goose Creek General Crook, with one thousand three hundred mounted men and two hundred and fifty friendly Indians, came upon a force of Sioux warriors two thousand five hundred strong, under the command of Sitting Bull,[4] near the head waters of Rosebud Creek, a tributary of the Yellowstone River. The attack was begun by the Sioux, who rolled back the Indian scouts on the main body. We judge that the friendly Crows and Snakes precipitated the fight before the troops could take position, in their haste to attack their traditional foes, the Sioux. The latter, who appear to have acted bravely, and to have been superbly handled, soon repulsed this Indian rush, and then took up commanding positions on the lower ridges above Rosebud Creek, from which they were dislodged only at great exposure to the troops, and retreated only to take up better positions on the higher ridges. In thus driving the Indians the troops had become dangerously sepa-

---

4. The *Herald* made the common, but erroneous assumption that Indians had an organized command structure comparable to that used by the whites. In fact, no particular chief was in charge, and Plains Indian culture rarely permitted any person to hold that much power.

rated and in danger of having their flanks turned, necessitating a reconcentration in face of a galling fire. The strenuous effort made by the Sioux to prevent this junction of the separated forces shows that their leader thoroughly understands the art of mountain warfare; and, although his warriors were finally dislodged from their highest points, the absence of pursuit, and the fact that his prompt attack on the column saved the great Sioux village, proclaim him the victor. That he was able to cope successfully with such a force of regular troops backed by Indian allies and to march off free to choose his next battle ground marks out Sitting Bull as a formidable foe. There is no necessity to lay blame at present upon General Crook, whose decision not to pursue the Sioux into a dangerous country was probably the best under the circumstances. Whether he blundered in the fight we do not presume to say until he has been heard from at length.

While Crook's forces have been practically brought to a standstill for three weeks at least, he having returned to his headquarters on Goose Creek, and while Sitting Bull is free to move his village off where it may take two months to find him, we must revert to the other two bodies of troops moving against him under General Gibbons [sic] and General Terry. It has been reported that Gibbons was checked in his attempt to cross the Yellowstone by probably a detachment of the same band that stopped Crook. General Terry at last accounts was in a quandary on the Little Missouri River, whither he went to seek Sitting Bull, and although he may have effected a junction or established communication with Gibbons it seems extremely doubtful that he even now knows in what direction to seek the Sioux. The best fortune we can hope for is that Terry shall find Sitting Bull and prevent his running East, so that by the time Crook is ready to advance there may be a chance of co-operating with him. The war now looks as though it would be protracted, bloody and very costly. Ten killed and twenty wounded on our side against thirteen Sioux scalps is not an encouraging beginning.

Bibliography

Government Documents

Heitman, Francis B. *Historical Register and Dictionary of the United States Army, From Its Organization, September 29, 1789, to March 2, 1903.* 2 vols. Washington: Government Printing Office, 1903.

United States Department of the Interior. Board of Indian Commissioners. *Peace with the Apaches of New Mexico and Arizona. Report of Vincent Colyer, Member of the Board of Indian Commissioners. 1871.* 1872. Reprint. Tucson: Territorial Press, 1964.

United States Department of War. Office of the Adjutant General. RG 393. Special File. Military Division of the Missouri. National Archives Microfilm Publication 1495. Washington: National Archives and Record Service, n.d. As follows:

Roll 2. "Citizens Expeditions" to the Black Hills.

Rolls 2-4. Sioux War, 1876-77.

—. *Report of the Secretary of War: Being Part of the Message and Documents Communicated to the Two Houses of Congress at the Beginnine of the Second Session of the Forty-fourth Congress.* Vol. 1. Washington: Government Printing Office, 1876.

Manuscript Sources

Bourke, John Gregory. Diaries. 124 vols. United States Military Academy Library, West Point, New York. Microfilm in possession of the editor.

Capron, Thaddeus. Diary. American Heritage Center. University of Wyoming, Laramie. MS 1694.

Carr, Eugene Asa. Papers. United States Army Military History Institute. Carlisle Barracks, Pa.

Crook, George. Collection. Microfilm edition. Rutherford B. Hayes Library, Rutherford B. Hayes Presidential Center. Fremont, Ohio.

Kennon, Lyman Walter Vere. Diary. George Crook and Lyman W.V. Kennon Papers. United States Army Military History Institute. Carlisle Barracks, Pa.

Nickerson, Azor Howitt. "Major General George Crook and the Indians." Typescript. Walter Scribner Schuyler Papers. Henry E. Huntington Library and Art Gallery, San Marino, Calif.

Books—Primary

Bourke, John Gregory. *An Apache Campaign in the Sierra Madre: An Account of the Expedition in Pursuit of the Hostile Chiricahua Apaches in the Spring of 1883.* 1886. Reprint. Lincoln: University of Nebraska Press, 1987.

—. *Apache Medicine-Men.* 1892. Reprint. New York: Dover Publications, Inc., 1993.

—. *On the Border With Crook.* 1891. Reprint. Alexandria, Virginia: Time-Life Books, 1980.

Carter, Robert Goldthwaite. *On the Border With Mackenzie, or Winning the West from the Comanches.* 1935. Reprint. New York: Antiquarian Press, 1961.

Dodge, Richard Irving. *Our Wild Indians: Thirty-three Years' Personal Experience Among the Red Men of the Great West.* Hartford, CT: A.D. Worthington and Company, 1882.

Finerty, John F. *War-Path and Bivouac: The Big Horn and Yellowstone Expedition.* 1890. Reprint. Lincoln: University of Nebraska Press, 1966.

Greene, Jerome A., comp. *Battles and Skirmishes of the Great Sioux War, 1876-1877: The Military View.* Norman: University of Oklahoma Press, 1993.

—. *Lakota and Cheyenne: Indian Views of the Great Sioux War, 1876-1877.* Norman: University of Oklahoma Press, 1994.

Howard, Oliver Otis. *My Life and Experiences Among Our Hostile Indians.* 1907. Reprint. New York: Da Capo Press, Inc., 1972.

Hunt, Frazier, and Robert Hunt. *I Fought With Custer: The Story of Sergeant Windolph, Last Survivor of the Battle of the Little Big Horn*. New York: Charles Scribner's Sons, 1947.

Kime, Wayne R., ed. *The Black Hills Journals of Colonel Richard Irving Dodge*. Norman: University of Oklahoma Press, 1996.

—. *The Powder River Expedition Journals of Colonel Richard Irving Dodge*. Norman: University of Oklahoma Press, 1997.

Mills, Anson. *My Story*. 2nd ed. Washington: Press of Byron S. Adams, 1921.

Schmitt, Martin F., ed. *General George Crook, His Autobiography*. Norman: University of Oklahoma Press, 1946. Reprinted, 1986.

Summerhayes, Martha. *Vanished Arizona: Recollections of the Army Life of a New England Woman*. 1911. Reprint. Lincoln: University of Nebraska Press, 1979.

Sweeney, Edwin R., ed. *Making Peace with Cochise: The 1872 Journal of Captain Joseph Alton Sladen*. Norman: University of Oklahoma Press, 1997.

Willert, James, ed. *Bourke's Diary: From Journals of 1st Lt. John Gregory Bourke, June 27-Sept. 15, 1876*. La Miranda, California: James Willert, 1986.

Books—Secondary

Altshuler, Constance Wynn. *Cavalry Yellow & Infantry Blue: Army Officers in Arizona Between 1851 and 1886*. Tucson: The Arizona Historical Society, 1991.

—. *Chains of Command: Arizona and the Army, 1856-1875*. Tucson: The Arizona Historical Society, 1981.

—. *Starting with Defiance: Nineteenth Century Arizona Military Posts*. Tucson: The Arizona Historical Society, 1983.

Bancroft, Hubert Howe. *History of Arizona and New Mexico, 1530-1888*. The Works of Hubert Howe Bancroft 17. San Francisco: The History Company, 1889.

—. *Register of Pioneer Inhabitants of California 1542 to 1848 and Index to Information Concerning Them in Bancroft's History of California Volumes I-V*. Los Angeles: Dawson's Book Shop, 1964.

Bigler, David L. *Forgotten Kingdom: The Mormon Theocracy in the American West, 1847-1896*. Kingdom in the West: The Mormons and the American Frontier, Vol. 2. Spokane: The Arthur H. Clark Co., 1998.

Brown, Dee. *The Fetterman Massacre*. Originally published as *Fort Phil Kearny: An American Saga*. 1962. Reprint. Lincoln: University of Nebraska Press, 1971.

Buecker, Thomas R. *Fort Robinson and the American West 1874-1899*. Lincoln: Nebraska State Historical Society, 1999.

Clum, Woodworth. *Apache Agent: The Story of John P. Clum*. Boston: Houghton Mifflin Co., 1936.

Cordell, Linda S. *Ancient Pueblo Peoples*. Washington: Smithsonian Books, 1994.

Crawford, Lewis F. *The Exploits of Ben Arnold, Indian Fighter, Gold Miner, Cowboy, Hunter, and Army Scout*. Originally published as *Rekindling Camp Fires*. 1926. Reprint. Norman: University of Oklahoma Press, 1999.

DeBarthe, Joe. *The Life and Adventures of Frank Grouard, Chief of Scouts, U.S.A.* 1894. Reprint. Alexandria, Va.: Time-Life Books, 1982.

Dunlay, Thomas W. *Wolves for the Blue Soldiers: Indian Scouts and Auxiliaries with the United States Army, 1860-90*. Lincoln: University of Nebraska Press, 1982. Reprinted 1987.

Faulk, Odie B. *Crimson Desert: Indian Wars of the American Southwest*. New York: Oxford University Press, 1974.

Fontana, Bernard L. *Entrada: The Legacy of Spain and Mexico in the United States*. Tucson: Southwest Parks and Monuments Association, 1994.

Frazer, Robert W. *Forts of the West: Military Forts and Presidios and Posts Commonly Called Forts West of the Mississippi River to 1898*. Norman: University of Oklahoma Press, 1965. Reprinted 1972.

Gilbert, Hila, with George Harris and Bernice Pourier Harris. *"Big Bat" Pourier*. Sheridan, Wyo.: The Mills Company, 1968.

Gray, John S. *Centennial Campaign: The Sioux War of 1876*. 1976. Reprint, Norman: University of Oklahoma Press, 1988.

Hardorff, Richard G. *Hokahey! A Good Day to Die! The Indian Casualties of the Custer Fight*. Spokane: The Arthur H. Clark Company, 1993.

Hedren, Paul L. *Fort Laramie in 1876: Chronicle of a Frontier Post at War*. Lincoln: University of Nebraska Press, 1988.

Herr, John K. and Edward S. Wallace. *The Story of the U.S. Cavalry: 1775-1942*. 1953. Reprint. New York: Bonanza Books, 1984.

Hoig, Stan. *The Battle of the Washita: The Sheridan-Custer Indian Campaign of 1867-69*. Garden City: Doubleday & Company, 1976.

Hoogenboom, Ari. *Rutherford B. Hayes, Warrior and President*. Lawrence, Kans.: University Press of Kansas, 1995.

Houk, Walter. *The Botanical Gardens at the Huntington*. New York: Harry N. Abrams, Inc., 1996.

Hoxie, Frederick E., ed. *Encyclopedia of North American Indians*. Boston: Houghton Mifflin Company, 1996.

Hyde, George E. *Red Cloud's Folk: A History of the Oglala Sioux Indians*. Norman: University of Oklahoma Press, 1957. Reprinted 1975.

—. *Spotted Tail's Folk: A History of the Brulé Sioux*. Norman: University of Oklahoma Press, 1961. Reprinted 1987.

Jackson, Donald. *Custer's Gold: The United States Cavalry Expedition of 1874*. New Haven: Yale University Press, 1966.

Johnson, Allen, and Dumas Malone, eds. *Dictionary of American Biography*. 20 vols. New York: Charles Scribner's Sons, 1928-38.

King, James T. *War Eagle: A Life of General Eugene A. Carr*. Lincoln: University of Nebraska Press, 1963.

Knight, Oliver. *Following the Indian Wars: The Story of the Newspaper Correspondents among the Indian Campaigners*. Norman: University of Oklahoma Press, 1960. Reprinted 1993.

Krause, Herbert, and Gary D. Olson. *Prelude to Glory: A Newspaper Accounting of Custer's 1874 Expedition to the Black Hills*. Sioux Falls, S.D.: Brevet Press, 1974.

Kroeker, Marvin E. *Great Plains Command: William B. Hazen in the Frontier West*. Norman: University of Oklahoma Press, 1976.

Lamar, Howard R., ed. *The New Encyclopedia of the American West*. New Haven: Yale University Press, 1998.

Larson, Robert W. *Red Cloud, Warrior-Statesman of the Lakota Sioux*. Norman: University of Oklahoma Press, 1997.

Lazarus, Edward. *Black Hills/White Justice: The Sioux Nation Versus the United States, 1775 to the Present*. New York: HarperCollins Publishers, 1991.

Loughmiller, Campbell, and Lynn Loughmiller. *Texas Wildflowers: A Field Guide*. Austin: University of Texas Press, 1984.

McFeely, William S. *Grant, A Biography*. New York: W.W. Norton & Company, 1981.

Mangum, Neil C. *Battle of the Rosebud: Prelude to the Little Bighorn.* El Segundo, CA: Upton & Sons, 1996.

Marston, Daniel. *The Seven Years' War.* Essential Histories. Oxford: Osprey Publishing, 2001.

Moorehead, Alan. *The White Nile.* New York: Harper & Brothers, 1960.

Noble, David Grant. *Ancient Ruins of the Southwest: An Archaeological Guide.* 2nd rev. ed. Flagstaff, Ariz.: Northland Publishing Company, 2000.

Nye, Wilbur Sturtevant. *Carbine & Lance: The Story of Old Fort Sill.* 3rd ed. Norman: University of Oklahoma Pres, 1969. Reprinted 1983.

Olson, James C. *Red Cloud and the Sioux Problem.* Lincoln: Unversity of Nebraska Press, 1965.

O'Neal, Bill. *Fighting Men of the Indian Wars: A Biographical Encyclopedia of the Mountain Men, Soldiers, Cowboys, and Pioneers Who Took Up Arms During America's Westward Expansion.* Stillwater, OK: Barbed Wire Press, 1991.

Parkman, Francis. *The Jesuits in North America in the Seventeenth Century.* Frontenac Edition. 2 vols. Boston: Little, Brown, and Company, 1902.

Pierce, Michael D. *The Most Promising Young Officer: A Life of Ranald Slidell Mackenzie.* Norman: University of Oklahoma Press, 1993.

Porter, Joseph. *Paper Medicine Man: John Gregory Bourke and His American West.* Norman: University of Oklahoma: 1986. Reprinted 1989.

Priest, Loring Benson. *Uncle Sam's Stepchildren: The Reformation of United States Indian Policy, 1867-1887.* 1942. Reprint. New York: Octagon Books, 1972.

Prucha, Francis Paul. *The Great Father: The United States Government and the American Indians.* Abridged ed. Lincoln: University of Nebraska Press, 1986.

Rice, Edward. *Captain Sir Richard Francis Burton.*1990. Reprint. New York: Barnes & Noble, Inc., 1999.

Rickey, Don, Jr. *Forty Miles a Day on Beans and Hay: The Enlisted Soldier Fighting the Indian Wars.* Norman: University of Oklahoma Press, 1963. Reprinted 1985.

Robinson, Charles M., III. *Bad Hand: A Biography of General Ranald S. Mackenzie.* Austin: State House Press, 1993.

—. *The Court Martial of Lieutenant Henry Flipper*. El Paso: Texas Western Press, 1994.

—. *General Crook and the Western Frontier*. Norman: University of Oklahoma Press, 2001.

—. *A Good Year to Die: The Story of the Great Sioux War*. New York: Random House, 1995.

Schubert, Frank N. *Outpost of the Sioux Wars: A History of Fort Robinson*. Originally published as *Buffalo Soldiers, Braves, and Brass: The Story of Fort Robinson, Nebraska*. 1993. Reprint. Lincoln: University of Nebraska Press, 1995.

Spellenberg, Richard. *National Audubon Society Field Guide to North American Wildflowers: Western Region*. New York: Alfred A. Knopf, 1979.

Sweeney, Edwin R. *Cochise, Chiricahua Apache Chief*. Norman: University of Oklahoma Press, 1991.

Thrapp, Dan L. *Al Sieber, Chief of Scouts*. Norman: University of Oklahoma Press, 1964. Reprinted 1995.

—. *Encyclopedia of Frontier Biography*. 3 vols. 1988. Reprint. Lincoln: University of Nebraska Press, 1991.

—. *The Conquest of Apacheria*. Norman: University of Oklahoma Press, 1968. Reprinted 1988.

Utley, Robert M. *Cavalier in Buckskin: George Armstrong Custer and the Western Military Frontier*. Norman: University of Oklahoma Press, 1988.

—. *A Clash of Cultures: Fort Bowie and the Chiricahua Apaches*. Washington: National Park Service, 1977.

—, ed. *Encyclopedia of the American West*. New York: Wing Books, 1997.

—. *Frontier Regulars: The United States Army and the Indian 1866-1891*. 1973. Reprint. Lincoln: University of Nebraska Press, 1984.

—. *The Lance and the Shield: The Life and Times of Sitting Bull*. New York: Henry Holt & Co., 1993.

Vaughn, J.W. *With Crook at the Rosebud*. 1956. Reprint. Lincoln: University of Nebraska Press, 1988.

Warner, Ezra J. *Generals in Blue: Lives of the Union Commanders*. Baton Rouge: Louisiana State University Press, 1964.

Willem, John M. *The United States Trade Dollar*. 2nd ed. Racine, Wisc.: Whitman Publishing Co., 1965.

Worcester, Donald E. *The Apaches: Eagles of the Southwest*. Norman: University of Oklahoma Press, 1979.

Articles and Pamphlets—Primary

Bloom, Lansing B., ed. "Bourke on the Southwest." *New Mexico Historical Review*. Vol. 8, no. 1 (January 1933): 1-30; Vol. 9, no. 1 (January 1934): 33-77; Vol. 9, no. 2 (April 1934): 159-83; Vol. 9, no. 3 (July 1934): 273-89; Vol. 9, no. 4 (October 1934): 375-435; Vol. 10, no. 1 (January 1935): 1-35; Vol. 10, no. 2 (April 1935); Vol. 10, no. 3 (July 1935).

Bourke, John Gregory. "The American Congo." *Scribner's Magazine*. 15 (May 1894): 590-610. Reprint, n.p. n.d.

—. "General Crook in the Indian Country." *The Century Magazine*. Vol. 41, no. 5 (March 1891): 643-660.

Lemly, Henry Rowan. "The Fight on the Rosebud." John M. Carroll, intro. *The Papers of the Order of the Indian Wars*. (Fort Collins, Colorado, 1975): 13-18.

Articles and Pamphlets—Secondary

Adams, William Y. "The Development of San Carlos Apache Wage Labor to 1954." Keith H. Basso and Morris E. Opler, eds. *Apachean Culture History and Ethnology*. Anthropological Papers of the University of Arizona No. 21. (Tucson: University of Arizona Press, 1971): 116-28.

Farnsworth, Janet Webb. "The Day the Southwest Shook." *True West*. Vol. 42, no. 7 (June 1995): 35-39.

Hedren, Paul. "*Paper Medicine Man* and the Renaissance in Frontier Military History: A Review Essay." *New Mexico Historical Review*. Vol. 62, no. 1 (January 1987): 95-102.

Hicks, Sam. "Aparajo, the Perfect Packsaddle." *The American West*. Vol. 6, no. 1 (January 1969): 28-32.

McDermott, John D. "The Military Problem and the Black Hills, 1874-75." John D. McDermott, comp. *Gold Rush: The Black Hills Story*. (Pierre: South Dakota Historical Society Press, 2001): 4-26.

Ortiz, Alfonso. "Farmers and Raiders of the Southwest." *The World of the American Indian*. (Washington: National Geographic Society, 1974): 157-201.

Robinson, Charles M., III. "Fort Ringgold: A Well-Preserved Frontier Post Begins to Decay." *Old West*. Vol. 27, no. 3 (Spring 1991): 46-49.

—. "On the Border With Bourke: Two Borderlands Pamphlets of the 1890s." *Journal of South Texas*. Vol. 15, no. 1 (Spring 2002): 38-46.

Russell, Francis. "Apostle to the Indians." *American Heritage*. Vol. 9, no. 1 (December 1957): 4-9, 117-19.

Turcheneske, John Anthony, Jr. "Historical Manuscripts as Sources for Anthropological Study: The Ethnological Correspondence of John Gregory Bourke." *New Mexico Historical Review*. Vol. 59, no. 3 (July 1984): 267-86.

"War Against Peace or A New Attila. Contemporaneous episodes on the frontier of Texas, attested by facts compiled by 'El Bien Publico's publishers." Rio Grande City, TX: Jesús T. Recio, Publisher, 1895.

Index